DAMA-DMBOK

DATA MANAGEMENT BODY OF KNOWLEDGE
SECOND EDITION

DAMA International

Technics Publications
BASKING RIDGE, NEW JERSEY

Dedicated to the memory of

Patricia Cupoli, MLS, MBA, CCP, CDMP

(May 25, 1948 – July 28, 2015)

for her lifelong commitment to the Data Management profession
and her contributions to this publication.

Published by:

2 Lindsley Road
Basking Ridge, NJ 07920 USA

https://www.TechnicsPub.com

Senior Editor:	Deborah Henderson, CDMP
Editor:	Susan Earley, CDMP
Production Editor:	Laura Sebastian-Coleman, CDMP, IQCP
Bibliography Researcher:	Elena Sykora, DGSP
Collaboration Tool Manager:	Eva Smith, CDMP

Cover design by Lorena Molinari

Second Edition

First Printing 2017

Copyright © 2017 DAMA International

ISBN, Print ed.	9781634622349
ISBN, PDF ed.	9781634622363
ISBN, Server ed.	9781634622486
ISBN, Enterprise ed.	9781634622479
Library of Congress Control Number:	2017941854

Contents

Chapter 9: Document and Content Management _____ 287

Chapter 10: Reference and Master Data _____ 327

Chapter 13: Data Quality _____423

Figures

Tables

Preface

DAMA International is pleased to release the second edition of the DAMA Guide to the Data Management Body of Knowledge (DAMA-DMBOK2). Since the publication of the first edition in 2009, significant developments have taken place in the field of data management. Data Governance has become a standard structure in many organizations, new technologies have enabled the collection and use of 'Big Data' (semi-structured and unstructured data in a wide range of formats), and the importance of data ethics has grown along with our ability to explore and exploit the vast amount of data and information produced as part of our daily lives.

These changes are exciting. They also place new and increasing demands on our profession. DAMA has responded to these changes by reformulating the DAMA Data Management Framework (the DAMA Wheel), adding detail and clarification, and expanding the scope of the DMBOK:

- Context diagrams for all Knowledge Areas have been improved and updated.

- Data Integration and Interoperability has been added as a new Knowledge Area to highlight its importance (Chapter 8).

- Data Ethics has been called out as a separate chapter due to the increasing necessity of an ethical approach to all aspects of data management (Chapter 2).

- The role of governance has been described both as a function (Chapter 3) and in relation to each Knowledge Area.

- A similar approach has been taken with organizational change management, which is described in Chapter 17 and incorporated into the Knowledge Area chapters.

- New chapters on Big Data and Data Science (Chapter 14) and Data Management Maturity Assessment (Chapter 15) help organizations understand where they want to go and give them the tools to get there.

- The second edition also includes a newly formulated set of data management principles to support the ability of organizations to manage their data effectively and get value from their data assets (Chapter 1).

We hope the DMBOK2 will serve data management professionals across the globe as a valuable resource and guide. Nevertheless, we also recognize it is only a starting point. Real advancement will come as we apply and learn from these ideas. DAMA exists to enable members to learn continuously, by sharing ideas, trends, problems, and solutions.

Sue Geuens   Laura Sebastian-Coleman
President   Publications Officer
DAMA International   DAMA International

CHAPTER 1

Data Management

1. Introduction

Many organizations recognize that their data is a vital enterprise asset. Data and information can give them insight about their customers, products, and services. It can help them innovate and reach strategic goals. Despite that recognition, few organizations actively manage data as an asset from which they can derive ongoing value (Evans and Price, 2012). Deriving value from data does not happen in a vacuum or by accident. It requires intention, planning, coordination, and commitment. It requires management and leadership.

Data Management is the development, execution, and supervision of plans, policies, programs, and practices that deliver, control, protect, and enhance the value of data and information assets throughout their lifecycles.

A *Data Management Professional* is any person who works in any facet of data management (from technical management of data throughout its lifecycle to ensuring that data is properly utilized and leveraged) to meet strategic organizational goals. Data management professionals fill numerous roles, from the highly technical (e.g., database administrators, network administrators, programmers) to strategic business (e.g., Data Stewards, Data Strategists, Chief Data Officers).

Data management activities are wide-ranging. They include everything from the ability to make consistent decisions about how to get strategic value from data to the technical deployment and performance of databases. Thus data management requires both technical and non-technical (i.e., 'business') skills. Responsibility for managing data must be shared between business and information technology roles, and people in both areas must be able to collaborate to ensure an organization has high quality data that meets its strategic needs.

Data and information are not just assets in the sense that organizations invest in them in order to derive future value. Data and information are also vital to the day-to-day operations of most organizations. They have been called the 'currency', the 'life blood', and even the 'new oil' of the information economy.[1] Whether or not an organization gets value from its analytics, it cannot even transact business without data.

To support the data management professionals who carry out the work, DAMA International (The Data Management Association) has produced this book, the second edition of *The DAMA Guide to the Data*

---

[1] Google 'data as currency', 'data as life blood', and 'the new oil', for numerous references.

Management Body of Knowledge (DMBOK2). This edition builds on the first one, published in 2009, which provided foundational knowledge on which to build as the profession advanced and matured.

This chapter outlines a set of principles for data management. It discusses challenges related to following those principles and suggests approaches for meeting these challenges. The chapter also describes the DAMA Data Management Framework, which provides the context for the work carried out by data management professionals within various Data Management Knowledge Areas.

1.1 Business Drivers

Information and knowledge hold the key to competitive advantage. Organizations that have reliable, high quality data about their customers, products, services, and operations can make better decisions than those without data or with unreliable data. Failure to manage data is similar to failure to manage capital. It results in waste and lost opportunity. The primary driver for data management is to enable organizations to get value from their data assets, just as effective management of financial and physical assets enables organizations to get value from those assets.

1.2 Goals

Within an organization, data management goals include:

- Understanding and supporting the information needs of the enterprise and its stakeholders, including customers, employees, and business partners
- Capturing, storing, protecting, and ensuring the integrity of data assets
- Ensuring the quality of data and information
- Ensuring the privacy and confidentiality of stakeholder data
- Preventing unauthorized or inappropriate access, manipulation, or use of data and information
- Ensuring data can be used effectively to add value to the enterprise

2. Essential Concepts

2.1 Data

Long-standing definitions of *data* emphasize its role in representing facts about the world.[2] In relation to information technology, *data* is also understood as information that has been stored in digital form (though data is

---

[2] The New Oxford American Dictionary defines data as "facts and statistics collected together for analysis." The American Society for Quality (ASQ) defines data as "A set of collected facts" and describes two kinds of numerical data: measured or variable and counted or attributed. The International Standards Organization (ISO) defines data as "re-interpretable

not limited to information that has been digitized and data management principles apply to data captured on paper as well as in databases). Still, because today we can capture so much information electronically, we call many things 'data' that would not have been called 'data' in earlier times – things like names, addresses, birthdates, what one ate for dinner on Saturday, the most recent book one purchased.

Such facts about individual people can be aggregated, analyzed, and used to make a profit, improve health, or influence public policy. Moreover our technological capacity to measure a wide range of events and activities (from the repercussions of the Big Bang to our own heartbeats) and to collect, store, and analyze electronic versions of things that were not previously thought of as data (videos, pictures, sound recordings, documents) is close to surpassing our ability to synthesize these data into usable information.[3] To take advantage of the variety of data without being overwhelmed by its volume and velocity requires reliable, extensible data management practices.

Most people assume that, because data represents facts, it is a form of truth about the world and that the facts will fit together. But 'facts' are not always simple or straightforward. Data is a means of representation. It stands for things other than itself (Chisholm, 2010). Data is both an interpretation of the objects it represents and an object that must be interpreted (Sebastian-Coleman, 2013). This is another way of saying that we need context for data to be meaningful. Context can be thought of as data's representational system; such a system includes a common vocabulary and a set of relationships between components. If we know the conventions of such a system, then we can interpret the data within it.[4] These conventions are often documented in a specific kind of data referred to as Metadata.

However, because people often make different choices about how to represent concepts, they create different ways of representing the same concepts. From these choices, data takes on different shapes. Think of the range of ways we have to represent calendar dates, a concept about which there is an agreed-to definition. Now consider more complex concepts (such as customer or product), where the granularity and level of detail of what needs to be represented is not always self-evident, and the process of representation grows more complex, as does the process of managing that information over time. (See Chapter 10).

Even within a single organization, there are often multiple ways of representing the same idea. Hence the need for Data Architecture, modeling, governance, and stewardship, and Metadata and Data Quality management, all of which help people understand and use data. Across organizations, the problem of multiplicity multiplies. Hence the need for industry-level data standards that can bring more consistency to data.

Organizations have always needed to manage their data, but changes in technology have expanded the scope of this management need as they have changed people's understanding of what data is. These changes have enabled organizations to use data in new ways to create products, share information, create knowledge, and improve

---

representation of information in a formalized manner suitable for communication, interpretation, or processing" (ISO 11179). This definition emphasizes the electronic nature of data and assumes, correctly, that data requires standards because it is managed through information technology systems. That said, it does not speak to the challenges of formalizing data in a consistent way, across disparate systems. Nor does it account well for the concept of unstructured data.

[3] http://ubm.io/2c4yPOJ (Accessed 20016-12-04). http://bit.ly/1rOQktl (Accessed 20016-12-04).

[4] For additional information on the constructed-ness of data see: Kent, *Data and Reality* (2012) and Devlin, *Business Unintelligence* (2013).

organizational success. But the rapid growth of technology and with it human capacity to produce, capture, and mine data for meaning has intensified the need to manage data effectively.

2.2 Data and Information

Much ink has been spilled over the relationship between data and information. Data has been called the "raw material of information" and information has been called "data in context".[5] Often a layered pyramid is used to describe the relationship between data (at the base), information, knowledge, and wisdom (at the very top). While the pyramid can be helpful in describing why data needs to be well-managed, this representation presents several challenges for data management.

- It is based on the assumption that data simply exists. But data does not simply exist. Data has to be created.

- By describing a linear sequence from data through wisdom, it fails to recognize that it takes knowledge to create data in the first place.

- It implies that data and information are separate things, when in reality, the two concepts are intertwined with and dependent on each other. Data is a form of information and information is a form of data.

Within an organization, it may be helpful to draw a line between information and data for purposes of clear communication about the requirements and expectations of different uses by different stakeholders. ("Here is a sales report for the last quarter [information]. It is based on data from our data warehouse [data]. Next quarter these results [data] will be used to generate our quarter-over-quarter performance measures [information]"). Recognizing data and information need to be prepared for different purposes drives home a central tenet of data management: Both data and information need to be managed. Both will be of higher quality if they are managed together with uses and customer requirements in mind. Throughout the DMBOK, the terms will be used interchangeably.

2.3 Data as an Organizational Asset

An *asset* is an economic resource, that can be owned or controlled, and that holds or produces value. Assets can be converted to money. Data is widely recognized as an enterprise asset, though understanding of what it means to manage data as an asset is still evolving. In the early 1990s, some organizations found it questionable whether the value of goodwill should be given a monetary value. Now, the 'value of goodwill' commonly shows up as an item on the Profit and Loss Statement (P&L). Similarly, while not universally adopted, monetization of data is becoming increasingly common. It will not be too long before we see this as a feature of P&Ls. (See Chapter 3.)

Today's organizations rely on their data assets to make more effective decisions and to operate more efficiently. Businesses use data to understand their customers, create new products and services, and improve operational efficiency by cutting costs and controlling risks. Government agencies, educational institutions, and not-for-profit

---

[5] See English, 1999 and DAMA, 2009.

organizations also need high quality data to guide their operational, tactical, and strategic activities. As organizations increasingly depend on data, the value of data assets can be more clearly established.

Many organizations identify themselves as 'data-driven'. Businesses aiming to stay competitive must stop making decisions based on gut feelings or instincts, and instead use event triggers and apply analytics to gain actionable insight. Being data-driven includes the recognition that data must be managed efficiently and with professional discipline, through a partnership of business leadership and technical expertise.

Furthermore, the pace of business today means that change is no longer optional; digital disruption is the norm. To react to this, business must co-create information solutions with technical data professionals working alongside line-of-business counterparts. They must plan for how to obtain and manage data that they know they need to support business strategy. They must also position themselves to take advantage of opportunities to leverage data in new ways.

2.4 Data Management Principles

Data management shares characteristics with other forms of asset management, as seen in Figure 1. It involves knowing what data an organization has and what might be accomplished with it, then determining how best to use data assets to reach organizational goals.

Like other management processes, it must balance strategic and operational needs. This balance can best be struck by following a set of principles that recognize salient features of data management and guide data management practice.

- **Data is an asset with unique properties**: Data is an asset, but it differs from other assets in important ways that influence how it is managed. The most obvious of these properties is that data is not consumed when it is used, as are financial and physical assets.

- **The value of data can and should be expressed in economic terms**: Calling data an asset implies that it has value. While there are techniques for measuring data's qualitative and quantitative value, there are not yet standards for doing so. Organizations that want to make better decisions about their data should develop consistent ways to quantify that value. They should also measure both the costs of low quality data and the benefits of high quality data.

- **Managing data means managing the quality of data**: Ensuring that data is fit for purpose is a primary goal of data management. To manage quality, organizations must ensure they understand stakeholders' requirements for quality and measure data against these requirements.

- **It takes Metadata to manage data**: Managing any asset requires having data about that asset (number of employees, accounting codes, etc.). The data used to manage and use data is called *Metadata*. Because data cannot be held or touched, to understand what it is and how to use it requires definition and knowledge in the form of Metadata. Metadata originates from a range of processes related to data creation, processing, and use, including architecture, modeling, stewardship, governance, Data Quality management, systems development, IT and business operations, and analytics.

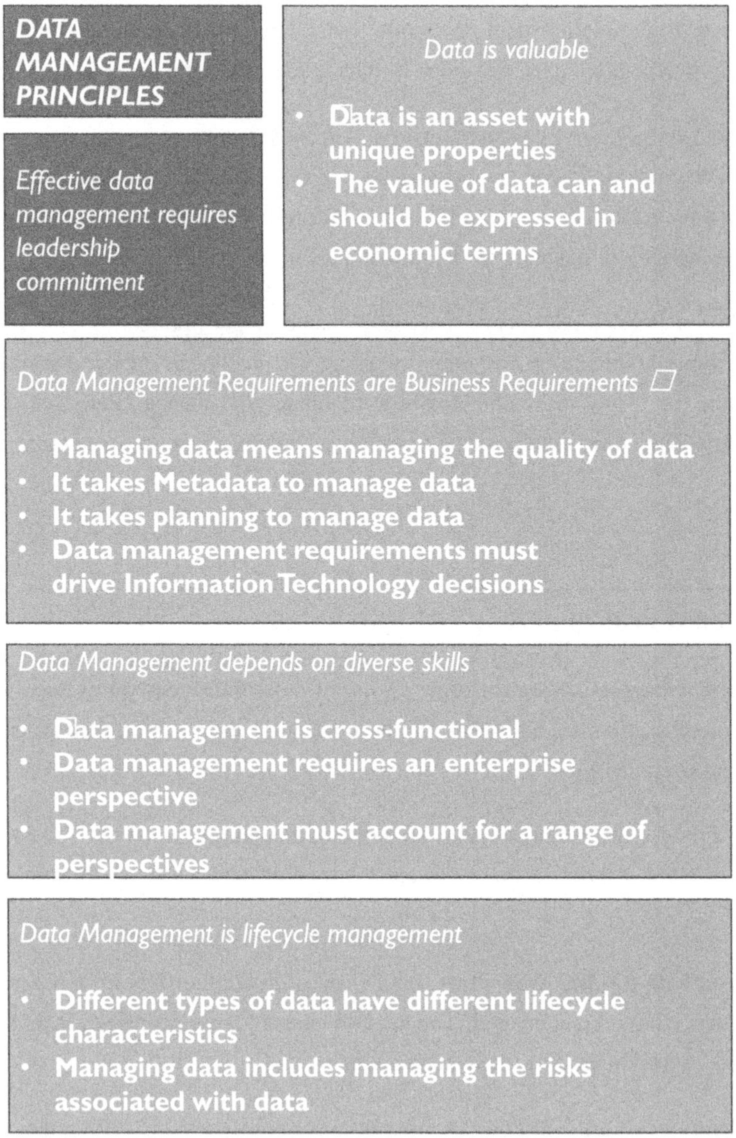

DATA MANAGEMENT PRINCIPLES

Effective data management requires leadership commitment

Data is valuable

- Data is an asset with unique properties
- The value of data can and should be expressed in economic terms

Data Management Requirements are Business Requirements ▱

- Managing data means managing the quality of data
- It takes Metadata to manage data
- It takes planning to manage data
- Data management requirements must drive Information Technology decisions

Data Management depends on diverse skills

- Data management is cross-functional
- Data management requires an enterprise perspective
- Data management must account for a range of perspectives

Data Management is lifecycle management

- Different types of data have different lifecycle characteristics
- Managing data includes managing the risks associated with data

Figure 1 Data Management Principles

- **It takes planning to manage data**: Even small organizations can have complex technical and business process landscapes. Data is created in many places and is moved between places for use. To coordinate work and keep the end results aligned requires planning from an architectural and process perspective.

- **Data management is cross-functional; it requires a range of skills and expertise**: A single team cannot manage all of an organization's data. Data management requires both technical and non-technical skills and the ability to collaborate.

- **Data management requires an enterprise perspective**: Data management has local applications, but it must be applied across the enterprise to be as effective as possible. This is one reason why data management and data governance are intertwined.

- **Data management must account for a range of perspectives**: Data is fluid. Data management must constantly evolve to keep up with the ways data is created and used and the data consumers who use it.

- **Data management is lifecycle management**: Data has a lifecycle and managing data requires managing its lifecycle. Because data begets more data, the data lifecycle itself can be very complex. Data management practices need to account for the data lifecycle.

- **Different types of data have different lifecycle characteristics**: And for this reason, they have different management requirements. Data management practices have to recognize these differences and be flexible enough to meet different kinds of data lifecycle requirements.

- **Managing data includes managing the risks associated with data**: In addition to being an asset, data also represents risk to an organization. Data can be lost, stolen, or misused. Organizations must consider the ethical implications of their uses of data. Data-related risks must be managed as part of the data lifecycle.

- **Data management requirements must drive Information Technology decisions**: Data and data management are deeply intertwined with information technology and information technology management. Managing data requires an approach that ensures technology serves, rather than drives, an organization's strategic data needs.

- **Effective data management requires leadership commitment**: Data management involves a complex set of processes that, to be effective, require coordination, collaboration, and commitment. Getting there requires not only management skills, but also the vision and purpose that come from committed leadership.

2.5 Data Management Challenges

Because data management has distinct characteristics derived from the properties of data itself, it also presents challenges in following these principles. Details of these challenges are discussed in Sections 2.5.1 through 2.5.13. Many of these challenges refer to more than one principle.

2.5.1 Data Differs from Other Assets[6]

Physical assets can be pointed to, touched, and moved around. They can be in only one place at a time. Financial assets must be accounted for on a balance sheet. However, data is different. Data is not tangible. Yet it is durable; it does not wear out, though the value of data often changes as it ages. Data is easy to copy and transport. But it is not easy to reproduce if it is lost or destroyed. Because it is not consumed when used, it can even be stolen without being gone. Data is dynamic and can be used for multiple purposes. The same data can even be used by multiple people at the same time – something that is impossible with physical or financial assets. Many uses of data beget more data. Most organizations must manage increasing volumes of data and the relation between data sets.

---

[6] This section derives from Redman, Thomas. *Data Quality for the Information Age* (1996) pp. 41-42, 232-36; and *Data Driven* (2008), Chapter One, "The Wondrous and Perilous Properties of Data and Information."

These differences make it challenging to put a monetary value on data. Without this monetary value, it is difficult to measure how data contributes to organizational success. These differences also raise other issues that affect data management, such as defining data ownership, inventorying how much data an organization has, protecting against the misuse of data, managing risk associated with data redundancy, and defining and enforcing standards for Data Quality.

Despite the challenges with measuring the value of data, most people recognize that data, indeed, has value. An organization's data is unique to itself. Were organizationally unique data (such as customer lists, product inventories, or claim history) to be lost or destroyed, replacing it would be impossible or extremely costly. Data is also the means by which an organization knows itself – it is a meta-asset that describes other assets. As such, it provides the foundation for organizational insight.

Within and between organizations, data and information are essential to conducting business. Most operational business transactions involve the exchange of information. Most information is exchanged electronically, creating a data trail. This data trail can serve purposes in addition to marking the exchanges that have taken place. It can provide information about how an organization functions.

Because of the important role that data plays in any organization, it needs to be managed with care.

2.5.2 Data Valuation

Value is the difference between the cost of a thing and the benefit derived from that thing. For some assets, like stock, calculating value is easy. It is the difference between what the stock cost when it was purchased and what it was sold for. But for data, these calculations are more complicated, because neither the costs nor the benefits of data are standardized.

Since each organization's data is unique to itself, an approach to data valuation needs to begin by articulating general cost and benefit categories that can be applied consistently within an organization. Sample categories include[7]:

- Cost of obtaining and storing data
- Cost of replacing data if it were lost
- Impact to the organization if data were missing
- Cost of risk mitigation and potential cost of risks associated with data
- Cost of improving data
- Benefits of higher quality data
- What competitors would pay for data
- What the data could be sold for
- Expected revenue from innovative uses of data

---

[7] While the DMBOK2 was preparing to go to press, another means of valuing data was in the news: Wannacry ransomware attack (17 May 2017) impacted more than 100K organizations in 150 countries. The culprits used the software to hold data hostage until victims paid ransom to get their data released. http://bit.ly/2tNoyQ7.

A primary challenge to data asset valuation is that the value of data is contextual (what is of value to one organization may not be of value to another) and often temporal (what was valuable yesterday may not be valuable today). That said, within an organization, certain types of data are likely to be consistently valuable over time. Take reliable customer information, for example. Customer information may even grow more valuable over time, as more data accumulates related to customer activity.

In relation to data management, establishing ways to associate financial value with data is critical, since organizations need to understand assets in financial terms in order to make consistent decisions. Putting value on data becomes the basis of putting value on data management activities.[8] The process of data valuation can also be used a means of change management. Asking data management professionals and the stakeholders they support to understand the financial meaning of their work can help an organization transform its understanding of its own data and, through that, its approach to data management.

2.5.3 Data Quality

Ensuring that data is of high quality is central to data management. Organizations manage their data because they want to use it. If they cannot rely on it to meet business needs, then the effort to collect, store, secure, and enable access to it is wasted. To ensure data meets business needs, they must work with data consumers to define these needs, including characteristics that make data of high quality.

Largely because data has been associated so closely with information technology, managing Data Quality has historically been treated as an afterthought. IT teams are often dismissive of the data that the systems they create are supposed to store. It was probably a programmer who first observed 'garbage in, garbage out' – and who no doubt wanted to let it go at that. But the people who want to use the data cannot afford to be dismissive of quality. They generally assume data is reliable and trustworthy, until they have a reason to doubt these things. Once they lose trust, it is difficult to regain it.

Most uses of data involve learning from it in order to apply that learning and create value. Examples include understanding customer habits in order to improve a product or service and assessing organizational performance or market trends in order to develop a better business strategy, etc. Poor quality data will have a negative impact on these decisions.

As importantly, poor quality data is simply costly to any organization. Estimates differ, but experts think organizations spend between 10-30% of revenue handling data quality issues. IBM estimated the cost of poor quality data in the US in 2016 was $3.1 Trillion.[9] Many of the costs of poor quality data are hidden, indirect, and therefore hard to measure. Others, like fines, are direct and easy to calculate. Costs come from:

- Scrap and rework
- Work-arounds and hidden correction processes

---

[8] For case studies and examples, see Aiken and Billings, *Monetizing Data Management* (2014).

[9] Reported in Redman, Thomas. "Bad Data Costs U.S. $3 Trillion per Year." Harvard Business Review. 22 September 2016. https://hbr.org/2016/09/bad-data-costs-the-u-s-3-trillion-per-year.

- Organizational inefficiencies or low productivity
- Organizational conflict
- Low job satisfaction
- Customer dissatisfaction
- Opportunity costs, including inability to innovate
- Compliance costs or fines
- Reputational costs

The corresponding benefits of high quality data include:

- Improved customer experience
- Higher productivity
- Reduced risk
- Ability to act on opportunities
- Increased revenue
- Competitive advantage gained from insights on customers, products, processes, and opportunities

As these costs and benefits imply, managing Data Quality is not a one-time job. Producing high quality data requires planning, commitment, and a mindset that builds quality into processes and systems. All data management functions can influence Data Quality, for good or bad, so all of them must account for it as they execute their work. (See Chapter 13).

2.5.4 Planning for Better Data

As stated in the chapter introduction, deriving value from data does not happen by accident. It requires planning in many forms. It starts with the recognition that organizations can control how they obtain and create data. If they view data as a product that they create, they will make better decisions about it throughout its lifecycle. These decisions require systems thinking because they involve:

- The ways data connects business processes that might otherwise be seen as separate
- The relationship between business processes and the technology that supports them
- The design and architecture of systems and the data they produce and store
- The ways data might be used to advance organizational strategy

Planning for better data requires a strategic approach to architecture, modeling, and other design functions. It also depends on strategic collaboration between business and IT leadership. And, of course, it depends on the ability to execute effectively on individual projects.

The challenge is that there are usually organizational pressures, as well as the perennial pressures of time and money, that get in the way of better planning. Organizations must balance long- and short-term goals as they execute their strategies. Having clarity about the trade-offs leads to better decisions.

2.5.5 Metadata and Data Management

Organizations require reliable Metadata to manage data as an asset. Metadata in this sense should be understood comprehensively. It includes not only the business, technical, and operational Metadata described in Chapter 12, but also the Metadata embedded in Data Architecture, data models, data security requirements, data integration standards, and data operational processes. (See Chapters 4 – 11.)

Metadata describes what data an organization has, what it represents, how it is classified, where it came from, how it moves within the organization, how it evolves through use, who can and cannot use it, and whether it is of high quality. Data is abstract. Definitions and other descriptions of context enable it to be understood. They make data, the data lifecycle, and the complex systems that contain data comprehensible.

The challenge is that Metadata is a form of data and needs to be managed as such. Organizations that do not manage their data well generally do not manage their Metadata at all. Metadata management often provides a starting point for improvements in data management overall.

2.5.6 Data Management is Cross-functional

Data management is a complex process. Data is managed in different places within an organization by teams that have responsibility for different phases of the data lifecycle. Data management requires design skills to plan for systems, highly technical skills to administer hardware and build software, data analysis skills to understand issues and problems, analytic skills to interpret data, language skills to bring consensus to definitions and models, as well as strategic thinking to see opportunities to serve customers and meet goals.

The challenge is getting people with this range of skills and perspectives to recognize how the pieces fit together so that they collaborate well as they work toward common goals.

2.5.7 Establishing an Enterprise Perspective

Managing data requires understanding the scope and range of data within an organization. Data is one of the 'horizontals' of an organization. It moves across verticals, such as sales, marketing, and operations… Or at least it should. Data is not only unique to an organization; sometimes it is unique to a department or other sub-part of an organization. Because data is often viewed simply as a by-product of operational processes (for example, sales transaction records are the by-product of the selling process), it is not always planned for beyond the immediate need.

Even within an organization, data can be disparate. Data originates in multiple places within an organization. Different departments may have different ways of representing the same concept (e.g., customer, product, vendor). As anyone involved in a data integration or Master Data Management project can testify, subtle (or blatant) differences in representational choices present challenges in managing data across an organization. At the same time, stakeholders assume that an organization's data should be coherent, and a goal of managing data is to make it fit together in common sense ways so that it is usable by a wide range of data consumers.

One reason data governance has become increasingly important is to help organizations make decisions about data across verticals. (See Chapter 3.)

2.5.8 Accounting for Other Perspectives

Today's organizations use data that they create internally, as well as data that they acquire from external sources. They have to account for different legal and compliance requirements across national and industry lines. People who create data often forget that someone else will use that data later. Knowledge of the potential uses of data enables better planning for the data lifecycle and, with that, for better quality data. Data can also be misused. Accounting for this risk reduces the likelihood of misuse.

2.5.9 The Data Lifecycle

Like other assets, data has a lifecycle. To effectively manage data assets, organizations need to understand and plan for the data lifecycle. Well-managed data is managed strategically, with a vision of how the organization will use its data. A strategic organization will define not only its data content requirements, but also its data management requirements. These include policies and expectations for use, quality, controls, and security; an enterprise approach to architecture and design; and a sustainable approach to both infrastructure and software development.

The data lifecycle is based on the product lifecycle. It should not be confused with the systems development lifecycle. Conceptually, the data lifecycle is easy to describe (see Figure 2). It includes processes that create or obtain data, those that move, transform, and store it and enable it to be maintained and shared, and those that use or apply it, as well as those that dispose of it.[10] Throughout its lifecycle, data may be cleansed, transformed, merged, enhanced, or aggregated. As data is used or enhanced, new data is often created, so the lifecycle has internal iterations that are not shown on the diagram. Data is rarely static. Managing data involves a set of interconnected processes aligned with the data lifecycle.

The specifics of the data lifecycle within a given organization can be quite complicated, because data not only has a lifecycle, it also has lineage (i.e., a pathway along which it moves from its point of origin to its point of usage, sometimes called the *data chain*). Understanding the data lineage requires documenting the origin of data sets, as well as their movement and transformation through systems where they are accessed and used. Lifecycle and lineage intersect and can be understood in relation to each other. The better an organization understands the lifecycle and lineage of its data, the better able it will be to manage its data.

The focus of data management on the data lifecycle has several important implications:

- **Creation and usage are the most critical points in the data lifecycle**: Data management must be executed with an understanding of how data is produced, or obtained, as well as how data is used. It costs money to produce data. Data is valuable only when it is consumed or applied. (See Chapters 5, 6, 8, 11, and 14.)

---

[10] See McGilvray (2008) and English (1999) for information on the product lifecycle and data.

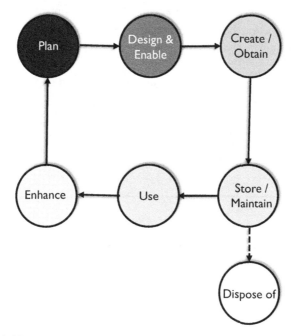

Figure 2 Data Lifecycle Key Activities

- **Data Quality must be managed throughout the data lifecycle**: Data Quality Management is central to data management. Low quality data represents cost and risk, rather than value. Organizations often find it challenging to manage the quality of data because, as described previously, data is often created as a by-product or operational processes and organizations often do not set explicit standards for quality. Because the quality of quality can be impacted by a range of lifecycle events, quality must be planned for as part of the data lifecycle (see Chapter 13).

- **Metadata Quality must be managed through the data lifecycle**: Because Metadata is a form of data, and because organizations rely on it to manage other data, Metadata quality must be managed in the same way as the quality of other data (see Chapter 12).

- **Data Security must be managed throughout the data lifecycle**: Data management also includes ensuring that data is secure and that risks associated with data are mitigated. Data that requires protection must be protected throughout its lifecycle, from creation to disposal (see Chapter 7 Data Security).

- **Data Management efforts should focus on the most critical data**: Organizations produce a lot of data, a large portion of which is never actually used. Trying to manage every piece of data is not possible. Lifecycle management requires focusing on an organization's most critical data and minimizing data ROT (Data that is Redundant, Obsolete, Trivial) (Aiken, 2014).

2.5.10 Different Types of Data

Managing data is made more complicated by the fact that there are different types of data that have different lifecycle management requirements. Any management system needs to classify the objects that are managed. Data can be classified by type of data (e.g., transactional data, Reference Data, Master Data, Metadata; alternatively category data, resource data, event data, detailed transaction data) or by content (e.g., data domains, subject areas) or by format or by the level of protection the data requires. Data can also be classified by how and where it is stored or accessed. (See Chapters 5 and 10.)

Because different types of data have different requirements, are associated with different risks, and play different roles within an organization, many of the tools of data management are focused on aspects of classification and control (Bryce, 2005). For example, Master Data has different uses and consequently different management requirements than does transactional data. (See Chapters 9, 10, 12, and 14.)

2.5.11 Data and Risk

Data not only represents value, it also represents risk. Low quality data (inaccurate, incomplete, or out-of-date) obviously represents risk because its information is not right. But data is also risky because it can be misunderstood and misused.

Organizations get the most value from the highest quality data – available, relevant, complete, accurate, consistent, timely, usable, meaningful, and understood. Yet, for many important decisions, we have information gaps – the difference between what we know and what we need to know to make an effective decision. Information gaps represent enterprise liabilities with potentially profound impacts on operational effectiveness and profitability. Organizations that recognize the value of high quality data can take concrete, proactive steps to improve the quality and usability of data and information within regulatory and ethical cultural frameworks.

The increased role of information as an organizational asset across all sectors has led to an increased focus by regulators and legislators on the potential uses and abuses of information. From Sarbanes-Oxley (focusing on controls over accuracy and validity of financial transaction data from transaction to balance sheet) to Solvency II (focusing on data lineage and quality of data underpinning risk models and capital adequacy in the insurance sector), to the rapid growth in the last decade of data privacy regulations (covering the processing of data about people across a wide range of industries and jurisdictions), it is clear that, while we are still waiting for Accounting to put Information on the balance sheet as an asset, the regulatory environment increasingly expects to see it on the risk register, with appropriate mitigations and controls being applied.

Likewise, as consumers become more aware of how their data is used, they expect not only smoother and more efficient operation of processes, but also protection of their information and respect for their privacy. This means the scope of who our strategic stakeholders are as data management professionals can often be broader than might have traditionally been the case. (See Chapters 2 Data Handling Ethics and 7 Data Security.)

Increasingly, the balance sheet impact of information management, unfortunately, all too often arises when these risks are not managed and shareholders vote with their share portfolios, regulators impose fines or restrictions on operations, and customers vote with their wallets.

2.5.12 Data Management and Technology

As noted in the chapter introduction and elsewhere, data management activities are wide-ranging and require both technical and business skills. Because almost all of today's data is stored electronically, data management tactics are strongly influenced by technology. From its inception, the concept of data management has been deeply intertwined with management of technology. That legacy continues. In many organizations, there is ongoing tension between the drive to build new technology and the desire to have more reliable data – as if the two were opposed to each other instead of necessary to each other.

Successful data management requires sound decisions about technology, but managing technology is not the same as managing data. Organizations need to understand the impact of technology on data, in order to prevent technological temptation from driving their decisions about data. Instead, data requirements aligned with business strategy should drive decisions about technology.

2.5.13 Effective Data Management Requires Leadership and Commitment

The Leader's Data Manifesto (2017) recognized that an "organization's best opportunities for organic growth lie in data." Although most organizations recognize their data as an asset, they are far from being data-driven. Many don't know what data they have or what data is most critical to their business. They confuse data and information technology and mismanage both. They do not approach data strategically. And they underestimate the work involved with data management. These conditions add to the challenges of managing data and point to a factor critical to an organization's potential for success: committed leadership and the involvement of everyone at all levels of the organization.[11]

The challenges outlined here should drive this point home: Data management is neither easy nor simple. But because few organizations do it well, it is a source of largely untapped opportunity. To become better at it requires vision, planning, and willingness to change. (See Chapters 15-17.)

Advocacy for the role of Chief Data Officer (CDO) stems from a recognition that managing data presents unique challenges and that successful data management must be business-driven, rather than IT-driven. A CDO can lead data management initiatives and enable an organization to leverage its data assets and gain competitive advantage from them. However, a CDO not only leads initiatives. He or she must also lead cultural change that enables an organization to have a more strategic approach to its data.

2.6 Data Management Strategy

A strategy is a set of choices and decisions that together chart a high-level course of action to achieve high-level goals. In the game of chess, a strategy is a sequenced set of moves to win by checkmate or to survive by stalemate. A strategic *plan* is a high-level course of action to achieve high-level goals.

---

[11] The full text of *The Leader's Data Manifesto* can be found at: http://bit.ly/2sQhcy7.

A data strategy should include business plans to use information to competitive advantage and support enterprise goals. Data strategy must come from an understanding of the data needs inherent in the business strategy: what data the organization needs, how it will get the data, how it will manage it and ensure its reliability over time, and how it will utilize it.

Typically, a data strategy requires a supporting Data Management program strategy – a plan for maintaining and improving the quality of data, data integrity, access, and security while mitigating known and implied risks. The strategy must also address known challenges related to data management.

In many organizations, the data management strategy is owned and maintained by the CDO and enacted through a data governance team, supported by a Data Governance Council. Often, the CDO will draft an initial data strategy and data management strategy even before a Data Governance Council is formed, in order to gain senior management's commitment to establishing data stewardship and governance.

The components of a data management strategy should include:

- A compelling vision for data management

- A summary business case for data management, with selected examples

- Guiding principles, values, and management perspectives

- The mission and long-term directional goals of data management

- Proposed measures of data management success

- Short-term (12-24 months) Data Management program objectives that are SMART (specific, measurable, actionable, realistic, time-bound)

- Descriptions of data management roles and organizations, along with a summary of their responsibilities and decision rights

- Descriptions of Data Management program components and initiatives

- A prioritized program of work with scope boundaries

- A draft implementation roadmap with projects and action items

Deliverables from strategic planning for data management include:

- **A Data Management Charter**: Overall vision, business case, goals, guiding principles, measures of success, critical success factors, recognized risks, operating model, etc.

- **A Data Management Scope Statement**: Goals and objectives for some planning horizon (usually 3 years) and the roles, organizations, and individual leaders accountable for achieving these objectives.

- **A Data Management Implementation Roadmap**: Identifying specific programs, projects, task assignments, and delivery milestones (see Chapter 15).

The data management strategy should address all DAMA Data Management Framework Knowledge Areas relevant to the organization. (See Figure 5 Figure 5 The DAMA-DMBOK2 Data Management Framework (The DAMA Wheeland Sections 3.3 and 4.)

3. Data Management Frameworks

Data management involves a set of interdependent functions, each with its own goals, activities, and responsibilities. Data management professionals need to account for the challenges inherent in trying to derive value from an abstract enterprise asset while balancing strategic and operational goals, specific business and technical requirements, risk and compliance demands, and conflicting understandings of what the data represents and whether it is of high quality.

There is a lot to keep track of, which is why it helps to have a framework to understand the data management comprehensively and see relationships between its component pieces. Because the functions depend on one another and need to be aligned, in any organization, people responsible for the different aspects of data management need to collaborate if the organization is to derive value from its data.

Frameworks developed at different levels of abstraction provide a range of perspectives on how to approach data management. These perspectives provide insight that can be used to clarify strategy, develop roadmaps, organize teams, and align functions.

The ideas and concepts presented in the DMBOK2 will be applied differently across organizations. An organization's approach to data management depends on key factors such as its industry, the range of data it uses, its culture, maturity level, strategy, vision, and the specific challenges it is addressing. The frameworks described in this section provide some lenses through which to see data management and apply concepts presented in the DMBOK.

- The first two, the Strategic Alignment Model and the Amsterdam Information Model show high-level relationships that influence how an organization manages data.

- The DAMA DMBOK Framework (The DAMA Wheel, Hexagon, and Context Diagram) describes Data Management Knowledge Areas, as defined by DAMA, and explains how their visual representation within the DMBOK.

- The final two take the DAMA Wheel as a starting point and rearrange the pieces in order to better understand and describe the relationships between them.

3.1 Strategic Alignment Model

The Strategic Alignment Model (Henderson and Venkatraman, 1999) abstracts the fundamental drivers for any approach to data management. At its center is the relationship between data and information. Information is most often associated with business strategy and the operational use of data. Data is associated with information technology and processes which support physical management of systems that make data accessible for use. Surrounding this concept are the four fundamental domains of strategic choice: business strategy, information technology strategy, organizational infrastructure and processes, and information technology infrastructure and processes.

The fully articulated Strategic Alignment Model is more complex than is illustrated in Figure 3. Each of the corner hexagons has its own underlying dimensions. For example, within both Business and IT strategy, there is a need to account for scope, competencies, and governance. Operations must account for infrastructure, processes, and skills. The relationships between the pieces help an organization understand both the strategic fit of the different components and the functional integration of the pieces. Even the high-level depiction of the model is useful in understanding the organizational factors that influence decisions about data and data management.

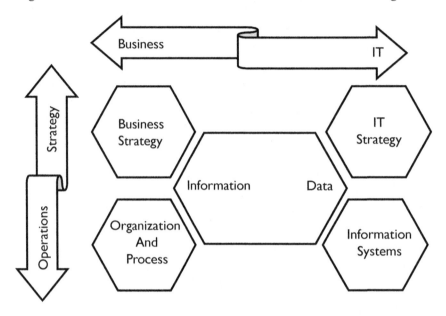

Figure 3 Strategic Alignment Model[12]

3.2 The Amsterdam Information Model

The Amsterdam Information Model, like the Strategic Alignment Model, takes a strategic perspective on business and IT alignment (Abcouwer, Maes, and Truijens, 1997),[13] Known as the 9-cell, it recognizes a middle layer that focuses on structure and tactics, including planning and architecture. Moreover, it recognizes the necessity of information communication (expressed as the information governance and data quality pillar in Figure 4).

The creators of both the SAM and AIM frameworks describe in detail the relation between the components, from both a horizontal (Business / IT strategy) and vertical (Business Strategy / Business Operations) perspective.

---

[12] Adapted by Henderson and Venkatraman.

[13] See also: Business IT Alignment Blog, *The Amsterdam Information Model (AIM) 9-Cells* (posted 2010-12-08). https://businessitalignment.wordpress.com/tag/amsterdam-information-model/ *Frameworks for IT Management*, Chapter 13. Van Haren Publishing, 2006. http://bit.ly/2sq2Ow1.

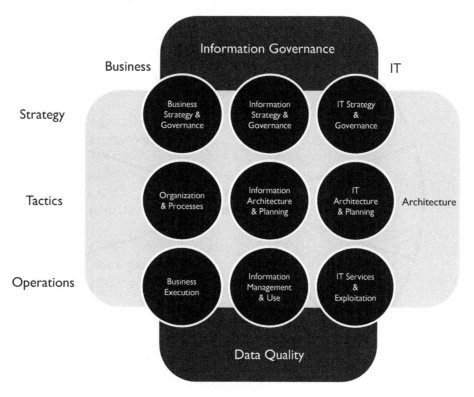

Figure 4 Amsterdam Information Model[14]

3.3 The DAMA-DMBOK Framework

The DAMA-DMBOK Framework goes into more depth about the Knowledge Areas that make up the overall scope of data management. Three visuals depict DAMA's Data Management Framework:

- The DAMA Wheel (Figure 5)
- The Environmental Factors hexagon (Figure 6)
- The Knowledge Area Context Diagram (Figure 7)

The DAMA Wheel defines the Data Management Knowledge Areas. It places data governance at the center of data management activities, since governance is required for consistency within and balance between the functions. The other Knowledge Areas (Data Architecture, Data Modeling, etc.) are balanced around the Wheel. They are all necessary parts of a mature data management function, but they may be implemented at different times, depending on the requirements of the organization. These Knowledge Areas are the focus of Chapters 3 – 13 of the DMBOK2. (See Figure 5.)

The Environmental Factors hexagon shows the relationship between people, process, and technology and provides a key for reading the DMBOK context diagrams. It puts goals and principles at the center, since these provide guidance for how people should execute activities and effectively use the tools required for successful data management. (See Figure 6.)

---

[14] Adapted from Maas.

Figure 5 The DAMA-DMBOK2 Data Management Framework (The DAMA Wheel)

Figure 6 DAMA Environmental Factors Hexagon

The Knowledge Area Context Diagrams (See Figure 7) describe the detail of the Knowledge Areas, including detail related to people, processes and technology. They are based on the concept of a SIPOC diagram used for product management (Suppliers, Inputs, Processes, Outputs, and Consumers). Context Diagrams put activities at the center, since they produce the deliverables that meet the requirements of stakeholders.

Each context diagram begins with the Knowledge Area's definition and goals. Activities that drive the goals (center) are classified into four phases: Plan (P), Develop (D), Operate (O), and Control (C). On the left side (flowing into the activities) are the Inputs and Suppliers. On the right side (flowing out of the activities) are Deliverables and Consumers. Participants are listed below the Activities. On the bottom are Tools, Techniques, and Metrics that influence aspects of the Knowledge Area.

Lists in the context diagram are illustrative, not exhaustive. Items will apply differently to different organizations. The high-level role lists include only the most important roles. Each organization can adapt this pattern to address its own needs.

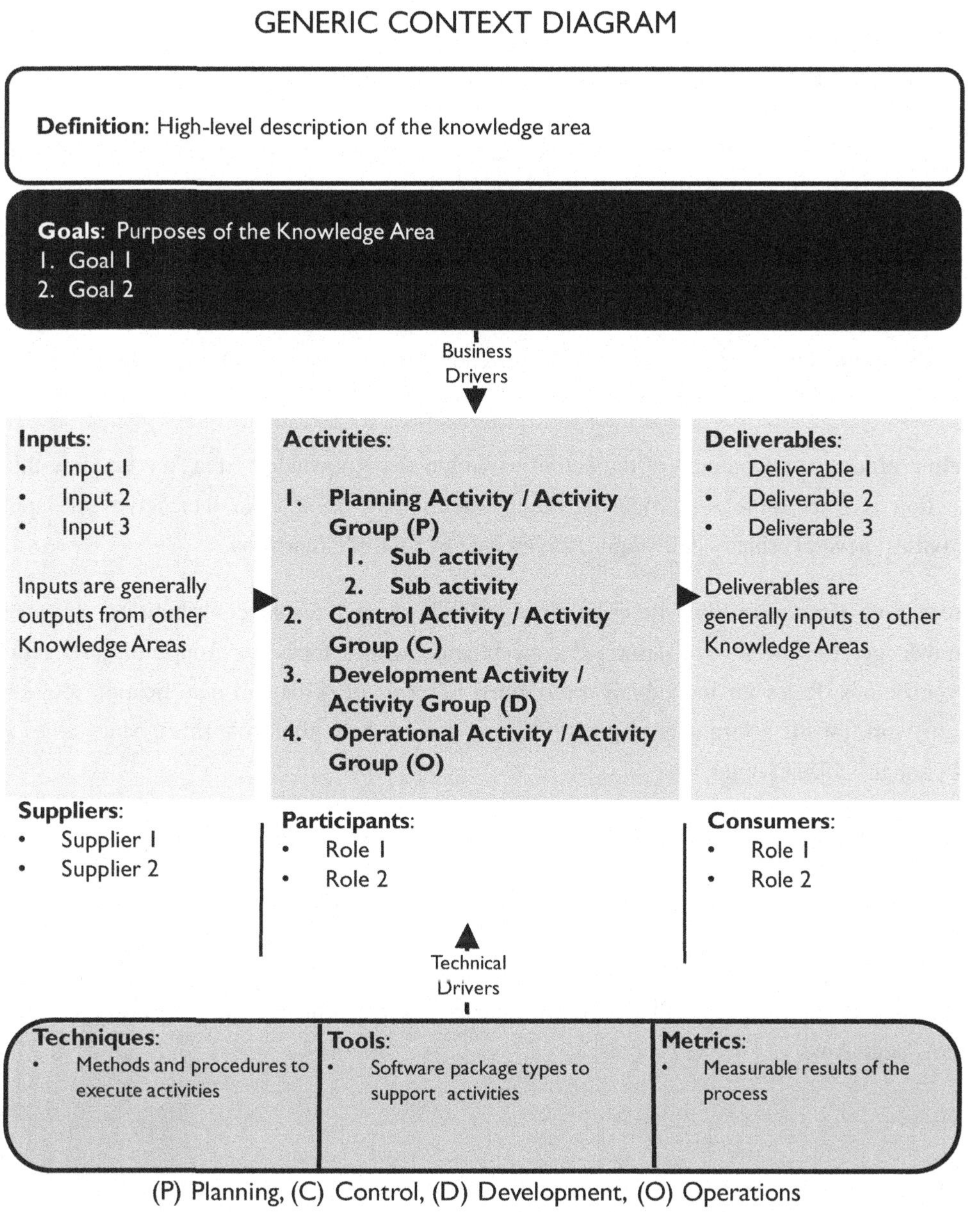

GENERIC CONTEXT DIAGRAM

Definition: High-level description of the knowledge area

Goals: Purposes of the Knowledge Area
1. Goal 1
2. Goal 2

Business Drivers

Inputs:
- Input 1
- Input 2
- Input 3

Inputs are generally outputs from other Knowledge Areas

Activities:

1. **Planning Activity / Activity Group (P)**
   1. Sub activity
   2. Sub activity
2. **Control Activity / Activity Group (C)**
3. **Development Activity / Activity Group (D)**
4. **Operational Activity / Activity Group (O)**

Deliverables:
- Deliverable 1
- Deliverable 2
- Deliverable 3

Deliverables are generally inputs to other Knowledge Areas

Suppliers:
- Supplier 1
- Supplier 2

Participants:
- Role 1
- Role 2

Consumers:
- Role 1
- Role 2

Technical Drivers

Techniques:
- Methods and procedures to execute activities

Tools:
- Software package types to support activities

Metrics:
- Measurable results of the process

(P) Planning, (C) Control, (D) Development, (O) Operations

Figure 7 Knowledge Area Context Diagram

The component pieces of the context diagram include:

1. **Definition**: This section concisely defines the Knowledge Area.

2. **Goals** describe the purpose the Knowledge Area and the fundamental principles that guide performance of activities within each Knowledge Area.

3. **Activities** are the actions and tasks required to meet the goals of the Knowledge Area. Some activities are described in terms of sub-activities, tasks, and steps. Activities are classified into four categories: Plan, Develop, Operate, and Control.

   a. **(P) Planning Activities** set the strategic and tactical course for meeting data management goals. Planning activities occur on a recurring basis.

   b. **(D) Development Activities** are organized around the system development lifecycle (SDLC) (analysis, design, build, test, preparation, and deployment).

   c. **(C) Control Activities** ensure the ongoing quality of data and the integrity, reliability, and security of systems through which data is accessed and used.

   d. **(O) Operational Activities** support the use, maintenance, and enhancement of systems and processes through which data is accessed and used.

4. **Inputs** are the tangible things that each Knowledge Area requires to initiate its activities. Many activities require the same inputs. For example, many require knowledge of the Business Strategy as input.

5. **Deliverables** are the outputs of the activities within the Knowledge Area, the tangible things that each function is responsible for producing. Deliverables may be ends in themselves or inputs into other activities. Several primary deliverables are created by multiple functions.

6. **Roles and Responsibilities** describe how individuals and teams contribute to activities within the Knowledge Area. Roles are described conceptually, with a focus on groups of roles required in most organizations. Roles for individuals are defined in terms of skills and qualification requirements. Skills Framework for the Information Age (SFIA) was used to help align role titles. Many roles will be cross-functional.[15] (See Chapter 16).

7. **Suppliers** are the people responsible for providing or enabling access to inputs for the activities.

8. **Consumers** those that directly benefit from the primary deliverables created by the data management activities.

9. **Participants** are the people that perform, manage the performance of, or approve the activities in the Knowledge Area.

---

[15] http://bit.ly/2sTusD0.

10. **Tools** are the applications and other technologies that enable the goals of the Knowledge Area.[16]

11. **Techniques** are the methods and procedures used to perform activities and produce deliverables within a Knowledge Area. Techniques include common conventions, best practice recommendations, standards and protocols, and, where applicable, emerging alternative approaches.

12. **Metrics** are standards for measurement or evaluation of performance, progress, quality, efficiency, or other effect. The metrics sections identify measurable facets of the work that is done within each Knowledge Area. Metrics may also measure more abstract characteristics, like improvement or value.

While the DAMA Wheel presents the set of Knowledge Areas at a high level, the Hexagon recognizes components of the structure of Knowledge Areas, and the Context Diagrams present the detail within each Knowledge Area. None of the pieces of the existing DAMA Data Management framework describe the relationship between the different Knowledge Areas. Efforts to address that question have resulted in reformulations of the DAMA Framework, which are described in the next two sections.

3.4 DMBOK Pyramid (Aiken)

If asked, many organizations would say that they want to get the most of out of their data – they are striving for that golden pyramid of advanced practices (data mining, analytics, etc.). But that pyramid is only the top of a larger structure, a pinnacle on a foundation. Most organizations do not have the luxury of defining a data management strategy before they start having to manage data. Instead, they build toward that capability, most times under less than optimal conditions.

Peter Aiken's framework uses the DMBOK functional areas to describe the situation in which many organizations find themselves. An organization can use it to define a way forward to a state where they have reliable data and processes to support strategic business goals. In trying to reach this goal, many organizations go through a similar logical progression of steps (See Figure 8):

- **Phase 1**: The organization purchases an application that includes database capabilities. This means the organization has a starting point for data modeling / design, data storage, and data security (e.g., let some people in and keep others out). To get the system functioning within their environment and with their data requires work on integration and interoperability.

- **Phase 2**: Once they start using the application, they will find challenges with the quality of their data. But getting to higher quality data depends on reliable Metadata and consistent Data Architecture. These provide clarity on how data from different systems works together.

- **Phase 3**: Disciplined practices for managing Data Quality, Metadata, and architecture require Data Governance that provides structural support for data management activities. Data Governance also enables execution of strategic initiatives, such as Document and Content Management, Reference Data

---

[16] DAMA International does not endorse specific tools or vendors.

Management, Master Data Management, Data Warehousing, and Business Intelligence, which fully enable the advanced practices within the golden pyramid.

- **Phase 4**: The organization leverages the benefits of well-managed data and advances its analytic capabilities.

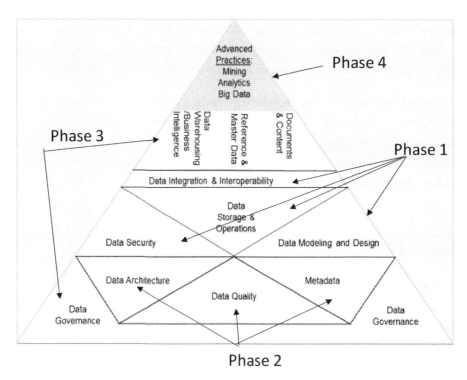

Figure 8 Purchased or Built Database Capability[17]

Aiken's pyramid draws from the DAMA Wheel, but also informs it by showing the relation between the Knowledge Areas. They are not all interchangeable; they have various kinds of interdependencies. The Pyramid framework has two drivers. First, the idea of building on a foundation, using components that need to be in the right places to support each other. Second, the somewhat contradictory idea that these may be put in place in an arbitrary order.

3.5 DAMA Data Management Framework Evolved

Aiken's pyramid describes how organizations evolve toward better data management practices. Another way to look at the DAMA Knowledge Areas is to explore the dependencies between them. Developed by Sue Geuens, the framework in Figure 9 recognizes that Business Intelligence and Analytic functions have dependencies on all other data management functions. They depend directly on Master Data and data warehouse solutions. But those, in turn, are dependent on feeding systems and applications. Reliable Data Quality, data design, and data interoperability practices are at the foundation of reliable systems and applications. In addition, data governance, which within this

---

[17] Golden Pyramid figure copyright Data BluePrint, used with permission.

model includes Metadata Management, data security, Data Architecture and Reference Data Management, provides a foundation on which all other functions are dependent.

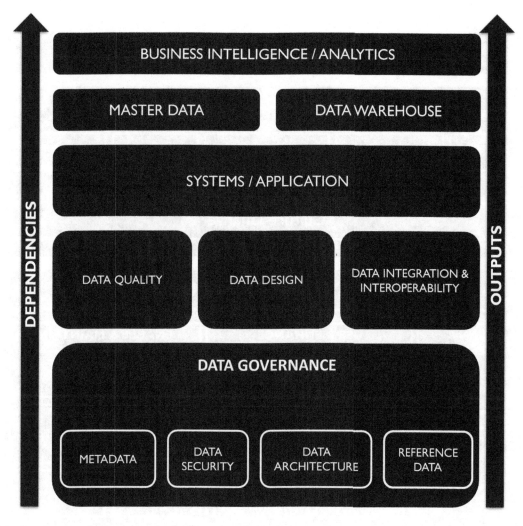

Figure 9 DAMA Functional Area Dependencies

A third alternative to DAMA Wheel is depicted in Figure 10. This also draws on architectural concepts to propose a set of relationships between the DAMA Knowledge Areas. It provides additional detail about the content of some Knowledge Areas in order to clarify these relationships.

The framework starts with the guiding purpose of data management: To enable organizations to get value from their data assets as they do from other assets. Deriving value requires lifecycle management, so data management functions related to the data lifecycle are depicted in the center of the diagram. These include planning and designing for reliable, high quality data; establishing processes and functions through which data can be enabled for use and also maintained; and, finally, using the data in various types of analysis and through those processes, enhancing its value.

The lifecycle management section depicts the data management design and operational functions (modeling, architecture, storage and operations, etc.) that are required to support traditional uses of data (Business Intelligence, document and content management). It also recognizes emerging data management functions (Big Data storage) that support emerging uses of data (Data Science, predictive analytics, etc.). In cases where data is truly managed as an asset, organizations may be able to get direct value from their data by selling it to other organizations (data monetization).

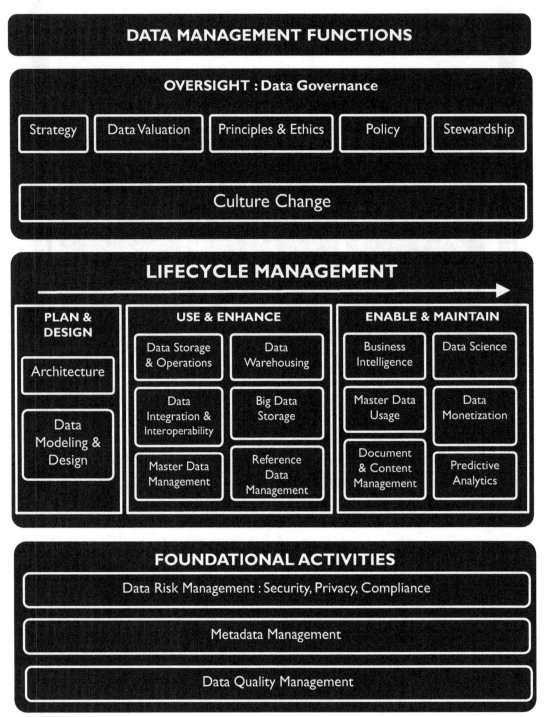

Figure 10 DAMA Data Management Function Framework

Organizations that focus only on direct lifecycle functions will not get as much value from their data as those that support the data lifecycle through foundational and oversight activities. Foundational activities, like data risk management, Metadata, and Data Quality management, span the data lifecycle. They enable better design decisions and make data easier to use. If these are executed well, data is less expensive to maintain, data consumers have more confidence in it, and the opportunities for using it expand.

To successfully support data production and use and to ensure that foundational activities are executed with discipline, many organizations establish oversight in the form of data governance. A data governance program enables an organization to be data-driven, by putting in place the strategy and supporting principles, policies, and stewardship practices that ensure the organization recognizes and acts on opportunities to get value from its data. A data governance program should also engage in organizational change management activities to educate the organization and encourage behaviors that enable strategic uses of data. Thus, the necessity of culture change spans the breadth of data governance responsibilities, especially as an organization matures its data management practices.

The DAMA Data Management Framework can also be depicted as an evolution of the DAMA Wheel, with core activities surrounded by lifecycle and usage activities, contained within the strictures of governance. (See Figure 11.)

Core activities, including Metadata Management, Data Quality Management, and data structure definition (architecture) are at the center of the framework.

Lifecycle management activities may be defined from a planning perspective (risk management, modeling, data design, Reference Data Management) and an enablement perspective (Master Data Management, data technology development, data integration and interoperability, data warehousing, and data storage and operations).

Usages emerge from the lifecycle management activities: Master data usage, Document and content management, Business Intelligence, Data Science, predictive analytics, data visualization. Many of these create more data by enhancing or developing insights about existing data. Opportunities for data monetization may be identified as uses of data.

Data governance activities provide oversight and containment, through strategy, principles, policy, and stewardship. They enable consistency through data classification and data valuation.

The intention in presenting different visual depictions of the DAMA Data Management Framework is to provide additional perspective and to open discussion about how to apply the concepts presented in DMBOK. As the importance of data management grows, such frameworks become useful communications tools both within the data management community and between the data management community and our stakeholders.

4. DAMA and the DMBOK

While data management presents many challenges, few of them are new. Since at least the 1980s, organizations have recognized that managing data is central to their success. As our ability and desire to create and exploit data has increased, so too has the need for reliable data management practices.

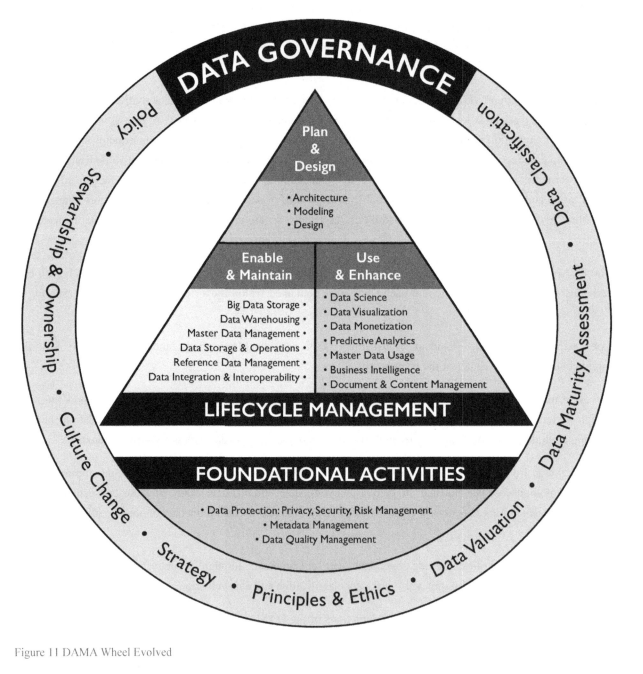

Figure 11 DAMA Wheel Evolved

DAMA was founded to address these challenges. The DMBOK, an accessible, authoritative reference book for data management professionals, supports DAMA's mission by:

- **Providing a functional framework** for the implementation of enterprise data management practices; including guiding principles, widely adopted practices, methods and techniques, functions, roles, deliverables and metrics.

- **Establishing a common vocabulary** for data management concepts and serving as the basis for best practices for data management professionals.

- **Serving as the fundamental reference guide** for the CDMP (Certified Data Management Professional) and other certification exams.

The DMBOK is structured around the eleven Knowledge Areas of the DAMA-DMBOK Data Management Framework (also known as the DAMA Wheel, see Figure 5). Chapters 3 – 13 are focused on Knowledge Areas. Each Knowledge Area chapter follows a common structure:

1. Introduction
    - Business Drivers
    - Goals and Principles
    - Essential Concepts
2. Activities
3. Tools
4. Techniques
5. Implementation Guidelines
6. Relation to Data Governance
7. Metrics

Knowledge Areas describe the scope and context of sets of data management activities. Embedded in the Knowledge Areas are the fundamental goals and principles of data management. Because data moves horizontally within organizations, Knowledge Area activities intersect with each other and with other organizational functions.

1. **Data Governance** provides direction and oversight for data management by establishing a system of decision rights over data that accounts for the needs of the enterprise. (Chapter 3)

2. **Data Architecture** defines the blueprint for managing data assets by aligning with organizational strategy to establish strategic data requirements and designs to meet these requirements. (Chapter 4)

3. **Data Modeling and Design** is the process of discovering, analyzing, representing, and communicating data requirements in a precise form called the *data model*. (Chapter 5)

4. **Data Storage and Operations** includes the design, implementation, and support of stored data to maximize its value. Operations provide support throughout the data lifecycle from planning for to disposal of data. (Chapter 6)

5. **Data Security** ensures that data privacy and confidentiality are maintained, that data is not breached, and that data is accessed appropriately. (Chapter 7)

6. **Data Integration and Interoperability** includes processes related to the movement and consolidation of data within and between data stores, applications, and organizations. (Chapter 8)

7. **Document and Content Management** includes planning, implementation, and control activities used to manage the lifecycle of data and information found in a range of unstructured media, especially documents needed to support legal and regulatory compliance requirements. (Chapter 9)

8. **Reference and Master Data** includes ongoing reconciliation and maintenance of core critical shared data to enable consistent use across systems of the most accurate, timely, and relevant version of truth about essential business entities. (Chapter 10)

9. **Data Warehousing and Business Intelligence** includes the planning, implementation, and control processes to manage decision support data and to enable knowledge workers to get value from data via analysis and reporting. (Chapter 11)

10. **Metadata** includes planning, implementation, and control activities to enable access to high quality, integrated Metadata, including definitions, models, data flows, and other information critical to understanding data and the systems through which it is created, maintained, and accessed. (Chapter 12)

11. **Data Quality** includes the planning and implementation of quality management techniques to measure, assess, and improve the fitness of data for use within an organization. (Chapter 13)

In addition to chapters on the Knowledge Areas, the DAMA-DMBOK contains chapters on the following topics:

- **Data Handling Ethics** describes the central role that data ethics plays in making informed, socially responsible decisions about data and its uses. Awareness of the ethics of data collection, analysis, and use should guide all data management professionals. (Chapter 2)

- **Big Data and Data Science** describes the technologies and business processes that emerge as our ability to collect and analyze large and diverse data sets increases. (Chapter 14.)

- **Data Management Maturity Assessment** outlines an approach to evaluating and improving an organization's data management capabilities. (Chapter 15)

- **Data Management Organization and Role Expectations** provide best practices and considerations for organizing data management teams and enabling successful data management practices. (Chapter 16)

- **Data Management and Organizational Change Management** describes how to plan for and successfully move through the cultural changes that are necessary to embed effective data management practices within an organization. (Chapter 17)

How a particular organization manages its data depends on its goals, size, resources, and complexity, as well as its perception of how data supports it overall strategy. Most enterprises do not perform all the activities described in each Knowledge Area. However, understanding the wider context of data management will enable organizations to make better decisions about where to focus as they work to improve practices within and across these related functions.

5. Works Cited / Recommended

Abcouwer, A. W., Maes, R., Truijens, J.: "Contouren van een generiek Model voor Informatiemanagement." Primavera Working Paper 97-07, 1997. http://bit.ly/2rV5dLx.

Adelman, Sid, Larissa Moss, and Majid Abai. *Data Strategy*. Addison-Wesley Professional, 2005. Print.

Aiken, Peter and Billings, Juanita. *Monetizing Data Management*. Technics Publishing, LLC, 2014. Print.

Aiken, Peter and Harbour, Todd. *Data Strategy and the Enterprise Data Executive*. Technics Publishing, LLC. 2017. Print.

APRA (Australian Prudential Regulation Authority). *Prudential Practice Guide CPG 234, Management of Security Risk in Information and Information Technology*. May 2013. http://bit.ly/2sAKe2y.

APRA (Australian Prudential Regulation Authority). *Prudential Practice Guide CPG 235, Managing Data Risk*. September 2013. http://bit.ly/2sVIFil.

Borek, Alexander et al. *Total Information Risk Management: Maximizing the Value of Data and Information Assets*. Morgan Kaufmann, 2013. Print.

Brackett, Michael. *Data Resource Design: Reality Beyond Illusion*. Technics Publishing, LLC. 2014. Print.

Bryce, Tim. *Benefits of a Data Taxonomy*. Blog 2005-07-11. http://bit.ly/2sTeU1U.

Chisholm, Malcolm and Roblyn-Lee, Diane. *Definitions in Data Management: A Guide to Fundamental Semantic Metadata*. Design Media, 2008. Print.

Devlin, Barry. *Business Unintelligence*. Technics Publishing, LLC. 2013. Print.

English, Larry. *Improving Data Warehouse and Business Information Quality: Methods For Reducing Costs And Increasing Profits*. John Wiley and Sons, 1999. Print.

Evans, Nina and Price, James. "Barriers to the Effective Deployment of Information Assets: An Executive Management Perspective." *Interdisciplinary Journal of Information, Knowledge, and Management* Volume 7, 2012. Accessed from http://bit.ly/2sVwvG4.

Fisher, Tony. *The Data Asset: How Smart Companies Govern Their Data for Business Success*. Wiley, 2009. Print. Wiley and SAS Business Ser.

Henderson, J.C., H Venkatraman, H. "Leveraging information technology for transforming Organizations." *IBM System Journal*. Volume 38, Issue 2.3, 1999. [1993 Reprint] http://bit.ly/2sV86Ay and http://bit.ly/1uW8jMQ.

Kent, William. *Data and Reality: A Timeless Perspective on Perceiving and Managing Information in Our Imprecise World*. 3d ed. Technics Publications, LLC, 2012. Print.

Kring, Kenneth L. *Business Strategy Mapping - The Power of Knowing How it All Fits Together*. Langdon Street Press (a division of Hillcrest Publishing Group, Inc.), 2009. Print.

Loh, Steve. *Data-ism: The Revolution Transforming Decision Making, Consumer Behavior, and Almost Everything Else*. HarperBusiness, 2015. Print.

Loshin, David. *Enterprise Knowledge Management: The Data Quality Approach*. Morgan Kaufmann, 2001. Print.

Maes, R.: "A Generic Framework for Information Management." PrimaVera Working Paper 99-02, 1999.

McGilvray, Danette. *Executing Data Quality Projects: Ten Steps to Quality Data and Trusted Information*. Morgan Kaufmann, 2008. Print.

McKnight, William. *Information Management: Strategies for Gaining a Competitive Advantage with Data*. Morgan Kaufmann, 2013. Print. The Savvy Manager's Guides.

Moody, Daniel and Walsh, Peter. "Measuring The Value Of Information: An Asset Valuation Approach." *European Conference on Information Systems (ECIS)*, 1999. http://bit.ly/29JucLO.

Olson, Jack E. *Data Quality: The Accuracy Dimension*. Morgan Kaufmann, 2003. Print.

Redman, Thomas. "Bad Data Costs U.S. $3 Trillion per Year." *Harvard Business Review*. 22 September 2016. Web.

Redman, Thomas. Data Driven: Profiting from Your Most Important Business Asset. *Harvard Business Review Press*. 2008. Print.

Redman, Thomas. *Data Quality: The Field Guide*. Digital Press, 2001. Print.

Reid, Roger, Gareth Fraser-King, and W. David Schwaderer. *Data Lifecycles: Managing Data for Strategic Advantage*. Wiley, 2007. Print.

Rockley, Ann and Charles Cooper. *Managing Enterprise Content: A Unified Content Strategy*. 2nd ed. New Riders, 2012. Print. Voices That Matter.

Sebastian-Coleman, Laura. *Measuring Data Quality for Ongoing Improvement: A Data Quality Assessment Framework*. Morgan Kaufmann, 2013. Print. The Morgan Kaufmann Series on Business Intelligence.

Simsion, Graeme. *Data Modeling: Theory and Practice*. Technics Publications, LLC, 2007. Print.

Surdak, Christopher. *Data Crush: How the Information Tidal Wave is Driving New Business Opportunities*. AMACOM, 2014. Print.

Waclawski, Janine. *Organization Development: A Data-Driven Approach to Organizational Change*. Pfeiffer, 2001. Print.

White, Stephen. *Show Me the Proof: Tools and Strategies to Make Data Work for the Common Core State Standards*. 2nd ed. Advanced Learning Press, 2011. Print.

CHAPTER 2

Data Handling Ethics

1. Introduction

Defined simply, *ethics* are principles of behavior based on ideas of right and wrong. Ethical principles often focus on ideas such as fairness, respect, responsibility, integrity, quality, reliability, transparency, and trust. Data handling ethics are concerned with how to procure, store, manage, use, and dispose of data in ways that are aligned with ethical principles. Handling data in an ethical manner is necessary to the long-term success of any organization that wants to get value from its data. Unethical data handling can result in the loss of reputation and customers, because it puts at risk people whose data is exposed. In some cases, unethical practices are also illegal.[18] Ultimately, for data management professionals and the organizations for which they work, data ethics are a matter of social responsibility.

The ethics of data handling are complex, but they center on several core concepts:

- **Impact on people**: Because data represents characteristics of individuals and is used to make decisions that affect people's lives, there is an imperative to manage its quality and reliability.

- **Potential for misuse**: Misusing data can negatively affect people and organizations, so there is an ethical imperative to prevent the misuse of data.

- **Economic value of data**: Data has economic value. Ethics of data ownership should determine how that value can be accessed and by whom.

Organizations protect data based largely on laws and regulatory requirements. Nevertheless, because data represents people (customers, employees, patients, vendors, etc.), data management professionals should recognize that there are ethical (as well as legal) reasons to protect data and ensure it is not misused. Even data that does not directly represent individuals can still be used to make decisions that affect people's lives.

There is an ethical imperative not only to protect data, but also to manage its quality. People making decisions, as well as those impacted by decisions, expect data to be complete and accurate. From both a business and a technical perspective, data management professionals have an ethical responsibility to manage data in a way that reduces the

---

[18] HIPAA (Health Insurance Portability and Accountability Act) in the US, PIPEDA (Personal Information Protection and Electronic Documents Act) in Canada, the EU General Data Protection Regulation (GDPR) and other data protection / information privacy laws describe obligations toward the handling of personal identifying data (e.g., name, addresses, religious affiliation, or sexual orientation) and privacy (access or restriction to this information).

risk that it may misrepresent, be misused, or be misunderstood. This responsibility extends across the data lifecycle, from creation to destruction of data.

Data Handling Ethics

Definition: Data handling ethics are concerned with how to procure, store, manage, interpret, analyze / apply and dispose of data in ways that are aligned with ethical principles, including community responsibility.

Goals:
1. To define ethical handling of data in the organization.
2. To educate staff on the organization risks of improper data handling.
3. To change/instill preferred culture and behaviors on handling data.
4. To monitor regulatory environment, measure, monitor, and adjust organization approaches for ethics in data.

Business Drivers

Inputs:
- Existing and Preferred Organization Ethics
- Business Strategy & Goals
- Organizational Structure
- Business Culture
- Regulations
- Existing Corporate Policies

Activities:
1. Review Data-Handling Practices (P)
2. Identify Principles, Practices, and Risk Factors (P)
3. Create and Ethical Data Handling Strategy
4. Address Practices Gaps (D)
5. Communicate and Educate Staff (D)
6. Monitor and Maintain Alignment (C)

Deliverables:
- Current Practices and Gaps
- Ethical Data Handling Strategy
- Communication Plan
- Ethics Training Program
- Ethical Corporate Statements on Data
- Awareness to Ethical Data Issues
- Aligned Incentives, KPIs, and Targets
- Updated Policies
- Ethical Data Handling Reporting

Suppliers:
- Executives
- Data Stewards
- Executive Data Stewards
- IT Executives
- Data Providers
- Regulators

Participants:
- Data Governance Bodies
- CDO / CIO
- Executives
- Coordinating Data Stewards
- Subject Matter Experts
- Change Managers
- DM Services

Consumers:
- Employees
- Executives
- Regulators

Technical Drivers

Techniques:
- Communication Plan Checklists
- Annual Ethics Statement Affirmations

Tools:
- Wikis, Knowledge Bases, Intranet Sites
- Microblogs, other internal communication tools

Metrics:
- Number of Employees Trained
- Compliance /non-compliance Incidents
- Corporate Executive Involvement

(P) Planning, (C) Control, (D) Development, (O) Operations

Figure 12 Context Diagram: Data Handling Ethics

Unfortunately, many organizations fail to recognize and respond to the ethical obligations inherent in data management. They may adopt a traditional technical perspective and profess not to understand the data; or they assume that if they follow the letter of the law, they have no risk related to data handling. This is a dangerous assumption.

The data environment is evolving rapidly. Organizations are using data in ways they would not have imagined even a few years ago. While laws codify some ethical principles, legislation cannot keep up with the risks associated with evolution of the data environment. Organizations must recognize and respond to their ethical obligation to protect data entrusted to them by fostering and sustaining a culture that values the ethical handling of information.

2. Business Drivers

Like W. Edward Deming's statements on quality, ethics means "doing it right when no one is looking." An ethical approach to data use is increasingly being recognized as a competitive business advantage (Hasselbalch and Tranberg, 2016). Ethical data handling can increase the trustworthiness of an organization and the organization's data and process outcomes. This can create better relationships between the organization and its stakeholders. Creating an ethical culture entails introducing proper governance, including institution of controls to ensure that both intended and resulting outcomes of data processing are ethical and do not violate trust or infringe on human dignity.

Data handling doesn't happen in a vacuum, and customers and stakeholders expect ethical behavior and outcomes from businesses and their data processes. Reducing the risk that data for which the organization is responsible will be misused by employees, customers, or partners is a primary reason for an organization to cultivate ethical principles for data handling. There is also an ethical responsibility to secure data from criminals (i.e., to protect against hacking and potential data breaches. (See Chapter 7.)

Different models of data ownership influence the ethics of data handling. For example, technology has improved the ability of organizations to share data with each other. This ability means organizations need to make ethical decisions about their responsibility for sharing data that does not belong to them.

The emerging roles of Chief Data Officer, Chief Risk Officer, Chief Privacy Officer, and Chief Analytics Officer are focused on controlling risk by establishing acceptable practices for data handling. But responsibility extends beyond people in these roles. Handling data ethically requires organization-wide recognition of the risks associated with misuse of data and organizational commitment to handling data based on principles that protect individuals and respect the imperatives related to data ownership.

3. Essential Concepts

3.1 Ethical Principles for Data

The accepted tenets of bioethics, which focus on preserving human dignity, provide a good general starting point for principles of data ethics. For example, the Belmont Principles for medical research may be adapted in Information Management disciplines (US-HSS, 1979).

- **Respect for Persons**: This principle reflects the fundamental ethical requirement that people be treated in a way that respects their dignity and autonomy as human individuals. It also requires that in cases where people have 'diminished autonomy', extra care be taken to protect their dignity and rights.

When we consider data as an asset, do we keep in mind that data also affects, represents, or touches people? Personal data is different from other raw 'assets', like oil or coal. Unethical use of personal data can directly influence people's interactions, employment opportunities, and place in the community. Do we design information systems in a way that limits autonomy or freedom of choice? Have we considered how processing data may affect people with mental or physical disabilities? Have we accounted for how they will access and utilize data? Does data processing take place on the basis of informed, valid consent?

- **Beneficence**: This principle has two elements: first, do not harm; second, maximize possible benefits and minimize possible harms.

The ethical principle of 'do not harm' has a long history in medical ethics, but also has clear application in the context of data and information management. Ethical data and information practitioners should identify stakeholders and consider the outcomes of data processing and work to maximize benefit and minimize risk of harm caused by the processes designed. Is a process designed in a way that assumes a zero-sum outcome rather than a win-win situation? Is data processing unnecessarily invasive and is there a less risky way to meet the requirements of the business need? Is the data handling in question lacking transparency in a way that might hide possible harm to people?

- **Justice**: This principle considers the fair and equitable treatment of people.

Some questions that might be asked regarding this principle: Are people or groups of people being treated unequally under similar circumstances? Does the outcome of a process or algorithm result in effects that disproportionately benefit or harm a certain group of people? Is machine learning being trained using datasets that contain data inadvertently reinforcing cultural prejudices?

The United States Department of Homeland Security's Menlo Report adapts the Belmont Principles to Information and Communication Technology Research, adding a fourth principle: Respect for Law and Public Interest (US-DHS, 2012).

In 2015, the European Data Protection Supervisor published an opinion on digital ethics highlighting the "engineering, philosophical, legal, and moral implications" of developments in data processing and Big Data. It called for a focus on data processing that upholds human dignity, and set out four pillars required for an information ecosystem that ensures ethical treatment of data (EDPS, 2015):

- Future-oriented regulation of data processing and respect for the rights to privacy and to data protection
- Accountable controllers who determine personal information processing
- Privacy conscious engineering and design of data processing products and services
- Empowered individuals

These principles map broadly to the principle set out in the Belmont Report, focusing on promoting human dignity and autonomy. The EDPS states that privacy is a fundamental human right. It challenges innovators to see dignity, privacy, and autonomy as a platform on which a sustainable digital environment is shaped, rather than an obstacle to development, and calls for transparency and communication with stakeholders.

Data Governance is a vital tool for ensuring these principles are considered in deciding who can do what with which data and under what circumstances processing is appropriate or necessary. The ethical impacts and risks of data processing on all stakeholders must be considered by practitioners, and managed in a similar manner to data quality.

3.2 Principles Behind Data Privacy Law

Public policy and law try to codify right and wrong based on ethical principles. But they cannot codify every circumstance. For example, privacy laws in the European Union, Canada, and the United States show different approaches to codifying data ethics. These principles can also provide a framework for organizational policy.

Privacy law is not new. Privacy and information privacy as concepts are firmly linked to the ethical imperative to respect human rights. In 1890, American legal scholars Samuel Warren and Louis Brandeis described privacy and information privacy as human rights with protections in common law that underpin several rights in the US constitution. In 1973, a code of Fair Information Practice was proposed, and the concept of information privacy as a fundamental right was reaffirmed in the US Privacy Act of 1974, which states that "the right to privacy is a personal and fundamental right protected by the Constitution of the United States".

In the wake of human rights violations during the Second World War, the European Convention of Human Rights (1950) established both the general right to privacy and the specific right to information privacy (or the right to protection of one's personal data) as human rights which are fundamental to upholding the right to Human Dignity. In 1980, the Organization for Economic Co-operation and Development (OECD) established Guidelines and Principles for Fair Information Processing that became the basis for the European Union's data protection laws.

OECD's eight core principles, the Fair Information Processing Standards, are intended to ensure that personal data is processed in a manner that respects individuals' right to privacy. They include: limitations on data collection; an expectation that data will be of high quality; the requirement that when data is collected, it is done for a specific purpose; limitations on data usage; security safeguards; an expectation of openness and transparency; the right of an individual to challenge the accuracy of data related to himself or herself; and accountability for organizations to follow the guidelines.

The OECD principles have since been superseded by principles underlying the General Data Protection Regulation of the EU, (GDPR, 2016). See Table 1.

Table 1 GDPR Principles

GDPR Principle	Description of Principle
Fairness, Lawfulness, Transparency	Personal data shall be processed lawfully, fairly, and in a transparent manner in relation to the data subject.
Purpose Limitation	Personal data must be collected for specified, explicit, and legitimate purposes, and not processed in a manner that is incompatible with those purposes.
Data Minimization	Personal data must be adequate, relevant, and limited to what is necessary in relation to the purposes for which they are processed.
Accuracy	Personal data must be accurate, and where necessary, kept up-to-date. Every reasonable step must be taken to ensure that personal data that are inaccurate, having regard to the purpose for which they are processed, are erased or rectified without delay.
Storage Limitation	Data must be kept in a form that permits identification of data subjects [individuals] for no longer than is necessary for the purposes for which the personal data are processed.
Integrity and Confidentiality	Data must be processed in a manner that ensures appropriate security of the personal data, including protection against unauthorized or unlawful processing and against accidental loss, destruction or damage, using appropriate technical or organizational measures.
Accountability	Data Controllers shall be responsible for, and be able to demonstrate compliance with [these principles].

These principles are balanced by and support certain qualified rights individuals have to their data, including the rights to access, rectification of inaccurate data, portability, the right to object to processing of personal data that may cause damage or distress, and erasure. When processing of personal data is done based on consent, that consent must be an affirmative action that is freely given, specific, informed, and unambiguous. The GDPR requires effective governance and documentation to enable and demonstrate compliance and mandates Privacy by Design.

Canadian privacy law combines a comprehensive regime of privacy protection with industry self-regulation. PIPEDA (Personal Information Protection and Electronic Documents Act) applies to every organization that collects, uses, and disseminates personal information in the course of commercial activities. It stipulates rules, with exceptions, that organizations must follow in their use of consumers' personal information. Table 2 describes statutory obligations based on PIPEDA.[19]

In Canada, the Federal Privacy Commissioner has the sole responsibility for handling privacy complaints against organizations. However, they fill an ombudsman role; their decisions are only recommendations (not legally binding and with no precedential value, even within the commissioner's office).

---

[19] http://bit.ly/2tNM53c.

Table 2 Canadian Privacy Statutory Obligations

PIPEDA Principle	Description of Principle
Accountability	An organization is responsible for personal information under its control and must designate an individual to be accountable for the organization's compliance with the principle.
Identifying Purposes	An organization must identify the purposes for which personal information is collected at or before the time the information is collected.
Consent	An organization must obtain the knowledge and consent of the individual for the collection, use, or disclosure of personal information, except where inappropriate.
Limiting Collection, Use, Disclosure, and Retention	The collection of personal information must be limited to that which is necessary for the purposes identified by the organization. Information shall be collected by fair and lawful means. Personal information shall not be used or disclosed for purposes other than those for which it was collected, except with the consent of the individual or as required by law. Personal information shall be retained only as long as necessary for the fulfillment of those purposes.
Accuracy	Personal information must be as accurate, complete, and up-to-date as is necessary for the purposes for which it is to be used.
Safeguards	Personal information must be protected by security safeguards appropriate to the sensitivity of the information.
Openness	An organization must make specific information about its policies and practices relating to the management of their personal information readily available to individuals.
Individual Access	Upon request, an individual shall be informed of the existence, use, and disclosure of his or her personal information, and shall be given access to that information. An individual shall be able to challenge the accuracy and completeness of the information and have it amended as appropriate.
Compliance Challenges	An individual shall be able to address a challenge concerning compliance with the above principles to the designated individual or individuals accountable for the organization's compliance.

In March 2012, the US Federal Trade Commission (FTC) issued a report recommending organizations design and implement their own privacy programs based on best practices described in the report (i.e., Privacy by Design) (FTC 2012). The report reaffirms the FTC's focus on Fair Information Processing Principles (see Table 3).

Table 3 United States Privacy Program Criteria

Principle	Description of Principle
Notice / Awareness	Data collectors must disclose their information practices before collecting personal information from consumers.
Choice / Consent	Consumers must be given options with respect to whether and how personal information collected from them may be used for purposes beyond those for which the information was provided.
Access / Participation	Consumers should be able to view and contest the accuracy and completeness of data collected about them.
Integrity / Security	Data collectors must take reasonable steps to assure that information collected from consumers is accurate and secure from unauthorized use.
Enforcement / Redress	The use of a reliable mechanism to impose sanctions for noncompliance with these fair information practices.

These principles are developed to embody the concepts in the OECD Fair Information Processing Guidelines, including emphasis on data minimization (reasonable collection limitation) and storage limitation (sound retention), accuracy, and the requirement that companies must provide reasonable security for consumer data. Other focuses for fair information practices include:

- Simplified consumer choice to reduce the burden placed on consumers
- The recommendation to maintain comprehensive data management procedure throughout the information lifecycle
- Do Not Track option
- Requirements for affirmative express consent
- Concerns regarding the data collection capabilities of large platform providers; transparency and clear privacy notices and policies
- Individuals' access to data
- Educating consumers about data privacy practices
- Privacy by Design

There is a global trend towards increasing legislative protection of individuals' information privacy, following the standards set by EU legislation. Laws around the world place different kinds of restrictions on the movement of data across international boundaries. Even within a multinational organization, there will be legal limits to sharing information globally. It is therefore important that organizations have policies and guidelines that enable staff to follow legal requirements as well as use data within the risk appetite of the organization.

3.3 Online Data in an Ethical Context

There are now emerging dozens of initiatives and programs designed to create a codified set of principles to inform ethical behaviors online in the United States (Davis, 2012). Topics include:

- **Ownership of data**: The rights to control one's personal data in relation to social media sites and data brokers. Downstream aggregators of personal data can embed data into deep profiles that individuals are not aware of.

- **The Right to be Forgotten**: To have information about an individual be erased from the web, particularly to adjust online reputation. This topic is part of data retention practices in general.

- **Identity**: Having the right to expect one identity and a correct identity, and to opt for a private identity.

- **Freedom of speech online**: Expressing one's opinions versus bullying, terror inciting, 'trolling,' or insulting.

3.4 Risks of Unethical Data Handling Practices

Most people who work with data know that it is possible to use data to misrepresent facts. The classic book *How to Lie with Statistics* by Darrell Huff (1954) describes a range of ways that data can be used to misrepresent facts while creating a veneer of factuality. Methods include judicious data selection, manipulation of scale, and omission of some data points. These approaches are still at work today.

One way to understand the implications of ethical handling of data is to examine practices that most people would agree are unethical. Ethical data handling entails a positive duty to handle data according to ethical principles such as trustworthiness. Ensuring data is trustworthy may include measuring is against Data Quality dimensions such as accuracy and timeliness. It also includes a base level of truthfulness and transparency – not using data to lie or mislead, and being transparent regarding the sources, uses, and intent behind an organization's data handling. The following scenarios describe unethical data practices that violate these principles among others.

3.4.1 Timing

It is possible to lie through omission or inclusion of certain data points in a report or activity based on timing. Equity market manipulation through 'end of day' stock trades can artificially raise a stock price at closing of the market giving an artificial view of the stock's worth. This is called market timing and is illegal.

Business Intelligence staff may be the first to notice anomalies. In fact, they are now seen as valuable players in the stock trading centers of the world recreating trading patterns looking for such problems as well as analyzing reports and reviewing and monitoring rules and alerts. Ethical Business Intelligence staff may need to alert appropriate governance or management functions to such anomalies.

3.4.2 Misleading Visualizations

Charts and graphs can be used to present data in a misleading manner. For instance, changing scale can make a trend line look better or worse. Leaving data points out, comparing two facts without clarifying their relationship, or ignoring accepted visual conventions (such as that the numbers in a pie chart representing percentages must add up to 100 and only 100), can also be used to trick people into interpreting visualizations in ways that are not supported by the data itself.[20]

3.4.3 Unclear Definitions or Invalid Comparisons

A US news outlet reported, based on 2011 US Census Bureau data, that 108.6 million people in the US were on welfare yet only 101.7 million people had full time jobs, making it seem that a disproportionate percentage of the overall population was on welfare.[21] Media Matters explained the discrepancy: The 108.6 million figure for the number of "people on welfare" comes from a Census Bureau's account ... of participation in means-tested

---

[20] How To Statistics (Website). *Misleading Graphs: Real Life Examples.* 24 January 2014. http://bit.ly/1jRLgRH See also io9 (Website). *The Most Useless and Misleading Infographics on the Internet.* http://bit.ly/1YDgURl See http://bit.ly/2tNktve Google "misleading data visualization" for additional examples. For counter examples, i.e., visuals with an ethical base, see Tufte (2001).

[21] As of 2015, the overall population of the US is estimated to be 321.4 million people. http://bit.ly/2iMlP58

programs, which include "anyone residing in a household in which one or more people received benefits" in the fourth quarter of 2011, thus including individuals who did not themselves receive government benefits. On the other hand, the "people with a full time job" figure ... included only individuals who worked, not individuals residing in a household where at least one person works.[22]

The ethical thing to do, in presenting information, is to provide context that informs its meaning, such as a clear, unambiguous definition of the population being measured and what it means to be "on welfare." When required context is left out, the surface of the presentation may imply meaning that the data does not support. Whether this effect is gained through the intent to deceive or through simply clumsiness, it is an unethical use of data.

It is also simply necessary, from an ethical perspective, not to misuse statistics.

Statistical 'smoothing' of numbers over a period could completely change perception of the number. 'Data mining snooping' is a recently coined term for a phenomenon in data mining statistical investigations where exhaustive correlations are performed on a data set, essentially over training a statistical model. Because of the behavior of 'statistical significance', it is reasonable to expect some statistically significant-looking results that are actually random results. The untrained can be misled. This is common in the financial and medical sectors (Jensen, 2000; ma.utexas.edu, 2012).[23]

3.4.4 Bias

Bias refers to an inclination of outlook. On the personal level, the term is associated with unreasoned judgments or prejudices. In statistics, bias refers to deviations from expected values. These are often introduced through systematic errors in sampling or data selection.[24] Bias can be introduced at different points in the data lifecycle: when data is collected or created, when it is selected for inclusion in analysis, through the methods by which it is analyzed, and in how the results of analysis are presented.

The ethical principle of justice creates a positive duty to be aware of possible biases that might influence data collection, processing, analysis, or interpretation. This is particularly important in the case of large-scale data processing that might disproportionately affect groups of people that have been historically subjected to prejudice or unfair treatment. Using data without addressing the ways in which bias may be introduced can compound prejudice while reducing transparency in process, giving the resulting outcomes the veneer of impartiality or neutrality when they are not neutral. There are several types of bias:

- **Data Collection for pre-defined result**: The analyst is pressured to collect data and produce results in order to reach a pre-defined conclusion, rather than as an effort to draw an objective conclusion.

---

[22] http://mm4a.org/2spKToU The example also demonstrates misleading visuals, as on the bar graph, the 108.6 million bar was shown as approximately 5 times larger than the 101.7 million column.

[23] See also numerous articles by W. Edwards Deming at: http://bit.ly/2tNnlZh

[24] http://bit.ly/2lOzJqU

- **Biased use of data collected**: Data may be collected with limited bias, but an analyst is pressured to use it to confirm a pre-determined approach. Data may even be manipulated to this end (i.e., some data may be discarded if it does not confirm the approach).

- **Hunch and search**: The analyst has a hunch and wants to satisfy that hunch, but uses only the data that confirms the hunch and does not account for other possibilities that the data may surface.

- **Biased sampling methodology**: Sampling is often a necessary part of data collection. But bias can be introduced by the method used to select the sample set. It is virtually impossible for humans to sample without bias of some sort. To limit bias, use statistical tools to select samples and establish adequate sample sizes. Awareness of bias in data sets used for training is particularly important.

- **Context and Culture**: Biases are often culturally or contextually-based, so stepping outside that culture or context is required for a neutral look at the situation.

Questions of bias are dependent on many factors, such as the type of data processing in question, the stakeholders involved, how data sets are populated, the business need being fulfilled, and the expected outcomes of the process. However, it is not always possible or even desirable to remove all bias. Business bias against poor customers (customers with whom no further business is sought) is a foundational piece to many scenarios built by business analysts; they are de-selected from samples, or ignored in the analysis. In such a case, analysts should document the criteria they used to define the population they are studying. In contrast, predictive algorithms determining 'criminal risk' of individuals or predictive policing sending resources to specific neighborhoods would have a much higher risk of violating ethical principles of justice or fairness, and should have greater precautions to ensure algorithmic transparency and accountability and to counter bias in data sets training any predictive algorithms.[25]

3.4.5 Transforming and Integrating Data

Data integration presents ethical challenges because data is changed as it moves from system to system. If data is not integrated with care, it presents risk for unethical or even illegal data handling. These ethical risks intersect with fundamental problems in data management, including:

- **Limited knowledge of data's origin and lineage**: If an organization does not know where data came from and how it has changed as it has moved between systems, then the organization cannot prove that the data represents what they claim it represents.

- **Data of poor quality**: Organizations should have clear, measurable standards for data quality, and should measure their data to confirm that it meets standards for quality. Without this confirmation, an organization cannot vouch for the data and data consumers may be at risk or put others at risk when they use the data.

---

[25] For examples of machine learning bias see Brennan (2015) and the Ford Foundation and ProPublica websites. In addition to bias, there is the problem of opaqueness. As predictive algorithms of learning machines become more complex, it is difficult to track the logic and lineage of their decisions. See Lewis and Monett (2017). http://bit.ly/1Om41ap; http://bit.ly/2oYmNRu.

- **Unreliable Metadata**: Data consumers depend on reliable Metadata, including consistent definitions of individual data elements, documentation of data's origin, and documentation of lineage (e.g., rules by which data is integrated). Without reliable Metadata, data may be misunderstood and potentially misused. In cases where data may move between organizations and especially where it may move across borders, Metadata should include tags that indicate its provenance, who owns it, and if it requires specific protection.

- **No documentation of data remediation history**: Organizations should also have auditable information related to the ways data has been changed. Even if the intention of data remediation is to improve the quality of data, doing so may be illegal. Data remediation should always follow a formal, auditable change control process.

3.4.6 Obfuscation / Redaction of Data

Obfuscating or redacting data is the practice of making information anonymous, or removing sensitive information. But obfuscation alone may not be sufficient to protect data if a downstream activity (analysis or combination with other datasets) can expose the data. This risk is present in the following instances:

- **Data aggregation**: When aggregating data across some set of dimensions, and removing identifying data, a dataset can still serve an analytic purpose without concern for disclosing personal identifying information (PII). Aggregations into geographic areas are a common practice (see Chapters 7 and 14).

- **Data marking**: Data marking is used to classify data sensitivity (secret, confidential, personal, etc.) and to control release to appropriate communities such as the public or vendors, or even vendors from certain countries or other community considerations.

- **Data masking**: Data masking is a practice where only appropriate submitted data will unlock processes. Operators cannot see what the appropriate data might be; they simply type in responses given to them, and if those responses are correct, further activities are permitted. Business processes using data masking include outsourced call centers, or sub-contractors who should only have partial access to information.

The use of extremely large data sets in Data Science analyses raises practical rather than merely theoretical concerns about the effectiveness of anonymization. Within large data sets, it is possible to combine data in ways enable individuals to be specifically identified, even if input data sets have been anonymized. The first concern when data lands in a data lake is to analyze it for sensitive data and apply accepted protection methods. These alone may not offer enough safeguard, however; this is why it is vital that organizations have strong governance and a commitment to ethical data handling. (See Chapter 14.)

3.5 Establishing an Ethical Data Culture

Establishing a culture of ethical data handling requires understanding existing practices, defining expected behaviors, codifying these in policies and a code of ethics, and providing training and oversight to enforce expected behaviors. As with other initiatives related to governing data and to changing culture, this process requires strong leadership.

Ethical handling of data obviously includes following the law, but also influences how data is analyzed and interpreted, as well as how it is leveraged internally and externally. An organizational culture that clearly values ethical behavior will not only have codes of conduct, but will ensure that clear communication and governance controls are in place to support employees with queries and proper escalation paths so that if employees become aware of unethical practices or ethical risk they are able to highlight the problem or stop the process without fear of retaliation. Improving an organization's ethical behavior regarding data requires a formal Organizational Change Management (OCM) process. (See Chapter 17.)

3.5.1 Review Current State Data Handling Practices

The first step to improvement is understanding the current state. The purpose of reviewing existing data handling practices is to understand the degree to which they are directly and explicitly connected to ethical and compliance drivers. This review should also identify how well employees understand the ethical implications of existing practices in building and preserving the trust of customers, partners, and other stakeholders. The deliverable from the review should document ethical principles that underlie the organization's collection, use, and oversight of data, throughout the data lifecycle, including data sharing activities.

3.5.2 Identify Principles, Practices, and Risk Factors

The purpose of formalizing ethical practices around data handling is to reduce the risk that data might be misused and cause harm to customers, employees, vendors, other stakeholders, or the organization as a whole. An organization trying to improve its practices should be aware of general principles, such as the necessity of protecting the privacy of individuals, as well as industry-specific concerns, such as the need to protect financial or health-related information.

An organization's approach to data ethics must align with legal and regulatory compliance requirements. For example, organizations that operate globally need to have a broad knowledge of the ethical principles at the foundation of the laws of the countries in which they operate, as well as specific knowledge of the agreements between countries. In addition, most organizations have specific risks, which may be related to their technology footprint, their rate of employee turnover, the means by which they collect customer data, or other factors.

Principles should be aligned with risks (bad things that can happen if the principles are not adhered to) and practices (the right ways of doing things so that risks are avoided). Practices should be supported by controls, as illustrated in the following example:

- **Guiding principle**: People have a right to privacy with respect to information about their health. Therefore, the personal health data of patients should not be accessed except by people who are authorized to access it as part of caring for patients.

- **Risk**: If there is wide access to the personal health data of patients, then information about individuals could become public knowledge, thereby jeopardizing their right to privacy.

- **Practice**: Only nurses and doctors will be allowed to access the personal health data of patients and only for purposes of providing care.

- **Control**: There will be an annual review of all users of the systems that contain personal health information of patients to ensure that only those people who need to have access do have access.

3.5.3 Create an Ethical Data Handling Strategy and Roadmap

After a review of current state and the development of a set of principles, an organization can formalize a strategy to improve its data handling practices. This strategy must express both ethical principles and expected behavior related to data, expressed in values statements and a code of ethical behavior. The component pieces of such a strategy include:

- **Values statements**: Values statements describe what the organization believes in. Examples might include truth, fairness, or justice. These statements provide a framework for ethical handling of data and decision-making.

- **Ethical data handling principles**: Ethical data handling principles describe how an organization approaches challenges presented by data; for example, how to respect the right of individuals to privacy. Principles and expected behaviors can be summarized in a code of ethics and supported through an ethics policy. Socialization of the code and policy should be included in the training and communications plan.

- **Compliance framework**: A compliance framework includes factors that drive organizational obligations. Ethical behaviors should enable the organization to meet compliance requirements. Compliance requirements are influenced by geographic and sector concerns.

- **Risk assessments**: Risk assessments identify the likelihood and the implications of specific problems arising within the organization. These should be used to prioritize actions related to mitigation, including employee compliance with ethical principles.

- **Training and communications**: Training should include review of the code of ethics. Employee must sign off that they are familiar with the code and the implications of unethical handling of data. Training needs to be ongoing; for example, through a requirement for an annual ethics statement affirmation. Communications should reach all employees.

- **Roadmap**: The roadmap should include a timeline with activities that can be approved by management. Activities will include execution of the training and communications plan, identification and remediation of gaps in existing practices, risk mitigation, and monitoring plans. Develop detailed statements that reflect the target position of the organization on the appropriate handling of data, include roles, responsibilities, and processes, and references to experts for more information. The roadmap should cover all applicable laws, and cultural factors.

- **Approach to auditing and monitoring**: Ethical ideas and the code of ethics can be reinforced through training. It is also advisable to monitor specific activities to ensure that they are being executed in compliance with ethical principles.

3.5.4 Adopt a Socially Responsible Ethical Risk Model

Data professionals involved in Business Intelligence, analytics, and Data Science are often responsible for data that describes:

- Who people are, including their countries of origin and their racial, ethnic, and religious characteristics
- What people do, including political, social, and potentially criminal activities
- Where people live, how much money they have, what they buy, who they talk with or text or send email to
- How people are treated, including outcomes of analysis, such as scoring and preference tracking that will tag them as ultimately privileged or not for future business

This data can be misused and counteract the principles underlying data ethics: respect for persons, beneficence, and justice.

Executing BI, analytics, and Data Science activities fairly requires an ethical perspective that looks beyond the boundaries of the organization for which people work and accounts for implications to the wider community. An ethical perspective is necessary not only because data can easily be misused but also because organizations have a social responsibility not to do harm with their data.

For example, an organization might set criteria for what it considers 'bad' customers in order to stop doing business with those individuals. But if that organization has a monopoly on an essential service in a particular geographic area, then some of those individuals may find themselves without that essential service and they will be in harm's way because of the organization's decision.

Projects that use personal data should have a disciplined approach to the use of that data. See Figure 13. They should account for:

- How they select their populations for study (arrow 1)
- How data will be captured (arrow 2)
- What activities analytics will focus on (arrow 3)
- How the results will be made accessible (arrow 4)

Within each area of consideration, they should address potential ethical risks, with a particular focus on possible negative effects on customers or citizens.

A risk model can be used to determine whether to execute the project. It will also influence how to execute the project. For example, the data will be made anonymous, the private information removed from the file, the security on the files tightened or confirmed, and a review of the local and other applicable privacy law reviewed with legal. Dropping customers may not be permitted under law if the organization is a monopoly in a jurisdiction, and citizens have no other provider options such as energy or water.

Because data analytics projects are complex, people may not see the ethical challenges. Organizations need to actively identify potential risks. They also need to protect whistleblowers who do see risks and raise concerns. Automated monitoring is not sufficient protection from unethical activities. People – the analysts themselves – need to reflect on possible bias. Cultural norms and ethics in the workplace influence corporate behavior – learn and use the ethical risk model. DAMA International encourages data professionals to take a professional stand, and present the risk situation to business leaders who may not have recognized the implications of particular uses of data and these implications in their work.

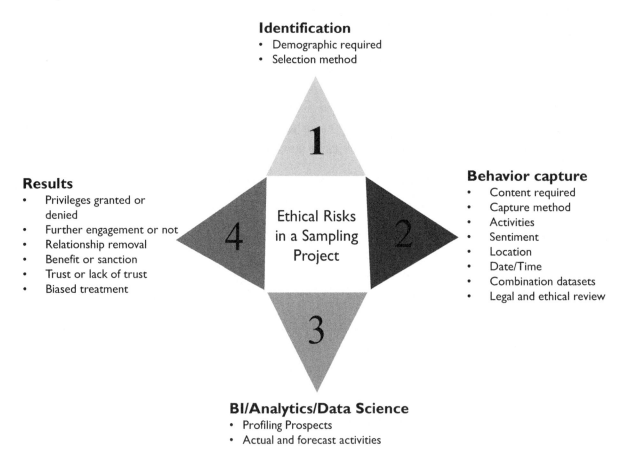

Figure 13 Ethical Risk Model for Sampling Projects

3.6 Data Ethics and Governance

Oversight for the appropriate handling of data falls under both data governance and legal counsel. Together they are required to keep up-to-date on legal changes, and reduce the risk of ethical impropriety by ensuring employees are aware of their obligations. Data Governance must set standards and policies for and provide oversight of data handling practices. Employees must expect fair handling, protection from reporting possible breaches, and non-interference in their personal lives. Data Governance has a particular oversight requirement to review plans and decisions proposed by BI, analytics and Data Science studies.

DAMA International's Certified Data Management Professional (CDMP) certification requires that data management professional subscribe to a formal code of ethics, including an obligation to handle data ethically for the sake of society beyond the organization that employs them.

---

4. Works Cited / Recommended

Blann, Andrew. *Data Handling and Analysis.* Oxford University Press, 2015. Print. Fundamentals of Biomedical Science.

Council for Big Data, Ethics, and Society (website) http://bit.ly/2sYAGAq.

Davis, Kord. *Ethics of Big Data: Balancing Risk and Innovation.* O'Reilly Media, 2012. Print.

European Data Protection Supervisor (EDPS). Opinion 4/2015 "Towards a new digital ethics: Data, dignity and technology." http://bit.ly/2sTFVlI.

Federal Trade Commission, US (FTC). *Federal Trade Commission Report Protecting Consumer Privacy in an Era of Rapid Change.* March 2012. http://bit.ly/2rVgTxQ and http://bit.ly/1SHOpRB.

GDPR REGULATION (EU) 2016/679 OF THE EUROPEAN PARLIAMENT AND OF THE COUNCIL of 27 April 2016 on the protection of natural persons with regard to the processing of personal data and on the free movement of such data, and repealing Directive 95/46/EC (General Data Protection Regulation).

Hasselbalch, Gry and Pernille Tranberg. *Data Ethics: The New Competitive Advantage.* Publishare. 2016.

Huff, Darrell. *How to Lie with Statistics.* Norton, 1954. Print.

Jensen, David. "Data Snooping, Dredging and Fishing: The Dark Side of Data Mining A SIGKDD99 Panel Report." *SIGKDD Explorations.* ACM SIGKDD, Vol. 1, Issue 2. January 2000. http://bit.ly/2tNThMK.

Johnson, Deborah G. *Computer Ethics.* 4th ed. Pearson, 2009. Print.

Kaunert, C. and S. Leonard, eds. *European Security, Terrorism and Intelligence: Tackling New Security Challenges in Europe.* Palgrave Macmillan, 2013. Print. Palgrave Studies in European Union Politics.

Kim, Jae Kwan and Jun Shao. *Statistical Methods for Handling Incomplete Data.* Chapman and Hall/CRC, 2013. Chapman and Hall/CRC Texts in Statistical Science.

Lake, Peter. *A Guide to Handling Data Using Hadoop: An exploration of Hadoop, Hive, Pig, Sqoop and Flume.* Peter Lake, 2015.

Lewis, Colin and Dagmar Monett. *AI and Machine Learning Black Boxes: The Need for Transparency and Accountability.* KD Nuggets (website), April 2017. http://bit.ly/2q3jXLr.

Lipschultz, Jeremy Harris. *Social Media Communication: Concepts, Practices, Data, Law and Ethics.* Routledge, 2014. Print.

Mayfield, M.I. *On Handling the Data.* CreateSpace Independent Publishing Platform, 2015. Print.

Mazurczyk, Wojciech et al. *Information Hiding in Communication Networks: Fundamentals, Mechanisms, and Applications.* Wiley-IEEE Press, 2016. Print. IEEE Press Series on Information and Communication Networks Security.

Naes, T. and E. Risvik eds. *Multivariate Analysis of Data in Sensory Science.* Volume 16. Elsevier Science, 1996. Print. Data Handling in Science and Technology (Book 16).

Olivieri, Alejandro C. et al, eds. *Fundamentals and Analytical Applications of Multi-way Calibration.* Volume 29. Elsevier, 2015. Print. Data Handling in Science and Technology (Book 29).

ProPublica (website). "Machine Bias: Algorithmic injustice and the formulas that increasingly influence our lives." May 2016 http://bit.ly/2oYmNRu.

Provost, Foster and Tom Fawcett. *Data Science for Business: What you need to know about data mining and data-analytic thinking*. O'Reilly Media, 2013. Print.

Quinn, Michael J. *Ethics for the Information Age*. 6th ed. Pearson, 2014. Print.

Richards, Lyn. *Handling Qualitative Data: A Practical Guide*. 3 Pap/Psc ed. SAGE Publications Ltd, 2014. Print.

Thomas, Liisa M. *Thomas on Data Breach: A Practical Guide to Handling Data Breach Notifications Worldwide*. LegalWorks, 2015. Print.

Tufte, Edward R. *The Visual Display of Quantitative Information*. 2nd ed. Graphics Pr., 2001. Print.

University of Texas at Austin, Department of Mathematics (website). *Common Misteaks Mistakes in Using Statistics*. http://bit.ly/2tsWthM. Web.

US Department of Health and Human Services. *The Belmont Report*. 1979. http://bit.ly/2tNjb3u (US-HSS, 2012).

US Department of Homeland Security. "Applying Principles to Information and Communication Technology Research: A Companion to the Department of Homeland Security Menlo Report". January 3, 2012. http://bit.ly/2rV2mSR (US-DHS, 1979).

Witten, Ian H., Eibe Frank and Mark A. Hall. *Data Mining: Practical Machine Learning Tools and Techniques*. 3rd ed. Morgan Kaufmann, 2011. Print. Morgan Kaufmann Series in Data Management Systems.

CHAPTER 3

Data Governance

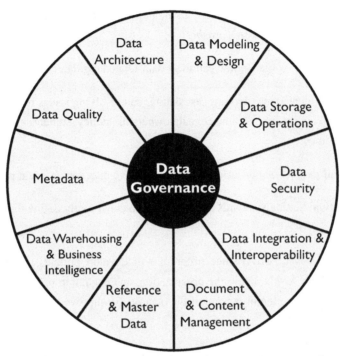

DAMA-DMBOK2 Data Management Framework

Copyright © 2017 by DAMA International

1. Introduction

Data Governance (DG) is defined as the exercise of authority and control (planning, monitoring, and enforcement) over the management of data assets. All organizations make decisions about data, regardless of whether they have a formal Data Governance function. Those that establish a formal Data Governance program exercise authority and control with greater intentionality (Seiner, 2014). Such organizations are better able to increase the value they get from their data assets.

The Data Governance function guides all other data management functions. The purpose of Data Governance is to ensure that data is managed properly, according to policies and best practices (Ladley, 2012). While the driver of data management overall is to ensure an organization gets value out of its data, Data Governance focuses on how decisions are made about data and how people and processes are expected to behave in relation to data. The scope and focus of a particular data governance program will depend on organizational needs, but most programs include:

- **Strategy**: Defining, communicating, and driving execution of Data Strategy and Data Governance Strategy

- **Policy**: Setting and enforcing policies related to data and Metadata management, access, usage, security, and quality

- **Standards and quality**: Setting and enforcing Data Quality and Data Architecture standards

- **Oversight**: Providing hands-on observation, audit, and correction in key areas of quality, policy, and data management (often referred to as *stewardship)*

- **Compliance**: Ensuring the organization can meet data-related regulatory compliance requirements

- **Issue management**: Identifying, defining, escalating, and resolving issues related to data security, data access, data quality, regulatory compliance, data ownership, policy, standards, terminology, or data governance procedures

- **Data management projects**: Sponsoring efforts to improve data management practices

- **Data asset valuation**: Setting standards and processes to consistently define the business value of data assets

To accomplish these goals, a Data Governance program will develop policies and procedures, cultivate data stewardship practices at multiple levels within the organization, and engage in organizational change management efforts that actively communicate to the organization the benefits of improved data governance and the behaviors necessary to successfully manage data as an asset.

For most organizations, adopting formal Data Governance requires the support of organizational change management (see Chapter 17), as well as sponsorship from a C-level executive, such as Chief Risk Officer, Chief Financial Officer, or Chief Data Officer.

The ability to create and share data and information has transformed our personal and economic interactions. Dynamic market conditions and a heightened awareness of data as a competitive differentiator are causing organizations to realign data management responsibilities. This type of change is clear in the financial, ecommerce, government, and retail sectors. Organizations increasingly strive to become data-driven – proactively considering data requirements as part of strategy development, program planning, and technology implementation. However, doing so often entails significant cultural challenges. Moreover, because culture can derail any strategy, Data Governance efforts need to include a cultural change component – again, supported by strong leadership.

To benefit from data as a corporate asset, the organizational *culture* must learn to value data and data management activities. Even with the best data strategy, data governance and data management plans will not succeed unless the organization accepts and manages change. For many organizations, cultural change is a major challenge. One of the foundational tenets of change management is that organizational change requires individual change (Hiatt and

Creasey, 2012). When data governance and data management demand significant behavioral changes, formal change management is required for success.

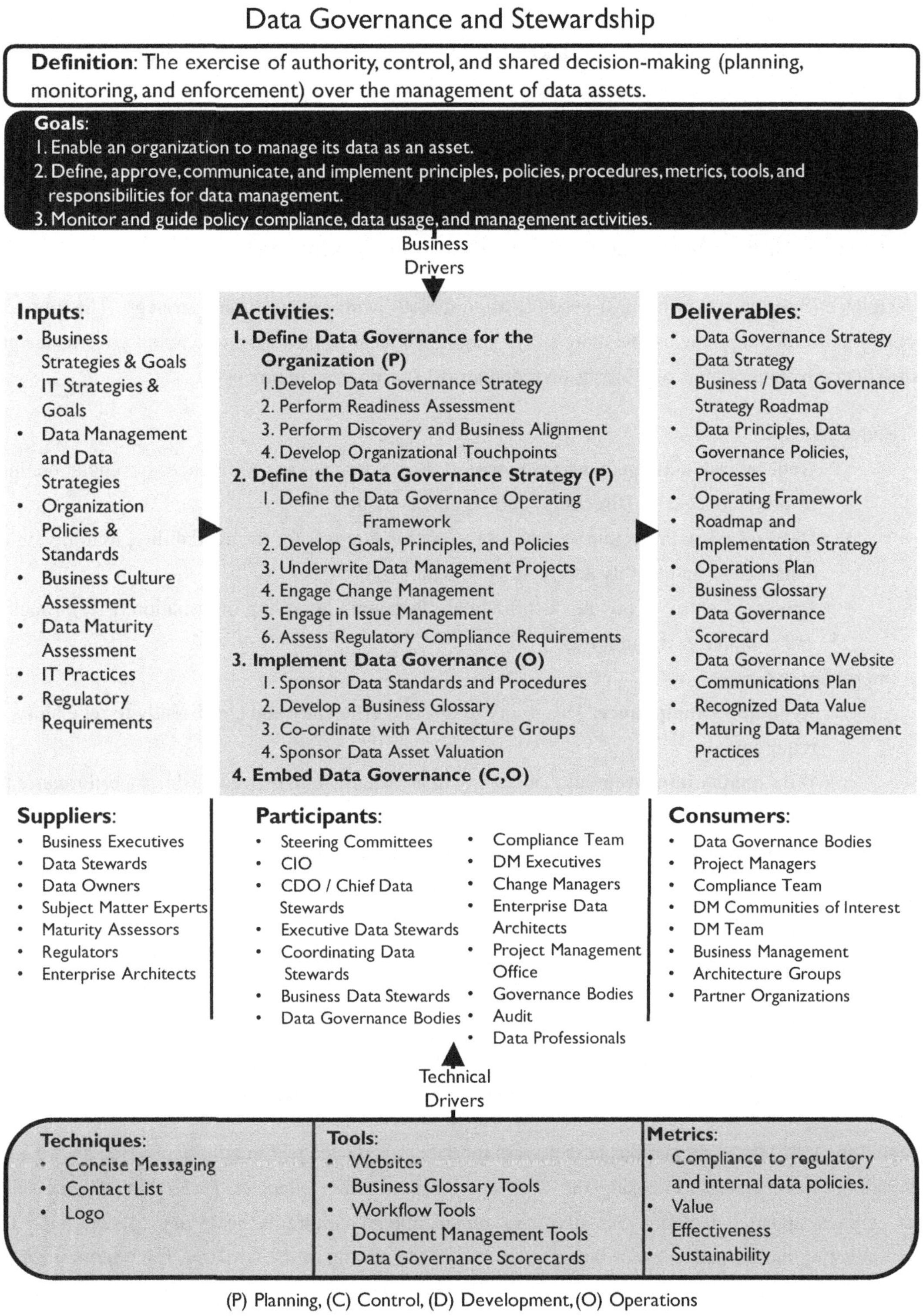

Data Governance and Stewardship

Definition: The exercise of authority, control, and shared decision-making (planning, monitoring, and enforcement) over the management of data assets.

Goals:
1. Enable an organization to manage its data as an asset.
2. Define, approve, communicate, and implement principles, policies, procedures, metrics, tools, and responsibilities for data management.
3. Monitor and guide policy compliance, data usage, and management activities.

Business Drivers

Inputs:
- Business Strategies & Goals
- IT Strategies & Goals
- Data Management and Data Strategies
- Organization Policies & Standards
- Business Culture Assessment
- Data Maturity Assessment
- IT Practices
- Regulatory Requirements

Activities:
1. **Define Data Governance for the Organization (P)**
   1. Develop Data Governance Strategy
   2. Perform Readiness Assessment
   3. Perform Discovery and Business Alignment
   4. Develop Organizational Touchpoints
2. **Define the Data Governance Strategy (P)**
   1. Define the Data Governance Operating Framework
   2. Develop Goals, Principles, and Policies
   3. Underwrite Data Management Projects
   4. Engage Change Management
   5. Engage in Issue Management
   6. Assess Regulatory Compliance Requirements
3. **Implement Data Governance (O)**
   1. Sponsor Data Standards and Procedures
   2. Develop a Business Glossary
   3. Co-ordinate with Architecture Groups
   4. Sponsor Data Asset Valuation
4. **Embed Data Governance (C,O)**

Deliverables:
- Data Governance Strategy
- Data Strategy
- Business / Data Governance Strategy Roadmap
- Data Principles, Data Governance Policies, Processes
- Operating Framework
- Roadmap and Implementation Strategy
- Operations Plan
- Business Glossary
- Data Governance Scorecard
- Data Governance Website
- Communications Plan
- Recognized Data Value
- Maturing Data Management Practices

Suppliers:
- Business Executives
- Data Stewards
- Data Owners
- Subject Matter Experts
- Maturity Assessors
- Regulators
- Enterprise Architects

Participants:
- Steering Committees
- CIO
- CDO / Chief Data Stewards
- Executive Data Stewards
- Coordinating Data Stewards
- Business Data Stewards
- Data Governance Bodies
- Compliance Team
- DM Executives
- Change Managers
- Enterprise Data Architects
- Project Management Office
- Governance Bodies
- Audit
- Data Professionals

Consumers:
- Data Governance Bodies
- Project Managers
- Compliance Team
- DM Communities of Interest
- DM Team
- Business Management
- Architecture Groups
- Partner Organizations

Technical Drivers

Techniques:
- Concise Messaging
- Contact List
- Logo

Tools:
- Websites
- Business Glossary Tools
- Workflow Tools
- Document Management Tools
- Data Governance Scorecards

Metrics:
- Compliance to regulatory and internal data policies.
- Value
- Effectiveness
- Sustainability

(P) Planning, (C) Control, (D) Development, (O) Operations

Figure 14 Context Diagram: Data Governance and Stewardship

1.1 Business Drivers

The most common driver for data governance is often regulatory compliance, especially for heavily regulated industries, such as financial services and healthcare. Responding to evolving legislation requires strict data governance processes. The explosion in advanced analytics and Data Science has created an additional driving force.

While compliance or analytics may drive governance, many organizations back into data governance via an information management program driven by other business needs, such as Master Data Management (MDM), by major data problems, or both. A typical scenario: a company needs better customer data, it chooses to develop Customer MDM, and then it realizes successful MDM requires data governance.

Data governance is not an end in itself. It needs to align directly with organizational strategy. The more clearly it helps solve organizational problems, the more likely people will change behaviors and adopt governance practices. Drivers for data governance most often focus on reducing risks or improving processes.

- Reducing Risk
    - o **General risk management**: Oversight of the risks data poses to finances or reputation, including response to legal (E-Discovery) and regulatory issues.
    - o **Data security**: Protection of data assets through controls for the availability, usability, integrity, consistency, auditability and security of data.
    - o **Privacy**: Control of private / confidential / Personal Identifying Information (PII) through policy and compliance monitoring.
- Improving Processes
    - o **Regulatory compliance**: The ability to respond efficiently and consistently to regulatory requirements.
    - o **Data quality improvement**: The ability to contribute to improved business performance by making data more reliable.
    - o **Metadata Management**: Establishment of a business glossary to define and locate data in the organization; ensuring the wide range of other Metadata is managed and made available to the organization.
    - o **Efficiency in development projects**: SDLC improvements to address issues and opportunities in data management across the organization, including management of data-specific technical debt through governance of the data lifecycle.
    - o **Vendor management**: Control of contracts dealing with data, such as cloud storage, external data purchase, sales of data as a product, and outsourcing data operations.

It is essential to clarify the particular business drivers for data governance within an organization and to align them with overall business strategy. Focusing the 'DG organization' often alienates leadership who perceive extra overhead without apparent benefits. Sensitivity to organizational culture is necessary to determine the right language, operating model, and roles for the program. As of the writing of the DMBOK2, the term *organization* is being replaced with terms like *operating model* or *operating framework*.

While people sometimes claim it is difficult to understand what data governance is, *governance* itself is a common concept. Rather than inventing new approaches, data management professionals can apply the concepts and principles of other types of governance to the governance of data. A common analogy is to equate data governance to auditing and accounting. Auditors and controllers set the rules for managing financial assets. Data governance professionals set rules for managing data assets. Other areas carry out these rules.

Data governance is not a one-time thing. Governing data requires an ongoing program focused on ensuring that an organization gets value from its data and reduces risks related to data. A Data Governance team can be a virtual organization or a line organization with specific accountabilities. To be effective, the roles and activities within data governance need to be well understood. They should be built around an operating framework that functions well in the organization. A data governance program should take into account distinctive organizational and cultural issues and the specific data management challenges and opportunities within the organization. (See Chapters 1 and 16.)

Data governance is separate from IT governance. IT governance makes decisions about IT investments, the IT application portfolio, and the IT project portfolio – in other words, hardware, software, and overall technical architecture. IT governance aligns the IT strategies and investments with enterprise goals and strategies. The COBIT (Control Objectives for Information and Related Technology) framework provides standards for IT governance, but only a small portion of the COBIT framework addresses managing data and information. Some critical topics, such as Sarbanes-Oxley compliance (U.S.A.), span the concerns of corporate governance, IT governance, and data governance. In contrast, Data Governance focuses exclusively on the management of data assets and of data as an asset.

1.2 Goals and Principles

The goal of Data Governance is to enable an organization to manage data as an asset. DG provides the principles, policy, processes, framework, metrics, and oversight to manage data as an asset and to guide data management activities at all levels. To achieve this overall goal, a DG program must be:

- **Sustainable**: The DG program needs to be 'sticky'. DG is not a project with a defined end; it is an ongoing process that requires organizational commitment. DG necessitates changes in how data is managed and used. This does not always mean massive new organizations and upheaval. It does mean managing change in a way that is sustainable beyond the initial implementation of any data governance component. Sustainable data governance depends on business leadership, sponsorship, and ownership.

- **Embedded**: DG is not an add-on process. DG activities need to be incorporated into development methods for software, use of data for analytics, management of Master Data, and risk management.

- **Measured**: DG done well has positive financial impact, but demonstrating this impact requires understanding the starting point and planning for measurable improvement.

Implementing a DG program requires commitment to change. The following principles, developed since the early 2000s, can help set a strong foundation for data governance.[26]

---

26 The Data Governance Institute. http://bit.ly/1ef0tnb.

- **Leadership and strategy**: Successful Data Governance starts with visionary and committed leadership. Data management activities are guided by a data strategy that is itself driven by the enterprise business strategy.

- **Business-driven**: Data Governance is a business program, and, as such, must govern IT decisions related to data as much as it governs business interaction with data.

- **Shared responsibility**: Across all Data Management Knowledge Areas, data governance is a shared responsibility between business data stewards and technical data management professionals.

- **Multi-layered**: Data governance occurs at both the enterprise and local levels and often at levels in between.

- **Framework-based**: Because data governance activities require coordination across functional areas, the DG program must establish an operating framework that defines accountabilities and interactions.

- **Principle-based**: Guiding principles are the foundation of DG activities, and especially of DG policy. Often, organizations develop policy without formal principles – they are trying to solve particular problems. Principles can sometimes be reverse-engineered from policy. However, it is best to articulate a core set of principles and best practices as part of policy work. Reference to principles can mitigate potential resistance. Additional guiding principles will emerge over time within an organization. Publish them in a shared internal environment along with other data governance artifacts.

1.3 Essential Concepts

Just as an auditor controls financial processes but does not actually execute financial management, data governance ensures data is properly managed without directly executing data management (see Figure 15). Data governance represents an *inherent separation of duty between oversight and execution.*

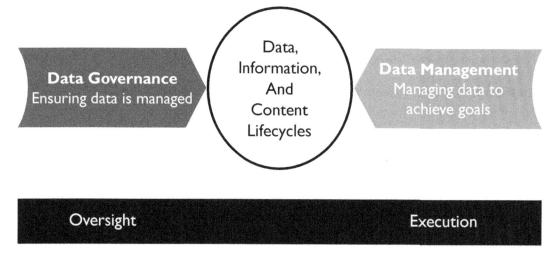

Figure 15 Data Governance and Data Management

1.3.1 Data-centric Organization

A data-centric organization values data as an asset and manages data through all phases of its lifecycle, including project development and ongoing operations. To become data-centric, an organization must change the way it translates strategy into action. Data is no longer treated as a by-product of process and applications. Ensuring data is of high quality is a goal of business processes. As organizations strive to make decisions based on insights gained from analytics, effective data management becomes a very high priority.

People tend to conflate data and information technology. To become data-centric, organizations need to think differently and recognize that managing data is different from managing IT. This shift is not easy. Existing culture, with its internal politics, ambiguity about ownership, budgetary competition, and legacy systems, can be a huge obstacle to establishing an enterprise vision of data governance and data management.

While each organization needs to evolve its own principles, those that seek to get more value from their data are likely to share the following:

- Data should be managed as a corporate asset
- Data management best practices should be incented across the organization
- Enterprise data strategy must be directly aligned with overall business strategy
- Data management processes should be continuously improved

1.3.2 Data Governance Organization

The core word in governance is *govern*. Data governance can be understood in terms of political governance. It includes legislative-like functions (defining policies, standards, and the Enterprise Data Architecture), judicial-like functions (issue management and escalation), and executive functions (protecting and serving, administrative responsibilities). To better manage risk, most organizations adopt a representative form of data governance, so that all stakeholders can be heard.

Each organization should adopt a governance model that supports its business strategy and is likely to succeed within its own cultural context. Organizations should also be prepared to evolve that model to meet new challenges. Models differ with respect to their organizational structure, level of formality, and approach to decision-making. Some models are centrally organized, while others are distributed.

Data governance organizations may also have multiple layers to address concerns at different levels within an enterprise – local, divisional, and enterprise-wide. The work of governance is often divided among multiple committees, each with a purpose and level of oversight different from the others.

Figure 16 represents a generic data governance model, with activities at different levels within the organization (vertical axis), as well as separation of governance responsibilities within organizational functions and between technical (IT) and business areas. Table 4 describes the typical committees that might be established within a data governance operating framework. Note this is not an organization chart. The diagram explains how various areas work together to carry out DG, in-line with the aforementioned trend to de-emphasize the term *organization*.

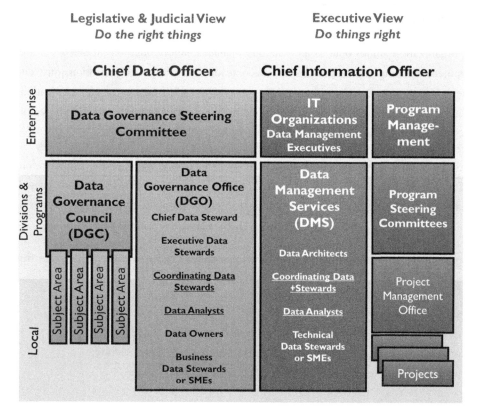

Figure 16 Data Governance Organization Parts

Table 4 Typical Data Governance Committees / Bodies

Data Governance Body	Description
Data Governance Steering Committee	The primary and highest authority organization for data governance in an organization, responsible for oversight, support, and funding of data governance activities. Consists of a cross-functional group of senior executives.
	Typically releases funding for data governance and data governance-sponsored activities as recommended by the DGC and CDO. This committee may in turn have oversight from higher-level funding or initiative-based steering committees.
Data Governance Council (DGC)	Manages data governance initiatives (e.g., development of policies or metrics), issues, and escalations. Consists of executive according to the operating model used. See Figure 17.
Data Governance Office (DGO)	Ongoing focus on enterprise-level data definitions and data management standards across all DAMA-DMBOK Knowledge Areas. Consists of coordinating roles that are labelled as *data stewards* or *custodians,* and *data owners.*
Data Stewardship Teams	Communities of interest focused on one or more specific subject-areas or projects, collaborating or consulting with project teams on data definitions and data management standards related to the focus. Consists of business and technical data stewards and data analysts.
Local Data Governance Committee	Large organizations may have divisional or departmental data governance councils working under the auspices of an Enterprise DGC. Smaller organizations should try to avoid such complexity.

1.3.3 Data Governance Operating Model Types

In a centralized model, one Data Governance organization oversees all activities in all subject areas. In a replicated model, the same DG operating model and standards are adopted by each business unit. In a federated model, one Data Governance organization coordinates with multiple Business Units to maintain consistent definitions and standards. (See Figure 17 and Chapter 16.)

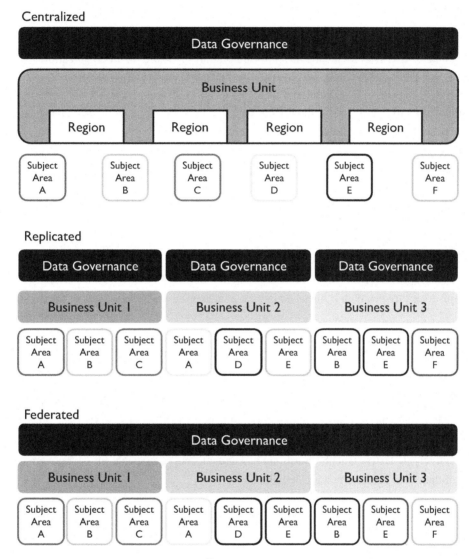

Figure 17 Enterprise DG Operating Framework Examples[27]

1.3.4 Data Stewardship

Data Stewardship is the most common label to describe accountability and responsibility for data and processes that ensure effective control and use of data assets. Stewardship can be formalized through job titles and

---

[27] Adapted from Ladley (2012).

descriptions, or it can be a less formal function driven by people trying to help an organization get value from its data. Often terms like *custodian* or *trustee* are synonyms for those who carry out steward-like functions.

The focus of stewardship activities will differ from organization to organization, depending on organizational strategy, culture, the problems an organization is trying to solve, its level of data management maturity, and the formality of its stewardship program. However, in most cases, data stewardship activities will focus on some, if not all, of the following:

- **Creating and managing core Metadata**: Definition and management of business terminology, valid data values, and other critical Metadata. Stewards are often responsible for an organization's Business Glossary, which becomes the system of record for business terms related to data.

- **Documenting rules and standards**: Definition/documentation of business rules, data standards, and data quality rules. Expectations used to define high quality data are often formulated in terms of rules rooted in the business processes that create or consume data. Stewards help surface these rules in order to ensure that there is consensus about them within the organization and that they are used consistently.

- **Managing data quality issues**: Stewards are often involved with the identification and resolution of data related issues or in facilitating the process of resolution.

- **Executing operational data governance activities**: Stewards are responsible for ensuring that, day-to-day and project-by-project, data governance policies and initiatives are adhered to. They should influence decisions to ensure that data is managed in ways that support the overall goals of the organization.

1.3.5 Types of Data Stewards

A *steward* is a person whose job it is to manage the property of another person. Data Stewards manage data assets on behalf of others and in the best interests of the organization (McGilvray, 2008). Data Stewards represent the interests of all stakeholders and must take an enterprise perspective to ensure enterprise data is of high quality and can be used effectively. Effective Data Stewards are accountable and responsible for data governance activities and have a portion of their time dedicate to these activities.

Depending on the complexity of the organization and the goals of its DG program, formally appointed Data Stewards may be differentiated by their place within an organization, by the focus of their work, or by both. For example:

- **Chief Data Stewards** may chair data governance bodies in lieu of the CDO or may act as a CDO in a virtual (committee-based) or distributed data governance organization. They may also be Executive Sponsors.

- **Executive Data Stewards** are senior managers who serve on a Data Governance Council.

- **Enterprise Data Stewards** have oversight of a data domain across business functions.

- **Business Data Stewards** are business professionals, most often recognized subject matter experts, accountable for a subset of data. They work with stakeholders to define and control data.

- **A Data Owner** is a business Data Steward, who has approval authority for decisions about data within their domain.

- **Technical Data Stewards** are IT professionals operating within one of the Knowledge Areas, such as Data Integration Specialists, Database Administrators, Business Intelligence Specialists, Data Quality Analysts or Metadata Administrators.

- **Coordinating Data Stewards** lead and represent teams of business and technical Data Stewards in discussions across teams and with executive Data Stewards. Coordinating Data Stewards are particularly important in large organizations.

The first edition of the DAMA-DMBOK stated that "the best Data Stewards are often found, not made" (DAMA, 2009). This assertion acknowledges that in most organizations, there are people who steward data, even in the absence of a formal data governance program. Such individuals are already involved in helping the organization reduce data-related risks and get more value from its data. Formalizing their stewardship accountabilities recognizes the work they are doing and enables them to be more successful and to contribute more. All of that said, Data Stewards can be 'made'; people can be trained to be Data Stewards. And people who are already stewarding data can develop their skills and knowledge so that they become better at the work of stewardship (Plotkin, 2014).

1.3.6 Data Policies

Data policies are directives that codify principles and management intent into fundamental rules governing the creation, acquisition, integrity, security, quality, and use of data and information.

Data policies are global. They support data standards, as well as expected behaviors related to key aspects of data management and use. Data policies vary widely across organizations. Data policies describe the 'what' of data governances (what to do and what not to do), while standards and procedures describe 'how' to do data governance. There should be relatively few data policies, and they should be stated briefly and directly.

1.3.7 Data Asset Valuation

Data asset valuation is the process of understanding and calculating the economic value of data to an organization. Because data, information, and even Business Intelligence are abstract concepts, people have difficulty aligning them with economic impact. The key to understanding the value of a non-fungible item (like data) is understanding how it is used and the value brought by its usage (Redman, 1996). Unlike many other assets (e.g., money, physical equipment), data sets are not interchangeable (fungible). One organization's customer data differs from another organization's in important ways; not only the customers themselves, but the data associated with them (purchasing history, preferences, etc.) How an organization gets value from customer data (i.e., what it learns about its customers from this data and how it applies what it learns) can be a competitive differentiator.

Most phases of the data lifecycle involve costs (including acquiring, storing, administering, and disposing of data). Data only brings value when it is used. When used, data also creates costs related to risk management. So value comes when the economic benefit of using data outweighs the costs of acquiring and storing it, as well as managing risk related to usage.

Some other ways to measure value include:

- **Replacement cost**: The replacement or recovery cost of data lost in a disaster or data breach, including the transactions, domains, catalogs, documents and metrics within an organization.

- **Market value**: The value as a business asset at the time of a merger or acquisition.

- **Identified opportunities**: The value of income that can be gained from opportunities identified in the data (in Business Intelligence), by using the data for transactions, or by selling the data.

- **Selling data**: Some organizations package data as a product or sell insights gained from their data.

- **Risk cost**: A valuation based on potential penalties, remediation costs, and litigation expenses, derived from legal or regulatory risk from:

  - The absence of data that is required to be present.
  - The presence of data that should not be present (e.g., unexpected data found during legal discovery; data that is required to be purged but has not been purged).
  - Data that is incorrect, causing damage to customers, company finances, and reputation in addition to the above costs.
  - Reduction in risk and risk cost is offset by the operational intervention costs to improve and certify data

To describe the concept of information asset value, one can translate Generally Accepted Accounting Principles into Generally Accepted Information Principles[28] (see Table 5).

Table 5 Principles for Data Asset Accounting

Principle	Description
Accountability Principle	An organization must identify individuals who are ultimately accountable for data and content of all types.
Asset Principle	Data and content of all types are assets and have characteristics of other assets. They should be managed, secured, and accounted for as other material or financial assets.
Audit Principle	The accuracy of data and content is subject to periodic audit by an independent body.
Due Diligence Principle	If a risk is known, it must be reported. If a risk is possible, it must be confirmed. Data risks include risks related to poor data management practices.
Going Concern Principle	Data and content are critical to successful, ongoing business operations and management (i.e., they are not viewed as temporary means to achieve results or merely as a business by-product).

---

[28] Adapted from Ladley (2010). See pp 108-09, Generally Accepted Information Principles.

Principle	Description
Level of Valuation Principle	Value the data as an asset at a level that makes the most sense, or is the easiest to measure.
Liability Principle	There is a financial liability connected to data or content based on regulatory and ethical misuse or mismanagement.
Quality Principle	The meaning, accuracy, and lifecycle of data and content can affect the financial status of the organization.
Risk Principle	There is risk associated with data and content. This risk must be formally recognized, either as a liability or through incurring costs to manage and reduce the inherent risk.
Value Principle	There is value in data and content, based on the ways these are used to meet an organization's objectives, their intrinsic marketability, and/or their contribution to the organization's goodwill (balance sheet) valuation. The value of information reflects its contribution to the organization offset by the cost of maintenance and movement.

2. Activities

2.1 Define Data Governance for the Organization

Data Governance efforts must support business strategy and goals. An organization's business strategy and goals inform both the enterprise data strategy and how data governance and data management activities need to be operationalized in the organization.

Data governance enables shared responsibility for data-related decisions. Data governance activities cross organizational and system boundaries in support of an integrated view of data. Successful data governance requires a clear understanding of what is being governed and who is being governed, as well as who is governing.

Data governance is most effective when it is an enterprise effort, rather than isolated to a particular functional area. Defining the scope of data governance in an enterprise usually entails defining what *enterprise* means. Data governance, in turn, governs that defined enterprise.

2.2 Perform Readiness Assessment

Assessments that describe the current state of an organization's information management capabilities, maturity, and effectiveness are crucial to planning a DG program. Because they can be used to measure a program's effectiveness, assessments are also valuable in managing and sustaining a DG program. Typical assessments include:

- **Data management maturity**: Understand what the organization does with data; measure its current data management capabilities and capacity. The focus is on the impressions business personnel have about how well the company manages data and uses data to its advantage, as well as on objective criteria, such as use of tools, levels of reporting, etc. (See Chapter 15.)

- **Capacity to change**: Since DG requires behavioral change, it is important to measure the capacity for the organization to change behaviors required for adapting DG. Secondarily, this activity will help identify potential resistance points. Often DG requires formal organizational change management. In assessing the capacity to change, the change management process will evaluate existing organizational structure, perceptions of culture, and the change management process itself (Hiatt and Creasey, 2012). (See Chapter 17.)

- **Collaborative readiness**: This assessment characterizes the organization's ability to collaborate in the management and use of data. Since stewardship by definition crosses functional areas, it is collaborative in nature. If an organization does not know how to collaborate, culture will be an obstacle to stewardship. Never assume an organization knows how to collaborate. When done in conjunction with change capacity this assessment offers insight into the cultural capacity for implementing DG.

- **Business alignment**: Sometimes included with the change capacity, a business alignment assessment examines how well the organization aligns uses of data with business strategy. It is often surprising to discover how ad hoc data-related activities can be.

2.3 Perform Discovery and Business Alignment

A DG program must contribute to the organization by identifying and delivering on specific benefits (e.g., reduce fines paid to regulators). Discovery activity will identify and assess the effectiveness of existing policies and guidelines – what risks they address, what behaviors they encourage, and how well they have been implemented. Discovery can also identify opportunities for DG to improve the usefulness of data and content. Business alignment attaches business benefits to DG program elements.

Data Quality (DQ) analysis is part of discovery. DQ assessment will provide insight into existing issues and obstacles, as well as the impact and risks associated with poor quality data. DQ assessment can identify business processes that are at risk if executed using poor quality data, as well as the financial and other benefits of creating a Data Quality program as part of data governance efforts. (See Chapter 13.)

Assessment of data management practices is another key aspect of the data governance discovery process. For example, this might mean identifying power users to create an initial list of potential agents for ongoing DG activity.

Derive a list of DG requirements from the discovery and alignment activities. For example, if regulatory risks generate a financial concern to the business, then specify DG activities that support risk management. These requirements will drive DG strategy and tactics.

2.4 Develop Organizational Touch Points

Part of alignment includes developing organizational touchpoints for Data Governance work. Figure 18 illustrates examples of touch points that support alignment and cohesiveness of an enterprise data governance and data management approach in areas outside the direct authority of the Chief Data Officer.

- **Procurement and Contracts**: The CDO works with Vendor/Partner Management or Procurement to develop and enforce standard contract language vis-à-vis data management contracts. These could include Data-as-a-Service (DaaS) and cloud-related procurements, other outsourcing arrangements, third-party development efforts, or content acquisition/ licensing deals, and possibly data-centric IT tools acquisitions and upgrades.

- **Budget and Funding**: If the CDO is not directly in control of all data acquisition-related budgets, then the office can be a focal point for preventing duplicate efforts and ensuring optimization of acquired data assets.

- **Regulatory Compliance**: The CDO understands and works within required local, national, and international regulatory environments, and how these impact the organization and their data management activities. Ongoing monitoring is performed to identify and track new and potential impacts and requirements.

- **SDLC / development framework**: The data governance program identifies control points where enterprise policies, processes, and standards can be developed in the system or application development lifecycles.

The touch points that the CDO influences support the organization's cohesiveness in managing its data, therefore, increasing its nimbleness to use its data. In essence, this is a vision of how DG will be perceived by the organization.

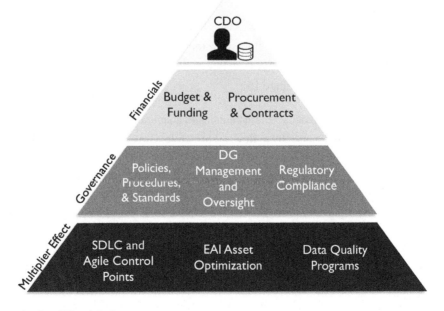

Figure 18 CDO Organizational Touch Points

2.5 Develop Data Governance Strategy

A data governance strategy defines the scope and approach to governance efforts. DG strategy should be defined comprehensively and articulated in relation to the overall business strategy, as well as to data management and IT strategies. It should be implemented iteratively as the pieces are developed and approved. The specific content will be tailored to each organization, but the deliverables include:

- **Charter**: Identifies the business drivers, vision, mission, and principles for data governance, including readiness assessment, internal process discovery, and current issues or success criteria

- **Operating framework and accountabilities**: Defines structure and responsibility for data governance activities

- **Implementation roadmap**: Timeframes for the roll out of policies and directives, business glossary, architecture, asset valuation, standards and procedures, expected changes to business and technology processes, and deliverables to support auditing activities and regulatory compliance

- **Plan for operational success**: Describing a target state of sustainable data governance activities

2.6 Define the DG Operating Framework

While developing a basic definition of DG is easy, creating an operating model that an organization will adopt can be difficult. Consider these areas when constructing an organization's operating model:

- **Value of data to the organization**: If an organization sells data, obviously DG has a huge business impact. Organizations that use data as a crucial commodity (e.g., Facebook, Amazon) will need an operating model that reflects the role of data. For organizations where data is an operational lubricant, the form of DG will be less intense.

- **Business model**: Decentralized business vs. centralized, local vs. international, etc. are factors that influence how business occurs, and therefore, how the DG operating model is defined. Links with specific IT strategy, Data Architecture, and application integration functions should be reflected in the target operating framework design (per Figure 16).

- **Cultural factors**: Such as acceptance of discipline and adaptability to change. Some organizations will resist the imposition of governance by policy and principle. Governance strategy will need to advocate for an operating model that fits with organizational culture, while still progressing change.

- **Impact of regulation**: Highly regulated organizations will have a different mindset and operating model of DG than those less regulated. There may be links to the Risk Management group or Legal as well.

Layers of data governance are often part of the solution. This means determining where accountability should reside for stewardship activities, who owns the data, etc. The operating model also defines the interaction between the governance organization and the people responsible for data management projects or initiatives, the engagement of change management activities to introduce this new program, and the model for issue management resolution pathways through governance. Figure 19 shows an example of an operating framework. The example is illustrative. This kind of artifact must be customized to meet the needs of a specific organization.

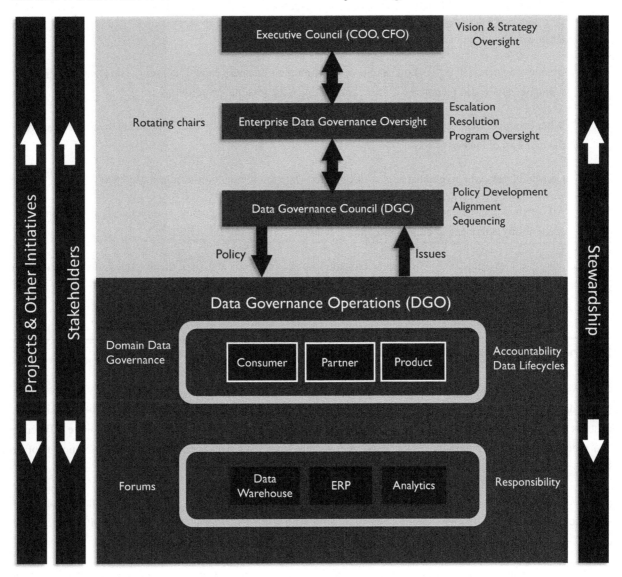

Figure 19 An Example of an Operating Framework

2.7 Develop Goals, Principles, and Policies

Development of goals, principles, and policies derived from the Data Governance Strategy will guide the organization into the desired future state.

Goals, principles, and policies are typically drafted by either by data management professionals, business policy staff, or a combination, under the auspices of data governance. Next, Data Stewards and management review and refine them. Then, the Data Governance Council (or similar body) conducts the final review, revision, and adoption.

Policies may take different shapes, as in the following examples:

- The Data Governance Office (DGO) will certify data for use by the organization.

- Business owners will be approved by the Data Governance Office.

- Business owners will designate Data Stewards from their business capability areas. The Data Stewards will have day-to-day responsibility for coordinating data governance activities.

- Whenever possible, standardized reporting and/or dashboards/scorecards will be made available to serve the majority of business needs.

- Certified Users will be granted access to Certified Data for ad hoc /non-standard reporting.

- All certified data will be evaluated on a regular basis to assess its accuracy, completeness, consistency, accessibility, uniqueness, compliance, and efficiency.

Data policies must be effectively communicated, monitored, enforced, and periodically re-evaluated. The Data Governance Council may delegate this authority to the Data Stewardship Steering Committee.

2.8 Underwrite Data Management Projects

Initiatives to improve data management capabilities provide enterprise-wide benefits. These usually require cross-functional sponsorship or visibility from the DGC. They can be hard to sell because they can be perceived as obstacles to 'just getting things done'. The key to promoting them is to articulate the ways they improve efficiency and reduce risk. Organizations that want to get more value from their data need to prioritize development of or improvement of data management capabilities.

The DGC helps define the business case and oversees project status and progress on data management improvement projects. The DGC coordinates its efforts with a Project Management Office (PMO), where one exists. Data management projects may be considered part of the overall IT project portfolio.

The DGC may also coordinate data management improvement efforts with large programs with enterprise-wide scope. Master Data Management projects, such as Enterprise Resource Planning (ERP), Customer or Citizen Relationship Management (CRM), global parts lists, are good candidates for this kind of coordination.

Data management activity in other projects must be accommodated by the internal SDLC, service delivery management, other Information Technology Infrastructure Library (ITIL) components, and PMO processes.[29] Every project with a significant data component (and almost every project has these) should capture data management requirements *early* in the SDLC (planning and design phases). These include architecture, regulatory compliance, system-of-record identification and analysis, and data quality inspection and remediation. There may also be data management support activities, including requirements verification testing using standard test beds.

---

[29] http://bit.ly/2spRr7e.

2.9 Engage Change Management

Organizational Change Management (OCM) is the vehicle for bringing about change in an organization's systems and processes. The Change Management Institute posits that organizational change management is more than just the 'people side of projects'. It should be viewed as the approach the whole organization uses to manage change well. Organizations often manage the transitions of projects rather than the evolution of the organization (Anderson and Ackerson, 2012). An organization that is mature in its management of change builds a clear organizational vision, actively leads and monitors change from the top, and designs and manages smaller change efforts. It adapts change initiatives based on the feedback and collaboration of the whole organization (Change Management Institute, 2012). (See Chapter 17.)

For many organizations, the formality and discipline inherent in DG differ from existing practices. Adopting them requires that people change their behaviors and interactions. A formal OCM program, with the right executive sponsor, is critical to driving the behavioral changes required to sustain DG. Organizations should create a team responsible for:

- **Planning**: Planning change management, including performing stakeholder analysis, gaining sponsorship, and establishing a communications approach to overcome resistance to change.

- **Training**: Creating and executing training plans for data governance programs.

- **Influencing systems development**: Engaging with the PMO to add data governance steps the SDLC.

- **Policy implementation**: Communicating data policies and the organization's commitment to data management activities.

- **Communications**: Increasing awareness of the role and responsibilities of Data Stewards and other data governance professionals, as well as the objectives and expectations for data management projects.

Communications are vital to the change management process. A change management program supporting formal Data Governance should focus communications on:

- **Promoting the value of data assets**: Educate and inform employees about the role data plays in achieving organizational goals.

- **Monitoring and acting on feedback about data governance activities**: In addition to sharing information, communications plans should elicit feedback that can guide both the DG program and the change management process. Actively seeking and using input from stakeholders can build commitment to the program's goals, while also identifying successes and opportunities for improvement.

- **Implementing data management training**: Training at all levels of the organization increases awareness of data management best practices and processes.

- Measuring the effects of change management on in five key areas:[30]

---

[30] http://bit.ly/1qKvLyJ. See also Hiatt and Creasey (2012).

      o   Awareness of the need to change

      o   Desire to participate and support the change

      o   Knowledge about how to change

      o   Ability to implement new skills and behaviors

      o   Reinforcement to keep the change in place

- **Implementing new metrics and KPIs**: Employee incentives should be realigned to support behaviors connected to data management best practices. Since enterprise data governance requires cross-functional cooperation, incentives should encourage cross-unit activities and collaboration.

2.10 Engage in Issue Management

Issue management is the process for identifying, quantifying, prioritizing, and resolving data governance-related issues, including:

- **Authority**: Questions regarding decision rights and procedures

- **Change management escalations**: Issues arising from the change management process

- **Compliance**: Issues with meeting compliance requirements

- **Conflicts**: Conflicting policies, procedures, business rules, names, definitions, standards, architecture, data ownerships and conflicting stakeholder interests in data and information

- **Conformance**: Issue related to conformance to policies, standards, architecture, and procedures

- **Contracts**: Negotiation and review of data sharing agreements, buying and selling data, and cloud storage

- **Data security and identity**: Privacy and confidentiality issues, including breach investigations

- **Data quality**: Detection and resolution of data quality issues, including disasters or security breaches

Many issues can be resolved locally in Data Stewardship teams. Issues requiring communication and / or escalation must be logged, and may be escalated to the Data Stewardship teams, or higher to the DGC, as shown in Figure 20. A Data Governance Scorecard can be used to identify trends related to issues, such as where within the organization they occur, what their root causes are, etc. Issues that cannot be resolved by the DGC should be escalated to corporate governance and / or management.

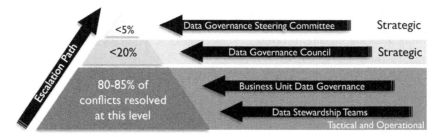

Figure 20 Data Issue Escalation Path

Data governance requires control mechanisms and procedures for:

- Identifying, capturing, logging, tracking, and updating issues
- Assignment and tracking of action items
- Documenting stakeholder viewpoints and resolution alternatives
- Determining, documenting, and communicating issue resolutions
- Facilitating objective, neutral discussions where all viewpoints are heard
- Escalating issues to higher levels of authority

Data issue management is very important. It builds credibility for the DG team, has direct, positive effects on data consumers, and relieves the burden on production support teams. Solving issues also proves that data can be managed and its quality improved. Successful issue management requires control mechanisms that demonstrate the work effort and impact of resolution.

2.11 Assess Regulatory Compliance Requirements

Every enterprise is affected by governmental and industry regulations, including regulations that dictate how data and information are to be managed. Part of the data governance function is to monitor and ensure regulatory compliance. Regulatory compliance is often the initial reason for implementing data governance. Data governance guides the implementation of adequate controls to monitor and document compliance with data-related regulations.

Several global regulations have significant implications on data management practices. For example:

- **Accounting Standards**: The Government Accounting Standards Board (GASB) and the Financial Accounting Standards Board (FASB) accounting standards also have significant implications on how information assets are managed (in the US).

- **BCBS 239** (Basel Committee on Banking Supervision) and **Basel II** refer to Principles for Effective Risk Data Aggregation and risk reporting, a wide ranging set of regulations for banks. Since 2006, financial institutions doing business in European Union countries are required to report standard information proving liquidity.

- **CPG 235**: The Australian Prudential Regulation Authority (APRA) provides oversight of banking and insurance entities. It publishes standards and guides to assist in meeting these standards. Among these is CGP 235, a standard for managing data risk. It focuses on addressing the sources of data risk and on managing data throughout its lifecycle.

- **PCI-DSS**: The Payment Card Industry Data Security Standards (PCI-DSS).

- **Solvency II**: European Union regulations, similar to Basel II, for the insurance industry.

- **Privacy laws**: Local, sovereign, and international laws all apply.

Data governance organizations work with other business and technical leadership to evaluate the implications of regulations. The organization must determine, for example,

- In what ways is a regulation relevant to the organization?
- What constitutes compliance? What policies and procedures will be required to achieve compliance?
- When is compliance required? How and when is compliance monitored?
- Can the organization adopt industry standards to achieve compliance?
- How is compliance demonstrated?
- What is the risk of and penalty for non-compliance?
- How is non-compliance identified and reported? How is non-compliance managed and rectified?

DG monitors the organization's response to regulatory requirements or audit undertakings involving data and data practices (for example, certifying the quality of data in regulatory reporting). (See Chapter 6.)

2.12 Implement Data Governance

Data governance cannot be implemented overnight. It requires planning – not only to account for organizational change, but also simply because it includes many complex activities that need to be coordinated. It is best to create an implementation roadmap that illustrates the timeframes for and relationship between different activities. For example, if the DG program is focused on improving compliance, priorities may be driven by specific regulatory requirements. In a federated DG organization, implementation in various lines of business can occur on different schedules, based on their level of engagement and maturity, as well as funding.

Some DG work is foundational. Other work depends on it. This work has an initial release and ongoing cultivation. Prioritized activities in the early stages include:

- Defining data governance procedures required to meet high priority goals

- Establishing a business glossary and documenting terminology and standards

- Coordinating with Enterprise Architecture and Data Architecture to support better understanding of the data and the systems

- Assigning financial value to data assets to enable better decision-making and to increase understanding of the role that data plays in organizational success

2.13 Sponsor Data Standards and Procedures

A standard is defined as "something that is very good and that is used to make judgments about the quality of other things" or as "something set up and established by authority as a rule for the measure of quantity, weight, extent, value, or quality."[31] Standards help define quality because they provide a means of comparison. They also offer the potential to simplify processes. By adopting a standard, an organization makes a decision once and codifies it in a

---

[31] http://bit.ly/2sTfugb

set of assertions (the standard). It does not need to make the same decision all over again for each project. Enforcing standards should promote consistent results from the processes using them.

Unfortunately, creating or adopting standards is often a politicized process and these goals get lost. Most organizations are not well-practiced at developing or enforcing data or data governance standards. In some cases, they have not recognized the value in doing so and therefore have not taken the time to do so. Other times they simply don't know how to. Consequently, 'standards' vary widely within and across organizations, as do expectations for conformance. DG standards should be mandatory.

Data standards can take different forms depending on what they describe: assertions about how a field must be populated, rules governing the relationships between fields, detailed documentation of acceptable and unacceptable values, format, etc. They are usually drafted by data management professionals. Data standards should be reviewed, approved and adopted by the DGC, or a delegated workgroup, such as a Data Standards Steering Committee. The level of detail in data standards documentation depends, in part, on organizational culture. Keep in mind that documenting data standards presents an opportunity to capture details and knowledge that otherwise may be lost. Recreating or reverse engineering to access this knowledge is very expensive, compared to documenting it up front.

Data standards must be effectively communicated, monitored, and periodically reviewed and updated. Most importantly, there must be a means to enforce them. Data can be measured against standards. Data management activities can be audited for standards compliance by the DGC or the Data Standards Steering Committee on a defined schedule or as part of SDLC approval processes.

Data management procedures are the documented methods, techniques, and steps followed to accomplish specific activities that produce certain outcomes and supporting artifacts. Like policies and standards, procedures vary widely across organizations. As is the case with data standards, procedural documents capture organizational knowledge in an explicit form. Procedural documentation is usually drafted by data management professionals.

Examples of concepts that can be standardized within the Data Management Knowledge Areas include:

- **Data Architecture**: Enterprise data models, tool standards, and system naming conventions

- **Data Modeling and Design**: Data model management procedures, data modeling naming conventions, definition standards, standard domains, and standard abbreviations

- **Data Storage and Operations**: Tool standards, standards for database recovery and business continuity, database performance, data retention, and external data acquisition

- **Data Security**: Data access security standards, monitoring and audit procedures, storage security standards, and training requirements

- **Data Integration**: Standard methods and tools used for data integration and interoperability

- **Documents and Content**: Content management standards and procedures, including use of enterprise taxonomies, support for legal discovery, document and email retention periods, electronic signatures, and report distribution approaches

- **Reference and Master Data**: Reference Data Management control procedures, systems of data record, assertions establishing and mandating use, standards for entity resolution

- **Data Warehousing and Business Intelligence**: Tool standard, processing standards and procedures, report and visualization formatting standards, standards for Big Data handling

- **Metadata**: Standard business and technical Metadata to be captured, Metadata integration procedures and usage

- **Data Quality**: Data quality rules, standard measurement methodologies, data remediation standards and procedures

- **Big Data and Data Science**: Data source identification, authority, acquisition, system of record, sharing and refresh

2.14 Develop a Business Glossary

Data Stewards are generally responsible for business glossary content. A glossary is necessary because people use words differently. It is particularly important to have clear definitions for data, because data represents things other than itself (Chisholm, 2010). In addition, many organizations develop their own internal vocabulary. A glossary is a means of sharing this vocabulary within the organization. Developing and documenting standard data definitions reduces ambiguity and improves communication. Definitions must be clear, rigorous in wording, and explain any exceptions, synonyms or variants. Approvers of terminology should include representatives from core user groups. Data Architecture often can supply draft definitions and type breakouts from subject area models.

Business glossaries have the following objectives:

- Enable common understanding of the core business concepts and terminology

- Reduce the risk that data will be misused due to inconsistent understanding of the business concepts

- Improve the alignment between technology assets (with their technical naming conventions) and the business organization

- Maximize search capability and enable access to documented institutional knowledge

A business glossary is not merely a list of terms and definitions. Each term will also be associated with other valuable Metadata: synonyms, metrics, lineage, business rules, the steward responsible for the term, etc.

2.15 Coordinate with Architecture Groups

The DGC sponsors and approves data architecture artifacts, such as a business-oriented enterprise data model. The DGC may appoint or interact with an Enterprise Data Architecture Steering Committee or Architecture Review Board (ARB) to oversee the program and its iterative projects. The enterprise data model should be developed and maintained jointly by data architects and Data Stewards working together in subject area teams. Depending on the organization, this work can be coordinated either by the Enterprise Data Architect or by the steward. As business requirements evolve, the Data Stewardship teams should propose changes and develop extensions to the enterprise data model.

The enterprise data model should be reviewed, approved, and formally adopted by the DGC. This model must align with key business strategies, processes, organizations, and systems. Data strategy and Data Architecture are central to coordination between the 'Doing things right' and 'Doing the right things' when managing data assets.

2.16 Sponsor Data Asset Valuation

Data and information are assets because they have or can create value. Today's accounting practices consider data an intangible asset, much like software, documentation, expert knowledge, trade secrets, and other intellectual property. That said, organizations find it challenging to put monetary value on data. The DGC should organize the effort and set standards for doing so.

Some organizations start by estimating the value of business losses due to inadequate information. Information gaps – the difference between what information is needed and what is available – represent business liabilities. The cost of closing or preventing gaps can be used to estimate of business value of the missing data. From there, the organization can develop models to estimate the value of the information that does exist.

Value estimates can be built into a data strategy roadmap that will justify business cases for root cause solutions to quality issues, as well as for other governance initiatives.

2.17 Embed Data Governance

One goal of the data governance organization is to embed in a range of processes behaviors related to managing data as an asset. The ongoing operation of DG requires planning. The operations plan contains the list of events required to implement and operate DG activities. It outlines activities, timing, and techniques necessary to sustain success.

Sustainability means acting to ensure that processes and funding are in place to enable the continued performance of the DG organizational framework. Central to this requirement is that the organization *accepts* the governance of data; that the function is managed, its results are monitored and measured, and the obstacles that so often cause DG programs to falter or fail are overcome.

In order to deepen the organization's understanding of data governance in general, its application locally, and to learn from each other, create a Data Governance Community of Interest. This is particularly useful in the first years of governance, and will likely taper off as the DG operations become mature.

3. Tools and Techniques

Data governance is fundamentally about organizational behavior. This is not a problem that can be solved through technology. However, there are tools that support the overall process. For example, DG requires ongoing communication. A DG program should take advantage of existing communications channels to communicate key messages in a consistent manner and to keep stakeholders informed about policies, standards, and requirements.

In addition, a DG program must manage its own work and its own data effectively. Tools help not only with these tasks, but also with the metrics that support them. Before choosing a tool for a specific function, like a business glossary solution, an organization should define its overall governance goals and requirements with an eye to building out a tool set. For example, some glossary solutions include additional components for policy and workflow management. If such additional functionality is desired, requirements should be clarified and tested before a tool is adopted. Otherwise, the organization will have multiple tools, none of which may meet its needs.

3.1 Online Presence / Websites

The Data Governance program should have an online presence. It can make core documents available via a central website or a collaboration portal. Websites can house documentation libraries, give access to search capabilities, and help manage simple workflow. A website can also help establish a brand for the program through logos and a consistent visual representation. A DG program website should include:

- The Data Governance strategy and program charter, including vision, benefits, goals, principles, and implementation roadmap
- Data policies and data standards
- Descriptions of data stewardship roles and responsibilities
- Program news announcements
- Links to forums for a Data Governance Community of Interest
- Links to executive messages regarding data governance topics
- Reports on Data Quality measurements
- Procedures for issue identification and escalation
- Links to request services or capture issues
- Documents, presentations, and training programs with links to related online resources
- Data Governance program contact information

3.2 Business Glossary

A Business Glossary is a core DG tool. It houses agreed-upon definitions of business terms and relates these to data. There are many business glossary tools available, some as part of larger ERP systems, data integration tools, or Metadata management tools, and some as standalone tools.

3.3 Workflow Tools

Larger organizations may want to consider a robust workflow tool to manage processes, such as the implementation of new data governance policies. These tools connect processes to documents, and can be useful in policy administration and issue resolution.

3.4 Document Management Tools

Very often, a document management tool is used by governance teams to assist in managing policies and procedures.

3.5 Data Governance Scorecards

The collection of metrics to track data governance activities and compliance with policies can be reported up to the Data Governance Council and Data Governance Steering Committees on an automated scorecard.

4. Implementation Guidelines

Once the data governance program is defined, an operating plan developed, and an implementation roadmap prepared with the support of information gathered in the data maturity assessment (see Chapter 15), the organization can begin to implement processes and policies. Most rollout strategies are incremental, either applying DG first to a large effort, such as MDM, or by a region or division. Rarely is DG deployed enterprise-wide as a first effort.

4.1 Organization and Culture

As noted in Section 2.9, the formality and discipline inherent in data governance will be new and different for many organizations. Data governance adds value by bringing about changes in behavior. There may be resistance to change and a learning or adoption curve for new methods of making decisions and governing projects.

Effective and long-lasting data governance programs require a cultural shift in organizational thinking and behavior about data, as well as an ongoing program of change management to support the new thinking, behaviors, policies, and processes to achieve the desired future state of behavior around data. No matter how precise or exotic the data governance strategy, ignoring culture will diminish chances for success. Focus on managing change must be part of the implementation strategy.

The target of organization change is sustainability. *Sustainability* is a quality of a process that measures how easy it is for the process to continue to add value. Sustaining a data governance program requires planning for change. (See Chapter 17.)

4.2 Adjustment and Communication

Data Governance programs are implemented incrementally within the context of a wider business and data management strategy. Success requires keeping the wider goals in mind while putting the pieces in place. The DG team will need to be flexible and adjust its approach as conditions shift. Tools required to manage and communicate changes include:

- **Business / DG strategy map**: This map connects DG activity with business needs. Periodically measuring and communicating how DG is helping the business is vital to obtain ongoing support for the program.

- **DG roadmap**: The roadmap to DG should not be rigid. It should be adapted to changes in business environment or priorities.

- **Ongoing business case for DG**: The business case must be adjusted periodically to reflect changing priorities and financial realities of the organization.

- **DG metrics**: Metrics will need to grow and change as the DG program matures.

5. Metrics

To counter resistance or the challenge of a long learning curve, a DG program must be able to measure progress and success through metrics that demonstrate how DG participants have added business value and attained objectives.

In order to manage the behavior changes required, it is important to measure progress of the rollout of data governance, compliance with the data governance requirements, and the value data governance is bringing to the organization. Metrics that reinforce DG's value and those that verify the organization has the resources required to support DG after it is rolled out are also important to sustaining a DG program. Sample metrics include:

- Value
  - Contributions to business objectives
  - Reduction of risk
  - Improved efficiency in operations
- Effectiveness
  - Achievement of goals and objectives
  - Extent stewards are using the relevant tools
  - Effectiveness of communication
  - Effectiveness of education/training

- o   Speed of change adoption
- Sustainability
  - o   Performance of policies and processes (i.e., are they working appropriately?)
  - o   Conformance to standards and procedures (i.e., are staff following the guidance and changing behavior as necessary?)

---

6. Works Cited / Recommended

Adelman, Sid, Larissa Moss and Majid Abai. *Data Strategy*. Addison-Wesley Professional, 2005. Print.

Anderson, Dean and Anderson, Linda Ackerson. *Beyond Change Management*. Pfeiffer, 2012.

Avramov, Lucien and Maurizio Portolani. *The Policy Driven Data Center with ACI: Architecture, Concepts, and Methodology*. Cisco Press, 2014. Print. Networking Technology.

Axelos Global Best Practice (ITIL website). http://bit.ly/1H6SwxC.

Brzezinski, Robert. *HIPAA Privacy and Security Compliance - Simplified: Practical Guide for Healthcare Providers and Practice Managers*. CreateSpace Independent Publishing Platform, 2014. Print.

Calder, Alan. *IT Governance: Implementing Frameworks and Standards for the Corporate Governance of IT*. IT Governance Publishing, 2009. Print.

Change Management Institute and Carbon Group. *Organizational Change Maturity Model*, 2012. http://bit.ly/1Q62tR1.

Change Management Institute (website). http://bit.ly/1Q62tR1.

Chisholm, Malcolm and Roblyn-Lee, Diane. *Definitions in Data Management: A Guide to Fundamental Semantic Metadata*. Design Media, 2008. Print.

Cokins, Gary et al. *CIO Best Practices: Enabling Strategic Value with Information Technology*, 2nd ed. Wiley, 2010. Print.

De Haes, Steven and Wim Van Grembergen. *Enterprise Governance of Information Technology: Achieving Alignment and Value, Featuring COBIT 5*. 2nd ed. Springer, 2015. Print. Management for Professionals.

DiStefano, Robert S. *Asset Data Integrity Is Serious Business*. Industrial Press, Inc., 2010. Print.

Doan, AnHai, Alon Halevy and Zachary Ives. *Principles of Data Integration*. Morgan Kaufmann, 2012. Print.

Fisher, Tony. *The Data Asset: How Smart Companies Govern Their Data for Business Success*. Wiley, 2009. Print.

Giordano, Anthony David. *Performing Information Governance: A Step-by-step Guide to Making Information Governance Work*. IBM Press, 2014. Print. IBM Press.

Hiatt, Jeff and Creasey, Timothy. *Change Management: The People Side of Change*. Prosci, 2012.

Huwe, Ruth A. *Metrics 2.0: Creating Scorecards for High-Performance Work Teams and Organizations*. Praeger, 2010. Print.

Ladley, John. *Data Governance: How to Design, Deploy and Sustain an Effective Data Governance Program*. Morgan Kaufmann, 2012. Print. The Morgan Kaufmann Series on Business Intelligence.

Ladley, John. *Making Enterprise Information Management (EIM) Work for Business: A Guide to Understanding Information as an Asset*. Morgan Kaufmann, 2010. Print.

Marz, Nathan and James Warren. *Big Data: Principles and best practices of scalable realtime data systems*. Manning Publications, 2015. Print.

McGilvray, Danette. *Executing Data Quality Projects: Ten Steps to Quality Data and Trusted Information.* Morgan Kaufmann, 2008. Print.

Osborne, Jason W. *Best Practices in Data Cleaning: A Complete Guide to Everything You Need to Do Before and After Collecting Your Data.* SAGE Publications, Inc, 2013. Print.

Plotkin, David. *Data Stewardship: An Actionable Guide to Effective Data Management and Data Governance.* Morgan Kaufmann, 2013. Print.

PROSCI (website). http://bit.ly/2tt1bf9.

Razavi, Behzad. *Principles of Data Conversion System Design.* Wiley-IEEE Press, 1994. Print.

Redman, Thomas C. *Data Driven: Profiting from Your Most Important Business Asset.* Harvard Business Review Press, 2008. Print.

Reinke, Guido. *The Regulatory Compliance Matrix: Regulation of Financial Services, Information and Communication Technology, and Generally Related Matters.* GOLD RUSH Publishing, 2015. Print. Regulatory Compliance.

Seiner, Robert S. *Non-Invasive Data Governance.* Technics Publications, LLC, 2014. Print.

Selig, Gad. *Implementing IT Governance: A Practical Guide to Global Best Practices in IT Management.* Van Haren Publishing, 2008. Print. Best Practice.

Smallwood, Robert F. *Information Governance: Concepts, Strategies, and Best Practices.* Wiley, 2014. Print. Wiley CIO.

Soares, Sunil. *Selling Information Governance to the Business: Best Practices by Industry and Job Function.* Mc Press, 2011. Print.

Tarantino, Anthony. *The Governance, Risk, and Compliance Handbook: Technology, Finance, Environmental, and International Guidance and Best Practices.* Wiley, 2008. Print.

The Data Governance Institute (website). http://bit.ly/1ef0tnb.

The KPI Institute and Aurel Brudan, ed. *The Governance, Compliance and Risk KPI Dictionary: 130+ Key Performance Indicator Definitions.* CreateSpace Independent Publishing Platform, 2015. Print.

CHAPTER 4

Data Architecture

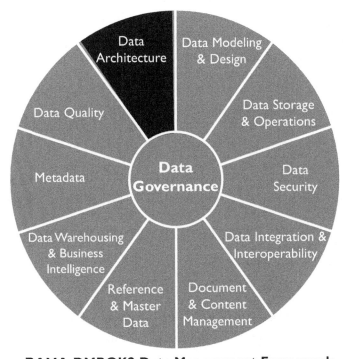

DAMA-DMBOK2 Data Management Framework

Copyright © 2017 by DAMA International

1. Introduction

*A*rchitecture refers to the art and science of building things (especially habitable structures) and to the results of the process of building – the buildings themselves. In a more general sense, architecture refers to an organized arrangement of component elements intended to optimize the function, performance, feasibility, cost, and aesthetics of an overall structure or system.

The term *architecture* has been adopted to describe several facets of information systems design. ISO/IEC 42010:2007 *Systems and Software Engineering – Architecture Description* (2011) defines *architecture* as "the fundamental organization of a system, embodied in its components, their relationships to each other and the environment, and the principles governing its design and evolution." However, depending on context, the word *architecture* can refer to a description of the current state of systems, the components of a set of systems, the discipline of designing systems (architecture practice), the intentional design of a system or a set of systems (future state or proposed architecture), the artifacts that describe a system (architecture documentation), or the team that does the design work (the Architects or the Architecture team).

Architecture practice is carried out at different levels within an organization (enterprise, domain, project, etc.) and with different areas of focus (infrastructure, application, and data). Exactly what architects do can be confusing to people who are not architects and who do not recognize the distinctions implied by these levels and focus areas. One reason architectural frameworks are valuable is that they enable non-architects to understand these relationships.

The discipline of Enterprise Architecture encompasses domain architectures, including business, data, application, and technology. Well-managed enterprise architecture practices help organizations understand the current state of their systems, promote desirable change toward future state, enable regulatory compliance, and improve effectiveness. Effective management of data and the systems in which data is stored and used is a common goal of the breadth of architecture disciplines.

In this chapter, Data Architecture will be considered from the following perspectives:

- **Data Architecture outcomes**, such models, definitions and data flows on various levels, usually referred as Data Architecture artifacts

- **Data Architecture activities**, to form, deploy and fulfill Data Architecture intentions

- **Data Architecture behavior**, such as collaborations, mindsets, and skills among the various roles that affect the enterprise's Data Architecture

Together, these three form the essential components of Data Architecture.

Data Architecture is fundamental to data management. Because most organizations have more data than individual people can comprehend, it is necessary to represent organizational data at different levels of abstraction so that it can be understood and management can make decisions about it.

Data Architecture artifacts includes specifications used to describe existing state, define data requirements, guide data integration, and control data assets as put forth in a data strategy. An organization's Data Architecture is described by an integrated collection of master design documents at different levels of abstraction, including standards that govern how data is collected, stored, arranged, used, and removed. It is also classified by descriptions of all the containers and paths that data takes through an organization's systems.

The most detailed Data Architecture design document is a formal enterprise data model, containing data names, comprehensive data and Metadata definitions, conceptual and logical entities and relationships, and business rules. Physical data models are included, but as a product of data modeling and design, rather than Data Architecture.

Data Architecture is most valuable when it fully supports the needs of the entire enterprise. Enterprise Data Architecture enables consistent data standardization and integration across the enterprise.

The artifacts that architects create constitute valuable Metadata. Ideally, architectural artifacts should be stored and managed in an enterprise architecture artifact repository.

We are in the middle of the third wave of end customer digitalization. Banks and financial transactions came first; various digital service interactions were in the second wave; and the internet of things and telematics drive the third. Traditional industries, like automotive, health care equipment, and tooling, are going digital in this third wave.

This happens in almost every industry. New Volvo cars have now on-call 24/7 service, not only for vehicle-related matters, but also to locate restaurants and shopping. Overhead cranes, pallet loaders, and anesthesia equipment are collecting and sending operational data that enables up-time services. Offerings have moved from suppling equipment to pay-per-use or availability contracts. Many of these companies have little if any experience in these areas, since they were previously taken care of by retailers or aftermarket service providers.

Forward-looking organizations should include data management professionals (e.g., Enterprise Data Architects or a strategic Data Stewards) when they are designing new market offerings, because nowadays these usually include hardware, software, and services that capture data, depend on data access, or both.

1.1 Business Drivers

The goal of Data Architecture is to be a bridge between business strategy and technology execution. As part of Enterprise Architecture, Data Architects:

- Strategically prepare organizations to quickly evolve their products, services, and data to take advantage of business opportunities inherent in emerging technologies

- Translate business needs into data and system requirements so that processes consistently have the data they require

- Manage complex data and information delivery throughout the enterprise

- Facilitate alignment between Business and IT

- Act as agents for change, transformation, and agility

These business drivers should influence measures of the value of Data Architecture.

Data architects create and maintain organizational knowledge about data and the systems through which it moves. This knowledge enables an organization to manage its data as an asset and increase the value it gets from its data by identifying opportunities for data usage, cost reduction, and risk mitigation.

1.2 Data Architecture Outcomes and Practices

Primary Data Architecture outcomes include:

- Data storage and processing requirements
- Designs of structures and plans that meet the current and long-term data requirements of the enterprise

Data Architecture

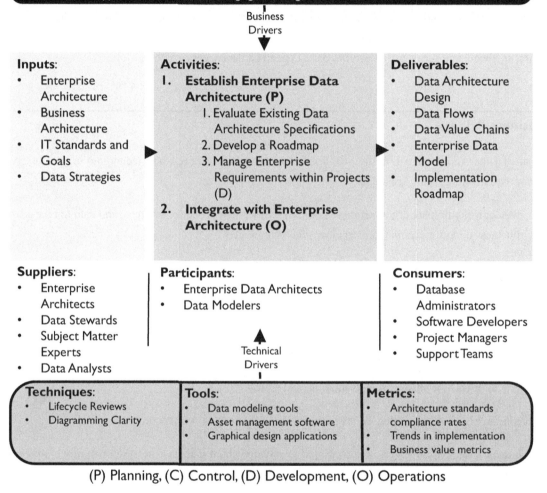

Definition: Identifying the data needs of the enterprise (regardless of structure), and designing and maintaining the master blueprints to meet those needs. Using master blueprints to guide data integration, control data assets, and align data investments with business strategy.

Goals:
1. Identify data storage and processing requirements.
2. Design structures and plans to meet the current and long-term data requirements of the enterprise.
3. Strategically prepare organizations to quickly evolve their products, services, and data to take advantage of business opportunities inherent in emerging technologies.

Business Drivers

Inputs:
- Enterprise Architecture
- Business Architecture
- IT Standards and Goals
- Data Strategies

Activities:
1. **Establish Enterprise Data Architecture (P)**
   1. Evaluate Existing Data Architecture Specifications
   2. Develop a Roadmap
   3. Manage Enterprise Requirements within Projects (D)
2. **Integrate with Enterprise Architecture (O)**

Deliverables:
- Data Architecture Design
- Data Flows
- Data Value Chains
- Enterprise Data Model
- Implementation Roadmap

Suppliers:
- Enterprise Architects
- Data Stewards
- Subject Matter Experts
- Data Analysts

Participants:
- Enterprise Data Architects
- Data Modelers

Consumers:
- Database Administrators
- Software Developers
- Project Managers
- Support Teams

Technical Drivers

Techniques:
- Lifecycle Reviews
- Diagramming Clarity

Tools:
- Data modeling tools
- Asset management software
- Graphical design applications

Metrics:
- Architecture standards compliance rates
- Trends in implementation
- Business value metrics

(P) Planning, (C) Control, (D) Development, (O) Operations

Figure 21 Context Diagram: Data Architecture

Architects seek to design in a way that brings value to the organization. This value comes through an optimal technical footprint, operational and project efficiencies, and the increased ability of the organization to use its data. To get there requires good design, planning, and the ability to ensure that the designs and plans are executed effectively.

To reach these goals, Data Architects define and maintain specifications that:

- Define the current state of data in the organization
- Provide a standard business vocabulary for data and components

- Align Data Architecture with enterprise strategy and business architecture
- Express strategic data requirements
- Outline high-level integrated designs to meet these requirements
- Integrate with overall enterprise architecture roadmap

An overall Data Architecture practice includes:

- Using Data Architecture artifacts (master blueprints) to define data requirements, guide data integration, control data assets, and align data investments with business strategy
- Collaborating with, learning from and influencing various stakeholders that are engaged with improving the business or IT systems development
- Using Data Architecture to establish the semantics of an enterprise, via a common business vocabulary

1.3 Essential Concepts

1.3.1 Enterprise Architecture Domains

Data Architecture operates in context of other architecture domains, including business, application, and technical architecture. Table 6 describes and compares these domains. Architects from different domains must address development directions and requirements collaboratively, as each domain influences and put constraints on the other domains. (See also Figure 22.)

Table 6 Architecture Domains

Domain	Enterprise Business Architecture	Enterprise Data Architecture	Enterprise Applications Architecture	Enterprise Technology Architecture
Purpose	To identify how an enterprise creates value for customers and other stakeholders	To describe how data should be organized and managed	To describe the structure and functionality of applications in an enterprise	To describe the physical technology needed to enable systems to function and deliver value
Elements	Business models, processes, capabilities, services, events, strategies, vocabulary	Data models, data definitions, data mapping specifications, data flows, structured data APIs	Business systems, software packages, databases	Technical platforms, networks, security, integration tools
Dependencies	Establishes requirements for the other domains	Manages data created and required by business architecture	Acts on specified data according to business requirements	Hosts and executes the application architecture
Roles	Business architects and analysts, business data stewards	Data architects and modelers, data stewards	Applications architects	Infrastructure architects

1.3.2 Enterprise Architecture Frameworks

An architecture framework is a foundational structure used to develop a broad range of related architectures. Architectural frameworks provide ways of thinking about and understanding architecture. They represent an overall 'architecture for architecture.'

IEEE Computer Society maintains a standard for Enterprise Architecture Frameworks, ISO/IEC/IEEE 42010:2011, Systems and software engineering — Architecture description and a comparison table.[32] Common frameworks and methods include Data Architecture as one of the architectural domains.

1.3.2.1 Zachman Framework for Enterprise Architecture

The most well-known enterprise architectural framework, the Zachman Framework, was developed by John A. Zachman in the 1980s. (See Figure 22.) It has continued to evolve. Zachman recognized that in creating buildings, airplanes, enterprises, value chains, projects, or systems, there are many audiences, and each has a different perspective about architecture. He applied this concept to the requirements for different types and levels of architecture within an enterprise.

The Zachman Framework is an ontology – the 6x6 matrix comprises the complete set of models required to describe an enterprise and the relationships between them. It does not define how to create the models. It simply shows what models should exist.

	What	How	Where	Who	When	Why	
Executive	Inventory Identification	Process Identification	Distribution Identification	Responsibility Identification	Timing Identification	Motivation Identification	**Scope Context**
Business Management	Inventory definition	Process Definition	Distribution Definition	Responsibility Definition	Timing Definition	Motivation Definition	**Business Concepts**
Architect	Inventory Representation	Process Representation	Distribution Representation	Responsibility Representation	Timing Representation	Motivation Representation	**System Logic**
Engineer	Inventory Specification	Process Specification	Distribution Specification	Responsibility Specification	Timing Specification	Motivation Specification	**Technology Physics**
Technician	Inventory Configuration	Process Configuration	Distribution Configuration	Responsibility Configuration	Timing Configuration	Motivation Configuration	**Tool Components**
Enterprise	Inventory Instantiations	Process Instantiations	Distribution Instantiations	Responsibility Instantiations	Timing Instantiations	Motivation Instantiations	**Operational Instances**
	Inventory Sets	**Process Flows**	**Distribution Networks**	**Responsibility Assignments**	**Timing Cycles**	**Motivation Intentions**	

Figure 22 Simplified Zachman Framework

The two dimensions in the matrix framework are the *communication interrogatives* (i.e., what, how, where, who, when, why) as columns and the *reification transformations* (Identification, Definition, Representation, Specification, Configuration, and Instantiation) as rows. The framework classifications are represented by the cells

---

[32] http://bit.ly/2tNnD2j; http://bit.ly/2rVinIq.

(the intersection between the interrogatives and the transformations). Each cell in the Zachman Framework represents a unique type of design artifact.

Communication interrogatives are the fundamental questions that can be asked about any entity. Translated to enterprise architecture, the columns can be understood as follows:

- **What** (the inventory column): Entities used to build the architecture
- **How** (the process column): Activities performed
- **Where** (the distribution column): Business location and technology location
- **Who** (the responsibility column): Roles and organizations
- **When** (the timing column): Intervals, events, cycles, and schedules
- **Why** (the motivation column): Goals, strategies, and means

Reification transformations represent the steps necessary to translate an abstract idea into a concrete instance (an instantiation). These are represented in the rows: planner, owner, designer, builder, implementer, and user. Each has a different perspective on the overall process and different problems to solve. These perspectives are depicted as rows. For example, each perspective has a different relation to the **What** (inventory or data) column:

- **The executive perspective** (business context): Lists of business elements defining scope in identification models.

- **The business management perspective** (business concepts): Clarification of the relationships between business concepts defined by Executive Leaders as Owners in definition models.

- **The architect perspective** (business logic): System logical models detailing system requirements and unconstrained design represented by Architects as Designers in representation models.

- **The engineer perspective** (business physics): Physical models optimizing the design for implementation for specific use under the constraints of specific technology, people, costs, and timeframes specified by Engineers as Builders in specification models.

- **The technician perspective** (component assemblies): A technology-specific, out-of-context view of how components are assembled and operate configured by Technicians as Implementers in configuration models.

- **The user perspective** (operations classes): Actual functioning instances used by Workers as Participants. There are no models in this perspective.

As noted previously, each cell in the Zachman Framework represents a unique type of design artifact, defined by the intersection of its row and column. Each artifact represents how the specific perspective answers the fundamental questions.

1.3.3 Enterprise Data Architecture

Enterprise Data Architecture defines standard terms and designs for the elements that are important to the organization. The design of an Enterprise Data Architecture includes depiction of the business data as such, including the collection, storage, integration, movement, and distribution of data.

As data flows in an organization through feeds or interfaces, it is secured, integrated, stored, recorded, catalogued, shared, reported on, analyzed, and delivered to stakeholders. Along the way, the data may be verified, enhanced, linked, certified, aggregated, anonymized, and used for analytics until archived or purged. The Enterprise Data Architecture descriptions must therefore include both Enterprise Data Models (e.g., data structures and data specifications), as well as Data Flow Design:

- **Enterprise Data Model (EDM)**: The EDM is a holistic, enterprise-level, implementation-independent conceptual or logical data model providing a common consistent view of data across the enterprise. It is common to use the term to mean a high-level, simplified data model, but that is a question of abstraction for presentation. An EDM includes key enterprise data entities (i.e., business concepts), their relationships, critical guiding business rules, and some critical attributes. It sets forth the foundation for all data and data-related projects. Any project-level data model must be based on the EDM. The EDM should be reviewed by stakeholders, so that there is consensus that it effectively represents the enterprise.

- **Data Flow Design**: Defines the requirements and master blueprint for storage and processing across databases, applications, platforms, and networks (the components). These data flows map the movement of data to business processes, locations, business roles, and to technical components.

These two types of specifications need to fit well together. As mentioned, both need to be reflected in current state and target state (architecture perspective), and also in transition state (project perspective).

1.3.3.1 Enterprise Data Model

Some organizations create an EDM as a stand-alone artifact. In other organizations, it is understood as composed of data models from different perspectives and at different levels of detail, that consistently describe an organization's understanding of data entities, data attributes, and their relationships across the enterprise. An EDM includes both universal (Enterprise-wide Conceptual and Logical Models) and application- or project-specific data models, along with definitions, specifications, mappings, and business rules.

Adopting an industry standard model can jumpstart the process of developing an EDM. These models provide a useful guide and references. However, even if an organization starts with a purchased data model, producing enterprise-wide data models requires a significant investment. Work includes defining and documenting an organization's vocabulary, business rules, and business knowledge. Maintaining and enriching an EDM requires an ongoing commitment of time and effort.

An organization that recognizes the need for an enterprise data model must decide how much time and effort it can devote to building and maintaining it. EDMs can be built at different levels of detail, so resource availability will influence initial scope. Over time, as the needs of the enterprise demand, the scope and level of detail captured within an enterprise data model typically expands. Most successful enterprise data models are built incrementally and iteratively, using layers. Figure 23 shows how different types of models are related and how conceptual models are ultimately linkable to physical application data models. It distinguishes:

- A conceptual overview over the enterprise's subject areas
- Views of entities and relationships for each subject area
- Detailed, partially attributed logical views of these same subject areas
- Logical and physical models specific to an application or project

All levels are part of the Enterprise Data Model, and linkages create paths to trace an entity from top to bottom and between models in the same level.

- **Vertical**: Models in each level map to models in other levels. Model lineage is created using these maps. For example, a table or file MobileDevice in a project-specific physical model may link to a MobileDevice entity in the project-specific logical model, a MobileDevice entity in the Product subject area in the Enterprise Logical Model, a Product conceptual entity in the Product Subject Area Model, and to the Product entity in the Enterprise Conceptual Model.

- **Horizontal**: Entities and relationships may appear in multiple models in the same level; entities in logical models centered on one topic may relate to entities in other topics, marked or noted as external to the subject area on the model images. A Product Part entity may appear in the Product subject area models and in the Sales Order, Inventory, and Marketing subject areas, related as external links.

An enterprise data model at all levels is developed using data modeling techniques. (See Chapter 5.)

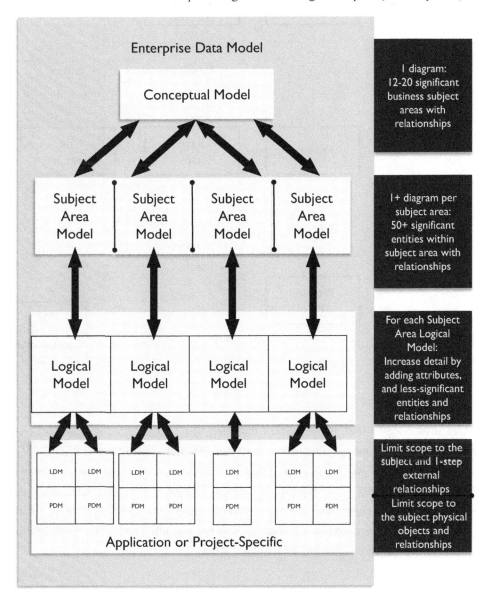

Figure 23 Enterprise Data Model

Figure 24 depicts three Subject Area diagrams (simplified examples), each containing a Conceptual Data Model with a set of entities. Relationships may cross Subject Area borders; each entity in an enterprise data model should reside in only one Subject Area, but can be related to entities in any other Subject Area.

Hence, the conceptual enterprise data model is built up by the combination of Subject Area models. The enterprise data model can be built using a top-down approach or using a bottom-up approach. The top-down approach means starting with forming the Subject Areas and then populating them with models. When using a bottom-up approach the Subject Area structure is based on existing data models. A combination of the approaches is usually recommended; starting with bottom-up using existing models and completing the enterprise data model by populating the models by delegating Subject Area modeling to projects.

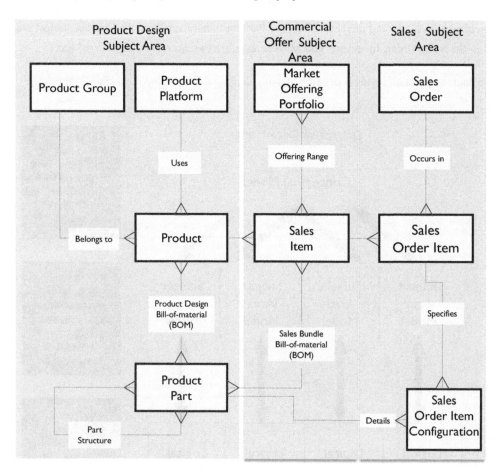

Figure 24 Subject Area Models Diagram Example

The Subject Area discriminator (i.e., the principles that form the Subject Area structure) must be consistent throughout the enterprise data model. Frequently used subject area discriminator principles include: using normalization rules, dividing Subject Areas from systems portfolios (i.e., funding), forming Subject Areas from data governance structure and data ownership (organizational), using top-level processes (based on the business value chains), or using business capabilities (enterprise architecture-based). The Subject Area structure is usually most effective for Data Architecture work if it is formed using normalization rules. The normalization process will establish the major entities that carry/constitute each Subject Area.

1.3.3.2 Data Flow Design

Data flows are a type of data lineage documentation that depicts how data moves through business processes and systems. End-to-end data flows illustrate where the data originated, where it is stored and used, and how it is transformed as it moves inside and between diverse processes and systems. Data lineage analysis can help explain the state of data at a given point in the data flow.

Data flows map and document relationships between data and

- Applications within a business process
- Data stores or databases in an environment
- Network segments (useful for security mapping)
- Business roles, depicting which roles have responsibility for creating, updating, using, and deleting data (CRUD)
- Locations where local differences occur

Data flows can be documented at different levels of detail: Subject Area, business entity, or even the attribute level. Systems can be represented by network segments, platforms, common application sets, or individual servers. Data flows can be represented by two-dimensional matrices (Figure 25) or in data flow diagrams (Figure 26).

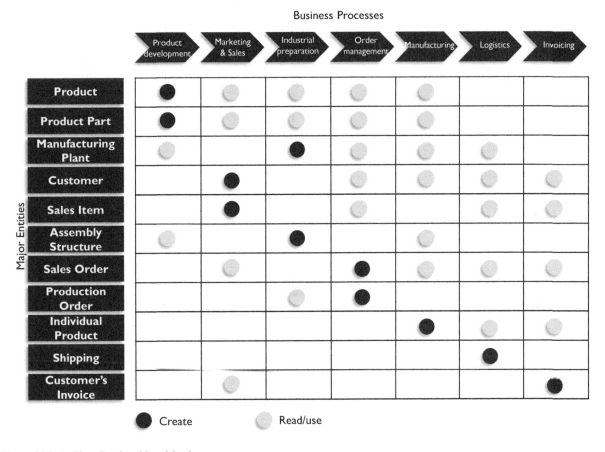

Figure 25 Data Flow Depicted in a Matrix

A matrix gives a clear overview of what data the processes create and use. The benefits of showing the data requirements in a matrix is that it takes into consideration that data does not flow in only one direction; the data exchange between processes are many-to-many in a quite complex way, where any data may appear anywhere. In addition, a matrix can be used to clarify the processes' data acquisition responsibilities and the data dependencies between the processes, which in turn improves the process documentation. Those who prefer working with business capabilities could show this in the same way – just exchanging the processes axis to capabilities. Building such matrices is a long-standing practice in enterprise modeling. IBM introduced this practice in its Business Systems Planning (BSP) method. James Martin later popularized it in his Information Systems Planning (ISP) method during the 1980's.

The data flow in Figure 26 is a traditional high-level data flow diagram depicting what kind of data flows between systems. Such diagrams can be described in many formats and detail levels.

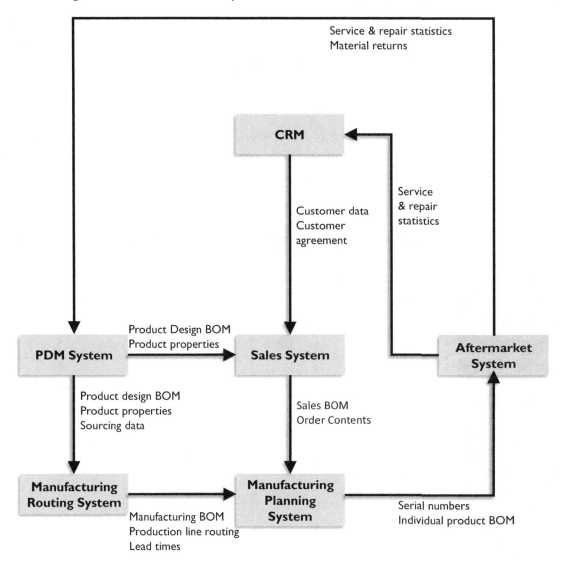

Figure 26 Data Flow Diagram Example

---

2. Activities

Data and enterprise architecture deal with complexity from two viewpoints:

- **Quality-oriented**: Focus on improving execution within business and IT development cycles. Unless architecture is managed, architecture will deteriorate. Systems will gradually become more complex and inflexible, creating risk for an organization. Uncontrolled data delivery, data copies, and interface 'spaghetti' relationships make organizations less efficient and reduce trust in the data.

- **Innovation-oriented**: Focus on transforming business and IT to address new expectations and opportunities. Driving innovation with disruptive technologies and data uses has become a role of the modern Enterprise Architect.

These two drivers require separate approaches. The quality-oriented approach aligns with traditional Data Architecture work where architectural quality improvements are accomplished incrementally. The architecture tasks are distributed to projects, where architects participate or the project carries out by delegation. Typically, the architect keeps the entirety of architecture in mind and focuses on long-term goals directly connected to governance, standardization, and structured development. The innovation-oriented approach can have a shorter-term perspective and be using unproven business logic and leading edge technologies. This orientation often requires architects make contact with people within the organization with whom IT professionals do not usually interact (e.g., product development representatives and business designers).

2.1 Establish Data Architecture Practice

Ideally, Data Architecture should be an integral part of enterprise architecture. If there is not an enterprise architecture function, a Data Architecture team can still be established. Under these conditions, an organization should adopt a framework that helps articulate the goals and drivers for Data Architecture. These drivers will influence approach, scope, and the priorities on the roadmap.

Choose a framework applicable to the business type (e.g., use a government framework for a governmental organization). The views and taxonomy in the framework must be useful in communication to the various stakeholders. This is especially important for Data Architecture initiatives, as they address business and systems terminology. Data Architecture has an inherently close relationship to business architecture.

An Enterprise Data Architecture practice generally includes the following work streams, executed serially or in parallel:

- **Strategy**: Select frameworks, state approaches, develop roadmap

- **Acceptance and culture**: Inform and motivate changes in behavior

- **Organization**: Organize Data Architecture work by assigning accountabilities and responsibilities

- **Working methods**: Define best practices and perform Data Architecture work within development projects, in coordination with Enterprise Architecture

- **Results**: Produce Data Architecture artifacts within an overall roadmap

Enterprise Data Architecture also influences the scope boundaries of projects and system releases:

- **Defining project data requirements**: Data Architects provide enterprise data requirements for individual projects.

- **Reviewing project data designs**: Design reviews ensure that conceptual, logical, and physical data models are consistent with architecture and in support of long-term organizational strategy.

- **Determining data lineage impact**: Ensures that business rules in the applications along the data flow are consistent and traceable.

- **Data replication control**: Replication is a common way to improve application performance and make data more readily available, but it can also create inconsistencies in the data. Data Architecture governance ensures that sufficient replication control (methods and mechanisms) are in place to achieve required consistency. (Not all applications need strict consistency.)

- **Enforcing Data Architecture standards**: Formulating and enforcing standards for the Enterprise Data Architecture lifecycle. Standards can be expressed as principles and procedures, guidelines and as well as blueprints with compliance expectations.

- **Guide data technology and renewal decisions**: The Data Architect works with Enterprise Architects to manage data technology versions, patches, and policies each application uses, as a roadmap for data technology.

2.1.1 Evaluate Existing Data Architecture Specifications

Every organization has some form of documentation for its existing systems. Identify these documents and evaluate them for accuracy, completeness, and level of detail. If necessary, update them to reflect the current state.

2.1.2 Develop a Roadmap

If an enterprise were developed from scratch (free from dependence on existing processes), an optimal architecture would be based solely on the data required to run the enterprise, priorities would be set by business strategy, and decisions could be made unencumbered by the past. Very few organizations are ever in this state. Even in an ideal situation, data dependencies would quickly arise and need to be managed. A roadmap provides a means to manage these dependencies and make forward-looking decisions. A roadmap helps an organization see trade-offs and formulate a pragmatic plan, aligned with business needs and opportunities, external requirements, and available resources.

A roadmap for Enterprise Data Architecture describes the architecture's 3-5 year development path. Together with the business requirements, consideration of actual conditions, and technical assessments, the roadmap describes how the target architecture will become reality. The Enterprise Data Architecture roadmap must be integrated into an overall enterprise architecture roadmap that includes high-level milestones, resources needed, and costs estimations, divided in business capability work streams. The roadmap should be guided by a data management maturity assessment. (See Chapter 15.)

Most business capabilities require data as an input; others also produce data on which other business capabilities are dependent. The enterprise architecture and the Enterprise Data Architecture can be formed coherently by resolving this data flow in a chain of dependencies between business capabilities.

A business-data-driven roadmap starts with the business capabilities that are most independent (i.e., have the least dependency from other activities), and ends with those who are most dependent on others. Dealing with each business capability in sequence will follow an overall business data origination order. Figure 27 shows an example chain of dependency, with the lowest dependency at the top. Product Management and Customer Management do not depend on anything else and thus constitute Master Data. The highest dependency items are on the bottom where Customer's Invoice Management depends on Customer Management and Sales Order Management, which in turn depends on two others.

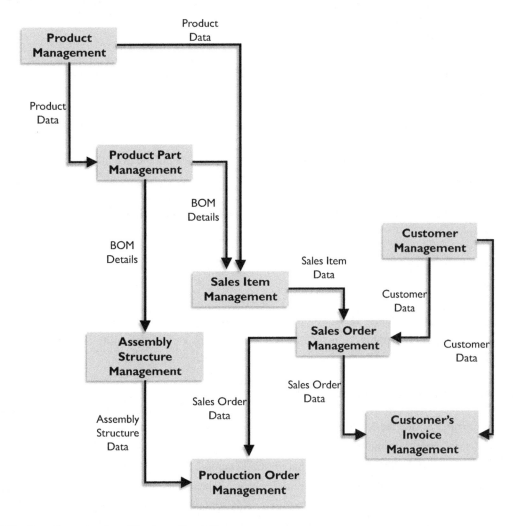

Figure 27 The Data Dependencies of Business Capabilities

Therefore, the roadmap would ideally advise starting at Product Management and Customer Management capabilities and then resolve each dependency in steps from top to bottom.

2.1.3 Manage Enterprise Requirements within Projects

Architecture should not be locked into the limitations that prevail at the time it is developed. Data models and other specifications describing an organization's Data Architecture must be flexible enough to accommodate future requirements. A data model at the architectural level should have a global view of the enterprise along with clear definitions that can be understood throughout the organization.

Development projects implement solutions for capturing, storing, and distributing data based on business requirements and the standards established by the Enterprise Data Architecture. This process, by its nature, is accomplished incrementally.

At the project level, the process of specifying requirements via a data model begins with review of business needs. Often these needs will be specific to the goals of the project and will not have enterprise implications. The process should still include developing definitions of terms and other activities that support use of the data.

Importantly, data architects must be able to understand requirements in relation to the overall architecture. When a project specification is completed, the data architects should determine:

- Whether enterprise-wide entities represented in the specification conform to agreed-upon standards

- What entities in the requirements specification should be included in the overall Enterprise Data Architecture

- Whether entities and definitions in this specification need to be generalized or improved upon to handle future trends

- Whether new data delivery architectures are indicated or whether to point the developers in the direction of reuse

Organizations often wait to address Data Architecture concerns until projects need to design data storage and integration. However, it is preferable to include these considerations early in planning and throughout the entire project lifecycle.

Enterprise Data Architecture project-related activities include:

- **Define scope**: Ensure the scope and interface are aligned with the enterprise data model. Understand the project's potential contribution to the overall Enterprise Data Architecture, with respect to what the project will model and design and in terms of what existing components should (or can) be reused. In those areas that should be designed, the project needs to determine dependencies with stakeholders outside the project scope, such as down-stream processes. The data artifacts that the project determines to be shareable or reusable need to be incorporated into the enterprise logical data model and designated repositories.

- **Understand business requirements**: Capture data-related requirements such as entity, source(s), availability, quality, and pain points, and estimate the business value of meeting these requirements.

- **Design**: Form detailed target specifications, including business rules in a data lifecycle perspective. Validate the outcome and, when needed, address needs for extended and improved standardized models. The enterprise logical data model and enterprise architecture repository are good places for project data architects to look and reuse constructs that are shareable across the enterprise. Review and use data technology standards.

- **Implement**:

    o **When buying,** reverse engineer purchased applications (Commercial Off the Shelf – COTS) and map against data structure. Identify and document gaps and differences in structures, definitions, and rules. Ideally, vendors will supply data models for their products; however, many do not, as they consider these proprietary. If possible, negotiate for a model with in-depth definitions.

    o **When reusing data,** map application data models against common data structures and existing and new processes to understand CRUD operations. Enforce the use of system of record or other authoritative data. Identify and document gaps.

    o **When building,** implement data storage according to the data structure. Integrate according to standardized or designed specifications. (See Chapter 8.)

The role of Enterprise Data Architects in projects depends on the development methodology. The process of building architectural activities into projects also differs between methodologies.

- **Waterfall methods**: Understand the requirements and construct systems in sequential phases as part of an overall enterprise design. This method includes tollgates designed to control change. It is usually no problem to include Data Architecture activities in such models. Be sure to include an enterprise perspective.

- **Incremental methods**: Learn and construct in gradual steps (i.e., mini-waterfalls). This method creates prototypes based on vague overall requirements. The initiation phase is crucial; it is best to create a comprehensive data design in early iterations.

- **Agile, iterative, methods**: Learn, construct, and test in discrete delivery packages (called 'sprints') that are small enough that if work needs to be discarded, not much is lost. Agile methods (Scrum, Rapid Development, and Unified Process) promote object-oriented modeling that emphasizes user interface design, software design, and systems behavior. Complete such methods with specifications for data models, data capture, data storage, and data distribution. Experience from DevOps, an emerging and popular agile approach, testifies about improved data design and effective design choices when programmers and data architects have a strong working relationship and both comply with standards and guidelines.

2.2 Integrate with Enterprise Architecture

The work of developing Enterprise Data Architecture specifications from the subject area level to more detailed levels and in relation to other architecture domains is typically performed within funded projects. Funded projects generally drive architecture priorities. Nevertheless, enterprise-wide Data Architecture matters should be addressed proactively. In fact, Data Architecture may influence the scope of projects. It is best, therefore, to integrate Enterprise Data Architecture matters with project portfolio management. Doing so enables implementation of the roadmap and contributes to better project outcomes.

Likewise, the Enterprise Data Architects need to be included with enterprise application development and integration planning. Apply the Data Architecture view on the target application landscape and the roadmap to that landscape.

3. Tools

3.1 Data Modeling Tools

Data modeling tools and model repositories are necessary for managing the enterprise data model in all levels. Most data modeling tools include lineage and relation tracking functions, which enable architects to manage linkages between models created for different purposes and at different levels of abstraction. (See Chapter 5.)

3.2 Asset Management Software

Asset management software is used to inventory systems, describe their content, and track the relationships between them. Among other things, these tools enable an organization to ensure that it follows contractual obligations related to software licenses and to collect data related to assets that can be used to minimize costs and optimize their IT footprint. Because they compile an inventory of IT assets, such tools collect and contain valuable Metadata about systems and the data they contain. This Metadata is very helpful when creating data flows or researching current state.

3.3 Graphical Design Applications

Graphical design applications are used to create architectural design diagrams, data flows, data value chains, and other architectural artifacts.

4. Techniques

4.1 Lifecycle Projections

Architecture designs can be aspirational or future-looking, implemented and active, or plans for retirement. What they represent should be clearly documented. For example:

- **Current**: Products currently supported and used
- **Deployment period**: Products deployed for use in the next 1-2 years

- **Strategic period**: Products expected to be available for use in the next 2+ years
- **Retirement**: Products the organization has retired or intends to retire within a year
- **Preferred**: Products preferred for use by most applications
- **Containment**: Products limited to use by certain applications
- **Emerging**: Products being researched and piloted for possible future deployment
- **Reviewed**: Products that have been evaluated, the evaluation results and are currently not in any other status above

See Chapter 6 for more about managing data technologies.

4.2 Diagramming Clarity

Models and diagrams present information based on an established set of visual conventions. These need to be used consistently or they will be misunderstood and may, in fact, be incorrect. Characteristics that minimize distractions, and maximize useful information include:

- **A clear and consistent legend**: The legend should identify all objects and lines and what they signify. The legend should be placed in the same spot in all diagrams.

- **A match between all diagram objects and the legend**: In legends that are used as templates, not all legend objects may appear in the diagram, but all diagram objects should match a legend objects.

- **A clear and consistent line direction**: All flows should start at one side or corner (generally the left) and flow toward the opposite side or corner as much as possible. Loops and circles will occur, so make the lines going backward flow out and around to be clear.

- **A consistent line cross display method**: Lines can cross as long as it is clear that the crossing point is not a join. Use line jumps for all lines in one direction. Do not join lines to lines. Minimize the number of lines that cross.

- **Consistent object attributes**: Any difference in sizes, colors, line thickness, etc. should signify something, otherwise differences are distracting.

- **Linear symmetry**: Diagrams with objects placed in lines and columns are more readable than those with random placement. While it is rarely possible to align all objects, lining up at least half (horizontally and/or vertically) will greatly improve readability of any diagram.

5. Implementation Guidelines

As stated in the chapter introduction, Data Architecture is about artifacts, activities and behavior. Implementing Enterprise Data Architecture is therefore about:

- Organizing the Enterprise Data Architecture teams and forums

- Producing the initial versions of Data Architecture artifacts, such as enterprise data model, enterprise-wide data flow and road maps

- Forming and establishing a data architectural way of working in development projects

- Creating awareness throughout the organization of the value of Data Architecture efforts

A Data Architecture implementation should include at least two of these as they benefit from being launched simultaneously, or at least as parallel activities. The implementation can begin in a part of the organization, or, in a data domain, such as product data or customer data. After learning and maturing, the implementation may grow wider.

Data models and other Data Architecture artifacts are usually captured within development projects, and then standardized and managed by data architects. Therefore, the first projects will have larger portions of Data Architecture work before there are any artifacts to reuse. These early projects could benefit from special architecture funding.

The Enterprise Data Architect collaborates with other business and technology architects who share the common goal of improving organizational effectiveness and agility. The business drivers for the overall enterprise architecture also influence Enterprise Data Architecture implementation strategy significantly.

Establishing an Enterprise Data Architecture in a solution-oriented culture where new inventions are tried using disruptive technology will require an agile implementation approach. This can include having an outlined subject area model on an overall level while participating on a detail level in agile sprints. Thus, the Enterprise Data Architecture will evolve incrementally. However, this agile approach needs to ensure that data architects are engaged early in development initiatives, as these evolve rapidly in an inventive culture.

Having a quality driver for enterprise architecture may force some initial Data Architecture work on an enterprise level for planned development projects. Typically, the Enterprise Data Architecture starts with Master Data areas that are in great need for improvements and, once established and accepted, expands to include business event oriented data (i.e., transactional data). This is the traditional implementation approach where Enterprise Data Architects produce blueprints and templates to be used throughout the system landscape, and ensuring compliance using various governance means.

5.1 Readiness Assessment / Risk Assessment

Architecture initiation projects expose more risks than other projects, especially during the first attempt within the organization. The most significant risks are:

- **Lack of management support**: Any reorganization of the enterprise during the planned execution of the project will affect the architecture process. For example, new decision makers may question the process and be tempted to withdraw from opportunities for participants to continue their work on the Data Architecture. It is by establishing support among management that an architecture process can survive reorganization. Therefore, be certain to enlist into the Data Architecture development process more than one member of top-level management, or at least senior management, who understand the benefits of Data Architecture.

- **No proven record of accomplishment**: Having a sponsor is essential to the success of the effort, as is his or her confidence in those carrying out the Data Architecture function. Enlist the help of a senior architect colleague to help carry out the most important steps.

- **Apprehensive sponsor**: If the sponsor requires all communication to pass through them, it may be an indication that that person is uncertain of their role, has interests other than the objectives of the Data Architecture process, or is uncertain of the data architect's capability. Regardless of the reason, the sponsor must allow the project manager and data architect to take the leading roles in the project. Try to establish independence in the workplace, along with the sponsor's confidence.

- **Counter-productive executive decisions**: It may be the case that although management understands the value of a well-organized Data Architecture, they do not know how to achieve it. Therefore, they may make decisions that counteract the data architect's efforts. This is not a sign of disloyal management but rather an indication that the data architect needs to communicate more clearly or frequently with management.

- **Culture shock**: Consider how the working culture will change among those who will be affected by the Data Architecture. Try to imagine how easy or difficult it will be for the employees to change their behavior within the organization.

- **Inexperienced project leader**: Make sure that the project manager has experience with Enterprise Data Architecture particularly if the project has a heavy data component. If this is not the case, encourage the sponsor to change or educate the project manager (Edvinsson, 2013).

- **Dominance of a one-dimensional view**: Sometimes the owner(s) of one business application might tend to dictate their view about the overall enterprise-level Data Architecture (e.g., the owners of an ERP system) at the expense of a more well-balanced, all-inclusive view.

5.2 Organization and Cultural Change

The speed with which an organization adopts architectural practices depends on how adaptive its culture is. The nature of design work requires that architects collaborate with developers and other creative thinkers throughout the organization. Often such people are used to working in their own ways. They may embrace or resist the change required to adopt formal architecture principles and tools.

Output-oriented, strategically aligned organizations are in the best position to adopt architectural practices. These organizations are most often goal-oriented, aware of customer and partner challenges, and capable of prioritizing based on common objectives.

The ability of an organization to adopt Data Architecture practices depends on several factors:

- Cultural receptivity to architectural approach (developing an architecture-friendly culture)
- Organizational recognition of data as a business asset, not just an IT concern
- Organizational ability to let go of a local perspective and adopt an enterprise perspective on data
- Organizational ability to integrate architectural deliverables into project methodology
- Level of acceptance of formal data governance

- Ability to look holistically at the enterprise, rather than being focused solely on project delivery and IT solutioning (Edvinsson, 2013)

6. Data Architecture Governance

Data Architecture activities directly support the alignment and control of data. Data architects often act as business liaisons for data governance activities. Therefore, Enterprise Data Architecture and the Data Governance organization have to be well aligned. Ideally, both a data architect and a Data Steward should be assigned to each subject area and even to each entity within a subject area. In addition, business oversight should be aligned to process oversight. Business event subject areas should be aligned with business process governance as each event entity usually corresponds to a business process. Data Architecture governance activities include:

- **Overseeing Projects**: This includes ensuring that projects comply with required Data Architecture activities, use and improve architectural assets, and implement according to stated architectural standards.
- **Managing architectural designs, lifecycle, and tools**: Architectural designs must be defined, evaluated and maintained. Enterprise Data Architecture serves as a 'zoning plan' for long-term integration. Future state architecture affects project objectives and influences the priority of the projects in the project portfolio.
- **Defining standards**: Setting the rules, guidelines, and specifications for how data is used within the organization.
- **Creating data-related artifacts**: Artifacts that enable compliance with governance directives.

6.1 Metrics

Performance metrics on Enterprise Data Architecture reflect the architectural goals: architectural compliance, implementation trends, and business value from Data Architecture. Data Architecture metrics are often monitored annually as part of overall business customer satisfaction with projects.

- **Architecture standard compliance rate** measures how closely projects comply with established Data Architectures and how well projects adhere to processes for engaging with enterprise architecture. Metrics that track project exceptions may also be useful as a means of understanding obstacles to adoption.

- **Implementation trends** track the degree to which enterprise architecture has improved the organization's ability to implement projects, along at least two lines:

  - **Use/reuse/replace/retire measurements**: Determine the proportion of new architecture artifacts versus reused, replaced, or retired artifacts.
  - **Project execution efficiency measurements**: These measure lead times for projects and their resource costs for delivery improvements with reusable artifacts and guiding artifacts.

- **Business value measurements** track progress toward expected business effects and benefits.

- o **Business agility improvements**: Measurements that account for the benefits of lifecycle improvements or alternative, the cost of delay.
- o **Business quality**: Measurements of whether business cases are fulfilled as intended; measuring whether projects actually deliver changes that lead to business improvements based on newly created or integrated data.
- o **Business operation quality**: Measurements of improved efficiency. Examples include improved accuracy, and reducing the time and expense of correcting mistakes due to data errors.
- o **Business environment improvements**: Examples include improved client retention rate related to reducing data errors, and reduced incidence of remarks from authorities on submitted reports.

7. Works Cited / Recommended

Ahlemann, Frederik, Eric Stettiner, Marcus Messerschmidt, and Christine Legner, eds. *Strategic Enterprise Architecture Management: Challenges, Best Practices, and Future Developments*. Springer, 2012. Print. Management for Professionals.

Bernard, Scott A. *An Introduction to Enterprise Architecture*. 2nd ed. Authorhouse, 2005. Print.

Brackett, Michael H. *Data Sharing Using a Common Data Architecture*. John Wiley and Sons, 1994. Print.

Carbone, Jane. *IT Architecture Toolkit*. Prentice Hall, 2004. Print.

Cook, Melissa. *Building Enterprise Information Architectures: Re-Engineering Information Systems*. Prentice Hall, 1996. Print.

Edvinsson, Hakan and Lottie Aderinne. *Enterprise Architecture Made Simple Using the Ready, Set, Go Approach to Achieving Information Centricity*. Technics Publications, LCC, 2013. Print.

Executive Office of the President of the United States. *The Common Approach to Federal Enterprise Architecture*. whitehouse.gov, 2012. Web.

Fong, Joseph. *Information Systems Reengineering and Integration*. 2nd ed. Springer, 2006. Print.

Gane, Chris and Trish Sarson. *Structured Systems Analysis: Tools and Techniques*. Prentice Hall, 1979. Print.

Hagan, Paula J., ed. *EABOK: Guide to the (Evolving) Enterprise Architecture Body of Knowledge*. mitre.org MITRE Corporation, 2004. Web.

Harrison, Rachel. *TOGAF Version 8.1.1 Enterprise Edition - Study Guide*. The Open Group. 2nd ed. Van Haren Publishing, 2007. Print. TOGAF.

Hoberman, Steve, Donna Burbank, and Chris Bradley. *Data Modeling for the Business: A Handbook for Aligning the Business with IT using High-Level Data Models*. Technics Publications, LLC, 2009. Print. Take It with You Guides.

Hoberman, Steve. *Data Modeling Made Simple: A Practical Guide for Business and Information Technology Professionals*. 2nd ed. Technics Publications, LLC, 2009. Print.

Hoogervorst, Jan A. P. *Enterprise Governance and Enterprise Engineering*. Springer, 2009. Print. The Enterprise Engineering Ser.

ISO (website). http://bit.ly/2sTp2rA, http://bit.ly/2ri8Gqk.

Inmon, W. H., John A. Zachman, and Jonathan G. Geiger. *Data Stores, Data Warehousing and the Zachman Framework: Managing Enterprise Knowledge*. McGraw-Hill, 1997. Print.

Lankhorst, Marc. Enterprise Architecture at Work: Modeling, Communication and Analysis. Springer, 2005. Print.

Martin, James and Joe Leben. *Strategic Information Planning Methodologies*, 2nd ed. Prentice Hall, 1989. Print.

Osterwalder, Alexander and Yves Pigneur. *Business Model Generation: A Handbook for Visionaries, Game Changers, and Challengers*. Wiley, 2010. Print.

Perks, Col and Tony Beveridge. *Guide to Enterprise IT Architecture*. Springer, 2003. Print. Springer Professional Computing.

Poole, John, Dan Chang, Douglas Tolbert, and David Mellor. *Common Warehouse Metamodel*. Wiley, 2001. Print. OMG (Book 17).

Radhakrishnan, Rakesh. *Identity and Security: A Common Architecture and Framework For SOA and Network Convergence*. futuretext, 2007. Print.

Ross, Jeanne W., Peter Weill, and David Robertson. *Enterprise Architecture As Strategy: Creating a Foundation For Business Execution*. Harvard Business School Press, 2006. Print.

Schekkerman, Jaap. *How to Survive in the Jungle of Enterprise Architecture Frameworks: Creating or Choosing an Enterprise Architecture Framework*. Trafford Publishing, 2006. Print.

Spewak, Steven and Steven C. Hill. *Enterprise Architecture Planning: Developing a Blueprint for Data, Applications, and Technology*. 2nd ed. A Wiley-QED Publication, 1993. Print.

Ulrich, William M. and Philip Newcomb. *Information Systems Transformation: Architecture-Driven Modernization Case Studies*. Morgan Kaufmann, 2010. Print. The MK/OMG Press.

CHAPTER 5

Data Modeling and Design

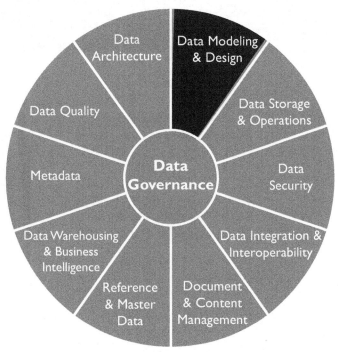

DAMA-DMBOK2 Data Management Framework

Copyright © 2017 by DAMA International

1. Introduction

Data modeling is the process of discovering, analyzing, and scoping data requirements, and then representing and communicating these data requirements in a precise form called the *data model*. Data modeling is a critical component of data management. The modeling process requires that organizations discover and document how their data fits together. The modeling process itself designs how data fits together (Simsion, 2013). Data models depict and enable an organization to understand its data assets.

There are a number of different schemes used to represent data. The six most commonly used schemes are: Relational, Dimensional, Object-Oriented, Fact-Based, Time-Based, and NoSQL. Models of these schemes exist at three levels of detail: conceptual, logical, and physical. Each model contains a set of components. Examples of components are entities, relationships, facts, keys, and attributes. Once a model is built, it needs to be reviewed and once approved, maintained.

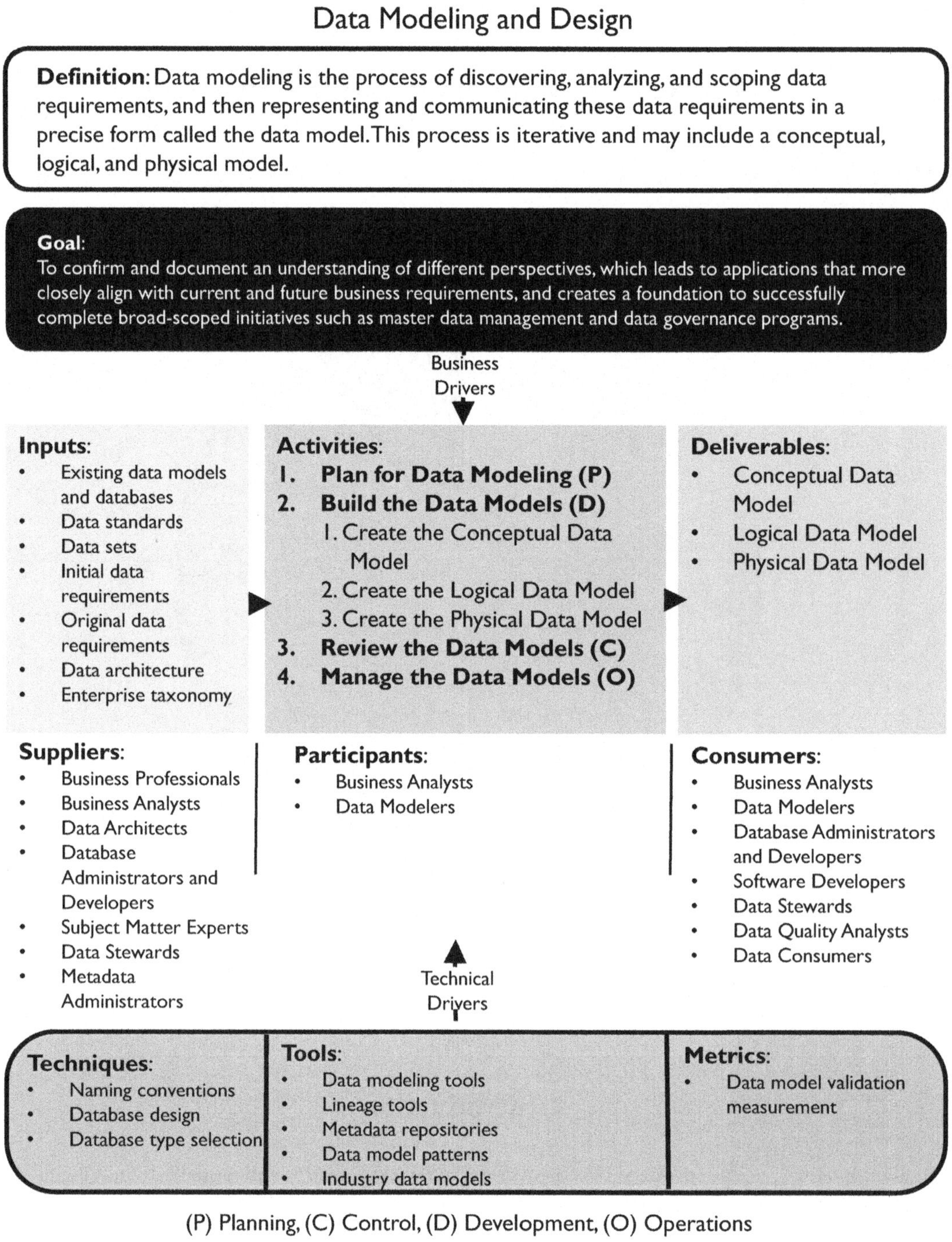

Data Modeling and Design

Definition: Data modeling is the process of discovering, analyzing, and scoping data requirements, and then representing and communicating these data requirements in a precise form called the data model. This process is iterative and may include a conceptual, logical, and physical model.

Goal:
To confirm and document an understanding of different perspectives, which leads to applications that more closely align with current and future business requirements, and creates a foundation to successfully complete broad-scoped initiatives such as master data management and data governance programs.

Business Drivers

Inputs:
- Existing data models and databases
- Data standards
- Data sets
- Initial data requirements
- Original data requirements
- Data architecture
- Enterprise taxonomy

Activities:
1. **Plan for Data Modeling (P)**
2. **Build the Data Models (D)**
   1. Create the Conceptual Data Model
   2. Create the Logical Data Model
   3. Create the Physical Data Model
3. **Review the Data Models (C)**
4. **Manage the Data Models (O)**

Deliverables:
- Conceptual Data Model
- Logical Data Model
- Physical Data Model

Suppliers:
- Business Professionals
- Business Analysts
- Data Architects
- Database Administrators and Developers
- Subject Matter Experts
- Data Stewards
- Metadata Administrators

Participants:
- Business Analysts
- Data Modelers

Consumers:
- Business Analysts
- Data Modelers
- Database Administrators and Developers
- Software Developers
- Data Stewards
- Data Quality Analysts
- Data Consumers

Technical Drivers

Techniques:
- Naming conventions
- Database design
- Database type selection

Tools:
- Data modeling tools
- Lineage tools
- Metadata repositories
- Data model patterns
- Industry data models

Metrics:
- Data model validation measurement

(P) Planning, (C) Control, (D) Development, (O) Operations

Figure 28 Context Diagram: Data Modeling and Design

Data models comprise and contain Metadata essential to data consumers. Much of this Metadata uncovered during the data modeling process is essential to other data management functions. For example, definitions for data governance and lineage for data warehousing and analytics.

This chapter will describe the purpose of data models, the essential concepts and common vocabulary used in data modeling, and data modeling goals and principles. It will use a set of examples from data related to education to illustrate how data models work and to show differences between them.

1.1 Business Drivers

Data models are critical to effective management of data. They:

- Provide a common vocabulary around data
- Capture and document explicit knowledge about an organization's data and systems
- Serve as a primary communications tool during projects
- Provide the starting point for customization, integration, or even replacement of an application

1.2 Goals and Principles

The goal of data modeling is to confirm and document understanding of different perspectives, which leads to applications that more closely align with current and future business requirements, and creates a foundation to successfully complete broad-scoped initiatives such as Master Data Management and data governance programs. Proper data modeling leads to lower support costs and increases the reusability opportunities for future initiatives, thereby reducing the costs of building new applications. Data models are an important form of Metadata.

Confirming and documenting understanding of different perspectives facilitates:

- **Formalization**: A data model documents a concise definition of data structures and relationships. It enables assessment of how data is affected by implemented business rules, for current as-is states or desired target states. Formal definition imposes a disciplined structure to data that reduces the possibility of data anomalies occurring when accessing and persisting data. By illustrating the structures and relationships in the data, a data model makes data easier to consume.

- **Scope definition**: A data model can help explain the boundaries for data context and implementation of purchased application packages, projects, initiatives, or existing systems.

- **Knowledge retention/documentation**: A data model can preserve corporate memory regarding a system or project by capturing knowledge in an explicit form. It serves as documentation for future projects to use as the as-is version. Data models help us understand an organization or business area, an existing application, or the impact of modifying an existing data structure. The data model becomes a reusable map to help business professionals, project managers, analysts, modelers, and developers understand data structure within the environment. In much the same way as the mapmaker learned and documented a geographic landscape for others to use for navigation, the modeler enables others to understand an information landscape (Hoberman, 2009).

1.3 Essential Concepts

This section will explain the different types of data that can be modeled, the component pieces of data models, the types of data models that can be developed, and the reasons for choosing different types in different situations. This set of definitions is extensive, in part, because data modeling itself is about the process of definition. It is important to understand the vocabulary that supports the practice.

1.3.1 Data Modeling and Data Models

Data modeling is most frequently performed in the context of systems development and maintenance efforts, known as the system development lifecycle (SDLC). Data modeling can also be performed for broad-scoped initiatives (e.g., Business and Data Architecture, Master Data Management, and data governance initiatives) where the immediate end result is not a database but an understanding of organizational data.

A model is a representation of something that exists or a pattern for something to be made. A model can contain one or more diagrams. Model diagrams make use of standard symbols that allow one to understand content. Maps, organization charts, and building blueprints are examples of models in use every day.

A data model describes an organization's data as the organization understands it, or as the organization wants it to be. A data model contains a set of symbols with text labels that attempts visually to represent data requirements as communicated to the data modeler, for a specific set of data that can range in size from small, for a project, to large, for an organization. The model is a form of documentation for data requirements and data definitions resulting from the modeling process. Data models are the main medium used to communicate data requirements from business to IT and within IT from analysts, modelers, and architects, to database designers and developers.

1.3.2 Types of Data that are Modeled

Four main types of data can be modeled (Edvinsson, 2013). The types of data being modeled in any given organization reflect the priorities of the organization or the project that requires a data model:

- **Category information**: Data used to classify and assign types to things. For example, customers classified by market categories or business sectors; products classified by color, model, size, etc.; orders classified by whether they are open or closed.

- **Resource information**: Basic profiles of resources needed conduct operational processes such as Product, Customer, Supplier, Facility, Organization, and Account. Among IT professionals, resource entities are sometimes referred to as Reference Data.

- **Business event information**: Data created while operational processes are in progress. Examples include Customer Orders, Supplier Invoices, Cash Withdrawal, and Business Meetings. Among IT professionals, event entities are sometimes referred to as transactional business data.

- **Detail transaction information**: Detailed transaction information is often produced through point-of-sale systems (either in stores or online). It is also produced through social media systems, other Internet interactions (clickstream, etc.), and by sensors in machines, which can be parts of vessels and vehicles, industrial components, or personal devices (GPS, RFID, Wi-Fi, etc.). This type of detailed information can be aggregated, used to derive other data, and analyzed for trends, similar to how the business information events are used. This type of data (large volume and/or rapidly changing) is usually referred to as Big Data.

These types refer to 'data at rest'. Data in motion can also be modeled, for example, in schemes for systems, including protocols, and schemes for messaging and event-based systems.

1.3.3 Data Model Components

As will be discussed later in the chapter, different types of data models represent data through different conventions (See Section 1.3.4). However, most data models contain the same basic building blocks: entities, relationships, attributes, and domains.

1.3.3.1 Entity

Outside of data modeling, the definition of *entity* is a thing that exists separate from other things. Within data modeling, an entity is a thing about which an organization collects information. Entities are sometimes referred to as the nouns of an organization. An entity can be thought of as the answer to a fundamental question – who, what, when, where, why, or how – or to a combination of these questions (see Chapter 4). Table 7 defines and gives examples of commonly used entity categories (Hoberman, 2009).

Table 7 Commonly Used Entity Categories

Category	Definition	Examples
Who	Person or organization of interest. That is, *Who* is important to the business? Often a 'who' is associated with a party generalization, or role such as Customer or Vendor. Persons or organizations can have multiple roles or be included in multiple parties.	Employee, Patient, Player, Suspect, Customer, Vendor, Student, Passenger, Competitor, Author
What	Product or service of interest to the enterprise. It often refers to what the organization makes or what service it provides. That is, *What* is important to the business? Attributes for categories, types, etc. are very important here.	Product, Service, Raw Material, Finished Good, Course, Song, Photograph, Book
When	Calendar or time interval of interest to the enterprise. That is, *When* is the business in operation?	Time, Date, Month, Quarter, Year, Calendar, Semester, Fiscal Period, Minute, Departure Time
Where	Location of interest to the enterprise. Location can refer to actual places as well as electronic places. That is, *Where* is business conducted?	Mailing Address, Distribution Point, Website URL, IP Address
Why	Event or transaction of interest to the enterprise. These events keep the business afloat. That is, *Why* is the business in business?	Order, Return, Complaint, Withdrawal, Deposit, Compliment, Inquiry, Trade, Claim

Category	Definition	Examples
How	Documentation of the event of interest to the enterprise. Documents provide the evidence that the events occurred, such as a Purchase Order recording an Order event. That is, *How* do we know that an event occurred?	Invoice, Contract, Agreement, Account, Purchase Order, Speeding Ticket, Packing Slip, Trade Confirmation
Measurement	Counts, sums, etc. of the other categories (what, where) at or over points in time (when).	Sales, Item Count, Payments, Balance

1.3.3.1.1 Entity Aliases

The generic term *entity* can go by other names. The most common is *entity-type*, as a type of something is being represented (e.g., Jane is of type Employee), therefore Jane is the entity and Employee is the entity type. However, in widespread use today is using the term *entity* for Employee and *entity instance* for Jane.

Table 8 Entity, Entity Type, and Entity Instance

Usage	Entity	Entity Type	Entity Instance
Common Use	Jane	Employee	
Recommended Use	Employee		Jane

Entity instances are the occurrences or values of a particular entity. The entity **Student** may have multiple student instances, with names Bob Jones, Joe Jackson, Jane Smith, and so forth. The entity **Course** can have instances of Data Modeling Fundamentals, Advanced Geology, and English Literature in the 17th Century.

Entity aliases can also vary based on scheme. (Schemes will be discussed in Section 1.3.4.) In relational schemes the term *entity* is often used, in dimensional schemes the terms *dimension* and *fact table* are often used, in object-oriented schemes the terms *class* or *object* are often used, in time-based schemes the terms *hub, satellite,* and *link* are often used, and in NoSQL schemes terms such as *document* or *node* are used.

Entity aliases can also vary based on level of detail. (The three levels of detail will be discussed in Section 1.3.5.) An entity at the conceptual level can be called a *concept* or *term*, an entity at the logical level is called an *entity* (or a different term depending on the scheme), and at the physical level the terms vary based on database technology, the most common term being *table*.

1.3.3.1.2 Graphic Representation of Entities

In data models, entities are generally depicted as rectangles (or rectangles with rounded edges) with their names inside, such as in Figure 29, where there are three entities: **Student, Course,** and **Instructor**.

Student		Course		Instructor

Figure 29 Entities

1.3.3.1.3 Definition of Entities

Entity definitions are essential contributors to the business value of any data model. They are core Metadata. High quality definitions clarify the meaning of business vocabulary and provide rigor to the business rules governing entity relationships. They assist business and IT professionals in making intelligent business and application design decisions. High quality data definitions exhibit three essential characteristics:

- **Clarity**: The definition should be easy to read and grasp. Simple, well-written sentences without obscure acronyms or unexplained ambiguous terms such as *sometimes* or *normally*.

- **Accuracy**: The definition is a precise and correct description of the entity. Definitions should be reviewed by experts in the relevant business areas to ensure that they are accurate.

- **Completeness**: All of the parts of the definition are present. For example, in defining a code, examples of the code values are included. In defining an identifier, the scope of uniqueness in included in the definition.

1.3.3.2 Relationship

A relationship is an association between entities (Chen, 1976). A relationship captures the high-level interactions between conceptual entities, the detailed interactions between logical entities, and the constraints between physical entities.

1.3.3.2.1 Relationship Aliases

The generic term *relationship* can go by other names. Relationship aliases can vary based on scheme. In relational schemes the term *relationship* is often used, dimensional schemes the term *navigation path* is often used, and in NoSQL schemes terms such as *edge* or *link* are used, for example. Relationship aliases can also vary based on level of detail. A relationship at the conceptual and logical levels is called a *relationship*, but a relationship at the physical level may be called by other names, such as *constraint* or *reference*, depending on the database technology.

1.3.3.2.2 Graphic Representation of Relationships

Relationships are shown as lines on the data modeling diagram. See Figure 30 for an Information Engineering example.

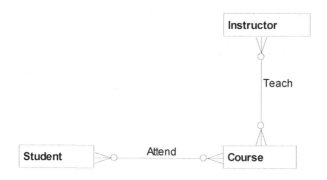

Figure 30 Relationships

In this example, the relationship between **Student** and **Course** captures the rule that a Student may attend Courses. The relationship between **Instructor** and **Course** captures the rule than an Instructor may teach Courses. The symbols on the line (called cardinality) capture the rules in a precise syntax. (These will be explained in Section 1.3.3.2.3.) A relationship is represented through foreign keys in a relational database and through alternative methods for NoSQL databases such as through edges or links.

1.3.3.2.3 Relationship Cardinality

In a relationship between two entities, *cardinality* captures how many of one entity (entity instances) participates in the relationship with how many of the other entity. Cardinality is represented by the symbols that appear on both ends of a relationship line. Data rules are specified and enforced through cardinality. Without cardinality, the most one can say about a relationship is that two entities are connected in some way.

For cardinality, the choices are simple: zero, one, or many. Each side of a relationship can have any combination of zero, one, or many ('many' means could be more than 'one'). Specifying zero or one allows us to capture whether or not an entity instance is required in a relationship. Specifying one or many allows us to capture how many of a particular instance participates in a given relationship.

These cardinality symbols are illustrated in the following information engineering example of **Student** and **Course**.

Figure 31 Cardinality Symbols

The business rules are:

- Each **Student** may attend one or many **Courses**.
- Each **Course** may be attended by one or many **Students**.

1.3.3.2.4 Arity of Relationships

The number of entities in a relationship is the 'arity' of the relationship. The most common are unary, binary, and ternary relationships.

1.3.3.2.4.1 Unary (Recursive) Relationship

A unary (also known as a recursive or self-referencing) relationship involves only one entity. A one-to-many recursive relationship describes a hierarchy, whereas a many-to-many relationship describes a network or graph. In a hierarchy, an entity instance has at most one parent (or higher-level entity). In relational modeling, child entities are on the many side of the relationship, with parent entities on the one side of the relationship. In a network, an entity instance can have more than one parent.

For example, a Course can require prerequisites. If, in order to take the Biology Workshop, one would first need to complete the Biology Lecture, the Biology Lecture is the prerequisite for the Biology Workshop. In the following relational data models, which use information engineering notation, one can model this recursive relationship as either a hierarchy or network:

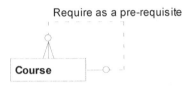

Figure 32 Unary Relationship - Hierarchy

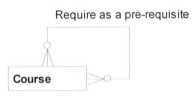

Figure 33 Unary Relationship - Network

This first example (Figure 32) is a hierarchy and the second (Figure 33) is a network. In the first example, the Biology Workshop requires first taking the Biology Lecture and the Chemistry Lecture. Once the Biology Lecture is chosen as the prerequisite for the Biology Workshop, the Biology Lecture cannot be the prerequisite for any other courses. The second example allows the Biology Lecture to be the prerequisite for other courses as well.

1.3.3.2.4.2 Binary Relationship

An arity of two is also known as binary. A binary relationship, the most common on a traditional data model diagram, involves two entities. Figure 34, a UML class diagram, shows that both **Student** and **Course** are entities participating in a binary relationship.

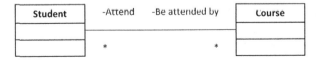

Figure 34 Binary Relationship

1.3.3.2.4.3 Ternary Relationship

An arity of three, known as ternary, is a relationship that includes three entities. An example in fact-based modeling (object-role notation) appears in Figure 35. Here **Student** can register for a particular **Course** in a given **Semester**.

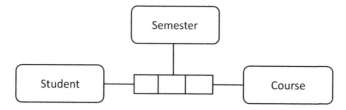

Figure 35 Ternary Relationship

1.3.3.2.5 Foreign Key

A foreign key is used in physical and sometimes logical relational data modeling schemes to represent a relationship. A foreign key may be created implicitly when a relationship is defined between two entities, depending on the database technology or data modeling tool, and whether the two entities involved have mutual dependencies.

In the example shown in Figure 36, Registration contains two foreign keys, **Student Number** from **Student** and **Course Code** from **Course**. Foreign keys appear in the entity on the many side of the relationship, often called the child entity. **Student** and **Course** are parent entities and **Registration** is the child entity.

Figure 36 Foreign Keys

1.3.3.3 Attribute

An attribute is a property that identifies, describes, or measures an entity. Attributes may have domains, which will be discussed in Section 1.3.3.4. The physical correspondent of an attribute in an entity is a column, field, tag, or node in a table, view, document, graph, or file.

1.3.3.3.1 Graphic Representation of Attributes

In data models, attributes are generally depicted as a list within the entity rectangle, as shown in Figure 37, where the attributes of the entity **Student** include **Student Number**, **Student First Name**, **Student Last Name**, and **Student Birth Date**.

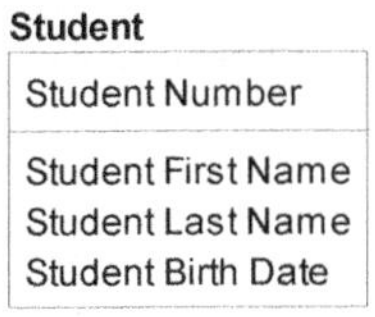

Student

Student Number
Student First Name
Student Last Name
Student Birth Date

Figure 37 Attributes

1.3.3.3.2 Identifiers

An identifier (also called a *key*) is a set of one or more attributes that uniquely defines an instance of an entity. This section defines types of keys by construction (simple, compound, composite, surrogate) and function (candidate, primary, alternate).

1.3.3.3.2.1 Construction-type Keys

A *simple key* is one attribute that uniquely identifies an entity instance. Universal Product Codes (UPCs) and Vehicle Identification Numbers (VINs) are examples of simple keys. A *surrogate key* is also an example of a simple key. A surrogate key is a unique identifier for a table. Often a counter and always system-generated without intelligence, a surrogate key is an integer whose meaning is unrelated to its face value. (In other words, a Month Identifier of 1 cannot be assumed to represent January.) Surrogate keys serve technical functions and should not be visible to end users of a database. They remain behind the scenes to help maintain uniqueness, allow for more efficient navigation across structures, and facilitate integration across applications.

A *compound key* is a set of two or more attributes that together uniquely identify an entity instance. Examples are US phone number (area code + exchange + local number) and credit card number (issuer ID + account ID + check digit).

A *composite key* contains one compound key and at least one other simple or compound key or non-key attribute. An example is a key on a multi-dimensional fact table, which may contain several compound keys, simple keys, and optionally a load timestamp.

1.3.3.3.2.2 Function-type Keys

A *super key* is any set of attributes that uniquely identify an entity instance. A *candidate key* is a minimal set of one or more attributes (i.e., a simple or compound key) that identifies the entity instance to which it belongs. Minimal means that no subset of the candidate key uniquely identifies the entity instance. An entity may have multiple candidate keys. Examples of candidate keys for a customer entity are email address, cell phone number, and customer account number. Candidate keys can be business keys (sometimes called *natural keys*). A *business key* is one or more attributes that a business professional would use to retrieve a single entity instance. Business keys and surrogate keys are mutually exclusive.

A *primary key* is the candidate key that is chosen to be *the* unique identifier for an entity. Even though an entity may contain more than one candidate key, only one candidate key can serve as the primary key for an entity. An *alternate key* is a candidate key that although unique, was not chosen as the primary key. An alternate key can still be used to find specific entity instances. Often the primary key is a surrogate key and the alternate keys are business keys.

1.3.3.3.2.3 Identifying vs. Non-Identifying Relationships

An independent entity is one where the primary key contains only attributes that belong to that entity. A dependent entity is one where the primary key contains at least one attribute from another entity. In relational schemes, most notations depict independent entities on the data modeling diagram as rectangles and dependent entities as rectangles with rounded corners.

In the student example shown in Figure 38, **Student** and **Course** are independent entities and **Registration** is a dependent entity.

Figure 38 Dependent and Independent Entity

Dependent entities have at least one identifying relationship. An identifying relationship is one where the primary key of the parent (the entity on the one side of the relationship) is migrated as a foreign key to the child's primary key, as can be seen with the relationship from **Student** to **Registration**, and from **Course** to **Registration**. In non-identifying relationships, the primary key of the parent is migrated as a non-primary foreign key attribute to the child.

1.3.3.4 Domain

In data modeling, a *domain* is the complete set of possible values that an attribute can be assigned. A domain may be articulated in different ways (see points at the end of this section). A domain provides a means of standardizing the characteristics of the attributes. For example, the domain **Date**, which contains all possible valid dates, can be assigned to any date attribute in a logical data model or date columns/fields in a physical data model, such as:

- EmployeeHireDate
- OrderEntryDate
- ClaimSubmitDate
- CourseStartDate

All values inside the domain are valid values. Those outside the domain are referred to as invalid values. An attribute should not contain values outside of its assigned domain. **EmployeeGenderCode**, for example, may be limited to the domain of female and male. The domain for **EmployeeHireDate** may be defined simply as valid dates. Under this rule, the domain for **EmployeeHireDate** does not include February 30 of any year.

One can restrict a domain with additional rules, called *constraints*. Rules can relate to format, logic, or both. For example, by restricting the **EmployeeHireDate** domain to dates earlier than today's date, one would eliminate

March 10, 2050 from the domain of valid values, even though it is a valid date. **EmployeeHireDate** could also be restricted to days in a typical workweek (e.g., dates that fall on a Monday, Tuesday, Wednesday, Thursday, or Friday).

Domains can be defined in different ways.

- **Data Type**: Domains that specify the standard types of data one can have in an attribute assigned to that domain. For example, Integer, Character(30), and Date are all data type domains.

- **Data Format**: Domains that use patterns including templates and masks, such as are found in postal codes and phone numbers, and character limitations (alphanumeric only, alphanumeric with certain special characters allowed, etc.) to define valid values.

- **List**: Domains that contain a finite set of values. These are familiar to many people from functionality like dropdown lists. For example, the list domain for **OrderStatusCode** can restrict values to only {Open, Shipped, Closed, Returned}.

- **Range**: Domains that allow all values of the same data type that are between one or more minimum and/or maximum values. Some ranges can be open-ended. For example, **OrderDeliveryDate** must be between **OrderDate** and three months in the future.

- **Rule-based**: Domains defined by the rules that values must comply with in order to be valid. These include rules comparing values to calculated values or other attribute values in a relation or set. For example, **ItemPrice** must be greater than **ItemCost**.

1.3.4 Data Modeling Schemes

The six most common schemes used to represent data are: Relational, Dimensional, Object-Oriented, Fact-Based, Time-Based, and NoSQL. Each scheme uses specific diagramming notations (see Table 9).

Table 9 Modeling Schemes and Notations

Scheme	Sample Notations
Relational	Information Engineering (IE) Integration Definition for Information Modeling (IDEF1X) Barker Notation Chen
Dimensional	Dimensional
Object-Oriented	Unified Modeling Language (UML)
Fact-Based	Object Role Modeling (ORM or ORM2) Fully Communication Oriented Modeling (FCO-IM)
Time-Based	Data Vault Anchor Modeling
NoSQL	Document Column Graph Key-Value

This section will briefly explain each of these schemes and notations. The use of schemes depends in part on the database being built, as some are suited to particular technologies, as shown in Table 10.

For the relational scheme, all three levels of models can be built for RDBMS, but only conceptual and logical models can be built for the other types of databases. This is true for the fact-based scheme as well. For the dimensional scheme, all three levels of models can be built for both RDBMS and MDBMS databases. The object-oriented scheme works well for RDBMS and object databases.

The time-based scheme is a physical data modeling technique primarily for data warehouses in a RDBMS environment. The NoSQL scheme is heavily dependent on the underlying database structure (document, column, graph, or key-value), and is therefore a physical data modeling technique. Table 10 illustrates several important points including that even with a non-traditional database such as one that is document-based, a relational CDM and LDM can be built followed by a document PDM.

Table 10 Scheme to Database Cross Reference

Scheme	Relational Database Management System (RDBMS)	Multidimensional Database Management System (MDBMS)	Object Databases	Document	Column	Graph	Key-Value
Relational	CDM LDM PDM	CDM LDM	CDM LDM	CDM LDM	CDM LDM	CDM LDM	CDM LDM
Dimensional	CDM LDM PDM	CDM LDM PDM					
Object-Oriented	CDM LDM PDM		CDM LDM PDM				
Fact-Based	CDM LDM PDM	CDM LDM	CDM LDM	CDM LDM	CDM LDM	CDM LDM	CDM LDM
Time-Based	PDM						
NoSQL			PDM	PDM	PDM	PDM	PDM

1.3.4.1 Relational

First articulated by Dr. Edward Codd in 1970, relational theory provides a systematic way to organize data so that they reflected their meaning (Codd, 1970). This approach had the additional effect of reducing redundancy in data storage. Codd's insight was that data could most effectively be managed in terms of two-dimensional *relations*. The term *relation* was derived from the mathematics (set theory) upon which his approach was based. (See Chapter 6.)

The design objectives for the relational model are to have an exact expression of business data and to have one fact in one place (the removal of redundancy). Relational modeling is ideal for the design of operational systems, which require entering information quickly and having it stored accurately (Hay, 2011).

There are several different kinds of notation to express the association between entities in relational modeling, including Information Engineering (IE), Integration Definition for Information Modeling (IDEF1X), Barker Notation, and Chen Notation. The most common form is IE syntax, with its familiar tridents or 'crow's feet' to depict cardinality. (See Figure 39.)

Figure 39 IE Notation

1.3.4.2 Dimensional

The concept of dimensional modeling started from a joint research project conducted by General Mills and Dartmouth College in the 1960's.[33] In dimensional models, data is structured to optimize the query and analysis of large amounts of data. In contrast, operational systems that support transaction processing are optimized for fast processing of individual transactions.

Dimensional data models capture business questions focused on a particular business process. The process being measured on the dimensional model in Figure 40 is Admissions. Admissions can be viewed by the Zone the student is from, School Name, Semester, and whether the student is receiving financial aid. Navigation can be made from Zone up to Region and Country, from Semester up to Year, and from School Name up to School Level.

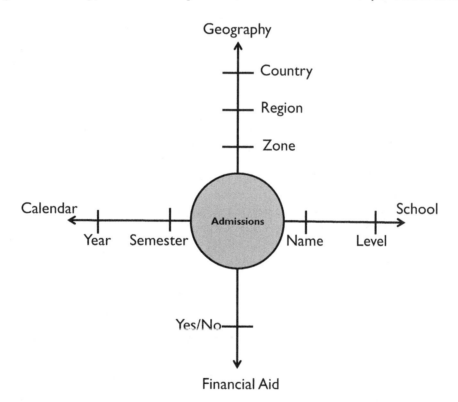

Figure 40 Axis Notation for Dimensional Models

---

[33] http://bit.ly/2tsSP7w.

The diagramming notation used to build this model – the 'axis notation' – can be a very effective communication tool with those who prefer not to read traditional data modeling syntax.

Both the relational and dimensional conceptual data models can be based on the same business process (as in this example with Admissions). The difference is in the meaning of the relationships, where on the relational model the relationship lines capture business rules, and on the dimensional model, they capture the navigation paths needed to answer business questions.

1.3.4.2.1 Fact Tables

Within a dimensional scheme, the rows of a fact table correspond to particular measurements and are numeric, such as amounts, quantities, or counts. Some measurements are the results of algorithms, in which case Metadata is critical to proper understanding and usage. Fact tables take up the most space in the database (90% is a reasonable rule of thumb), and tend to have large numbers of rows.

1.3.4.2.2 Dimension Tables

Dimension tables represent the important objects of the business and contain mostly textual descriptions. Dimensions serve as the primary source for 'query by' or 'report by' constraints, by acting as the entry points or links into the fact tables. Dimensions are typically highly denormalized and typically account for about 10% of the total data.

Dimensions must have a unique identifier for each row. The two main approaches to identifying keys for dimension tables are surrogate keys and natural keys.

Dimensions also have attributes that change at different rates. Slowly changing dimensions (SCDs) manage changes based on the rate and type of change. The three main types of change are sometimes known by ORC.

- **Overwrite (Type 1)**: The new value overwrites the old value in place.

- **New Row (Type 2)**: The new values are written in a new row, and the old row is marked as not current.

- **New Column (Type 3)**: Multiple instances of a value are listed in columns on the same row, and a new value means writing the values in the series one spot down to make space at the front for the new value. The last value is discarded.

1.3.4.2.3 Snowflaking

Snowflaking is the term given to normalizing the flat, single-table, dimensional structure in a star schema into the respective component hierarchical or network structures.

1.3.4.2.4 Grain

The term *grain* stands for the meaning or description of a single row of data in a fact table; this is the most detail any row will have. Defining the grain of a fact table is one of the key steps in dimensional design. For example, if a dimensional model is measuring the student registration process, the grain may be student, day, and class.

1.3.4.2.5 Conformed Dimensions

Conformed dimensions are built with the entire organization in mind instead of just a particular project; this allows these dimensions to be shared across dimensional models, due to containing consistent terminology and values. For example, if **Calendar** is a conformed dimension, a dimensional model built to count student applicants by **Semester** will contain the same values and definition of **Semester** as a dimensional model built to count student graduates.

1.3.4.2.6 Conformed Facts

Conformed facts use standardized definitions of terms across individual marts. Different business users may use the same term in different ways. 'Customer additions' may be different from 'gross additions' or 'adjusted additions.' Developers need to be keenly aware of things that may be named the same but actually represent different concepts across organizations, or conversely things that are named differently but are actually the same concept across organizations.

1.3.4.3 Object-Oriented (UML)

The Unified Modeling Language (UML) is a graphical language for modeling software. The UML has a variety of notations of which one (the class model) concerns databases. The UML class model specifies classes (entity types) and their relationship types (Blaha, 2013).

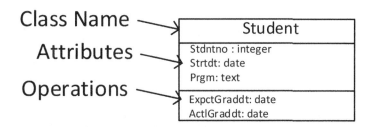

Figure 41 UML Class Model

Figure 41 illustrates the characteristics of a UML Class Model:

- A Class diagram resembles an ER diagram except that the Operations or Methods section is not present in ER.
- In ER, the closest equivalent to Operations would be Stored Procedures.

- Attribute types (e.g., Date, Minutes) are expressed in the implementable application code language and not in the physical database implementable terminology.
- Default values can be optionally shown in the notation.
- Access to data is through the class' exposed interface. Encapsulation or data hiding is based on a 'localization effect'. A class and the instances that it maintains are exposed through Operations.

The class has Operations or Methods (also called its "behavior"). Class behavior is only loosely connected to business logic because it still needs to be sequenced and timed. In ER terms, the table has stored procedures/triggers.

Class Operations can be:

- Public: Externally visible
- Internally Visible: Visible to children Objects
- Private: Hidden

In comparison, ER Physical models only offer Public access; all data is equally exposed to processes, queries, or manipulations.

1.3.4.4 Fact-Based Modeling (FBM)

Fact-Based Modeling, a family of conceptual modeling languages, originated in the late 1970s. These languages are based in the analysis of natural verbalization (plausible sentences) that might occur in the business domain. Fact-based languages view the world in terms of objects, the facts that relate or characterize those objects, and each role that each object plays in each fact. An extensive and powerful constraint system relies on fluent automatic verbalization and automatic checking against the concrete examples. Fact-based models do not use attributes, reducing the need for intuitive or expert judgment by expressing the exact relationships between objects (both entities and values). The most widely used of the FBM variants is Object Role Modeling (ORM), which was formalized as a first-order logic by Terry Halpin in 1989.

1.3.4.4.1 Object Role Modeling (ORM or ORM2)

Object-Role Modeling (ORM) is a model-driven engineering approach that starts with typical examples of required information or queries presented in any external formulation familiar to users, and then verbalizes these examples at the conceptual level, in terms of simple facts expressed in a controlled natural language. This language is a restricted version of natural language that is unambiguous, so the semantics are readily grasped by humans; it is also formal, so it can be used to automatically map the structures to lower levels for implementation (Halpin, 2015).

Figure 42 illustrates an ORM model.

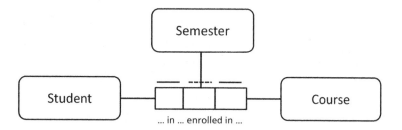

Figure 42 ORM Model

1.3.4.4.2 Fully Communication Oriented Modeling (FCO-IM)

FCO-IM is similar in notation and approach to ORM. The numbers in Figure 43 are references to verbalizations of facts. For example, 2 might refer to several verbalizations including "Student 1234 has first name Bill."

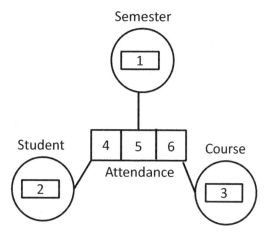

Figure 43 FCO-IM Model

1.3.4.5 Time-Based

Time-based patterns are used when data values must be associated in chronological order and with specific time values.

1.3.4.5.1 Data Vault

The Data Vault is a detail-oriented, time-based, and uniquely linked set of normalized tables that support one or more functional areas of business. It is a hybrid approach, encompassing the best of breed between third normal form (3NF, to be discussed in Section 1.3.6) and star schema. Data Vaults are designed specifically to meet the needs of enterprise data warehouses. There are three types of entities: hubs, links, and satellites. The Data Vault design is focused around the functional areas of business with the hub representing the primary key. The links provide transaction integration between the hubs. The satellites provide the context of the hub primary key (Linstedt, 2012).

In Figure 44, **Student** and **Course** are hubs, which represent the main concepts within a subject. Attendance is a link, which relates two hubs to each other. **Student Contact, Student Characteristics,** and **Course Description** are satellites that provide the descriptive information on the hub concepts and can support varying types of history.

Anchor Modeling is a technique suited for information that changes over time in both structure and content. It provides graphical notation used for conceptual modeling similar to traditional data modeling, with extensions for working with temporal data. Anchor Modeling has four basic modeling concepts: anchors, attributes, ties, and knots. Anchors model entities and events, attributes model properties of anchors, ties model the relationships between anchors, and knots are used to model shared properties, such as states.

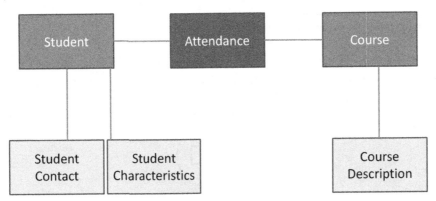

Figure 44 Data Vault Model

1.3.4.5.2 Anchor Modeling

On the anchor model in Figure 45, **Student, Course,** and **Attendance** are anchors, the gray diamonds represent ties, and the circles represent attributes.

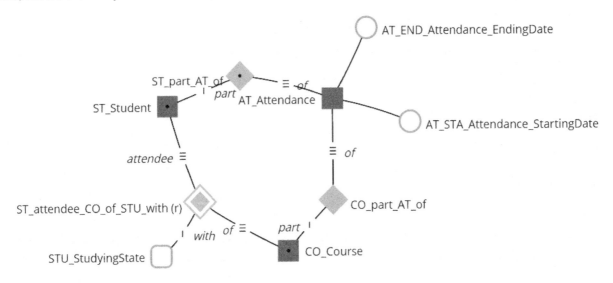

Figure 45 Anchor Model

1.3.4.6 NoSQL

NoSQL is a name for the category of databases built on non-relational technology. Some believe that NoSQL is not a good name for what it represents, as it is less about how to query the database (which is where SQL comes in) and more about how the data is stored (which is where relational structures comes in).

There are four main types of NoSQL databases: document, key-value, column-oriented, and graph.

1.3.4.6.1 Document

Instead of taking a business subject and breaking it up into multiple relational structures, document databases frequently store the business subject in one structure called a *document*. For example, instead of storing **Student**, **Course**, and **Registration** information in three distinct relational structures, properties from all three will exist in a single document called **Registration**.

1.3.4.6.2 Key-value

Key-value databases allow an application to store its data in only two columns ('key' and 'value'), with the feature of storing both simple (e.g., dates, numbers, codes) and complex information (unformatted text, video, music, documents, photos) stored within the 'value' column.

1.3.4.6.3 Column-oriented

Out of the four types of NoSQL databases, column-oriented is closest to the RDBMS. Both have a similar way of looking at data as rows and values. The difference, though, is that RDBMSs work with a predefined structure and simple data types, such as amounts and dates, whereas column-oriented databases, such as Cassandra, can work with more complex data types including unformatted text and imagery. In addition, column-oriented databases store each column in its own structure.

1.3.4.6.4 Graph

A graph database is designed for data whose relations are well represented as a set of nodes with an undetermined number of connections between these nodes. Examples where a graph database can work best are social relations (where nodes are people), public transport links (where nodes could be bus or train stations), or roadmaps (where nodes could be street intersections or highway exits). Often requirements lead to traversing the graph to find the shortest routes, nearest neighbors, etc., all of which can be complex and time-consuming to navigate with a traditional RDMBS. Graph databases include Neo4J, Allegro, and Virtuoso.

1.3.5 Data Model Levels of Detail

In 1975, the American National Standards Institute's Standards Planning and Requirements Committee (SPARC) published their three-schema approach to database management. The three key components were:

- **Conceptual**: This embodies the 'real world' view of the enterprise being modeled in the database. It represents the current 'best model' or 'way of doing business' for the enterprise.

- **External**: The various users of the database management system operate on sub-sets of the total enterprise model that are relevant to their particular needs. These subsets are represented as 'external schemas'.

- **Internal**: The 'machine view' of the data is described by the internal schema. This schema describes the stored representation of the enterprise's information (Hay, 2011).

These three levels most commonly translate into the conceptual, logical, and physical levels of detail, respectively. Within projects, conceptual data modeling and logical data modeling are part of requirements planning and analysis activities, while physical data modeling is a design activity. This section provides an overview of conceptual, logical, and physical data modeling. In addition, each level will be illustrated with examples from two schemes: relational and dimensional.

1.3.5.1 Conceptual

A conceptual data model captures the high-level data requirements as a collection of related concepts. It contains only the basic and critical business entities within a given realm and function, with a description of each entity and the relationships between entities.

For example, if we were to model the relationship between students and a school, as a relational conceptual data model using the IE notation, it might look like Figure 46.

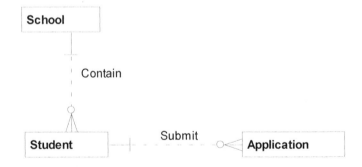

Figure 46 Relational Conceptual Model

Each **School** may contain one or many **Students**, and each **Student** must come from one **School**. In addition, each **Student** may submit one or many **Applications**, and each **Application** must be submitted by one **Student**.

The relationship lines capture business rules on a relational data model. For example, Bob the student can attend County High School or Queens College, but cannot attend both when applying to this particular university. In addition, an application must be submitted by a single student, not two and not zero.

Recall Figure 40, which is reproduced below as Figure 47. This dimensional conceptual data model using the Axis notation, illustrates concepts related to school:

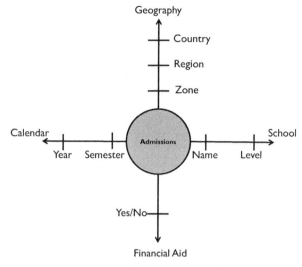

Figure 47 Dimensional Conceptual Model

1.3.5.2 Logical

A logical data model is a detailed representation of data requirements, usually in support of a specific usage context, such as application requirements. Logical data models are still independent of any technology or specific implementation constraints. A logical data model often begins as an extension of a conceptual data model.

In a relational logical data model, the conceptual data model is extended by adding attributes. Attributes are assigned to entities by applying the technique of normalization (see Section 1.3.6), as shown in Figure 48. There is a very strong relationship between each attribute and the primary key of the entity in which it resides. For instance, **School Name** has a strong relationship to **School Code**. For example, each value of a **School Code** brings back at most one value of a **School Name**.

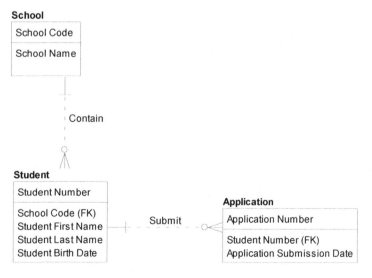

Figure 48 Relational Logical Data Model

A dimensional logical data model is in many cases a fully-attributed perspective of the dimensional conceptual data model, as illustrated in Figure 49. Whereas the logical relational data model captures the business rules of a business process, the logical dimensional captures the business questions to determine the health and performance of a business process.

Admissions Count in Figure 49 is the measure that answers the business questions related to **Admissions**. The entities surrounding the **Admissions** provide the context to view **Admissions Count** at different levels of granularity, such as by **Semester** and **Year**.

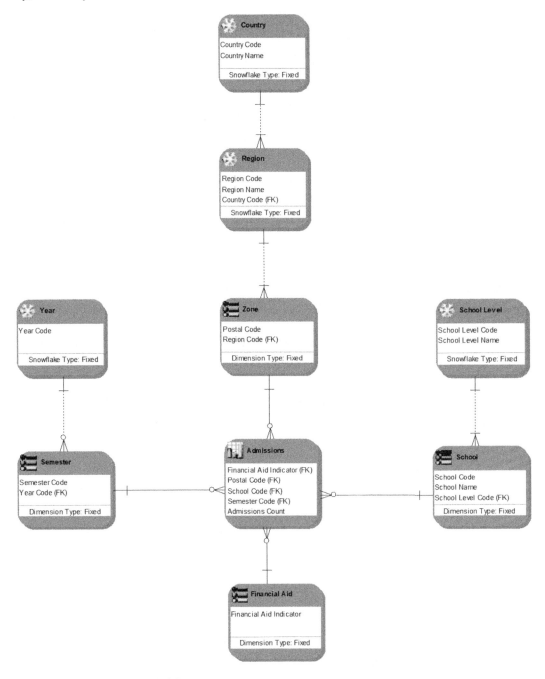

Figure 49 Dimensional Logical Data Model

1.3.5.3 Physical

A physical data model (PDM) represents a detailed technical solution, often using the logical data model as a starting point and then adapted to work within a set of hardware, software, and network tools. Physical data models are built for a particular technology. Relational DBMSs, for example, should be designed with the specific capabilities of a database management system in mind (e.g., IBM DB2, UDB, Oracle, Teradata, Sybase, Microsoft SQL Server, or Microsoft Access).

Figure 50 illustrates a relational physical data model. In this data model, School has been denormalized into the **Student** entity to accommodate a particular technology. Perhaps whenever a Student is accessed, their school information is as well and therefore storing school information with **Student** is a more performant structure than having two separate structures.

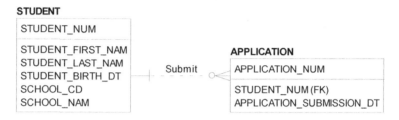

Figure 50 Relational Physical Data Model

Because the physical data model accommodates technology limitations, structures are often combined (denormalized) to improve retrieval performance, as shown in this example with **Student** and **School**.

Figure 51 illustrates a dimensional physical data model (usually a star schema, meaning there is one structure for each dimension).

Similar to the relational physical data model, this structure has been modified from its logical counterpart to work with a particular technology to ensure business questions can be answered with simplicity and speed.

1.3.5.3.1 Canonical

A variant of a physical scheme is a Canonical Model, used for data in motion between systems. This model describes the structure of data being passed between systems as packets or messages. When sending data through web services, an Enterprise Service Bus (ESB), or through Enterprise Application Integration (EAI), the canonical model describes what data structure the sending service and any receiving services should use. These structures should be designed to be as generic as possible to enable re-use and simplify interface requirements.

This structure may only be instantiated as a buffer or queue structure on an intermediary messaging system (middleware) to hold message contents temporarily.

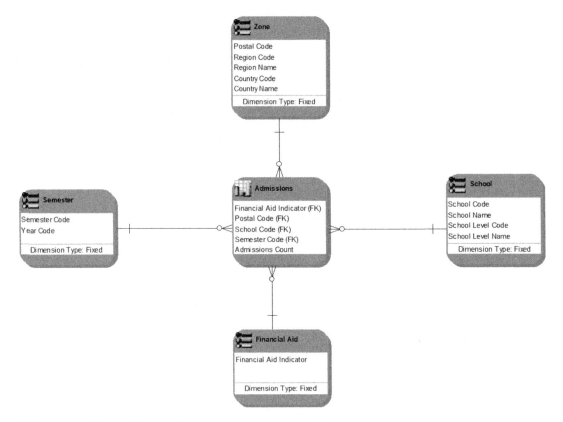

Figure 51 Dimensional Physical Data Model

1.3.5.3.2 Views

A view is a virtual table. Views provide a means to look at data from one or many tables that contain or reference the actual attributes. A standard view runs SQL to retrieve data at the point when an attribute in the view is requested. An instantiated (often called 'materialized') view runs at a predetermined time. Views are used to simplify queries, control data access, and rename columns, without the redundancy and loss of referential integrity due to denormalization.

1.3.5.3.3 Partitioning

Partitioning refers to the process of splitting a table. It is performed to facilitate archiving and to improve retrieval performance. Partitioning can be either vertical (separating groups of columns) or horizontal (separating groups of rows).

- **Vertically split**: To reduce query sets, create subset tables that contain subsets of columns. For example, split a customer table in two based on whether the fields are mostly static or mostly volatile (to improve load / index performance), or based on whether the fields are commonly or uncommonly included in queries (to improve table scan performance).

- **Horizontally split**: To reduce query sets, create subset tables using the value of a column as the differentiator. For example, create regional customer tables that contain only customers in a specific region.

1.3.5.3.4 Denormalization

Denormalization is the deliberate transformation of normalized logical data model entities into physical tables with redundant or duplicate data structures. In other words, denormalization intentionally puts one attribute in multiple places. There are several reasons to denormalize data. The first is to improve performance by:

- Combining data from multiple other tables in advance to avoid costly run-time joins

- Creating smaller, pre-filtered copies of data to reduce costly run-time calculations and/or table scans of large tables

- Pre-calculating and storing costly data calculations to avoid run-time system resource competition

Denormalization can also be used to enforce user security by segregating data into multiple views or copies of tables according to access needs.

This process does introduce a risk of data errors due to duplication. Therefore, denormalization is frequently chosen if structures such as views and partitions fall short in producing an efficient physical design. It is good practice to implement data quality checks to ensure that the copies of the attributes are correctly stored. In general, denormalize only to improve database query performance or to facilitate enforcement of user security.

Although the term *denormalization* is used in this section, the process does not apply just to relational data models. For example, one can denormalize in a document database, but it would be called something different – such as *embedding*.

In dimensional data modeling, denormalization is called *collapsing* or *combining*. If each dimension is collapsed into a single structure, the resulting data model is called a *Star Schema* (see Figure 51). If the dimensions are not collapsed, the resulting data model is called a *Snowflake* (See Figure 49).

1.3.6 Normalization

Normalization is the process of applying rules in order to organize business complexity into stable data structures. The basic goal of normalization is to keep each attribute in only one place to eliminate redundancy and the inconsistencies that can result from redundancy. The process requires a deep understanding of each attribute and each attribute's relationship to its primary key.

Normalization rules sort attributes according to primary and foreign keys. Normalization rules sort into levels, with each level applying granularity and specificity in search of the correct primary and foreign keys. Each level comprises a separate normal form, and each successive level does not need to include previous levels. Normalization levels include:

- **First normal form (1NF)**: Ensures each entity has a valid primary key, and every attribute depends on the primary key; removes repeating groups, and ensures each attribute is atomic (not multi-valued). 1NF includes the resolution of many-to-many relationships with an additional entity often called an associative entity.

- **Second normal form (2NF)**: Ensures each entity has the minimal primary key and that every attribute depends on the complete primary key.

- **Third normal form (3NF)**: Ensures each entity has no hidden primary keys and that each attribute depends on no attributes outside the key ("the key, the whole key and nothing but the key").

- **Boyce / Codd normal form (BCNF)**: Resolves overlapping composite candidate keys. A candidate key is either a primary or an alternate key. 'Composite' means more than one (i.e., two or more attributes in an entity's primary or alternate keys), and 'overlapping' means there are hidden business rules between the keys.

- **Fourth normal form (4NF)**: Resolves all many-to-many-to-many relationships (and beyond) in pairs until they cannot be broken down into any smaller pieces.

- **Fifth normal form (5NF)**: Resolves inter-entity dependencies into basic pairs, and all join dependencies use parts of primary keys.

The term *normalized model* usually means the data is in 3NF. Situations requiring BCNF, 4NF, and 5NF occur rarely.

1.3.7 Abstraction

Abstraction is the removal of details in such a way as to broaden applicability to a wide class of situations while preserving the important properties and essential nature from concepts or subjects. An example of abstraction is the **Party/Role** structure, which can be used to capture how people and organizations play certain roles (e.g., employee and customer). Not all modelers or developers are comfortable with, or have the ability to work with abstraction. The modeler needs to weigh the cost of developing and maintaining an abstract structure versus the amount of rework required if the unabstracted structure needs to be modified in the future (Giles 2011).

Abstraction includes *generalization* and *specialization*. Generalization groups the common attributes and relationships of entities into *supertype* entities, while specialization separates distinguishing attributes within an entity into *subtype* entities. This specialization is usually based on attribute values within an entity instance.

Subtypes can also be created using *roles* or *classification* to separate instances of an entity into groups by function. An example is **Party**, which can have subtypes of **Individual** and **Organization**.

The *subtyping relationship* implies that all of the properties from the supertype are inherited by the subtype. In the relational example shown in Figure 52, **University** and **High School** are subtypes of **School**.

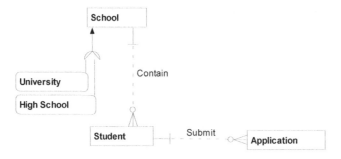

Figure 52 Supertype and Subtype Relationships

Subtyping reduces redundancy on a data model. It also makes it easier to communicate similarities across what otherwise would appear to be distinct and separate entities.

---

2. Activities

This section will briefly cover the steps for building conceptual, logical, and physical data models, as well as maintaining and reviewing data models. Both forward engineering and reverse engineering will be discussed.

2.1 Plan for Data Modeling

A plan for data modeling contains tasks such as evaluating organizational requirements, creating standards, and determining data model storage.

The deliverables of the data modeling process include:

- **Diagram**: A data model contains one or more diagrams. The diagram is the visual that captures the requirements in a precise form. It depicts a level of detail (e.g., conceptual, logical, or physical), a scheme (relational, dimensional, object-oriented, fact-based, time-based, or NoSQL), and a notation within that scheme (e.g., information engineering, unified modeling language, object-role modeling).

- **Definitions**: Definitions for entities, attributes, and relationships are essential to maintaining the precision on a data model.

- **Issues and outstanding questions**: Frequently the data modeling process raises issues and questions that may not be addressed during the data modeling phase. In addition, often the people or groups responsible for resolving these issues or answering these questions reside outside of the group building the data model. Therefore, often a document is delivered that contains the current set of issues and outstanding questions. An example of an outstanding issue for the student model might be, "If a **Student** leaves and then returns, are they assigned a different **Student Number** or do they keep their original **Student Number**?"

- **Lineage**: For physical and sometimes logical data models, it is important to know the data lineage, that is, where the data comes from. Often lineage takes the form of a source/target mapping, where one can capture the source system attributes and how they populate the target system attributes. Lineage can also trace the data modeling components from conceptual to logical to physical within the same modeling effort. There are two reasons why lineage is important to capture during the data modeling. First, the data modeler will obtain a very strong understanding of the data requirements and therefore is in the best position to determine the source attributes. Second, determining the source attributes can be an effective tool to validate the accuracy of the model and the mapping (i.e., a reality check).

2.2 Build the Data Model

To build the models, modelers often rely heavily on previous analysis and modeling work. They may study existing data models and databases, refer to published standards, and incorporate any data requirements. After studying these inputs, they start building the model. Modeling is a very iterative process (Figure 53). Modelers draft the model, and then return to business professionals and business analysts to clarify terms and business rules. They then update the model and ask more questions (Hoberman, 2014).

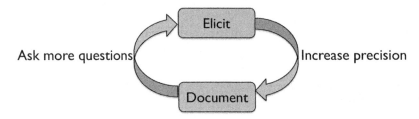

Figure 53 Modeling is Iterative

2.2.1 Forward Engineering

Forward engineering is the process of building a new application beginning with the requirements. The CDM is completed first to understand the scope of the initiative and the key terminology within that scope. Then the LDM is completed to document the business solution, followed by the PDM to document the technical solution.

2.2.1.1 Conceptual Data Modeling

Creating the CDM involves the following steps:

- **Select Scheme**: Decide whether the data model should be built following a relational, dimensional, fact-based, or NoSQL scheme. Refer to the earlier discussion on scheme and when to choose each scheme (see Section 1.3.4).

- **Select Notation**: Once the scheme is selected, choose the appropriate notation, such as information engineering or object role modeling. Choosing a notation depends on standards within an organization and the familiarity of users of a particular model with a particular notation.

- **Complete Initial CDM**: The initial CDM should capture the viewpoint of a user group. It should not complicate the process by trying to figure out how their viewpoint fits with other departments or with the organization as a whole.

  o Collect the highest-level concepts (nouns) that exist for the organization. Common concepts are **Time, Geography, Customer/Member/Client, Product/Service**, and **Transaction**.
  o Then collect the activities (verbs) that connect these concepts. Relationships can go both ways, or involve more than two concepts. Examples are: **Customers** have multiple **Geographic Locations** (home, work, etc.), **Geographic Locations** have many **Customers**. **Transactions** occur at a **Time**, at a **Facility**, for a **Customer**, selling a **Product**.

- **Incorporate Enterprise Terminology**: Once the data modeler has captured the users' view in the boxes and lines, the data modeler next captures the enterprise perspective by ensuring consistency with enterprise terminology and rules. For example, there would be some reconciliation work involved if the audience conceptual data model had an entity called **Client**, and the enterprise perspective called this same concept **Customer**.

- **Obtain Sign-off**: After the initial model is complete, make sure the model is reviewed for data modeling best practices as well as its ability to meet the requirements. Usually email verification that the model looks accurate will suffice.

2.2.1.2 Logical Data Modeling

A logical data model (LDM) captures the detailed data requirements within the scope of a CDM.

2.2.1.2.1 Analyze Information Requirements

To identify information requirements, one must first identify business information needs, in the context of one or more business processes. As their input, business processes require information products that are themselves the output from other business processes. The names of these information products often identify an essential business vocabulary that serves as the basis for data modeling. Regardless of whether processes or data are modeled sequentially (in either order), or concurrently, effective analysis and design should ensure a relatively balanced view of data (nouns) and processes (verbs), with equal emphasis on both process and data modeling.

Requirements analysis includes the elicitation, organization, documentation, review, refinement, approval, and change control of business requirements. Some of these requirements identify business needs for data and information. Express requirement specifications in both words and diagrams.

Logical data modeling is an important means of expressing business data requirements. For many people, as the old saying goes, 'a picture is worth a thousand words'. However, some people do not relate easily to pictures; they relate better to reports and tables created by data modeling tools.

Many organizations have formal requirements. Management may guide drafting and refining formal requirement statements, such as "The system shall…" Written data requirement specification documents may be maintained using requirements management tools. The specifications gathered through the contents of any such documentation should carefully synchronize with the requirements captured with data models to facilitate impact analysis so one can answer questions like "Which parts of my data models represent or implement Requirement X?" or "Why is this entity here?"

2.2.1.2.2 Analyze Existing Documentation

It can often be a great jump-start to use pre-existing data artifacts, including already built data models and databases. Even if the data models are out-of-date, parts can be useful to start a new model. Make sure however, that any work done based on existing artifacts is validated by the SMEs for accuracy and currency. Companies often use packaged applications, such as Enterprise Resource Planning (ERP) systems, that have their own data models. Creation of the LDM should take into account these data models and either use them, where applicable, or map them to the new enterprise data model. In addition, there could be useful data modeling patterns, such as a standard way of modeling the Party Role concept. Numerous industry data models capture how a generic industry, such as retail or manufacturing, should be modeled. These patterns or industry data models can then be customized to work for the particular project or initiative.

2.2.1.2.3 Add Associative Entities

Associative entities are used to describe Many-to-Many (or Many-to-Many-to-Many, etc.) relationships. An associative entity takes the identifying attributes from the entities involved in the relationship, and puts them into a new entity that just describes the relationship between the entities. This allows the addition of attributes to describe that relationship, like in effective and expiration dates. Associative entities may have more than two parents. Associative entities may become nodes in graph databases. In dimensional modeling, associative entities usually become fact tables.

2.2.1.2.4 Add Attributes

Add attributes to the conceptual entities. An attribute in a logical data model should be atomic. It should contain one and only one piece of data (fact) that cannot be divided into smaller pieces. For example, a conceptual attribute called phone number divides into several logical attributes for phone type code (home, office, fax, mobile, etc.), country code, (1 for US and Canada), area code, prefix, base phone number, and extension.

2.2.1.2.5 Assign Domains

Domains, which were discussed in Section 1.3.3.4, allow for consistency in format and value sets within and across projects. **Student Tuition Amount** and **Instructor Salary Amount** can both be assigned the **Amount** domain, for example, which will be a standard currency domain.

2.2.1.2.6 Assign Keys

Attributes assigned to entities are either key or non-key attributes. A key attribute helps identify one unique entity instance from all others, either fully (by itself) or partially (in combination with other key elements). Non-key attributes describe the entity instance but do not help uniquely identify it. Identify primary and alternate keys.

2.2.1.3 Physical Data Modeling

Logical data models require modifications and adaptations in order to have the resulting design perform well within storage applications. For example, changes required to accommodate Microsoft Access would be different from changes required to accommodate Teradata. Going forward, the term *table* will be used to refer to tables, files, and schemas; the term *column* to refer to columns, fields, and elements; and the term *row* to refer to rows, records, or instances.

2.2.1.3.1 Resolve Logical Abstractions

Logical abstraction entities (supertypes and subtypes) become separate objects in the physical database design using one of two methods.

- **Subtype absorption**: The subtype entity attributes are included as nullable columns into a table representing the supertype entity.
- **Supertype partition**: The supertype entity's attributes are included in separate tables created for each subtype.

2.2.1.3.2 Add Attribute Details

Add details to the physical model, such as the technical name of each table and column (relational databases), or file and field (non-relational databases), or schema and element (XML databases).

Define the physical domain, physical data type, and length of each column or field. Add appropriate constraints (e.g., nullability and default values) for columns or fields, especially for NOT NULL constraints.

2.2.1.3.3 Add Reference Data Objects

Small Reference Data value sets in the logical data model can be implemented in a physical model in three common ways:

- **Create a matching separate code table**: Depending on the model, these can be unmanageably numerous.
- **Create a master shared code table**: For models with a large number of code tables, this can collapse them into one table; however, this means that a change to one reference list will change the entire table. Take care to avoid code value collisions as well.
- **Embed rules or valid codes into the appropriate object's definition**: Create a constraint in the object definition code that embeds the rule or list. For code lists that are only used as reference for one other object, this can be a good solution.

2.2.1.3.4 Assign Surrogate Keys

Assign unique key values that are not visible to the business and have no meaning or relationship with the data with which they are matched. This is an optional step and depends primarily on whether the natural key is large, composite, and whose attributes are assigned values that could change over time.

If a surrogate key is assigned to be the primary key of a table, make sure there is an alternate key on the original primary key. For example, if on the LDM the primary key for **Student** was **Student First Name**, **Student Last Name**, and **Student Birth Date** (i.e., a composite primary key), on the PDM the primary key for **Student** may be the surrogate key **Student ID**. In this case, there should be an alternate key defined on the original primary key of **Student First Name**, **Student Last Name**, and **Student Birth Date**.

2.2.1.3.5 Denormalize for Performance

In some circumstances, denormalizing or adding redundancy can improve performance so much that it outweighs the cost of the duplicate storage and synchronization processing. Dimensional structures are the main means of denormalization.

2.2.1.3.6 Index for Performance

An index is an alternate path for accessing data in the database to optimize query (data retrieval) performance. Indexing can improve query performance in many cases. The database administrator or database developer must select and define appropriate indexes for database tables. Major RDBMS products support many types of indexes. Indexes can be unique or non-unique, clustered or non-clustered, partitioned or non-partitioned, single column or multi-column, b-tree or bitmap or hashed. Without an appropriate index, the DBMS will revert to reading every row in the table (table scan) to retrieve any data. On large tables, this is very costly. Try to build indexes on large tables to support the most frequently run queries, using the most frequently referenced columns, particularly keys (primary, alternate, and foreign).

2.2.1.3.7 Partition for Performance

Great consideration must be given to the partitioning strategy of the overall data model (dimensional) especially when facts contain many optional dimensional keys (sparse). Ideally, partitioning on a date key is recommended; when this is not possible, a study is required based on profiled results and workload analysis to propose and refine the subsequent partitioning model.

2.2.1.3.8 Create Views

Views can be used to control access to certain data elements, or to embed common join conditions or filters to standardize common objects or queries. Views themselves should be requirements-driven. In many cases, they will need to be developed via a process that mirrors the development of the LDM and PDM.

2.2.2 Reverse Engineering

Reverse engineering is the process of documenting an existing database. The PDM is completed first to understand the technical design of an existing system, followed by an LDM to document the business solution that the existing system meets, followed by the CDM to document the scope and key terminology within the existing system. Most data modeling tools support reverse engineering from a variety of databases; however, creating a readable layout of the model elements still requires a modeler. There are several common layouts (orthogonal, dimensional, and hierarchical) which can be selected to get the process started, but contextual organization (grouping entities by subject area or function) is still largely a manual process.

2.3 Review the Data Models

As do other areas of IT, models require quality control. Continuous improvement practices should be employed. Techniques such as time-to-value, support costs, and data model quality validators such as the Data Model Scorecard® (Hoberman, 2009), can all be used to evaluate the model for correctness, completeness, and consistency. Once the CDM, LDM, and PDM are complete, they become very useful tools for any roles that need to understand the model, ranging from business analysts through developers.

2.4 Maintain the Data Models

Once the data models are built, they need to be kept current. Updates to the data model need to be made when requirements change and frequently when business processes change. Within a specific project, often when one model level needs to change, a corresponding higher level of model needs to change. For example, if a new column is added to a physical data model, that column frequently needs to be added as an attribute to the corresponding logical data model. A good practice at the end of each development iteration is to reverse engineer the latest physical data model and make sure it is still consistent with its corresponding logical data model. Many data modeling tools help automate this process of comparing physical with logical.

3. Tools

There are many types of tools that can assist data modelers in completing their work, including data modeling, lineage, data profiling tools, and Metadata repositories.

3.1 Data Modeling Tools

Data modeling tools are software that automate many of the tasks the data modeler performs. Entry-level data modeling tools provide basic drawing functionality including a data modeling pallet so that the user can easily create entities and relationships. These entry-level tools also support *rubber banding,* which is the automatic redrawing of relationship lines when entities are moved. More sophisticated data modeling tools support forward engineering from conceptual to logical to physical to database structures, allowing the generation of database data definition language (DDL). Most will also support reverse engineering from database up to conceptual data model. These more sophisticated tools often support functionality such as naming standards validation, spellcheckers, a place to store Metadata (e.g., definitions and lineage), and sharing features (such as publishing to the Web).

3.2 Lineage Tools

A lineage tool is software that allows the capture and maintenance of the source structures for each attribute on the data model. These tools enable impact analysis; that is, one can use them to see if a change in one system or part of system has effects in another system. For example, the attribute **Gross Sales Amount** might be sourced from several applications and require a calculation to populate – lineage tools would store this information. Microsoft Excel® is a frequently-used lineage tool. Although easy to use and relatively inexpensive, Excel does not enable real impact analysis and leads to manually managing Metadata. Lineage is also frequently captured in a data modeling tool, Metadata repository, or data integration tool. (See Chapters 11 and 12.)

3.3 Data Profiling Tools

A data profiling tool can help explore the data content, validate it against existing Metadata, and identify Data Quality gaps/deficiencies, as well as deficiencies in existing data artifacts, such as logical and physical models, DDL, and model descriptions. For example, if the business expects that an Employee can have only one job position at a time, but the system shows Employees have more than one job position in the same timeframe, this will be logged as a data anomaly. (See Chapters 8 and 13.)

3.4 Metadata Repositories

A Metadata repository is a software tool that stores descriptive information about the data model, including the diagram and accompanying text such as definitions, along with Metadata imported from other tools and processes (software development and BPM tools, system catalogs, etc.). The repository itself should enable Metadata integration and exchange. Even more important than storing the Metadata is sharing the Metadata. Metadata repositories must have an easily accessible way for people to view and navigate the contents of the repository. Data modeling tools generally include a limited repository. (See Chapter 13.)

3.5 Data Model Patterns

Data model patterns are reusable modeling structures that can be applied to a wide class of situations. There are elementary, assembly, and integration data model patterns. Elementary patterns are the 'nuts and bolts' of data modeling. They include ways to resolve many-to-many relationships, and to construct self-referencing hierarchies. Assembly patterns represent the building blocks that span the business and data modeler worlds. Business people can understand them – assets, documents, people and organizations, and the like. Equally importantly, they are often the subject of published data model patterns that can give the modeler proven, robust, extensible, and implementable designs. Integration patterns provide the framework for linking the assembly patterns in common ways (Giles, 2011).

3.6 Industry Data Models

Industry data models are data models pre-built for an entire industry, such as healthcare, telecom, insurance, banking, or manufacturing. These models are often both broad in scope and very detailed. Some industry data models contain thousands of entities and attributes. Industry data models can be purchased through vendors or obtained through industry groups such as ARTS (for retail), SID (for communications), or ACORD (for insurance).

Any purchased data model will need to be customized to fit an organization, as it will have been developed from multiple other organizations' needs. The level of customization required will depend on how close the model is to an organization's needs, and how detailed the most important parts are. In some cases, it can be a reference for an organization's in-progress efforts to help the modelers make models that are more complete. In others, it can merely save the data modeler some data entry effort for annotated common elements.

4. Best Practices

4.1 Best Practices in Naming Conventions

The ISO 11179 Metadata Registry, an international standard for representing Metadata in an organization, contains several sections related to data standards, including naming attributes and writing definitions.

Data modeling and database design standards serve as the guiding principles to effectively meet business data needs, conform to Enterprise and Data Architecture (see Chapter 4) and ensure the quality of data (see Chapter 14). Data architects, data analysts, and database administrators must jointly develop these standards. They must complement and not conflict with related IT standards.

Publish data model and database naming standards for each type of modeling object and database object. Naming standards are particularly important for entities, tables, attributes, keys, views, and indexes. Names should be unique and as descriptive as possible.

Logical names should be meaningful to business users, using full words as much as possible and avoiding all but the most familiar abbreviations. Physical names must conform to the maximum length allowed by the DBMS, so use abbreviations where necessary. While logical names use blank spaces as separators between words, physical names typically use underscores as word separators.

Naming standards should minimize name changes across environments. Names should not reflect their specific environment, such as test, QA, or production. Class words, which are the last terms in attribute names such as Quantity, Name, and Code, can be used to distinguish attributes from entities and column names from table names. They can also show which attributes and columns are quantitative rather than qualitative, which can be important when analyzing the contents of those columns.

4.2 Best Practices in Database Design

In designing and building the database, the DBA should keep the following design principles in mind (remember the acronym PRISM):

- **Performance and ease of use**: Ensure quick and easy access to data by approved users in a usable and business-relevant form, maximizing the business value of both applications and data.

- **Reusability**: The database structure should ensure that, where appropriate, multiple applications can use the data and that the data can serve multiple purposes (e.g., business analysis, quality improvement, strategic planning, customer relationship management, and process improvement). Avoid coupling a database, data structure, or data object to a single application.

- **Integrity**: The data should always have a valid business meaning and value, regardless of context, and should always reflect a valid state of the business. Enforce data integrity constraints as close to the data as possible, and immediately detect and report violations of data integrity constraints.

- **Security**: True and accurate data should always be immediately available to authorized users, but only to authorized users. The privacy concerns of all stakeholders, including customers, business partners, and government regulators, must be met. Enforce data security, like data integrity, as close to the data as possible, and immediately detect and report security violations.

- **Maintainability**: Perform all data work at a cost that yields value by ensuring that the cost of creating, storing, maintaining, using, and disposing of data does not exceed its value to the organization. Ensure the fastest possible response to changes in business processes and new business requirements.

5. Data Model Governance

5.1 Data Model and Design Quality Management

Data analysts and designers act as intermediaries between information consumers (the people with business requirements for data) and the data producers who capture the data in usable form. Data professionals must balance the data requirements of the information consumers and the application requirements of data producers.

Data professionals must also balance the short-term versus long-term business interests. Information consumers need data in a timely fashion to meet short-term business obligations and to take advantage of current business opportunities. System-development project teams must meet time and budget constraints. However, they must also meet the long-term interests of all stakeholders by ensuring that an organization's data resides in data structures that are secure, recoverable, sharable, and reusable, and that this data is as correct, timely, relevant, and usable as possible. Therefore, data models and database designs should be a reasonable balance between the short-term needs and the long-term needs of the enterprise.

5.1.1 Develop Data Modeling and Design Standards

As previously noted (in Section 4.1) data modeling and database design standards provide guiding principles to meet business data requirements, conform to Enterprise and Data Architecture standards, and ensure the quality of data. Data modeling and database design standards should include the following:

- A list and description of standard data modeling and database design deliverables
- A list of standard names, acceptable abbreviations, and abbreviation rules for uncommon words, that apply to all data model objects
- A list of standard naming formats for all data model objects, including attribute and column class words
- A list and description of standard methods for creating and maintaining these deliverables
- A list and description of data modeling and database design roles and responsibilities
- A list and description of all Metadata properties captured in data modeling and database design, including both business Metadata and technical Metadata. For example, guidelines may set the expectation that the data model captures lineage for each attribute.
- Metadata quality expectations and requirements (see Chapter 13)
- Guidelines for how to use data modeling tools
- Guidelines for preparing for and leading design reviews
- Guidelines for versioning of data models
- Practices that are discouraged

5.1.2 Review Data Model and Database Design Quality

Project teams should conduct requirements reviews and design reviews of the conceptual data model, logical data model, and physical database design. The agenda for review meetings should include items for reviewing the starting model (if any), the changes made to the model and any other options that were considered and rejected, and how well the new model conforms to any modeling or architecture standards in place.

Conduct design reviews with a group of subject matter experts representing different backgrounds, skills, expectations, and opinions. It may require executive mandate to get expert resources allocated to these reviews. Participants must be able to discuss different viewpoints and reach group consensus without personal conflict, as all participants share the common goal of promoting the most practical, best performing and most usable design. Chair each design review with one leader who facilitates the meeting. The leader creates and follows an agenda, ensures all required documentation is available and distributed, solicits input from all participants, maintains order and keeps the meeting moving, and summarizes the group's consensus findings. Many design reviews also use a scribe to capture points of discussion.

In reviews where there is no approval, the modeler must rework the design to resolve the issues. If there are issues that the modeler cannot resolve on their own, the final say should be given by the owner of the system reflected by the model.

5.1.3 Manage Data Model Versioning and Integration

Data models and other design specifications require careful change control, just like requirements specifications and other SDLC deliverables. Note each change to a data model to preserve the lineage of changes over time. If a change affects the logical data model, such as a new or changed business data requirement, the data analyst or architect must review and approve the change to the model.

Each change should note:

- **Why** the project or situation required the change
- **What** and **How** the object(s) changed, including which tables had columns added, modified, or removed, etc.
- **When** the change was approved and when the change was made to the model (not necessarily when the change was implemented in a system)
- **Who** made the change
- **Where** the change was made (in which models)

Some data modeling tools include repositories that provide data model versioning and integration functionality. Otherwise, preserve data models in DDL exports or XML files, checking them in and out of a standard source code management system just like application code.

5.2 Data Modeling Metrics

There are several ways of measuring a data model's quality, and all require a standard for comparison. One method that will be used to provide an example of data model validation is The Data Model Scorecard®, which provides 11 data model quality metrics: one for each of ten categories that make up the Scorecard and an overall score across all ten categories (Hoberman, 2015). Table 11 contains the Scorecard template.

Table 11 Data Model Scorecard® Template

#	Category	Total score	Model score	%	Comments
1	How well does the model capture the requirements?	15			
2	How complete is the model?	15			
3	How well does the model match its scheme?	10			
4	How structurally sound is the model?	15			
5	How well does the model leverage generic structures?	10			
6	How well does the model follow naming standards?	5			
7	How well has the model been arranged for readability?	5			
8	How good are the definitions?	10			
9	How consistent is the model with the enterprise?	5			
10	How well does the metadata match the data?	10			
	TOTAL SCORE	100			

The model score column contains the reviewer's assessment of how well a particular model met the scoring criteria, with a maximum score being the value that appears in the total score column. For example, a reviewer might give a model a score of 10 on "How well does the model capture the requirements?" The % column presents the Model Score for the category divided by the Total Score for the category. For example, receiving 10 out of 15 would lead to 66%. The comments column should document information that explains the score in more detail or captures the action items required to fix the model. The last row contains the overall score assigned to the model, a sum of each of the columns.

A brief description of each category follows:

1. **How well does the model capture the requirements?** Here we ensure that the data model represents the requirements. If there is a requirement to capture order information, in this category we check the model to make sure it captures order information. If there is a requirement to view **Student Count** by **Semester** and **Major**, in this category we make sure the data model supports this query.

2. **How complete is the model?** Here completeness means two things: completeness of requirements and completeness of Metadata. Completeness of requirements means that each requirement that has been requested appears on the model. It also means that the data model only contains what is being asked for and nothing extra. It's easy to add structures to the model anticipating that they will be used in the near future; we note these sections of the model during the review. The project may become too hard to deliver if the modeler includes something that was never asked for. We need to consider the likely cost of including a future requirement in the case that it never eventuates. Completeness of Metadata means that all of the descriptive information surrounding the model is present as well; for example, if we are reviewing a physical data model, we would expect formatting and nullability to appear on the data model.

3. **How well does the model match its scheme?** Here we ensure that the model level of detail (conceptual, logical, or physical), and the scheme (e.g., relational, dimensional, NoSQL) of the model being reviewed matches the definition for this type of model.

4. **How structurally sound is the model?** Here we validate the design practices employed to build the model to ensure one can eventually build a database from the data model. This includes avoiding design issues such as having two attributes with the same exact name in the same entity or having a null attribute in a primary key.

5. **How well does the model leverage generic structures?** Here we confirm an appropriate use of abstraction. Going from **Customer Location** to a more generic **Location**, for example, allows the design to more easily handle other types of locations such as warehouses and distribution centers.

6. **How well does the model follow naming standards?** Here we ensure correct and consistent naming standards have been applied to the data model. We focus on naming standard structure, term, and style. Structure means that the proper building blocks are being used for entities, relationships, and attributes. For example, a building block for an attribute would be the subject of the attribute such as 'Customer' or 'Product'. Term means that the proper name is given to the attribute or entity. Term also includes proper spelling and abbreviation. Style means that the appearance, such as upper case or camel case, is consistent with standard practices.

7. **How well has the model been arranged for readability?** Here we ensure the data model is easy to read. This question is not the most important of the ten categories. However, if your model is hard to read, you may not accurately address the more important categories on the scorecard. Placing parent entities above

their child entities, displaying related entities together, and minimizing relationship line length all improve model readability.

8. **How good are the definitions?** Here we ensure the definitions are clear, complete, and accurate.

9. **How consistent is the model with the enterprise?** Here we ensure the structures on the data model are represented in a broad and consistent context, so that one set of terminology and rules can be spoken in the organization. The structures that appear in a data model should be consistent in terminology and usage with structures that appear in related data models, and ideally with the enterprise data model (EDM), if one exists.

10. **How well does the Metadata match the data?** Here we confirm that the model and the actual data that will be stored within the resulting structures are consistent. Does the column **Customer_Last_Name** really contain the customer's last name, for example? The Data category is designed to reduce these surprises and help ensure the structures on the model match the data these structures will be holding.

The scorecard provides an overall assessment of the quality of the model and identifies specific areas for improvement.

---

6. Works Cited / Recommended

Ambler, Scott. *Agile Database Techniques: Effective Strategies for the Agile Software Developer.* Wiley and Sons, 2003. Print.

Avison, David and Christine Cuthbertson. *A Management Approach to Database Applications.* McGraw-Hill Publishing Co., 2002. Print. Information systems ser.

Blaha, Michael. *UML Database Modeling Workbook.* Technics Publications, LLC, 2013. Print.

Brackett, Michael H. *Data Resource Design: Reality Beyond Illusion.* Technics Publications, LLC, 2012. Print.

Brackett, Michael H. *Data Resource Integration: Understanding and Resolving a Disparate Data Resource.* Technics Publications, LLC, 2012. Print.

Brackett, Michael H. *Data Resource Simplexity: How Organizations Choose Data Resource Success or Failure.* Technics Publications, LLC, 2011. Print.

Bruce, Thomas A. *Designing Quality Databases with IDEF1X Information Models.* Dorset House, 1991. Print.

Burns, Larry. *Building the Agile Database: How to Build a Successful Application Using Agile Without Sacrificing Data Management.* Technics Publications, LLC, 2011. Print.

Carlis, John and Joseph Maguire. *Mastering Data Modeling - A User-Driven Approach.* Addison-Wesley Professional, 2000. Print.

Codd, Edward F. "A Relational Model of Data for Large Shared Data Banks". *Communications of the ACM,* 13, No. 6 (June 1970).

DAMA International. *The DAMA Dictionary of Data Management. 2nd Edition: Over 2,000 Terms Defined for IT and Business Professionals.* 2nd ed. Technics Publications, LLC, 2011. Print.

Daoust, Norman. *UML Requirements Modeling for Business Analysts: Steps to Modeling Success.* Technics Publications, LLC, 2012. Print.

Date, C. J. *An Introduction to Database Systems.* 8th ed. Addison-Wesley, 2003. Print.

Date, C. J. and Hugh Darwen. *Databases, Types and the Relational Model*. 3d ed. Addison Wesley, 2006. Print.

Date, Chris J. *The Relational Database Dictionary: A Comprehensive Glossary of Relational Terms and Concepts, with Illustrative Examples*. O'Reilly Media, 2006. Print.

Dorsey, Paul. *Enterprise Data Modeling Using UML*. McGraw-Hill Osborne Media, 2009. Print.

Edvinsson, Håkan and Lottie Aderinne. *Enterprise Architecture Made Simple: Using the Ready, Set, Go Approach to Achieving Information Centricity*. Technics Publications, LLC, 2013. Print.

Fleming, Candace C. and Barbara Von Halle. The Handbook of Relational Database Design. Addison Wesley, 1989. Print.

Giles, John. *The Nimble Elephant: Agile Delivery of Data Models using a Pattern-based Approach*. Technics Publications, LLC, 2012. Print.

Golden, Charles. *Data Modeling 152 Success Secrets - 152 Most Asked Questions On Data Modeling - What You Need to Know*. Emereo Publishing, 2015. Print. Success Secrets.

Halpin, Terry, Ken Evans, Pat Hallock, and Bill McLean. *Database Modeling with Microsoft Visio for Enterprise Architects*. Morgan Kaufmann, 2003. Print. The Morgan Kaufmann Series in Data Management Systems.

Halpin, Terry. *Information Modeling and Relational Databases*. Morgan Kaufmann, 2001. Print. The Morgan Kaufmann Series in Data Management Systems.

Halpin, Terry. *Information Modeling and Relational Databases: From Conceptual Analysis to Logical Design*. Morgan Kaufmann, 2001. Print. The Morgan Kaufmann Series in Data Management Systems.

Harrington, Jan L. *Relational Database Design Clearly Explained*. 2nd ed. Morgan Kaufmann, 2002. Print. The Morgan Kaufmann Series in Data Management Systems.

Hay, David C. *Data Model Patterns: A Metadata Map*. Morgan Kaufmann, 2006. Print. The Morgan Kaufmann Series in Data Management Systems.

Hay, David C. *Enterprise Model Patterns: Describing the World (UML Version)*. Technics Publications, LLC, 2011. Print.

Hay, David C. *Requirements Analysis from Business Views to Architecture*. Prentice Hall, 2002. Print.

Hay, David C. *UML and Data Modeling: A Reconciliation*. Technics Publications, LLC, 2011. Print.

Hernandez, Michael J. *Database Design for Mere Mortals: A Hands-On Guide to Relational Database Design*. 2nd ed. Addison-Wesley Professional, 2003. Print.

Hoberman, Steve, Donna Burbank, Chris Bradley, et al. *Data Modeling for the Business: A Handbook for Aligning the Business with IT using High-Level Data Models*. Technics Publications, LLC, 2009. Print. Take It with You Guides.

Hoberman, Steve. *Data Model Scorecard*. Technics Publications, LLC, 2015. Print.

Hoberman, Steve. *Data Modeling Made Simple with ER/Studio Data Architect*. Technics Publications, LLC, 2013. Print.

Hoberman, Steve. *Data Modeling Made Simple: A Practical Guide for Business and IT Professionals*. 2nd ed. Technics Publications, LLC, 2009. Print.

Hoberman, Steve. *Data Modeling Master Class Training Manual*. 7th ed. Technics Publications, LLC, 2017. Print.

Hoberman, Steve. *The Data Modeler's Workbench. Tools and Techniques for Analysis and Design*. Wiley, 2001. Print.

Hoffer, Jeffrey A., Joey F. George, and Joseph S. Valacich. *Modern Systems Analysis and Design*. 7th ed. Prentice Hall, 2013. Print.

IIBA and Kevin Brennan, ed. *A Guide to the Business Analysis Body of Knowledge (BABOK Guide)*. International Institute of Business Analysis, 2009. Print.

Kent, William. *Data and Reality: A Timeless Perspective on Perceiving and Managing Information in Our Imprecise World*. 3d ed. Technics Publications, LLC, 2012. Print.

Krogstie, John, Terry Halpin, and Keng Siau, eds. *Information Modeling Methods and Methodologies: Advanced Topics in Database Research*. Idea Group Publishing, 2005. Print. Advanced Topics in Database Research.

Linstedt, Dan. *Super Charge Your Data Warehouse: Invaluable Data Modeling Rules to Implement Your Data Vault*. Amazon Digital Services. 2012. Data Warehouse Architecture Book 1.

Muller, Robert. J. *Database Design for Smarties: Using UML for Data Modeling*. Morgan Kaufmann, 1999. Print. The Morgan Kaufmann Series in Data Management Systems.

Needham, Doug. *Data Structure Graphs: The structure of your data has meaning*. Doug Needham Amazon Digital Services, 2015. Kindle.

Newton, Judith J. and Daniel Wahl, eds. *Manual for Data Administration*. NIST Special Publications, 1993. Print.

Pascal, Fabian. *Practical Issues in Database Management: A Reference for The Thinking Practitioner*. Addison-Wesley Professional, 2000. Print.

Reingruber, Michael. C. and William W. Gregory. *The Data Modeling Handbook: A Best-Practice Approach to Building Quality Data Models*. Wiley, 1994. Print.

Riordan, Rebecca M. *Designing Effective Database Systems*. Addison-Wesley Professional, 2005. Print.

Rob, Peter and Carlos Coronel. *Database Systems: Design, Implementation, and Management*. 7th ed. Cengage Learning, 2006. Print.

Schmidt, Bob. *Data Modeling for Information Professionals*. Prentice Hall, 1998. Print.

Silverston, Len and Paul Agnew. *The Data Model Resource Book, Volume 3: Universal Patterns for Data Modeling*. Wiley, 2008. Print.

Silverston, Len. *The Data Model Resource Book, Volume 1: A Library of Universal Data Models for All Enterprises*. Rev. ed. Wiley, 2001. Print.

Silverston, Len. *The Data Model Resource Book, Volume 2: A Library of Data Models for Specific Industries*. Rev. ed. Wiley, 2001. Print.

Simsion, Graeme C. and Graham C. Witt. *Data Modeling Essentials*. 3rd ed. Morgan Kaufmann, 2004. Print.

Simsion, Graeme. *Data Modeling: Theory and Practice*. Technics Publications, LLC, 2007. Print.

Teorey, Toby, et al. *Database Modeling and Design: Logical Design*, 4th ed. Morgan Kaufmann, 2010. Print. The Morgan Kaufmann Series in Data Management Systems.

Thalheim, Bernhard. *Entity-Relationship Modeling: Foundations of Database Technology*. Springer, 2000. Print.

Watson, Richard T. *Data Management: Databases and Organizations*. 5th ed. Wiley, 2005. Print.

CHAPTER 6

Data Storage and Operations

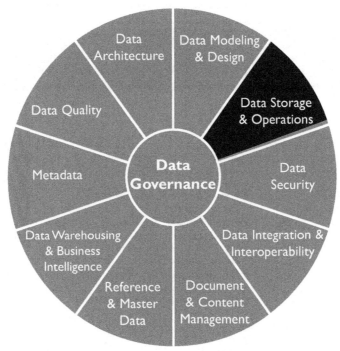

DAMA-DMBOK2 Data Management Framework

Copyright © 2017 by DAMA International

---

1. Introduction

Data Storage and Operations includes the design, implementation, and support of stored data, to maximize its value throughout its lifecycle, from creation/acquisition to disposal (see Chapter 1). Data Storage and Operations includes two sub-activities:

- **Database support** focuses on activities related to the data lifecycle, from initial implementation of a database environment, through obtaining, backing up, and purging data. It also includes ensuring the database performs well. Monitoring and tuning are critical to database support.

- **Database technology support** includes defining technical requirements that will meet organizational needs, defining technical architecture, installing and administering technology, and resolving issues related to technology.

Database administrators (DBAs) play key roles in both aspects of data storage and operations. The role of DBA is the most established and most widely adopted data professional role, and database administration practices are perhaps the most mature of all data management practices. DBAs also play dominant roles in data operations and data security. (See Chapter 7.)

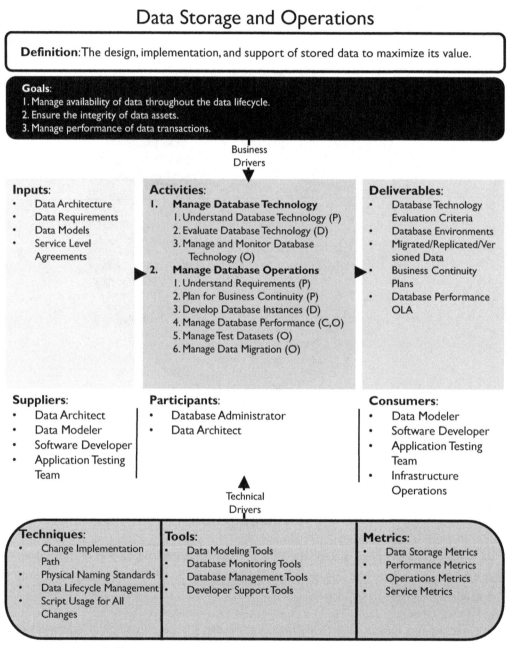

Data Storage and Operations

Definition: The design, implementation, and support of stored data to maximize its value.

Goals:
1. Manage availability of data throughout the data lifecycle.
2. Ensure the integrity of data assets.
3. Manage performance of data transactions.

Business Drivers

Inputs:
- Data Architecture
- Data Requirements
- Data Models
- Service Level Agreements

Activities:
1. **Manage Database Technology**
   1. Understand Database Technology (P)
   2. Evaluate Database Technology (D)
   3. Manage and Monitor Database Technology (O)
2. **Manage Database Operations**
   1. Understand Requirements (P)
   2. Plan for Business Continuity (P)
   3. Develop Database Instances (D)
   4. Manage Database Performance (C,O)
   5. Manage Test Datasets (O)
   6. Manage Data Migration (O)

Deliverables:
- Database Technology Evaluation Criteria
- Database Environments
- Migrated/Replicated/Versioned Data
- Business Continuity Plans
- Database Performance OLA

Suppliers:
- Data Architect
- Data Modeler
- Software Developer
- Application Testing Team

Participants:
- Database Administrator
- Data Architect

Consumers:
- Data Modeler
- Software Developer
- Application Testing Team
- Infrastructure Operations

Technical Drivers

Techniques:
- Change Implementation Path
- Physical Naming Standards
- Data Lifecycle Management
- Script Usage for All Changes

Tools:
- Data Modeling Tools
- Database Monitoring Tools
- Database Management Tools
- Developer Support Tools

Metrics:
- Data Storage Metrics
- Performance Metrics
- Operations Metrics
- Service Metrics

(P) Planning, (C) Control, (D) Development, (O) Operations

Figure 54 Context Diagram: Data Storage and Operations

1.1 Business Drivers

Companies rely on their information systems to run their operations. Data Storage and Operations activities are crucial to organizations that rely on data. Business continuity is the primary driver of these activities. If a system becomes unavailable, company operations may be impaired or stopped completely. A reliable data storage infrastructure for IT operations minimizes the risk of disruption.

1.2 Goals and Principles

The goals of data storage and operations include:

- Managing the availability of data throughout the data lifecycle
- Ensuring the integrity of data assets
- Managing the performance of data transactions

Data Storage and Operations represent a highly technical side of data management. DBAs and others involved in this work can do their jobs better and help the overall work of data management when they follow these guiding principles:

- **Identify and act on automation opportunities**: Automate database development processes, developing tools, and processes that shorten each development cycle, reduce errors and rework, and minimize the impact on the development team. In this way, DBAs can adapt to more iterative (agile) approaches to application development. This improvement work should be done in collaboration with data modeling and Data Architecture.

- **Build with reuse in mind**: Develop and promote the use of abstracted and reusable data objects that prevent applications from being tightly coupled to database schemas (the so-called 'object-relational impedance mismatch'). A number of mechanisms exist to this end, including database views, triggers, functions and stored procedures, application data objects and data-access layers, XML and XSLT, ADO.NET typed data sets, and web services. The DBA should be able to assess the best approach virtualizing data. The end goal is to make using the database as quick, easy, and painless as possible.

- **Understand and appropriately apply best practices**: DBAs should promote database standards and best practices as requirements, but be flexible enough to deviate from them if given acceptable reasons for these deviations. Database standards should never be a threat to the success of a project.

- **Connect database standards to support requirements**: For example, the Service Level Agreement (SLA) can reflect DBA-recommended and developer-accepted methods of ensuring data integrity and data security. The SLA should reflect the transfer of responsibility from the DBAs to the development team if the development team will be coding their own database update procedures or data access layer. This prevents an 'all or nothing' approach to standards.

- **Set expectations for the DBA role in project work**: Ensuring project methodology includes onboarding the DBA in project definition phase can help throughout the SDLC. The DBA can understand project needs and support requirements up-front. This will improve communication by clarifying the project team's expectations from the data group. Having a dedicated primary and secondary DBA during analysis and design clarify expectations about DBA tasks, standards, work effort, and timelines for development work. Teams should also clarify expectations for support after implementation.

1.3 Essential Concepts

1.3.1 Database Terms

Database terminology is specific and technical. In working as a DBA or with DBAs, it is important to understand the specifics of this technical language:

- **Database**: Any collection of stored data, regardless of structure or content. Some large databases refer to instances and schema.
- **Instance**: An execution of database software controlling access to a certain area of storage. An organization will usually have multiple instances executing concurrently, using different areas of storage. Each instance is independent of all other instances.
- **Schema**: A subset of a database objects contained within the database or an instance. Schemas are used to organize objects into more manageable parts. Usually, a schema has an owner and an access list particular to the schema's contents. Common uses of schemas are to isolate objects containing sensitive data from the general user base, or to isolate read-only views from the underlying tables in relational databases. Schema can also be used to refer to a collection of database structures with something in common.
- **Node**: An individual computer hosting either processing or data as part of a distributed database.
- **Database abstraction** means that a common application interface (API) is used to call database functions, such that an application can connect to multiple different databases without the programmer having to know all function calls for all possible databases. ODBC (Open Database Connectivity) is an example of an API that enables database abstraction. Advantages include portability; disadvantages include inability to use specific database functions that are not common across databases.

1.3.2 Data Lifecycle Management

DBAs maintain and assure the accuracy and consistency of data over its entire lifecycle through the design, implementation, and usage of any system that stores, processes, or retrieves data. The DBA is the custodian of all database changes. While many parties may request changes, the DBA defines the precise changes to make to the database, implements the changes, and controls the changes.

Data lifecycle management includes implementing policies and procedures for acquisition, migration, retention, expiration, and disposition of data. It is prudent to prepare checklists to ensure all tasks are performed at a high level of quality. DBAs should use a controlled, documented, and auditable process for moving application database changes to the Quality Assurance or Certification (QA) and Production environments. A manager-approved service request or change request usually initiates the process. The DBA should have a back out plan to reverse changes in case of problems.

1.3.3 Administrators

The role of Database Administrator (DBA) is the most established and the most widely adopted data professional role. DBAs play the dominant roles in Data Storage and Operations, and critical roles in Data Security (see Chapter 7), the physical side of data modeling, and database design (see Chapter 5). DBAs provide support for development, test, QA, and special use database environments.

DBAs do not exclusively perform all the activities of Data Storage and Operations. Data stewards, data architects, network administrators, data analysts, and security analysts participate in planning for performance, retention, and recovery. These teams may also participate in obtaining and processing data from external sources.

Many DBAs specialize as Production, Application, Procedural and Development DBAs. Some organizations also have Network Storage Administrators (NSA) who specialize in supporting the data storage system separately from the data storage applications or structures.

In some organizations, each specialized role reports to a different organization within IT. Production DBAs may be part of production infrastructure or application operations support groups. Application, Development, and Procedural DBAs are sometimes integrated into application development organizations. NSAs usually are connected to Infrastructure organizations.

1.3.3.1 Production DBA

Production DBAs take primary responsibility for data operations management, including:

- Ensuring the performance and reliability of the database, through performance tuning, monitoring, error reporting, and other activities

- Implementing backup and recovery mechanisms to ensure data can be recovered if lost in any circumstance

- Implementing mechanisms for clustering and failover of the database, if continual data availability data is a requirement

- Executing other database maintenance activities, such as implementing mechanisms for archiving data

As part of managing data operations, Production DBAs create the following deliverables:

- A production database environment, including an instance of the DBMS (Database Management System) on the supporting server, of a sufficient size and capacity to ensure adequate performance, configured for the appropriate level of security, reliability, and availability. Database System Administration is responsible for the DBMS environment.

- Mechanisms and processes for controlled implementation of changes to databases in the production environment

- Mechanisms for ensuring the availability, integrity, and recoverability of data in response to all circumstances that could result in loss or corruption of data

- Mechanisms for detecting and reporting any error that occurs in the database, the DBMS, or the data server

- Database availability, recovery, and performance in accordance with service level agreements

- Mechanisms and processes for monitoring database performance as workloads and data volumes vary

1.3.3.2 Application DBA

An application DBA is responsible for one or more databases in all environments (development / test, QA, and production), as opposed to database systems administration for any of these environments. Sometimes, application DBAs report to the organizational units responsible for development and maintenance of the applications supported by their databases. There are pros and cons to staffing application DBAs.

Application DBAs are viewed as integral members of an application support team. By focusing on a specific database, they can provide better service to application developers. However, application DBAs can easily become isolated and lose sight of the organization's overall data needs and common DBA practices. Application DBAs collaborate closely with data analysts, modelers, and architects.

1.3.3.3 Procedural and Development DBAs

Procedural DBAs lead the review and administration of procedural database objects. A procedural DBA specializes in development and support of procedural logic controlled and execute by the DBMS: stored procedures, triggers, and user-defined functions (UDFs). The procedural DBA ensures this procedural logic is planned, implemented, tested, and shared (reused).

Development DBAs focus on data design activities including creating and managing special use databases, such as 'sandbox' or exploration areas.

In many cases, these two functions are combined under one position.

1.3.3.4 NSA

Network Storage Administrators are concerned with the hardware and software supporting data storage arrays. Multiple network storage array systems have different needs and monitoring requirements than simple database systems.

1.3.4 Database Architecture Types

A database can be classified as either centralized or distributed. A centralized system manages a single database, while a distributed system manages multiple databases on multiple systems. A distributed system's components can be classified depending on the autonomy of the component systems into two types: federated (autonomous) or non-federated (non-autonomous). Figure 55 illustrates the difference between centralized and distributed.

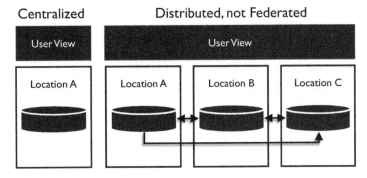

Figure 55 Centralized vs. Distributed

1.3.4.1 Centralized Databases

Centralized databases have all the data in one system in one place. All users come to the one system to access the data. For certain restricted data, centralization can be ideal, but for data that needs to be widely available, centralized databases have risks. For example, if the centralized system is unavailable, there are no other alternatives for accessing the data.

1.3.4.2 Distributed Databases

Distributed databases make possible quick access to data over a large number of nodes. Popular distributed database technologies are based on using commodity hardware servers. They are designed to scale out from single servers to thousands of machines, each offering local computation and storage. Rather than rely on hardware to deliver high-availability, the database management software itself is designed to replicate data amongst the servers, thereby delivering a highly available service on top of a cluster of computers. Database management software is also designed to detect and handle failures. While any given computer may fail, the system overall is unlikely to.

Some distributed databases implement a computational paradigm named MapReduce to further improve performance. In MapReduce, the data request is divided into many small fragments of work, each of which may be executed or re-executed on any node in the cluster. In addition, data is co-located on the compute nodes, providing very high aggregate bandwidth across the cluster. Both the filesystem and the application are designed to automatically handle node failures.

1.3.4.2.1 Federated Databases

Federation provisions data without additional persistence or duplication of source data. A federated database system maps multiple autonomous database systems into a single federated database. The constituent databases, sometimes geographically separated, are interconnected via a computer network. They remain autonomous yet participate in a federation to allow partial and controlled sharing of their data. Federation provides an alternative to merging disparate databases. There is no actual data integration in the constituent databases because of data federation; instead, data interoperability manages the view of the federated databases as one large object (see Chapter 8). In contrast, a non-federated database system is an integration of component DBMS's that are not autonomous; they are controlled, managed and governed by a centralized DBMS.

Federated databases are best for heterogeneous and distributed integration projects such as enterprise information integration, data virtualization, schema matching, and Master Data Management.

Federated architectures differ based on levels of integration with the component database systems and the extent of services offered by the federation. A FDBMS can be categorized as either loosely or tightly coupled.

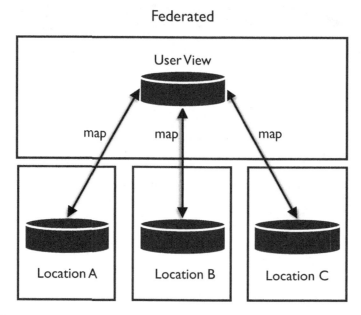

Figure 56 Federated Databases

Loosely coupled systems require component databases to construct their own federated schema. A user will typically access other component database systems by using a multi-database language, but this removes any levels of location transparency, forcing the user to have direct knowledge of the federated schema. A user imports the data required from other component databases, and integrates it with their own to form a federated schema.

Tightly coupled systems consist of component systems that use independent processes to construct and publish an integrated federated schema, as illustrated in Figure 57. The same schema can apply to all parts of the federation, with no data replication.

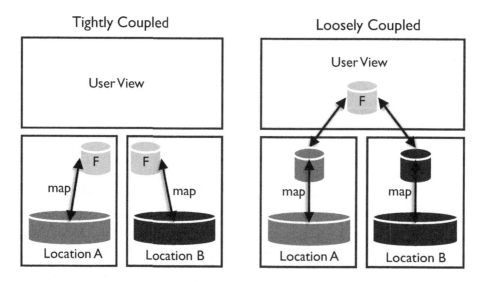

Figure 57 Coupling

1.3.4.2.2 Blockchain Database

Blockchain databases are a type of federated database used to securely manage financial transactions. They can also be used for contract management or exchange of health information. There are two types of structures: individual records and blocks. Each transaction has a record. The database creates chains of time-bound groups of transactions (blocks) that also contain information from the previous block in the chain. Hash algorithms are used to create information about transactions to store in blocks while the block is the end of the chain. Once a new block is created, the old block hash should never change, which means that no transactions contained within that block may change. Any change to transactions or blocks (tampering) will be apparent when the hash values no longer match.

1.3.4.3 Virtualization / Cloud Platforms

Virtualization (also called 'cloud computing') provides computation, software, data access, and storage services that do not require end-user knowledge of the physical location and configuration of the system that delivers the service(s). Parallels are often drawn between the concept of cloud computing and the electricity grid: end users consume power without needing to understand the component devices or infrastructure required to provide the service. However, virtualization can be on-premises or off-premises.

Cloud computing is a natural evolution of the widespread adoption of virtualization, service oriented architectures, and utility computing. Here are some methods for implementing databases on the cloud:

- **Virtual machine image**: Cloud platforms allow users to purchase virtual machine instances for a limited time. It is possible to run a database on these virtual machines. Users can either upload their own machine image with a database installed on it, or use ready-made machine images that already include an optimized installation of a database.

- **Database-as-a-service (DaaS)**: Some cloud platforms offer options for using a database-as-a-service, without physically launching a virtual machine instance for the database. In this configuration, application owners do not have to install and maintain the database on their own. Instead, the database service provider is responsible for installing and maintaining the database, and application owners pay according to their usage.

- **Managed database hosting on the cloud**: Here the database is not offered as a service; instead, the cloud provider hosts the database and manages it on the application owner's behalf.

DBAs, in coordination with network and system administrators, need to establish a systematic integrated project approach to include standardization, consolidation, virtualization, and automation of data backup and recovery functions, as well as security of these functions.

- **Standardization/consolidation**: Consolidation reduces the number of data storage locations an organization has, including the number of data stores and processes within a data center. Based on Data Governance policy, Data Architects and DBAs may develop the standard procedures that include identifying mission critical data, duration of data retention, data encryption procedures, and data replication policies.

- **Server virtualization**: Virtualization technologies allow equipment, such as servers from multiple data centers, to be replaced or consolidated. Virtualization lowers capital and operational expenses and reduces energy consumption. Virtualization technologies are also used to create virtual desktops, which can then be hosted in data centers and rented out on a subscription basis. Gartner views virtualization as a catalyst for modernization (Bittman, 2009). Virtualization provides data storage operations much more flexibility in provisioning storage at local or cloud environment.

- **Automation**: Data automation involves automating tasks such as provisioning, configuration, patching, release management, and compliance.

- **Security**: The security of data on virtual systems needs to be integrated with existing security of physical infrastructures (see Chapter 7).

1.3.5 Database Processing Types

There are two basic types of database processing. ACID and BASE are on opposite ends of a spectrum, so the coincidental names matching ends of a pH spectrum are helpful. The CAP Theorem is used to define how closely a distributed system may match either ACID or BASE.

1.3.5.1 ACID

The acronym ACID was coined in the early 1980's as the indispensable constraint for achieving reliability within database transactions. For decades, it has provided transaction processing with a reliable foundation on which to build.[34]

- **Atomicity**: All operations are performed, or none of them is, so that if one part of the transaction fails, then the entire transaction fails.

- **Consistency**: The transaction must meet all rules defined by the system at all times and must void half-completed transactions.

- **Isolation**: Each transaction is independent unto itself.

- **Durability**: Once complete, the transaction cannot be undone.

Relational ACID technologies are the dominant tools in relational database storage; most use SQL as the interface.

1.3.5.2 BASE

The unprecedented increase in data volumes and variability, the need to document and store unstructured data, the need for read-optimized data workloads, and subsequent need for greater flexibility in scaling, design, processing, cost, and disaster recovery gave rise to the diametric opposite of ACID, appropriately termed BASE:

---

[34] Jim Gray established the concept. Haerder and Rueter (1983) coined the term ACID.

- **Basically Available**: The system guarantees some level of availability to the data even when there are node failures. The data may be stale, but the system will still give and accept responses.

- **Soft State**: The data is in a constant state of flux; while a response may be given, the data is not guaranteed to be current.

- **Eventual Consistency**: The data will eventually be consistent through all nodes and in all databases, but not every transaction will be consistent at every moment.

BASE-type systems are common in Big Data environments. Large online organizations and social media companies commonly use BASE implementations, as immediate accuracy of all data elements at all times is not necessary. Table 12 summarizes the differences between ACID and BASE.

Table 12 ACID vs BASE

Item	ACID	BASE
Casting (data structure)	Schema must exist	Dynamic
	Table structure exists	Adjust on the fly
	Columns data typed	Store dissimilar data
Consistency	Strong Consistency Available	Strong, Eventual, or None
Processing Focus	Transactional	Key-value stores
Processing Focus	Row/Column	Wide-column stores
History	1970s application storage	2000s unstructured storage
Scaling	Product Dependent	Automatically spreads data across commodity servers
Origin	Mixture	Open-source
Transaction	Yes	Possible

1.3.5.3 CAP

The CAP Theorem (or Brewer's Theorem) was developed in response to a shift toward more distributed systems (Brewer, 2000). The theorem asserts that a distributed system cannot comply with all parts of ACID at all time. The larger the system, the lower the compliance. A distributed system must instead trade-off between properties.

- **Consistency**: The system must operate as designed and expected at all times.
- **Availability**: The system must be available when requested and must respond to each request.
- **Partition Tolerance**: The system must be able to continue operations during occasions of data loss or partial system failure.

The CAP Theorem states that at most two of the three properties can exist in any shared-data system. This is usually stated with a 'pick two' statement, illustrated in Figure 58.

An interesting use of this theorem drives the Lambda Architecture design discussed in Chapter 14. Lambda Architecture uses two paths for data: a Speed path where availability and partition tolerance are most important, and a Batch path where consistency and availability are most important.

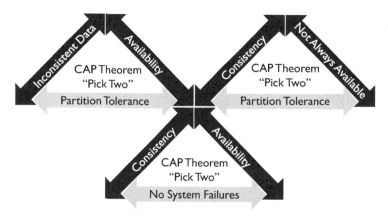

Figure 58 CAP Theorem

1.3.6 Data Storage Media

Data can be stored on a variety of media, including disks, volatile memory, and flash drives. Some systems can combine multiple storage types. The most commonly used are Disk and Storage Area Networks (SAN), In-Memory, Columnar Compression Solutions, Virtual Storage Area Network VSAN, Cloud-based storage solutions, Radio Frequency Identification (RFID), Digital wallets, Data centers and Private, Public, and Hybrid Cloud Storage. (See Chapter 14.)

1.3.6.1 Disk and Storage Area Networks (SAN)

Disk storage is a very stable method of storing data persistently. Multiple types of disk can exist in the same system. Data can be stored according to usage patterns, with less-used data stored on slower-access disks, which are usually cheaper than high performance disk systems.

Disk arrays can be collected into Storage Area Networks (SAN). Data movement on a SAN may not require a network, as data can be moved on the backplane.

1.3.6.2 In-Memory

In-Memory databases (IMDB) are loaded from permanent storage into volatile memory when the system is turned on, and all processing occurs within the memory array, providing faster response time than disk-based systems. Most in-memory databases also have features to set and configure durability in case of unexpected shutdown.

If the application can be reasonably assured to fit most/all data into memory, then significant optimization can be made available from in-memory database systems. These IMDB's provide more predictable access time to data than do disk storage mechanisms, but they require a much larger investment. IMDB's provide functionality for real-time processing of analytics and are generally reserved for this due to the investment required.

1.3.6.3 Columnar Compression Solutions

Columnar-based databases are designed to handle data sets in which data values are repeated to a great extent. For example, in a table with 256 columns, a lookup for a value that exists in a row will retrieve all the data in the row (and be somewhat disk-bound). Columnar storage reduces this I/O bandwidth by storing column data using compression – where the state (for example) is stored as a pointer to a table of states, compressing the master table significantly.

1.3.6.4 Flash Memory

Recent advances in memory storage have made flash memory or solid state drives (SSDs) an attractive alternative to disks. Flash memory combines the access speed of memory-based storage with the persistence of disk-based storage.

1.3.7 Database Environments

Databases are used in a variety of environments during the systems development lifecycle. When testing changes, DBAs should be involved in designing the data structures in the Development environment. The DBA team should implement any changes to the QA environment, and must be the only team implementing changes to the Production environment. Production changes must adhere strictly to standard processes and procedures.

While most data technology is software running on general purpose hardware, occasionally specialized hardware is used to support unique data management requirements. Types of specialized hardware include data appliances – servers built specifically for data transformation and distribution. These servers integrate with existing infrastructure either directly as a plug-in, or peripherally as a network connection.

1.3.7.1 Production Environment

The production environment is the technical environment where all business processes occur. Production is mission-critical – if this environment ceases to operate, business processes will stop, resulting in bottom-line losses, as well as a negative impact on customers who are unable to access services. In an emergency, or for public service systems, unexpected loss of function can be disastrous.

The production environment is the 'real' environment from a business perspective. However, in order to have a reliable production environment, other non-production environments must exist and be used appropriately. For example, production environments should not be used for development and testing as these activities put production processes and data at risk.

1.3.7.2 Pre-production Environments

Pre-production environments are used to develop and test changes before such changes are introduced to the production environment. In pre-production environments, issues with changes can be detected and addressed without affecting normal business processes. In order to detect potential issues, the configuration of pre-production environments must closely resemble the production environment.

Due to space and cost, it is usually not possible to exactly replicate production in the pre-production environments. The closer on the development path the non-production environment is to the production environment, the more closely the non-production environment needs to match the production environment. Any deviation from the production system equipment and configuration can itself create issues or errors that are unrelated to the change, complicating issue research and resolution.

Common types of pre-production environments include development, test, support, and special use environments.

1.3.7.2.1 Development

The development environment is usually a slimmer version of the production environment. It generally has less disk space, fewer CPUs, less RAM, etc. Developers use this environment to create and test code for changes in separate environments, which then are combined in the QA environment for full integration testing. Development can have many copies of production data models, depending on how development projects are managed. Larger organizations may give individual developers their own environments to manage with all appropriate rights.

The development environment should be the first place any patches or updates are applied for testing. This environment should be isolated from and on different physical hardware than the production environments. Due to the isolation, data from production systems may need to be copied to the development environments. However, in many industries, production data is protected through regulation. Do not move data from production environments without first determining what restrictions there are on doing so. (See Chapter 7.)

1.3.7.2.2 Test

The test environment is used to execute quality assurance and user acceptance testing and, in some cases, stress or performance tests. In order to prevent test results from being distorted due to environmental differences, the test environment ideally also has the same software and hardware as the production environment. This is especially important for performance testing. Test may or may not be connected via network to production systems in order to read production data. Test environments should *never* write to production systems.

Test environments serve many uses:

- **Quality Assurance Testing (QA)**: Used to test functionality against requirements.
- **Integration Testing**: Used for testing as a whole multiple parts of a system that have been developed or upgraded independently.
- **User Acceptance Testing (UAT)**: Used for testing the system functionality from a user perspective. Use Cases are the most common inputs for testing performed in this environment.
- **Performance Testing**: Used to perform high-volume or high-complexity tests at any time, rather than having to wait for off hours, or adversely affecting production system peak time.

1.3.7.2.3 Sandboxes or Experimental Environments

A sandbox is an alternate environment that allows read-only connections to production data and can be managed by the users. Sandboxes are used to experiment with development options and test hypotheses about data or merge production data with user-developed data or supplemental data obtained from external sources. Sandboxes are valuable, for example, when performing a Proof-of-Concept.

A sandbox environment can either be a sub-set of the production system, walled off from production processing, or a completely separate environment. Sandbox users often have CRUD rights over their own space so that they can quickly validate ideas and options for changes to the system. The DBAs usually have little to do with these environments other than setting them up, granting access, and monitoring usage. If the Sandbox areas are situated in production database systems, they must be isolated in order to avoid adversely affecting production operations. These environments should never write back to the production systems.

Sandbox environments could be handled by virtual machines (VMs), unless licensing costs for separate instances becomes prohibitive.

1.3.8 Database Organization

Data storage systems provide a way to encapsulate the instructions necessary to put data on disks and manage processing, so developers can simply use instructions to manipulate data. Databases are organized in three general ways: Hierarchical, Relational, and Non-Relational. These classes are not mutually exclusive (see Figure 59). Some database systems can read and write data organized in relational and non-relational structures. Hierarchical databases can be mapped to relational tables. Flat files with line delimiters can be read as tables with rows, and one or more columns can be defined to describe the row contents.

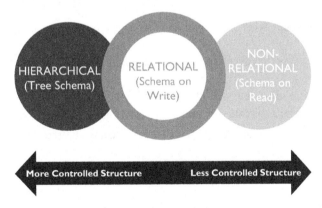

Figure 59 Database Organization Spectrum

1.3.8.1 Hierarchical

Hierarchical database organization is the oldest database model, used in early mainframe DBMS, and is the most rigid of structures. In hierarchical databases, data is organized into a tree-like structure with mandatory parent/child relationships: each parent can have many children, but each child has only one parent (also known as a 1-to-many relationship). Directory trees are an example of a hierarchy. XML also uses a hierarchical model. It can be represented as a relational database, although the actual structure is that of a tree traversal path.

1.3.8.2 Relational

People sometimes think that relational databases are named for the relation between tables. This is not the case. Relational databases are based on set theory and relational algebra, where data elements or attributes (columns) are related into tuples (rows). (See Chapter 5.) Tables are sets of relations with identical structure. Set operations (like union, intersect, and minus) are used to organize and retrieve data from relational databases, in the form of Structured Query Language (SQL). In order to write data, the structure (schema) has to be known in advance (schema on write). Relational databases are row-oriented.

The database management system (DBMS) of a relational database is called RDBMS. A relational database is the predominant choice in storing data that constantly changes. Variations on relational databases include Multidimensional and Temporal.

1.3.8.2.1 Multidimensional

Multidimensional database technologies store data in a structure that allows searching using several data element filters simultaneously. This type of structure is used most frequently in Data Warehousing and Business Intelligence. Some of these database types are proprietary, although most large databases have cube technology built in as objects. Access to the data uses a variant of SQL called MDX or Multidimensional eXpression.

1.3.8.2.2 Temporal

A temporal database is a relational database with built-in support for handling data involving time. The temporal aspects usually include valid time and transaction time. These attributes can be combined to form bi-temporal data.

- **Valid time** is the timeframe when a fact is true with respect to the entity it represents in the real world.

- **Transaction time** is the period during which a fact stored in the database is considered true.

It is possible to have timelines other than Valid Time and Transaction Time, such as Decision Time, in the database. In that case, the database is called a multi-temporal database as opposed to a bi-temporal database. Temporal databases enable application developers and DBAs to manage current, proposed, and historical versions of data in the same database.

1.3.8.3 Non-relational

Non-relational databases can store data as simple strings or complete files. Data in these files can be read in different ways, depending on the need (this characteristic is referred to as 'schema on read'). Non-relational databases may be row-oriented, but this is not required.

A non-relational database provides a mechanism for storage and retrieval of data that employs less constrained consistency models than traditional relational databases. Motivations for this approach include simplicity of design, horizontal scaling, and finer control over availability.

Non-relational databases are usually referred to as NoSQL (which stands for "Not Only SQL"). The primary differentiating factor is the storage structure itself, where the data structure is no longer bound to a tabular relational design. It could be a tree, a graph, a network, or a key-value pairing. The NoSQL tag emphasizes that some editions may in fact support conventional SQL directives. These databases are often highly optimized data stores intended for simple retrieval and appending operations. The goal is improved performance, especially with respect to latency and throughput. NoSQL databases are used increasingly in Big Data and real-time web applications. (See Chapter 5.)

1.3.8.3.1 Column-oriented

Column-oriented databases are used mostly in Business Intelligence applications because they can compress redundant data. For example, a state ID column only has unique values, instead of one value for each of a million rows.

There are trade-offs between column-oriented (non-relational) and row-oriented (usually relational) organization.

- Column-oriented organization is more efficient when an aggregate needs to be computed over many rows. This only holds true for a notably smaller subset of all columns of data, because reading that smaller subset of data can be faster than reading all data.

- Column-oriented organization is more efficient when new values of a column are supplied for all rows at once, because that column data can be written efficiently to replace old column data without touching any other columns for the rows.

- Row-oriented organization is more efficient when many columns of a single row are required at the same time, and when row-size is relatively small, as the entire row can be retrieved with a single disk seek.

- Row-oriented organization is more efficient when writing a new row if all of the row data is supplied at the same time; the entire row can be written with a single disk seek.

- In practice, row-oriented storage layouts are well suited for Online Transaction Processing (OLTP)-like workloads, which are more heavily loaded with interactive transactions. Column-oriented storage layouts are well suited for Online Analytical Processing (OLAP)-like workloads (e.g., data warehouses) which typically involve a smaller number of highly complex queries over all data (possibly terabytes).

1.3.8.3.2 Spatial

A spatial database is optimized to store and query data that represents objects defined in a geometric space. Spatial databases support several primitive types (simple geometric shapes such as box, rectangle, cube, cylinder, etc.) and geometries composed of collections of points, lines, and shapes.

Spatial database systems use indexes to quickly look up values; the way that most databases index data is not optimal for spatial queries. Instead, spatial databases use a spatial index to speed up database operations.

Spatial databases can perform a wide variety of spatial operations. As per the Open Geospatial Consortium standard, a spatial database may perform one or more of the following operations:

- **Spatial Measurements**: Computes line length, polygon area, the distance between geometries, etc.

- **Spatial Functions**: Modifies existing features to create new ones; for example, by providing a buffer around them, intersecting features, etc.

- **Spatial Predicates**: Allows true/false queries about spatial relationships between geometries. Examples include "Do two polygons overlap?" or "Is there a residence located within a mile of the area of the proposed landfill?"

- **Geometry Constructors**: Creates new geometries, usually by specifying the vertices (points or nodes) which define the shape.

- **Observer Functions**: Queries that return specific information about a feature such as the location of the center of a circle.

1.3.8.3.3 Object / Multi-media

A multimedia database includes a Hierarchical Storage Management system for the efficient management of a hierarchy of magnetic and optical storage media. It also includes a collection of objects classes, which represents the foundation of the system.

1.3.8.3.4 Flat File Database

A flat file database describes any of various means to encode a data set as a single file. A flat file can be a plain text file or a binary file. Strictly, a flat file database consists of nothing but data, and contains records that may vary in length and delimiters. More broadly, the term refers to any database that exists in a single file in the form of rows and columns, with no relationships or links between records and fields except the structure. Plain text files usually contain one record per line. A list of names, addresses, and phone numbers, written by hand on a sheet of paper, is an example of a flat file database. Flat files are used not only as data storage tools in DBMS systems, but also as data transfer tools. Hadoop databases use flat file storage.

1.3.8.3.5 Key-Value Pair

Key-Value pair databases contain sets of two items: a key identifier and a value. There are a few specific uses of these types of databases.

- **Document Databases**: Document-oriented databases contain collections of files including both structure and data. Each document is assigned a key. More advanced document-oriented databases also can store attributes for the document's contents, such as dates or tags. This type of database can store both complete and incomplete documents. Document databases may use XML or JSON (Java Script Object Notation) structures.

- **Graph Databases**: Graph databases store key-value pairs where the focus is on the relationship between the nodes, rather than on the nodes themselves.

1.3.8.3.6 Triplestore

A data entity composed of subject-predicate-object is known as a triplestore. In Resource Description Framework (RDF) terminology, a triplestore is composed of a subject that denotes a resource, the predicate that expresses a relationship between the subject and the object, and the object itself. A triplestore is a purpose-built database for the storage and retrieval of triples in the form of subject-predicate-object expressions.

Triplestores can be broadly classified into three categories: Native triplestores, RDBMS-backed triplestores and NoSQL triplestores.

- **Native triplestores** are those that are implemented from scratch and exploit the RDF data model to efficiently store and access the RDF data.
- **RDBMS-backed triplestores** are built by adding an RDF specific layer to an existing RDBMS.
- **NoSQL Triplestores** are currently being investigated as possible storage managers for RDF.

Triplestore databases are best for taxonomy and thesaurus management, linked data integration, and knowledge portals.

1.3.9 Specialized Databases

Some specialized situations require specialized types of databases that are managed differently from traditional relational databases. Examples include:

- **Computer Assisted Design and Manufacturing (CAD / CAM)** applications require an Object database, as will most embedded real-time applications.

- **Geographical Information Systems (GIS)** make use of specialized geospatial databases, which have at least annual updates to their Reference Data. Some specialized GIS are used for utilities (electric grid, gas lines, etc.), for telecom in network management, or for ocean navigation.

- **Shopping-cart applications** found on most online retail websites, make use of XML databases to initially store the customer order data, and may be used real-time by social media databases for ad placement on other websites.

Some of this data is then copied into one or more traditional OLTP (Online Transaction Processing) databases or data warehouses. In addition, many off-the-shelf vendor applications may use their own proprietary databases. At the very least, their schemas will be proprietary and mostly concealed, even if they sit on top of traditional relational DBMSs.

1.3.10 Common Database Processes

All databases, no matter the type, share the following processes in some way.

1.3.10.1 Archiving

Archiving is the process of moving data off immediately accessible storage media and onto media with lower retrieval performance. Archives can be restored to the originating system for short-term use. Data that is not actively needed to support application processes should be moved to an archive on less-expensive disk, tape, or a CD / DVD jukebox. Restoring from an archive should be a matter of simply copying the data from the archive back into the system.

Archival processes must be aligned with the partitioning strategy to ensure optimal availability and retention. A robust approach involves:

- Creating a secondary storage area, preferably on a secondary database server
- Partitioning existing database tables into archival blocks
- Replicating the data that is needed less often to the separate database
- Creating tape or disk backups
- Creating database jobs that periodically purge unneeded data

It is wise to schedule regular tests of archive restoration to ensure avoid surprises in an emergency.

When changes are made to the technology or structure of a production system, the archive also needs to be evaluated to ensure that data moved from the archive into current storage will be readable. There are several ways of handling out-of-synch archives:

- Determine if or how much of the archive is required to be preserved. What is not required can be considered purged.

- For major changes in technology, restore the archives to the originating system before the technology change, upgrade or migrate to the new technology, and re-archive the data using the new technology.

- For high-value archives where the source database structures change, restore the archive, make any changes to the data structures, and re-archive the data with the new structure.

- For infrequent-access archives where the source technology or structure changes, keep a small version of the old system running with limited access, and extract from the archives using the old system as needed.

Archives that are not recoverable with current technology are useless, and keeping old machinery around to read archives that cannot be otherwise read, is not efficient or cost-effective.

1.3.10.2 Capacity and Growth Projections

Think of a database as a box, the data as fruit, and overhead (indexes, etc.) as packing material. The box has dividers, and fruit and packing material go in the cells:

- First, decide the size of the box that will hold all the fruit and any packing material needed – that is the Capacity.
- How much fruit goes into the box, and how quickly?
- How much fruit comes out of the box, and how quickly?

Decide if the box will stay the same size over time, or must be expanded over time to hold more fruit. This projection of how much and how quickly the box must expand to hold incoming fruit and packing material is the growth projection. If the box cannot expand, the fruit must be taken out as fast as it is put in, and the growth projection is zero.

How long should the fruit stay in the cells? If the fruit in one cell gets dehydrated over time, or for any reason becomes not as useful, should that fruit be put in a separate box for longer term storage (i.e., archived)? Will there ever be a need to bring that dehydrated fruit back into the main box? Moving the fruit to another box with the ability to move it back into the first box is an important part of archiving. This allows the box to not have to be expanded quite as often or as much.

If a fruit becomes too stagnant to use, throw that fruit away (i.e., purge the data).

1.3.10.3 Change Data Capture (CDC)

Change data capture refers to the process of detecting that data has changed and ensuring that information relevant to the change is stored appropriately. Often referred to as log-based replication, CDC is a non-invasive way to replicate data changes to a target without affecting the source. In a simplified CDC context, one computer system has data that may have changed from a previous point in time, and a second computer system needs to reflect the same change. Rather than sending the entire database over the network to reflect just a few minor changes, the idea is to just send what changed (deltas), so that the receiving system can make appropriate updates.

There are two different methods to detect and collect changes: data versioning, which evaluates columns that identify rows that have changed (e.g., last-update-timestamp columns, version-number columns, status-indicator columns), or by reading logs that document the changes and enable them to be replicated in secondary systems.

1.3.10.4 Purging

It is incorrect to assume that all data will reside forever in primary storage. Eventually, the data will fill the available space, and performance will begin to degrade. At that point, data will need to be archived, purged, or both. Just as importantly, some data will degrade in value and is not worth keeping. Purging is the process of completely removing data from storage media such that it cannot be recovered. A principal goal of data management is that the cost of maintaining data should not exceed its value to the organization. Purging data reduces costs and risks. Data to be purged is generally deemed obsolete and unnecessary, even for regulatory purposes. Some data may become a liability if kept longer than necessary. Purging it reduces the risks that it may be misused.

1.3.10.5 Replication

Data replication means same data is stored on multiple storage devices. In some situations, having duplicate databases is useful, such as in a high-availability environment where spreading the workload among identical databases in different hardware or even data centers can preserve functionality during peak usage times or disasters.

Replication can be active or passive:

- **Active replication** is performed by recreating and storing the same data at every replica from every other replica.
- **Passive replication** involves recreating and storing data on a single primary replica and then transforming its resultant state to other secondary replicas.

Replication has two dimensions of scaling:

- Horizontal data scaling has more data replicas.
- Vertical data scaling has data replicas located further away in distance geographically.

Multi-master replication, where updates can be submitted to any database node and then ripple through to other servers, is often desired, but increases complexity and cost.

Replication transparency occurs when data is replicated between database servers so that the information remains consistent throughout the database system and users cannot tell or even know which database copy they are using.

The two primary replication patterns are mirroring and log shipping (see Figure 60).

- In mirroring, updates to the primary database are replicated immediately (relatively speaking) to the secondary database, as part of a two-phase commit process.

- In log shipping, a secondary server receives and applies copies of the primary database's transaction logs at regular intervals.

The choice of replication method depends on how critical the data is, and how important it is that failover to the secondary server be immediate. Mirroring is usually a more expensive option than log shipping. For one secondary server, mirroring is effective; log shipping may be used to update additional secondary servers.

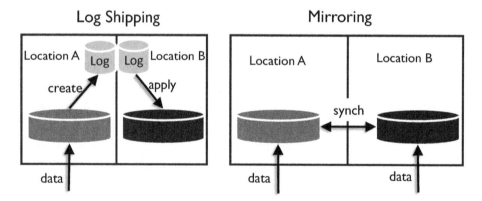

Figure 60 Log Shipping vs. Mirroring

1.3.10.6 Resiliency and Recovery

Resiliency in databases is the measurement of how tolerant a system is to error conditions. If a system can tolerate a high level of processing errors and still function as expected, it is highly resilient. If an application crashes upon the first unexpected condition, that system is not resilient. If the database can detect and either abort or automatically recover from common processing errors (runaway query, for example), it is considered resilient. There are always some conditions that no system can detect in advance, such as a power failure, and those conditions are considered disasters.

Three recovery types provide guidelines for how quickly recovery takes place and what it focuses on:

- **Immediate recovery** from some issues sometimes can be resolved through design; for example, predicting and automatically resolving issues, such as those that might be caused by a failover to backup system.

- **Critical recovery** refers to a plan to restore the system as quickly as possible in order to minimize delays or shut downs of business processes.

- **Non-critical recovery** means that restoration of function can be delayed until systems that are more critical have been restored.

Data processing errors include data load failures, query return failures, and obstacles to completing ETL or other processes. Common ways of increasing resilience in data processing systems are to trap and re-route data causing errors, detect and ignore data causing errors, and implement flags in processing for completed steps to avoid reprocessing data or repeating completed steps when restarting a process.

Each system should require a certain level of resiliency (high or low). Some applications may require that any error halts all processing (low resiliency), while others may only require that the errors be trapped and re-routed for review, if not outright ignored.

For extremely critical data, the DBA will need to implement a replication pattern in which data moves to another copy of the database on a remote server. In the event of database failure, applications can then 'fail over' to the remote database and continue processing.

1.3.10.7 Retention

Data Retention refers to how long data is kept available. Data retention planning should be part of the physical database design. Retention requirements also affect capacity planning.

Data Security also affects data retention plans, as some data needs to be retained for specific timeframes for legal reasons. Failure to retain data for the appropriate length of time can have legal consequences. Likewise, there are also regulations related to purging data. Data can become a liability if kept longer than specified. Organizations should formulate retention policies based on regulatory requirements and risk management guidelines. These policies should drive specifications for purging and archiving of data.

1.3.10.8 Sharding

Sharding is a process where small chunks of the database are isolated and can be updated independently of other shards, so replication is merely a file copy. Because the shards are small, refreshes/overwrites may be optimal.

2. Activities

The two main activities in Data Operations and Storage are Database Technology Support and Database Operations Support. Database Technology Support is specific to selecting and maintaining the software that stores and manages the data. Database Operations Support is specific to the data and processes that the software manages.

2.1 Manage Database Technology

Managing database technology should follow the same principles and standards for managing any technology.

The leading reference model for technology management is the Information Technology Infrastructure Library (ITIL), a technology management process model developed in the United Kingdom. ITIL principles apply to managing data technology.[35]

2.1.1 Understand Database Technology Characteristics

It is important to understand how technology works, and how it can provide value in the context of a particular business. The DBA, along with the rest of the data services teams, works closely with business users and managers to understand the data and information needs of the business. DBAs and Database Architects combine their knowledge of available tools with the business requirements in order to suggest the best possible applications of technology to meet organizational needs.

Data professionals must first understand the characteristics of a candidate database technology before determining which to recommend as a solution. For example, database technologies that do not have transaction-based capabilities (e.g., commit and rollback) are not suitable for operational situations supporting Point-of-Sale processes.

Do not assume that a single type of database architecture or DBMS works for every need. Most organizations have multiple database tools installed, to perform a range of functions, from performance tuning to backups, to managing the database itself. Only a few of these tool sets have mandated standards.

2.1.2 Evaluate Database Technology

Selecting strategic DBMS software is particularly important. DBMS software has a major impact on data integration, application performance, and business productivity. Some of the factors to consider when selecting DBMS software include:

- Product architecture and complexity
- Volume and velocity limits, including streaming rate
- Application profile, such as transaction processing, Business Intelligence, and personal profiles

---

[35] http://bit.ly/1gA4mpr.

- Specific functionality, such as temporal calculation support
- Hardware platform and operating system support
- Availability of supporting software tools
- Performance benchmarks, including real-time statistics
- Scalability
- Software, memory, and storage requirements
- Resiliency, including error handling and reporting

Some factors are not directly related to the technology itself, but rather to the purchasing organization and to the tool vendors. For example:

- Organizational appetite for technical risk
- Available supply of trained technical professionals
- Cost of ownership, such as licensing, maintenance, and computing resources
- Vendor reputation
- Vendor support policy and release schedule
- Customer references

The expense of the product, including administration, licensing, and support, should not exceed the product's value to the business. Ideally, the technology should be as user friendly, self-monitoring, and self-administering as possible. If it is not, then it may be necessary to bring in staff with experience using the tool.

It is a good idea to start with a small pilot project or a proof-of-concept (POC), to get a good idea of the true costs and benefits before proceeding with a full-blown production implementation.

2.1.3 Manage and Monitor Database Technology

DBAs often serve as Level 2 technical support, working with help desks and technology vendor support to understand, analyze, and resolve user problems. The key to effective understanding and use of any technology is training. Organizations should make sure they have training plans and budgets in place for everyone involved in implementing, supporting, and using data and database technology. Training plans should include appropriate levels of cross-training to better support application development, especially Agile development. DBAs should have working knowledge of application development skills, such as data modeling, use-case analysis, and application data access.

The DBA will be responsible for ensuring databases have regular backups and for performing recovery tests. However, if data from these databases needs to be merged with other existing data in one or more databases, there may be a data integration challenge. DBAs should not simply merge data. Instead, they should work with other stakeholders to ensure that data can be integrated correctly and effectively.

When a business requires new technology, the DBAs will work with business users and application developers to ensure the most effective use of the technology, to explore new applications of the technology, and to address any problems or issues that surface from its use. The DBAs then deploy new technology products in pre-production and production environments. They will need to create and document processes and procedures for administering the product with the least amount of effort and expense.

2.2 Manage Databases

Database support, as provided by DBAs and Network Storage Administrators (NSAs), is at the heart of data management. Databases reside on managed storage areas. Managed storage can be as small as a disk drive on a personal computer (managed by the OS), or as large as RAID arrays on a storage area network or SAN. Backup media is also managed storage.

DBAs manage various data storage applications by assigning storage structures, maintaining physical databases (including physical data models and physical layouts of the data, such as assignments to specific files or disk areas), and establishing DBMS environments on servers.

2.2.1 Understand Requirements

2.2.1.1 Define Storage Requirements

DBAs establish storage systems for DBMS applications and file storage systems to support NoSQL. NSAs and DBAs together play a vital role in establishing file storage systems. Data enters the storage media during normal business operations and, depending on the requirements, can stay permanently or temporarily. It is important to plan for adding additional space well in advance of when that space is actually needed. Doing any sort of maintenance in an emergency is a risk.

All projects should have an initial capacity estimate for the first year of operations, and a growth projection for the following few years. Capacity and growth should be estimated not only for the space the data itself holds, but also for indexes, logs, and any redundant images such as mirrors.

Data storage requirements must account for regulation related to data retention. For legal reasons, organizations are required to retain some data for set periods (see Chapter 9). In some cases, they may also be required to purge data after a defined period. It's a good idea to discuss data retention needs with the data owners at design time and reach agreement on how to treat data through its lifecycle.

The DBAs will work with application developers and other operations staff, including server and storage administrators, to implement the approved data retention plan.

2.2.1.2 Identify Usage Patterns

Databases have predictable usage patterns. Basic types of patterns include:

- Transaction-based
- Large data set write- or retrieval-based
- Time-based (heavier at month end, lighter on weekends, etc.),
- Location-based (more densely populated areas have more transactions, etc.)
- Priority-based (some departments or batch IDs have higher priority than others)

Some systems will have a combination of these basic patterns. DBAs need to be able to predict ebbs and flows of usage patterns and have processes in place to handle peaks (such as query governors or priority management) as well as to take advantage of valleys (delay processes that need large amounts of resources until a valley pattern exists). This information can be used to maintain database performance.

2.2.1.3 Define Access Requirements

Data access includes activities related to storing, retrieving, or acting on data housed in a database or other repository. Data Access is simply the authorization to access different data files.

Various standard languages, methods, and formats exist for accessing data from databases and other repositories: SQL, ODBC, JDBC, XQJ, ADO.NET, XML, X Query, X Path, and Web Services for ACID-type systems. BASE-type access method standards include C, C++, REST, XML, and Java[36]. Some standards enable translation of data from unstructured (such as HTML or free-text files) to structured (such as XML or SOL).

Data architects and DBAs can assist organizations to select appropriate methods and tools required for data access.

2.2.2 Plan for Business Continuity

Organizations need to plan for business continuity in the event of disaster or adverse event that impacts their systems and their ability to use their data. DBAs must make sure a recovery plan exists for all databases and database servers, covering scenarios that could result in loss or corruption of data, such as:

- Loss of the physical database server
- Loss of one or more disk storage devices
- Loss of a database, including the DBMS Master Database, temporary storage database, transaction log segment, etc.
- Corruption of database index or data pages
- Loss of the database or log segment filesystems
- Loss of database or transaction log backup files

Each database should be evaluated for criticality so that its restoration can be prioritized. Some databases will be essential to business operations and will need to be restored immediately. Less critical databases will not be restored until primary systems are up and running. Still other may not need to be restored at all; for example, if they are merely copies that are refreshed when loaded.

Management and the organization's business continuity group, if one exists, should review and approve the data recovery plan. The DBA group should regularly review the plans for accuracy and comprehensiveness. Keep a copy of the plan, along with all the software needed to install and configure the DBMS, instructions, and security codes (e.g., the administrator password) in a secure, off-site location in the event of a disaster.

No system can be recovered from a disaster if the backups are unavailable or unreadable. Regular backups are essential to any recovery effort, but if they are unreadable, they are worse than useless; processing time making the

---

[36] http://bit.ly/1rWAUxS (accessed 2/28/2016) has a list of all data access methods for BASE-type systems.

unreadable backups will have been wasted, along with the opportunity for fixing the issue that made the backups unreadable. Keep all backups in a secure, off-site location.

2.2.2.1 Make Backups

Make backups of databases and, if appropriate, the database transaction logs. The system's Service Level Agreement (SLA) should specify backup frequency. Balance the importance of the data against the cost of protecting it. For large databases, frequent backups can consume large amounts of disk storage and server resources. In addition to incremental backups, periodically make a complete backup of each database. Furthermore, databases should reside on a managed storage area, ideally a RAID array on a storage area network or SAN, with daily back up to separate storage media. For OLTP databases, the frequency of transaction log backups will depend on the frequency of updating, and the amount of data involved. For frequently updated databases, more frequent log dumps will not only provide greater protection, but will also reduce the impact of the backups on server resources and applications.

Backup files should be kept on a separate filesystem from the databases, and should be backed up to some separate storage medium as specified in the SLA. Store copies of the daily backups in a secure off-site facility. Most DBMSs support hot backups of the database – backups taken while applications are running. When some updates occur in transit, they will roll either forward to completion, or roll back when the backup reloads. The alternative is a cold backup taken when the database is off-line. However, a cold backup may not be a viable option if applications need to be continuously available.

2.2.2.2 Recover Data

Most backup software includes the option to read from the backup into the system. The DBA works with the infrastructure team to re-mount the media containing the backup and to execute the restoration. The specific utilities used to execute the restoration of the data depend on the type of databased.

Data in file system databases may be easier to restore than those in relational database management systems, which may have catalog information that needs to be updated during the data recovery, especially if the recovery is from logs instead of a full backup.

It is critical to periodically test recovery of data. Doing so will reduce bad surprises during a disaster or emergency. Practice runs can be executed on non-production system copies with identical infrastructure and configuration, or if the system has a failover, on the secondary system.

2.2.3 Develop Database Instances

DBAs are responsible for the creation of database instances. Related activities include:

- **Installing and updating DBMS software**: DBAs install new versions of the DBMS software and apply maintenance patches supplied by the DBMS vendor in all environments (from development to production) as indicated by the vendor and vetted by and prioritized by DBA specialists, security specialists, and management. This is a critical activity to ensure against vulnerability to attacks, as well as to ensure ongoing data integrity in centralized and decentralized installations.

- **Maintaining multiple environment installations, including different DBMS versions**: DBAs may install and maintain multiple instances of DBMS software in sandbox, development, testing, user acceptance testing, system acceptance testing, quality assurance, pre-production, hot-fix, disaster recovery environments, and production, and manage migration of the DBMS software versions through environments relative to applications and systems versioning and changes.

- **Installing and administering related data technology**: DBAs may be involved in installing data integration software and third party data administration tools.

2.2.3.1 Manage the Physical Storage Environment

Storage environment management needs to follow traditional Software Configuration Management (SCM) processes or Information Technology Infrastructure Library (ITIL) methods to record modification to the database configuration, structures, constraints, permissions, thresholds, etc. DBAs need to update the physical data model to reflect the changes to the storage objects as part of a standard configuration management process. With agile development and extreme programming methods, updates to the physical data model play important roles in preventing design or development errors.

DBAs need to apply the SCM process to trace changes and to verify that the databases in the development, test, and production environments have all of the enhancements included in each release – even if the changes are cosmetic or only in a virtualized data layer.

The four procedures required to ensure a sound SCM process are configuration identification, configuration change control, configuration status accounting, and configuration audits.

- During the **configuration identification** process, DBAs will work with data stewards, data architects, and data modelers to identify the attributes that define every aspect of a configuration for end-user purposes. These attributes are recorded in configuration documentation and baselined. Once an attribute is baselined a formal configuration change control processes is required to change the attribute.

- **Configuration change control** is a set of processes and approval stages required to change a configuration item's attributes and to re-baseline them.

- **Configuration status accounting** is the ability to record and report on the configuration baseline associated with each configuration item at any point in time.

- **Configuration audits** occur both at delivery and when effecting a change. There are two types. A physical configuration audit ensures that a configuration item is installed in accordance with the requirements of its detailed design documentation, while a functional configuration audit ensures that performance attributes of a configuration item are achieved.

To maintain data integrity and traceability throughout the data lifecycle, DBAs communicate the changes to physical database attributes to modelers, developers, and Metadata managers.

DBAs must also maintain metrics on data volume, capacity projections, and query performance, as well as statistics on physical objects, in order to identify data replication needs, data migration volumes, and data recovery checkpoints. Larger databases will also have object partitioning, which must be monitored and maintained over time to ensure that the object maintains the desired distribution of data.

2.2.3.2 Manage Database Access Controls

DBAs are responsible for managing the controls that enable access to the data. DBAs oversee the following functions to protect data assets and data integrity:

- **Controlled environment**: DBAs work with NSAs to manage a controlled environment for data assets; this includes network roles and permissions management, 24x7 monitoring and network health monitoring, firewall management, patch management, and Microsoft Baseline Security Analyzer (MBSA) integration.

- **Physical security**: The physical security of data assets is managed by Simple Network Management Protocol (SNMP)-based monitoring, data audit logging, disaster management, and database backup planning. DBAs configure and monitor these protocols. Monitoring is especially important for security protocols.

- **Monitoring**: Database systems are made available by continuous hardware and software monitoring of critical servers.

- **Controls**: DBAs maintain information security by access controls, database auditing, intrusion detection, and vulnerability assessment tools.

Concepts and activities involved in setting up data security are discussed in Chapter 7.

2.2.3.3 Create Storage Containers

All data must be stored on a physical drive and organized for ease of load, search, and retrieval. Storage containers themselves may contain storage objects, and each level must be maintained appropriate to the level of the object. For example, relational databases have schemas that contain tables, and non-relational databases have filesystems that contain files.

2.2.3.4 Implement Physical Data Models

DBAs are typically responsible for creating and managing the complete physical data storage environment based on the physical data model. The physical data model includes storage objects, indexing objects, and any encapsulated code objects required to enforce data quality rules, connect database objects, and achieve database performance.

Depending on the organization, data modelers may provide the data model and the DBAs implement the physical layout of the data model in storage. In other organizations, DBAs may take a skeleton of a physical model and add all the database-specific implementation details, including indexes, constraints, partitions or clusters, capacity estimates, and storage allocation details.

For third-party database structures provided as part of an application, most data modeling tools allow reverse engineering of Commercial Off the Shelf (COTS) or Enterprise Resource Planning (ERP) system databases, as long as the modeling tool can read the storage tool catalog. These can be used to develop a Physical Model. DBAs or data modelers will still need to review and potentially update the physical model for application-based constraints or relationships; not all constraints and relationships are installed in database catalogs, especially for older applications where database abstraction was desired.

Well-maintained physical models are necessary when DBAs are providing Data-as-a-Service.

2.2.3.5 Load Data

When first built, databases are empty. DBAs fill them. If the data to be loaded has been exported using a database utility, it may not be necessary to use a data integration tool to load it into the new database. Most database systems have bulk load capabilities, requiring that the data be in a format that matches the target database object, or having a simple mapping function to link data in the source to the target object.

Most organizations also obtain some data from external third-party sources, such as lists of potential customers purchased from an information broker, postal and address information, or product data provided by a supplier. The data can be licensed or provided as an open data service, free of charge; provided in a number of different formats (CD, DVD, EDI, XML, RSS feeds, text files); or provided upon request or regularly updated via a subscription service. Some acquisitions require legal agreements. DBAs need to be aware of these restrictions before loading data.

DBAs may be asked to handle these types of loads, or to create the initial load map. Limit manual execution of these loads to installations or other one-time situations, or ensure they are automated and scheduled.

A managed approach to data acquisition centralizes responsibility for data subscription services with data analysts. The data analyst will need to document the external data source in the logical data model and data dictionary. A developer may design and create scripts or programs to read the data and load it into a database. The DBA will be responsible for implementing the necessary processes to load the data into the database and / or make it available to the application.

2.2.3.6 Manage Data Replication

DBAs can influence decisions about the data replication process by advising on:

- Active or passive replication
- Distributed concurrency control from distributed data systems
- The appropriate methods to identify updates to data through either timestamp or version numbers under Change Data Control process

For small systems or data objects, complete data refreshes may satisfy the requirements for concurrency. For larger objects where most of the data does NOT change, merging changes into the data object is more efficient than completely copying all data for every change. For large objects where most of the data is changed, it may still be better to do a refresh than to incur the overhead of so many updates.

2.2.4 Manage Database Performance

The Database performance depends on two interdependent facets: availability and speed. Performance includes ensuring availability of space, query optimization, and other factors that enable a database to return data in an efficient way. Performance cannot be measured without availability. An unavailable database has a performance measure of zero. DBAs and NSAs manage database performance by:

- Setting and tuning operating system and application parameters.

- Managing database connectivity. NSAs and DBAs provide technical guidance and support for IT and business users requiring database connectivity based on policies enforced through standards and protocols of the organization.

- Working with system programmers and network administrators to tune operating systems, networks, and transaction processing middleware to work with the database.

- Dedicating appropriate storage and enabling the database to work with storage devices and storage management software. Storage management software optimizes the use of different storage technologies for cost-effective storage of older, less-frequently referenced data, by migrating that data to less expensive storage devices. This results in more rapid retrieval time for core data. DBAs work with storage administrators to set up and monitor effective storage management procedures.

- Providing volumetric growth studies to support storage acquisition and general data lifecycle management activities of retention, tuning, archiving, backup, purging, and disaster recovery.

- Working with system administrators to provide operating workloads and benchmarks of deployed data assets that support SLA management, charge-back calculations, server capacity, and lifecycle rotation within the prescribed planning horizon.

2.2.4.1 Set Database Performance Service Levels

System performance, data availability and recovery expectations, and expectations for teams to respond to issues are usually governed through Service Level Agreements (SLAs) between IT data management services organizations and data owners (Figure 61).

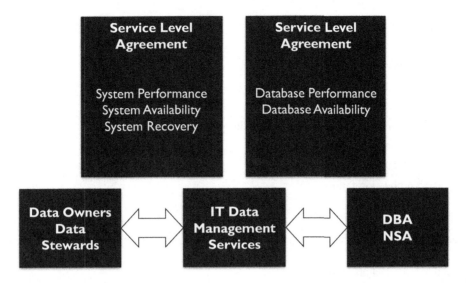

Figure 61 SLAs for System and Database Performance

Typically, an SLA will identify the timeframes during which the database is expected to be available for use. Often an SLA will identify a specified maximum allowable execution time for a few application transactions (a mix of complex queries and updates). If the database is not available as agreed to, or if process execution times violate the SLA, the data owners will ask the DBA to identify and remediate the causes of the problem.

2.2.4.2 Manage Database Availability

Availability is the percentage of time that a system or database can be used for productive work. As organizations increase their uses of data, availability requirements increase, as do the risks and costs of unavailable data. To meet higher demand, maintenance windows are shrinking. Four related factors affect availability:

- **Manageability**: The ability to create and maintain an environment
- **Recoverability**: The ability to reestablish service after interruption, and correct errors caused by unforeseen events or component failures
- **Reliability**: The ability to deliver service at specified levels for a stated period
- **Serviceability**: The ability to identify the existence of problems, diagnose their causes, and repair / solve them

Many things may prevent databases from being available, including:

- Planned outages
    - o   For maintenance
    - o   For upgrades
- Unplanned outages
    - o   Loss of the server hardware
    - o   Disk hardware failure
    - o   Operating system failure
    - o   DBMS software failure
    - o   Data center site loss
    - o   Network failure

- Application problems
  - o Security and authorization problems
  - o Severe performance problems
  - o Recovery failures
- Data problems
  - o Corruption of data (due to bugs, poor design, or user error)
  - o Loss of database objects
  - o Loss of data
  - o Data replication failure
- Human error

DBAs are responsible for doing everything possible to ensure databases stay online and operational, including:

- Running database backup utilities
- Running database reorganization utilities
- Running statistics gathering utilities
- Running integrity checking utilities
- Automating the execution of these utilities
- Exploiting table space clustering and partitioning
- Replicating data across mirror databases to ensure high availability

2.2.4.3 Manage Database Execution

DBAs also establish and monitor database execution, use of data change logs, and synchronization of duplicated environments. Log sizes and locations require space and in some cases can be treated like file-based databases on their own. Other applications that consume logs must also be managed, to ensure use of the correct logs at the required logging level. The more detail that is logged, the more space and processing required, which may adversely affect performance.

2.2.4.4 Maintain Database Performance Service Levels

DBAs optimize database performance both proactively and reactively, by monitoring performance and by responding to problems quickly and competently. Most DBMSs provide the capability of monitoring performance, allowing DBAs to generate analysis reports. Most server operating systems have similar monitoring and reporting capabilities. DBAs should run activity and performance reports against both the DBMS and the server on a regular basis, including during periods of heavy activity. They should compare these reports to previous reports to identify any negative trends and save them to help analyze problems over time.

2.2.4.4.1 Transaction Performance vs. Batch Performance

Data movement may occur in real time through online transactions. However, many data movement and transformation activities are performed through batch programs, which may move data between systems, or merely perform operations on data within a system. These batch jobs must complete within specified windows in the operating schedule. DBAs and data integration specialists monitor the performance of batch data jobs, noting exceptional completion times and errors, determining the root cause of errors, and resolving these issues.

2.2.4.4.2 Issue Remediation

When performance problems occur, the DBA, NSA, and Server Administration teams should use the monitoring and administration tools of the DBMS to help identify the source of the problem. Common reasons for poor database performance include:

- **Memory allocation or contention**: A buffer or cache for data.

- **Locking and blocking**: In some cases, a process running in the database may lock up database resources, such as tables or data pages, and block another process that needs them. If the problem persists, the DBA can kill the blocking process. In some cases, two processes may 'deadlock', with each process locking resources needed by the other. Most DBMSs will automatically terminate one of these processes after an interval of time. These types of problems are often the result of poor coding, either in the database or in the application.

- **Inaccurate database statistics**: Most relational DBMSs have a built-in query optimizer, which relies on stored statistics about the data and indexes to make decisions about how to execute a given query most effectively. These statistics should be updated frequently, especially in active databases. Failure to do so will result in poorly performing queries.

- **Poor coding**: Perhaps the most common cause of poor database performance is poorly coded SQL. Query coders need a basic understanding of how the SQL query optimizer works. They should code SQL in a way that takes maximum advantage of the optimizer's capabilities. Some systems allow encapsulation of complex SQL in stored procedures, which can be pre-compiled and pre-optimized, rather than embedded in application code or in script files.

- **Inefficient complex table joins**: Use views to pre-define complex table joins. In addition, avoid using complex SQL (e.g., table joins) in database functions; unlike stored procedures, these are opaque to the query optimizer.

- **Insufficient indexing**: Code complex queries and queries involving large tables to use indexes built on the tables. Create the indexes necessary to support these queries. Be careful about creating too many indexes on heavily updated tables, as this will slow down update processing.

- **Application activity**: Ideally, applications should be running on a server separate from the DBMS, so that they are not competing for resources. Configure and tune database servers for maximum performance. In addition, the new DBMSs allow application objects, such as Java and .NET classes, to be encapsulated in database objects and executed in the DBMS. Be careful about making use of this capability. It can be very useful in certain cases, but executing application code on the database server may affect the interoperability, application architecture, and performance of database processes.

- **Overloaded servers**: For DBMSs that support multiple databases and applications, there may be a breaking point where the addition of more databases has an adverse effect on the performance of existing databases. In this case, create a new database server. In addition, relocate databases that have grown very large, or that are being used more heavily than before, to a different server. In some cases, address problems with large databases by archiving less-used data to another location, or by deleting expired or obsolete data.

- **Database volatility**: In some cases, large numbers of table inserts and deletes over a short while can create inaccurate database distribution statistics. In these cases, turn off updating database statistics for these tables, as the incorrect statistics will adversely affect the query optimizer.

- **Runaway queries**: Users may unintentionally submit queries that use a majority of the system's shared resources. Use rankings or query governors to kill or pause these queries until they can be evaluated and improved.

After the cause of the problem is identified, the DBA will take whatever action is needed to resolve the problem, including working with application developers to improve and optimize the database code, and archiving or deleting data that is no longer actively needed by application processes. In exceptional cases for OLTP-type databases, the DBA may consider working with the data modeler restructure the affected portion of the database. Do this only after other measures (e.g., the creation of views and indexes and the rewriting of SQL code) have been tried, and only after careful consideration of the possible consequences, such as loss of data integrity or the increase in complexity of SQL queries against denormalized tables.

For read-only reporting and analytical databases, denormalization for performance and ease of access is the rule rather than the exception, and poses no threat or risk.

2.2.4.5 Maintain Alternate Environments

Databases do not appear once and remain unchanged. Business rules change, business processes change, and technology changes. Development and test environments enable changes to be tested before they are brought into a production environment. DBAs can make whole or subset copies of database structures and data onto other environments to enable development and testing of system changes. There are several types of alternate environments.

- **Development environments** are used to create and test changes that will be implemented in production. Development must be maintained to closely resemble the production environment, though with scaled down resources.

- **Test environments** serve several purposes: QA, integration testing, UAT, and performance testing. The test environment ideally also has the same software and hardware as production. In particular, environments used for performance testing should not be scaled down in resources.

- **Sandboxes** or experimental environments are used to test hypotheses and develop new uses of data. The DBAs generally set up, grant access to, and monitor usage of these environments. They should also ensure that sandboxes are isolated and do not adversely affecting production operations.

- **Alternate production environments** are required to support offline backups, failover, and resiliency support systems. These systems should be identical to the production systems, although the backup (and recovery) system can be scaled down in compute capacity, since it is mostly dedicated to I/O activities.

2.2.5 Manage Test Data Sets

Software testing is labor-intensive and accounts for nearly half of the cost of the system development. Efficient testing requires high quality test data, and this data must be managed. Test data generation is a critical step in software testing.

Test data is data that has been specifically identified to test a system. Testing can include verifying that a given set of input produces expected output or challenging the ability of programming to respond to unusual, extreme, exceptional, or unexpected input. Test data can be completely fabricated or generated using meaningless values or it can be sample data. Sample data can be a subset of actual production data (by either content or structure), or generated from production data. Production data can be filtered or aggregated to create multiple sample data sets, depending on the need. In cases where production data contains protected or restricted data, sample data must be masked.

Test data may be produced in a focused or systematic way (as is typically the case in functionality testing) using statistics or filters, or by using other, less-focused approaches (as is typically the case in high-volume randomized automated tests). Test data may be produced by the tester, by a program or function that aids the tester, or by a copy of production data that has been selected and screened for the purpose. Test data may be recorded for short-term re-use, created and managed to support regression tests, or used once and then removed – although in most organizations, cleanup after projects does not include this step. DBAs should monitor project test data and ensure that obsolete test data is purged regularly to preserve capacity.

It is not always possible to produce enough data for some tests, especially performance tests. The amount of test data to be generated is determined or limited by considerations such as time, cost, and quality. It is also impacted by regulation that limits the use of production data in a test environment. (See Chapter 7.)

2.2.6 Manage Data Migration

Data migration is the process of transferring data between storage types, formats, or computer systems, with as little change as possible. Changing data during migration is discussed in Chapter 8.

Data migration is a key consideration for any system implementation, upgrade, or consolidation. It is usually performed programmatically, being automated based on rules. However, people need to ensure that the rules and programs are executed correctly. Data migration occurs for a variety of reasons, including server or storage equipment replacements or upgrades, website consolidation, server maintenance, or data center relocation. Most implementations allow this to be done in a non-disruptive manner, such as concurrently while the host continues to perform I/O to the logical disk (or LUN).

The mapping granularity dictates how quickly the Metadata can be updated, how much extra capacity is required during the migration, and how quickly the previous location is marked as free. Smaller granularity means faster update, less space required, and quicker freeing up of old storage.

Many day-to-day tasks a storage administrator has to perform can be simply and concurrently completed using data migration techniques:

- Moving data off an over-used storage device to a separate environment

- Moving data onto a faster storage device as needs require
- Implementing an Information Lifecycle Management policy
- Migrating data off older storage devices (either being scrapped or off-lease) to offline or cloud storage

Automated and manual data remediation is commonly performed in migration to improve the quality of data, eliminate redundant or obsolete information, and match the requirements of the new system. Data migration phases (design, extraction, remediation, load, verification) for applications of moderate to high complexity are commonly repeated several times before the new system is deployed.

3. Tools

In addition to the database management systems themselves, DBAs use multiple other tools to manage databases. For example, modeling and other application development tools, interfaces that allow users to write and execute queries, data evaluation and modification tools for data quality improvement, and performance load monitoring tools.

3.1 Data Modeling Tools

Data modeling tools automate many of the tasks the data modeler performs. Some data modeling tools allow the generation of database data definition language (DDL). Most support reverse engineering from database into a data model. Tools that are more sophisticated validate naming standards, check spelling, store Metadata such as definitions and lineage, and even enable publishing to the web. (See Chapter 5.)

3.2 Database Monitoring Tools

Database monitoring tools automate monitoring of key metrics, such as capacity, availability, cache performance, user statistics, etc., and alert DBAs and NSAs to database issues. Most such tools can simultaneously monitor multiple database types.

3.3 Database Management Tools

Database systems have often included management tools. In addition, several third-party software packages allow DBAs to manage multiple databases. These applications include functions for configuration, installation of patches and upgrades, backup and restore, database cloning, test management, and data clean-up routines.

3.4 Developer Support Tools

Developer Support tools contain a visual interface for connecting to and executing commands on a database. Some are included with the database management software. Others include third-party applications.

4. Techniques

4.1 Test in Lower Environments

For upgrades and patches to operating systems, database software, database changes, and code changes, install and test on the lowest level environment first – usually development. Once tested on the lowest level, install on the next higher levels, and install on the production environment last. This ensures that the installers have experience with the upgrade or patch, and can minimize disruption to the production environments.

4.2 Physical Naming Standards

Consistency in naming speeds understanding. Data architects, database developers, and DBAs can use naming standards for defining Metadata or creating rules for exchanging documents between organizations.

ISO/IEC 11179 – Metadata registries (MDR), addresses the semantics of data, the representation of data, and the registration of the descriptions of that data. It is through these descriptions that an accurate understanding of the semantics and a useful depiction of the data are found.

The significant section for physical databases within that standards is Part 5 – Naming and Identification Principles, which describes how to form conventions for naming data elements and their components.

4.3 Script Usage for All Changes

It is extremely risky to directly change data in a database. However, there may be a need, such as an annual change in the chart of accounts structures, or in mergers and acquisitions, or emergencies, where these are indicated due to the 'one-off' nature of the request and/or the lack of appropriate tools for these circumstances. It is helpful to place changes to be made into update script files and test them thoroughly in non-production environments before applying to production.

5. Implementation Guidelines

5.1 Readiness Assessment / Risk Assessment

A risk and readiness assessment revolves around two central ideas: risk of data loss and risks related to technology readiness.

- **Data loss**: Data can be lost through technical or procedural errors, or through malicious intent. Organizations need to put in place strategies to mitigate these risks. Service Level Agreements often specify the general requirements for protection. SLAs need to be supported by well-documented procedures. Ongoing assessment is required to ensure robust technical responses are in place to prevent data loss through malicious intent, as cyber threats are ever evolving. SLA audit and data audits are recommended to assess and plan risk mitigations.

- **Technology readiness**: Newer technologies such as NoSQL, Big Data, triple stores, and FDMS require skills and experience readiness in IT. Many organizations do not have the skill sets needed to take advantage of these new technologies. DBAs, systems engineers and application developers, and business users must be ready to use the benefits from these in the BI and other applications.

5.2 Organization and Cultural Change

DBAs often do not effectively promote the value of their work to the organization. They need to recognize the legitimate concerns of data owners and data consumers, balance short-term and long-term data needs, educate others in the organization about the importance of good data management practices, and optimize data development practices to ensure maximum benefit to the organization and minimal impact on data consumers. By regarding data work as an abstract set of principles and practices, and disregarding the human elements involved, DBAs risk propagating an 'us versus them' mentality, and being regarded as dogmatic, impractical, unhelpful, and obstructionist.

Many disconnects – mostly clashes in frames of reference – contribute to this problem. Organizations generally regard information technology in terms of specific applications, not data, and usually see data from an application-centric point of view. The long-term value to organizations of secure, reusable, high quality data, such as data as a corporate resource, is not as easily recognized or appreciated.

Application development often sees data management as an impediment to application development, as something that makes development projects take longer and cost more without providing additional benefit. DBAs have been slow to adapt to changes in technology (e.g., XML, objects, and service-oriented architectures) and new methods of application development (e.g., Agile Development, XP, and Scrum). Developers, on the other hand, often fail to recognize how good data management practices can help them achieve their long-term goals of object and application reuse, and true service-oriented application architecture.

DBAs and other data management practitioners can help overcome these organizational and cultural obstacles. They can promote a more helpful and collaborative approach to meeting the organization's data and information needs by following the guiding principles to identify and act on automation opportunities, building with reuse in mind, applying best practices, connecting databased standards to support requirements, and setting expectations for DBAs in project work. In addition, they should:

- **Proactively communicate**: DBAs should be in close communication with project teams, both during development and after implementation, to detect and resolve any issues as early as possible. They should review data access code, stored procedures, views, and database functions written by development teams and help surface any problems with database design.

- **Communicate with people on their level and in their terms**: It is better to talk with business people in terms of business needs and ROI, and with developers in terms of object-orientation, loose coupling, and ease of development.

- **Stay business-focused**: The objective of application development is to meet business requirements and derive maximum value from the project.

- **Be helpful**: Always telling people 'no' encourages them to ignore standards and find another path. Recognize that people need to do whatever they need to do and not helping them succeed becomes mutually detrimental.

- **Learn continually**: Assess setbacks encountered during a project for lessons learned and apply these to future projects. If problems arise from having done things wrong, point to them later as reasons for doing things right.

To sum up, understand stakeholders and their needs. Develop clear, concise, practical, business-focused standards for doing the best possible work in the best possible way. Moreover, teach and implement those standards in a way that provides maximum value to stakeholders and earns their respect.

6. Data Storage and Operations Governance

6.1 Metrics

Data Storage metrics may include:

- Count of databases by type
- Aggregated transaction statistics
- Capacity metrics, such as
  - Amount of storage used
  - Number of storage containers
  - Number of data objects in terms of committed and uncommitted block or pages
  - Data in queue
- Storage service usage
- Requests made against the storage services

- Improvements to performance of the applications that use a service

Performance metrics may be used to measure:

- Transaction frequency and quantity
- Query performance
- API (application programming interface) service performance

Operational metrics may consist of:

- Aggregated statistics about data retrieval time
- Backup size
- Data quality measurement
- Availability

Service metrics may include

- Issue submission, resolution, and escalation count by type
- Issue resolution time

DBAs need to discuss the need for metrics with data architects, Data Quality teams.

6.2 Information Asset Tracking

Part of data storage governance includes ensuring that an organization complies with all licensing agreements and regulatory requirements. Carefully track and conduct yearly audits of software license and annual support costs, as well as server lease agreements and other fixed costs. Being out of compliance with licensing agreements poses serious financial and legal risks for an organization.

Audit data can help determine the total cost-of-ownership (TCO) for each type of technology and technology product. Regularly evaluate technologies and products that are becoming obsolete, unsupported, less useful, or too expensive.

6.3 Data Audits and Data Validation

A data audit is the evaluation of a data set based on defined criteria. Typically, an audit is performed to investigate specific concerns about a data set and is designed to determine whether the data was stored in compliance with contractual and methodological requirements. The data audit approach may include a project-specific and comprehensive checklist, required deliverables, and quality control criteria.

Data validation is the process of evaluating stored data against established acceptance criteria to determine its quality and usability. Data validation procedures depend on the criteria established by the Data Quality team (if one is in place) or other data consumer requirements. DBAs support part of data audits and validation by:

- Helping develop and review the approach
- Performing preliminary data screening and review

- Developing data monitoring methods
- Applying statistical, geo-statistical, and bio-statistical techniques to optimize analysis of data
- Supporting sampling and analysis
- Reviewing data
- Providing support for data discovery
- Acting as SMEs for questions related to database administration

7. Works Cited / Recommended

Amir, Obaid. *Storage Data Migration Guide.* 2012. Kindle.

Armistead, Leigh. *Information Operations Matters: Best Practices.* Potomac Books Inc., 2010. Print.

Axelos Global Best Practice (ITIL website). http://bit.ly/1H6SwxC.

Bittman, Tom. "Virtualization with VMWare or HyperV: What you need to know." Gartner Webinar, 25 November, 2009. http://gtnr.it/2rRl2aP, Web.

Brewer, Eric. "Toward Robust Distributed Systems." PODC Keynote 2000. http://bit.ly/2sVsYYv Web.

Dunham, Jeff. *Database Performance Tuning Handbook.* McGraw-Hill, 1998. Print.

Dwivedi, Himanshu. *Securing Storage: A Practical Guide to SAN and NAS Security.* Addison-Wesley Professional, 2005. Print.

EMC Education Services, ed. *Information Storage and Management: Storing, Managing, and Protecting Digital Information in Classic, Virtualized, and Cloud Environments.* 2nd ed. Wiley, 2012. Print.

Finn, Aidan, et al. *Microsoft Private Cloud Computing.* Sybex, 2013. Print.

Finn, Aidan. *Mastering Hyper-V Deployment.* Sybex. 2010. Print.

Fitzsimmons, James A. and Mona J. Fitzsimmons. *Service Management: Operations, Strategy, Information Technology.* 6th ed. Irwin/McGraw-Hill, 2007. Print with CDROM.

Gallagher, Simon, et al. *VMware Private Cloud Computing with vCloud Director.* Sybex. 2013. Print.

Haerder, T. and A Reuter. "Principles of transaction-oriented database recovery". *ACM Computing Surveys* 15 (4) (1983). https://web.stanford.edu/class/cs340v/papers/recovery.pdf Web.

Hitachi Data Systems Academy, *Storage Concepts: Storing and Managing Digital Data.* Volume 1. HDS Academy, Hitachi Data Systems, 2012. Print.

Hoffer, Jeffrey, Mary Prescott, and Fred McFadden. *Modern Database Management.* 7th Edition. Prentice Hall, 2004. Print.

Khalil, Mostafa. *Storage Implementation in vSphere 5.0.* VMware Press, 2012. Print.

Kotwal, Nitin. *Data Storage Backup and Replication: Effective Data Management to Ensure Optimum Performance and Business Continuity.* Nitin Kotwal, 2015. Amazon Digital Services LLC.

Kroenke, D. M. *Database Processing: Fundamentals, Design, and Implementation.* 10th Edition. Pearson Prentice Hall, 2005. Print.

Liebowitz, Matt et al. *VMware vSphere Performance: Designing CPU, Memory, Storage, and Networking for Performance-Intensive Workloads.* Sybex, 2014. Print.

Matthews, Jeanna N. et al. *Running Xen: A Hands-On Guide to the Art of Virtualization.* Prentice Hall, 2008. Print.

Mattison, Rob. *Understanding Database Management Systems.* 2nd Edition. McGraw-Hill, 1998. Print.

McNamara, Michael J. *Scale-Out Storage: The Next Frontier in Enterprise Data Management.* FriesenPress, 2014. Kindle.

Mullins, Craig S. *Database Administration: The Complete Guide to Practices and Procedures.* Addison-Wesley, 2002. Print.

Parsaye, Kamran and Mark Chignell. *Intelligent Database Tools and Applications: Hyperinformation Access, Data Quality, Visualization, Automatic Discovery.* John Wiley and Sons, 1993. Print.

Pascal, Fabian. *Practical Issues in Database Management: A Reference for The Thinking Practitioner.* Addison-Wesley, 2000. Print.

Paulsen, Karl. *Moving Media Storage Technologies: Applications and Workflows for Video and Media Server Platforms.* Focal Press, 2011. Print.

Piedad, Floyd, and Michael Hawkins. *High Availability: Design, Techniques and Processes.* Prentice Hall, 2001. Print.

Rob, Peter, and Carlos Coronel. *Database Systems: Design, Implementation, and Management.* 7th Edition. Course Technology, 2006. Print.

Sadalage, Pramod J., and Martin Fowler. *NoSQL Distilled: A Brief Guide to the Emerging World of Polyglot Persistence.* Addison-Wesley, 2012. Print. Addison-Wesley Professional.

Santana, Gustavo A. *Data Center Virtualization Fundamentals: Understanding Techniques and Designs for Highly Efficient Data Centers with Cisco Nexus, UCS, MDS, and Beyond.* Cisco Press, 2013. Print. Fundamentals.

Schulz, Greg. *Cloud and Virtual Data Storage Networking.* Auerbach Publications, 2011. Print.

Simitci, Huseyin. *Storage Network Performance Analysis.* Wiley, 2003. Print.

Tran, Duc A. *Data Storage for Social Networks: A Socially Aware Approach.* 2013 ed. Springer, 2012. Print. Springer Briefs in Optimization.

Troppens, Ulf, et al. *Storage Networks Explained: Basics and Application of Fibre Channel SAN, NAS, iSCSI, InfiniBand and FCoE.* Wiley, 2009. Print.

US Department of Defense. *Information Operations: Doctrine, Tactics, Techniques, and Procedures.* 2011. Kindle.

VMware. *VMware vCloud Architecture Toolkit (vCAT): Technical and Operational Guidance for Cloud Success.* VMware Press, 2013. Print.

Wicker, Stephen B. *Error Control Systems for Digital Communication and Storage.* US ed. Prentice-Hall, 1994. Print.

Zarra, Marcus S. *Core Data: Data Storage and Management for iOS, OS X, and iCloud.* 2nd ed. Pragmatic Bookshelf, 2013. Print. Pragmatic Programmers.

CHAPTER 7

Data Security

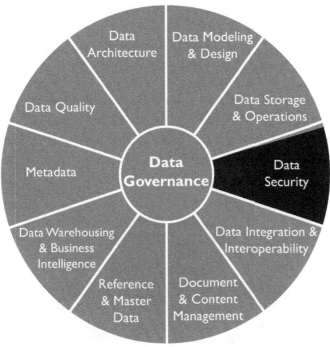

DAMA-DMBOK2 Data Management Framework

Copyright © 2017 by DAMA International

1. Introduction

Data Security includes the planning, development, and execution of security policies and procedures to provide proper authentication, authorization, access, and auditing of data and information assets. The specifics of data security (which data needs to be protected, for example) differ between industries and countries. Nevertheless, the goal of data security practices is the same: To protect information assets in alignment with privacy and confidentiality regulations, contractual agreements, and business requirements. These requirements come from:

- **Stakeholders**: Organizations must recognize the privacy and confidentiality needs of their stakeholders, including clients, patients, students, citizens, suppliers, or business partners. Everyone in an organization must be a responsible trustee of data about stakeholders.

- **Government regulations**: Government regulations are in place to protect the interests of some stakeholders. Regulations have different goals. Some restrict access to information, while others ensure openness, transparency, and accountability.

- **Proprietary business concerns**: Each organization has proprietary data to protect. An organization's data provides insight into its customers and, when leveraged effectively, can provide a competitive advantage. If confidential data is stolen or breached, an organization can lose competitive advantage.

- **Legitimate access needs**: When securing data, organizations must also enable legitimate access. Business processes require individuals in certain roles be able to access, use, and maintain data.

- **Contractual obligations**: Contractual and non-disclosure agreements also influence data security requirements. For example, the PCI Standard, an agreement among credit card companies and individual business enterprises, demands that certain types of data be protected in defined ways (e.g., mandatory encryption for customer passwords).

Effective data security policies and procedures ensure that the right people can use and update data in the right way, and that all inappropriate access and update is restricted (Ray, 2012) (see Figure 62). Understanding and complying with the privacy and confidentiality interests and needs of all stakeholders is in the best interest of every organization. Client, supplier, and constituent relationships all trust in, and depend on, the responsible use of data.

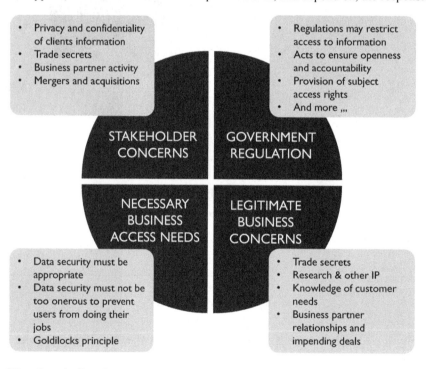

Figure 62 Sources of Data Security Requirements

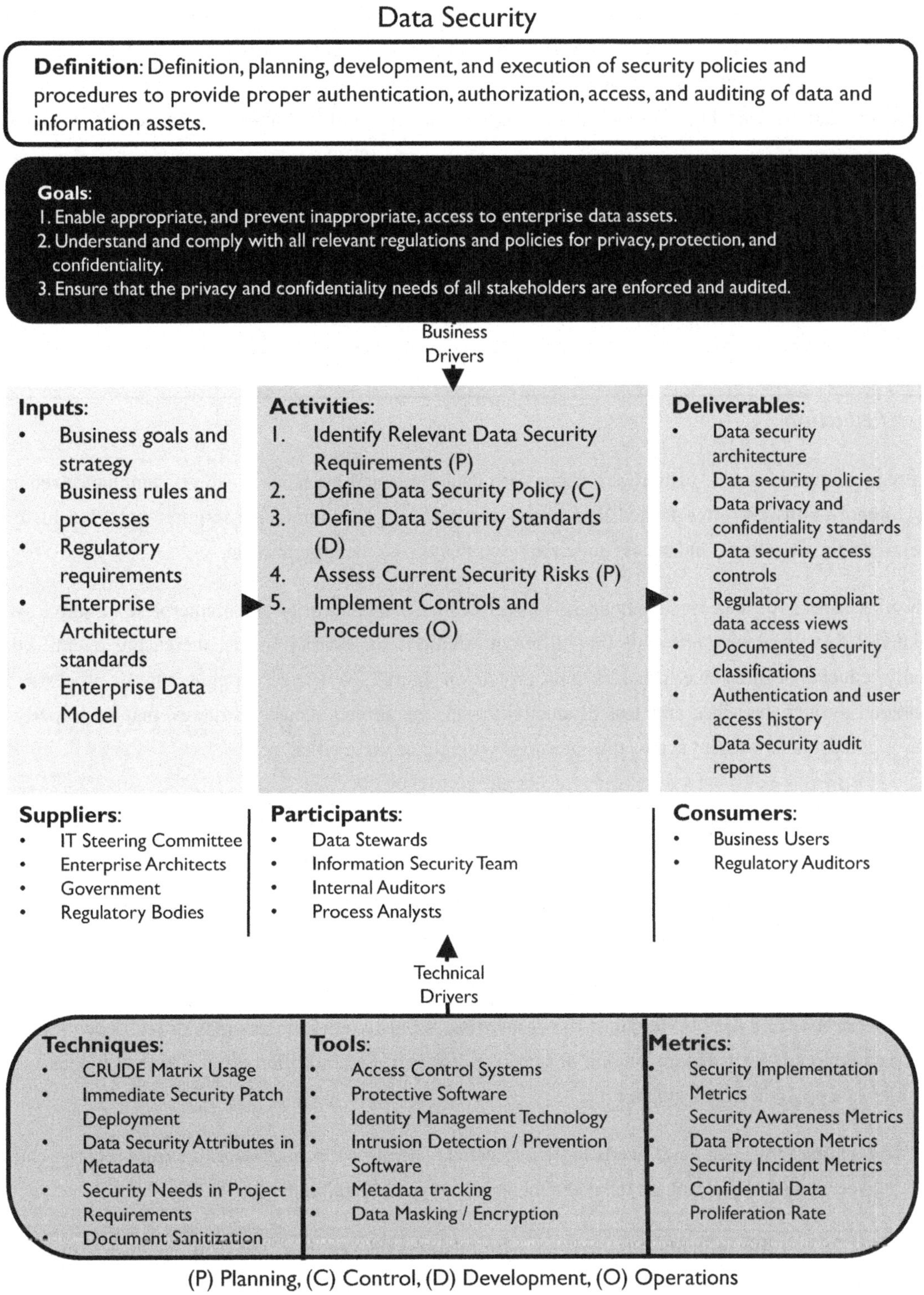

Data Security

Definition: Definition, planning, development, and execution of security policies and procedures to provide proper authentication, authorization, access, and auditing of data and information assets.

Goals:
1. Enable appropriate, and prevent inappropriate, access to enterprise data assets.
2. Understand and comply with all relevant regulations and policies for privacy, protection, and confidentiality.
3. Ensure that the privacy and confidentiality needs of all stakeholders are enforced and audited.

Business Drivers

Inputs:
- Business goals and strategy
- Business rules and processes
- Regulatory requirements
- Enterprise Architecture standards
- Enterprise Data Model

Activities:
1. Identify Relevant Data Security Requirements (P)
2. Define Data Security Policy (C)
3. Define Data Security Standards (D)
4. Assess Current Security Risks (P)
5. Implement Controls and Procedures (O)

Deliverables:
- Data security architecture
- Data security policies
- Data privacy and confidentiality standards
- Data security access controls
- Regulatory compliant data access views
- Documented security classifications
- Authentication and user access history
- Data Security audit reports

Suppliers:
- IT Steering Committee
- Enterprise Architects
- Government
- Regulatory Bodies

Participants:
- Data Stewards
- Information Security Team
- Internal Auditors
- Process Analysts

Consumers:
- Business Users
- Regulatory Auditors

Technical Drivers

Techniques:
- CRUDE Matrix Usage
- Immediate Security Patch Deployment
- Data Security Attributes in Metadata
- Security Needs in Project Requirements
- Document Sanitization

Tools:
- Access Control Systems
- Protective Software
- Identity Management Technology
- Intrusion Detection / Prevention Software
- Metadata tracking
- Data Masking / Encryption

Metrics:
- Security Implementation Metrics
- Security Awareness Metrics
- Data Protection Metrics
- Security Incident Metrics
- Confidential Data Proliferation Rate

(P) Planning, (C) Control, (D) Development, (O) Operations

Figure 63 Context Diagram: Data Security

1.1 Business Drivers

Risk reduction and business growth are the primary drivers of data security activities. Ensuring that an organization's data is secure reduces risk and adds competitive advantage. Security itself is a valuable asset.

Data security risks are associated with regulatory compliance, fiduciary responsibility for the enterprise and stockholders, reputation, and a legal and moral responsibility to protect the private and sensitive information of employees, business partners, and customers. Organizations can be fined for failure to comply with regulations and contractual obligations. Data breaches can cause a loss of reputation and customer confidence. (See Chapter 2.)

Business growth includes attaining and sustaining operational business goals. Data security issues, breaches, and unwarranted restrictions on employee access to data can directly impact operational success.

The goals of mitigating risks and growing the business can be complementary and mutually supportive if they are integrated into a coherent strategy of information management and protection.

1.1.1 Risk Reduction

As data regulations increase — usually in response to data thefts and breaches — so do compliance requirements. Security organizations are often tasked with managing not only IT compliance requirements, but also policies, practices, data classifications, and access authorization rules across the organization.

As with other aspects of data management, it is best to address data security as an enterprise initiative. Without a coordinated effort, business units will find different solutions to security needs, increasing overall cost while potentially reducing security due to inconsistent protection. Ineffective security architecture or processes can cost organizations through breaches and lost productivity. An operational security strategy that is properly funded, systems-oriented, and consistent across the enterprise will reduce these risks.

Information security begins by classifying an organization's data in order to identify which data requires protection. The overall process includes the following steps:

- **Identify and classify sensitive data assets**: Depending on the industry and organization, there can be few or many assets, and a range of sensitive data (including personal identification, medical, financial, and more).

- **Locate sensitive data throughout the enterprise**: Security requirements may differ, depending on where data is stored. A significant amount of sensitive data in a single location poses a high risk due to the damage possible from a single breach.

- **Determine how each asset needs to be protected**: The measures necessary to ensure security can vary between assets, depending on data content and the type of technology.

- **Identify how this information interacts with business processes**: Analysis of business processes is required to determine what access is allowed and under what conditions.

In addition to classifying the data itself, it is necessary to assess external threats (such as those from hackers and criminals) and internal risks (posed by employees and processes). Much data is lost or exposed through the ignorance of employees who did not realize that the information was highly sensitive or who bypassed security policies.[37] The customer sales data left on a web server that is hacked, the employee database downloaded onto a

---

[37] One survey stated, "70 percent of IT professionals believe the use of unauthorized programs resulted in as many as half of their companies' data loss incidents. This belief was most common in the United States (74 percent), Brazil (75 percent), and

contractor's laptop that is subsequently stolen, and trade secrets left unencrypted in an executive's computer that goes missing, all result from missing or unenforced security controls.

The impact of security breaches on well-established brands in recent years has resulted in huge financial losses and a drop in customer trust. Not only are the external threats from the criminal hacking community becoming more sophisticated and targeted, the amount of damage done by external and internal threats, intentional or unintentional, has also been steadily increasing over the years (Kark, 2009).

In a world of almost all-electronic, business infrastructure, trustworthy information systems have become a business differentiator.

1.1.2 Business Growth

Globally, electronic technology is pervasive in the office, the marketplace, and the home. Desktop and laptop computers, smart phones, tablets, and other devices are important elements of most business and government operations. The explosive growth of e-commerce has changed how organizations offer goods and services. In their personal lives, individuals have become accustomed to conducting business online with goods providers, medical agencies, utilities, governmental offices, and financial institutions. Trusted e-commerce drives profit and growth. Product and service quality relate to information security in a quite direct fashion: Robust information security enables transactions and builds customer confidence.

1.1.3 Security as an Asset

One approach to managing sensitive data is via Metadata. Security classifications and regulatory sensitivity can be captured at the data element and data set level. Technology exists to tag data so that Metadata travel with the information as it flows across the enterprise. Developing a master repository of data characteristics means all parts of the enterprise can know precisely what level of protection sensitive information requires.

If a common standard is enforced, this approach enables multiple departments, business units, and vendors to use the same Metadata. Standard security Metadata can optimize data protection and guide business usage and technical support processes, leading to lower costs. This layer of information security can help prevent unauthorized access to and misuse of data assets. When sensitive data is correctly identified as such, organizations build trust with their customers and partners. Security-related Metadata itself becomes a strategic asset, increasing the quality of transactions, reporting, and business analysis, while reducing the cost of protection and associated risks that lost or stolen information cause.

India (79 percent)." A report from the Ponomon group and Symantic Anti-Virus found that, "human errors and system problems caused two-thirds of data breaches in 2012. http://bit.ly/1dGChAz, http://symc.ly/1FzNo5l, http://bit.ly/2sQ68Ba, http://bit.ly/2tNEkKY.

1.2 Goals and Principles

1.2.1 Goals

The goals of data security activities include:

- Enabling appropriate access and preventing inappropriate access to enterprise data assets
- Enabling compliance with regulations and policies for privacy, protection, and confidentiality
- Ensuring that stakeholder requirements for privacy and confidentiality are met

1.2.2 Principles

Data security in an organization follows these guiding principles:

- **Collaboration**: Data Security is a collaborative effort involving IT security administrators, data stewards/data governance, internal and external audit teams, and the legal department.

- **Enterprise approach**: Data Security standards and policies must be applied consistently across the entire organization.

- **Proactive management**: Success in data security management depends on being proactive and dynamic, engaging all stakeholders, managing change, and overcoming organizational or cultural bottlenecks such as traditional separation of responsibilities between information security, information technology, data administration, and business stakeholders.

- **Clear accountability**: Roles and responsibilities must be clearly defined, including the 'chain of custody' for data across organizations and roles.

- **Metadata-driven**: Security classification for data elements is an essential part of data definitions.

- **Reduce risk by reducing exposure**: Minimize sensitive/confidential data proliferation, especially to non-production environments.

1.3 Essential Concepts

Information security has a specific vocabulary. Knowledge of key terms enables clearer articulation of governance requirements.

1.3.1 Vulnerability

A *vulnerability* is a weaknesses or defect in a system that allows it to be successfully attacked and compromised – essentially a hole in an organization's defenses. Some vulnerabilities are called *exploits*.

Examples include network computers with out-of-date security patches, web pages not protected with robust passwords, users not trained to ignore email attachments from unknown senders, or corporate software unprotected against technical commands that will give the attacker control of the system.

In many cases, non-production environments are more vulnerable to threats than production environments. Thus, it is critical to keep production data out of non-production environments.

1.3.2 Threat

A *threat* is a potential offensive action that could be taken against an organization. Threats can be internal or external. They are not always malicious. An uniformed insider can take offensive actions again the organization without even knowing it. Threats may relate to specific vulnerabilities, which then can be prioritized for remediation. Each threat should match to a capability that either prevents the threat or limits the damage it might cause. An occurrence of a threat is also called an *attack surface*.

Examples of threats include virus-infected email attachments being sent to the organization, processes that overwhelm network servers and result in an inability to perform business transactions (also called denial-of-service attacks), and exploitation of known vulnerabilities.

1.3.3 Risk

The term *risk* refers both to the possibility of loss and to the thing or condition that poses the potential loss. Risk can be calculated for each possible threat using the following factors.

- Probability that the threat will occur and its likely frequency
- The type and amount of damage created each occurrence might cause, including damage to reputation
- The effect damage will have on revenue or business operations
- The cost to fix the damage after an occurrence
- The cost to prevent the threat, including by remediation of vulnerabilities
- The goal or intent of the probable attacker

Risks can be prioritized by potential severity of damage to the company, or by likelihood of occurrence, with easily exploited vulnerabilities creating a higher likelihood of occurrence. Often a priority list combines both metrics. Prioritization of risk must be a formal process among the stakeholders.

1.3.4 Risk Classifications

Risk classifications describe the sensitivity of the data and the likelihood that it might be sought after for malicious purposes. Classifications are used to determine who (i.e., people in which roles) can access the data. The highest security classification of any datum within a user entitlement determines the security classification of the entire aggregation. Example classifications include:

- **Critical Risk Data (CRD)**: Personal information aggressively sought for unauthorized use by both internal and external parties due to its high direct financial value. Compromise of CRD would not only harm individuals, but would result in financial harm to the company from significant penalties, costs to retain customers and employees, as well as harm to brand and reputation.

- **High Risk Data (HRD)**: HRD is actively sought for unauthorized use due to its potential direct financial value. HRD provides the company with a competitive edge. If compromised, it could expose the company to financial harm through loss of opportunity. Loss of HRD can cause mistrust leading to the loss of business and may result in legal exposure, regulatory fines and penalties, as well as damage to brand and reputation.

- **Moderate Risk Data (MRD)**: Company information that has little tangible value to unauthorized parties; however, the unauthorized use of this non-public information would likely have a negative effect on the company.

1.3.5 Data Security Organization

Depending on the size of the enterprise, the overall Information Security function may be the primary responsibility of a dedicated Information Security group, usually within the Information Technology (IT) area. Larger enterprises often have a Chief Information Security Officer (CISO) who reports to either the CIO or the CEO. In organizations without dedicated Information Security personnel, responsibility for data security will fall on data managers. In all cases, data managers need to be involved in data security efforts.

In large enterprises, the information security personnel may let specific data governance and user authorization functions be guided by the business managers. Examples include granting user authorizations and data regulatory compliance. Dedicated Information Security personnel are often most concerned with the technical aspects of information protection such as combating malicious software and system attacks. However, there is ample room for collaboration during development or an installation project.

This opportunity for synergy is often missed when the two governance entities, IT and Data Management, lack an organized process to share regulatory and security requirements. They need a standard procedure to inform each other of data regulations, data loss threats, and data protection requirements, and to do so at the commencement of every software development or installation project.

The first step in the NIST (National Institute of Standards and Technology) Risk Management Framework, for example, is to categorize all enterprise information.[38] Creating an enterprise data model is essential to this goal. Without clear visibility to the location of all sensitive information, it is impossible to create a comprehensive and effective data protection program.

Data managers need to be actively engaged with information technology developers and cyber security professionals so that regulated data may be identified, sensitive systems can be properly protected, and user access controls can be designed to enforce confidentiality, integrity, and data regulatory compliance. The larger the enterprise, the more important becomes the need for teamwork and reliance on a correct and updated enterprise data model.

---

[38] National Institute of Standards and Technology (US) http://bit.ly/1eQYolG.

1.3.6 Security Processes

Data security requirements and procedures are categorized into four groups, known as the four A's: Access, Audit, Authentication, and Authorization. Recently an E, Entitlement, has been included, for effective data regulatory compliance. Information classification, access rights, role groups, users, and passwords are the means to implementing policy and satisfying the four A's. Security Monitoring is also essential for proving the success of the other processes. Both monitoring and audit can be done continuously or intermittently. Formal audits must be done by a third party to be considered valid. The third party may be internal or external.

1.3.6.1 The Four A's

- **Access**: Enable individuals with authorization to access systems in a timely manner. Used as a verb, *access* means to actively connect to an information system and be working with the data. Used as a noun, *access* indicates that the person has a valid authorization to the data.

- **Audit**: Review security actions and user activity to ensure compliance with regulations and conformance with company policy and standards. Information security professionals periodically review logs and documents to validate compliance with security regulations, policies, and standards. Results of these audits are published periodically.

- **Authentication**: Validate users' access. When a user tries to log into a system, the system needs to verify that the person is who he or she claims to be. Passwords are one way of doing this. More stringent authentication methods include the person having a security token, answering questions, or submitting a fingerprint. All transmissions during authentication are encrypted to prevent theft of the authenticating information.

- **Authorization**: Grant individuals privileges to access specific views of data, appropriate to their role. After the authorization decision, the Access Control System checks each time a user logs in to see if they have a valid authorization token. Technically, this is an entry in a data field in the corporate Active Directory indicating that the person has been authorized by somebody to access the data. It further indicates that a responsible person made the decision to grant this authorization because the user is entitled to it by virtue of their job or corporate status.

- **Entitlement**: An Entitlement is the sum total of all the data elements that are exposed to a user by a single access authorization decision. A responsible manager must decide that a person is 'entitled' to access this information before an authorization request is generated. An inventory of all the data exposed by each entitlement is necessary in determining regulatory and confidentiality requirements for Entitlement decisions.

1.3.6.2 Monitoring

Systems should include monitoring controls that detect unexpected events, including potential security violations. Systems containing confidential information, such as salary or financial data, commonly implement active, real-time monitoring that alerts the security administrator to suspicious activity or inappropriate access.

Some security systems will actively interrupt activities that do not follow specific access profiles. The account or activity remains locked until security support personnel evaluate the details.

In contrast, passive monitoring tracks changes over time by taking snapshots of the system at regular intervals, and comparing trends against a benchmark or other criteria. The system sends reports to the data stewards or security administrator accountable for the data. While active monitoring is a detection mechanism, passive monitoring is an assessment mechanism.

1.3.7 Data Integrity

In security, *data integrity* is the state of being whole – protected from improper alteration, deletion, or addition. For example, in the U.S., Sarbanes-Oxley regulations are mostly concerned with protecting financial information integrity by identifying rules for how financial information can be created and edited.

1.3.8 Encryption

Encryption is the process of translating plain text into complex codes to hide privileged information, verify complete transmission, or verify the sender's identity. Encrypted data cannot be read without the decryption key or algorithm, which is usually stored separately and cannot be calculated based on other data elements in the same data set. There are four main methods of encryption – hash, symmetric, private-key, and public-key – with varying levels of complexity and key structure.

1.3.8.1 Hash

Hash encryption uses algorithms to convert data into a mathematical representation. The exact algorithms used and order of application must be known in order to reverse the encryption process and reveal the original data. Sometimes hashing is used as verification of transmission integrity or identity. Common hashing algorithms are Message Digest 5 (MD5) and Secure Hashing Algorithm (SHA).

1.3.8.2 Private-key

Private-key encryption uses one key to encrypt the data. Both the sender and the recipient must have the key to read the original data. Data can be encrypted one character at a time (as in a stream) or in blocks. Common private-key algorithms include Data Encryption Standard (DES), Triple DES (3DES), Advanced Encryption Standard (AES), and International Data Encryption Algorithm (IDEA). Cyphers Twofish and Serpent are also considered secure. The use of simple DES is unwise as it is susceptible to many easy attacks.

1.3.8.3 Public-key

In public-key encryption, the sender and the receiver have different keys. The sender uses a public key that is freely available, and the receiver uses a private key to reveal the original data. This type of encryption is useful when many data sources must send protected information to just a few recipients, such as when submitting data to clearinghouses. Public-key methods include Rivest-Shamir-Adelman (RSA) Key Exchange and Diffie-Hellman Key Agreement. PGP (Pretty Good Privacy) is a freely available application of public-key encryption.

1.3.9 Obfuscation or Masking

Data can be made less available by obfuscation (making obscure or unclear) or masking, which removes, shuffles, or otherwise changes the appearance of the data, without losing the meaning of the data or the relationships the data has to other data sets, such as foreign key relationships to other objects or systems. The values within the attributes may change, but the new values are still valid for those attributes. Obfuscation is useful when displaying sensitive information on screens for reference, or creating test data sets from production data that comply with expected application logic.

Data masking is a type of data-centric security. There are two types of data masking, persistent and dynamic. Persistent masking can be executed in-flight or in-place.

1.3.9.1 Persistent Data Masking

Persistent data masking permanently and irreversibly alters the data. This type of masking is not typically used in production environments, but rather between a production environment and development or test environments. Persistent masking changes the data, but the data must still be viable for use to test processes, application, report, etc.

- **In-flight persistent masking** occurs when the data is masked or obfuscated while it is moving between the source (typically production) and destination (typically non-production) environment. In-flight masking is very secure when properly executed because it does not leave an intermediate file or database with unmasked data. Another benefit is that it is re-runnable if issues are encountered part way through the masking.

- **In-place persistent masking** is used when the source and destination are the same. The unmasked data is read from the source, masked, and then used to overwrite the unmasked data. In-place masking assumes the sensitive data is in a location where it should not exist and the risk needs to be mitigated, or that there is an extra copy of the data in a secure location to mask before moving it to the non-secure location. There are risks to this process. If the masking process fails mid-masking, it can be difficult to restore the data to a useable format. This technique has a few niche uses, but in general, in-flight masking will more securely meet project needs.

1.3.9.2 Dynamic Data Masking

Dynamic data masking changes the appearance of the data to the end user or system without changing the underlying data. This can be extremely useful when users need access to some sensitive production data, but not all of it. For example, in a database the social security number is stored as 123456789, but to the call center associate that needs to verify who they are speaking to, the data shows up as ***-**-6789.

1.3.9.3 Masking Methods

There are several methods for masking or obfuscating data.

- **Substitution**: Replace characters or whole values with those in a lookup or as a standard pattern. For example, first names can be replaced with random values from a list.

- **Shuffling**: Swap data elements of the same type within a record, or swap data elements of one attribute between rows. For example, mixing vendor names among supplier invoices such that the original supplier is replaced with a different valid supplier on an invoice.

- **Temporal variance**: Move dates +/– a number of days – small enough to preserve trends, but significant enough to render them non-identifiable.

- **Value variance**: Apply a random factor +/– a percent, again small enough to preserve trends, but significant enough to be non-identifiable.

- **Nulling or deleting**: Remove data that should not be present in a test system.

- **Randomization**: Replace part or all of data elements with either random characters or a series of a single character.

- **Encryption**: Convert a recognizably meaningful character stream to an unrecognizable character stream by means of a cipher code. An extreme version of obfuscation in-place.

- **Expression masking**: Change all values to the result of an expression. For example, a simple expression would just hard code all values in a large free form database field (that could potentially contain confidential data) to be 'This is a comment field'.

- **Key masking**: Designate that the result of the masking algorithm/process must be unique and repeatable because it is being used mask a database key field (or similar). This type of masking is extremely important for testing to maintain integrity around the organization.

1.3.10 Network Security Terms

Data security includes both data-at-rest and data-in-motion. Data-in-motion requires a network in order to move between systems. It is no longer sufficient for an organization to wholly trust in the firewall to protect it from malicious software, poisoned email, or social engineering attacks. Each machine on the network needs to have a line of defense, and web servers need sophisticated protection as they are continually exposed to the entire world on the Internet.

1.3.10.1 Backdoor

A *backdoor* refers to an overlooked or hidden entry into a computer system or application. It allows unauthorized users to bypass the password requirement to gain access. Backdoors are often created by developers for maintenance purposes. Any backdoor is a security risk. Other backdoors are put in place by the creators of commercial software packages.

Default passwords left unchanged when installing any software system or web page package is a backdoor and will undoubtedly be known to hackers. Any backdoor is a security risk.

1.3.10.2 Bot or Zombie

A *bot* (short for robot) or *Zombie* is a workstation that has been taken over by a malicious hacker using a Trojan, a Virus, a Phish, or a download of an infected file. Remotely controlled, bots are used to perform malicious tasks, such as sending large amounts of spam, attacking legitimate businesses with network-clogging Internet packets, performing illegal money transfers, and hosting fraudulent websites. A *Bot-Net* is a network of robot computers (infected machines).[39]

It was estimated in 2012 that globally 17% of all computers (approximately 187 million of 1.1 Billion computers) do not have anti-virus protection.[40] In the USA that year, 19.32% of users surfed unprotected. A large percentage of them are Zombies. Estimates are that two billion computers are in operation as of 2016.[41] Considering that desktop and laptop computers are being eclipsed in number by smart phones, tablets, wearables, and other devices, many of which are used for business transactions, the risks for data exposure will only increase.[42]

1.3.10.3 Cookie

A *cookie* is a small data file that a website installs on a computer's hard drive, to identify returning visitors and profile their preferences. Cookies are used for Internet commerce. However, they are also controversial, as they raise questions of privacy because spyware sometimes uses them.

---

[39] http://bit.ly/1FrKWR8, http://bit.ly/2rQQuWJ.

[40] http://tcrn.ch/2rRnsGr (17% globally lack AV), http://bit.ly/2rUE2R4, http://bit.ly/2sPLBN4, http://ubm.io/1157kyO (Windows 8 lack of AV).

[41] http://bit.ly/2tNLO0i (2016 number reaches 2 billion.), http://bit.ly/2rCzDCV, http://bit.ly/2tNpwfg.

[42] Cisco Corporation estimated that "By 2018, there will be 8.2 billion handheld or personal mobile-ready devices and 2 billion machine-to-machine connections (e.g., GPS systems in cars, asset tracking systems in shipping and manufacturing sectors, or medical applications making patient records and health status more readily available.)" http://bit.ly/Msevdw (future numbers of computers and devices).

1.3.10.4 Firewall

A *firewall* is software and/or hardware that filters network traffic to protect an individual computer or an entire network from unauthorized attempts to access or attack the system. A firewall may scan both incoming and outgoing communications for restricted or regulated information and prevent it from passing without permission (Data Loss Prevention). Some firewalls also restrict access to specific external websites.

1.3.10.5 Perimeter

A *perimeter* is the boundary between an organization's environments and exterior systems. Typically, a firewall will be in place between all internal and external environments.

1.3.10.6 DMZ

Short for de-militarized zone, a *DMZ* is an area on the edge or perimeter of an organization, with a firewall between it and the organization. A DMZ environment will always have a firewall between it and the internet (see Figure 64). DMZ environments are used to pass or temporarily store data moving between organizations.

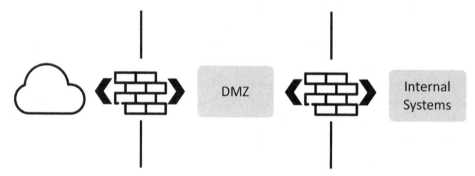

Figure 64 DMZ Example

1.3.10.7 Super User Account

A *Super User Account* is an account that has administrator or root access to a system to be used only in an emergency. Credentials for these accounts are highly secured, only released in an emergency with appropriate documentation and approvals, and expire within a short time. For example, the staff assigned to production control might require access authorizations to multiple large systems, but these authorizations should be tightly controlled by time, user ID, location, or other requirement to prevent abuse.

1.3.10.8 Key Logger

Key Loggers are a type of attack software that records all the keystrokes that a person types into their keyboard, then sends them elsewhere on the Internet. Thus, every password, memo, formula, document, and web address is captured. Often an infected website or malicious software download will install a key logger. Some types of document downloads will allow this to happen as well.

1.3.10.9 Penetration Testing

Setting up a secure network and website is incomplete without testing it to make certain that it truly is secure. In Penetration Testing (sometimes called 'penn test'), an ethical hacker, either from the organization itself or hired from an external security firm, attempts to break into the system from outside, as would a malicious hacker, in order to identify system vulnerabilities. Vulnerabilities found through penetration tests can be addressed before the application is released.

Some people are threatened by ethical hacking audits because they believe these audits will result only in finger pointing. The reality is that in the fast-moving conflict between business security and criminal hacking, all purchased and internally-developed software contains potential vulnerabilities that were not known at the time of their creation. Thus, all software implementations must be challenged periodically. Finding vulnerabilities is an ongoing procedure and no blame should be applied – only security patches.

As proof of the need for continual software vulnerability mitigation, observe a constant stream of security patches arriving from software vendors. This continual security patch update process is a sign of due diligence and professional customer support from these vendors. Many of these patches are the result of ethical hacking performed on behalf of the vendors.

1.3.10.10 Virtual Private Network (VPN)

VPN connections use the unsecured internet to create a secure path or 'tunnel' into an organization's environment. The tunnel is highly encrypted. It allows communication between users and the internal network by using multiple authentication elements to connect with a firewall on the perimeter of an organization's environment. Then it strongly encrypts all transmitted data.

1.3.11 Types of Data Security

Data security involves not just preventing inappropriate access, but also enabling appropriate access to data. Access to sensitive data should be controlled by granting permissions (opt-in). Without permission, a user should not be allowed to see data or take action within the system. 'Least Privilege' is an important security principle. A user, process, or program should be allowed to access only the information allowed by its legitimate purpose.

1.3.11.1 Facility Security

Facility security is the first line of defense against bad actors. Facilities should have, at a minimum, a locked data center with access restricted to authorized employees. Social threats to security (See Section 1.3.15) recognize humans as the weakest point in facility security. Ensure that employees have the tools and training to protect data in facilities.

1.3.11.2 Device Security

Mobile devices, including laptops, tablets, and smartphones, are inherently insecure, as they can be lost, stolen, and physically and electronically attacked by criminal hackers. They often contain corporate emails, spreadsheets, addresses, and documents that, if exposed, can be damaging to the organization, its employees, or its customers.

With the explosion of portable devices and media, a plan to manage the security of these devices (both company-owned and personal) must be part of any company's overall strategic security architecture. This plan should include both software and hardware tools.

Device security standards include:

- Access policies regarding connections using mobile devices
- Storage of data on portable devices such as laptops, DVDs, CDs, or USB drives
- Data wiping and disposal of devices in compliance with records management policies
- Installation of anti-malware and encryption software
- Awareness of security vulnerabilities

1.3.11.3 Credential Security

Each user is assigned credentials to use when obtaining access to a system. Most credentials are a combination of a User ID and a Password. There is a spectrum of how credentials are used across systems within an environment, depending on the sensitivity of the system's data, and the system's capabilities to link to credential repositories.

1.3.11.3.1 Identity Management Systems

Traditionally, users have had different accounts and passwords for each individual resource, platform, application system, or workstation. This approach requires users to manage several passwords and accounts. Organizations with enterprise user directories may have a synchronization mechanism established between the heterogeneous resources to ease user password management. In such cases, the user is required to enter the password only once, usually when logging into the workstation, after which all authentication and authorization executes through a reference to the enterprise user directory. An identity management system implementing this capability is known as 'single-sign-on', and is optimal from a user perspective.

1.3.11.3.2 User ID Standards for Email Systems

User IDs should be unique within the email domain. Most companies use some first name or initial, and full or partial last name as the email or network ID, with a number to differentiate collisions. Names are generally known and are more useful for business contact reasons.

Email or network IDs containing system employee ID numbers are discouraged, as that information is not generally available outside the organization, and provides data that should be secure within the systems.

1.3.11.3.3 Password Standards

Passwords are the first line of defense in protecting access to data. Every user account should be required to have a password set by the user (account owner) with a sufficient level of password complexity defined in the security standards, commonly referred to as 'strong' passwords.

When creating a new user account, the generated temporary password should be set to expire immediately after the first use and the user must choose a new password for subsequent access. Do not permit blank passwords.

Most security experts recommend requiring users to change their passwords every 45 to 180 days, depending on the nature of the system, the type of data, and the sensitivity of the enterprise. However, changing passwords too frequently introduces risk, since it often causes employees write down their new passwords.

1.3.11.3.4 Multiple Factor Identification

Some systems require additional identification procedures. These can include a return call to the user's mobile device that contains a code, the use of a hardware item that must be used for login, or a biometric factor such as fingerprint, facial recognition, or retinal scan. Two-factor identification makes it much harder to break into an account or to log into a user's device. All users with authorization entitlement to highly sensitive information should use two-factor identification to log into the network.

1.3.11.4 Electronic Communication Security

Users must be trained to avoid sending their personal information or any restricted or confidential company information over email or direct communication applications. These insecure methods of communication can be read or intercepted by outside sources. Once a user sends an email, he or she no longer controls the information in it. It can be forwarded to other people without the sender's knowledge or consent.

Social media also applies here. Blogs, portals, wikis, forums, and other Internet or Intranet social media should be considered insecure and should not contain confidential or restricted information.

1.3.12 Types of Data Security Restrictions

Two concepts drive security restrictions: the level of confidentiality of data and regulation related to data.

- **Confidentiality level**: *Confidential* means secret or private. Organizations determine which types of data should not be known outside the organization, or even within certain parts of the organization. Confidential information is shared only on a 'need-to-know' basis. Levels of confidentiality depend on who needs to know certain kinds of information.

- **Regulation**: Regulatory categories are assigned based on external rules, such as laws, treaties, customs agreements, and industry regulations. Regulatory information is shared on an 'allowed-to-know' basis. The ways in which data can be shared are governed by the details of the regulation.

The main difference between confidential and regulatory restrictions is where the restriction originates: confidentiality restrictions originate internally, while regulatory restrictions are externally defined.

Another difference is that any data set, such as a document or a database view, can only have one confidentiality level. This level is established based on the most sensitive (and highest classified) item in the data set. Regulatory categorizations, however, are additive. A single data set may have data restricted based on multiple regulatory categories. To assure regulatory compliance, enforce all actions required for each category, along with the confidentiality requirements.

When applied to the user entitlement (the aggregation of the particular data elements to which a user authorization provides access), all protection policies must be followed, regardless of whether they originated internally or externally.

1.3.12.1 Confidential Data

Confidentiality requirements range from high (very few people have access, for example, to data about employee compensation) to low (everyone has access to product catalogs). A typical classification schema might include two or more of the five confidentiality classification levels listed here:

- **For general audiences**: Information available to anyone, including the public.

- **Internal use only**: Information limited to employees or members, but with minimal risk if shared. For internal use only; may be shown or discussed, but not copied, outside the organization.

- **Confidential**: Information that cannot be shared outside the organization without a properly executed non-disclosure agreement or similar in place. Client confidential information may not be shared with other clients.

- **Restricted confidential**: Information limited to individuals performing certain roles with the 'need to know.' Restricted confidential may require individuals to qualify through clearance.

- **Registered confidential**: Information so confidential that anyone accessing the information must sign a legal agreement to access the data and assume responsibility for its secrecy.

The confidentiality level does not imply any details about restrictions due to regulatory requirements. For example, it does not inform the data manager that data may not be exposed outside its country of origin, or that some employees are prohibited from seeing certain information based on regulations like HIPAA.

1.3.12.2 Regulated Data

Certain types of information are regulated by external laws, industry standards, or contracts that influence how data can be used, as well as who can access it and for what purposes. As there are many overlapping regulations, it is easier to collect them by subject area into a few regulatory categories or families to better inform data managers of regulatory requirements.

Each enterprise, of course, must develop regulatory categories that meet their own compliance needs. Further, it is important that this process and the categories be as simple as possible to allow for an actionable protection capability. When category protective actions are similar, they should be combined into a regulation 'family'. Each regulatory category should include auditable protective actions. This is not an organizational tool but an enforcement method.

Since different industries are affected by different types of regulations, the organization needs to develop regulatory groupings that meet their operational needs. For example, companies that do no business outside of their native land may not need to incorporate regulations pertaining to exports.

However, since all nations have some mixture of personal data privacy laws, and customers are likely to be from anywhere in the world, it may be wise and easier to gather all customer data privacy regulations into a single regulatory family, and comply with the requirements for all the nations. Doing so ensures compliance everywhere, and offers a single standard to enforce.

An example of the possible detail of regulatory compliance is one that prohibits by law a single type of data element in the database to travel outside the physical borders of the originating nation. Several regulations, both domestic and international, have this as a requirement.

An optimal number of regulatory action categories is nine or fewer. Sample regulatory categories follow.

1.3.12.2.1 Sample Regulatory Families

Certain government regulations specify data elements by name, and demand that they be protected in specific ways. Each element does not need a different category; instead, use a single family of actions to protect all specifically targeted data fields. Some PCI data may be included in these categories even though it is a contractual obligation and not a governmental regulation. PCI contractual obligations are mostly uniform around the globe.

- **Personal Identification Information (PII)**: Also known as Personally Private Information (PPI), includes any information that can personally identify the individual (individually or as a set), such as name, address, phone numbers, schedule, government ID number, account numbers, age, race, religion, ethnicity, birthday, family members' names or friends' names, employment information (HR data), and in many cases, remuneration. Highly similar protective actions will satisfy the EU Privacy Directives, Canadian Privacy law (PIPEDA), PIP Act 2003 in Japan, PCI standards, US FTC requirements, GLB, FTC standards, and most Security Breach of Information Acts.

- **Financially Sensitive Data**: All financial information, including what may be termed 'shareholder' or 'insider' data, including all current financial information that has not yet been reported publicly. It also includes any future business plans not made public, planned mergers, acquisitions, or spin-offs, non-public reports of significant company problems, unexpected changes in senior management, comprehensive sales, orders, and billing data. All of these can be captured within this one category, and protected by the same policies. In the US, this is covered under Insider Trading Laws, SOX (Sarbanes-Oxley Act), or GLBA (Gramm-Leach-Bliley/Financial Services Modernization Act). Note: Sarbanes-Oxley act restricts and manages who can change financial data, thus assuring data integrity, while Insider Trading laws affect all those who can see financial data.

- **Medically Sensitive Data/Personal Health Information (PHI)**: All information regarding a person's health or medical treatments. In the US, this is covered by HIPAA (Health Information Portability and Accountability Act). Other nations also have restrictive laws regarding protection of personal and medical information. As these are evolving, ensure Corporate Counsel is aware of the need to follow legal requirements in a nation in which the organization does business or has customers.

- **Educational Records**: All information regarding a person's education. In the US, this is covered by FERPA (Family Educational Rights and Privacy Act).

1.3.12.2.2 Industry or Contract-based Regulation

Some industries have specific standards for how to record, retain, and encrypt information. Some also disallow deletion, editing, or distributing to prohibited locations. For example, regulations for pharmaceuticals, other dangerous substances, food, cosmetics, and advanced technology prevent the transmission or storage of certain information outside the country of origin, or require data to be encrypted during transport.

- **Payment Card Industry Data Security Standard (PCI-DSS)**: PCI-DSS is the most widely known industry data security standard. It addresses any information that can identify an individual with an account at a financial organization, such as name, credit card number (any number on the card), bank account number, or account expiration date. Most of these data fields are regulated by laws and policies. Any data with this classification in its Metadata definition automatically should be carefully reviewed by data stewards when included in any database, application, report, dashboard, or user view.

- **Competitive advantage or trade secrets**: Companies that use proprietary methods, mixtures, formulas, sources, designs, tools, recipes, or operational techniques to achieve a competitive advantage may be protected by industry regulations and/or intellectual property laws.

- **Contractual restrictions**: In its contracts with vendors and partners, an organization may stipulate how specific pieces of information may or may not be used, and which information can and cannot be shared. For example, environmental records, hazardous materials reports, batch numbers, cooking times, points of origin, customer passwords, account numbers, and certain national identity numbers of non-US nationals. Specific technical companies may need to include certain restricted products or ingredients in this category.

1.3.13 System Security Risks

The first step in identifying risk is identifying where sensitive data is stored, and what protections are required for that data. It is also necessary to identify risks inherent in systems. System security risks include elements that can compromise a network or database. These threats allow legitimate employees to misuse information, either intentionally or accidentally, and enable malicious hacker success.

1.3.13.1 Abuse of Excessive Privilege

In granting access to data, the principle of least privilege should be applied. A user, process, or program should be allowed to access only the information allowed by its legitimate purpose. The risk is that users with privileges that exceed the requirements of their job function may abuse these privileges for malicious purpose or accidentally. Users may be granted more access than they should have (excessive privilege) simply because it is challenging to manage user entitlements. The DBA may not have the time or Metadata to define and update granular access privilege control mechanisms for each user entitlement. As a result, many users receive generic default access privileges that far exceed specific job requirements. This lack of oversight to user entitlements is one reason why many data regulations specify data management security.

The solution to excessive privileges is query-level access control, a mechanism that restricts database privileges to minimum-required SQL operations and data. The granularity of data access control must extend beyond the table to specific rows and columns within a table. Query-level access control is useful for detecting excessive privilege abuse by malicious employees.

Most database software implementations integrate some level of query-level access control (triggers, row-level security, table security, views), but the manual nature of these 'built-in' features make them impractical for all but the most limited deployments. The process of manually defining a query-level access control policy for all users across database rows, columns, and operations is time consuming. To make matters worse, as user roles change over time, query policies must be updated to reflect those new roles. Most database administrators would have a hard time defining a useful query policy for a handful of users at a single point in time, much less hundreds of users over time. As a result, in a large number of organizations, automated tools are usually necessary to make real query-level access control functional.

1.3.13.2 Abuse of Legitimate Privilege

Users may abuse legitimate database privileges for unauthorized purposes. Consider a criminally inclined healthcare worker with privileges to view individual patient records via a custom Web application.

The structure of corporate Web applications normally limits users to viewing an individual patient's healthcare history, where multiple records cannot be viewed simultaneously and electronic copies are not allowed. However, the worker may circumvent these limitations by connecting to the database using an alternative system such as MS-Excel. Using MS-Excel and his legitimate login credentials, the worker might retrieve and save all patient records.

There are two risks to consider: intentional and unintentional abuse. Intentional abuse occurs when an employee deliberately misuses organizational data. For example, an errant worker who wants to trade patient records for money or for intentional damage, such as releasing (or threatening to release) sensitive information publicly. Unintentional abuse is a more common risk: The diligent employee who retrieves and stores large amounts of patient information to a work machine for what he or she considers legitimate work purposes. Once the data exists on an endpoint machine, it becomes vulnerable to laptop theft and loss.

The partial solution to the abuse of legitimate privilege is database access control that not only applies to specific queries, but also enforces policies for end-point machines using time of day, location monitoring, and amount of information downloaded, and reduces the ability of any user to have unlimited access to all records containing sensitive information unless it is specifically demanded by their job and approved by their supervisor. For example while it may be necessary for a field agent to access their customer's personal records, they might not be allowed to download the entire customer database to their laptop just to 'save time'.

1.3.13.3 Unauthorized Privilege Elevation

Attackers may take advantage of database platform software vulnerabilities to convert access privileges from those of an ordinary user to those of an administrator. Vulnerabilities may occur in stored procedures, built-in functions, protocol implementations, and even SQL statements. For example, a software developer at a financial institution might take advantage of a vulnerable function to gain the database administrative privilege. With administrative privilege, the offending developer may turn off audit mechanisms, create bogus accounts, transfer funds, or close accounts.

Prevent privilege elevation exploits with a combination of traditional intrusion prevention systems (IPS) and query-level access control intrusion prevention. These systems inspect database traffic to identify patterns that correspond to known vulnerabilities. For example, if a given function is vulnerable to an attack, an IPS may either block all access to the procedure, or block those procedures allowing embedded attacks.

Combine IPS with alternative attack indicators, such as query access control, to improve accuracy in identifying attacks. IPS can detect whether a database request accesses a vulnerable function while query access control detects whether the request matches normal user behavior. If a single request indicates both access to a vulnerable function and unusual behavior, then an attack is almost certainly occurring.

1.3.13.4 Service Account or Shared Account Abuse

Use of service accounts (batch IDs) and shared accounts (generic IDs) increases the risk of data security breaches and complicates the ability to trace the breach to its source. Some organizations further increase their risk when they configure monitoring systems to ignore any alerts related to these accounts. Information security managers should consider adopting tools to manage service accounts securely.

1.3.13.4.1 Service Accounts

Service accounts are convenient because they can tailor enhanced access for the processes that use them. However, if they are used for other purposes, they are untraceable to a particular user or administrator. Unless they have access to decryption keys, service accounts do not threaten encrypted data. This may be especially important for data held on servers storing legal documents, medical information, trade secrets, or confidential executive planning.

Restrict the use of service accounts to specific tasks or commands on specific systems, and require documentation and approval for distributing the credentials. Consider assigning a new password every time distribution occurs, using processes such as those in place for Super User accounts.

1.3.13.4.2 Shared Accounts

Shared accounts are created when an application cannot handle the number of user accounts needed or when adding specific users requires a large effort or incurs additional licensing costs. For shared accounts, credentials are given to multiple users, and the password is rarely changed due to the effort to notify all users. Because they provide essentially ungoverned access, any use of shared accounts should be carefully evaluated. They should never be used by default.

1.3.13.5 Platform Intrusion Attacks

Software updates and intrusion prevention protection of database assets requires a combination of regular software updates (patches) and the implementation of a dedicated Intrusion Prevention Systems (IPS). An IPS is usually, but not always, implemented alongside of an Intrusion Detection System (IDS). The goal is to prevent the vast majority of network intrusion attempts and to respond quickly to any intrusion that has succeeded in working its way past a prevention system. The most primitive form of intrusion protection is a firewall, but with mobile users, web access, and mobile computing equipment a part of most enterprise environments, a simple firewall, while still necessary, is no longer sufficient.

Vendor-provided updates reduce vulnerabilities found in database platforms over time. Unfortunately, software updates are often implemented by enterprises according to periodic maintenance cycles rather than as soon as possible after the patches are made available. In between update cycles, databases are not protected. In addition, compatibility problems sometimes prevent software updates altogether. To address these problems, implement IPS.

1.3.13.6 SQL Injection Vulnerability

In a SQL injection attack, a perpetrator inserts (or 'injects') unauthorized database statements into a vulnerable SQL data channel, such as stored procedures and Web application input spaces. These injected SQL statements are passed to the database, where they are often executed as legitimate commands. Using SQL injection, attackers may gain unrestricted access to an entire database.

SQL injections are also used to attack the DBMS, by passing SQL commands as a parameter of a function or stored procedure. For example, a component that provides backup functionality usually runs at a high privilege; calling a SQL injection vulnerable function in that specific component could allow a regular user to escalate their privileges, become a DBA and take over the database.

Mitigate this risk by sanitizing all inputs before passing them back to the server.

1.3.13.7 Default Passwords

It is a long-standing practice in the software industry to create default accounts during the installation of software packages. Some are used in the installation itself. Others provide users with a means to test the software out of the box.

Default passwords are part of many demo packages. Installation of third party software creates others. For example, a CRM package might create several accounts in the backend database, for install, test, and admin and for regular users. SAP creates a number of default database users at the time of installation. The DBMS industry also engages in this practice.

Attackers are constantly looking for an easy way to steal sensitive data. Mitigate threats to sensitive data by creating the required username and password combinations, and ensuring the no default passwords are left in place in the DBMS. Eliminating the default passwords is an important security step after every implementation.

1.3.13.8 Backup Data Abuse

Backups are made to reduce the risks associated with data loss, but backups also represent a security risk. The news offers many stories about lost backup media. Encrypt all database backups. Encryption prevents loss of a backup either in tangible media or in electronic transit. Securely manage backup decryption keys. Keys must be available off-site to be useful for disaster recovery.

1.3.14 Hacking / Hacker

The term *hacking* came from an era when finding clever ways to perform some computer task was the goal. A hacker is a person who finds unknown operations and pathways within complex computer systems. Hackers can be good or bad.

An ethical or 'White Hat' hacker works to improve a system. ('White Hat' refers to American western movies in which the hero always wore a white hat.) Without ethical hackers, system vulnerabilities that could be corrected would be discovered only by accident. The systematic patching (updating) of computers to increase security results from ethical hacking.

A malicious hacker is someone who intentionally breaches or 'hacks' into a computer system to steal confidential information or to cause damage. Malicious Hackers usually look for financial or personal information in order to steal money or identities. They try to guess simple passwords, and seek to find undocumented weaknesses and backdoors in existing systems. They are sometimes called 'Black Hat hackers'. (In those same American westerns where the heroes wore white hats, the villains wore black hats.)

1.3.15 Social Threats to Security / Phishing

Social threats to security often involve direct communications (whether in person, by phone, or over the internet) designed to trick people who have access to protected data into providing that information (or access to the information) to people who will use it for criminal or malicious purposes.

Social engineering refers to how malicious hackers try to trick people into giving them either information or access. Hackers use any information they obtain to convince other employees that they have legitimate requests. Sometimes hackers will contact several people in sequence, collecting information at each step useful for gaining the trust of the next higher employee.

Phishing refers to a phone call, instant message, or email meant to lure recipients into giving out valuable or private information without realizing they are doing so. Often these calls or messages appear to be from a legitimate source. For example, sometimes they are framed as sales pitches for discounts or lowered interest rates. But they ask for personal information such as names, passwords, Social Security numbers, or credit card information. To reduce suspicion, these messages often request the recipient to 'update' or 'confirm' information. Phishing instant messages and emails might also direct users to phony websites to trick them into providing personal information. Of special danger are fake emails specifically targeted to senior executives by name. This is called 'Spear-phishing for whales'. In addition to phoning and spoofing, hackers have been known to physically go to target sites and speak directly with employees, sometimes using disguises or posing as vendors, in order to gain access to sensitive information.[43]

1.3.16 Malware

Malware refers to any malicious software created to damage, change, or improperly access a computer or network. Computer viruses, worms, spyware, key loggers, and adware are all examples of malware. Any software installed without authorization can be considered malware, if for no other reason than that it takes up disk space and possibly processing cycles that the system owner did not authorize. Malware can take many forms, depending on its purpose (replication, destruction, information or processing theft, or behavior monitoring).

1.3.16.1 Adware

Adware is a form of spyware that enters a computer from an Internet download. Adware monitors a computer's use, such as what websites are visited. Adware also may insert objects and tool bars in the user's browser. Adware is not illegal, but is used to develop complete profiles of the user's browsing and buying habits to sell to other marketing firms. It can also be easily leveraged by malicious software for identity theft.

1.3.16.2 Spyware

Spyware refers to any software program that slips into a computer without consent, in order to track online activity. These programs tend to piggyback on other software programs. When a user downloads and installs free software from a site on the Internet, spyware can also install, usually without the user's knowledge. Different forms of spyware track different types of activity. Some programs monitor what websites are visited, while others record the user's keystrokes to steal personal information, such as credit card numbers, bank account information, and passwords.

Many legitimate websites, including search engines, install tracking spyware, which is a form of Adware.

---

[43] The FBI report on Russian Hacking during the 2016 US Presidential Election outlines how these techniques were used in that instance. http://bit.ly/2iKStXO.

1.3.16.3 Trojan Horse

The Trojan horse was a large wooden 'gift statue' of a horse that the Greeks gave to the people of Troy, who quickly brought it inside the city walls. Unfortunately for them, it concealed Greek soldiers, who, once inside the Troy, slipped out and attacked the city.

In computer security terms, a Trojan horse refers to a malicious program that enters a computer system disguised or embedded within legitimate software. Once installed, a Trojan horse will delete files, access personal information, install malware, reconfigure the computer, install a key logger, or even allow hackers to use the computer as a weapon (Bot or Zombie) against other computers on a network.

1.3.16.4 Virus

A *virus* is a program that attaches itself to an executable file or vulnerable application and delivers a payload that ranges from annoying to extremely destructive. A file virus executes when an infected file opens. A virus always needs to accompany another program. Opening downloaded and infected programs can release a virus.

1.3.16.5 Worm

A computer *worm* is a program built to reproduce and spread across a network by itself. A worm-infected computer will send out a continuous stream of infected messages. A worm may perform several different malicious activities, although the main function is to harm networks by consuming large amounts of bandwidth, potentially shutting the network down.

1.3.16.6 Malware Sources

1.3.16.6.1 Instant Messaging (IM)

IM allows users to relay messages to each other in real-time. IM is also becoming a new threat to network security. Because many IM systems have been slow to add security features, malicious hackers have found IM a useful means of spreading viruses, spyware, phishing scams, and a wide variety of worms. Typically, these threats infiltrate systems through contaminated attachments and messages.

1.3.16.6.2 Social Networking Sites

Social networking sites, such as Facebook, Twitter, Vimeo, Google+, LinkedIn, Xanga, Instagram, Pinterest, or MySpace, where users build online profiles and share personal information, opinions, photographs, blog entries, and other information, have become targets of online predators, spammers, and identity thieves.

In addition to representing a threat from malicious people, these sites pose risks from employees who may post information sensitive to the enterprise or 'insider' knowledge that might affect the price of a public organization's stock. Inform users of the dangers and the reality that whatever they post will become permanent on the Internet. Even if they later remove the data, many will have made copies. Some companies block these sites at their firewall.

1.3.16.6.3 Spam

Spam refers to unsolicited, commercial email messages sent out in bulk, usually to tens of millions of users in hopes that a few may reply. A return rate of 1% can net millions of dollars. Most email routing systems have traps to filter out known spam message patterns to reduce internal traffic. These exclusion patterns include:

- Domains known for spam transmission
- CC: or BCC: address count above certain limits
- Email body has only an image as a hyperlink
- Specific text strings or words

Responding to a spam message will confirm to the sender that they have reached a legitimate email address and will increase future spam because lists of valid emails can be sold to other spammers.

Spam messages may also be Internet hoaxes or include malware attachments, with attachment names and extensions, message text, and images giving the appearance of a legitimate communication. One way to detect spam email is to hover the pointer over any hyperlinks, which will show the actual link that has nothing in common with the company shown in the text. Another way is the lack of a way to unsubscribe. In the US, advertising emails are required to list an unsubscribe link to stop further emails.

2. Activities

There is no one prescribed way of implementing data security to meet all necessary privacy and confidentiality requirements. Regulations focus on the ends of security, not the means for achieving it. Organizations should design their own security controls, demonstrate that the controls meet or exceed the requirements of the laws or regulations, document the implementation of those controls, and monitor and measure them over time. As in other Knowledge Areas, the activities include identifying requirements, assessing the current environment for gaps or risks, implementing security tools and processes, and auditing data security measures to ensure they are effective.

2.1 Identify Data Security Requirements

It is important to distinguish between business requirements, external regulatory restrictions, and the rules imposed by application software products. While application systems serve as vehicles to enforce business rules and procedures, it is common for these systems to have their own data security requirements over and above those required for business processes. These requirements are becoming more common with packaged and off-the-shelf systems. It is necessary, however, to see that they support organizational data security standards as well.

2.1.1 Business Requirements

Implementing data security within an enterprise begins with a thorough understanding of business requirements. The business needs of an enterprise, its mission, strategy and size, and the industry to which it belongs define the degree of rigidity required for data security. For example, financial and securities enterprises in the United States are highly regulated and required to maintain stringent data security standards. In contrast, a small-scale retail enterprise may choose not to have the same kind of data security function that a large retailer has, even though both of them have similar core business activities.

Analyze business rules and processes to identify security touch points. Every event in the business workflow may have its own security requirements. Data-to-process and data-to-role relationship matrices are useful tools to map these needs and guide definition of data security role-groups, parameters, and permissions. Plan to address short-term and long-term goals to achieve a balanced and effective data security function.

2.1.2 Regulatory Requirements

Today's fast changing and global environment requires organizations to comply with a growing set of laws and regulations. The ethical and legal issues facing organizations in the Information Age are leading governments to establish new laws and standards. These have all imposed strict security controls on information management. (See Chapter 2.)

Create a central inventory of all relevant data regulations and the data subject area affected by each regulation. Add links to the corresponding security policies developed for compliance to these regulations (see Table 13), and the controls implemented. Regulations, policies, required actions, and data affected will change over time, so this inventory should be in a format that is simple to manage and maintain.

Table 13 Sample Regulation Inventory Table

Regulation	Subject Area Affected	Security Policy Links	Controls Implemented

Examples of laws that influence data security include:

- US
    - Sarbanes-Oxley Act of 2002
    - Health Information Technology for Economic and Clinical Health (HITECH) Act, enacted as part of the American Recovery and Reinvestment Act of 2009
    - Health Insurance Portability and Accountability Act of 1996 (HIPAA) Security Regulations
    - Gramm-Leach-Bliley I and II
    - SEC laws and Corporate Information Security Accountability Act
    - Homeland Security Act and USA Patriot Act
    - Federal Information Security Management Act (FISMA)
    - California: SB 1386, California Security Breach Information Act
- EU
    - Data Protection Directive (EU DPD 95/46/) AB 1901, Theft of electronic files or databases

- Canada
  - o Canadian Bill 198
- Australia
  - o The CLERP Act of Australia

Regulations that impact data security include:

- Payment Card Industry Data Security Standard (PCI DSS), in the form of a contractual agreement for all companies working with credit cards
- EU: The Basel II Accord, which imposes information controls for all financial institutions doing business in its related countries
- US: FTC Standards for Safeguarding Customer Info

Compliance with company policies or regulatory restrictions will often require adjustments to business processes. For example, the need to authorize access to health information (regulated data elements) to multiple unique groups of users, in order to accommodate HIPAA.

2.2 Define Data Security Policy

Organizations should create data security policies based on business and regulatory requirements. A policy is a statement of a selected course of action and high-level description of desired behavior to achieve a set of goals. Data security policies describe behaviors that are determined to be in the best interests of an organization that wishes to protect its data. For policies to have a measurable impact, they must be auditable and audited.

Corporate policies often have legal implications. A court may consider a policy instituted to support a legal regulatory requirement to be an intrinsic part of the organization's effort to comply with that legal requirement. Failure to comply with a corporate policy might have negative legal ramifications after a data breach.

Defining security policy requires collaboration between IT security administrators, Security Architects, Data Governance committees, Data Stewards, internal and external audit teams, and the legal department. Data Stewards must also collaborate with all Privacy Officers (Sarbanes-Oxley supervisors, HIPAA Officers, etc.), and business managers having data expertise, to develop regulatory category Metadata and apply proper security classifications consistently. All data regulation compliance actions must be coordinated to reduce cost, work instruction confusion, and needless turf battles.

2.2.1 Security Policy Contents

Different levels of policy are required to govern behavior related to enterprise security. For example:

- **Enterprise Security Policy**: Global policies for employee access to facilities and other assets, email standards and policies, security access levels based on position or title, and security breach reporting policies

- **IT Security Policy**: Directory structures standards, password policies, and an identity management framework

- **Data Security Policy**: Categories for individual application, database roles, user groups, and information sensitivity

Commonly, the IT Security Policy and Data Security Policy are part of a combined security policy. The preference, however, should be to separate them. Data security policies are more granular in nature, specific to content, and require different controls and procedures. The Data Governance Council should review and approve the Data Security Policy. The Data Management Executive owns and maintains the policy.

Employees need to understand and follow security policies. Develop security policies so that the required processes and the reasons behind them are clearly defined and achievable. Compliance should be made easier than non-compliance. Policies need to protect and secure data without stifling user access.

Security policies should be in a format easily accessible by the suppliers, consumers, and other stakeholders. They should be available and maintained on the company intranet or a similar collaboration portal.

Data security policies, procedures, and activities should be periodically reevaluated to strike the best possible balance between the data security requirements of all stakeholders.

2.3 Define Data Security Standards

Policies provide guidelines for behavior. They do not outline every possible contingency. Standards supplement policies and provide additional detail on how to meet the intention of the policies. For example, a policy may state that passwords must follow guidelines for strong passwords; the standards for strong passwords would be detailed separately; and the policy would be enforced through technology that prevents passwords from being created if they do not meet the standards for strong passwords.

2.3.1 Define Data Confidentiality Levels

Confidentiality classification is an important Metadata characteristic, guiding how users are granted access privileges. Each organization should create or adopt a classification scheme that meets its business requirements. Any classification method should be clear and easy to apply. It will contain a range of levels, from the least to the most confidential (e.g., from "for general use" to "registered confidential"). (See Section 1.3.12.1.)

2.3.2 Define Data Regulatory Categories

A growing number of highly publicized data breaches, in which sensitive personal information has been compromised, have resulted in data-specific laws to being introduced. Financially-focused data incidents have spurred governments across the globe to implement additional regulations.

This has created a new class of data, which might be called 'Regulated Information'. Regulatory requirements are an extension of information security. Additional measures are required to manage regulatory requirements effectively. Consultation with corporate counsel is often helpful in determining what actions certain regulations require from the enterprise. Often the regulations imply a goal, and it is up to the corporation to determine the means for reaching that information protection goal. Actions that can be audited provide legal proof of compliance.

A useful way to handle the data-specific regulations is by analyzing and grouping similar regulations into categories, as was been done by grouping various risks into a few security classifications.

With more than one-hundred different data-specific ordinances around the world, it would be useless to develop a different category for each regulation. Most data regulations, imposed as they are by separate legal entities, seek to do the same thing. For example, the contractual obligations for protecting confidential customer data are remarkably similar to U.S., Japanese, and Canadian government regulations for protecting Personally Identifiable Information, and similar for compliance with EU privacy requirements. This pattern is easy to see when the auditable compliance actions for each regulation are listed and compared. Thus, they may all be managed properly by using the same protective action category.

A key principle for both security classification and regulatory categorization is that most information can be aggregated so that it has greater or lesser sensitivity. Developers need to know how aggregations affect the overall security classification and regulatory categories. When a developer of a dashboard, report, or database view knows that some of the data that is required may be personally private or insider or related to competitive advantage, the system can then be designed to eliminate aspects of that from the entitlement, or, if the data must remain in the user-entitlement, to enforce all the security and regulatory requirements at the time of user authorization.

The results of this classification work will be a formally approved set of security classifications and regulatory categories and a process for capturing this Metadata in a central repository so that employees, both business and technical, know the sensitivity if the information they are handling, transmitting, and authorizing

2.3.3 Define Security Roles

Data access control can be organized at an individual or group level, depending on the need. That said, granting access and update privileges to individual user accounts entails a great deal of redundant effort. Smaller organizations may find it acceptable to manage data access at the individual level. However, larger organizations will benefit greatly from role-based access control, granting permissions to role groups and thereby to each group member.

Role groups enable security administrators to define privileges by role and to grant these privileges by enrolling users in the appropriate role group. While it is technically possible to enroll a user in more than one group, this practice may make it difficult to understand the privileges granted to a specific user. Whenever possible, try to assign each user to only one role group. This may require the creation of different user views of certain data entitlements to comply with regulations.

Data consistency in user and role management is a challenge. User information such as name, title, and employee ID must be stored redundantly in several locations. These islands of data often conflict, representing multiple versions of the 'truth'. To avoid data integrity issues, manage user identity data and role-group membership centrally. This is a requirement for the quality of data used for effective access control. Security administrators create, modify, and delete user accounts and role groups. Changes made to the group taxonomy and membership should receive appropriate approval. Changes should be tracked via a change management system.

Applying data security measures inconsistently or improperly within an organization can lead to employee dissatisfaction and significant risk to the organization. Role-based security depends on clearly defined, consistently assigned roles.

There are two ways to define and organize roles: as a grid (starting from the data), or in a hierarchy (starting from the user).

2.3.3.1 Role Assignment Grid

A grid can be useful for mapping out access roles for data, based on data confidentiality, regulations, and user functions. The Public User role can have access to all data ranked for General Audiences and not subject to any regulations. A Marketing role may have access to some PII information for use in developing campaigns, but not to any restricted data, or Client Confidential data. Table 14 shows a very simplified example.

Table 14 Role Assignment Grid Example

	Confidentiality Level		
	General Audience	**Client Confidential**	**Restricted Confidential**
Not Regulated	Public User Role	Client Manager Role	Restricted Access Role
PII	Marketing Role	Client Marketing Role	HR Role
PCI	Financial Role	Client Financial Role	Restricted Financial Role

2.3.3.2 Role Assignment Hierarchy

Construct group definitions at a workgroup or business unit level. Organize these roles in a hierarchy, so that child roles further restrict the privileges of parent roles. The ongoing maintenance of these hierarchies is a complex operation requiring reporting systems capable of granular drill down to individual user privileges. A security role hierarchy example is shown in Figure 65.

2.3.4 Assess Current Security Risks

Security risks include elements that can compromise a network and/or database. The first step in identifying risk is identifying where sensitive data is stored, and what protections are required for that data. Evaluate each system for the following:

- The sensitivity of the data stored or in transit
- The requirements to protect that data, and
- The current security protections in place

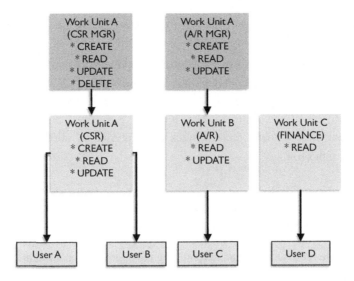

Figure 65 Security Role Hierarchy Example Diagram

Document the findings, as they create a baseline for future evaluations. This documentation may also be a requirement for privacy compliance, such as in the European Union. Gaps must be remediated through improved security processes supported by technology. The impact of improvements should be measured and monitored to ensure risks are mitigated.

In larger organizations, white-hat hackers may be hired to assess vulnerabilities. A white hat exercise can be used as proof of an organization's impenetrability, which can be used in publicity for market reputation.

2.3.5 Implement Controls and Procedures

Implementation and administration of data security policy is primarily the responsibility of security administrators, in coordination with data stewards and technical teams. For example, database security is often a DBA responsibility.

Organizations must implement proper controls to meet the security policy requirements. Controls and procedures should (at a minimum) cover:

- How users gain and lose access to systems and/or applications
- How users are assigned to and removed from roles
- How privilege levels are monitored
- How requests for access changes are handled and monitored
- How data is classified according to confidentiality and applicable regulations
- How data breaches are handled once detected

Document the requirements for allowing original user authorizations so de-authorization may happen when these conditions no longer apply.

For instance, a policy to 'maintain appropriate user privileges' could have a control objective of '*Review DBA and User rights and privileges on a monthly basis*'. The organization's procedure to satisfy this control might be to implement and maintain processes to:

- Validate assigned permissions against a change management system used for tracking all user permission requests
- Require a workflow approval process or signed paper form to record and document each change request
- Include a procedure for eliminating authorizations for people whose job status or department no longer qualifies them to have certain access rights

Some level of management must formally request, track, and approve all initial authorizations and subsequent changes to user and group authorizations

2.3.5.1 Assign Confidentiality Levels

Data Stewards are responsible for evaluating and determining the appropriate confidentiality level for data based on the organization's classification scheme.

The classification for documents and reports should be based on the highest level of confidentiality for any information found within the document. (See Chapter 9.) Label each page or screen with the classification in the header or footer. Information products classified as least confidential (e.g., "For General Audiences") do not need labels. Assume any unlabeled products to be for General Audiences.

Document authors and information product designers are responsible for evaluating, correctly classifying, and labeling the appropriate confidentiality level for each document, as well as each database, including relational tables, columns, and user entitlement views.

In larger organizations, much of the security classification and protective effort will be the responsibility of a dedicated information security organization. While Information Security will be happy to have the Data Stewards work with these classifications, they usually take responsibility for enforcement and for physically protecting the network.

2.3.5.2 Assign Regulatory Categories

Organizations should create or adopt a classification approach to ensure that they can meet the demands of regulatory compliance. (See Section 3.3.) This classification scheme provides a foundation for responding to internal and external audits. Once it is in place, information needs to be assessed and classified within the schema. Security staff may not be familiar with this concept, as they do not work with individual data regulations, but with infrastructure systems. They will need to have documented requirements for data protection relating to these categories defining actions they can implement.

2.3.5.3 Manage and Maintain Data Security

Once all the requirements, policies, and procedures are in place, the main task is to ensure that security breaches do not occur, and if they do, to detect them as soon as possible. Continual monitoring of systems and auditing of the execution of security procedures are crucial to preserving data security.

2.3.5.3.1 Control Data Availability / Data-centric Security

Controlling data availability requires management of user entitlements and of the structures (data masking, view creation, etc.) that technically control access based on entitlements. Some databases are better than others in providing structures and processes to protect data in storage. (See Section 3.7.)

Security Compliance managers may have direct responsibility for designing user entitlement profiles that allow the business to function smoothly, while following relevant restrictions.

Defining entitlements and granting authorizations requires an inventory of data, careful analysis of data needs, and documentation of the data exposed in each user entitlement. Often highly sensitive information is mixed with non-sensitive information. An enterprise data model is essential to identifying and locating sensitive data. (See Section 1.1.1.)

Data masking can protect data even if it is inadvertently exposed. Certain data regulations require encryption, an extreme version of in-place masking. Authorization to the decryption keys can be part of the user authorization process. Users authorized to access the decryption keys can see the unencrypted data, while others only see random characters.

Relational database views can used to enforce data security levels. Views can restrict access to certain rows based on data values or restrict access to certain columns, limiting access to confidential or regulated fields.

2.3.5.3.2 Monitor User Authentication and Access Behavior

Reporting on access is a basic requirement for compliance audits. Monitoring authentication and access behavior provides information about who is connecting and accessing information assets. Monitoring also helps detect unusual, unforeseen, or suspicious transactions that warrant investigation. In this way, it compensates for gaps in data security planning, design, and implementation.

Deciding what needs monitoring, for how long, and what actions to take in the event of an alert, requires careful analysis driven by business and regulatory requirements. Monitoring entails a wide range of activities. It can be specific to certain data sets, users, or roles. It can be used to validate data integrity, configurations, or core Metadata. It can be implemented within a system or across dependent heterogeneous systems. It can focus on specific privileges, such as the ability to download large sets of data or to access data at off hours.

Monitoring can be automated or executed manually or executed through a combination of automation and oversight. Automated monitoring does impose overhead on the underlying systems and may affect system performance. Periodic snapshots of activity can be useful in understanding trends and comparing against standards criteria. Iterative configuration changes may be required to achieve the optimal parameters for proper monitoring.

Automated recording of sensitive or unusual database transactions should be part of any database deployment. Lack of automated monitoring represents serious risks:

- **Regulatory risk**: Organizations with weak database audit mechanisms will increasingly find that they are at odds with government regulatory requirements. Sarbanes-Oxley (SOX) in the financial services sector and the Healthcare Information Portability and Accountability Act (HIPAA) in the healthcare sector are just two examples of US government regulation with clear database audit requirements.

- **Detection and recovery risk**: Audit mechanisms represent the last line of defense. If an attacker circumvents other defenses, audit data can identify the existence of a violation after the fact. Audit data can also be used to link a violation to a particular user or as a guide to repair the system.

- **Administrative and audit duties risk**: Users with administrative access to the database server – whether that access was obtained legitimately or maliciously – can turn off auditing to hide fraudulent activity. Audit duties should ideally be separate from both database administrators and the database server platform support staff.

- **Risk of reliance on inadequate native audit tools**: Database software platforms often try to integrate basic audit capabilities but they often suffer from multiple weaknesses that limit or preclude deployment. When users access the database via Web applications (such as SAP, Oracle E-Business Suite, or PeopleSoft), native audit mechanisms have no awareness of specific user identities and all user activity is associated with the Web application account name. Therefore, when native audit logs reveal fraudulent database transactions, there is no link to the responsible user.

To mitigate the risks, implement a network-based audit appliance, which can address most of the weaknesses associated with native audit tools, but which does not take place of regular audits by trained auditors. This kind of appliance has the following benefits:

- **High performance**: Network-based audit appliances can operate at line speed with little impact on database performance.

- **Separation of duties**: Network-based audit appliances should operate independently of database administrators making it possible to separate audit duties from administrative duties as appropriate.

- **Granular transaction tracking** supports advanced fraud detection, forensics, and recovery. Logs include details such as source application name, complete query text, query response attributes, source OS, time, and source name.

2.3.5.4 Manage Security Policy Compliance

Managing security policy compliance includes ongoing activities to ensure policies are followed and controls are effectively maintained. Management also includes providing recommendations to meet new requirements. In many cases, Data Stewards will act in conjunction with Information Security and Corporate Counsel so that operational policies and technical controls are aligned.

2.3.5.4.1 Manage Regulatory Compliance

Managing regulatory compliance includes:

- Measuring compliance with authorization standards and procedures
- Ensuring that all data requirements are measurable and therefore auditable (i.e., assertions like "be careful" are not measurable)
- Ensuring regulated data in storage and in motion is protected using standard tools and processes

- Using escalation procedures and notification mechanisms when potential non-compliance issues are discovered, and in the event of a regulatory compliance breach

Compliance controls require audit trails. For example, if policy states that users must take training before accessing certain data, then the organization must be able to prove that any given user took the training. Without an audit trail, there is no evidence of compliance. Controls should be designed to ensure they are auditable.

2.3.5.4.2 Audit Data Security and Compliance Activities

Internal audits of activities to ensure data security and regulatory compliance policies are followed should be conducted regularly and consistently. Compliance controls themselves must be revisited when new data regulation is enacted, when existing regulation changes, and periodically to ensure usefulness. Internal or external auditors may perform audits. In all cases, auditors must be independent of the data and / or process involved in the audit to avoid any conflict of interest and to ensure the integrity of the auditing activity and results.

Auditing is not a fault-finding mission. The goal of auditing is to provide management and the data governance council with objective, unbiased assessments, and rational, practical recommendations.

Data security policy statements, standards documents, implementation guides, change requests, access monitoring logs, report outputs, and other records (electronic or hard copy) form the input to an audit. In addition to examining existing evidence, audits often include performing tests and checks, such as:

- Analyzing policy and standards to assure that compliance controls are defined clearly and fulfill regulatory requirements

- Analyzing implementation procedures and user-authorization practices to ensure compliance with regulatory goals, policies, standards, and desired outcomes

- Assessing whether authorization standards and procedures are adequate and in alignment with technology requirements

- Evaluating escalation procedures and notification mechanisms to be executed when potential non-compliance issues are discovered or in the event of a regulatory compliance breach

- Reviewing contracts, data sharing agreements, and regulatory compliance obligations of outsourced and external vendors, that ensure business partners meet their obligations and that the organization meets its legal obligations for protecting regulated data

- Assessing the maturity of security practices within the organization and reporting to senior management and other stakeholders on the 'State of Regulatory Compliance'

- Recommending Regulatory Compliance policy changes and operational compliance improvements

Auditing data security is not a substitute for management of data security. It is a supporting process that objectively assesses whether management is meeting goals.

3. Tools

The tools used for managing information security depend, in large part, on the size of the organization, the network architecture, and the policies and standards used by a security organization.

3.1 Anti-Virus Software / Security Software

Anti-virus software protects computers from viruses encountered on the Web. New viruses and other malware appear every day, so it is important to update security software regularly.

3.2 HTTPS

If a Web address begins with https://, it indicates that the website is equipped with an encrypted security layer. Typically, users must provide a password or other means of authentication to access the site. Making payments online or accessing classified information uses this encryption protection. Train users to look for this in the URL address when they are performing sensitive operations over the Internet, or even within the enterprise. Without encryption, people on the same network segment can read the plain text information.

3.3 Identity Management Technology

Identity management technology stores assigned credentials and shares them with systems upon request, such as when a user logs into a system. Some applications manage their own credential repository, although it is more convenient for users to have most or all applications use a central credential repository. There are protocols for managing credentials: Lightweight Directory Access Protocol (LDAP) is one.

Some companies choose and provide an enterprise approved 'Password Safe' product that creates an encrypted password file on each user's computer. Users only need to learn one long pass-phrase to open the program and they can store all their passwords safely in the encrypted file. A single-sign-on system also can perform this role.

3.4 Intrusion Detection and Prevention Software

Tools that can detect incursions and dynamically deny access are necessary for when hackers do penetrate firewalls or other security measures.

An Intrusion Detection System (IDS) will notify appropriate people when an inappropriate incident happens. IDS should optimally be connected with an intrusion Prevention System (IPS) that automatically responds to known attacks and illogical combinations of user commands. Detection is often accomplished by analysis of patterns within the organization. Knowledge of expected patterns allows detection of out-of-the-ordinary events. When these take place, the system can send alerts.

3.5 Firewalls (Prevention)

Secure and sophisticated firewalls, with capacity to allow full speed data transmission while still performing detailed packet analysis, should be placed at the enterprise gateway. For web servers exposed to the Internet, a more complex firewall structure is advised, as many malicious hacker attacks exploit legitimate appearing traffic that is intentionally malformed to exploit database and web server vulnerabilities.

3.6 Metadata Tracking

Tools that track Metadata can help an organization track the movement of sensitive data. These tools create a risk that outside agents can detect internal information from metadata associated with documents. Identification of sensitive information using Metadata provides the best way to ensure that data is protected properly. Since the largest number of data loss incidents result from the lack of sensitive data protection due to ignorance of its sensitivity, Metadata documentation completely overshadows any hypothetical risk that might occur if the Metadata were to be somehow exposed from the Metadata repository. This risk is made more negligible since it is trivial for an experienced hacker to locate unprotected sensitive data on the network. The people most likely unaware of the need to protect sensitive data appear to be employees and managers.

3.7 Data Masking/Encryption

Tools that perform masking or encryption are useful for restricting movement of sensitive data. (See Section 1.3.9.)

4. Techniques

Techniques for managing information security depend on the size of the organization, the architecture of the network, the type of data that must be secured, and the policies and standards used by a security organization.

4.1 CRUD Matrix Usage

Creating and using data-to-process and data-to-role relationship (CRUD–Create, Read, Update, Delete) matrices help map data access needs and guide definition of data security role groups, parameters, and permissions. Some versions add an E for Execute to make CRUDE.

4.2 Immediate Security Patch Deployment

A process for installing security patches as quickly as possible on all machines should be in place. A malicious hacker only needs root access to one machine in order to conduct his attack successfully on the network. Users should not be able to delay this update.

4.3 Data Security Attributes in Metadata

A Metadata repository is essential to assure the integrity and consistent use of an Enterprise Data Model across business processes. Metadata should include security and regulatory classifications for data. (See Section 1.1.3.) Having security Metadata in place protects an organization from employees who may not recognize the data as sensitive. When Data Stewards apply confidentiality and regulatory categories, category information should be documented in the Metadata repository and, if technology allows, tagged to the data. (See Sections 3.3.1 and 3.3.2.) These classifications can be used to define and manage user entitlements and authorizations, as well as to inform development teams about risks related to sensitive data.

4.4 Metrics

It is essential to measure information protection processes to ensure that they are functioning as required. Metrics also enable improvement of these processes. Some metrics measure progress on processes: the number of audits performed, security systems installed, incidents reported, and the amount of unexamined data in systems. More sophisticated metrics will focus on findings from audits or the movement of the organization along a maturity model.

In larger organizations with existing information security staff, a significant number of these metrics may already exist. It is helpful to reuse existing metrics as a part of an overall threat management measurement process, and to prevent duplication of effort. Create a baseline (initial reading) of each metric to show progress over time.

While a great number of security activities and conditions can be measured and tracked, focus on actionable metrics. A few key metrics in organized groups are easier to manage than pages of apparently unrelated indicators. Improvement actions may include awareness training on data regulatory policies and compliance actions.

Many organizations face similar data security challenges. The following lists may assist in selecting applicable metrics.

4.4.1 Security Implementation Metrics

These general security metrics can be framed as positive value percentages:

*   Percentage of enterprise computers having the most recent security patches installed
*   Percentage of computers having up-to-date anti-malware software installed and running
*   Percentage of new-hires who have had successful background checks
*   Percentage of employees scoring more than 80% on annual security practices quiz
*   Percentage of business units for which a formal risk assessment analysis has been completed
*   Percentage of business processes successfully tested for disaster recovery in the event of fire, earthquake, storm, flood, explosion or other disaster
*   Percentage of audit findings that have been successfully resolved

Trends can be tracked on metrics framed as lists or statistics:

*   Performance metrics of all security systems

- Background investigations and results
- Contingency planning and business continuity plan status
- Criminal incidents and investigations
- Due diligence examinations for compliance, and number of findings that need to be addressed
- Informational risk management analysis performed and number of those resulting in actionable changes
- Policy audit implications and results, such as clean desk policy checks, performed by evening-shift security officers during rounds
- Security operations, physical security, and premises protection statistics
- Number of documented, accessible security standards (a.k.a. policies)
- The motivation of relevant parties to comply with security policies can also be measured
- Business conduct and reputational risk analysis, including employee training
- Business hygiene and insider risk potential based on specific types of data such as financial, medical, trade secrets, and insider information
- Confidence and influence indicators among managers and employees as an indication of how data information security efforts and policies are perceived

Select and maintain a reasonable number of actionable metrics in appropriate categories over time to assure compliance, spot issues before they become crises, and indicate to senior management a determination to protect valuable corporate information.

4.4.2 Security Awareness Metrics

Consider these general areas to select appropriate metrics:

- **Risk assessment findings** provide qualitative data that needs to be fed back to appropriate business units to make them more aware of their accountability.

- **Risk events and profiles** identify unmanaged exposures that need correction. Determine the absence or degree of measurable improvement in risk exposure or conformance to policy by conducting follow-up testing of the awareness initiative to see how well the messages got across.

- **Formal feedback surveys and interviews** identify the level of security awareness. Also, measure the number of employees who have successfully completed security awareness training within targeted populations.

- **Incident post mortems, lessons learned, and victim interviews** provide a rich source of information on gaps in security awareness. Measures may include how much vulnerability has been mitigated.

- **Patching effectiveness audits** involve specific machines that work with confidential and regulated information to assess the effectiveness of security patching. (An automated patching system is advised whenever possible.)

4.4.3 Data Protection Metrics

Requirements will dictate which of these are pertinent to an organization:

- **Criticality ranking** of specific data types and information systems that, if made inoperable, would have profound impact on the enterprise.

- **Annualized loss expectancy** of mishaps, hacks, thefts, or disasters related to data loss, compromise, or corruption.

- **Risk of specific data losses** related to certain categories of regulated information, and remediation priority ranking.

- **Risk mapping of data to specific business processes**. Risks associated with Point of Sale devices would be included in the risk profile of the financial payment system.

- **Threat assessments** performed based on the likelihood of an attack against certain valuable data resources and the media through which they travel.

- **Vulnerability assessments** of specific parts of the business process where sensitive information could be exposed, either accidentally or intentionally.

Auditable list of locations where sensitive data is propagated throughout the organization.

4.4.4 Security Incident Metrics

- Intrusion attempts detected and prevented
- Return on Investment for security costs using savings from prevented intrusions

4.4.5 Confidential Data Proliferation

The number of copies of confidential data should be measured in order to reduce this proliferation. The more places confidential data is stored, the higher the risk of a breach.

4.5 Security Needs in Project Requirements

Every project that involves data must address system and data security. Identify detailed data and application security requirements in the analysis phase. Identification up front guides the design and prevents having to retrofit security processes. If implementation teams understand data protection requirements from the start, they can build compliance into the basic architecture of the system. This information can also be used for selecting appropriate vendor/purchased software packages.

4.6 Efficient Search of Encrypted Data

Searching encrypted data obviously includes the need to decrypt the data. One way to reduce the amount of data that needs decryption is to encrypt the search criteria (such as a string) using the same encryption method used for the data, and then seek matches. The amount of data matching the encrypted search criteria will be much less, and therefore less costly (and risky) to decrypt. Then search using clear text on the result set to get exact matches.

4.7 Document Sanitization

Document sanitization is the process of cleaning Metadata, such as tracked change history, from documents before sharing. Sanitization mitigates the risk of sharing confidential information that might be embedded in comments. In contracts especially, access to this information may negatively affect negotiations.

5. Implementation Guidelines

Implementation of data security practices depends on corporate culture, the nature of the risks, the sensitivity of what data the company manages, and the types of systems in place. Implementation system components should be guided by a strategic security plan and supporting architecture.

5.1 Readiness Assessment / Risk Assessment

Keeping data secure is deeply connected to corporate culture. Organizations often end up reacting to crises, rather than proactively managing accountability and ensuring auditability. While perfect data security is next to impossible, the best way to avoid data security breaches is to build awareness and understanding of security requirements, policies, and procedures. Organizations can increase compliance through:

- **Training**: Promotion of standards through training on security initiatives at all levels of the organization. Follow training with evaluation mechanisms such as online tests focused on improving employee awareness. Such training and testing should be mandatory and a prerequisite for employee performance evaluation.

- **Consistent policies**: Definition of data security policies and regulatory compliance policies for workgroups and departments that complement and align with enterprise policies. Adopting an 'act local' mindset helps engage people more actively.

- **Measure the benefits of security**: Link data security benefits to organizational initiatives. Organizations should include objective metrics for data security activities in their balanced scorecard measurements and project evaluations.

- **Set security requirements for vendors**: Include data security requirements in service level agreements and outsourcing contractual obligations. SLA agreements must include all data protection actions.

- **Build a sense of urgency**: Emphasize legal, contractual, and regulatory requirements to build a sense of urgency and an internal framework for data security management.

- **Ongoing communications**: Supporting a continual employee security-training program informing workers of safe computing practices and current threats. An ongoing program communicates that safe computing is important enough for management to support it.

5.2 Organization and Cultural Change

Organizations need to develop data policies that enable them to meet their goals while protecting sensitive and regulated information from misuse or unauthorized exposure. They must account for the interests of all stakeholders as they balance risks with ease of access. Often the technical architecture must accommodate the Data Architecture to balance these needs to create an effective and secure electronic environment. In most organizations, the behavior of both management and employees will need to change if they are to successfully protect their data.

In many larger companies, the existing information security group will have in place policies, safeguards, security tools, access control systems, and information protection devices and systems. There should be a clear understanding and appreciation where these elements complement the work done by the Data Stewards and data administrators. Data Stewards are generally responsible for data categorization. Information security teams assist with compliance enforcement and establish operational procedures based on data protection policies, and security and regulatory categorization.

Implementing data security measures without regard for the expectations of customers and employees can result in employee dissatisfaction, customer dissatisfaction, and organizational risk. To promote compliance, data security measures must account for the viewpoint of those who will be working with the data and systems. Well-planned and comprehensive technical security measures should make secure access easier for stakeholders.

5.3 Visibility into User Data Entitlement

Each user data entitlement, which is the sum total of all the data made available by a single authorization, must be reviewed during system implementation to determine if it contains any regulated information. Knowing who can see which data requires management of Metadata that describes the confidentiality and regulatory classifications of the data, as well as management of the entitlements and authorizations themselves. Classification of regulatory sensitivity should be a standard part of the data definition process.

5.4 Data Security in an Outsourced World

Anything can be outsourced except liability.

Outsourcing IT operations introduces additional data security challenges and responsibilities. Outsourcing increases the number of people who share accountability for data across organizational and geographic boundaries. Previously informal roles and responsibilities must be explicitly defined as contractual obligations. Outsourcing contracts must specify the responsibilities and expectations of each role.

Any form of outsourcing increases risk to the organization, including some loss of control over the technical environment and the people working with the organization's data. Data security measures and processes must look at the risk from the outsource vendor as both an external and internal risk.

The maturity of IT outsourcing has enabled organizations to re-look at outsourced services. A broad consensus has emerged that architecture and ownership of IT, which includes data security architecture, should be an in-sourced function. In other words, the internal organization owns and manages the enterprise and security architecture. The outsourced partner may take the responsibility for implementing the architecture.

Transferring control, but not accountability, requires tighter risk management and control mechanisms. Some of these mechanisms include:

- Service level agreements
- Limited liability provisions in the outsourcing contract
- Right-to-audit clauses in the contract
- Clearly defined consequences to breaching contractual obligations
- Frequent data security reports from the service vendor
- Independent monitoring of vendor system activity
- Frequent and thorough data security auditing
- Constant communication with the service vendor
- Awareness of legal differences in contract law should the vendor be located in another country and a dispute arises

In an outsourced environment, it is critical to track the lineage, or flow, of data across systems and individuals to maintain a 'chain of custody'. Outsourcing organizations especially benefit from developing CRUD (Create, Read, Update, and Delete) matrices that map data responsibilities across business processes, applications, roles, and organizations, tracing the transformation, lineage, and chain of custody for data. Additionally, the ability to execute business decisions or application functionality such as approving checks or orders, must be included as part of the matrix.

Responsible, Accountable, Consulted, and Informed (RACI) matrices also help clarify roles, the separation of duties, and responsibilities of different roles, including their data security obligations.

The RACI matrix can become part of the contractual agreements and data security policies. Defining responsibility matrices like RACI will establish clear accountability and ownership among the parties involved in the outsourcing engagement, leading to support of the overall data security policies and their implementation.

In outsourcing information technology operations, the accountability for maintaining data still lies with the organization. It is critical to have appropriate compliance mechanisms in place and have realistic expectations from parties entering into the outsourcing agreements.

5.5 Data Security in Cloud Environments

The rapid emergence of web computing and business-to-business and business-to-consumer interaction has caused the boundaries of data to extend beyond the four walls of the organization. The recent advances in cloud computing have extended the boundaries a step further. The 'as-a-service' nomenclature is now common across all stacks of technology and business. 'Data-as-a-Service', 'Software-as-a-Service', 'Platform-as-a-Service' are commonly used terms today. Cloud computing, or having resources distributed over the internet to process data and information, is complementing the 'X-as-a-Service' provisioning.

Data security policies need to account for the distribution of data across the different service models. This includes the need to leverage external data security standards.

Shared responsibility, defining chain of custody of data and defining ownership and custodianship rights, is especially important in cloud computing. Infrastructure considerations (e.g., Who is responsible for the firewall when the cloud provider delivers the software over the web? Who is accountable for access rights on the servers?) have direct impacts to data security management and data policies.

Fine-tuning or even creating a new data security management policy geared towards cloud computing is necessary for organizations of all sizes. Even if an organization has not directly implemented resources in the cloud, business partners may. In a connected world of data, having a business partner use cloud computing means putting the organization's data in the cloud. The same data proliferation security principles apply to sensitive/confidential production data.

Internal cloud data-center architecture, including virtual machines even though potentially more secure, should follow the same security policy as the rest of the enterprise.

6. Data Security Governance

Securing enterprise systems and the data they store requires cooperation between IT and business stakeholders. Strong, clear policies and procedures are at the foundation of security governance.

6.1 Data Security and Enterprise Architecture

Enterprise Architecture defines the information assets and components of an enterprise, their interrelationships, and business rules regarding transformation, principles, and guidelines. Data Security architecture is the component of enterprise architecture that describes how data security is implemented within the enterprise to satisfy the business rules and external regulations. Architecture influences:

- Tools used to manage data security
- Data encryption standards and mechanisms
- Access guidelines to external vendors and contractors
- Data transmission protocols over the internet
- Documentation requirements
- Remote access standards
- Security breach incident-reporting procedures

Security architecture is particularly important for the integration of data between:

- Internal systems and business units

- An organization and its external business partners
- An organization and regulatory agencies

For example, an architectural pattern of a service-oriented integration mechanism between internal and external parties would call for a data security implementation different from traditional electronic data interchange (EDI) integration architecture.

For a large enterprise, the formal liaison function between these disciplines is essential to protecting information from misuse, theft, exposure, and loss. Each party must be aware of elements that concern the others, so they can speak a common language and work toward shared goals.

7. Works Cited / Recommended

Andress, Jason. *The Basics of Information Security: Understanding the Fundamentals of InfoSec in Theory and Practice.* Syngress, 2011. Print.

Calder, Alan, and Steve Watkins. *IT Governance: An International Guide to Data Security and ISO27001/ISO27002.* 5th ed. Kogan Page, 2012. Print.

Fuster, Gloria González. *The Emergence of Personal Data Protection as a Fundamental Right of the EU.* Springer, 2014. Print. Law, Governance and Technology Series / Issues in Privacy and Data Protection.

Harkins, Malcolm. *Managing Risk and Information Security: Protect to Enable (Expert's Voice in Information Technology).* Apress, 2012. Kindle.

Hayden, Lance. *IT Security Metrics: A Practical Framework for Measuring Security and Protecting Data.* McGraw-Hill Osborne Media, 2010. Print.

Kark, Khalid. "Building A Business Case for Information Security". *Computer World.* 2009-08-10 http://bit.ly/2rCu7QQ Web.

Kennedy, Gwen, and Leighton Peter Prabhu. *Data Privacy: A Practical Guide.* Interstice Consulting LLP, 2014. Kindle. Amazon Digital Services.

Murdoch, Don GSE. *Blue Team Handbook: Incident Response Edition: A condensed field guide for the Cyber Security Incident Responder.* 2nd ed. CreateSpace Independent Publishing Platform, 2014. Print.

National Institute for Standards and Technology (US Department of Commerce website) http://bit.ly/1eQYolG.

Rao, Umesh Hodeghatta and Umesha Nayak. *The InfoSec Handbook: An Introduction to Information Security.* Apress, 2014. Kindle. Amazon Digital Services.

Ray, Dewey E. *The IT professional's merger and acquisition handbook.* Cognitive Diligence, 2012.

Schlesinger, David. *The Hidden Corporation: A Data Management Security Novel.* Technics Publications, LLC, 2011. Print.

Singer, P.W. and Allan Friedman. *Cybersecurity and Cyberwar: What Everyone Needs to Know®.* Oxford University Press, 2014. Print. What Everyone Needs to Know.

Watts, John. *Certified Information Privacy Professional Study Guide: Pass the IAPP's Certification Foundation Exam with Ease!* CreateSpace Independent Publishing Platform, 2014. Print.

Williams, Branden R., Anton Chuvakin Ph.D. *PCI Compliance: Understand and Implement Effective PCI Data Security Standard Compliance.* 4th ed. Syngress, 2014. Print.

CHAPTER 8

Data Integration and Interoperability

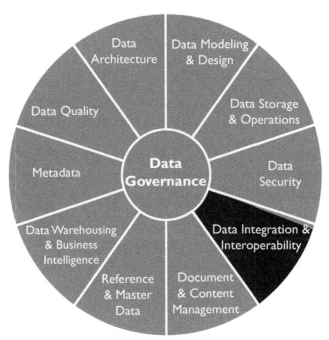

DAMA-DMBOK2 Data Management Framework

Copyright © 2017 by DAMA International

1. Introduction

Data Integration and Interoperability (DII) describes processes related to the movement and consolidation of data within and between data stores, applications and organizations. Integration consolidates data into consistent forms, either physical or virtual. Data Interoperability is the ability for multiple systems to communicate. DII solutions enable basic data management functions on which most organizations depend:

- Data migration and conversion
- Data consolidation into hubs or marts
- Integration of vendor packages into an organization's application portfolio
- Data sharing between applications and across organizations
- Distributing data across data stores and data centers
- Archiving data

- Managing data interfaces
- Obtaining and ingesting external data
- Integrating structured and unstructured data
- Providing operational intelligence and management decision support

DII is dependent on these other areas of data management:

- **Data Governance**: For governing the transformation rules and message structures
- **Data Architecture**: For designing solutions
- **Data Security**: For ensuring solutions appropriately protect the security of data, whether it is persistent, virtual, or in motion between applications and organizations
- **Metadata**: For tracking the technical inventory of data (persistent, virtual, and in motion), the business meaning of the data, the business rules for transforming the data, and the operational history and lineage of the data
- **Data Storage and Operations**: For managing the physical instantiation of the solutions
- **Data Modeling and Design**: For designing the data structures including physical persistence in databases, virtual data structures, and messages passing information between applications and organizations

Data Integration and Interoperability is critical to Data Warehousing and Business Intelligence, as well as Reference Data and Master Data Management, because all of these focus on transforming and integrating data from source systems to consolidated data hubs and from hubs to the target systems where it can be delivered to data consumers, both system and human.

Data Integration and Interoperability is central to the emerging area of Big Data management. Big Data seeks to integrate various types of data, including data structured and stored in databases, unstructured text data in documents or files, other types of unstructured data such as audio, video, and streaming data. This integrated data can be mined, used to develop predictive models, and deployed in operational intelligence activities.

1.1 Business Drivers

The need to manage data movement efficiently is a primary driver for DII. Since most organizations have hundreds or thousands of databases and stores, managing the processes for moving data between the data stores within the organization and to and from other organizations has become a central responsibility of every information technology organization. If not managed properly, the process of moving data can overwhelm IT resources and capabilities and dwarf the support requirements of traditional application and data management areas.

The advent of organizations purchasing applications from software vendors, rather than developing custom applications, has amplified the need for enterprise data integration and interoperability. Each purchased application comes with its own set of Master Data stores, transaction data stores, and reporting data stores that must integrate with the other data stores in the organization. Even Enterprise Resource Planning (ERP) systems that run the common functions of the organization, rarely, if ever, encompass all the data stores in the organization. They, too, have to have their data integrated with other organizational data.

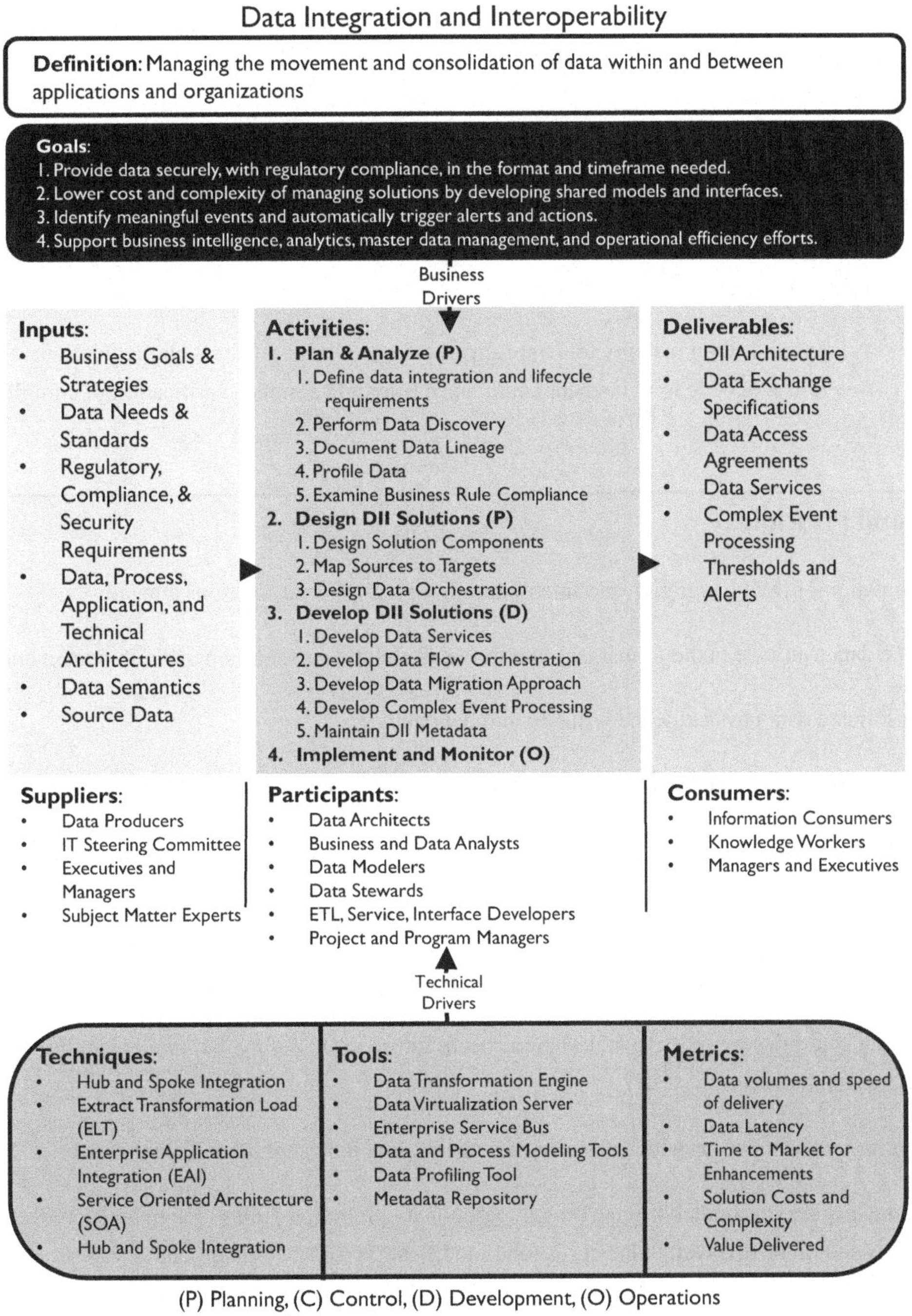

Data Integration and Interoperability

Definition: Managing the movement and consolidation of data within and between applications and organizations

Goals:
1. Provide data securely, with regulatory compliance, in the format and timeframe needed.
2. Lower cost and complexity of managing solutions by developing shared models and interfaces.
3. Identify meaningful events and automatically trigger alerts and actions.
4. Support business intelligence, analytics, master data management, and operational efficiency efforts.

Business Drivers

Inputs:
- Business Goals & Strategies
- Data Needs & Standards
- Regulatory, Compliance, & Security Requirements
- Data, Process, Application, and Technical Architectures
- Data Semantics
- Source Data

Activities:
1. **Plan & Analyze (P)**
   1. Define data integration and lifecycle requirements
   2. Perform Data Discovery
   3. Document Data Lineage
   4. Profile Data
   5. Examine Business Rule Compliance
2. **Design DII Solutions (P)**
   1. Design Solution Components
   2. Map Sources to Targets
   3. Design Data Orchestration
3. **Develop DII Solutions (D)**
   1. Develop Data Services
   2. Develop Data Flow Orchestration
   3. Develop Data Migration Approach
   4. Develop Complex Event Processing
   5. Maintain DII Metadata
4. **Implement and Monitor (O)**

Deliverables:
- DII Architecture
- Data Exchange Specifications
- Data Access Agreements
- Data Services
- Complex Event Processing Thresholds and Alerts

Suppliers:
- Data Producers
- IT Steering Committee
- Executives and Managers
- Subject Matter Experts

Participants:
- Data Architects
- Business and Data Analysts
- Data Modelers
- Data Stewards
- ETL, Service, Interface Developers
- Project and Program Managers

Consumers:
- Information Consumers
- Knowledge Workers
- Managers and Executives

Technical Drivers

Techniques:
- Hub and Spoke Integration
- Extract Transformation Load (ELT)
- Enterprise Application Integration (EAI)
- Service Oriented Architecture (SOA)
- Hub and Spoke Integration

Tools:
- Data Transformation Engine
- Data Virtualization Server
- Enterprise Service Bus
- Data and Process Modeling Tools
- Data Profiling Tool
- Metadata Repository

Metrics:
- Data volumes and speed of delivery
- Data Latency
- Time to Market for Enhancements
- Solution Costs and Complexity
- Value Delivered

(P) Planning, (C) Control, (D) Development, (O) Operations

Figure 66 Context Diagram: Data Integration and Interoperability

The need to manage complexity and the costs associated with complexity are reasons to architect data integration from an enterprise perspective. An enterprise design of data integration is demonstrably more efficient and cost effective than distributed or point-to-point solutions. Developing point-to-point solutions between applications can result in thousands to millions of interfaces and can quickly overwhelm the capabilities of even the most effective and efficient IT support organization.

Data hubs such as data warehouses and Master Data solutions help to alleviate this problem by consolidating the data needed by many applications and providing those applications with consistent views of the data. Similarly, the complexity of managing operational and transactional data that needs to be shared across the organization can be greatly simplified using enterprise data integration techniques such as hub-and-spoke integration and canonical message models.

Another business driver is managing the cost of support. Moving data using multiple technologies, each requiring specific development and maintenance skills, can drive support costs up. Standard tool implementations can reduce support and staffing costs and improve the efficiency of troubleshooting efforts. Reducing the complexity of interface management can lower the cost of interface maintenance, and allow support resources to be more effectively deployed on other organizational priorities.

DII also supports an organization's ability to comply with data handling standards and regulations. Enterprise-level DII systems enable re-use of code to implement compliance rules and simplify verification of compliance.

1.2 Goals and Principles

The implementation of Data Integration and Interoperability practices and solutions aims to:

* Make data available in the format and timeframe needed by data consumers, both human and system

* Consolidate data physically and virtually into data hubs

* Lower cost and complexity of managing solutions by developing shared models and interfaces

* Identify meaningful events (opportunities and threats) and automatically trigger alerts and actions

* Support Business Intelligence, analytics, Master Data Management, and operational efficiency efforts

When implementing DII, an organization should follow these principles:

* Take an enterprise perspective in design to ensure future extensibility, but implement through iterative and incremental delivery

* Balance local data needs with enterprise data needs, including support and maintenance.

* Ensure business accountability for Data Integration and Interoperability design and activity. Business experts should be involved in the design and modification of data transformation rules, both persistent and virtual.

1.3 Essential Concepts

1.3.1 Extract, Transform, and Load

Central to all areas in Data Integration and Interoperability is the basic process of Extract, Transform, and Load (ETL). Whether executed physically or virtually, in batch or real-time, these are the essential steps in moving data around and between applications and organizations.

Depending on data integration requirements, ETL can be performed as a periodically scheduled event (batch) or whenever new or updated data is available (real-time or event-driven). Operational data processing tends to be real-time or near real-time, while data needed for analysis or reporting is often scheduled in batch jobs.

Data integration requirements also determine whether the extracted and transformed data is physically stored in staging structures. Physical staging allows for an audit trail of steps that have occurred with the data and potential process restarts from an intermediate point. However, staging structures take up disk space and take time to write and read. Data integration needs that require very low latency will usually not include physical staging of the intermediate data integration results.

1.3.1.1 Extract

The extract process includes selecting the required data and extracting it from its source. Extracted data is then staged, in a physical data store on disk or in memory. If physically staged on disk, the staging data store may be co-located with the source data store or with the target data store, or both.

Ideally, if this process executes on an operational system, it is designed to use as few resources as possible, in order to avoid negatively affecting the operational processes. Batch processing during off-peak hours is an option for extracts that include complex processing to perform the selection or identify changed data to extract.

1.3.1.2 Transform

The transform process makes the selected data compatible with the structure of the target data store. Transformation includes cases where data is removed from the source when it moves to the target, where data is copied to multiple targets, and where the data is used to trigger events but is not persisted.

Examples of transformation may include

- **Format changes**: Conversion of the technical format of the data; for example, from EBCDIC to ASCII format

- **Structure changes**: Changes to the structure of the data; for example, from denormalized to normalized records

- **Semantic conversion**: Conversion of data values to maintain consistent semantic representation. For example, the source gender codes might include 0, 1, 2, and 3, while the target gender codes might be represented as UNKNOWN, FEMALE, MALE, or NOT PROVIDED.

- **De-duping**: Ensuring that if rules require unique key values or records, a means for scanning the target, and detecting and removing duplicate rows, is included

- **Re-ordering**: Changing the order of the data elements or records to fit a defined pattern

Transformation may be performed in batch or real-time, either physically storing the result in a staging area, or virtually storing the transformed data in memory until ready to move to the load step. Data resulting from the transformation stage should be ready to integrate with data in the target structure.

1.3.1.3 Load

The load step of ETL is physically storing or presenting the result of the transformations in the target system. Depending on the transformations performed, the target system's purpose, and the intended use, the data may need further processing to be integrated with other data, or it may be in a final form, ready to present to consumers.

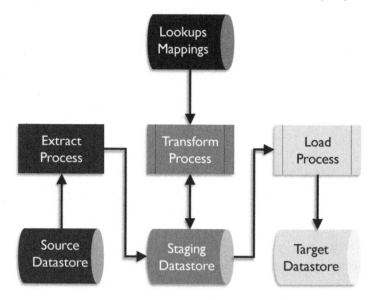

Figure 67 ETL Process Flow

1.3.1.4 ELT

If the target system has more transformation capability than either the source or an intermediary application system, the order of processes may be switched to ELT – Extract, Load, and Transform. ELT allows transformations to occur after the load to the target system, often as part of the process. ELT allows source data to be instantiated on the target system as raw data, which can be useful for other processes. This is common in Big Data environments where ELT loads the data lake. (See Chapter 14.)

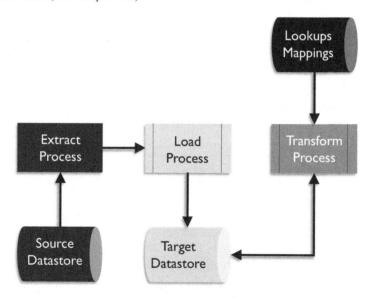

Figure 68 ELT Process Flow

1.3.1.5 Mapping

A synonym for transformation, a *mapping* is both the process of developing the lookup matrix from source to target structures and the result of that process. A mapping defines the sources to be extracted, the rules for identifying data for extraction, targets to be loaded, rules for identifying target rows for update (if any), and any transformation rules or calculations to be applied. Many data integration tools offer visualizations of mappings that enable developers to use graphical interfaces to create transformation code.

1.3.2 Latency

Latency is the time difference between when data is generated in the source system and when the data is available for use in the target system. Different approaches to data processing result in different degrees of data latency. Latency can be high (batch) or low (event-driven) to very low (real-time synchronous).

1.3.2.1 Batch

Most data moves between applications and organizations in clumps or files either on request by a human data consumer or automatically on a periodic schedule. This type of interaction is called *batch* or *ETL*.

Data moving in batch mode will represent either the full set of data at a given point in time, such as account balances at the end of a period, or data that has changed values since the last time the data was sent, such as address changes that have been made in a day. The set of changed data is called the *delta*, and the data from a point in time is called a *snapshot*.

With batch data integration solutions, there is often a significant delay between when data changes in the source and when it is updated in the target, resulting in high latency. Batch processing is very useful for processing very high volumes of data in a short time window. It tends to be used for data warehouse data integration solutions, even when lower latency solutions are available.

To achieve fast processing and lower latency, some data integration solutions use micro-batch processing which schedules batch processing to run on a much higher frequency than daily, such as every five minutes.

Batch data integration is used for data conversions, migrations, and archiving, as well as for extracting from and loading data warehouses and data marts. There are risks associated with the timing of batch processing. To minimize issues with application updates, schedule data movement between applications at the end of logical processing for the business day, or after special processing of the data has occurred at night. To avoid incomplete data sets, jobs moving data to a data warehouse should be scheduled based on the daily, weekly, or monthly reporting schedule.

1.3.2.2 Change Data Capture

Change Data Capture is a method of reducing bandwidth by filtering to include only data that has been changed within a defined timeframe. Change data capture monitors a data set for changes (inserts, changes, deletes) and then passes those changes (the deltas) to other data sets, applications, and organizations that consume the data. Data may also be tagged with identifiers such as flags or timestamps as part of the process. Change data capture may be data-based or log-based. (See Chapter 6.)

There are three techniques for data-based change data capture.

- The source system populates specific data elements, such as timestamps within a range, or codes or flags, which serve as change indicators. The extract process uses rules to identify rows to extract.

- The source system processes add to a simple list of objects and identifiers when changing data, which is then used to control selection of data for extraction.

- The source system processes copy data that has changed into a separate object as part of the transaction, which is then used for extract processing. This object does not need to be within the database management system.

These types of extraction use capabilities built into the source application, which may be resource intensive and require the ability to modify the source application.

In log-based change data captures, data activity logs created by the database management system are copied and processed, looking for specific changes that are then translated and applied to a target database. Complex translations may be difficult, but intermediary structures resembling the source object can be used as a way of staging the changes for further processing.

1.3.2.3 Near-real-time and Event-driven

Most data integration solutions that are not performed in batches use a near-real-time or event-driven solution. Data is processed in smaller sets spread across the day in a defined schedule, or data is processed when an event happens, such as a data update. Near-real-time processing has a lower latency than batch processing and often a lower system load as the work is distributed over time, but it is usually slower than a synchronized data integration solution. Near-real-time data integration solutions are usually implemented using an enterprise service bus.

State information and process dependencies must be monitored by the target application load process. Data coming into the target may not be available in the exact order that the target needs to build the correct target data. For example, process Master Data or dimensional data prior to transactional data that uses that Master Data.

1.3.2.4 Asynchronous

In an asynchronous data flow, the system providing data does not wait for the receiving system to acknowledge update before continuing processing. Asynchronous implies that either the sending or receiving system could be off-line for some period without the other system also being off-line.

Asynchronous data integration does not prevent the source application from continuing its processing, or cause the source application to be unavailable if any of the target applications are unavailable. Since the data updates made to applications in an asynchronous configuration are not immediate, the integration is called *near-real-time*. The delay between updates made in the source and relayed to target data sets in a near-real-time environment is usually measured in seconds or minutes.

1.3.2.5 Real-time, Synchronous

There are situations where no time delay or other differences between source and target data is acceptable. When data in one data set must be kept perfectly in synch with the data in another data set, then a real-time, synchronous solution must be used.

In a synchronous integration solution, an executing process waits to receive confirmation from other applications or processes prior to executing its next activity or transaction. This means that the solution can process fewer transactions because it has to spend time waiting for confirmation of data synchronization. If any of the applications that need the update are not available then the transaction cannot be completed in the primary application. This situation keeps data synchronized but has the potential to make strategic applications dependent on less critical applications.

Solutions using this type of architecture exist on a continuum based on how much difference between data sets might be possible and how much such a solution is worth. Data sets may be kept in synch through database capabilities such as two-phase commits, which ensure that all updates in a business transaction are all successful, or none is made. For example, financial institutions use two-phase commit solutions to ensure that financial transaction tables are absolutely synchronized with financial balance tables. Most programming does not use two-phase commit. There is a very small possibility that if an application is interrupted unexpectedly then one data set may be updated but not another.

Real-time, synchronous solutions require less state management than asynchronous solutions because the order in which transactions are processed is clearly managed by the updating applications. However, they also may lead to blocking and delay other transactions.

1.3.2.6 Low Latency or Streaming

Tremendous advances have been made in developing extremely fast data integration solutions. These solutions require a large investment in hardware and software. The extra costs of low latency solutions are justified if an organization requires extremely fast data movement across large distances. 'Streaming data' flows from computer systems on a real-time continuous basis immediately as events occur. Data streams capture events like the purchase of goods or financial securities, social media comments, and readouts from sensors monitoring location, temperature, usage, or other values.

Low latency data integration solutions are designed to minimize the response time to events. They may include the use of hardware solutions like solid-state disk or software solutions like in-memory databases so that the process does not have to slow down to read or write to traditional disk. The read and write processes to traditional disk drives is thousands of times slower than processing data in-memory or on solid-state disk drives.

Asynchronous solutions are usually used in low latency solutions so that transactions do not need to wait for confirmation from subsequent processes before processing the next piece of data.

Massive multi-processing, or simultaneous processing, is also a common configuration in low latency solutions so that the processing of incoming data can be spread out over many processors simultaneously, and not bottlenecked by a single or small number of processors.

1.3.3 Replication

To provide better response time for users located around the world, some applications maintain exact copies of data sets in multiple physical locations. Replication solutions minimize the performance impact of analytics and queries on the primary transactional operating environment.

Such a solution must synchronize the physically distributed data set copies. Most database management systems have replication utilities to do this work. These utilities work best when the data sets are all maintained in the same database management system technology. Replication solutions usually monitor the log of changes to the data set, not the data set itself. They minimize the impact on any operational applications because they do not compete with the applications for access to the data set. Only data from the change log passes between replicated copies. Standard replication solutions are near-real-time; there is a small delay between a change in one copy of the data set and another.

Because the benefits of replication solutions — minimal effect on the source data set and minimal amount of data being passed — are very desirable, replication is used in many data integration solutions, even those that do not include long distance physical distribution. The database management utilities do not require extensive programming, so there tend to be few programming bugs.

Replication utilities work optimally when source and target data sets are exact copies of each other. Differences between source and target introduce risks to synchronization. If the ultimate target is not an exact copy of the source then it is necessary to maintain a staging area to house an exact copy of the sources. This requires extra disk usage and possibly extra database technology.

Data replication solutions are not optimal if changes to the data may occur at multiple copy sites. If it is possible that the same piece of data is changed at two different sites, then there is a risk that the data might get unsynchronized, or one of the sites may have their changes overwritten without warning. (See Chapter 6.)

1.3.4 Archiving

Data that is used infrequently or not actively used may be moved to an alternate data structure or storage solution that is less costly to the organization. ETL functions can be used to transport and possibly transform the archive data to the data structures in the archive environment. Use archives to store data from applications that are being retired, as well as data from production operational systems that have not been used for a long time, to improve operational efficiency.

It is critical to monitor archive technology to ensure that the data is still accessible when technology changes. Having an archive in an older structure or format unreadable by newer technology can be a risk, especially for data that is still legally required. (See Chapter 9.)

1.3.5 Enterprise Message Format / Canonical Model

A canonical data model is a common model used by an organization or data exchange group that standardizes the format in which data will be shared. In a hub-and-spoke data interaction design pattern, all systems that want to provide or receive data interact only with a central information hub. Data is transformed from or to a sending or receiving system based on a common or enterprise message format for the organization (a canonical model). (See Chapter 5.) Use of a canonical model limits the number of data transformations needed by any system or organization exchanging data. Each system needs to transform data only to and from the central canonical model, rather than to the format of the multitude of systems with which it may want to exchange data.

Although developing and agreeing on a shared message format is a major undertaking, having a canonical model can significantly reduce the complexity of data interoperability in an enterprise, and thus greatly lower the cost of support. The creation and management of the common canonical data model for all data interactions is a complex item of overhead that is required in the implementation of an enterprise data integration solution using a hub-and-spoke interaction model. It is justifiable in support of managing the data interactions between more than three systems and critical for managing data interactions in environments of more than 100 application systems.

1.3.6 Interaction Models

Interaction models describe ways to make connections between systems in order to transfer data.

1.3.6.1 Point-to-point

The vast majority of interactions between systems that share data do so 'point-to-point'; they pass data directly to each other. This model makes sense in the context of a small set of systems. However, it becomes quickly inefficient and increases organizational risk when many systems require the same data from the same sources.

- **Impacts to processing**: If source systems are operational, then the workload from supplying data could affect processing.

- **Managing interfaces**: The number of interfaces needed in a point-to-point interaction model approaches the number of systems squared (s^2). Once they are built, these interfaces need to be maintained and supported. The workload to manage and support interfaces between the systems can quickly become greater than supporting the systems themselves.

- **Potential for inconsistency**: Design issues arise when multiple systems require different versions or formats of the data. The use of multiple interfaces to obtain data will lead to inconsistencies in the data sent to downstream systems.

1.3.6.2 Hub-and-spoke

The hub-and-spoke model, an alternative to point-to-point, consolidates shared data (either physically or virtually) in a central data hub that many applications can use. All systems that want to exchange data do so through a central common data control system, rather than directly with one another (point-to-point). Data Warehouses, Data Marts, Operational Data Stores, and Master Data Management hubs are the most well-known examples of data hubs.

The hubs provide consistent views of the data with limited performance impact on the source systems. Data hubs even minimize the number of systems and extracts that must access the data sources, thus minimizing the impact on the source system resources. Adding new systems to the portfolio only requires building interfaces to the data hub. Hub-and-spoke interaction is more efficient and can be cost-justified even if the number of systems involved is relatively small, but it becomes critical to managing a portfolio of systems in the hundreds or thousands.

Enterprise Service Buses (ESB) are the data integration solution for near real-time sharing of data between many systems, where the hub is a virtual concept of the standard format or the canonical model for sharing data in the organization.

Hub-and-spoke may not always be the best solution. Some hub-and-spoke model latency is unacceptable or performance is insufficient. The hub itself creates overhead in a hub-and-spoke architecture. A point-to-point solution would not require the hub. However, the benefits of the hub outweigh the drawbacks of the overhead as soon as three or more systems are involved in sharing data. Use of the hub-and-spoke design pattern for the interchange of data can drastically reduce the proliferation of data transformation and integration solutions and thus dramatically simplify the necessary organizational support.

1.3.6.3 Publish - Subscribe

A publish and subscribe model involves systems pushing data out (publish), and other systems pulling data in (subscribe). Systems providing data are listed in a catalog of data services, and systems looking to consume data subscribe to those services. When data is published, the data is automatically sent to the subscribers.

When multiple data consumers want a certain set of data or data in a certain format, developing that data set centrally and making it available to all who need it ensures that all constituents receive a consistent data set in a timely manner.

1.3.7 DII Architecture Concepts

1.3.7.1 Application Coupling

Coupling describes the degree to which two systems are entwined. Two systems that are tightly coupled usually have a synchronous interface, where one system waits for a response from the other. Tight coupling represents a riskier operation: if one system is unavailable then they are both effectively unavailable, and the business continuity plan for both have to be the same. (See Chapter 6.)

Where possible, loose coupling is a preferred interface design, where data is passed between systems without waiting for a response and one system may be unavailable without causing the other to be unavailable. Loose coupling can be implemented using various techniques with services, APIs, or message queues. Figure 69 illustrates a possible loose coupling design.

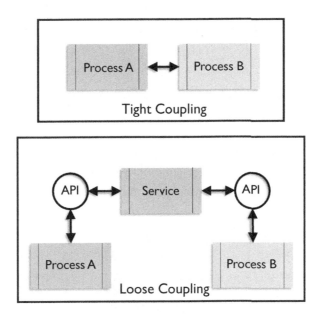

Figure 69 Application Coupling

Service Oriented Architecture using an Enterprise Service Bus is an example of a loosely coupled data interaction design pattern.

Where the systems are loosely coupled, replacement of systems in the application inventory can theoretically be performed without rewriting the systems with which they interact, because the interaction points are well-defined.

1.3.7.2 Orchestration and Process Controls

Orchestration is the term used to describe how multiple processes are organized and executed in a system. All systems handling messages or data packets must be able to manage the order of execution of those processes, in order to preserve consistency and continuity.

Process Controls are the components that ensure shipment, delivery, extraction, and loading of data is accurate and complete. An often-overlooked aspect of basic data movement architecture, controls include:

- Database activity logs
- Batch job logs
- Alerts
- Exception logs
- Job dependence charts with remediation options, standard responses
- Job 'clock' information, such as the timing of dependent jobs, the expected length of the jobs, and the computing (available) window time

1.3.7.3 Enterprise Application Integration (EAI)

In an enterprise application integration model (EAI), software modules interact with one another only through well-defined interface calls (application programming interfaces – APIs). Data stores are updated only by their own software modules and other software cannot reach in to the data in an application but only access through the defined APIs. EAI is built on object-oriented concepts, which emphasize reuse and the ability to replace any module without impact on any other.

1.3.7.4 Enterprise Service Bus (ESB)

An Enterprise Service Bus is a system that acts as an intermediary between systems, passing messages between them. Applications can send and receive messages or files using the ESB, and are encapsulated from other processes existing on the ESB. An example of loose coupling, the ESB acts as the service between the applications. (See Figure 70.)

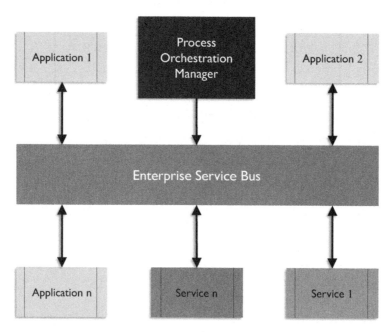

Figure 70 Enterprise Service Bus

1.3.7.5 Service-Oriented Architecture (SOA)

Most mature enterprise data integration strategies utilize the idea of service-oriented architecture (SOA), where the functionality of providing data or updating data (or other data services) can be provided through well-defined service calls between applications. With this approach, applications do not have to have direct interaction with or knowledge of the inner workings of other applications. SOA enables application independence and the ability for an organization to replace systems without needing to make significant changes to the systems that interfaced with them.

The goal of service-oriented architecture is to have well-defined interaction between self-contained software modules. Each module performs functions (a.k.a. provides services) to other software modules or to human consumers. The key concept is that SOA architecture provides independent services: the service has no fore knowledge of the calling application and the implementation of the service is a black box to the calling application. A service-oriented architecture may be implemented with various technologies including web services, messaging, RESTful APIs, etc. Services are usually implemented as APIs (application programming interfaces) that are available to be called by application systems (or human consumers). A well-defined API registry describes what options are available, parameters that need to be provided, and resulting information that is provided.

Data services, which may include the addition, deletion, update, and retrieval of data, are specified in a catalog of available services. To achieve the enterprise goals of scalability (supporting integrations between all applications in the enterprise without using unreasonable amounts of resources to do so) and reuse (having services that are leveraged by all requestors of data of a type), a strong governance model must be established around the design and registration of services and APIs. Prior to developing new data services, it is necessary to ensure that no service already exists that could provide the requested data. In addition, new services need to be designed to meet broad requirements so that they will not be limited to the immediate need but can be reused.

1.3.7.6 Complex Event Processing (CEP)

Event processing is a method of tracking and analyzing (processing) streams of information (data) about things that happen (events), and deriving a conclusion from them. Complex event processing (CEP) combines data from multiple sources to identify meaningful events (such as opportunities or threats) to predict behavior or activity and automatically trigger real-time response, such as suggesting a product for a consumer to purchase. Rules are set to guide the event processing and routing.

Organizations can use complex event processing to predict behavior or activity and automatically trigger real-time response. Events such as sales leads, web clicks, orders, or customer service calls may happen across the various layers of an organization. Alternatively, they may include news items, text messages, social media posts, stock market feeds, traffic reports, weather reports, or other kinds of data. An event may also be defined as a change of state, when a measurement exceeds a predefined threshold of time, temperature, or other value.

CEP presents some data challenges. In many cases, the rate at which events occur makes it impractical to retrieve the additional data necessary to interpret the event as it occurs. Efficient processing typically mandates pre-positioning some data in the CEP engine's memory.

Supporting complex event processing requires an environment that can integrate vast amounts of data of various types. Because of the volume and variety of data usually involved in creating predictions, complex event processing is often tied to Big Data. It often requires use of technologies that support ultra-low latency requirements such as processing real-time streaming data and in-memory databases. (See Chapter 14.)

1.3.7.7 Data Federation and Virtualization

When data exists in disparate data stores, it can be brought together in ways other than physical integration. Data Federation provides access to a combination of individual data stores, regardless of structure. Data Virtualization enables distributed databases, as well as multiple heterogeneous data stores, to be accessed and viewed as a single database. (See Chapter 6.)

1.3.7.8 Data-as-a-Service (DaaS)

Software-as-a-service (SaaS) is a delivery and licensing model. An application is licensed to provide services, but the software and data are located at a data center controlled by the software vendor, rather than in the data center of the licensing organization. There are similar concepts for providing various tiers of computing infrastructure-as-a-service (IT-as-a-service, platform-as-a-service, database-as-a-service).

One definition of Data-as-a-Service (DaaS) is data licensed from a vendor and provided on demand, rather than stored and maintained in the data center of the licensing organization. A common example includes information on the securities sold through a stock exchange and associated prices (current and historical).

Although Data-as-a-Service certainly lends itself to vendors that sell data to stakeholders within an industry, the 'service' concept is also used within an organization to provide enterprise data or data services to various functions and operational systems. Service organizations provide a catalog of services available, service levels, and pricing schedules.

1.3.7.9 Cloud-based Integration

Cloud-based integration (also known as integration platform-as-a-service or IPaaS) is a form of systems integration delivered as a cloud service that addresses data, process, service oriented architecture (SOA), and application integration use cases.

Prior to the emergence of cloud computing, integration could be categorized as either internal or business to business (B2B). Internal integration requirements are serviced through an on-premises middleware platform, and typically use a service bus (ESB) to manage exchange of data between systems. Business-to-business integration is serviced through EDI (electronic data interchange) gateways or value-added networks (VAN) or market places.

The advent of SaaS applications created a new kind of demand for integrating data located outside of an organization's data center, met through cloud-based integration. Since their emergence, many such services have also developed the capability to integrate on-premises applications as well as function as EDI gateways.

Cloud-based integration solutions are usually run as SaaS applications in the data centers of the vendors and not the organizations that own the data being integrated. Cloud-based integration involves interacting with the SaaS application data to be integrated using SOA interaction services. (See Chapter 6.)

1.3.8 Data Exchange Standards

Data Exchange Standards are formal rules for the structure of data elements. ISO (International Standards Organization) has developed data exchange standards, as have many industries. A data exchange specification is a common model used by an organization or data exchange group that standardizes the format in which data will be shared. An exchange pattern defines a structure for data transformations needed by any system or organization exchanging data. Data needs to be mapped to the exchange specification.

Although developing and agreeing on a shared message format is a major undertaking, having an agreed upon exchange format or data layout between systems can significantly simplify data interoperability in an enterprise, lowering the cost of support and enabling better understanding of the data.

The National Information Exchange Model (NIEM) was developed to exchange documents and transactions across government organizations in the United States. The intention is that the sender and receiver of information share a common, unambiguous understanding of the meaning of that information. Conformance to NIEM ensures that a basic set of information is well understood and carries the same consistent meaning across various communities, thus allowing interoperability.

NIEM uses Extensible Markup Language (XML) for schema definitions and element representation, which allows the structure and meaning of data to be defined through simple, but carefully defined XML syntax rules.

2. Data Integration Activities

Data Integration and Interoperability involves getting data where it is needed, when it is needed, and in the form in which it is needed. Data integration activities follow a development lifecycle. They begin with planning and move through design, development, testing, and implementation. Once implemented, integrated systems must be managed, monitored and enhanced.

2.1 Plan and Analyze

2.1.1 Define Data Integration and Lifecycle Requirements

Defining data integration requirements involves understanding the organization's business objectives, as well as the data required and the technology initiatives proposed to meet those objectives. It is also necessary to gather any relevant laws or regulations regarding the data to be used. Some activities may need to be restricted due to the data contents, and knowing up front will prevent issues later. Requirements must also account for organizational policy on data retention and other parts of the data lifecycle. Often requirements for data retention will differ by data domain and type.

Data integration and lifecycle requirements are usually defined by business analysts, data stewards, and architects in various functions, including IT, who have a desire to get data in a certain place, in a certain format, and integrated with other data. The requirements will determine the type of DII interaction model, which then determines the technology and services necessary to fulfill the requirements.

The process of defining requirements creates and uncovers valuable Metadata. This Metadata should be managed throughout the data lifecycle, from discovery through operations. The more complete and accurate an organization's Metadata, the better its ability to manage the risks and costs of data integration.

2.1.2 Perform Data Discovery

Data discovery should be performed prior to design. The goal of data discovery is to identify potential sources of data for the data integration effort. Discovery will identify where data might be acquired and where it might be integrated. The process combines a technical search, using tools that scan the Metadata and/or actual contents on an organization's data sets, with subject matter expertise (i.e., interviewing people who work with the data of interest).

Discovery also includes high-level assessment of data quality, to determine whether the data is fit for the purposes of the integration initiative. This assessment requires not only reviewing existing documentation, interviewing subject matter experts, but also verifying information gathered against the actual data through data profiling or other analysis. (See Section 2.1.4.) In almost all cases, there will be discrepancies between what is believed about a data set and what is actually found to be true.

Data discovery produces or adds to an inventory of organizational data. This inventory should be maintained in a Metadata repository. Ensure this inventory is maintained as a standard part of integration efforts: add or remove data stores, document structure changes.

Most organizations have a need to integrate data from their internal systems. However, data integration solutions may also involve the acquisition of data from outside the organization. There is a vast and ever growing amount of valuable information available for free, or from data vendors. Data from external sources can be extremely valuable when integrated with data from within an organization. However, acquiring and integrating external data takes planning.

2.1.3 Document Data Lineage

The process of data discovery will also uncover information about how data flows through an organization. This information can be used to document high-level data lineage: how the data under analysis is acquired or created by the organization, where it moves and is changed within the organization, and how the data is used by the organization for analytics, decision-making, or event triggering. Detailed lineage can include the rules according to which data is changed, and the frequency of changes.

Analysis of lineage may identify updates required to documentation of systems in use. Custom-coded ETL and other legacy data manipulation objects should be documented to ensure that the organization can analyze the impact of any changes in the data flow.

The analysis process may also identify opportunities for improvements in the existing data flow. For example, finding that code can be upgraded to a simple call to a function in a tool, or can be discarded as no longer relevant. Sometimes an old tool is performing a transformation that is undone later in the process. Finding and removing these inefficiencies can greatly help with the project's success and with an organization's overall ability to use its data.

2.1.4 Profile Data

Understanding data content and structure is essential to successful integration of data. Data profiling contributes to this end. Actual data structure and contents always differ from what is assumed. Sometimes differences are small;

other times they are large enough to derail an integration effort. Profiling can help integration teams discover these differences and use that knowledge to make better decisions about sourcing and design. If data profiling is skipped, then information that should influence design will not be discovered until testing or operations.

Basic profiling involves analysis of:

- Data format as defined in the data structures and inferred from the actual data
- Data population, including the levels of null, blank, or defaulted data
- Data values and how closely they correspond to a defined set of valid values
- Patterns and relationships internal to the data set, such as related fields and cardinality rules
- Relationships to other data sets

More extensive profiling of the potential source and target data sets is required to understand how well the data meets the requirements of the particular data integration initiative. Profile both the sources and targets to understand how to transform the data to match requirements.

One goal of profiling is to assess the quality of data. Assessing the fitness of the data for a particular use requires documenting business rules and measuring how well the data meets those business rules. Assessing accuracy requires comparing to a definitive set of data that has been determined to be correct. Such data sets are not always available, so measuring accuracy may not be possible, especially as part of a profiling effort.

As with high-level data discovery, data profiling includes verifying assumptions about the data against the actual data. Capture results of data profiling in a Metadata repository for use on later projects and use what is learned from the process to improve the accuracy of existing Metadata (Olson, 2003). (See Chapter 13.)

The requirement to profile data must be balanced with an organization's security and privacy regulations. (See Chapter 7.)

2.1.5 Collect Business Rules

Business rules are a critical subset of requirements. A business rule is a statement that defines or constrains an aspect of business processing. Business rules are intended to assert business structure or to control or influence the behavior of the business. Business rules fall into one of four categories: definitions of business terms, facts relating terms to each other, constraints or action assertions, and derivations.

Use business rules to support Data Integration and Interoperability at various points, to:

- Assess data in potential source and target data sets
- Direct the flow of data in the organization
- Monitor the organization's operational data
- Direct when to automatically trigger events and alerts

For Master Data Management, business rules include match rules, merge rules, survivorship rules, and trust rules. For data archiving, data warehousing, and other situations where a data store is in use, the business rules also include data retention rules.

Gathering business rules is also called rules harvesting or business rule mining. The business analyst or data steward can extract the rules from existing documentation (like use cases, specifications, or system code), or they may also organize workshops and interviews with subject matter experts (SMEs), or both.

2.2 Design Data Integration Solutions

2.2.1 Design Data Integration Architecture

Data integration solutions should be specified at both the enterprise level and the individual solution level (see Chapter 4). By establishing enterprise standards, the organization saves time in implementing individual solutions, because assessments and negotiations have been performed in advance of need. An enterprise approach saves money in the cost of licenses through group discounts and in the costs of operating a consistent and less complex set of solutions. Operational resources that support and back up one another can be part of a shared pool.

Design a solution to meet the requirements, reusing as many of the existing Data Integration and Interoperability components as is feasible. A solution architecture indicates the techniques and technologies that will be used. It will include an inventory of the involved data structures (both persistent and transitive, existing and required), an indication of the orchestration and frequency of data flow, regulatory and security concerns and remediation, and operating concerns around backup and recovery, availability, and data archive and retention.

2.2.1.1 Select Interaction Model

Determine which interaction model or combination will fulfill the requirements – hub-and-spoke, point-to-point, or publish-subscribe. If the requirements match an existing interaction pattern already implemented, re-use the existing system as much as possible, to reduce development efforts.

2.2.1.2 Design Data Services or Exchange Patterns

Create or re-use existing integration flows to move the data. These data services should be companions to existing similar data services, but be careful to not create multiple almost-identical services, as troubleshooting and support increasingly become difficult if services proliferate. If an existing data flow can be modified to support multiple needs, it may be worthwhile to make that change instead of creating a new service.

Any data exchange specification design should start with industry standards, or other exchange patterns already existing. When possible, make any changes to existing patterns generic enough to be useful to other systems; having specific exchange patterns that only relate to one exchange has the same issues as point-to-point connections.

2.2.2 Model Data Hubs, Interfaces, Messages, and Data Services

Data structures needed in Data Integration and Interoperability include those in which data persists, such as Master Data Management hubs, data warehouses and marts, and operational data stores, and those that are transient and used only for moving or transforming data, such as interfaces, message layouts, and canonical models. Both types should be modeled. (See Chapter 5.)

2.2.3 Map Data Sources to Targets

Almost all data integration solutions include transforming data from source to target structures. Mapping sources to targets involves specifying the rules for transforming data from one location and format to another.

For each attribute mapped, a mapping specification

- Indicates the technical format of the source and target
- Specifies transformations required for all intermediate staging points between source and target
- Describes how each attribute in a final or intermediate target data store will be populated
- Describes whether data values need to be transformed; for example, by looking up the source value in a table that indicates the appropriate target value
- Describes what calculations are required

Transformation may be performed on a batch schedule, or triggered by the occurrence of a real-time event. It may be accomplished through physical persistence of the target format or through virtual presentation of the data in the target format.

2.2.4 Design Data Orchestration

The flow of data in a data integration solution must be designed and documented. Data orchestration is the pattern of data flows from start to finish, including intermediate steps, required to complete the transformation and/or transaction.

Batch data integration orchestration will indicate the frequency of the data movement and transformation. Batch data integration is usually coded into a scheduler that triggers the start at a certain time, periodicity, or when an event occurs. The schedule may include multiple steps with dependencies.

Real-time data integration orchestration is usually triggered by an event, such as new or updated data. Real-time data integration orchestration is usually more complex and implemented across multiple tools. It may not be linear in nature.

2.3 Develop Data Integration Solutions

2.3.1 Develop Data Services

Develop services to access, transform, and deliver data as specified, matching the interaction model selected. Tools or vendor suites are most frequently used to implement data integration solutions, such as data transformation, Master Data Management, data warehousing, etc. Using consistent tools or standard vendor suites across the organization for these various purposes can simplify operational support and lower operating costs by enabling shared support solutions.

2.3.2 Develop Data Flows

Integration or ETL data flows will usually be developed within tools specialized to manage those flows in a proprietary way. Batch data flows will be developed in a scheduler (usually the enterprise standard scheduler) that will manage the order, frequency, and dependency of executing the data integration pieces that have been developed.

Interoperability requirements may include developing mappings or coordination points between data stores. Some organizations use an ESB to subscribe to data that is created or changed in the organization and other applications to publish changes to data. The enterprise service bus will poll the applications constantly to see if they have any data to publish and deliver to them new or changed data for which they have subscribed.

Developing real-time data integration flows involves monitoring for events that should trigger the execution of services to acquire, transform, or publish data. This is usually implemented within one or multiple proprietary technologies and is best implemented with a solution that can manage the operation across technologies.

2.3.3 Develop Data Migration Approach

Data needs to be moved when new applications are implemented or when applications are retired or merged. This process involves transformation of data to the format of the receiving application. Almost all application development projects involve some data migration, even if all that is involved is the population of Reference Data. Migration is not quite a one-time process, as it needs to be executed for testing phases as well as final implementation.

Data migration projects are frequently under-estimated or under-designed, because programmers are told to simply move the data; they do not engage in the analysis and design activities required for data integration. When data is migrated without proper analysis, it often looks different from the data that came in through the normal processing. Or the migrated data may not work with the application as anticipated. Profiling data of core operational applications will usually highlight data that has been migrated from one or more generations of previous operational systems and does not meet the standards of the data that enters the data set through the current application code. (See Chapter 6.)

2.3.4 Develop a Publication Approach

Systems where critical data is created or maintained need to make that data available to other systems in the organization. New or changed data should be pushed by data producing applications to other systems (especially data hubs and enterprise data buses) either at the time of data change (event-driven) or on a periodic schedule.

Best practice is to define common message definitions (canonical model) for the various types of data in the organization and let data consumers (either applications or individuals) who have appropriate access authority subscribe to receive notification of any changes to data of interest.

2.3.5 Develop Complex Event Processing Flows

Developing complex event processing solutions requires:

- Preparation of the historical data about an individual, organization, product, or market and pre-population of the predictive models
- Processing the real-time data stream to fully populate the predictive model and identify meaningful events (opportunities or threats)
- Executing the triggered action in response to the prediction

Preparation and pre-processing of the historical data needed in the predictive model may be performed in nightly batch processes or in near real-time. Usually some of the predictive model can be populated in advance of the triggering event, such as identifying what products are usually bought together in preparation of suggesting an additional item for purchase.

Some processing flows trigger a response to every event in the real-time stream, such as adding an item to a shopping cart; other processing flows attempt to identify particularly meaningful events that trigger action, such as a suspected fraudulent charge attempt on a credit card.

The response to the identification of a meaningful event may be as simple as a warning being sent out or as complex as the automatic deployment of armed forces.

2.3.6 Maintain DII Metadata

As previously noted (see Section 2.1), an organization will create and uncover valuable Metadata during the process of developing DII solutions. This Metadata should be managed and maintained to ensure proper understanding of the data in the system, and to prevent the need to rediscover it for future solutions. Reliable Metadata improves an organization's ability to manage risks, reduce costs, and obtain more value from its data.

Document the data structures of all systems involved in data integration as source, target, or staging. Include business definitions and technical definitions (structure, format, size), as well as the transformation of data between the persistent data stores. Whether data integration Metadata is stored in documents or a Metadata repository, it should not be changed without a review and approval process from both business and technical stakeholders.

Most ETL tool vendors package their Metadata repositories with additional functionality that enables governance and stewardship oversight. If the Metadata repository is utilized as an operational tool, then it may even include operational Metadata about when data was copied and transformed between systems.

Of particular importance for DII solutions is the SOA registry, which provides controlled access to an evolving catalog of information about the available services for accessing and using the data and functionality in an application.

2.4 Implement and Monitor

Activate the data services that have been developed and tested. Real-time data processing requires real-time monitoring for issues. Establish parameters that indicate potential problems with processing, as well as direct notification of issues. Automated as well as human monitoring for issues should be established, especially as the complexity and risk of the triggered responses rises. There are cases, for example, where issues with automated financial securities trading algorithms have triggered actions that have affected entire markets or bankrupted organizations.

Data interaction capabilities must be monitored and serviced at the same service level as the most demanding target application or data consumer.

3. Tools

3.1 Data Transformation Engine/ETL Tool

A data transformation engine (or ETL tool) is the primary tool in the data integration toolbox, central to every enterprise data integration program. These tools usually support the operation as well as the design of the data transformation activities.

Extremely sophisticated tools exist to develop and perform ETL, whether batch or real-time, physically or virtually. For single use point-to-point solutions, data integration processing is frequently implemented through custom coding. Enterprise level solutions usually require the use of tools to perform this processing in a standard way across the organization.

Basic considerations in selecting a data transformation engine should include whether it is necessary to handle batch as well as real-time functionality, and whether unstructured as well as structured data needs to be accommodated, as the most mature tools exist for batch-oriented processing of structured data only.

3.2 Data Virtualization Server

Data transformation engines usually perform extract, transform, and load physically on data; however, data virtualization servers perform data extract, transform, and integrate virtually. Data virtualization servers can combine structured and unstructured data. A data warehouse is frequently an input to a data virtualization server, but a data virtualization server does not replace the data warehouse in the enterprise information architecture.

3.3 Enterprise Service Bus

An enterprise service bus (ESB) refers to both a software architecture model and a type of message-oriented middleware used to implement near real-time messaging between heterogeneous data stores, applications, and servers that reside within the same organization. Most internal data integration solutions that need to execute more frequent than daily use this architecture and this technology. Most commonly, an ESB is used in asynchronous format to enable the free flow of data. An ESB can also be used synchronously in certain situations.

The enterprise service bus implements incoming and outgoing message queues on each of the systems participating in message interchange with an adapter or agent installed in each environment. The central processor for the ESB is usually implemented on a server separate from the other participating systems. The processor keeps track of which systems have subscribed interest in what kinds of messages. The central processor continuously polls each participating system for outgoing messages and deposits incoming messages into the message queue for subscribed types of messages and messages that have been directly addressed to that system.

This model is called 'near real-time' because the data can take up to a couple of minutes to get from sending system to receiving system. This is a loosely coupled model and the system sending data will not wait for confirmation of receipt and update from the receiving system before continuing processing.

3.4 Business Rules Engine

Many data integration solutions are dependent on business rules. An important form of Metadata, these rules can be used in basic integration and in solutions that incorporate complex event processing to enable an organization to respond to events in near real-time. A business rules engine that allows non-technical users to manage business rules implemented by software is a very valuable tool that will enable evolution of the solution at a lower cost, because a business rules engine can support changes to predictive models without technical code changes. For example, models that predict what a customer might want to purchase may be defined as business rules rather than code changes.

3.5 Data and Process Modeling Tools

Data modeling tools should be used to design not only the target but also the intermediate data structures needed in data integration solutions. The structure of the messages or streams of data that pass between systems and organizations, and are not usually persisted, should nevertheless be modeled. The flow of data between systems and organizations should also be designed, as should complex event processes.

3.6 Data Profiling Tool

Data profiling involves statistical analysis of data set contents to understand format, completeness, consistency, validity, and structure of the data. All data integration and interoperability development should include detailed assessment of potential data sources and targets to determine whether the actual data meets the needs of the proposed solution. Since most integration projects involve a significant amount of data, the most efficient means of conducting this analysis is to use a data profiling tool. (See Section 2.1.4 and Chapter 13.)

3.7 Metadata Repository

A Metadata repository contains information about the data in an organization, including data structure, content, and the business rules for managing the data. During data integration projects, one or more Metadata repositories may be used to document the technical structure and business meaning of the data being sourced, transformed, and targeted.

Usually the rules regarding data transformation, lineage, and processing used by the data integration tools are also stored in a Metadata repository as are the instructions for scheduled processes such as triggers and frequency.

Every tool usually has its own Metadata repository. Suites of tools from the same vendor may share a Metadata repository. One Metadata repository may be designated as a central point for consolidating data from the various operational tools. (See Chapter 12.)

4. Techniques

Several of the important techniques for designing data integration solutions are described in the Essential Concepts in this chapter. The basic goals are to keep the applications coupled loosely, limit the number of interfaces developed and requiring management by using a hub-and-spoke approach, and to create standard (or canonical) interfaces.

5. Implementation Guidelines

5.1 Readiness Assessment / Risk Assessment

All organizations have some form of DII already in place – so the readiness/risk assessment should be around enterprise integration tool implementation, or enhancing capabilities to allow interoperability.

Implementing *enterprise* data integration solutions is usually cost-justified based on implementation between many systems. Design an enterprise data integration solution to support the movement of data between many applications and organizations, and not just the first one to be implemented.

Many organizations spend their time reworking existing solutions instead of bringing additional value. Focus on implementing data integration solutions where none or limited integration currently exists, rather than replacing working data integration solutions with a common enterprise solution across the organization.

Certain data projects can justify a data integration solution focused only on a particular application, such as a data warehouse or Master Data Management hub. In those cases, any additional use of the data integration solution adds value to the investment, because the first system use already achieved the justification.

Application support teams prefer to manage data integration solutions locally. They will perceive that the cost of doing so is lower than leveraging an enterprise solution. The software vendors that support such teams will also prefer that they leverage the data integration tools that they sell. Therefore, it is necessary to sponsor the implementation of an enterprise data integration program from a level that has sufficient authority over solution design and technology purchase, such as from IT enterprise architecture. In addition, it may be necessary to encourage application systems to participate through positive incentives, such as funding the data integration technology centrally, and through negative incentives, such as refusing to approve the implementation of new alternative data integration technologies.

Development projects that implement new data integration technology frequently become focused on the technology and lose focus on the business goals. It is necessary to make sure that data integration solution implementation retain focus on the business goals and requirements, including making sure that some participants in every project are business- or application-oriented, and not just data integration tool experts.

5.2 Organization and Cultural Change

Organizations must determine whether responsibility for managing data integration implementations is centralized or whether it resides with decentralized application teams. Local teams understand the data in their applications. Central teams can build deep knowledge of tools and technologies. Many organizations develop a Center of Excellence specializing in the design and deployment of the enterprise data integration solutions. Local and central teams collaborate to develop solutions connecting an application into an enterprise data integration solution. The local team should take primary responsibility for managing the solution and resolving any problems, escalating to the Center of Excellence, if necessary.

Data integration solutions are frequently perceived as purely technical; however, to successfully deliver value, they must be developed based on deep business knowledge. The data analysis and modeling activities should be performed by business-oriented resources. Development of a canonical message model, or consistent standard for how data is shared in the organization, requires a large resource commitment that should involve business modeling resources as well as technical resources. Review all data transformation mapping design and changes with by business subject matter experts in each involved system.

6. DII Governance

Decisions about the design of data messages, data models, and data transformation rules have a direct impact on an organization's ability to use its data. These decisions must be business-driven. While there are many technical considerations in implementing business rules, a purely technical approach to DII can lead to errors in the data mappings and transformations as data flows into, through and out of an organization.

Business stakeholders are responsible for defining rules for how data should be modeled and transformed. Business stakeholders should approve changes to any of these business rules. Rules should be captured as Metadata and consolidated for cross-enterprise analysis. Identifying and verifying the predictive models and defining what actions should be automatically triggered by the predictions are also business functions.

Without trust that the integration or interoperable design will perform as promised, in a secure, reliable way, there can be no effective business value. In DII, the landscape of governance controls to support trust can be complex and detailed. One approach is to determine what events trigger governance reviews (exceptions or critical events). Map each trigger to reviews that engage with governance bodies. Event triggers may be part of the System Development Life Cycle (SDLC) at Stage Gates when moving from one phase to another or as part of User Stories. For example, architecture design compliance checklists may include such questions as: If possible, are you using the ESB and tools? Was there a search for reusable services?

Controls may come from governance-driven management routines, such as mandated reviews of models, auditing of Metadata, gating of deliverables, and required approvals for changes to transformation rules.

In Service Level Agreements, and in Business Continuity/Disaster Recovery plans, real-time operational data integration solutions must be included in the same backup and recovery tier as the most critical system to which they provide data.

Policies need to be established to ensure that the organization benefits from an enterprise approach to DII. For example, policies can be put in place to ensure that SOA principles are followed, that new services are created only after a review of existing services, and that all data flowing between systems goes through the enterprise service bus.

6.1 Data Sharing Agreements

Prior to the development of interfaces or the provision of data electronically, develop a data sharing agreement or memorandum of understanding (MOU) which stipulates the responsibilities and acceptable use of data to be exchanged, approved by the business data stewards of the data in question. The data sharing agreements should specify anticipated use and access to the data, restrictions on use, as well as expected service levels, including required system up times and response times. These agreements are especially critical for regulated industries, or when personal or secure information is involved.

6.2 DII and Data Lineage

Data lineage is useful to the development of DII solutions. It is also often required for data consumers to use data, but it is becoming even more important as data is integrated between organizations. Governance is required to ensure that knowledge of data origins and movement is documented. Data sharing agreements may stipulate limitations to the uses of data and in order to abide by these, it is necessary to know where data moves and persists. There are emerging compliance standards (for example, Solvency II regulation in Europe) that require organizations be able to describe where their data originated and how it has been changed as it has moved through various systems.

In addition, data lineage information is required when making changes to data flows. This information must be managed as a critical part of solution Metadata. Forward and backward data lineage (i.e., where did data get used and where did it come from) is critical as part of the impact analysis needed when making changes to data structures, data flows, or data processing.

6.3 Data Integration Metrics

To measure the scale and benefits from implementing Data Integration solutions, include metrics on availability, volume, speed, cost, and usage:

- Data Availability
  - Availability of data requested
- Data Volumes and Speed
  - Volumes of data transported and transformed
  - Volumes of data analyzed
  - Speed of transmission
  - Latency between data update and availability
  - Latency between event and triggered action
  - Time to availability of new data sources
- Solution Costs and Complexity
  - Cost of developing and managing solutions
  - Ease of acquiring new data
  - Complexity of solutions and operations
  - Number of systems using data integration solutions

7. Works Cited / Recommended

Aiken, P. and Allen, D. M. *XML in Data Management*. Morgan Kaufmann, 2004. Print.

Bahga, Arshdeep, and Vijay Madisetti. *Cloud Computing: A Hands-On Approach*. CreateSpace Independent Publishing Platform, 2013. Print.

Bobak, Angelo R. *Connecting the Data: Data Integration Techniques for Building an Operational Data Store (ODS)*. Technics Publications, LLC, 2012. Print.

Brackett, Michael. *Data Resource Integration: Understanding and Resolving a Disparate Data Resource*. Technics Publications, LLC, 2012. Print.

Carstensen, Jared, Bernard Golden, and JP Morgenthal. *Cloud Computing - Assessing the Risks*. IT Governance Publishing, 2012. Print.

Di Martino, Beniamino, Giuseppina Cretella, and Antonio Esposito. *Cloud Portability and Interoperability: Issues and Current Trend*. Springer, 2015. Print. SpringerBriefs in Computer Science.

Doan, AnHai, Alon Halevy, and Zachary Ives. *Principles of Data Integration*. Morgan Kaufmann, 2012. Print.

Erl, Thomas, Ricardo Puttini, and Zaigham Mahmood. *Cloud Computing: Concepts, Technology and Architecture*. Prentice Hall, 2013. Print. The Prentice Hall Service Technology Ser. from Thomas Erl.

Ferguson, M. *Maximizing the Business Value of Data Virtualization*. Enterprise Data World, 2012. Web. http://bit.ly/2sVAsui.

Giordano, Anthony David. *Data Integration Blueprint and Modeling: Techniques for a Scalable and Sustainable Architecture*. IBM Press, 2011. Print.

Haley, Beard. *Cloud Computing Best Practices for Managing and Measuring Processes for On-demand Computing, Applications and Data Centers in the Cloud with SLAs*. Emereo Publishing, 2008. Print.

Hohpe, Gregor and Bobby Woolf. *Enterprise Integration Patterns: Designing, Building, and Deploying Messaging Solutions*. Addison-Wesley Professional, 2003. Print.

Inmon, W. *Building the Data Warehouse*. 4th ed. Wiley, 2005. Print.

Inmon, W., Claudia Imhoff, and Ryan Sousa. *The Corporate Information Factory*. 2nd ed. Wiley 2001, Print.

Jamsa, Kris. *Cloud Computing: SaaS, PaaS, IaaS, Virtualization, Business Models, Mobile, Security and More*. Jones and Bartlett Learning, 2012. Print.

Kavis, Michael J. *Architecting the Cloud: Design Decisions for Cloud Computing Service Models (SaaS, PaaS, and IaaS)*. Wiley, 2014. Print. Wiley CIO.

Kimball, Ralph and Margy Ross. *The Data Warehouse Toolkit: The Complete Guide to Dimensional Modeling*. 2nd ed. Wiley, 2002. Print.

Linthicum, David S. *Cloud Computing and SOA Convergence in Your Enterprise: A Step-by-Step Guide*. Addison-Wesley Professional, 2009. Print.

Linthicum, David S. *Enterprise Application Integration*. Addison-Wesley Professional, 1999. Print.

Linthicum, David S. *Next Generation Application Integration: From Simple Information to Web Services*. Addison-Wesley Professional, 2003. Print.

Loshin, David. *Master Data Management*. Morgan Kaufmann, 2009. Print.

Majkic, Zoran. *Big Data Integration Theory: Theory and Methods of Database Mappings, Programming Languages, and Semantics*. Springer, 2014. Print. Texts in Computer Science.

Mather, Tim, Subra Kumaraswamy, and Shahed Latif. *Cloud Security and Privacy: An Enterprise Perspective on Risks and Compliance*. O'Reilly Media, 2009. Print. Theory in Practice.

Reese, George. *Cloud Application Architectures: Building Applications and Infrastructure in the Cloud*. O'Reilly Media, 2009. Print. Theory in Practice (O'Reilly).

Reeve, April. *Managing Data in Motion: Data Integration Best Practice Techniques and Technologies*. Morgan Kaufmann, 2013. Print. The Morgan Kaufmann Series on Business Intelligence.

Rhoton, John. *Cloud Computing Explained: Implementation Handbook for Enterprises*. Recursive Press, 2009. Print.

Sarkar, Pushpak. *Data as a Service: A Framework for Providing Reusable Enterprise Data Services*. Wiley-IEEE Computer Society Pr, 2015. Print.

Sears, Jonathan. *Data Integration 200 Success Secrets - 200 Most Asked Questions On Data Integration - What You Need to Know*. Emereo Publishing, 2014. Kindle.

Sherman, Rick. *Business Intelligence Guidebook: From Data Integration to Analytics*. Morgan Kaufmann, 2014. Print.

U.S. Department of Commerce. *Guidelines on Security and Privacy in Public Cloud Computing*. CreateSpace Independent Publishing Platform, 2014. Print.

Van der Lans, Rick. *Data Virtualization for Business Intelligence Systems: Revolutionizing Data Integration for Data Warehouses*. Morgan Kaufmann, 2012. Print. The Morgan Kaufmann Series on Business Intelligence.

Zhao, Liang, Sherif Sakr, Anna Liu, and Athman Bouguettaya. *Cloud Data Management*. Springer; 2014. Print.

CHAPTER 9

Document and Content Management

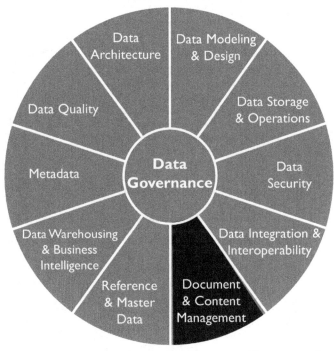

DAMA-DMBOK2 Data Management Framework

Copyright © 2017 by DAMA International

1. Introduction

Document and Content Management entails controlling the capture, storage, access, and use of data and information stored outside relational databases.[44] Its focus is on maintaining the integrity of and enabling access to documents and other unstructured or semi-structured information which makes it roughly equivalent to data operations management for relational databases. However, it also has strategic drivers. In many organizations, unstructured data has a direct relationship to structured data. Management decisions about such content should be applied consistently. In addition, as are other types of data, documents and unstructured content

---

[44] The types of unstructured data have evolved since the early 2000s, as the capacity to capture and store digital information has grown. The concept of *unstructured data* continues to refer to data that is not pre-defined through a data model, whether relational or otherwise.

are expected to be secure and of high quality. Ensuring security and quality requires governance, reliable architecture, and well-managed Metadata.

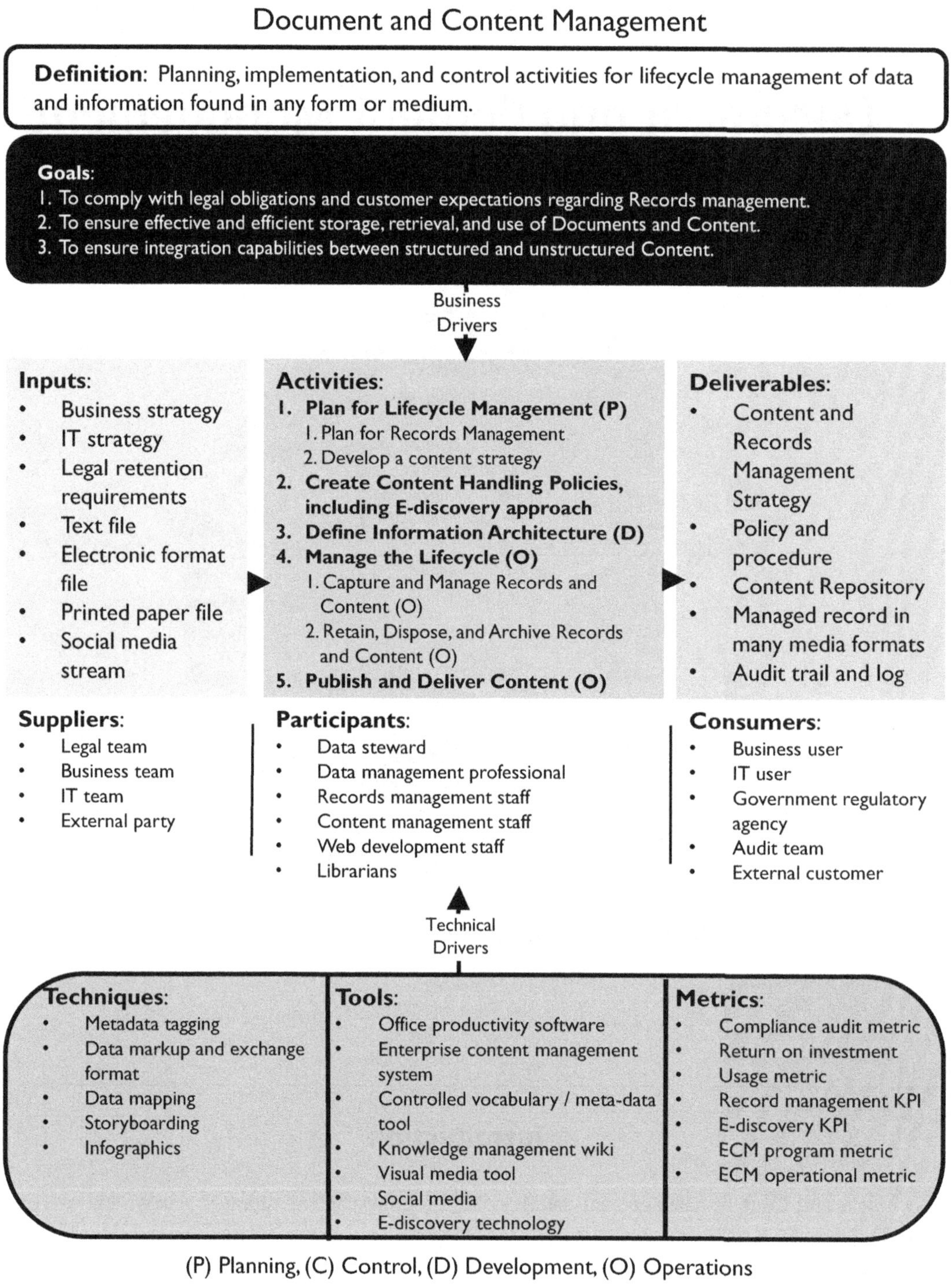

Document and Content Management

Definition: Planning, implementation, and control activities for lifecycle management of data and information found in any form or medium.

Goals:
1. To comply with legal obligations and customer expectations regarding Records management.
2. To ensure effective and efficient storage, retrieval, and use of Documents and Content.
3. To ensure integration capabilities between structured and unstructured Content.

Business Drivers

Inputs:
- Business strategy
- IT strategy
- Legal retention requirements
- Text file
- Electronic format file
- Printed paper file
- Social media stream

Activities:
1. **Plan for Lifecycle Management (P)**
   1. Plan for Records Management
   2. Develop a content strategy
2. **Create Content Handling Policies, including E-discovery approach**
3. **Define Information Architecture (D)**
4. **Manage the Lifecycle (O)**
   1. Capture and Manage Records and Content (O)
   2. Retain, Dispose, and Archive Records and Content (O)
5. **Publish and Deliver Content (O)**

Deliverables:
- Content and Records Management Strategy
- Policy and procedure
- Content Repository
- Managed record in many media formats
- Audit trail and log

Suppliers:
- Legal team
- Business team
- IT team
- External party

Participants:
- Data steward
- Data management professional
- Records management staff
- Content management staff
- Web development staff
- Librarians

Consumers:
- Business user
- IT user
- Government regulatory agency
- Audit team
- External customer

Technical Drivers

Techniques:
- Metadata tagging
- Data markup and exchange format
- Data mapping
- Storyboarding
- Infographics

Tools:
- Office productivity software
- Enterprise content management system
- Controlled vocabulary / meta-data tool
- Knowledge management wiki
- Visual media tool
- Social media
- E-discovery technology

Metrics:
- Compliance audit metric
- Return on investment
- Usage metric
- Record management KPI
- E-discovery KPI
- ECM program metric
- ECM operational metric

(P) Planning, (C) Control, (D) Development, (O) Operations

Figure 71 Context Diagram: Documents and Content

1.1 Business Drivers

The primary business drivers for document and content management include regulatory compliance, the ability to respond to litigation and e-discovery requests, and business continuity requirements. Good records management can also help organizations become more efficient. Well-organized, searchable websites that result from effective management of ontologies and other structures that facilitate searching help improve customer and employee satisfaction.

Laws and regulations require that organizations maintain records of certain kinds of activities. Most organizations also have policies, standards, and best practices for record keeping. Records include both paper documents and electronically stored information (ESI). Good records management is necessary for business continuity. It also enables an organization to respond in the case of litigation.

E-discovery is the process of finding electronic records that might serve as evidence in a legal action. As the technology for creating, storing, and using data has developed, the volume of ESI has increased exponentially. Some of this data will undoubtedly end up in litigation or regulatory requests.

The ability of an organization to respond to an e-discovery request depends on how proactively it has managed records such as email, chats, websites, and electronic documents, as well as raw application data and Metadata. Big Data has become a driver for more efficient e-discovery, records retention, and strong information governance.

Gaining efficiencies is a driver for improving document management. Technological advances in document management are helping organizations streamline processes, manage workflow, eliminate repetitive manual tasks, and enable collaboration. These technologies have the additional benefits of enabling people to locate, access, and share documents more quickly. They can also prevent documents from being lost. This is very important for e-discovery. Money is also saved by freeing up file cabinet space and reducing document handling costs.

1.2 Goals and Principles

The goals of implementing best practices around Document and Content Management include:

- Ensuring effective and efficient retrieval and use of data and information in unstructured formats

- Ensuring integration capabilities between structured and unstructured data

- Complying with legal obligations and customer expectations

Management of Documents and Content follows these guiding principles:

- Everyone in an organization has a role to play in protecting the organization's future. Everyone must create, use, retrieve, and dispose of records in accordance with the established policies and procedures.

- Experts in the handling of records and content should be fully engaged in policy and planning. Regulatory and best practices can vary significantly based on industry sector and legal jurisdiction.

Even if records management professionals are not available to the organization, everyone can be trained to understand the challenges, best practices, and issues. Once trained, business stewards and others can collaborate on an effective approach to records management.

In 2009, ARMA International, a not-for-profit professional association for managing records and information, published a set of Generally Acceptable Recordkeeping Principles® (GARP)[45] that describes how business records should be maintained. It also provides a recordkeeping and information governance framework with associated metrics. The first sentence of each principle is stated below. Further explanation can be found on the ARMA website.

- **Principle of Accountability**: An organization shall assign a senior executive to appropriate individuals, adopt policies and processes to guide staff, and ensure program auditability.

- **Principle of Integrity**: An information governance program shall be constructed so the records and information generated or managed by or for the organization have a reasonable and suitable guarantee of authenticity and reliability.

- **Principle of Protection**: An information governance program shall be constructed to ensure a reasonable level of protection to information that is personal or that otherwise requires protection.

- **Principle of Compliance**: An information governance program shall be constructed to comply with applicable laws and other binding authorities, as well as the organization's policies.

- **Principle of Availability**: An organization shall maintain its information in a manner that ensures timely, efficient, and accurate retrieval of its information.

- **Principle of Retention**: An organization shall retain its information for an appropriate time, taking into account all operational, legal, regulatory and fiscal requirements, and those of all relevant binding authorities.

- **Principle of Disposition**: An organization shall provide secure and appropriate disposition of information in accordance with its policies, and, applicable laws, regulations and other binding authorities.

- **Principle of Transparency**: An organization shall document its policies, processes and activities, including its information governance program, in a manner that is available to and understood by staff and appropriate interested parties.

1.3 Essential Concepts

1.3.1 Content

A document is to content what a bucket is to water: a container. *Content* refers to the data and information inside the file, document, or website. Content is often managed based on the concepts represented by the documents, as well as the type or status of the documents. Content also has a lifecycle. In its completed form, some content becomes a matter of record for an organization. Official records are treated differently from other content.

---

[45] ARMA International, ARMA Generally Accepted Recordkeeping Principles®, http://bit.ly/2tNF1E4.

1.3.1.1 Content Management

Content management includes the processes, techniques, and technologies for organizing, categorizing, and structuring information resources so that they can be stored, published, and reused in multiple ways.

The lifecycle of content can be active, with daily changes through controlled processes for creation and modification; or it can be more static with only minor, occasional changes. Content may be managed formally (strictly stored, managed, audited, retained or disposed of) or informally through ad hoc updates.

Content management is particularly important in websites and portals, but the techniques of indexing based on keywords and organizing based on taxonomies can be applied across technology platforms. When the scope of content management includes the entire enterprise, it is referred to as Enterprise Content Management (ECM).

1.3.1.2 Content Metadata

Metadata is essential to managing unstructured data, both what is traditionally thought of as content and documents and what we now understand as 'Big Data'. Without Metadata, it is not possible to inventory and organize content. Metadata for unstructured data content is based on:

- **Format**: Often the format of the data dictates the method to access the data (such as electronic index for electronic unstructured data).

- **Search-ability**: Whether search tools already exist for use with related unstructured data.

- **Self-documentation**: Whether the Metadata is self-documenting (as in filesystems). In this case, development is minimal, as the existing tool is simply adopted.

- **Existing patterns**: Whether existing methods and patterns can be adopted or adapted (as in library catalogs).

- **Content subjects**: The things people are likely to be looking for.

- **Requirements**: Need for thoroughness and detail in retrieval (as in the pharmaceutical or nuclear industry[46]). Therefore, detailed Metadata at the content level might be necessary, and a tool capable of content tagging might be necessary.

Generally, the maintenance of Metadata for unstructured data becomes the maintenance of a cross-reference between various local patterns and the official set of enterprise Metadata. Records managers and Metadata professionals recognize long-term embedded methods exist throughout the organization for documents, records, and other content that must be retained for many years, but that these methods are often costly to re-organize. In some organizations, a centralized team maintains cross-reference patterns between records management indexes, taxonomies, and even variant thesauri.

---

[46] These industries are responsible for supplying evidence of how certain kinds of materials are handled. Pharmacy manufacturers, for example, must keep detailed records of how a compound came to be and was then tested and handled, before being allowed to be used by people.

1.3.1.3 Content Modeling

Content modeling is the process of converting logical content concepts into content types, attributes, and data types with relationships. An attribute describes something specific and distinguishable about the content to which it relates. A data type restricts the type of data the attribute may hold, enabling validation and processing. Metadata management and data modeling techniques are used in the development of a content model.

There are two levels of content modeling. The first is at the information product level, which creates an actual deliverable like a website. The second is at the component level, which further details the elements that make up the information product model. The level of detail in the model depends on the granularity desired for reuse and structure.

Content models support the content strategy by guiding content creation and promoting reuse. They support adaptive content, which is format-free and device-independent. The models become the specifications for the content implemented in such structures such as XML schema definition (XSDs), forms, or stylesheets.

1.3.1.4 Content Delivery Methods

Content needs to be modular, structured, reusable, and device- and platform- independent. Delivery methods include web pages, print, and mobile apps as well as eBooks with interactive video and audio. Converting content into XML early in the workflow supports reuse across different media channels.

Content delivery systems are 'push', 'pull', or interactive.

- **Push**: In a push delivery system, users choose the type of content delivered to them on a pre-determined schedule. Syndication involves one party creating the content published in many places. Really Simple Syndication (RSS) is an example of a push content delivery mechanism. It distributes content (i.e., a feed) to syndicate news and other web content upon request.

- **Pull**: In a pull delivery system, users pull the content through the Internet. An example of a pull system is when shoppers visit online retail stores.

- **Interactive**: Interactive content delivery methods, such as third-party electronic point of sale (EPOS) apps or customer facing websites (e.g., for enrollment), need to exchange high volumes of real-time data between enterprise applications. Options for sharing data between applications include Enterprise Application Integration (EAI), Changed Data Capture, Data Integration and EII. (See Chapter 8.)

1.3.2 Controlled Vocabularies

A *controlled vocabulary* is a defined list of explicitly allowed terms used to index, categorize, tag, sort, and retrieve content through browsing and searching. A controlled vocabulary is necessary to systematically organize documents, records, and content. Vocabularies range in complexity from simple lists or pick lists, to the synonym rings or authority lists, to taxonomies, and, the most complex, thesauri and ontologies. An example of a controlled vocabulary is the Dublin Core, used to catalog publications.

Defined policies control over who adds terms to the vocabulary (e.g., a taxonomist or indexer, or librarian). Librarians are particularly trained in the theory and development of controlled vocabularies. Users of the list may only apply terms from the list for its scoped subject area. (See Chapter 10.)

Ideally, controlled vocabularies should be aligned with the entity names and definitions in an enterprise conceptual data model. A bottom up approach to collecting terms and concepts is to compile them in a folksonomy, which is a collection of terms and concepts obtained through social tagging.

Controlled vocabularies constitute a type of Reference Data. Like other Reference Data, their values and definitions need to be managed for completeness and currency. They can also be thought of as Metadata, as they help explain and support the use of other data. They are described in this chapter because Document and Content Management are primary use cases for controlled vocabularies.

1.3.2.1 Vocabulary Management

Because vocabularies evolve over time, they require management. ANSI/NISO Z39.19-2005 is an American standard, which provides guidelines for the Construction, Format, and Management of Monolingual Controlled Vocabularies, describes vocabulary management as a way to "to improve the effectiveness of information storage and retrieval systems, web navigation systems, and other environments that seek to both identify and locate desired content via some sort of description using language. The primary purpose of vocabulary control is to achieve consistency in the description of content objects and to facilitate retrieval."[47]

Vocabulary management is the function of defining, sourcing, importing, and maintaining any given vocabulary. Key questions to enable vocabulary management focus on uses, consumers, standards, and maintenance:

- What information concepts will this vocabulary support?

- Who is the audience for this vocabulary? What processes do they support? What roles do they play?

- Why is the vocabulary necessary? Will it support an application, content management, or analytics?

- What decision-making body is responsible for designating preferred terms?

- What existing vocabularies do different groups use to classify this information? Where are they located? How were they created? Who are their subject matter experts? Are there any security or privacy concerns for any of them?

- Is there an existing standard that can fulfill this need? Are there concerns of using an external standard vs. internal? How frequently is the standard updated and what is the degree of change of each update? Are standards accessible in an easy to import / maintain format, in a cost-efficient manner?

The results of this assessment will enable data integration. They will also help to establish internal standards, including associated preferred vocabulary through term and term relationship management functions.

---

[47] http://bit.ly/2sTaI2h.

If this kind of assessment is not done, preferred vocabularies would still be defined in an organization, except they would be done in silos, project by project, lead to a higher cost of integration and higher chances of data quality issues. (See Chapter 13.)

1.3.2.2 Vocabulary Views and Micro-controlled Vocabulary

A *vocabulary view* is a subset of a controlled vocabulary, covering a limited range of topics within the domain of the controlled vocabulary. Vocabulary views are necessary when the goal is to *use* a standard vocabulary containing a large number of terms, but not all terms are relevant to some consumers of the information. For example, a view that only contains terms relevant to a Marketing Business Unit would not contain terms relevant only to Finance.

Vocabulary views increase information's usability by limiting the content to what is appropriate to the users. Construct a vocabulary view of preferred vocabulary terms manually, or through business rules that act on preferred vocabulary term data or Metadata. Define rules for which terms are included in each vocabulary view.

A *micro-controlled vocabulary* is a vocabulary view containing highly specialized terms not present in the general vocabulary. An example of a micro-controlled vocabulary is a medical dictionary with subsets for medical disciplines. Such terms should map to the hierarchical structure of the broad controlled vocabulary. A micro-controlled vocabulary is internally consistent with respect to relationships among terms.

Micro-controlled vocabularies are necessary when the goal is to take advantage of a standard vocabulary, but the content is not sufficient and there is a need to manage additions/extensions for a specific group of information consumers. Building a micro-controlled vocabulary starts with the same steps as a vocabulary view, but it also includes addition or association of additional preferred terms that are differentiated from the pre-existing preferred terms by indicating a different source.

1.3.2.3 Term and Pick Lists

Lists of terms are just that: lists. They do not describe relationships between the terms. Pick lists, web pull-down lists, and lists of menu choices in information systems use term lists. They provide little or no guidance to the user, but they help to control ambiguity by reducing the domain of values.

Pick lists are often buried in applications. Content management software can help transform pick lists and controlled vocabularies into pick lists searchable from the home page. These pick lists are managed as faceted taxonomies inside the software.

1.3.2.4 Term Management

The standard ANSI/NISO Z39.19-2005 defines a *term* as "One or more words designating a concept."[48] Like vocabularies, individual terms also require management. Term Management includes specifying how terms are

---

[48] http://bit.ly/2sTaI2h.

initially defined and classified and how this information is maintained once it starts being used in different systems. Terms should be managed through a governance processes. Stewards may need to arbitrate to ensure stakeholder feedback is accounted for before terms are changed. Z39.19 defines a *preferred term* as one of two or more synonyms or lexical variants selected as a term for inclusion in a controlled vocabulary.

Term management includes establishing relationships between terms within a controlled vocabulary. There are three types of relationships:

- **Equivalent term relationship**: A relationship between or among terms in a controlled vocabulary that leads to one or more terms to use instead of the term from which the cross-reference is made. This is the most commonly used term mapping in IT functions, indicating a term or value from one system or vocabulary is the same as another, so integration technologies can perform their mapping and standardization.

- **Hierarchical relationship**: A relationship between or among terms in a controlled vocabulary that depicts broader (general) to narrower (specific) or whole-part relationships.

- **Related term relationship**: A term that is associatively but not hierarchically linked to another term in a controlled vocabulary.

1.3.2.5 Synonym Rings and Authority Lists

A *synonym ring* is a set of terms with roughly equivalent meaning. A synonym ring allows users who search on one of the terms to access content related to any of the terms. The manual development of synonym rings is for retrieval, not for indexing. They offer synonym control, and treat synonyms and near synonymous terms equally. Usage occurs where the indexing environment has an uncontrolled vocabulary or where there is no indexing. Search engines and different Metadata registries have synonym rings (See Chapter 13.) They can be difficult to implement on user interfaces.

An *authority list* is a controlled vocabulary of descriptive terms designed to facilitate retrieval of information within a specific domain or scope. Term treatment is not equal as it is within a synonym ring; instead, one term is preferred and the others are variants. An authority file cross-references synonyms and variants for each term to guide the user from a non-preferred to a preferred term. The list may or may not contain definitions of these terms. Authority lists should have designated managers. They may have structure. An example is the US Library of Congress' Subject Headings. (See Section 1.3.2.1.)

1.3.2.6 Taxonomies

Taxonomy is an umbrella term referring to any classification or controlled vocabulary. The best-known example of taxonomy is the classification system for all living things developed by the Swedish biologist Linnaeus.

In content management, a *taxonomy* is a naming structure containing a controlled vocabulary used for outlining topics and enabling navigation and search systems. Taxonomies help reduce ambiguity and control synonyms. A hierarchical taxonomy may contain different types of parent/child relationships useful for both indexers and searchers. Such taxonomies are used to create drill-down type interfaces.

Taxonomies can have different structures:

- A **flat taxonomy** has no relationships among the set of controlled categories. All the categories are equal. This is similar to a list; for example, a list of countries.

- A **hierarchical taxonomy** is a tree structure where nodes are related by a rule. A hierarchy has at least two levels and is bi-directional. Moving up the hierarchy expands the category; moving down refines the category. An example is geography, from continent down to street address.

- A **polyhierarchy** is a tree-like structure with more than one node relation rule. Child nodes may have multiple parents. Those parents may also share grandparents. As such, the traversal paths can be complicated and care must be taken to avoid potential invalid traversals: up the tree from a node that relates to the parent, but not to one of the grandparents. Complicated polyhierarchy structures may be better served with a facet taxonomy instead.

- A **facet taxonomy** looks like a star where each node is associated with the center node. Facets are attributes of the object in the center. An example is Metadata, where each attribute (creator, title, access rights, keywords, version, etc.) is a facet of a content object.

- A **network taxonomy** uses both hierarchical and facet structures. Any two nodes in network taxonomy establish linkages based on their associations. An example is a recommender engine (…if you liked that, you might also like this…). Another example is a thesaurus.

With the amount of data being generated, even with the best-defined taxonomies require automated flagging, correction, and routing rules. If taxonomies are not maintained, they will be underutilized or will produce incorrect results. This creates the risk that entities and staff governed by applicable regulations will be out of compliance. For example, in a financial taxonomy, the preferred term may be 'Postemployment'. Content may come from systems that classify it as 'Post-Employment', 'Post Employment', or even Post Retirement. To support such cases, appropriate synonym ring and related term relationships should be defined (US GAAP, 2008).

Organizations develop their own taxonomies to formalize collective thinking about topics specific to their work. Taxonomies are particularly important for presenting and finding information on websites, as many search engines rely on exact word matches and can only find items tagged or using the same words in the same way.

1.3.2.7 Classification Schemes and Tagging

Classification schemes are codes that represent controlled vocabulary. These schemes are often hierarchical and may have words associated with them, such as the Dewey Decimal System and the US Library of Congress Classification (main classes and subclasses). A number based taxonomy, the Dewey Decimal System is also a multi-lingual expression for subject coding, since numbers can be 'decoded' into any language.

Folksonomies are classification schemes for online content terms and names obtained through social tagging. Individual users and groups use them to annotate and categorize digital content. They typically do not have hierarchical structures or preferred terms. Folksonomies are not usually considered authoritative or applied to document indexing because experts do not compile them. However, because they directly reflect the vocabulary of users, they offer the potential to enhance information retrieval. Folksonomy terms can be linked to structured controlled vocabularies.

1.3.2.8 Thesauri

A *thesaurus* is type of controlled vocabulary used for content retrieval. It combines characteristics of synonym lists and taxonomies. A thesaurus provides information about each term and its relationship to other terms. Relationships are either hierarchical (parent/child or broad/narrower), associative ('see also') or equivalent (synonym or used/used from). Synonyms must be acceptably equivalent in all context scenarios. A thesaurus may also include definitions, citations, etc.

Thesauri can be used to organize unstructured content, uncover relationships between content from different media, improve website navigation, and optimize search. When a user inputs a term, a system can use a non-exposed thesaurus (one not directly available to the user) to automatically direct the search to a similar term. Alternatively, the system can suggest related terms with which a user could continue the search.

Standards that provide guidance on creating thesauri include ISO 25964 and ANSI/NISO Z39.19. 10.2.2.1.5 Ontologies.

1.3.2.9 Ontology

An *ontology* is a type of taxonomy that represents a set of concepts and their relationships within a domain. Ontologies provide the primary knowledge representation in the Semantic Web, and are used in the exchange of information between Semantic Web applications.[49]

Ontology languages such as Resource Description Framework Schema (RDFS) are used to develop ontologies by encoding the knowledge about specific domains. They may include reasoning rules to support processing of that knowledge. OWL (Web Ontology Language), an extension to RDFS, is a formal syntax for defining ontologies.

Ontologies describe classes (concepts), individuals (instances), attributes, relations, and events. An ontology can be a collection of taxonomies and thesauri of common vocabulary for knowledge representation and exchange of information. Ontologies often relate to a taxonomic hierarchy of classes and definitions with the subsumption relation, such as decomposing intelligent behavior into many simpler behavior modules and then layers.

There are two key differences between a taxonomy (like a data model) and an ontology:

- A taxonomy provides data content classifications for a given concept area. A data model specifically calls out the entity to which an attribute belongs and the valid for that attribute. In an ontology, though, entity, attribute, and content concepts can be completely mixed. Differences are identified through Metadata or other relationships.

- In a taxonomy or data model, what is defined is what is known – and nothing else. This is referred to as a closed-world assumption. In an ontology, possible relationships are inferred based on the nature of existing relationships, so something that is not explicitly declared can be true. This is referred to as the open-world assumption.

---

[49] Semantic Web, also known as Linked Data Web or Web 3.0, an enhancement of the current Web where meaning (i.e., semantics) is machine-process-able. Having a machine (computer) understand more makes it easier to find, share, and combine data / information more easily.

While taxonomy management evolved under the Library Sciences, today the art and science of taxonomy and ontology management fall under the semantics management space. (See Chapter 10.)

Because the process of modeling ontologies is somewhat subjective, it is important to avoid common pitfalls that cause ambiguity and confusion:

- Failure to distinguish between an instance-of relationship and a subclass-of relationship
- Modeling events as relations
- Lack of clarity and uniqueness of terms
- Modeling roles as classes
- Failure to reuse
- Mixing semantics of modeling language and concepts
- Use of a web-based, platform-independent tool (e.g., OOPS!) for ontology validation helps with diagnosis and repair of pitfalls

1.3.3 Documents and Records

Documents are electronic or paper objects that contain instructions for tasks, requirements for how and when to perform a task or function, and logs of task execution and decisions. Documents can communicate and share information and knowledge. Examples of documents include procedures, protocols, methods, and specifications.

Only a subset of documents will be designated as records. *Records* provide evidence that actions were taken and decisions were made in keeping with procedures; they can serve as evidence of the organization's business activities and regulatory compliance. People usually create records, but instruments and monitoring equipment could also provide data to generate records automatically.

1.3.3.1 Document Management

Document management encompasses the processes, techniques, and technologies for controlling and organizing documents and records throughout their lifecycle. It includes storage, inventory, and control, for both electronic and paper documents. More than 90% of the documents created today are electronic. While paperless documents are becoming more widely used, the world is still full of historical paper documents.

In general, document management concerns files, with little attention to file content. The information content within a file may guide how to manage that file, but document management treats the file as a single entity.

Both market and regulatory pressures put focus on records retention schedules, location, transport, and destruction. For example, some data about individuals cannot cross international boundaries.

Regulations and statutes, such as the U.S. Sarbanes-Oxley Act and E-Discovery Amendments to the Federal Rules of Civil Procedure and Canada's Bill 198, are now concerns of corporate compliance officers who push for standardization of records management practices within their organizations. Managing the lifecycle of documents and records includes:

- **Inventory**: Identification of existing and newly created documents / records.

- **Policy**: Creation, approval, and enforcement of documents / records policies, including a document / records retention policy.
- **Classification** of documents / records.
- **Storage**: Short- and long-term storage of physical and electronic documents / records.
- **Retrieval and Circulation**: Allowing access to and circulation of documents / records in accordance with policies, security and control standards, and legal requirements.
- **Preservation and Disposal**: Archiving and destroying documents / records according to organizational needs, statutes, and regulations.

Data management professionals are stakeholders in decisions about document classification and retention. They must support consistency between the base structured data and specific unstructured data. For example, if finished output reports are deemed appropriate historic documentation, the structured data in an OLTP or warehousing environment may be relieved of storing the report's base data.

Documents are often developed within a hierarchy with some documents more detailed than others are. Figure 72, based on text from ISO 9000 Introduction and Support Package: Guidance on the Documentation Requirements of ISO 9001, Clause 4.2, depicts a documentation-centric paradigm, appropriate for government or the military. ISO 9001 describes the minimal components of a basic quality management system. Commercial entities may have a different document hierarchies or flows to support business practices.

1.3.3.2 Records Management

Document management includes records management. Managing records has special requirements.[50] Records management includes the full lifecycle: from record creation or receipt through processing, distribution, organization, and retrieval, to disposition. Records can be physical (e.g., documents, memos, contracts, reports or microfiche); electronic (e.g., email content, attachments, and instant messaging); content on a website; documents on all types of media and hardware; and data captured in databases of all kinds. Hybrid records, such as aperture cards (paper record with a microfiche window imbedded with details or supporting material), combine formats. A *Vital Record* is type a record required to resume an organization's operations the event of a disaster.

Trustworthy records are important not only for record keeping but also for regulatory compliance. Having signatures on the record contributes to a record's integrity. Other integrity actions include verification of the event (i.e., witnessing in real time) and double-checking the information after the event.

Well-prepared records have characteristics such as:

- **Content**: Content must be accurate, complete and truthful.

- **Context**: Descriptive information (Metadata) about the record's creator, date of creation, or relationship to other records should be collected, structured and maintained with the record at the time of record creation.

- **Timeliness**: A record should be created promptly after the event, action or decision occurs.

---

[50] The ISO 15489 standard defines records management as "The field of management responsible for the efficient and systematic control of the creation, receipt, maintenance, use and disposition of records, including the processes for capturing and maintaining evidence of and information about business activities and transactions in the form of records." http://bit.ly/2sVG8EW.

- **Permanency**: Once they are designated as records, records cannot be changed for the legal length of their existence.

- **Structure**: The appearance and arrangement of a record's content should be clear. They should be recorded on the correct forms or templates. Content should be legible, terminology should be used consistently.

Figure 72 Document Hierarchy based on ISO 9001-4.2

Many records exist in both electronic and paper formats. Records Management requires the organization to know which copy (electronic or paper) is the official 'copy of record' to meet record keeping obligations. Once the copy of record is determined, the other copy can be safely destroyed.

1.3.3.3 Digital Asset Management

Digital Asset Management (DAM) is process similar to document management that focuses on the storage, tracking and use of rich media documents like video, logos, photographs, etc.

1.3.4 Data Map

A *Data Map* is an inventory of all ESI data sources, applications, and IT environments that includes the owners of the applications, custodians, relevant geographical locations, and data types.

1.3.5 E-discovery

Discovery is a legal term that refers to pre-trial phase of a lawsuit where both parties request information from each other to find facts for the case and to see how strong the arguments are on either side. The US Federal Rules of Civil Procedure (FRCP) have governed the discovery of evidence in lawsuits and other civil cases since 1938. For decades, paper-based discovery rules were applied to e-discovery. In 2006, amendments to the FRCP accommodated the discovery practice and requirements of ESI in the litigation process. Other global regulations have requirements specific to the ability of an organization to produce electronic evidence. Examples include the UK Bribery Act, Dodd-Frank Act, Foreign Account Tax Compliance Act (FATCA), Foreign Corrupt Practices Act, EU Data Protection Regulations and Rules, global anti-trust regulations, sector-specific regulations, and local court procedural rules.

Electronic documents usually have Metadata (which may not be available for paper documents) that plays an important part in evidence. Legal requirements come from the key legal processes such as e-discovery, as well as data and records retention practices, the legal hold notification (LHN) process, and legally defensible disposition practices. LHN includes identifying information that may be requested in a legal proceeding, locking that data or document down to prevent editing or deletion, and then notifying all parties in an organization that the data or document in question is subject to a legal hold. Figure 73 depicts a high-level Electronic Discovery Reference Model developed by EDRM, a standards and guidelines organization for e-discovery. This framework provides an approach to e-discovery that is handy for people involved in identifying how and where the relevant internal data is stored, what retention policies apply, what data is not accessible, and what tools are available to assist in the identification process.

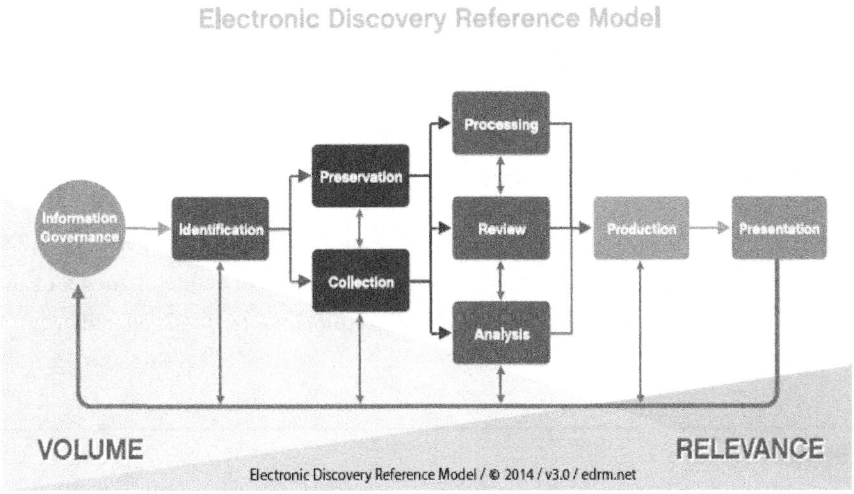

Figure 73 Electronic Discovery Reference Model[51]

---

[51] EDRM (edrm.net). Content posted at EDRM.net is licensed under a Creative Commons Attribution 3.0 Unported License.

The EDRM model assumes that data or information governance is in place. The model includes eight e-discovery phases that can be iterative. As e-discovery progresses, the volume of discoverable data and information is greatly reduced as their relevance is greatly increased.

The first phase, Identification, has two sub-phases: Early Case Assessment and Early Data Assessment (not depicted in the diagram). In Early Case Assessment, the legal case itself is assessed for pertinent information, called descriptive information or Metadata (e.g., keywords, date ranges, etc.). In Early Data Assessment, the types and location of data relevant to the case is assessed. Data assessment should identify policies related to the retention or destruction of relevant data so that ESI can be preserved. Interviews should be held with records management personnel, data custodians or data owners, and information technology personnel to obtain pertinent information. In addition, the involved personnel need to understand the case background, legal hold, and their role in the litigation.

The next phases in the model are the Preservation and Collection. Preservation ensures that the data that has been identified as potentially relevant is placed in a legal hold so it is not destroyed. Collection includes the acquisition and transfer of identified data from the company to their legal counsel in a legally defensible manner.

During the Processing phase data is de-duplicated, searched, and analyzed to determine which data items will move forward to the Review phase. In the Review phase, documents are identified to be presented in response to the request. Review also identifies privileged documents that will be withheld. Much of the selection depends on Metadata associated with the documents. Processing takes place after the Review phase because it addresses content analysis to understand the circumstances, facts and potential evidence in litigation or investigation and to enhance the search and review processes.

Processing and Review depend on analysis, but Analysis is called out as a separate phase with a focus on content. The goal of content analysis is to understand the circumstances, facts, and potential evidence in litigation or investigation, in order to formulate a strategy in response to the legal situation.

In the Production phase, data and information are turned over to opposing counsel, based on agreed-to specifications. Original sources of information may be files, spreadsheets, email, databases, drawings, photographs, data from proprietary applications, website data, voicemail, and much more. The ESI can be collected, processed and output to a variety of formats. *Native production* retains the original format of the files. *Near-native production* alters the original format through extraction and conversion. ESI can be produced in an image, or near paper, format. *Fielded data* is Metadata and other information extracted from native files when ESI is processed and produced in a text-delimited file or XML load file. The lineage of the materials provided during the Production phase is important, because no one wants to be accused of altering data or information provided.

Displaying the ESI at depositions, hearings, and trials is part of the Presentation phase. The ESI exhibits can be presented in paper, near paper, near-native and native formats to support or refute elements of the case. They may be used to elicit further information, validate existing facts or positions, or persuade an audience.

1.3.6 Information Architecture

Information Architecture is the process of creating structure for a body of information or content. It includes the following components:

- Controlled vocabularies

- Taxonomies and ontologies
- Navigation maps
- Metadata maps
- Search functionality specifications
- Use cases
- User flows

The information architecture and the content strategy together describe the 'what' – what content will be managed in a system. The design phases describe 'how' the content management strategy will be implemented.

For a document or content management system, the information architecture identifies the links and relationships between documents and content, specifies document requirements and attributes, and defines the structure of content in a document or content management system. Information architecture is central to developing effective websites. A storyboard provides a blueprint for a web project. It serves as an outline of the design approach, defines the elements that need to go on each web page, and shows the navigation and information flow of how the pages are to work together. This enables development of the navigational models, menus, and other components necessary for the management and use of the site.

1.3.7 Search Engine

A search engine is software that searches for information based on terms and retrieves websites that have those terms within their content. One example is Google. Search functionality requires several components: search engine software proper, spider software that roams the Web and stores the Uniform Resource Locators (URLs) of the content it finds, indexing of the encountered keywords and text, and rules for ranking.

1.3.8 Semantic Model

Semantic modeling is a type of knowledge modeling that describes a network of concepts (ideas or topics of concern) and their relationships. Incorporated into information systems, semantic models enable users to ask questions of the information in a non-technical way. For example, a semantic model can map database tables and views to concepts that are meaningful to business users.

Semantic models contain semantic objects and bindings. Semantic objects are things represented in the model. They can have attributes with cardinality and domains, and identifiers. Their structures can be simple, composite, compound, hybrid, association, parent / subtype, or archetype / version. Bindings represent associations or association classes in UML. These models help to identify patterns and trends and to discover relationships between pieces of information that might otherwise appear disparate. In doing so, they help enable integration of data across different knowledge domains or subject areas. Ontologies and controlled vocabularies are critical to semantic modeling.

Data integration uses ontologies in several different ways. A single ontology could be the reference model. If there are multiple data sources, then each individual data source is modeled using an ontology and later mapped to the other ontologies. The hybrid approach uses multiple ontologies that integrate with a common overall vocabulary.

1.3.9 Semantic Search

Semantic searching focuses on meaning and context rather than predetermined keywords. A semantic search engine can use artificial intelligence to identify query matches based on words and their context. Such a search engine can analyze by location, intent, word variations, synonyms, and concept matching.

Requirements for semantic search involve figuring out what users want which means thinking like the users. If users want search engines to work like natural language, most likely they will want web content to behave this way. The challenge for marketing organizations is to incorporated associations and keywords that are relevant to their users as well as their brands.

Web content optimized for semantics incorporates natural key words, rather than depending on rigid keyword insertion. Types of semantic keywords include: Core keywords that contain variations; thematic keywords for conceptually related terms; and stem keywords that anticipate what people might ask. Content can be further optimized through content relevancy and 'shareworthiness', and sharing content through social media integration.

Users of Business Intelligence (BI) and analytics tools often have semantic search requirements. The BI tools need to be flexible so that business users can find the information they need for analysis, reports and dashboards. Users of Big Data have a similar need to find common meaning in data from disparate formats.

1.3.10 Unstructured Data

It is estimated that as much as 80% of all stored data is maintained outside of relational databases. This unstructured data does not have a data model that enables users to understand its content or how it is organized; it is not tagged or structured into rows and columns. The term *unstructured* is somewhat misleading, as there often is structure in documents, graphics, and other formats, for instance, chapters or headers. Some refer to data stored outside relational databases as *non-tabular* or *semi-structured* data. No single term adequately describes the vast volume and diverse format of electronic information that is created and stored in today's world.

Unstructured data is found in various electronic formats: word processing documents, electronic mail, social media, chats, flat files, spreadsheets, XML files, transactional messages, reports, graphics, digital images, microfiche, video recordings, and audio recordings. An enormous amount of unstructured data also exists in paper files.

The fundamental principles of data management apply to both structured and unstructured data. Unstructured data is a valuable corporate asset. Storage, integrity, security, content quality, access, and effective use guide the management of unstructured data. Unstructured data requires data governance, architecture, security Metadata, and data quality.

Unstructured and semi-structured data have become more important to data warehousing and Business Intelligence. Data warehouses and their data models may include structured indexes to help users find and analyze unstructured data. Some databases include the capacity to handle URLs to unstructured data that perform as hyperlinks when retrieved from the database table. Unstructured data in data lakes is described in Chapter 14.

1.3.11 Workflow

Content development should be managed through a workflow that ensures content is created on schedule and receives proper approvals. Workflow components can include the creation, processing, routing, rules, administration, security, electronic signature, deadline, escalation (if problems occur), reporting and delivery. It should be automated through the use of a content management system (CMS) or a standalone system, rather than manual processes.

A CMS has the added benefit of providing version control. When content is checked into a CMS, it will be timestamped, assigned a version number, and tagged with the name of the person who made the updates.

The workflow needs to be repeatable, ideally containing process steps common across a variety of content. A set of workflows and templates may be necessary if there are significant differences between content types. Alignment of the stakeholders and distribution points (including technology) is important. Deadlines need to be refined to improve workflows, otherwise you can quickly find your work flows are out of date or there is confusion over which stakeholder is responsible for which piece.

2. Activities

2.1 Plan for Lifecycle Management

The practice of document management involves planning for a document's lifecycle, from its creation or receipt, through its distribution, storage, retrieval, archiving and potential destruction. Planning includes developing classification / indexing systems and taxonomies that enable storage and retrieval of documents. Importantly, lifecycle planning requires creating policy specifically for records.

First, identify the organizational unit responsible for managing the documents and records. That unit coordinates the access and distribution internally and externally, and integrates best practices and process flows with other departments throughout the organization. It also develops an overall document management plan that includes a business continuity plan for vital documents and records. The unit ensures it follows retention policies aligned with company standards and government regulations. It ensures that records required for long-term needs are properly archived and that others are properly destroyed at the end of their lifecycle in accordance with organizational requirements, statutes, and regulations.

2.1.1 Plan for Records Management

Records management starts with a clear definition of what constitutes a record. The team that defines records for a functional area should include SMEs from that area along with people who understand the systems that enable management of the records.

Managing electronic records requires decisions about where to store current, active records and how to archive older records. Despite the widespread use of electronic media, paper records are not going away in the near term. A records management approach should account for paper records and unstructured data as well as structured electronic records.

2.1.2 Develop a Content Strategy

Planning for content management should directly support the organization's approach to providing relevant and useful content in an efficient and comprehensive manner. A plan should account for content drivers (the reasons content is needed), content creation and delivery. Content requirements should drive technology decisions, such as the selection of a content management system.

A content strategy should start with an inventory of current state and a gap assessment. The strategy defines how content will be prioritized, organized, and accessed. Assessment often reveals ways to streamline production, workflow, and approval processes for content creation. A unified content strategy emphasizes designing modular content components for reusability rather than creating standalone content.

Enabling people to find different types of content through Metadata categorization and search engine optimization (SEO) is critical to any content strategy. Provide recommendations on content creation, publication, and governance. Policies, standards, and guidelines that apply to content and its lifecycle are useful to sustain and evolve an organization's content strategy.

2.1.3 Create Content Handling Policies

Policies codify requirements by describing principles, direction, and guidelines for action. They help employees understand and comply with the requirements for document and records management.

Most document management programs have policies related to:

- Scope and compliance with audits
- Identification and protection of vital records
- Purpose and schedule for retaining records (a.k.a retention schedule)
- How to respond to information hold orders (special protection orders); these are requirements for retaining information for a lawsuit, even if retention schedules have expired
- Requirements for onsite and offsite storage of records
- Use and maintenance of hard drive and shared network drives
- Email management, addressed from content management perspective
- Proper destruction methods for records (e.g., with pre-approved vendors and receipt of destruction certificates)

2.1.3.1 Social Media Policies

In addition to these standard topics, many organizations are developing policies to respond to new media. For example, an organization has to define if social media content posted on Facebook, Twitter, LinkedIn, chat rooms, blogs, wikis, or online forums constitutes a record, especially if employees post in the course of conducting business using organizational accounts.

2.1.3.2 Device Access Policies

Since the pendulum is swinging towards user driven IT with BYOD (bring-your-own-devices), BYOA (bring-your-own-apps), and WYOD (wear-your-own-devices), the content and records management functions need to work with these scenarios in order to ensure compliance, security and privacy.

Policies should distinguish between informal content (e.g., Dropbox or Evernote) and formal content (e.g., contracts and agreements), in order to put controls on formal content. Policies can also provide guidance on informal content.

2.1.3.3 Handling Sensitive Data

Organizations are legally required to protect privacy by identifying and protecting sensitive data. Data Security and/or Data Governance usually establish the confidentiality schemes and identify what assets are confidential or restricted. The people who produce or assemble content must apply these classifications. Documents, web pages, and other content components must be are marked as sensitive based on policies and legal requirements. Once marked, confidential data is either masked or deleted where appropriate. (See Chapter 7.)

2.1.3.4 Responding to Litigation

Organizations should prepare for the possibility of litigation requests through proactive e-discovery. (Hope for the best; prepare for the worst.) They should create and manage an inventory of their data sources and the risks associated with each. By identifying data sources that may have relevant information, they can respond in a timely manner to a litigation hold notice and prevent data loss. The appropriate technologies should be deployed to automate e-discovery processes.

2.1.4 Define Content Information Architecture

Many information systems such as the semantic web, search engines, web social mining, records compliance and risk management, geographic information systems (GIS), and Business Intelligence applications contain structured and unstructured data, documents, text, images, etc. Users have to submit their needs in a form understandable by the system retrieval mechanism to obtain information from these systems. Likewise, the inventory of documents and structured and unstructured data needs to be described / indexed in a format that allows the retrieval mechanism to identify the relevant matched data and information quickly. User queries may be imperfect in that they retrieve both relevant and irrelevant information, or do not retrieve all the relevant information.

Searches use either content-based indexing or Metadata. Indexing designs look at decision options for key aspects or attributes of indexes based on needs and preferences of users. They also look at the vocabulary management and the syntax for combining individual terms into headings or search statements.

Data management professionals may get involved with controlled vocabularies and terms in handling Reference Data (see Section 1.3.2.1) and Metadata for unstructured data and content. (See Chapter 12.) They should ensure that there is coordination with efforts to build controlled vocabularies, indexes, classification schemes for information retrieval, and data modeling and Metadata efforts executed as part of data management projects and applications.

2.2 Manage the Lifecycle

2.2.1 Capture Records and Content

Capturing content is the first step to managing it. Electronic content is often already in a format to be stored in electronic repositories. To reduce the risk of losing or damaging records, paper content needs to be scanned and then uploaded to the corporate system, indexed, and stored in the repository. Use electronic signatures if possible.

When content is captured, it should be tagged (indexed) with appropriate Metadata, such as (at minimum) a document or image identifier, the data and time of capture, the title and author(s). Metadata is necessary for retrieval of the information, as well as for understanding the context of the content. Automated workflows and recognition technologies can help with the capture and ingestion process, providing audit trails.

Some social media platforms offer the capability of capturing records. Saving the social media content in a repository makes it available for review, meta tagging and classification, and management as records. Web crawlers can capture versions of websites. Web capture tools, application-programming interfaces (APIs), and RSS feeds can capture content or social media export tools. Social media records can also be captured manually or via predefined, automated workflows.

2.2.2 Manage Versioning and Control

ANSI Standard 859 has three levels of control of data, based on the criticality of the data and the perceived harm that would occur if data were corrupted or otherwise unavailable: formal, revision, and custody:

- **Formal control** requires formal change initiation, thorough evaluation for impact, decision by a change authority, and full status accounting of implementation and validation to stakeholders

- **Revision control** is less formal, notifying stakeholders and incrementing versions when a change is required

- **Custody control** is the least formal, merely requiring safe storage and a means of retrieval

Table 15 shows a sample list of data assets and possible control levels.

ANSI 859 recommends taking into account the following criteria when determining which control level applies to a data asset:

- Cost of providing and updating the asset

- Project impact, if changes will have significant cost or schedule consequences
- Other consequences of change to the enterprise or project
- Need to reuse the asset or earlier versions of the asset
- Maintenance of a history of change (when required by the enterprise or the project)

Table 15 Levels of Control for Documents per ANSI-859

Data Asset	Formal	Revision	Custody
Action item lists		X	
Agendas			X
Audit findings		X	X
Budgets	X		
DD 250s			X
Final Proposal			X
Financial data and reports	X	X	X
Human Resources data		X	
Meeting minutes			X
Meeting notices and attendance lists		X	X
Project plans (including data management and configuration management plans)	X		
Proposal (in process)		X	
Schedules	X		
Statements of Work	X		
Trade studies		X	
Training material	X	X	
Working papers			X

2.2.3 Backup and Recovery

The document / record management system needs to be included in the organization's overall corporate backup and recovery activities, including business continuity and disaster recovery planning. A vital records program provides the organization with access to the records necessary to conduct its business during a disaster and to resume normal business afterward. Vital records must be identified, and plans for their protection and recovery must be developed and maintained. A records manager should be involved in risk mitigation and business continuity planning, to ensure these activities account for the security for vital records.

Disasters could include power outages, human error, network and hardware failure, software malfunction, malicious attack, as well as natural disasters. A Business Continuity Plan (or Disaster Recovery Plan) contains written policies, procedures, and information designed to mitigate the impact of threats to an organization's data, including documents, and to recover them as quickly as possible, with minimum disruption, in the event of a disaster.

2.2.4 Manage Retention and Disposal

Effective document / records management requires clear policies and procedures, especially regarding retention and disposal of records. A retention and disposition policy will define the timeframes during which documents for operational, legal, fiscal or historical value must be maintained. It defines when inactive documents can be transferred to a secondary storage facility, such as off-site storage. The policy specifies the processes for compliance and the methods and schedules for the disposition of documents. Legal and regulatory requirements must be considered when setting up retention schedules.

Records managers or information asset owners provide oversight to ensure that teams account for privacy and data protection requirements, and take actions to prevent in identify theft.

Document retention presents software considerations. Access to electronic records may require specific versions of software and operating systems. Technological changes as simple as the installation of new software can make documents unreadable or inaccessible.

Non-value-added information should be removed from the organization's holdings and disposed of to avoid wasting physical and electronic space, as well as the cost associated with its maintenance. There is also risk associated with retaining records past their legally required timeframes. This information remains discoverable for litigation.

Still, many organizations do not prioritize removal of non-value added information because:

- Policies are not adequate

- One person's non-valued-added information is another's valued information

- Inability to foresee future possible needs for current non-value-added physical and / or electronic records

- There is no buy-in for Records Management

- Inability to decide which records to delete

- Perceived cost of making a decision and removing physical and electronic records

- Electronic space is cheap. Buying more space when required is easier than archiving and removal processes

2.2.5 Audit Documents / Records

Document / records management requires periodic auditing to ensure that the right information is getting to the right people at the right time for decision-making or performing operational activities. Table 16 contains examples of audit measures.

An audit usually involves the following steps:

- Defining organizational drivers and identifying the stakeholders that comprise the 'why' of document / records management
- Gathering data on the process (the 'how'), once it is determined what to examine / measure and what tools to use (such as standards, benchmarks, interview surveys)
- Reporting the outcomes
- Developing an action plan of next steps and timeframes

Table 16 Sample Audit Measures

Document / Records Management Component	Sample Audit Measure
Inventory	Each location in the inventory is uniquely identified.
Storage	Storage areas for physical documents / records have adequate space to accommodate growth.
Reliability and Accuracy	Spot checks are executed to confirm that the documents / records are an adequate reflection of what has been created or received.
Classification and Indexing Schemes	Metadata and document file plans are well described.
Access and Retrieval	End users find and retrieve critical information easily.
Retention Processes	The retention schedule is structured in a logical way either by department, functional or major organizational functions.
Disposition Methods	Documents / records are disposed of as recommended.
Security and Confidentiality	Breaches of document / record confidentiality and loss of documents / records are recorded as security incidents and managed appropriately.
Organizational understanding of documents / records management	Appropriate training is provided to stakeholders and staff as to the roles and responsibilities related to document / records management.

2.3 Publish and Deliver Content

2.3.1 Provide Access, Search, and Retrieval

Once the content has been described by Metadata / key word tagging and classified within the appropriate information content architecture, it is available for retrieval and use. Portal technology that maintains profiles of users can help them find unstructured data. Search engines can return content based on keywords. Some organizations have professionals retrieve information through internal search tools.

2.3.2 Deliver Through Acceptable Channels

There is a shift in delivery expectations as the content users now want to consume or use content on a device of their choosing. Many organizations are still creating content in something like MS Word and moving it into HTML, or delivering content for a given platform, a certain screen resolution, or a given size on the screen. If another delivery channel is desired, this content has to be prepared for that channel (e.g., print). There is the potential that any changed content may need to be brought back into the original format.

When structured data from databases is formatted into HTML, it becomes difficult to recover the original structured data, as separating the data from the formatting is not always straightforward.

3. Tools

3.1 Enterprise Content Management Systems

An ECM may consist of a platform of core components or a set of applications that can be integrated wholly or used separately. These components, discussed below, can be in-house or outside the enterprise in the cloud.

Reports can be delivered through a number of tools, including printers, email, websites, portals, and messaging, as well as through a document management system interface. Depending on the tool, users can search by drill-down, view, download / check-in and out, and print reports on demand. The ability to add, change, or delete reports organized in folders facilitates report management. Report retention can be set for automatic purge or archival to other media, such as disk, CD-ROM, COLD (Computer Output to Laser Disk), etc. Reports can also be retained in cloud storage. As noted, retaining content in unreadable, outdated formats presents risk to the organization. (See Chapters 6 and 8, and Section 3.1.8.)

The boundaries between document management and content management are blurring as business processes and roles intertwine, and vendors try to widen the markets for their products.

3.1.1 Document Management

A *document management system* is an application used to track and store electronic documents and electronic images of paper documents. Document library systems, electronic mail systems and image management systems are specialized document management systems. Document management systems commonly provide storage, versioning, security, Metadata Management, content indexing, and retrieval capabilities. Extended capabilities of some systems can include Metadata views of documents.

Documents are created within a document management system, or captured via scanners or OCR software. These electronic documents must be indexed via keywords or text during the capture process so that the documents can be found. Metadata, such as the creator's name, and the dates the document was created, revised, stored, is typically stored for each document. Documents can be categorized for retrieval using a unique document identifier or by specifying partial search terms involving the document identifier and / or parts of the expected Metadata. Metadata can be extracted from the document automatically or added by the user. Bibliographic records of documents are descriptive structured data, typically in Machine-Readable Cataloging (MARC) standard format that are stored in library databases locally and made available through shared catalogues worldwide, as privacy and permissions allow.

Some systems have advanced capabilities such as compound document support and content replication. Word processing software creates the compound document and integrates non-text elements such as spreadsheets, videos, audio and other multimedia types. In addition, a compound document can be an organized collection of user interfaces to form a single, integrated view.

Document storage includes functions to manage documents. A document repository enables check-in and check-out features, versioning, collaboration, comparison, archiving, status state(s), migration from one storage media to another, and disposition. It may offer some access to and version management of documents external to its own repository (e.g., in a file share or cloud environment).

Some document management systems have a module that may support different types of workflows, such as:

- Manual workflows that indicate where the user sends the document
- Rules-based workflow, where rules are created that dictate the flow of the document within an organization
- Dynamic rules that allow for different workflows based on content

Document management systems have a rights management module where the administrator grants access based on document type and user credentials. Organizations may determine that certain types of documents require additional security or control procedures. Security restrictions, including privacy and confidentiality restrictions, apply during the document's creation and management, as well as during delivery. An electronic signature ensures the identity of the document sender and the authenticity of the message, among other things.

Some systems focus more on control and security of data and information, than on its access, use, or retrieval, particularly in the intelligence, military, and scientific research sectors. Highly competitive or highly regulated industries, such as the pharmaceutical and financial sectors, also implement extensive security and control measures.

3.1.1.1 Digital Asset Management

Since the functionality needed is similar, many document management systems include digital asset management. This is the management of digital assets such as audio, video, music, and digital photographs. Tasks involve cataloging, storage, and retrieval of digital assets.

3.1.1.2 Image Processing

An image processing system captures, transforms, and manages images of paper and electronic documents. The capturing capability uses technologies such as scanning, optical and intelligence character recognition, or form processing. Users can index or enter Metadata into the system and save the digitized image in a repository.

Recognition technologies include optical character recognition (OCR), which is the mechanical or electronic conversion of scanned (digitized) printed or handwritten text into a form that can be recognized by computer software. Intelligent character recognition (ICR) is a more advanced OCR system that can deal with printed and cursive handwriting. Both are important for converting large amounts of forms or unstructured data to a CMS format.

Forms processing is the capture of printed forms via scanning or recognition technologies. Forms submitted through a website can be captured as long as the system recognizes the layout, structure, logic, and contents.

Besides document images, other digitized images such as digital photographs, infographics, spatial or non-spatial data images may be stored in repositories. Some ECM systems are able to ingest diverse types of digitized documents and images such as COLD information, .wav and .wmv (audio) files, XML and healthcare HL7 messages into an integrated repository.

Images are often created by using computer software or cameras rather than on paper. Binary file formats include vector and raster (bitmap) types as well as MS Word .DOC format. Vector images use mathematical formulas rather than individual colored blocks, and are very good for creating graphics that frequently require resizing. File formats include .EPS, .AI or .PDF. Raster images use a fixed number of colored pixels to form a complete image, and cannot be resized easily without compromising their resolution. Examples of raster files include .JPEG, .GIF, .PNG, or .TIFF.

3.1.1.3 Records Management System

A records management system may offer capabilities such as automation of retention and disposition, e-discovery support, and long-term archiving to comply with legal and regulatory requirements. It should support a vital records program to retain critical business records. This type of system may be integrated with a documents management system.

3.1.2 Content Management System

A content management system is used to collect, organize, index, and retrieve content, storing it either as components or whole documents, while maintaining links between components. A CMS may also provide controls for revising content within documents. While a document management system may provide content management functionality over the documents under its control, a content management system is essentially independent of where and how the documents are stored.

Content management systems manage content through its lifecycle. For example, a web content management system controls website content through authoring, collaboration, and management tools based on core repository. It may contain user-friendly content creation, workflow and change management, and deployment functions to handle intranet, Internet, and extranet applications. Delivery functions may include responsive design and adaptive capabilities to support a range of client devices. Additional components may include search, document composition, e-signature, content analytics, and mobile applications.

3.1.3 Content and Document Workflow

Workflow tools support business processes, route content and documents, assign work tasks, track status, and create audit trails. A workflow provides for review and approval of content before it is published.

3.2 Collaboration Tools

Team collaboration tools enable the collection, storage, workflow, and management of documents pertinent to team activities. Social networking enables individual and teams to share documents and content inside the team and to reach out to an external group for input using blogs, wikis, RSS, and tagging.

3.3 Controlled Vocabulary and Metadata Tools

Tools that help develop or manage controlled vocabularies and Metadata range from office productivity software, Metadata repositories, and BI tools, to document and content management systems. For example:

- Data models used as guides to the data in an organization
- Document management systems and office productivity software
- Metadata repositories, glossaries, or directories
- Taxonomies and cross-reference schemes between taxonomies
- Indexes to collections (e.g., particular product, market or installation), filesystems, opinion polls, archives, locations, or offsite holdings
- Search engines
- BI tools that incorporate unstructured data
- Enterprise and departmental thesauri
- Published reports libraries, contents and bibliographies, and catalogs

3.4 Standard Markup and Exchange Formats

Computer applications cannot process unstructured data / content directly. Standard markup and exchange formats facilitate the sharing of data across information systems and the Internet.

3.4.1 XML

Extensible Markup Language (XML) provides a language for representing both structured and unstructured data and information. XML uses Metadata to describe the content, structure, and business rules of any document or database.

XML requires translating the structure of the data into a document structure for data exchange. XML tags data elements to identify the meaning of the data. Simple nesting and references provide the relationships between data elements.

XML namespaces provide a method to avoid a name conflict when two different documents use the same element names. Older methods of markup include HTML and SGML, to name a few.

The need for XML-capable content management has grown for several reasons:

- XML provides the capability of integrating structured data into relational databases with unstructured data. Unstructured data can be stored in a relational DBMS BLOB (binary large object) or in XML files.

- XML can integrate structured data with unstructured data in documents, reports, email, images, graphics, audio, and video files. Data modeling should take into account the generation of unstructured reports from structured data, and include them in creating error-correction workflows, backup, recovery, and archiving.

- XML also can build enterprise or corporate portals, (Business-to-Business [B2B], Business-to-Customer [B2C]), which provide users with a single access point to a variety of content.

- XML provides identification and labeling of unstructured data / content so that computer applications can understand and process them. In this way, structured data appends to unstructured content. An Extensible Markup Interface (XMI) specification consists of rules for generating the XML document containing the actual Metadata and thus is a 'structure' for XML.

3.4.2 JSON

JSON (JavaScript Object Notation) is an open, lightweight standard format for data interchange. Its text format is language-independent and easy to parse, but uses conventions from the C-family of languages. JSON has two structures: a collection of unordered name / value pairs known as objects and an ordered list of values realized as an array. It is emerging as the preferred format in web-centric, NoSQL databases.

An alternative to XML, JSON is used to transmit data between a server and web application. JSON is a similar but more compact way of representing, transmitting, and interpreting data than XML. Either XML or JSON content can be returned when using REST technology.

3.4.3 RDF and Related W3C Specifications

Resource Description Framework (RDF), a common framework used to describe information about any Web resource, is a standard model for data interchange on the Web. The RDF resources are saved in a triplestore, which is a database used to store and retrieve semantic queries using SPARQL.

RDF makes statements about a resource in the form of subject (resource)-predicate (property name)-object (property value) expressions or triples. Usually the subject-predicate-object is each described by a URI (Uniform Resource Identifier), but the subject and object could be blank nodes and the object could be a literal (null values and null strings are not supported). A URI names the relationship between resources as well as two ends of the link or triple. The most common form of URI is a URL (uniform resource locator). This allows structured and semi-structured data to be shared across applications.

The Semantic Web needs access to both data and relationships between data sets. The collection of interrelated data sets is also known as Linked Data. URIs provide a generic way to identify any entity that exists. HTML provides a means to structure and link documents on the Web. RDF provides a generic, graph-based data model to link data that describes things.

RDF uses XML as its encoding syntax. It views Metadata as data (e.g., author, date of creation, etc.). The described resources of RDF allow for the association of semantic meanings to resources. RDFS (RDF Schema) provides a data modeling vocabulary for RDF data and is an extension of the basic RDF vocabulary.

SKOS (Simple Knowledge Organization System) is a RDF vocabulary (i.e., an application of the RDF data model to capture data depicted as a hierarchy of concepts). Any type of classification, taxonomy, or thesaurus can be represented in SKOS.

OWL (W3C Web Ontology Language) is a vocabulary extension of RDF. It is a semantic markup language for publishing and sharing OWL documents (ontologies) on the Web. It is used when information contained in documents needs to be processed by applications rather than humans. Both RDF and OWL are Semantic Web standards that provide a framework for sharing and reuse of data, as well as enabling data integration and interoperability, on the Web.

RDF can help with the 'variety' characteristic of Big Data. If the data is accessible using the RDF triples model, data from different sources can be mixed and the SPARQL query language used to find connections and patterns without predefining a schema. As W3C describes it, "RDF has features that facilitate data merging even if the underlying schemas differ, and it specifically supports the evolution of schemas over time without requiring all the data consumers to be changed."[52] It can integrate disparate data from many sources and formats and then either reduce or replace the data sets (known as data fusion) through semantic alignment. (See Chapter 14.)

3.4.4 Schema.org

Labeling content with semantic markup (e.g., as defined by the open source Schema.org) makes it easier for semantic search engines to index content and for web crawlers to match content with a search query. Schema.org provides a collection of shared vocabularies or schemas for on-page markup so that the major search engines can understand them. It focuses on the meaning of the words on web pages as well as terms and keywords.

Snippets are the text that appears under every search result. Rich snippets are the detailed information on specific searches (e.g., gold star ratings under the link). To create rich snippets, the content on the web pages needs to be formatted properly with structured data like Microdata (a set of tags introduced with HTML5) and shared vocabularies from Schema.org.

The Schema.org vocabulary collection can also be used for structured data interoperability (e.g., with JSON).

3.5 E-discovery Technology

E-discovery often involves review of large volumes of documents. E-discovery technologies offer many capabilities and techniques such as early case assessment, collection, identification, preservation, processing, optical character recognition (OCR), culling, similarity analysis, and email thread analysis. Technology-assisted review (TAR) is a workflow or process where a team can review selected documents and mark them relevant or

---

[52] W3C, "Resource Description Framework (RDF)," http://bit.ly/1k9btZQ.

not. These decisions are become input for the predictive coding engine that reviews and sorts remaining documents according to relevancy. Support for information governance may be a feature as well.

4. Techniques

4.1 Litigation Response Playbook

E-discovery starts at the beginning of a lawsuit. However, an organization can plan for litigation response through the development of a playbook containing objectives, metrics and responsibilities before a major discovery project begins.

The playbook defines the target environment for e-discovery and assesses if gaps exist between current and target environments. It documents business processes for the lifecycle of e-discovery activities and identifies roles and responsibilities of the e-discovery team. A playbook can also enable an organization to identify risks and proactively prevent situations that might result in litigation.

To compile a playbook,

- Establish an inventory of policies and procedures for specific departments (Legal, Records Management, IT).
- Draft policies for topics, such as litigation holds, document retention, archiving, and backups.
- Evaluate IT tool capabilities such as e-discovery indexing, search and collection, data segregation and protection tools as well as the unstructured ESI sources / systems.
- Identify and analyze pertinent legal issues.
- Develop a communication and training plan to train employees on what is expected.
- Identify materials that may be prepared in advance for tailoring to a legal case.
- Analyze vendor services in case outside services are required.
- Develop processes on how to handle a notification and keep the playbook current.

4.2 Litigation Response Data Map

E-discovery often has a limited timeframe (e.g., 90 days). Providing attorneys with a data map of the IT and ESI environment available can enable an organization to respond more effectively. A data map is a catalog of information systems. It describes the systems and their uses, the information they contain, retention policies, and other characteristics. Catalogs often identify systems of record, originating applications, archives, disaster recovery copies, or backups, and media used for each. A data map should be comprehensive, containing all systems. Since email is often an object of scrutiny in litigation, the map should also describe how email is stored, processed, and consumed. Mapping business processes to the list of the systems and documenting user roles and privileges will enable assessment and documentation of information flows.

The process of creating the data map will demonstrate the value of creating Metadata as part of the document management process. Metadata is critical for searching. It also gives ESI documents context and enables cases, transcripts, undertakings, etc. to be associated with supporting documents.

An e-discovery data map should indicate which records are readily accessible and which are not. There are different e-discovery rules for these two categories. The inaccessible data needs to be identified and the reasons why it is inaccessible need to be documented. To respond appropriately to litigation, an organization should have an inventory of records in offsite storage, including external cloud storage.

Often, systems inventories already exist. For example, they may be maintained by Data Architecture, Metadata Management or IT Asset Management. The legal and / or records management functions should determine whether these can be extended for e-discovery purposes.

5. Implementation Guidelines

Implementing ECM is a long-term effort that can be perceived as expensive. As with any enterprise-wide effort, it requires buy-in from a wide range of stakeholders, and funding support from an executive committee for funding. With a large project, there is a risk that it will fall victim to budget cuts, business swings, management changes or inertia. To minimize risks, ensure that the content, not the technology, drives decisions for ECM implementation. Configure the workflow around the organizational needs to show value.

5.1 Readiness Assessment / Risk Assessment

The purpose of an ECM readiness assessment is to identify areas where content management improvement is needed and to determine how well adapted the organization is to changing its processes to meet these needs. A Data Management Maturity Assessment model can help in this process. (See Chapter 15.)

Some ECM critical success factors are similar to those in IT projects (e.g., executive support, involvement of users, user training, change management, corporate culture, and communication). Specific ECM critical success factors include content audit and classification for existing content, appropriate information architecture, support of the content lifecycle, definitions of appropriate Metadata tags, and the ability to customize functions in an ECM solution. Because ECM solutions involve technical and process complexity, the organization needs to ensure that it has the appropriate resources to support the process.

Risks can arise with ECM implementations due to project size, complexity in integrating with other software applications, process and organizational issues, and the effort required to migrate content. Lack of training for core team members and internal staff can lead to uneven use. Other risks include failure to put policies, processes, and procedures in place or lack of communication with stakeholders.

5.1.1 Records Management Maturity

ARMA's Generally Accepted Recordkeeping Principles® (See section 1.2) can guide an organization's assessment of it policies and practices for Records Management. Along with GARP, ARMA International has an Information Governance Maturity Model that can help assess an organization's recordkeeping program and practices.[53] This Maturity Model describes the characteristics of the information governance and recordkeeping environment at five levels of maturity for each of the eight GARP principles:

- **Level 1 Sub-Standard**: Information governance and recordkeeping concerns are not addressed or just minimally

- **Level 2 In Development**: Developing recognition that information governance and recordkeeping can have an impact on the organization

- **Level 3 Essential**: Minimum requirements that must be addressed to meet the legal and regulatory requirements

- **Level 4 Proactive**: A proactive information governance program has been established with a focus on continuous improvement

- **Level 5 Transformational**: Information governance is integrated into the corporate infrastructure and business processes

Several standards can be applied for technical assessments of records management systems and applications. For example,

- DoD 5015.2 Electronic Records Management Software Applications Design Criteria Standard
- ISO 16175, Principles and Functional Requirements for Records in Electronic Office Environments
- The Model Requirements for the Management of Electronic Records (MoReq2)
- The Records Management Services (RMS) specification from the Object Management Group (OMG)

Gaps and risks identified in records management readiness assessments should be analyzed their potential impact on the organization. Businesses are subject to laws that require maintenance and secure destruction of records. If an organization does not inventory its records, it is already at risk since it cannot know if records have been stolen or destroyed. An organization can spend a lot of time and money trying to find records if it lacks a functional record retention program. Lack of adherence to legal and regulatory requirements can lead to costly fines. Failure to identify and protect vital records can put a company out of business.

5.1.2 E-discovery Assessment

A readiness assessment should examine and identify improvement opportunities for the litigation response program. A mature program will specify clear roles and responsibilities, preservation protocols, data collection methodologies, and disclosure processes. Both the program and resulting processes should be documented, defensible, and auditable.

---

53 ARMA International, Information Governance Maturity Model, http://bit.ly/2sPWGOe.

The program needs to understand the organization's information lifecycle and develop an ESI data map for data sources (see Section 2.1.3.4). Since data preservation is a critical legal requirement, data retention policies should be proactively reviewed and assessed in anticipation of litigation. There should be a plan to work with IT to quickly implement litigation holds as required.

The risks of not having defined a proactive litigation response should be assessed and quantified. Sometimes organizations respond only if there is anticipated litigation, and then there is a scramble to find relevant documents and information to review. Most likely, this type of organization either over specifies the amount of data to be kept (i.e., everything) or does not have data deletion policies in place. Not having a retention schedule for data and information can lead to legal liabilities if older unpurged records are required for e-discovery, but not available.

5.2 Organization and Cultural Change

People can be a greater challenge than the technology. There may be issues in adapting the management practices in daily activities and getting people to use ECM. In that some cases, ECM can lead to more tasks; for example, scanning paper documents and defining required Metadata.

Often organizations manage information, including records, departmentally, creating information silos that hinder the sharing and proper management of data. A holistic enterprise approach to content and records management can eliminate users' perception that they need to store copies of the content. The ideal solution is a single repository, centrally and securely managed, with clearly defined policies and processes enforced across the enterprise. Training and communication about the processes, policies, and tools are critical to the success of a records management or ECM program.

Privacy, data protection, confidentiality, intellectual property, encryption, ethical use, and identity are the important issues that document and content management professionals must deal with in cooperation with other employees, management, and regulators. A centralized organization often deals with processes to improve access to information, control the growth of materials taking up office space, reduce operating costs, minimize litigation risks, safeguard vital information, and support better decision-making.

Both content and records management need to be elevated organizationally, and not seen as low-level or low-priority functions. In heavily regulated industries, the Records and Information Management (RIM) function needs to be closely aligned with the corporate legal function along with the e-discovery function. If the organization has objectives to improve operational efficiency by managing information better, then RIM should be aligned with marketing or an operational support group. If the organization sees RIM as part of IT, the RIM function should report directly to the CIO or CDO. Often the RIM function is found in ECM program or Enterprise Information Management (EIM) program.

6. Documents and Content Governance

6.1 Information Governance Frameworks

Documents, records, and other unstructured content represent risk to an organization. Managing this risk and getting value from this information both require governance. Drivers include:

- Legal and regulatory compliance
- Defensible disposition of records
- Proactive preparation for e-discovery
- Security of sensitive information
- Management of risk areas such as email and Big Data

Principles of successful Information Governance programs are emerging. One set of principles is the ARMA GARP® principles (see Section 1.2). Other principles include:

- Assign executive sponsorship for accountability
- Educate employees on information governance responsibilities
- Classify information under the correct record code or taxonomy category
- Ensure authenticity and integrity of information
- Determine that the official record is electronic unless specified differently
- Develop policies for alignment of business systems and third-parties to information governance standards
- Store, manage, make accessible, monitor, and audit approved enterprise repositories and systems for records and content
- Secure confidential or personally identifiable information
- Control unnecessary growth of information
- Dispose information when it reaches the end of its lifecycle
- Comply with requests for information (e.g., discovery, subpoena, etc.)
- Improve continuously

The Information Governance Reference Model (IGRM) (Figure 74) shows the relationship of Information Governance to other organizational functions. The outer ring includes the stakeholders who put policies, standards, processes, tools and infrastructure in place to manage information. The center shows a lifecycle diagram with each lifecycle component within the color or colors of the stakeholder(s) who executes that component. The IGRM complements ARMA's GARP®.

Sponsorship by someone close to or within the 'C' suite is a critical requirement for the formation and sustainability of the Information Governance program. A cross-functional senior level Information Council or Steering Committee is established that meets on a regular basis. The Council is responsible for an enterprise Information Governance strategy, operating procedures, guidance on technology and standards, communications and training, monitoring, and funding. Information Governance policies are written for the stakeholder areas, and then ideally technology is applied for enforcement.

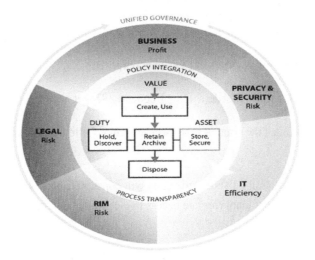

Figure 74 Information Governance Reference Model[54]

6.2 Proliferation of Information

Generally, unstructured data grows much faster than structured data. This adds to the challenge of governance. Unstructured data is not necessarily attached to a business function or department. Its ownership can be difficult to ascertain. It can also be difficult to classify the content of unstructured data, since the business purpose of the content cannot always be inferred from the system. Unmanaged unstructured data, without required Metadata, represents risk. It can be misinterpreted and, if content is not known, it may be mishandled or present privacy concerns. (See Chapter 14.)

6.3 Govern for Quality Content

Managing unstructured data requires effective partnership between data stewards and other data management professionals and records managers. For example, business data stewards can help define web portals, enterprise taxonomies, search engine indexes, and content management issues.

Document and content governance focuses on policies related to retention, electronic signatures, reporting formats, and report distribution. Policies will imply or state expectations about quality. Accurate, complete, and up-to-date

---

[54] EDRM (edrm.net). Content posted at EDRM.net is licensed under a Creative Commons Attribution 3.0 Unported License.

information will aid in making decisions. High quality information improves competitive advantage and increases organizational effectiveness. Defining quality content requires understanding the context of its production and use.

- **Producers**: Who creates the content and why do they create it?

- **Consumers**: Who uses the information and for what purposes?

- **Timing**: When is the information needed? How frequently does it need to be updated or accessed?

- **Format**: Do consumers need the content in a specific format for to meet their goals? Are there unacceptable formats?

- **Delivery**: How will information be delivered? How will consumers access the information? How will security be enforced to prevent inappropriate access to electronic content?

6.4 Metrics

Key Performance Indicators (KPIs) are both quantitative and qualitative measures used to review organizational performance against its goals. KPIs can be developed at the strategic and operational levels. Some KPIs may be appropriate for both levels, especially if they measure lifecycle functions or risks.

6.4.1 Records Management

At the strategic level, KPIs can be developed within such areas of records management compliance with regulatory requirements (e.g., time taken to meet requirements), and / or governance (e.g., compliance with policies). At the operational level, KPIs can be developed within such areas of records management resources (e.g., operational and capital costs), training (e.g., number of classes given, number of employees trained and at what level), delivery of daily records management services and operations (e.g., percentage meeting user SLAs), and / or integration of records management functions with other business systems (e.g., percentage of integration).

Criteria to measure success of a records management system implementation can include the following percentages:

- Percentage of total documents and email per user identified as corporate records
- Percentage of the identified corporate records declared as such and put under records control
- Percentage of total stored records that have the proper retention rules applied

These percentages can then be compared to determine best practice percentages.

Sometimes, measuring records management implementation success is a simple budgetary matter. A financial determination examines at what point the implementation of an electronic records management system becomes less expensive than acquiring more room to store paper records.

ARMA's GARP principle categories and maturity model can guide the definition of KPIs. ARMA's Information Governance Assessment software platform can identify information related compliance risks and develop metrics for governance program maturity in areas such as e-records and e-discovery (e.g., litigation holds).

6.4.2 E-discovery

One common KPI of e-discovery is cost reduction. Another KPI is efficiency gained in collecting information ahead of time rather reactively (e.g., average time in days to turn around e-discovery requests). How quickly an organization can implement a legal hold notification process (LHN) is third type of KPI.

Measurement of e-discovery is critical to a better rate of litigation wins. The EDRM model can guide development of KPIs based on what is required by each phase. ERDM also publishes a Metrics Model for e-discovery metrics.[55] The primary elements of Volume, Time, and Cost are in the center surrounded by the seven aspects of e-discovery work (Activities, Custodians, Systems, Media, Status, Format, and QA) which affect the outcome of the center elements.

6.4.3 ECM

KPIs should be developed to measure both tangible and intangible benefits of ECM. Tangible benefits include increased productivity, cost reduction, improved information quality, and improved compliance. Intangible benefits include improved collaboration, and simplification of job routines and workflow.

As ECM is being established, KPIs will focus on program and operational metrics. Program metrics include number of ECM projects, adoption, and user satisfaction levels. Operational metrics include the typical system type KPIs, such as the amount of downtime, number of users, etc.

Specific ECM metrics such as storage utilization (e.g., comparison of amount used with ECM implementation vs. amount used before ECM) and search retrieval performance can also be used as KPIs. Information retrieval is measured by precision and recall. Precision is the proportion of the retrieved documents that are actually relevant. Recall is a proportion of all relevant documents that are actually retrieved.

Over time, KPIs related to the value of business solutions can be developed.

- Financial KPIs can include the cost of ECM system, reduced costs related to physical storage, and percentage decrease in operational costs.

- Customer KPIs can include percentage incidents resolved at first contact and number of customer complaints.

- KPIs representing more effective and productive internal business processes can include percentage of paperwork reduced, percentage of error reduction using workflow and process automation.

- Training KPIs can include number of training sessions for management and non-management.

- Risk mitigation KPIs can include reduction of discovery costs, and number of audit trails tracking e-discovery requests.

---

[55] EDRM Metrics Model, http://bit.ly/2rURq7R.

7. Works Cited / Recommended

Boiko, Bob. *Content Management Bible*. 2nd ed. Wiley, 2004. Print.

Diamond, David. *Metadata for Content Management: Designing taxonomy, metadata, policy and workflow to make digital content systems better for users*. CreateSpace, 2016. Print.

Hedden, Heather. *The Accidental Taxonomist*. Information Today, Inc., 2010. Print.

Lambe, Patrick. *Organising Knowledge: Taxonomies, Knowledge and Organisational Effectiveness*. Chandos Publishing, 2007. Print. Chandos Knowledge Management.

Liu, Bing. *Web Data Mining: Exploring Hyperlinks, Contents, and Usage Data*. 2nd ed. Springer, 2011. Print. Data-Centric Systems and Applications.

Nichols, Kevin. *Enterprise Content Strategy: A Project Guide*. XML Press, 2015. Print.

Read, Judith and Mary Lea Ginn. *Records Management*. 9th ed. Cengage Learning, 2015. Print. Advanced Office Systems and Procedures.

Rockley, Ann and Charles Cooper. *Managing Enterprise Content: A Unified Content Strategy*. 2nd ed. New Riders, 2012. Print. Voices That Matter.

Smallwood, Robert F. *Information Governance: Concepts, Strategies, and Best Practices*. Wiley, 2014. Print. Wiley CIO.

US GAAP Financial Statement Taxonomy Project. *XBRL US GAAP Taxonomies*. v1.0 Technical Guide Document Number: SECOFM-USGAAPT-TechnicalGuide. Version 1.0. April 28, 2008 http://bit.ly/2rRauZt.

Reference and Master Data

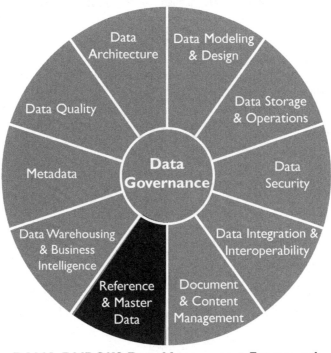

DAMA-DMBOK2 Data Management Framework

Copyright © 2017 by DAMA International

1. Introduction

In any organization, certain data is required across business areas, processes, and systems. The overall organization and its customers benefit if this data is shared and all business units can access the same customer lists, geographic location codes, business unit lists, delivery options, part lists, accounting cost center codes, governmental tax codes, and other data used to run the business. People using data generally assume a level of consistency exists across the organization, until they see disparate data.

In most organizations, systems and data evolve more organically than data management professionals would like. Particularly in large organizations, various projects and initiatives, mergers and acquisitions, and other business activities result in multiple systems executing essentially the same functions, isolated from each other. These conditions inevitably lead to inconsistencies in data structure and data values between systems. This variability increases costs and risks. Both can be reduced through the management of Master Data and Reference Data.

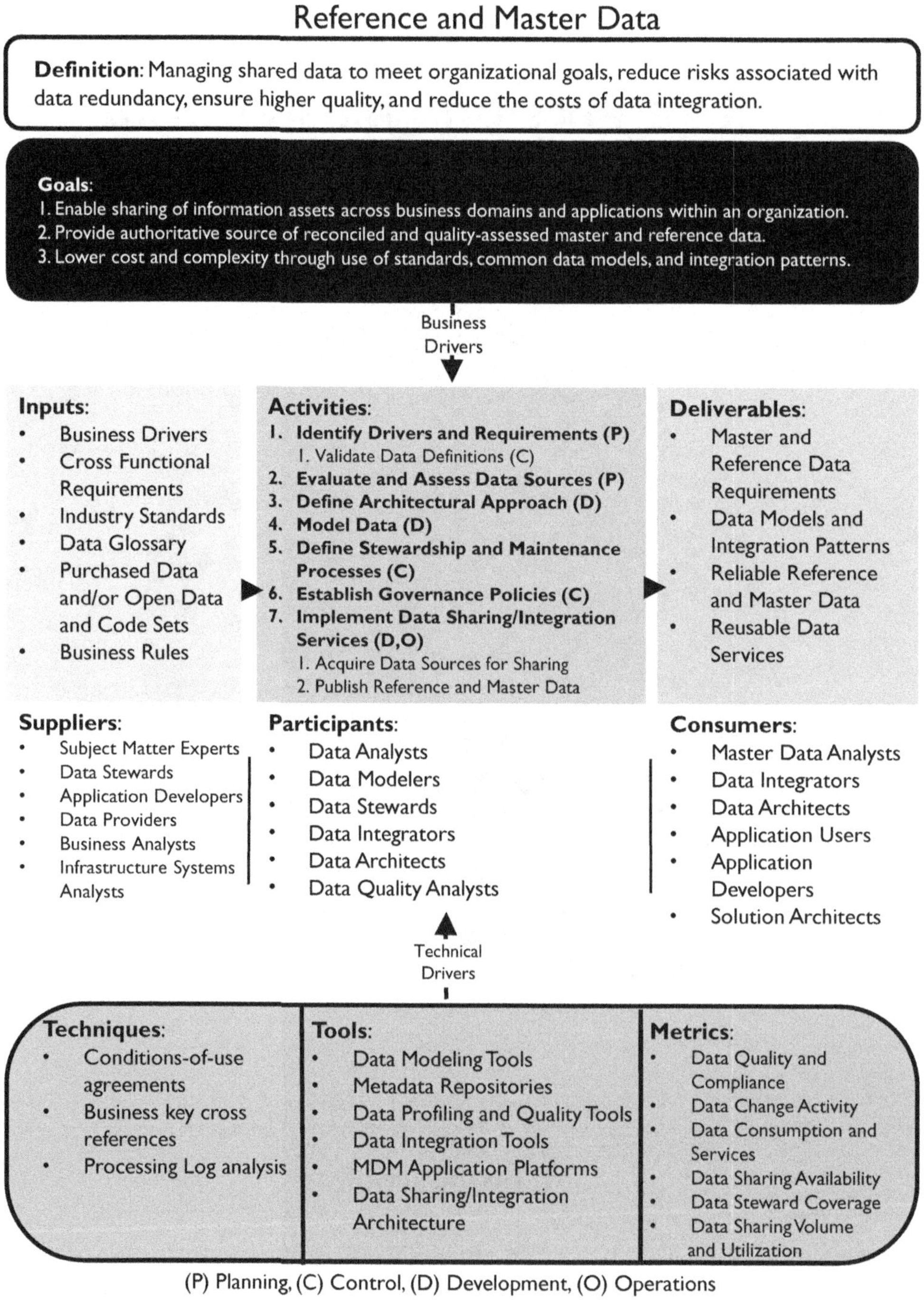

Reference and Master Data

Definition: Managing shared data to meet organizational goals, reduce risks associated with data redundancy, ensure higher quality, and reduce the costs of data integration.

Goals:
1. Enable sharing of information assets across business domains and applications within an organization.
2. Provide authoritative source of reconciled and quality-assessed master and reference data.
3. Lower cost and complexity through use of standards, common data models, and integration patterns.

Business Drivers

Inputs:
* Business Drivers
* Cross Functional Requirements
* Industry Standards
* Data Glossary
* Purchased Data and/or Open Data and Code Sets
* Business Rules

Activities:
1. **Identify Drivers and Requirements (P)**
   1. Validate Data Definitions (C)
2. **Evaluate and Assess Data Sources (P)**
3. **Define Architectural Approach (D)**
4. **Model Data (D)**
5. **Define Stewardship and Maintenance Processes (C)**
6. **Establish Governance Policies (C)**
7. **Implement Data Sharing/Integration Services (D,O)**
   1. Acquire Data Sources for Sharing
   2. Publish Reference and Master Data

Deliverables:
* Master and Reference Data Requirements
* Data Models and Integration Patterns
* Reliable Reference and Master Data
* Reusable Data Services

Suppliers:
* Subject Matter Experts
* Data Stewards
* Application Developers
* Data Providers
* Business Analysts
* Infrastructure Systems Analysts

Participants:
* Data Analysts
* Data Modelers
* Data Stewards
* Data Integrators
* Data Architects
* Data Quality Analysts

Consumers:
* Master Data Analysts
* Data Integrators
* Data Architects
* Application Users
* Application Developers
* Solution Architects

Technical Drivers

Techniques:
* Conditions-of-use agreements
* Business key cross references
* Processing Log analysis

Tools:
* Data Modeling Tools
* Metadata Repositories
* Data Profiling and Quality Tools
* Data Integration Tools
* MDM Application Platforms
* Data Sharing/Integration Architecture

Metrics:
* Data Quality and Compliance
* Data Change Activity
* Data Consumption and Services
* Data Sharing Availability
* Data Steward Coverage
* Data Sharing Volume and Utilization

(P) Planning, (C) Control, (D) Development, (O) Operations

Figure 75 Context Diagram: Reference and Master Data

1.1 Business Drivers

The most common drivers for initiating a Master Data Management program are:

- **Meeting organizational data requirements**: Multiple areas within an organization need access to the same data sets, with the confidence that the data sets are complete, current, and consistent. Master Data often form the basis of these data sets (e.g., determining whether an analysis includes all customers depends on having a consistently applied definition of a customer).

- **Managing data quality**: Data inconsistencies, quality issues, and gaps, lead to incorrect decisions or lost opportunities; Master Data Management reduces these risks by enabling a consistent representation of the entities critical to the organization.

- **Managing the costs of data integration**: The cost of integrating new data sources into an already complex environment are higher in the absence of Master Data, which reduces variation in how critical entities are defined and identified.

- **Reducing risk**: Master Data can enable simplification of data sharing architecture to reduce costs and risk associated with a complex environment.

The drivers for managing Reference Data are similar. Centrally managed Reference Data enables organizations to:

- Meet data requirements for multiple initiatives and reduce the risks and costs of data integration through use of consistent Reference Data

- Manage the quality of Reference Data

While data-driven organizational initiatives focus on transactional data (increasing sales or market share, reducing costs, demonstrating compliance), the ability to leverage such transactional data is highly dependent on the availability and quality of Reference and Master Data. Improving the availability and quality of Reference and Master Data has a dramatic impact on overall quality of the data and business confidence in data. These processes have additional benefits to an organization, including simplification of IT landscape, improved efficiency and productivity, and with these, the potential to improve the customer experience.

1.2 Goals and Principles

The goals of a Reference and Master Data Management program include:

- Ensuring the organization has complete, consistent, current, authoritative Master and Reference Data across organizational processes

- Enabling Master and Reference Data to be shared across enterprise functions and applications

- Lowering the cost and reducing the complexity of data usage and integration through standards, common data models, and integration patterns

Reference and Master Data Management follow these guiding principles:

- **Shared Data**: Reference and Master Data must be managed so that they are shareable across the organization.

- **Ownership**: Reference and Master Data belong to the organization, not to a particular application or department. Because they are widely shared, they require a high level of stewardship.

- **Quality**: Reference and Master Data Management require ongoing Data Quality monitoring and governance.

- **Stewardship**: Business Data Stewards are accountable for controlling and ensuring the quality of Reference Data.

- **Controlled Change**:

    o   At a given point of time, Master Data values should represent the organization's best understanding of what is accurate and current. Matching rules that change values should be applied with caution and oversight. Any identifier merged or split should be reversible.

    o   Changes to Reference Data values should follow a defined process; changes should be approved and communicated before they are implemented.

- **Authority**: Master Data values should be replicated only from the system of record. A system of reference may be required to enable sharing of Master Data across an organization.

1.3 Essential Concepts

1.3.1 Differences Between Master and Reference Data

Different types of data play different roles within an organization. They also have different management requirements. A distinction is often made between Transaction and Master Data, as well as between Master Data and Reference Data. Malcolm Chisholm has proposed a six-layer taxonomy of data that includes Metadata, Reference Data, enterprise structure data, transaction structure data, transaction activity data, and transaction audit data (Chisholm, 2008; Talburt and Zhou, 2015). Within this taxonomy, he defines Master Data as an aggregation of Reference Data, enterprise structure data, and transaction structure data:

- **Reference Data**, for example, code and description tables, is data that is used solely to characterize other data in an organization, or solely to relate data in a database to information beyond the boundaries of the organization.

- **Enterprise Structure Data**, for example, a chart of accounts, enables reporting of business activity by business responsibility.

- **Transaction Structure Data,** for example customer identifiers, describes the things must be present for a transaction to occur: products, customers, vendors.

Chisholm's definition distinguishes Master Data from transaction activity data that records details about transactions, and from transaction audit data that describes the state of transactions, as well as from Metadata, which describes other data (Chisholm, 2008). In this respect, Chisholm's definition is similar to the DAMA Dictionary's definition: *Master Data* is "the data that provides the context for business activity data in the form of common and abstract concepts that relate to the activity. It includes the details (definitions and identifiers) of internal and external objects involved in business transactions, such as customers, products, employees, vendors, and controlled domains (code values)" (DAMA, 2009).

Many people understand Master Data to include both transaction structure data and enterprise structure data. David Loshin's definition of Master Data aligns largely with these types. He describes Master Data objects as core business objects used in different applications across an organization, along with their associated Metadata, attributes, definitions, roles, connections, and taxonomies. Master Data objects represent those 'things' that matter most to an organization – those that are logged in transactions, reported on, measured, analyzed (Loshin, 2008).

Master Data requires identifying and / or developing a trusted version of truth for each instance of conceptual entities such as product, place, account, person, or organization and maintaining the currency of that version. The primary challenge with Master Data is entity resolution (also called identity management), the process of discerning and managing associations between data from different systems and processes. The entity instances represented by Master Data rows will be represented differently across systems. Master Data Management works to resolve these differences in order to consistently identify individual entity instances (i.e., specific customers, products, etc.) in different contexts. This process must also be managed over time, so that the identifiers for these Master Data entity instances remain consistent.[56]

Reference Data and Master Data share conceptually similar purposes. Both provide context critical to the creation and use of transactional data. (Reference Data also provides context for Master Data.) They enable data to be meaningfully understood. Importantly, both are shared resources that should be managed at the enterprise level. Having multiple instances of the same Reference Data is inefficient and inevitably leads to inconsistency between them. Inconsistency leads to ambiguity, and ambiguity introduces risk to an organization. A successful Reference Data or Master Data Management program involves the full range of data management functions (Data Governance, Data Quality, Metadata Management, Data Integration, etc.).

Reference Data also has characteristics that distinguish it from other kinds of Master Data (e.g., enterprise and transactional structure data). It is less volatile. Reference Data sets are generally less complex and smaller than either Transactional or Master Data sets. They have fewer columns and fewer rows. The challenges of entity resolution are not part of Reference Data Management.

The focus of data management differs between Reference and Master Data:

- **Master Data Management** (MDM) entails control over Master Data values and identifiers that enable consistent use, across systems, of the most accurate and timely data about essential business entities. The goals of MDM include ensuring availability of accurate, current values while reducing risks associated with ambiguous identifiers (those identified with more than one instance of an entity and those that refer to more than one entity).

- **Reference Data Management** (RDM) entails control over defined domain values and their definitions. The goal of RDM is to ensure the organization has access to a complete set of accurate and current values for each concept represented.

---

[56] John Talburt and Yinle Zhou (2015) describe the two step process in ER: first, determine whether two records refer to the same entity, then merge and reconcile data in the records in order to create a master record. They refer to Entity Identity Information Management (EIIM) as the process of ensuring that "an entity under management in the MDM system is consistently labeled with the same unique identifier from process to process."

One challenge of Reference Data Management is that of ownership or responsibility for definition and maintenance. Some Reference Data originates outside of the organizations that use it. Some crosses internal organizational boundaries and may not be owned by a single department. Other Reference Data may be created and maintained within a department but have potential value elsewhere in an organization. Determining responsibility for obtaining data and managing updates is part of RDM. Lack of accountability introduces risk, as differences in Reference Data may cause misunderstanding of data context (as when two business units have different values to classify the same concept). Because Master and Reference Data provide context for transactions, they shape the Transaction data entering an organization during operations (for example, in CRM and ERP systems). They also frame analysis performed on Transaction Data.

1.3.2 Reference Data

As noted, *Reference Data* is any data used to characterize or classify other data, or to relate data to information external to an organization (Chisholm, 2001). The most basic Reference Data consists of codes and descriptions, but some Reference Data can be more complex and incorporate mappings and hierarchies. Reference Data exists in virtually every data store. Classifications and categories may include statuses or types (e.g., Order Status: New, In Progress, Closed, Cancelled). External information may include geographic or standards information (e.g., Country Code: DE, US, TR).

Reference Data may be stored in different ways to meet the different needs. For example, data integration (e.g., data mappings for standardization or data quality checks), or other application functionality (e.g., synonym rings to enable search and discovery). It may also have device specific user interface considerations (e.g., multiple languages). Common storage techniques use:

- Code tables in relational databases, linked via foreign keys to other tables to maintain referential integrity functions within the database management system

- Reference Data Management systems that maintain business entities, allowed, future-state, or deprecated values, and term mapping rules to support broader application and data integration use

- Object attribute specific Metadata to specify permissible values with a focus on API or user interface access

Reference Data Management entails control and maintenance of defined domain values, definitions, and the relationships within and across domain values. The goal of Reference Data Management is to ensure values are consistent and current across different functions and that the data is accessible to the organization. Like other data, Reference Data requires Metadata. An important Metadata attribute for Reference Data includes its source. For example, the governing body for industry standard Reference Data.

1.3.2.1 Reference Data Structure

Depending on the granularity and complexity of what the Reference Data represents, it may be structured as a simple list, a cross-reference, or a taxonomy. The ability to use and maintain Reference Data should be accounted for when structuring it within a database or a Reference Data Management system.

1.3.2.1.1 Lists

The simplest form of Reference Data pairs a code value with a description in a list, such as in Table 17. The code value is the primary identifier, the short form reference value that appears in other contexts. The description states what the code represents. The description may be displayed in place of the code on screens, pages, drop-down lists, and reports. Note that in this example, the code value for United Kingdom is GB according to international standards, and not UK, even though UK is a common short form used in many forms of communication. Balance between standards compliance and usability when defining Reference Data requirements.

Table 17 Simple Reference List

Code Value	Description
US	United States of America
GB	United Kingdom (Great Britain)

Depending on the content and complexity of the Reference Data, additional attributes may be required to define the meaning of the code. Definitions provide information that the label alone does not provide. Definitions rarely appear on reports or drop-down lists. However, they do appear in places like Help functions for applications, which guide the appropriate use of codes in context.

Lists, like any Reference Data, must meet the requirements of data consumers, including requirements for the appropriate level of detail. If a list of values is intended to support data classification by casual users, a highly detailed list will likely cause data quality issues and adoption challenges. Similarly, a list of values that is too generic would prevent knowledge workers from capturing sufficient level of detail. To accommodate such cases, it is better to maintain distinct lists that are related vs. attempting to have a single list that is the standard for all user communities. Table 18 provides an example related to status codes for help desk tickets. Without the information provided by the definition, ticket status would be ambiguous to anyone unfamiliar with the system. This differentiation is especially necessary for classifications driving performance metrics or other Business Intelligence analytics.

Table 18 Simple Reference List Expanded

Code	Description	Definition
1	New	Indicates a newly created ticket without an assigned resource
2	Assigned	Indicates a ticket that has a named resource assigned
3	Work In Progress	Indicates the assigned resource started working on the ticket
4	Resolved	Indicates request is assumed to be fulfilled per the assigned resource
5	Cancelled	Indicates request was cancelled based on requester interaction
6	Pending	Indicates request cannot proceed without additional information
7	Fulfilled	Indicates request was fulfilled and verified by the requester

1.3.2.1.2 Cross-Reference Lists

Different applications may use different code sets to represent the same concept. These code sets may be at different granularities or the same granularity with different values. Cross-reference data sets translate between codes values. Table 19 presents a US State Code cross-reference (an example of multiple representations at the same level of grain). The US Postal Service State Codes are two character alpha codes. FIPS uses a numeric to express the same concept. The ISO State Code also includes a reference to the country.

Table 19 Cross-Reference List

USPS State Code	ISO State Code	FIPS Numeric State Code	State Abbreviation	State Name	Formal State Name
CA	US-CA	06	Calif.	California	State of California
KY	US-KY	21	Ky.	Kentucky	Commonwealth of Kentucky
WI	US-WI	55	Wis.	Wisconsin	State of Wisconsin

Language requirements may affect Reference Data structure. Multi-language lists are a specific instance of a cross-reference list. While code lists provide a standard, machine-readable format, language-specific glossaries provide usable content. Table 20 provides an example from the ISO 3166 standard. There are different ways to handle multi-language lists depending on how many languages and character sets are involved. Lists do not need to be normalized to be effective. The denormalized structure makes it somewhat easier to comprehend the relationships.

Table 20 Multi-Language Reference List

ISO 3166-1 Alpha 2 Country Code	English Name	Local Name	Local Name Local Alphabet	French Name	...
CN	China	Zhong Guo	中国/中國	Chine	

1.3.2.1.3 Taxonomies

Taxonomic Reference Data structures capture information at different levels of specificity. For example, a US ZIP Code may be a meaningful category itself, and it exists within a town, a county, and a state. These relationships can be expressed within reference table and multiple levels of analysis could be done using ZIP code as a driver.

Taxonomies enable content classification and multi-faceted navigation to support Business Intelligence. Taxonomic Reference Data can be stored in a recursive relationship. Taxonomy management tools also maintain hierarchical information. Table 21 and Table 22 show examples of two common hierarchical taxonomies. In both cases, the hierarchy includes a code, description, and a reference to a parent code that classifies the individual codes. For example, in Table 21, Floral plants (10161600) is a parent code to Roses, Poinsettias, and Orchids. In Table 22, Retail Trade (440000) is the parent to Food and Beverage Stores (445000), which is the parent to Specialty Food Stores (445200).

Table 21 UNSPSC (Universal Standard Products and Services Classification)[57]

Code Value	Description	Parent Code
10161600	Floral plants	10160000
10161601	Rose plants	10161600
10161602	Poinsettias plants	10161600
10161603	Orchid plants	10161600
10161700	Cut flowers	10160000
10161705	Cut roses	10161700

---

[57] http://bit.ly/2sAMU06.

Table 22 NAICS (North America Industry Classification System)[58]

Code Value	Description	Parent Code
440000	Retail Trade	440000
445000	Food and Beverage Stores	440000
445200	Specialty Food Stores	445000
445210	Meat Markets	445200
445220	Fish and Seafood Markets	445200
445290	Other Specialty Food Stores	445200
445291	Baked Goods Stores	445290
445292	Confectionary and Nut Stores	445290

1.3.2.1.4 Ontologies

Some organizations include ontologies used to manage website content as part of Reference Data. They fit this category in that they are used to characterize other data or to relate organizational data to information beyond the boundaries of the organization. Ontologies can also be understood as a form of Metadata. Ontologies and other complex taxonomies need to be managed in ways similar to how Reference Data is managed. Values need to be complete, current, and clearly defined. Best practices for maintaining ontologies are similar to those for Reference Data Management. One of the primary use cases for ontologies is content management. They are described in more detail in Chapter 9.

1.3.2.2 Proprietary or Internal Reference Data

Many organizations create Reference Data to support internal processes and applications. Often this proprietary reference data often grows organically over time. Part of RDM includes managing these data sets and, ideally, creating consistency between them, where this consistency serves the organization. For example, if different business units use different terms to describe the status of an account, then it is difficult for anyone in the organization to determine overall number of clients it serves at a point in time. In helping manage internal Reference Data sets, Data Stewards must balance between the need to have common words for the same information and the need for flexibility where processes differ from one another.

1.3.2.3 Industry Reference Data

Industry Reference Data is a broad term to describe data sets that are created and maintained by industry associations or government bodies, rather than by individual organizations, in order to provide a common standard for codifying important concepts. This codification leads to a common way to understand data, and is a prerequisite for data sharing and interoperability. For example, the International Classification of Diseases (ICD) codes provide a common way to classify health conditions (diagnoses) and treatments (procedures) and thus to have a consistent approach to delivering health care and understanding outcomes. If every doctor and hospital creates their own code set for diseases, it would be virtually impossible to understand trends and patterns.

---

[58] http://bit.ly/1mWACqg.

Industry Reference Data is produced and maintained external to the organizations that use it, but it is required to understand transactions within those organizations. It may be needed to support specific Data Quality Management efforts (e.g., third party business directories), business calculations (e.g., foreign exchange rates), or business data augmentation (e.g., marketing data). These data sets vary widely, depending on the industry and the individual code set. (See Chapter 10.)

1.3.2.4 Geographic or Geo-statistical Data

Geographic or geo-statistical reference enables classification or analysis based on geography. For example, census bureau reports describe population density and demographic shifts that support market planning and research. Weather history mapped to strict geographic classification can support inventory management and promotional planning.

1.3.2.5 Computational Reference Data

Many business activities rely on access to common, consistent calculations. For example, foreign exchange calculations rely on managed, time stamped exchange value tables. Computational Reference Data differs from other types because of the frequency with which it changes. Many organizations purchase this kind of data from third parties who ensure that it is complete and accurate. Attempting to maintain this data internally is likely to be fraught with latency issues.

1.3.2.6 Standard Reference Data Set Metadata

Reference Data, like other data, can change over time. Given its prevalence within any organization, it is important to maintain key Metadata about Reference Data sets to ensure their lineage and currency are understood and maintained. Table 23 provides examples of this Metadata.

Table 23 Critical Reference Data Metadata Attributes

Reference Data Set Key Information	Description
Formal Name	Official, especially if external name of the Reference Data set (e.g., ISO 3166-1991 Country Code List)
Internal Name	Name associated with the data set within the organization (e.g., Country Codes – ISO)
Data Provider	The party that provides and maintains the Reference Data set. This can be external (ISO), internal (a specific department), or external – extended (obtained from an external party but then extended and modified internally).
Data Provider Data Set Source	Description of where data provider's data sets can be obtained. This is likely a Universal Resource Identifier (URI) within or outside of the enterprise network.
Data Provider Latest Version Number	If available and maintained, this describes the latest version of the external data provider's data set where information may be added or deprecated from the version in the organization
Data Provider Latest Version Date	If available and maintained, this describes when the standard list was last updated

Reference Data Set Key Information	Description
Internal Version Number	Version number of the current Reference Data set or version number of the last update that was applied against the data set
Internal Version Reconciliation Date	Date when data set was last updated based on the external source
Internal Version Last Update Date	Date data set was last changed. This does not mean reconciliation with an external version.

1.3.3 Master Data

Master Data is data about the business entities (e.g., employees, customers, products, financial structures, assets, and locations) that provide context for business transactions and analysis. An entity is a real world object (person, organization, place, or thing). Entities are represented by entity instances, in the form of data / records. Master Data should represent the authoritative, most accurate data available about key business entities. When managed well, Master Data values are trusted and can be used with confidence.

Business rules typically dictate the format and allowable ranges of Master Data values. Common organizational Master Data includes data about:

- **Parties**, made up of individuals and organizations, and their roles, such as customers, citizens, patients, vendors, suppliers, agents, business partners, competitors, employees, or students
- **Products and Services**, both internal and external
- **Financial structures**, such as contracts, general ledger accounts, cost centers, or profit centers
- **Locations**, such as addresses and GPS coordinates

1.3.3.1 System of Record, System of Reference

When there are potentially different versions of 'the truth', it is necessary to distinguish between them. In order to do so, one must know where data originates or is accessed, and which data has been prepared for particular uses. A *System of Record* is an authoritative system where data is created/captured, and/or maintained through a defined set of rules and expectations (e.g., an ERP system may be the System of Record for sell-to customers). A *System of Reference* is an authoritative system where data consumers can obtain reliable data to support transactions and analysis, even if the information did not originate in the system of reference. MDM applications, Data Sharing Hubs, and Data Warehouses often serve as systems of reference.

1.3.3.2 Trusted Source, Golden Record

A *Trusted Source* is recognized as the 'best version of the truth' based on a combination of automated rules and manual stewardship of data content. A trusted source may also be referred to as a Single View, 360° View. Any MDM system should be managed so that it is a trusted source. Within a trusted source, records that represent the most accurate data about entity instances can be referred to as *Golden Records*.

The term *Golden Record* can be misleading. Tech Target defines a Golden Record as "the 'single version of the truth', where 'truth' is understood to mean the reference to which data users can turn when they want to ensure that they have the correct version of a piece of information. The golden record encompasses all the data in every system of record (SOR) within a particular organization."[59]

However, the two parts of this definition bring the concept into question, as data in different systems may not align into 'a single version of the truth'.

Within any Master Data effort, the merging/resolution of data from multiple sources into a 'Golden Record' does not mean that it is always a 100% complete and 100% accurate representation of all the entities within the organization (especially in organizations that have multiple SOR's supplying data to the Master Data environment). Promising that data is 'Golden' when it is not can undermine the confidence of data consumers.

This is why some prefer the term *Trusted Source* to refer to the "best version we have" of the Master Data. Doing so puts the emphasis on how data is defined and managed to get to a best version. It also helps different data consumers see the component pieces of the 'single version' that are important to them. Finance and Actuarial areas often have a different perspective of 'single version' of Customer than does the Marketing area. The *Trusted Source* provides multiple perspectives of business entities as identified and defined by Data Stewards.

1.3.3.3 Master Data Management

As described in the chapter introduction, Master Data Management entails control over Master Data values and identifiers that enable consistent use, across systems, of the most accurate and timely data about essential business entities. The goals include ensuring availability of accurate, current values while reducing the risk of ambiguous identifiers.

Gartner defines Master Data Management as "a technology-enabled discipline in which business and IT work together to ensure the uniformity, accuracy, stewardship, semantic consistency, and accountability of the enterprise's official shared Master Data assets. Master Data is the consistent and uniform set of identifiers and extended attributes that describes the core entities of the enterprise including customers, prospects, citizens, suppliers, sites, hierarchies, and chart of accounts."[60]

Gartner's definition stresses that MDM is a discipline, made up of people, processes, and technology. It is not a specific application solution. Unfortunately, the acronym MDM (Master Data Management) is often used to refer to systems or products used to manage Master Data.[61] MDM applications can facilitate the methods, and sometimes quite effectively, but using an MDM application does not guarantee that Master Data is being managed to meet the organizational needs. Assessing an organization's MDM requirements includes identifying:

- Which roles, organizations, places, and things are referenced repeatedly
- What data is used to describe people, organizations, places, and things

---

[59] http://bit.ly/2rRJI3b.

[60] http://gtnr.it/2rQOT33.

[61] Note that, throughout the DAMA-DMBOK, *MDM* refers to the overall process of managing Master Data, rather than to just the tools used to manage this data.

- How the data is defined and structured, including the granularity of the data
- Where the data is created/sourced, stored, made available, and accessed
- How the data changes as it moves through systems within the organization
- Who uses the data and for what purposes
- What criteria are used to understand the quality and reliability of the data and its sources

Master Data Management is challenging. It illustrates a fundamental challenge with data: People choose different ways to represent similar concepts and reconciliation between these representations is not always straightforward; as importantly, information changes over time and systematically accounting for these changes takes planning, data knowledge, and technical skills. In short, it takes work.

Any organization that has recognized the need for MDM probably already has a complex system landscape, with multiple ways of capturing and storing references to real world entities. Because of both organic growth over time or from mergers and acquisitions, the systems that provided input to the MDM process may have different definitions of the entities themselves and very likely have different standards for Data Quality. Because of this complexity, it is best to approach Master Data Management one data domain at a time. Start small, with a handful of attributes, and build out over time.

Planning for Master Data Management includes several basic steps. Within a domain:

- Identify candidate sources that will provide a comprehensive view of the Master Data entities
- Develop rules for accurately matching and merging entity instances
- Establish an approach to identify and restore inappropriately matched and merged data
- Establish an approach to distribute trusted data to systems across the enterprise

Executing the process, though, is not as simple as these steps imply, as MDM is a lifecycle management process. Activities critical to the lifecycle include:

- Establishing the context of Master Data entities, including definitions of associated attributes and the conditions of their use. This process requires governance.
- Identifying multiple instances of the same entity represented within and across data sources; building and maintaining identifiers and cross-references to enable information integration.
- Reconciling and consolidating data across sources to provide a master record or the best version of the truth. Consolidated records provide a merged view of information across systems and seek to address attribute naming and data value inconsistencies.
- Identifying improperly matched or merged instances and ensuring they are resolved and correctly associated with identifiers.
- Provisioning of access to trusted data across applications, either through direct reads, data services, or by replication feeds to transactional, warehousing or analytical data stores.
- Enforcing the use of Master Data values within the organization. This process also requires governance and change management to assure a shared enterprise perspective.

1.3.3.4 Master Data Management Key Processing Steps

Key processing steps for MDM are illustrated in Figure 76. They include data model management; data acquisition; data validation, standardization, and enrichment; entity resolution; and stewardship and sharing. In a comprehensive MDM environment, the logical data model will be physically instantiated in multiple platforms. It guides the implementation of the MDM solution, providing the basis of data integration services. It should guide how applications are configured to take advantage of data reconciliation and data quality verification capabilities.

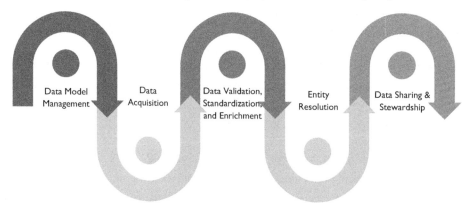

Figure 76 Key Processing Steps for MDM

1.3.3.4.1 Data Model Management

Master Data work brings to light the importance of clear and consistent logical data definitions. The model should help the organization overcome 'system speak'. Terms and definitions used within a source system may make sense within the confines of that system but they do not always make sense at an enterprise level. For Master Data, terms and definitions used at an enterprise level should be in context of the business conducted across the organization and not necessarily dependent on the source system contributing data values.

For attributes that make up Master Data, the granularity of the definition and associated data values must also make sense across the organization. Source systems may present the identical attribute name but the data values are in completely different contexts at the enterprise level. Similarly, source systems may present differently named attributes that at the enterprise level coalesce to a single attribute and the data values are in the proper context. Sometimes multiple attributes are presented from a single source and their respective data values are used to derive a single data value for an attribute defined at the enterprise level.

1.3.3.4.2 Data Acquisition

Even within a given source, data representing the same entity instance can look different, as illustrated in Table 24, where there are inconsistencies in how names, addresses, and telephone numbers are presented. This example will be referenced again later in the chapter.

Table 24 Source Data as Received by the MDM System

Source ID	Name	Address	Telephone
123	John Smith	123 Main, Dataland, SQ 98765	
234	J. Smith	123 Main, Dataland, DA	2345678900
345	Jane Smith	123 Main, Dataland, DA	234-567-8900

Planning for, evaluating, and incorporating new data sources into the Master Data Management solution must be a reliable, repeatable process. Data acquisition activities involve:

- Receiving and responding to new data source acquisition requests
- Performing rapid, ad-hoc, match and high-level data quality assessments using data cleansing and data profiling tools
- Assessing and communicating complexity of data integration to the requesters to help them with their cost-benefit analysis
- Piloting acquisition of data and its impact on match rules
- Finalizing data quality metrics for the new data source
- Determining who will be responsible for monitoring and maintaining the quality of a new source's data
- Completing integration into the overall data management environment

1.3.3.4.3 Data Validation, Standardization, and Enrichment

To enable entity resolution, data must be made as consistent as possible. This entails, at a minimum, reducing variation in format and reconciling values. Consistent input data reduces the chance or errors in associating records. Preparation processes include:

- **Validation**: Identifying data prove-ably erroneous or likely incorrect or defaulted (for example, removal of clearly fake email addresses)
- **Standardization**: Ensuring data content conforms to standard Reference Data values (e.g., country codes), formats (e.g., telephone numbers) or fields (e.g., addresses)
- **Enrichment**: Adding attributes that can improve entity resolution services (e.g., Dunn and Bradstreet DUNS Number and Ultimate DUNS Number for relating company records, Acxiom or Experian Consumer IDs for individual records)

Table 25 illustrates the results of the cleansing and standardization process on the example from Table 24. Addresses that had had different formats are now recognizably the same. Phone numbers include standard formatting.

Table 25 Standardized and Enriched Input Data

Source ID	Name	Address (Cleansed)	Telephone (Cleansed)
123	John Smith	123 Main, Dataland, SQ 98765	
234	J. Smith	123 Main, Dataland, SQ 98765	+1 234 567 8900
345	Jane Smith	123 Main, Dataland, SQ 98765	+1 234 567 8900

1.3.3.4.4 Entity Resolution and Identifier Management

Entity resolution is the process of determining whether two references to real world objects refer to the same object or to different objects (Talburt, 2011). Entity resolution is a decision-making process. Models for executing the process differ based on the approach they take to determining similarity between two references. While resolution always takes place between pairs of references, the process can be systematically extended to include large data sets. Entity resolution is critical to MDM, as the process of matching and merging records enables the construction of the Master Data set.

Entity resolution includes a set of activities (reference extraction, reference preparation, reference resolution, identity management, relationship analysis) that enable the identity of entity instances and the relationship between entity instances, to be managed over time. Within the process of reference resolution, two references may be identified as representing the same entity, through the process of determining equivalency. These references can then be linked through a value (a global identifier) that indicates that they are equivalent (Talburt, 2011).

1.3.3.4.4.1 Matching

Matching, or candidate identification, is the process of identifying how different records may relate to a single entity. The risks with this process are:

- **False positives**: Two references that do not represent the same entity are linked with a single identifier. This results in one identifier that refers to more than one real-world entity instance.

- **False negatives**: Two references represent the same entity but they are not linked with a single identifier. This results in multiple identifiers that refer to the same real-world entity when each instance is expected to have one-and-only-one identifier.

Both situations are addressed through a process called *similarity analysis* or *matching*, in which the degree of similarity between any two records is scored, often based on weighted approximate matching between corresponding attribute values. If the score is above a specified threshold, the two records are considered to represent the same entity (a match). Through similarity analysis, slight variations in data can be recognized and data values can be consolidated. Two basic approaches, which can be used together, are deterministic and probabilistic:

- **Deterministic** algorithms, like parsing and standardization, rely on defined patterns and rules for assigning weights and scores for determining similarity. Deterministic algorithms are predictable in that the patterns matched and the rules applied will always yield the same results. This type of matching works out-of-the-box with relatively good performance, but it is only as good as the situations anticipated by the people who developed the rules.

- **Probabilistic** algorithms rely on statistical techniques for assessing the probability that any pair of records represents the same entity. This relies on the ability to take data samples for training purposes by looking at the expected results for a subset of the records and tuning the matcher to self-adjust based on statistical analysis. These matchers are not reliant on rules, so the results may be nondeterministic. However, because the probabilities can be refined based on experience, probabilistic matchers are able to improve their matching precision as more data is analyzed.

1.3.3.4.4.2 Identity Resolution

Some matches occur with great confidence, based on exact data matches across multiple fields. Other matches are suggested with less confidence due to conflicting values. For example:

- If two records share the same last name, first name, birth date, and social security number, but the street address differs, is it safe to assume they refer to the same person who has changed their mailing address?

- If two records share the same social security number, street address, and first name, but the last name differs, is it safe to assume they refer to the same person who has changed their last name? Would the likelihood be increased or decreased based on gender and age?

- How do these examples change if the social security number is unknown for one record? What other identifiers are useful to determine the likelihood of a match? How much confidence is required for the organization to assert a match?

Table 26 illustrates the conclusion of the process for the sample records in Table 24 and Table 25. Here the second two entity instances (Source ID 234 and 345) are determined to represent the same person (Jane Smith), while the first one (Source ID 123) is identified as representing a different person (John Smith).

Table 26 Candidate Identification and Identity Resolution

Source ID	Name	Address (Cleansed)	Telephone (Cleansed)	Candidate ID	Party ID
123	John Smith	123 Main, Dataland, SQ 98765		XYZ	1
234	J. Smith	123 Main, Dataland, SQ 98765	+1 234 567 8900	XYZ, ABC	2
345	Jane Smith	123 Main, Dataland, SQ 98765	+1 234 567 8900	ABC	2

Despite the best efforts, match decisions sometimes prove to be incorrect. It is essential to maintain the history of matches so that matches can be undone when discovered to be incorrect. Match rate metrics enable organizations to monitor the impact and effectiveness of their matching inference rules. Reprocessing of match rules can help identify better match candidates as new information is received by the entity resolution process.

1.3.3.4.4.3 Matching Workflows / Reconciliation Types

Match rules for different scenarios require different workflows:

- **Duplicate identification match rules** focus on a specific set of data elements that uniquely identify an entity and identify merge opportunities without taking automatic action. Business Data Stewards can review these occurrences and decide to take action on a case-by-case basis.

- **Match-link rules** identify and cross-reference records that appear to relate to a master record without updating the content of the cross-referenced record. Match-link rules are easier to implement and much easier to reverse.

- **Match-merge rules** match records and merge the data from these records into a single, unified, reconciled, and comprehensive record. If the rules apply across data sources, create a single, unique, and comprehensive record in each data store. Minimally, use trusted data from one data store to supplement data in other data stores, replacing missing values or values thought to be inaccurate.

Match-merge rules are complex, and seek to provide the unified, reconciled version of information across multiple records and data sources. The complexity is due to the need to identify which field from which source can be trusted based on a series of rules. The introduction of each new source can change these rules over time. The challenges with match-merge rules include the operational complexity of reconciling the data and the cost of reversing the operation if there is a false merge.

Match-link is a simpler operation, as it acts on the cross-reference registry and not the individual attributes of the merged Master Data record, even though it may be more difficult to present comprehensive information from multiple records.

Periodically re-evaluate match-merge and match-link rules because confidence levels change over time. Many data matching engines provide statistical correlations of data values to help establish confidence levels. (See Chapter 13.)

1.3.3.4.4.4 Master Data ID Management

Managing Master Data involves managing identifiers. There are two types of identifiers that need to be managed across data sources in an MDM environment: Global IDs and Cross-Reference (x-Ref) information.

A *Global ID* is the MDM solution-assigned and -maintained unique identifier attached to reconciled records. Its purpose is to uniquely identify the entity instance. In the example in Table 26, when multiple records were determined to represent the same entity instance, the value 'ABC' was assigned to both as a candidate ID. The records were resolved to the single Party ID of '2'.

Global IDs should be generated by only one authorized solution, regardless of which technology is performing Master Data integration activities, to avoid any risk of duplicate values. Global IDs can be numbers or GUIDs (Global Unique Identifiers), as long as uniqueness can be maintained. The key complexity that needs to be handled for Global ID generation is to how to maintain the right global ID (to perform appropriate downstream data updates) due to an unmerge-remerge. *X-Ref Management* is management of the relationship between source IDs and the Global ID. X-Ref management should include capabilities to maintain history of such mappings to support match rate metrics, and to expose lookup services to enable data integration.

1.3.3.4.4.5 Affiliation Management

Affiliation Management is establishing and maintaining relationships between Master Data records of entities that have real-world relationships. Examples include ownership affiliations (e.g., Company X is a subsidiary of Company Y, a parent-child relationship) or other associations (e.g., Person XYZ works at Company X).

Data architecture design of an MDM solution must resolve whether to leverage parent-child relationships, affiliation relationships, or both for a given entity.

- **Affiliation relationships** provide the greatest flexibility through programming logic. The relationships type can be used to expose such data in a parent-child hierarchy. Many downstream solutions, such as reporting or account navigation tools would want to see a hierarchical view of the information.

- **Parent-Child relationships** require less programming logic as the navigation structure is implied. However, if the relationship changes and there isn't an available affiliation structure, this may influence the quality of the data and Business Intelligence dimensions.

1.3.3.4.5 Data Sharing and Stewardship

Although much of the work of Master Data Management can be automated through tools that enable processing of large numbers of records, it still requires stewardship to resolve situations where data is incorrectly matched. Ideally, lessons learned from the stewardship process can be used to improve matching algorithms and reduce instances of manual work. (See Chapters 3 and 8.)

1.3.3.5 Party Master Data

Party Master Data includes data about individuals, organizations, and the roles they play in business relationships. In the commercial environment, parties include customers, employees, vendors, partners, and competitors. In the public sector, parties are usually citizens. Law enforcement focuses on suspects, witnesses, and victims. Not-for-profit organizations focus on members and donors. While in healthcare, the focus is on patients and providers; in education, it is on students and faculty.

Customer Relationship Management (CRM) systems manage Master Data about customers. The goal of CRM is to provide complete and accurate information about each and every customer.

An essential aspect of CRM is identifying duplicate, redundant, or conflicting data from different systems and determining whether the data represents one or more than one customer. CRM must be able to resolve conflicting values, reconcile differences, and accurately represent current knowledge of the customer. This process requires robust rules as well as knowledge of the structure, granularity, lineage, and quality of data sources.

Specialized MDM systems perform similar functions for individuals, organizations and their roles, employees, and vendors. Regardless of industry or focus, managing business party Master Data poses unique challenges:

- The complexity of roles and relationships played by individuals and organizations
- Difficulties in unique identification
- The number of data sources and the differences between them
- The multiple mobile and social communications channels
- The importance of the data
- The expectations of how customers want to be engaged

Master Data is particularly challenging for parties playing multiple roles across an organization (e.g., an employee who is also a customer) and utilizing differing points of contact or engagement methods (e.g., interaction via mobile device application that is tied to a social media site).

1.3.3.6 Financial Master Data

Financial Master Data includes data about business units, cost centers, profit centers, general ledger accounts, budgets, projections, and projects. Typically, an Enterprise Resource Planning (ERP) system serves as the central hub for financial Master Data (chart of accounts), with project details and transactions created and maintained in one or more spoke applications. This is especially common in organizations with distributed back-office functions.

Financial Master Data solutions not only create, maintain, and share information; many can also simulate how changes to existing financial data may affect the organization's bottom line. Financial Master Data simulations are often part of Business Intelligence reporting, analysis, and planning modules, as well as more straightforward budgeting and projecting. Through these applications, versions of financial structures can be modeled to understand potential financial impacts. Once a decision is made, the agreed upon structural changes can be disseminated to all appropriate systems.

1.3.3.7 Legal Master Data

Legal Master Data includes data about contracts, regulations, and other legal matters. Legal Master Data allows analysis of contracts for different entities providing the same products or services, to enable better negotiation or to combine contracts into Master Agreements.

1.3.3.8 Product Master Data

Product Master Data can focus on an organization's internal products and services or on industry-wide (including competitor) products and services. Different types of product Master Data solutions support different business functions.

- **Product Lifecycle Management (PLM)** focuses on managing the lifecycle of a product or service from conception, through development, manufacturing, sale / delivery, service, and disposal. Organizations implement PLM systems to reduce time to market. In industries with long product development cycles (as much as 8 to 12 years in the pharmaceutical industry), PLM systems enable organizations to track cross-process cost and legal agreements as product concepts evolve from ideas to potential products under different names and potentially different licensing agreements.

- **Product Data Management (PDM)** supports engineering and manufacturing functions by capturing and enabling secure sharing of product information such as design documents (e.g., CAD drawings), recipes (manufacturing instructions), standard operating procedures, and bills of materials. PDM functionality can be enabled through specialized systems or ERP applications.

- **Product data in Enterprise Resource Planning (ERP)** systems focuses on SKUs to support order entry down to inventory level, where individual units can be identified through a variety of techniques.

- **Product data in Manufacturing Execution Systems (MES)** focus on raw inventory, semi-finished goods, and finished goods, where finished goods tie to products that can be stored and ordered through the ERP system. This data is also important across the supply chain and logistics systems.

- **Product data in a Customer Relationship Management (CRM)** system that supports marketing, sales, and support interactions can include product family and brands, sales rep association, and customer territory management, as well as marketing campaigns.

Many product masters closely tie to Reference Data Management systems.

1.3.3.9 Location Master Data

Location Master Data provides the ability to track and share geographic information and to create hierarchical relationships or territories based on geographic information. The distinction between reference and Master Data blurs for location data. Here is the difference:

- **Location Reference Data** typically includes geopolitical data, such as countries, states or provinces, counties, cities or towns, postal codes, and geographic positioning coordinates, such as latitude, longitude, and altitude. This data rarely changes, and changes are handled by external organizations. Location Reference Data may also include geographic regions and sales territories as defined by the organization.

- **Location Master Data** includes business party addresses and business party location, as well as facility addresses for locations owned by the organization. As organizations grow or contract, these addresses change more frequently than other Location Reference Data.

Different industries require specialized earth science data (geographic data about seismic faults, flood plains, soil, annual rainfall, and severe weather risk areas) and related sociological data (population, ethnicity, income, and terrorism risk), usually supplied from external sources.

1.3.3.10 Industry Master Data – Reference Directories

Reference Directories are authoritative listings of Master Data entities (companies, people, products, etc.) that organizations can purchase and use as the basis of their transactions. While reference directories are created by external organizations, a managed and reconciled version of the information is maintained in the organization's own systems.

Examples of licensed reference directories include Dun and Bradstreet's (D&B) Company Directory of worldwide Company Headquarters, Subsidiaries, and Branch locations, and the American Medical Association's Prescriber Database.

Reference directories enable Master Data use by:

- Providing a starting point for matching and linking new records. For example, in an environment with five data sources, each source can be compared against the directory (5 comparison points) vs. against each other (10 comparison points).
- Providing additional data elements that may not be as easily available at the time of record creation (e.g., for a physician, this may include medical license status; for a company, this may include a six digit NAICS industry classification).

As an organization's records match and reconcile with the reference directories, the trusted record will deviate from the reference directory with traceability to other source records, contributing attributes, and transformation rules.

1.3.4 Data Sharing Architecture

There are several basic architectural approaches to reference and Master Data integration. Each Master Data subject area will likely have its own system of record. For example, the human resource system usually serves as the system of record for employee data. A CRM system might serve as the system of record for customer data, while an ERP system might serve as the system of record for financial and product data.

The data sharing hub architecture model shown in Figure 77 represents a hub-and-spoke architecture for Master Data. The Master Data hub can handle interactions with spoke items such as source systems, business applications, and data stores while minimizing the number of integration points. A local data hub can extend and scale the Master Data hub. (See Chapter 8.)

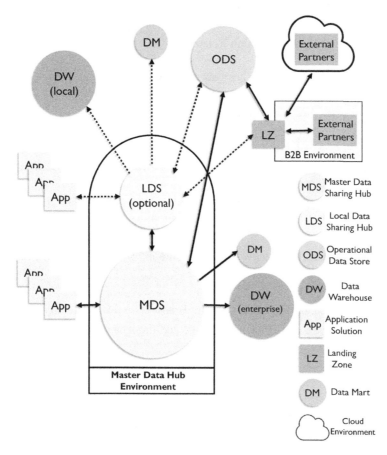

Figure 77 Master Data Sharing Architecture Example

Each of the three basic approaches to implementing a Master Data hub environment has pros and cons:

- A **Registry** is an index that points to Master Data in the various systems of record. The systems of record manage Master Data local to their applications. Access to Master Data comes from the master index. A registry is relatively easy to implement because it requires few changes in the systems of record. But often, complex queries are required to assemble Master Data from multiple systems. Moreover, multiple business rules need to be implemented to address semantic differences across systems in multiple places.

- In a **Transaction Hub**, applications interface with the hub to access and update Master Data. The Master Data exists within the Transaction Hub and not within any other applications. The Transaction Hub is the system of record for Master Data. Transaction Hubs enable better governance and provide a consistent source of Master Data. However, it is costly to remove the functionality to update Master Data from existing systems of record. Business rules are implemented in a single system: the Hub.

- **A Consolidated** approach is a hybrid of Registry and Transaction Hub. The systems of record manage Master Data local to their applications. Master Data is consolidated within a common repository and made available from a data-sharing hub, the system of reference for Master Data. This eliminates the need to access directly from the systems of record. The Consolidated approach provides an enterprise view with limited impact on systems of record. However, it entails replication of data and there will be latency between the hub and the systems of record.

2. Activities

As emphasized in Section 1.3.1, Master Data and Reference Data share certain characteristics (they are shared resources that provide context and meaning for other data and should be managed at the enterprise level), but they also differ in important ways (Reference Data sets are smaller, less volatile, do not require matching, merging, and linking, etc.). The activities section will first describe activities associated with MDM, and then describe those related to Reference Data.

2.1 MDM Activities

2.1.1 Define MDM Drivers and Requirements

Each organization has different MDM drivers and obstacles, influenced by the number and type of systems, their age, the business processes they support, and how data is used for both transactions and analytics. Drivers often include opportunities to improve customer service and/or operational efficiency, as well as to reduce risks related to privacy and compliance. Obstacles include differences in data meaning and structure between systems. These are often tied to cultural barriers – some business units may not want to incur the costs of changing their processes, even if change is presented as good for the enterprise as a whole.

It is relatively easy to define requirements for Master Data within an application. It is more difficult to define standard requirements across applications. Most organizations will want to approach one Master Data subject area, or even one entity, at a time. Prioritize Master Data efforts based on cost / benefit of proposed improvements and on the relative complexity of the Master Data subject area. Start with the simplest category in order to learn from the process.

2.1.2 Evaluate and Assess Data Sources

Data in existing applications forms the basis of a Master Data Management effort. It is important to understand the structure and content of this data and the processes through which it is collected or created. One outcome from an MDM effort can be improvements in Metadata generated through the effort to assess the quality of existing data.

One goal of assessment is to understand how complete data is with respect to the attributes that comprise Master Data. This process includes clarifying the definitions and granularity of those attributes. Semantic issues will arise at some point when defining and describing attributes. The Data Stewards will need to collaborate with the business areas on reconciliation and agreement on attribute naming and enterprise level definitions. (See Chapters 3 and 13.)

The other part of assessing sources is to understand the quality of the data. Data quality problems will complicate a Master Data project, so the assessment process should include addressing root causes of data issues. Never assume that data will be of high quality – it is safer to assume that is it not of high quality. Always assess its quality and suitability for a Master Data environment.

The biggest challenge, as noted, will be disparity between sources. Data may be of high quality within any given source, but still not fit together with data from other sources, due to structural differences and differences in the values by which similar attributes are represented. Master Data initiatives provide the opportunity to define and implement standards in applications in which data is created or collected.

For some Master Data entities, such as client, customer, or vendor, it is possible to purchase standardized data (such as Reference Directories) to enable the MDM effort. Several vendors have services that will supply cleansed data related to individual people or business entities or professions (e.g., health care professionals), that can be compared to an organization's internal data to improve contact information, addresses, and names (see Chapter 10). In addition to assessing the quality of existing data, it also necessary to understand the technology that supports the collection of inputs to an MDM effort. Existing technology will influence the architectural approach to MDM.

2.1.3 Define Architectural Approach

The architectural approach to MDM depends on business strategy, the platforms of existing data sources, and the data itself, particularly its lineage and volatility, and the implications of high or low latency. Architecture must account for data consumption and sharing models. Tooling for maintenance depends on both business requirements and architecture options. Tooling helps define and is dependent on the approach to stewardship and maintenance.

The number of source systems to be integrated into the Master Data solution and the platforms of those systems need to be accounted for when determining the approach to integration. The size and geographic spread of an organization will also influence the integration approach. Small organizations may effectively utilize a transaction hub whereas a global organization with multiple systems is more likely to utilize a registry. An organization with 'siloed' business units and various source systems may decide that a consolidated approach is the correct path to follow. Business domain experts, Data Architects, and Enterprise Architects should provide perspective on approach.

The data sharing hub architecture is particularly useful when there is no clear system of record for Master Data. In this case, multiple systems supply data. New data or updates from one system can be reconciled with data already supplied by another system. The data-sharing hub becomes the source of Master Data content for data warehouses or marts, reducing the complexity of extracts and the processing time for data transformation, remediation, and reconciliation. Of course, data warehouses must reflect changes made to the data-sharing hub for historical purposes, while the data-sharing hub itself may need to reflect just the current state.

2.1.4 Model Master Data

Master Data Management is a data integration process. To achieve consistent results and to manage the integration of new sources as an organization expands, it is necessary to model the data within subject areas. A logical or canonical model can be defined over the subject areas within the data-sharing hub. This would allow establishment of enterprise level definitions of subject area entities and attributes. (See Chapters 5 and 8.)

2.1.5 Define Stewardship and Maintenance Processes

Technical solutions can do remarkable work matching, merging, and managing identifiers for master records. However, the process also requires stewardship, not only to address records that fall out of the process, but also to remediate and improve the processes that cause them to fall out in the first place. MDM projects should account for resources required to support the ongoing quality of Master Data. There is a need to analyze records, provide feedback to source systems, and provide input that can be used to tune and improve the algorithms that drive the MDM solution.

2.1.6 Establish Governance Policies to Enforce Use of Master Data

The initial launch of a Master Data effort is challenging and takes a lot of focus. The real benefits (operational efficiency, higher quality, better customer service) come once people and systems start using the Master Data. The overall effort has to include a roadmap for systems to adopt master values and identifiers as input to processes. Establish unidirectional closed loops between systems to maintain consistency of values across systems.

2.2 Reference Data Activities

2.2.1 Define Drivers and Requirements

The primary drivers for Reference Data Management are operational efficiency and higher data quality. Managing Reference Data centrally is more cost effective than having multiple business units maintain their own data sets. It also reduces the risk of inconsistency between systems. That said, some Reference Data sets are more important than others; complex Reference Data sets take more work to set up and maintain than do simple ones. The most important Reference Data sets should drive requirements for a Reference Data Management system. Once such a system is in place, new Reference Data sets can be set up as part of projects. Existing Reference Data sets should be maintained based on a published schedule.

2.2.2 Assess Data Sources

Most industry standard Reference Data sets can be obtained from the organizations that create and maintain them. Some organizations supply such data free of charge. Others charge a fee. Intermediaries also package and sell Reference Data, often with value-added features. Depending on the number and type of Reference Data sets needed by an organization, it may be better to purchase from a vendor, especially if that vendor will guarantee the delivery of updates on a set schedule and will perform basic quality control on the data.

Most organizations also rely on Reference Data that is internally created and maintained. Determining the source for internal or local reference data is often more challenging than doing so for industry standard Reference Data. As is the case with Master Data, internal sources for Reference Data must be identified, compared, and assessed. Owners of existing data must understand the benefits of central management and agree to support processes to steward the data for the good of the enterprise.

2.2.3 Define Architectural Approach

Before purchasing or building a tool to manage Reference Data, it is critical to account for requirements and for the challenges posed by the Reference Data to be managed. For example, the volatility of data (most Reference Data is relatively static, but some is quite volatile), the frequency of updates, and the consumption models. Determine whether it is required to keep historical data on changes to the values or the definitions of the values. If the organization will purchase data from a vendor, account for the delivery and integration method.

The architectural approach needs to recognize that, invariably, some Reference Data will need to be updated manually. Ensure that the interface for updates is straightforward and can be configured to enforce basic data entry rules, such as ensuring parent/child relationships are maintained in Reference Data that includes hierarchies. The RDM tool should enable Stewards to make ad hoc updates without the need for technical support and should include workflows to ensure approvals and notifications are automated. Data Stewards should schedule known updates to align with the publication of new codes. Data consumers should be informed of all changes. In cases where Reference Data drives programming logic, the potential impact of changes should be assessed and accounted for before the changes are introduced.

2.2.4 Model Reference Data Sets

Many people think of Reference Data as simply codes and descriptions. However, much Reference Data is more complicated than that. For example, a ZIP Code data set will usually include information on state and county, as well as other geo-political attributes. For purposes of enabling long-term usage and establishing accurate Metadata, as well as for the maintenance process itself, it is valuable to create data models of Reference Data sets. Models help data consumers understand the relationships within the Reference Data set and they can be used to establish data quality rules.

2.2.5 Define Stewardship and Maintenance Processes

Reference Data requires stewardship to ensure that values are complete and current and that definitions are clear and understandable. In some cases, stewards will be directly responsible for hands-on maintenance of Reference Data; in other cases, they may facilitate the process. For example, if several different business units require Reference Data to support the same concept, a steward may facilitate discussions that define common values in a crosswalk.

As part of the stewardship process, it is helpful to capture basic Metadata about each Reference Data set. This could include: steward name, originating organization, expected frequency of updates, schedule for updates, processes using the Reference Data, whether historical versions of the data need to be retained, and more (see Section 1.3.2.6). Documenting what processes use Reference Data will enable more effective communication regarding changes to the data.

Many Reference Data Management tools include workflows to manage review and approval of changes to Reference Data. These workflows themselves depend on identifying who within an organization is responsible for Reference Data content.

2.2.6 Establish Reference Data Governance Policies

An organization only gets value from a centrally-managed Reference Data repository if people actually use the data from that repository. It is important to have policies in place that govern the quality and mandate the use of Reference Data from that repository, whether directly through publication from that repository or indirectly from a system of reference that is populated with data from the central repository.

3. Tools and Techniques

MDM requires tooling specifically designed to enable identity management. Master Data Management can be implemented through data integration tools, data remediation tools, operational data stores (ODS), data sharing hubs (DSH) or specialized MDM applications. Several vendors offer solutions that can cover one or more Master Data subject areas. Other vendors promote use of their data integration software products and implementation services to create custom Master Data solutions.

Packaged solutions for product, account and party as well as packaged data quality check services can jumpstart large programs. Incorporation of such services can enable organizations to use best-of-breed solutions, while integrating them to their overall business architecture to meet specific needs.

4. Implementation Guidelines

Master and Reference Data Management are forms of data integration. The implementation principles that apply to data integration and interoperability apply to MDM and RDM. (See Chapter 8.)

MDM and RDM capabilities cannot be implemented overnight. Solutions require specialized business and technical knowledge. Organizations should expect to implement Reference and Master Data solutions incrementally through a series of projects defined in an implementation roadmap, prioritized based on business needs and guided by an overall architecture.

Note that MDM programs will fail without proper governance. Data governance professionals must understand the challenges of MDM and RDM and assess the organization's maturity and ability to meet them. (See Chapter 15.)

4.1 Adhere to Master Data Architecture

Establishing and following proper reference architecture is critical to managing and sharing Master Data across an organization. The integration approach should take into account the organizational structure of the business, the number of distinct systems of record, the data governance implementation, the importance of access and latency of data values, and the number of consuming systems and applications.

4.2 Monitor Data Movement

Data integration processes for Master and Reference Data should be designed to ensure timely extraction and distribution of data across the organization. As data flows within a Reference or Master Data sharing environment, data flow should be monitored in order to:

- Show how data is shared and used across the organization
- Identify data lineage from / to administrative systems and applications
- Assist root cause analysis of issues
- Show effectiveness of data ingestion and consumption integration techniques
- Denote latency of data values from source systems through consumption
- Determine validity of business rules and transformations executed within integration components

4.3 Manage Reference Data Change

Since Reference Data is a shared resource, it cannot be changed arbitrarily. The key to successful Reference Data Management is organizational willingness to relinquish local control of shared data. To sustain this support, provide channels to receive and respond to requests for changes to Reference Data. The Data Governance Council should ensure that policies and procedures are implemented to handle changes to data within reference and Master Data environments.

Changes to Reference Data will need to be managed. Minor changes may affect a few rows of data. For example, when the Soviet Union broke into independent states, the term *Soviet Union* was deprecated and new codes were added. In the healthcare industry, procedure and diagnosis codes are updated annually to account for refinement of existing codes, obsoleting of codes, and the introduction of new codes. Major revisions to Reference Data impact data structure. For example, ICD-10 Diagnostic Codes are structured in ways very different from ICD-9. ICD10 has a different format. There are different values for the same concepts. More importantly, ICD-10 has additional principles of organization. ICD10 codes have a different granularity and are much more specific, so more information is conveyed in a single code. Consequently, there are many more of them (as of 2015, there were 68,000 ICD-10 codes, compared with 13,000 ICD-9s).[62]

The mandated use of ICD-10 codes in the US in 2015 required significant planning. Healthcare companies needed to make system changes as well as adjustments to impacted reporting to account for the new standard.

Types of changes include:

---

[62] http://bit.ly/1SSpds9 (accessed 8/13/16).

- Row level changes to external Reference Data sets
- Structural changes to external Reference Data sets
- Row level changes to internal Reference Data sets
- Structural changes to internal Reference Data sets
- Creation of new Reference Data sets

Changes can be planned / scheduled or ad hoc. Planned changes, such as monthly or annual updates to industry standard codes, require less governance than ad hoc updates. The process to request new Reference Data sets should account for potential uses beyond those of the original requestor.

Change requests should follow a defined process, as illustrated in Figure 78. When requests are received, stakeholders should be notified so that impacts can be assessed. If changes need approval, discussions should be held to get that approval. Changes should be communicated.

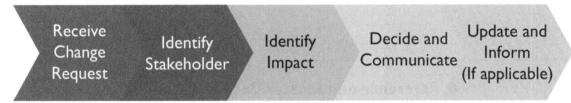

Figure 78 Reference Data Change Request Process

4.4 Data Sharing Agreements

Sharing and using Reference and Master Data across an organization requires collaboration between multiple parties internal to the organization and sometimes with parties external to it. To assure proper access and use, establish sharing agreements that stipulate what data can be shared and under what conditions. Having these agreements in place will help when issues arise regarding the availability of data within or quality of data brought into the data-sharing environment. This effort should be driven by the Data Governance program. It may involve Data Architects, Data Providers, Data Stewards, Application Developers, Business Analysts as well as Compliance / Privacy Officers and Security Officers.

Those responsible for the data-sharing environment have an obligation to downstream data consumers to provide high quality data. To fulfill this responsibility, they are dependent on upstream systems. SLA's and metrics should be established to measure the availability and quality of shared data. Processes should be put in place to address the root causes of issues with data quality or availability. A standard approach to communications should be put in place to keep all affected parties informed about the existence of issues and the status of remediation efforts. (See Chapter 8.)

5. Organization and Cultural Change

Reference and Master Data Management require people to relinquish control of some of their data and processes in order to create shared resources. It is not always easy to do this. While data management professionals can see that locally managed data is risky, the people who manage it locally need to get their work done and they may perceive MDM or RDM efforts as adding complication to their processes.

Fortunately, most people recognize that these efforts make fundamental sense. It is better to have one accurate and complete view of a single customer than to have multiple partial views.

Improving the availability and quality of reference and Master Data will undoubtedly require changes to procedures and traditional practices. Solutions should be scoped and implemented based on current organizational readiness and future needs tied to the organization's mission and vision.

Perhaps the most challenging cultural change is central to governance: Determining which individuals are accountable for which decisions – business Data Stewards, Architects, Managers, and Executives – and which decisions data stewardship teams, program steering committees, and the Data Governance Council should make collaboratively.

6. Reference and Master Data Governance

Because they are shared resources, Reference and Master Data require governance and stewardship. Not all data inconsistencies can be resolved through automation. Some require that people talk to each other. Without governance, Reference and Master Data solutions will just be additional data integration utilities, unable to deliver their full potential.

Governance processes will determine:

- The data sources to be integrated
- The data quality rules to be enforced
- The conditions of use rules to be followed
- The activities to be monitored and the frequency of monitoring
- The priority and response levels of data stewardships efforts
- How information is to be represented to meet stakeholder needs
- Standard approval gates, expectations in RDM and MDM deployment

Governance processes also bring compliance and legal stakeholders together with information consumers to ensure organizational risks are mitigated through definition and incorporation of privacy, security, and retention policies.

As an ongoing process, data governance must have the ability to review, receive, and consider new requirements and changes to existing rules, while making principles, rules, and guidelines available to those using Reference and Master Data.

6.1 Metrics

Certain metrics can be tied to Reference and Master Data quality and the processes that support these efforts:

- **Data quality and compliance**: DQ dashboards can describe the quality of Reference and Master Data. These metrics should denote the confidence (as a percentage) of a subject area entity or associated attribute and its fit-for-purpose for use across the organization.

- **Data change activity**: Auditing the lineage of trusted data is imperative to improving data quality in a data-sharing environment. Metrics should denote the rate of change of data values. These metrics will provide insight to the systems supplying data to the sharing environment, and can be used to tune algorithms in MDM processes.

- **Data ingestion and consumption**: Data is supplied by upstream systems and used by downstream systems and processes. These metrics should denote and track what systems are contributing data and what business areas are subscribing data from the sharing environment.

- **Service Level Agreements**: SLAs should be established and communicated to contributors and subscribers to ensure usage and adoption of the data-sharing environment. The level of adherence to SLAs can provide insight into both support processes and the technical and data problems that might slow down the MDM application.

- **Data Steward coverage**: These metrics should note the name or group responsible for data content, and how often the coverage is evaluated. They can be used to identify gaps in support.

- **Total Cost of Ownership**: There are multiple factors of this metric and different ways to represent it. From a solution view, costs can include environment infrastructure, software licenses, support staff, consulting fees, training, etc. Effectiveness of this metric is largely based on its consistent application across the organization.

- **Data sharing volume and usage**: Data ingestion and consumption volumes need to be tracked to determine the effectiveness of the data-sharing environment. These metrics should denote the volume and velocity of data defined, ingested, and subscribed to and from the data-sharing environment.

---

7. Works Cited / Recommended

Abbas, June. *Structures for Organizing Knowledge: Exploring Taxonomies, Ontologies, and Other Schema*. Neal-Schuman Publishers, 2010. Print.

Abernethy, Kenneth and J. Thomas Allen. *Exploring the Digital Domain: An Introduction to Computers and Information Fluency*. 2nd ed., 2004. Print.

Allen Mark and Dalton Cervo. *Multi-Domain Master Data Management: Advanced MDM and Data Governance in Practice*. Morgan Kaufmann, 2015. Print.

Bean, James. *XML for Data Architects: Designing for Reuse and Integration*. Morgan Kaufmann, 2003. Print. The Morgan Kaufmann Series in Data Management Systems.

Berson, Alex and Larry Dubov. *Master Data Management and Customer Data Integration for a Global Enterprise*. McGraw-Hill, 2007. Print.

Brackett, Michael. *Data Sharing Using a Common Data Architecture*. Wiley, 1994. Print. Wiley Professional Computing.

Cassell, Kay Ann and Uma Hiremath. *Reference and Information Services: An Introduction*. 3d ed. ALA Neal-Schuman, 2012. Print.

Cervo, Dalton and Mark Allen. *Master Data Management in Practice: Achieving True Customer MDM*. Wiley, 2011. Print.

Chisholm, Malcolm. "What is Master Data?" BeyeNetwork, February 6, 2008. http://bit.ly/2spTYOA Web.

Chisholm, Malcolm. *Managing Reference Data in Enterprise Databases: Binding Corporate Data to the Wider World*. Morgan Kaufmann, 2000. Print. The Morgan Kaufmann Series in Data Management Systems.

Dreibelbis, Allen, et al. *Enterprise Master Data Management: An SOA Approach to Managing Core Information*. IBM Press, 2008. Print.

Dyche, Jill and Evan Levy. *Customer Data Integration: Reaching a Single Version of the Truth*. John Wiley and Sons, 2006. Print.

Effingham, Nikk. *An Introduction to Ontology*. Polity, 2013. Print.

Finkelstein, Clive. *Enterprise Architecture for Integration: Rapid Delivery Methods and Techniques*. Artech House Print on Demand, 2006. Print. Artech House Mobile Communications Library.

Forte, Eric J., et al. *Fundamentals of Government Information: Mining, Finding, Evaluating, and Using Government Resources*. Neal-Schuman Publishers, 2011. Print.

Hadzic, Fedja, Henry Tan, Tharam S. Dillon. *Mining of Data with Complex Structures*. Springer, 2013. Print. Studies in Computational Intelligence.

Lambe, Patrick. *Organising Knowledge: Taxonomies, Knowledge and Organisational Effectiveness*. Chandos Publishing, 2007. Print. Chandos Knowledge Management.

Loshin, David. *Enterprise Knowledge Management: The Data Quality Approach*. Morgan Kaufmann, 2001. Print. The Morgan Kaufmann Series in Data Management Systems.

Loshin, David. *Master Data Management*. Morgan Kaufmann, 2008. Print. The MK/OMG Press.

Menzies, Tim, et al. *Sharing Data and Models in Software Engineering*. Morgan Kaufmann, 2014. Print.

Millett, Scott and Nick Tune. *Patterns, Principles, and Practices of Domain-Driven Design*. Wrox, 2015. Print.

Stewart, Darin L. *Building Enterprise Taxonomies*. Mokita Press, 2011. Print.

Talburt, John and Yinle Zhou. *Entity Information Management Lifecycle for Big Data*. Morgan Kauffman, 2015. Print.

Talburt, John. *Entity Resolution and Information Quality*. Morgan Kaufmann, 2011. Print.

Data Warehousing and Business Intelligence

DAMA-DMBOK2 Data Management Framework

Copyright © 2017 by DAMA International

---

1. Introduction

The concept of the Data Warehouse emerged in the 1980s as technology enabled organizations to integrate data from a range of sources into a common data model. Integrated data promised to provide insight into operational processes and open up new possibilities for leveraging data to make decisions and create organizational value. As importantly, data warehouses were seen as a means to reduce the proliferation of decision support systems (DSS), most of which drew on the same core enterprise data. The concept of an enterprise warehouse promised a way to reduce data redundancy, improve the consistency of information, and enable an enterprise to use its data to make better decisions.

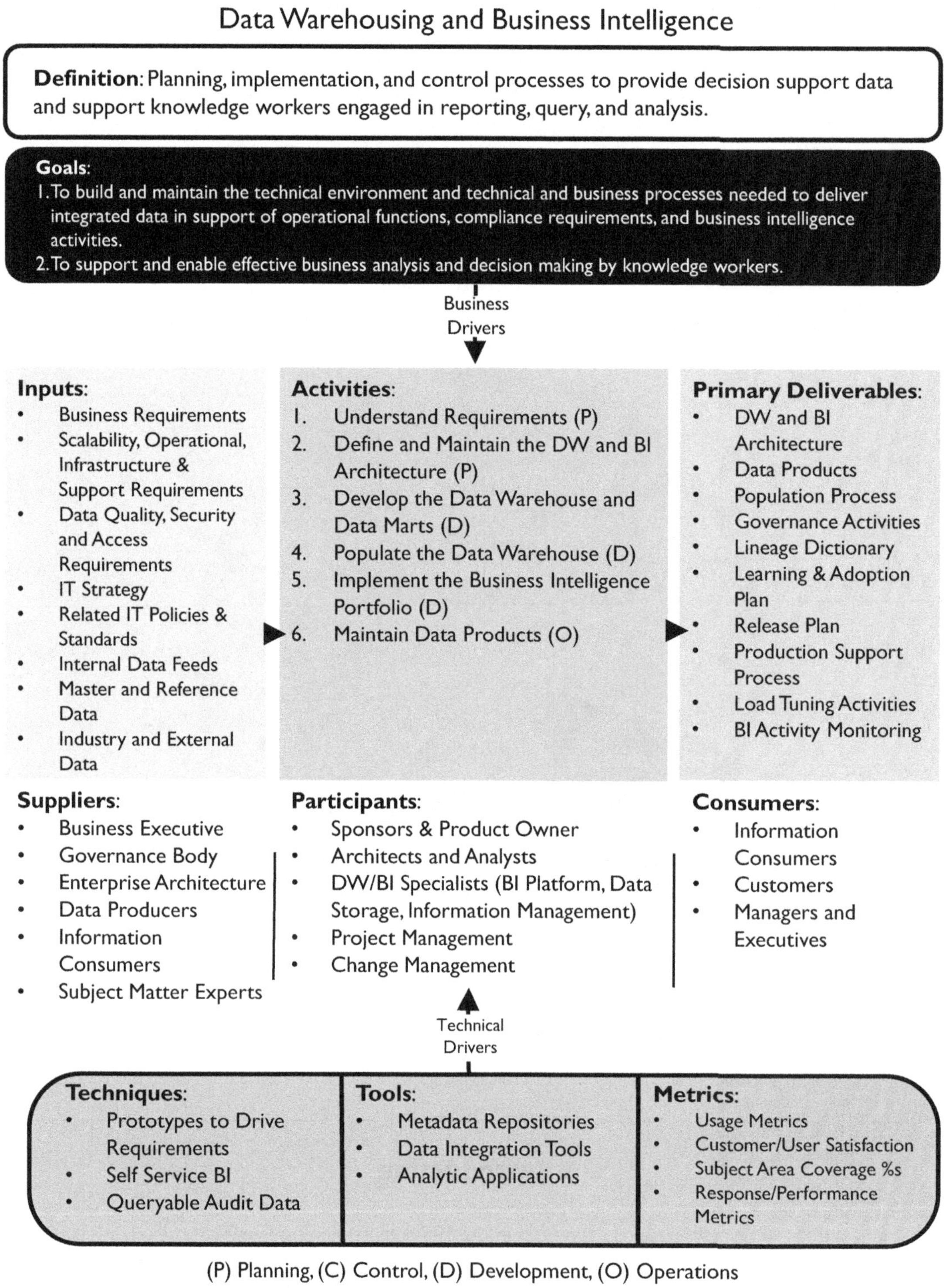

Data Warehousing and Business Intelligence

Definition: Planning, implementation, and control processes to provide decision support data and support knowledge workers engaged in reporting, query, and analysis.

Goals:
1. To build and maintain the technical environment and technical and business processes needed to deliver integrated data in support of operational functions, compliance requirements, and business intelligence activities.
2. To support and enable effective business analysis and decision making by knowledge workers.

Business
Drivers

Inputs:
- Business Requirements
- Scalability, Operational, Infrastructure & Support Requirements
- Data Quality, Security and Access Requirements
- IT Strategy
- Related IT Policies & Standards
- Internal Data Feeds
- Master and Reference Data
- Industry and External Data

Activities:
1. Understand Requirements (P)
2. Define and Maintain the DW and BI Architecture (P)
3. Develop the Data Warehouse and Data Marts (D)
4. Populate the Data Warehouse (D)
5. Implement the Business Intelligence Portfolio (D)
6. Maintain Data Products (O)

Primary Deliverables:
- DW and BI Architecture
- Data Products
- Population Process
- Governance Activities
- Lineage Dictionary
- Learning & Adoption Plan
- Release Plan
- Production Support Process
- Load Tuning Activities
- BI Activity Monitoring

Suppliers:
- Business Executive
- Governance Body
- Enterprise Architecture
- Data Producers
- Information Consumers
- Subject Matter Experts

Participants:
- Sponsors & Product Owner
- Architects and Analysts
- DW/BI Specialists (BI Platform, Data Storage, Information Management)
- Project Management
- Change Management

Consumers:
- Information Consumers
- Customers
- Managers and Executives

Technical
Drivers

Techniques:
- Prototypes to Drive Requirements
- Self Service BI
- Queryable Audit Data

Tools:
- Metadata Repositories
- Data Integration Tools
- Analytic Applications

Metrics:
- Usage Metrics
- Customer/User Satisfaction
- Subject Area Coverage %s
- Response/Performance Metrics

(P) Planning, (C) Control, (D) Development, (O) Operations

Figure 79 Context Diagram: DW/BI

Data warehouses began to be built in earnest in the 1990s. Since then (and especially with the co-evolution of Business Intelligence as a primary driver of business decision-making), data warehouses have become 'mainstream'. Most enterprises have data warehouses and warehousing is the recognized core of enterprise data management.[63] Even though well established, the data warehouse continues to evolve. As new forms of data are created with increasing velocity, new concepts, such as data lakes, are emerging that will influence the future of the data warehouse. See Chapters 8 and 15.

1.1 Business Drivers

The primary driver for data warehousing is to support operational functions, compliance requirements, and Business Intelligence (BI) activities (though not all BI activities depend on warehouse data). Increasingly organizations are being asked to provide data as evidence that they have complied with regulatory requirements. Because they contain historical data, warehouses are often the means to respond to such requests. Nevertheless, Business Intelligence support continues to be the primary reason for a warehouse. BI promises insight about the organization, its customers, and its products. An organization that acts on knowledge gained from BI can improve operational efficiency and competitive advantage. As more data has become available at a greater velocity, BI has evolved from retrospective assessment to predictive analytics.

1.2 Goals and Principles

Organizations implement data warehouses in order to:

- Support Business Intelligence activity
- Enable effective business analysis and decision-making
- Find ways to innovate based on insights from their data

The implementation of a Data Warehouse should follow these guiding principles:

- **Focus on business goals**: Make sure DW serves organizational priorities and solves business problems.

- **Start with the end in mind**: Let the business priority and scope of end-data-delivery in the BI space drive the creation of the DW content.

- **Think and design globally; act and build locally**: Let end-vision guide the architecture, but build and deliver incrementally, through focused projects or sprints that enable more immediate return on investment.

- **Summarize and optimize last, not first**: Build on the atomic data. Aggregate and summarize to meet requirements and ensure performance, not to replace the detail.

- **Promote transparency and self-service**: The more context (Metadata of all kinds) provided, the better able data consumers will be to get value out of the data. Keep stakeholders informed about the data and the processes by which it is integrated.

- **Build Metadata with the warehouse**: Critical to DW success is the ability to explain the data. For example, being able to answer basic questions like "Why is this sum X?" "How was that computed?" and

---

"Where did the data come from?" Metadata should be captured as part of the development cycle and managed as part of ongoing operations.

- **Collaborate**: Collaborate with other data initiatives, especially those for Data Governance, Data Quality, and Metadata.

- **One size does not fit all**: Use the right tools and products for each group of data consumers.

1.3 Essential Concepts

1.3.1 Business Intelligence

The term *Business Intelligence* (BI) has two meanings. First, it refers to a type of data analysis aimed at understanding organizational activities and opportunities. Results of such analysis are used to improve organizational success. When people say that data holds the key to competitive advantage, they are articulating the promise inherent in Business Intelligence activity: that if an organization asks the right questions of its own data, it can gain insights about its products, services, and customers that enable it to make better decisions about how to fulfill its strategic objectives. Secondly, *Business Intelligence* refers to a set of technologies that support this kind of data analysis. An evolution of decisions support tools, BI tools enable querying, data mining, statistical analysis, reporting, scenario modeling, data visualization, and dashboarding. They are used for everything from budgeting to advanced analytics.

1.3.2 Data Warehouse

A *Data Warehouse* (DW) is a combination of two primary components: An integrated decision support database and the related software programs used to collect, cleanse, transform, and store data from a variety of operational and external sources. To support historical, analytical, and BI requirements, a data warehouse may also include dependent data marts, which are subset copies of data from the warehouse. In its broadest context, a data warehouse includes any data stores or extracts used to support the delivery of data for BI purposes.

An *Enterprise Data Warehouse* (EDW) is a centralized data warehouse designed to service the BI needs of the entire organization. An EDW adheres to an enterprise data model to ensure consistency of decision support activities across the enterprise.

1.3.3 Data Warehousing

Data Warehousing describes the operational extract, cleansing, transformation, control, and load processes that maintain the data in a data warehouse. The data warehousing process focuses on enabling an integrated and historical business context on operational data by enforcing business rules and maintaining appropriate business data relationships. Data warehousing also includes processes that interact with Metadata repositories.

Traditionally, data warehousing focuses on structured data: elements in defined fields, whether in files or tables, as documented in data models. With recent advances in technology, the BI and DW space now embraces semi-structured and unstructured data. Semi-structured data, defined as electronic elements organized as semantic entities with no required attribute affinity, predates XML but not HTML; an EDI transfer could serve as an example. Unstructured data refers to data that is not predefined through a data model. Because unstructured data exists in a range of formats and encompasses items such as e-mail, free format text, business documents, videos, photos, and web pages to name a few, defining a feasible storage construct that sustains analytic workloads within warehousing governance has been a challenge yet to be overcome.

1.3.4 Approaches to Data Warehousing

Much of the conversation about what constitutes a data warehouse has been driven by two influential thought leaders – Bill Inmon and Ralph Kimball – who have different approaches to modeling and developing warehouses. Inmon defines a *data warehouse* as "a subject-oriented, integrated, time-variant and non-volatile collection of data in support of management's decision-making process."[64] A normalized relational model is used to store and manage data. Kimball defines a warehouse as "a copy of transaction data specifically structured for query and analysis." Kimball's approach calls for a dimensional model. (See Chapter 5.)

While Inmon and Kimball advocate different approaches to building warehouses, their definitions recognize similar core ideas:

- Warehouses store data from other systems
- The act of storage includes organizing the data in ways that increase its value
- Warehouses make data accessible and usable for analysis
- Organizations build warehouses because they need to make reliable, integrated data available to authorized stakeholders
- Warehouse data serves many purposes, from support of workflow to operational management to predictive analytics

1.3.5 Corporate Information Factory (Inmon)

Bill Inmon's Corporate Information Factory (CIF) is one of the two primary patterns for data warehousing. The component parts of Inmon's definition of a *data warehouse*, "a subject oriented, integrated, time variant, and nonvolatile collection of summary and detailed historical data," describe the concepts that support the CIF and point to the differences between warehouses and operational systems.

- **Subject-oriented**: The data warehouse is organized based on major business entities, rather than focusing on a functional or application.

- **Integrated**: Data in the warehouse is unified and cohesive. The same key structures, encoding and decoding of structures, data definitions, naming conventions are applied consistently throughout the

---

[64] http://bit.ly/1FtgeIL, last accessed 2/27/2016.

warehouse. Because data is integrated, Warehouse data is not simply a copy of operational data. Instead, the warehouse becomes a system of record for the data.

- **Time variant**: The data warehouse stores data as it exists in a set point in time. Records in the DW are like snapshots. Each one reflects the state of the data at a moment of time. This means that querying data based on a specific time period will always produce the same result, regardless of when the query is submitted.

- **Non-volatile**: In the DW, records are not normally updated as they are in operational systems. Instead, new data is appended to existing data. A set of records may represent different states of the same transaction.

- **Aggregate and detail data**: The data in the DW includes details of atomic level transactions, as well as summarized data. Operational systems rarely aggregate data. When warehouses were first established, cost and space considerations drove the need to summarize data. Summarized data can be persistent (stored in a table) or non-persistent (rendered in a view) in contemporary DW environments. The deciding factor in whether to persist data is usually performance.

- **Historical**: The focus of operational systems is current data. Warehouses contain historical data as well. Often they house vast amounts of it.

Inmon, Claudia Imhoff and Ryan Sousa describe data warehousing in the context of the Corporate Information Factory (CIF). See Figure 80. CIF components include:

- **Applications**: Applications perform operational processes. Detail data from applications is brought into the data warehouse and the operational data stores (ODS) where it can be analyzed.

- **Staging Area**: A database that stands between the operational source databases and the target databases. The data staging area is where the extract, transform, and load effort takes place. It is not used by end users. Most data in the data staging area is transient, although typically there is some relatively small amount of persistent data.

- **Integration and transformation**: In the integration layer, data from disparate sources is transformed so that it can be integrated into the standard corporate representation / model in the DW and ODS.

- **Operational Data Store (ODS)**: An ODS is integrated database of operational data. It may be sourced directly from applications or from other databases. ODS's generally contain current or near term data (30-90 days), while a DW contains historical data as well (often several years of data). Data in ODS's is volatile, while warehouse data is stable. Not all organizations use ODS's. They evolved as to meet the need for low latency data. An ODS may serve as the primary source for a data warehouse; it may also be used to audit a data warehouse.

- **Data marts**: Data marts provide data prepared for analysis. This data is often a sub-set of warehouse data designed to support particular kinds of analysis or a specific group of data consumers. For example, marts can aggregate data to support faster analysis. Dimensional modeling (using denormalization techniques) is often used to design user-oriented data marts.

- **Operational Data Mart (OpDM)**: An OpDM is a data mart focused on tactical decision support. It is sourced directly from an ODS, rather than from a DW. It shares characteristics of the ODS: it contains current or near-term data. Its contents are volatile.

- **Data Warehouse**: The DW provides a single integration point for corporate data to support management decision-making, and strategic analysis and planning. The data flows into a DW from the application systems and ODS, and flows out to the data marts, usually in one direction only. Data that needs correction is rejected, corrected at its source, and ideally re-fed through the system.

- **Operational reports**: Reports are output from the data stores.

- **Reference, Master, and external data**: In addition to transactional data from applications, the CIF also includes data required to understand transactions, such as reference and Master Data. Access to common data simplifies integration in the DW. While applications consume current master and Reference Data, the DW also requires historical values and the timeframes during which they were valid (see Chapter 10).

Figure 80 depicts movement within the CIF, from data collection and creation via applications (on the left) to the creation of information via marts and analysis (on the right). Movement from left to right includes other changes. For example,

- The purpose shifts from execution of operational functions to analysis
- End users of systems move from front line workers to decision-makers
- System usage moves from fixed operations to ad hoc uses
- Response time requirements are relaxed (strategic decisions take more time than do daily operations)
- Much more data is involved in each operation, query, or process

The data in DW and marts differs from that in applications:

- Data is organized by subject rather than function
- Data is integrated data rather than 'siloed'
- Data is time-variant vs. current-valued only
- Data has higher latency in DW than in applications
- Significantly more historical data is available in DW than in applications

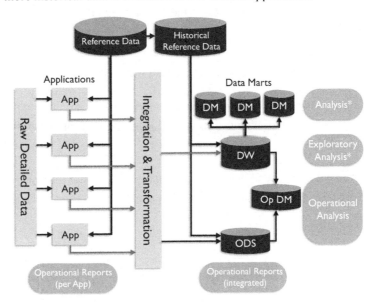

Figure 80 The Corporate Information Factory

1.3.6 Dimensional DW (Kimball)

Kimball's Dimensional Data Warehouse is the other primary pattern for DW development. Kimball defines a data warehouse simply as "a copy of transaction data specifically structured for query and analysis" (Kimball, 2002). The 'copy' is not exact, however. Warehouse data is stored in a dimensional data model. The dimensional model is designed to enable data consumers to understand and use the data, while also enabling query performance.[65] It is not normalized in the way an entity relationship model is.

Often referred to as *Star Schema*, dimensional models are comprised *facts*, which contain quantitative data about business processes (e.g., sales numbers), and *dimensions*, which store descriptive attributes related to fact data and allow data consumers to answer questions about the facts (e.g., how many units of product X were sold this quarter?) A fact table joins with many dimension tables, and when viewed as a diagram, appears as a star. (See Chapter 5.) Multiple fact tables will share the common, or conformed, dimensions via a 'bus', similar to a bus in a computer.[66] Multiple data marts can be integrated at an enterprise level by plugging into the bus of conformed dimensions.

The DW bus matrix shows the intersection of business processes that generate fact data and data subject areas that represent dimensions. Opportunities for conformed dimensions exist where multiple processes use the same data. Table 27 is a sample bus matrix. In this example, the business processes for Sales, Inventory, and Orders all require Date and Product data. Sales and Inventory both require Store data, while Inventory and Orders require Vendor data. Date, Product, Store and Vendor are all candidates for conformed dimensions. In contrast, Warehouse is not shared; it is used only by Inventory.

Table 27 DW-Bus Matrix Example

Business Processes	Subject Areas				
	Date	Product	Store	Vendor	Warehouse
Sales	X	X	X		
Inventory	X	X	X	X	X
Orders	X	X		X	
Conformed Dimension Candidate	*Yes*	*Yes*	*Yes*	*Yes*	*No*

The enterprise DW bus matrix can be used to represent the long-term data content requirements for the DW/BI system, independent of technology. This tool enables an organization to scope manageable development efforts. Each implementation builds an increment of the overall architecture. At some point, enough dimensional schemas exist to make good on the promise of an integrated enterprise data warehouse environment.

Figure 81 represents Kimball's Data Warehouse Chess Pieces view of DW/BI architecture. Note that Kimball's Data Warehouse is more expansive than Inmon's. The DW encompasses all components in the data staging and data presentation areas.

- **Operational source systems**: Operational / transactional applications of the Enterprise. These create the data that is integrated into the ODS and DW. This component is equivalent to the application systems in the CIF diagram.

---

[65] http://bit.ly/1udtNC8.

[66] The term *bus* came from Kimball's electrical engineering background, where a bus was something providing common power to a number of electrical components.

- **Data staging area**: Kimball's staging includes the set of processes needed to integrate and transform data for presentation. It can be compared to a combination of CIF's integration, transformation, and DW components. Kimball's focus is on efficient end-delivery of the analytical data, a scope smaller than Inmon's corporate management of data. Kimball's enterprise DW can fit into the architecture of the data staging area.

- **Data presentation area**: Similar to the Data Marts in the CIF. The key architectural difference being an integrating paradigm of a 'DW Bus,' such as shared or conformed dimensions unifying the multiple data marts.

- **Data access tools**: Kimball's approach focuses on end users' data requirements. These needs drive the adoption of appropriate data access tools.

1.3.7 DW Architecture Components

The data warehouse environment includes a collection of architectural components that need to be organized to meet the needs of the enterprise. Figure 82 depicts the architectural components of the DW/BI and Big Data Environment discussed in this section. The evolution of Big Data has changed the DW/BI landscape by adding another path through which data may be brought into an enterprise.

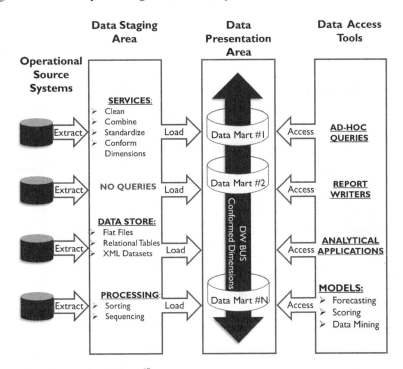

Figure 81 Kimball's Data Warehouse Chess Pieces[67]

Figure 82 also depicts aspects of the data lifecycle. Data moves from source systems, into a staging area where it may be cleansed and enriched as it is integrated and stored in the DW and/or an ODS. From the DW it may be accessed via marts or cubes and used for various kinds of reporting. Big Data goes through a similar process, but with a significant difference: while most warehouses integrate data before landing it in tables, Big Data solutions

---

[67] Adapted from Kimball and Ross (2002). Used with permission.

ingest data before integrating it. Big Data BI may include predictive analytics and data mining, as well as more traditional forms of reporting. (See Chapter 14.)

1.3.7.1 Source Systems

Source Systems, on the left side of Figure 82, include the operational systems and external data to be brought into the DW/BI environment. These typically include operational systems such as CRM, Accounting, and Human Resources applications, as well as operational systems that differ based on industry. Data from vendors and external sources may also be included, as may DaaS, web content, and any Big Data computation results.

1.3.7.2 Data Integration

Data integration covers Extract, Transform, and Load (ETL), data virtualization, and other techniques of getting data into a common form and location. In a SOA environment, the data services layers are part of this component. In Figure 82, all the arrows represent data integration processes. (See Chapter 8.)

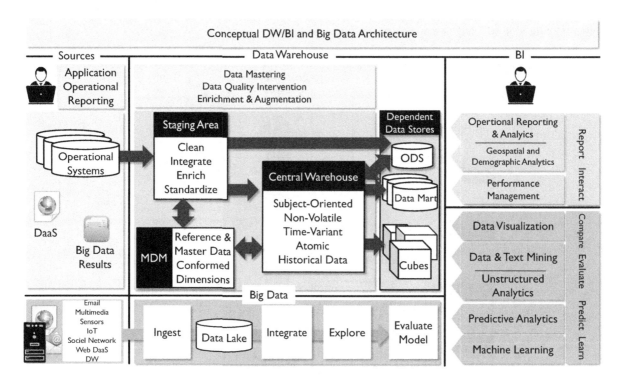

Figure 82 Conceptual DW/BI and Big Data Architecture

1.3.7.3 Data Storage Areas

The warehouse has a set of storage areas:

- **Staging area**: A staging area is an intermediate data store between an original data source and the centralized data repository. Data is staged so that it can be transformed, integrated, and prepped for loading to the warehouse.

- **Reference and Master Data conformed dimensions**: Reference and Master Data may be stored in separate repositories. The data warehouse feeds new Master Data and is fed by conformed dimension contents from the separate repositories.

- **Central Warehouse**: Once transformed and prepped, the DW data usually persists in the central or atomic layer. This layer maintains all historical atomic data as well as the latest instance of the batch run. The data structure of this area is developed and influenced based on performance needs and use patterns. Several design elements are brought to bear:
  - The relationship between the business key and surrogate keys for performance
  - Creation of indices and foreign keys to support dimensions
  - Change Data Capture (CDC) techniques that are used to detect, maintain, and store history

- **Operational Data Store (ODS)**: The ODS is a version of a central persisted store that supports lower latencies, and therefore operational use. Since the ODS contains a time window of data and not the history, it can be refreshed much more quickly than a warehouse. Sometimes real-time streams are snapshotted at predefined intervals into the ODS to enable integrated reporting and analysis. Over time, with the increasing frequency of updates driven by business needs, and growing technology and techniques to integrate real-time data into the DW, many installations have merged their ODS into the existing DW or Data Mart architecture.

- **Data marts**: A data mart is a type of data store often used to support presentation layers of the data warehouse environment. It is also used for presenting a departmental or functional sub-set of the DW for integrated reporting, query, and analysis of historical information. The data mart is oriented to a specific subject area, a single department, or a single business process. It can also form the basis of a virtualized warehouse where the combined marts comprise the resulting warehouse entity. Data integration processes will refresh, update or expand the contents of the various marts from the persistence layer.

- **Cubes**: Three classic implementation approaches support Online Analytical Processing (OLAP). Their names relate to underlying database types, such as Relational, Multi-dimensional, and Hybrid.

1.3.8 Types of Load Processing

Data warehousing involves two main types of data integration processes: historical loads and ongoing updates. Historical data is usually loaded only once, or a few times while working out data issues, and then never again. Ongoing updates are consistently scheduled and executed to keep the data in the warehouse up-to-date.

1.3.8.1 Historical Data

One advantage of a data warehouse is that it can capture detailed history of the data it stores. There are different methods to capture this detail. An organization that wants to capture history should design based on requirements. Being able to reproduce point-in-time snapshots requires a different approach than simply presenting current state.

The Inmon data warehouse suggests that all data is stored in a single data warehouse layer. This layer will store cleansed, standardized, and governed atomic level data. A common integration and transformation layer facilitates reuse across the delivery implementations. An enterprise data model is required for success. Once validated, this single store is available to different data consumers via a star structured data mart.

The Kimball data warehouse suggests that the data warehouse is composed of a combination of departmental data marts containing cleansed, standardized, and governed data. The data marts will store the history at the atomic level. Conformed dimensions and conformed facts will deliver enterprise level information.

Another approach, the Data Vault, also cleanses and standardizes as part of the staging process. History is stored in a normalized atomic structure, dimensional surrogate, primary and alternate keys are defined. Ensuring that the business and surrogate key relationship remains intact becomes the secondary role of the vault – this is the data mart history. Facts persisted here as atomic structures. The vault is then available to a variety of data consumers via data marts. By retaining the history inside the vault, reloading facts is possible when later increments introduce grain changes. It is possible to virtualize the presentation layer, facilitating agile incremental delivery and collaborative development with the business community. A final materialization process can implement a more traditional star data mart for production end user consumption.

1.3.8.2 Batch Change Data Capture

Data Warehouses are often loaded daily and serviced by a nightly batch window. The load process can accommodate a variety of change detection, as each source system may require differing change capture techniques.

Database log techniques are likely candidates for in-house developed applications as vendor purchased applications are unlikely to tolerate modification with triggers or additional overhead. Time stamped or log table loads are the most common. Full loads occur when dealing with legacy systems built without native time stamping capabilities (yes, there are applications without databases) or when certain batch recovery conditions apply.

Table 28 summarizes difference between change data capture techniques, including their relative complexity and speed. The overlap column identifies whether there may be data duplication between source system changes and the target environment. When Overlap is 'Yes' this change data may already be present. When the Delete indicator is set to 'Yes' that the Change Data Method will track any deletes that have occurred in the source system – useful for expiring dimensions no longer in use. When Deletes are not tracked by the source system, additional efforts are required to determine when they occur. (See Chapter 8.)

Table 28 CDC Technique Comparison

Method	Source System Requirement	Complexity	Fact Load	Dimension Load	Overlap	Deletes
Time stamped Delta Load	Changes in the source system are stamped with the system date and time.	Low	Fast	Fast	Yes	No
Log Table Delta Load	Source system changes are captured and stored in log tables	Medium	Nominal	Nominal	Yes	Yes
Database Transaction Log	Database captures changes in the transaction log	High	Nominal	Nominal	No	Yes

Method	Source System Requirement	Complexity	Fact Load	Dimension Load	Overlap	Deletes
Message Delta	Source system changes are published as [near] real-time messages	Extreme	Slow	Slow	No	Yes
Full Load	No change indicator, tables extracted in full and compared to identify change	Simple	Slow	Nominal	Yes	Yes

1.3.8.3 Near-real-time and Real-time

With the onset of Operational BI (or Operational Analytics) pushing for lower latency and more integration of real-time or near-real-time data into the data warehouse, new architectural approaches emerged to deal with the inclusion of volatile data. For example, a common application of operational BI is the automated banking machine data provisioning. When making a banking transaction, historical balances and new balances resulting from immediate banking actions need to be presented to the banking customer real-time. Two key design concepts that are required for provisioning data in near-real-time are isolation of change and alternatives to batch processing.

The impact of the changes from new volatile data must be isolated from the bulk of the historical, non-volatile DW data. Typical architectural approaches for isolation include a combination of building partitions and using union queries for the different partitions. Alternatives to batch processing handle the increasingly shorter latency requirements for data availability in the DW. There are three main types: trickle feeds, messaging, and streaming, which differ by where data is accumulated while waiting to be processed. (See Chapter 8.)

- **Trickle feeds (Source accumulation)**: Rather than run on a nightly schedule, trickle feeds execute batch loads on a more frequent schedule (e.g., hourly, every 5 minutes) or when a threshold is reached (e.g., 300 transactions, 1G of data). This allows some processing to happen during the day, but not as intensely as with a dedicated nightly batch process. Care is needed to ensure that if a trickle feed batch takes longer to complete than the time between feeds, the next feed is delayed so that the data is still loaded in proper order.

- **Messaging (Bus accumulation)**: Message interaction in real-time or near-real-time is useful when extremely small packets of data (messages, events, or transactions) are published to a bus as they occur. Target systems subscribe to the bus, and incrementally process the packets into the warehouse as needed. Source systems and target systems are independent of each other. Data-as-a-Service (DaaS) frequently uses this method.

- **Streaming (Target accumulation)**: Rather than wait on a source based schedule or threshold, a target system collects data as it is received into a buffer area or queue, and processes it in order. The result interaction or some aggregate may later appear as an additional feed to the warehouse.

2. Activities

2.1 Understand Requirements

Developing a data warehouse is different from developing an operational system. Operational systems depend on precise, specific requirements. Data warehouses bring together data that will be used in a range of different ways. Moreover, usage will evolve over time as users analyze and explore data. Take time in the initial phases to ask questions related to capabilities and sources of data to support these capabilities. This time to design pays off in reduced rework costs later when the data processing is being tested using the actual data sources.

In gathering requirements for DW/BI projects, begin with business goals and strategy. Identify and scope the business areas, then identify and interview the appropriate business people. Ask what they do and why. Capture specific questions they are asking now, and those they want to ask of the data. Document how they distinguish between and categorize important aspects of the information. Where possible, define and capture key performance metrics and calculations. These can uncover business rules that provide the foundation for automation of data quality expectations.

Catalog requirements and prioritize them into those necessary for production go-live and adoption of the warehouse and those that can wait. Look for items that are simple and valuable to jump-start the productivity of the initial project release. A DW/BI project requirements write-up should frame the whole context of the business areas and / or processes that are in scope.

2.2 Define and Maintain the DW/BI Architecture

The DW/BI architecture should describe where data comes from, where it goes, when it goes, why and how it goes into a warehouse. The 'how' includes the hardware and software detail and the organizing framework to bring all the activities together. Technical requirements should include performance, availability, and timing needs. (See Chapters 4 and 8.)

2.2.1 Define DW/BI Technical Architecture

The best DW/BI architectures will design a mechanism to connect back to transactional level and operational level reports in an atomic DW. This mechanism will protect the DW from having to carry every transactional detail. An example is providing a viewing mechanism for key operational reports or forms based on a transactional key, such as Invoice Number. Customers will always want all the detail available, but some of the operational data, such as long description fields, has value only in the context of the original report, and does not provide analytic value.

A conceptual architecture is a starting point. Many activities are necessary to correctly align the non-functional requirements to the business needs. Prototyping can quickly prove or disprove key points before making expensive commitments to technologies or architectures. In addition, empowering the business community with knowledge and adoption programs championed through a sanctioned change management team will assist in transition and ongoing operational success.

A natural extension to this transformation process is the maintenance, or at least validation, with the enterprise data model. Since the focus is on which data structures are in use by which organizational areas, check the physical deployment against the logical model. Make any updates if omissions or errors arise.

2.2.2 Define DW/BI Management Processes

Address production management with a coordinated and integrated maintenance process, delivering regular releases to the business community.

It is crucial to establish a standard release plan (see Section 2.6). Ideally, the warehouse project team should manage each update to the deployed data product as a software release that provisions additional functionality. Establishing a schedule for releases allows for an annual demand and resource plan and standard delivery schedule. Use the internal release to tweak this standardized schedule, the resource expectations and estimate sheets derived for it.

Establishing a functioning release process ensures that management understands this to be a data product-centric proactive process and not an installed product addressed through reactive issue resolution. It is critical to work pro-actively and collaboratively in a cross-functional team to continuously grow and enhancement features – reactive support systems reduce adoption.

2.3 Develop the Data Warehouse and Data Marts

Typically, DW/BI projects have three concurrent development tracks:

- **Data**: The data necessary to support the analysis the business wants to do. This track involves identifying the best sources for the data and designing rules for how the data is remediated, transformed, integrated, stored, and made available for use by the applications. This step also includes deciding how to handle data that doesn't fit expectations.

- **Technology**: The back-end systems and processes supporting the data storage and movement. Integration with the existing enterprise is fundamental, as the warehouse is not an island unto itself. Enterprise Architectures, specifically Technology and Application specialties, usually manage this track.

- **Business Intelligence tools**: The suite of applications necessary for data consumers to gain meaningful insight from deployed data products.

2.3.1 Map Sources to Targets

Source-to-target mapping establishes transformation rules for entities and data elements from individual sources to a target system. Such mapping also documents lineage for each data element available in the BI environment back to its respective source(s).

The most difficult part of any mapping effort is determining valid links or equivalencies between data elements in multiple systems. Consider the effort to consolidate data into a DW from multiple billing or order management systems. Chances are that tables and fields that contain equivalent data do not have the same names or structures.

A solid taxonomy is necessary to map data elements in different systems to a consistent structure in the DW. Most often, this taxonomy is the logical data model. The mapping process must also address whether data in different structures is to be appended, changed in place, or inserted.

2.3.2 Remediate and Transform Data

Data remediation or cleansing activities enforce standards and correct and enhance the domain values of individual data elements. Remediation is particularly necessary for initial loads where significant history is involved. To reduce the complexity of the target system, source systems should be made responsible for data remediation and correction.

Develop strategies for rows of data that are loaded but found to be incorrect. A policy for deleting old records may cause some havoc with related tables and surrogate keys, expiring a row and loading the new data as a completely new row may be a better option.

An optimistic load strategy may include creating dimension entries to accommodate fact data. Such a process must account for how to update and expire such entries. Pessimistic load strategies should include a recycle area for fact data that cannot be associated with corresponding dimension keys. These entries require appropriate notification, alerting and reporting to ensure they are tracked, and reloaded later. Fact jobs should consider first loading recycled entries, then processing newly arrived content.

Data transformation focuses on activities that implement business rules within a technical system. Data transformation is essential to data integration. Defining the correct rules by which to integrate data often requires direct involvement from Data Stewards and other SMEs. Rules should be documented so that they can be governed. Data integration tools perform these tasks. (See Chapter 8.)

2.4 Populate the Data Warehouse

The largest part of the work in any DW/BI effort is the preparation and processing of the data. The design decisions and principles for what data detail the DW contains are a key design priority for DW/BI architecture. Publishing clear rules for what data will be available via only operational reporting (such as in non-DW) is critical to the success of DW/BI efforts.

The key factors to consider when defining a population approach are required latency, availability of sources, batch windows or upload intervals, target databases, dimensional aspects, and timeframe consistency of the data warehouse and data mart. The approach must also address data quality processing, time to perform transformations, and late-arriving dimensions and data rejects.

Another aspect to defining a population approach centers around change data capture process – detecting changes in the source system, integrating those changes together, and aligning changes across time. Several databases now provision log capture functionality that data integration tools can operate on directly, so the database tells the user what has changed. Scripting processes can be written or generated where this function is not available. Several techniques are available to the design and build teams for integration and latency alignment across heterogeneous feeds.

The first increment paves the way for additional capability development and onboarding new business units. Many new technologies, processes, and skills are necessary, as well as careful planning and attention to detail. Downstream increments are to build on top of this foundational element, so more investments are recommended to sustain high quality data, technical architecture, and transitioning to production. Create processes to facilitate and automate timely identification of data errors with end user workflow integration.

2.5 Implement the Business Intelligence Portfolio

Implementing the BI Portfolio is about identifying the right tools for the right user communities within or across business units. Find similarities through alignment of common business processes, performance analysis, management styles, and requirements.

2.5.1 Group Users According to Needs

In defining the target user groups, there is a spectrum of BI needs. First, know the user groups and then match the tool to the user groups in the company. On one end of the spectrum are IT developers concerned with extracting data, who focus on advanced functionality. On the other end, information consumers may want fast access to previously developed and executed reports. These consumers may want some degree of interactivity such as drill, filter, sort, or may only want to see a static report.

Users may move from one class to another as their skills increase or as they perform different functions. A supply chain manager, for example, may want to view a static report on financials but a highly interactive report for analyzing inventory. A financial analyst and a line manager responsible for expenses may be power users when analyzing total expenses, but are satisfied with a static report of one phone bill. Executives and managers will use a combination of fixed reports, dashboards, and scorecards. Managers and power users tend to want to drill into these reports slice and dice the data to identify the root causes of problems. External customers may use any of these tools as part of their experience.

2.5.2 Match Tools to User Requirements

The marketplace offers an impressive range of reporting and analytics tools. Major BI vendors offer classic pixel-perfect report capabilities that were once the domain of application reports. Many application vendors offer embedded analytics with standard content fetched from pre-populated cubes or aggregate tables. Virtualization has blurred the lines between on-premises data sources and external purchased or open data, and in some cases provisions user-controlled report-centric integration on demand. In other words, it is prudent for companies to use common infrastructure and delivery mechanisms. These include the web, email, and applications for the delivery of all kinds of information and reports, of which DW/BI is a subset.

Many vendors are now combining related BI Tools, through mergers and acquisitions or net new development, and offering BI Suites. Suites are the primary option at the Enterprise Architecture level but given that most organizations have already purchased individual tools, or embraced open source tools, questions around replacement versus co-existence are likely to surface. Remember that every BI tool comes with a price, requiring system resources, support, training, and architectural integration.

2.6 Maintain Data Products

An implemented warehouse and its customer-facing BI tools is a data product. Enhancements (extensions, augmentations, or modifications) to an existing DW platform should be implemented incrementally.

Maintaining the scope for an increment, and executing a critical path for key work items, can be a challenge in a dynamic work environment. Set priorities with business partners and focus work on mandatory enhancements.

2.6.1 Release Management

Release Management is critical to an incremental development processes that grows new capabilities, enhances the production deployment, and ensures provision of regular maintenance across the deployed assets. This process will keep the warehouse up-to-date, clean, and operating at its best. However, this process requires the same alignment between IT and Business as between the Data Warehouse model and the BI capabilities. It is a continual improvement effort.

Figure 83 illustrates an example release process, based on a quarterly schedule. Over the year, there are three business-driven releases and one technology-based release (to address requirements internal to the warehouse). The process should enable incremental development of the warehouse and management of the backlog of requirements.

2.6.2 Manage Data Product Development Lifecycle

While data consumers are using the existing DW, the DW team is preparing for the next iteration, with the understanding that not all items will go to production. Align the iterations to releases with a backorder work list prioritized by the business units. Each iteration will extend an existing increment or add new functionality by onboarding a business unit. Releases will align functionality to the business unit, whereas the iteration will align the functionality to the configuration itself managed by the product manager.

Those items that business believes ready and feasible for further investigation can be reviewed, adjusted if necessary, and then promoted to a pilot or sandbox environment, where business users investigate new approaches, experiment with new techniques, or develop new models or learning algorithms. This area may see less governance and supervision than other business-facing areas but some form of sandbox prioritizing is necessary.

Akin to the traditional quality assurance or testing environment, scrutinize items in the pilot area for fit into the production world. How well pilot items perform determines their next steps. Take care not to promote blindly and without regard to downstream data quality or governance issues. The lifespan in production is just an existential measure: it must be of the highest practical quality to be in production.

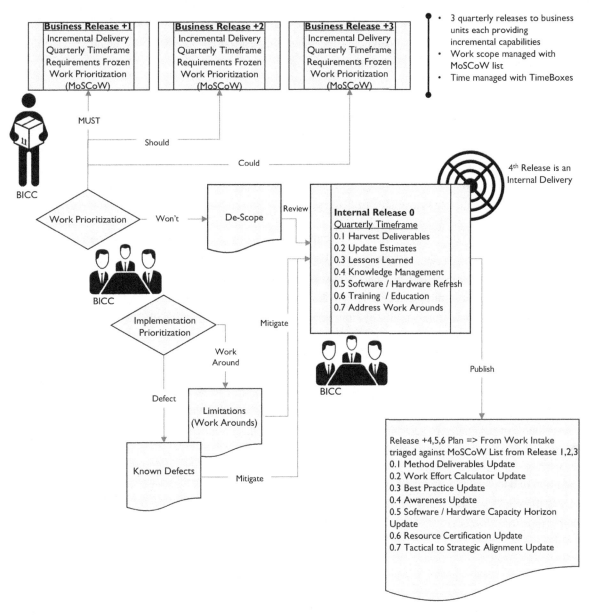

Figure 83 Release Process Example

Items passing the pilot and deemed production-ready by both business and IT representatives can be promoted to production as new data products. This completes one iteration.

Items not passing pilot can be rejected entirely or returned to development for fine-tuning. Perhaps additional support from the DW team is needed at this time to advance the item in the next promotion iteration.

2.6.3 Monitor and Tune Load Processes

Monitor load processing across the system for bottlenecks and dependencies. Employ database tuning techniques where and when needed, including partitioning, tuned backup, and recovery strategies. Archiving is a difficult subject in data warehousing.

Users often consider the data warehouse as an active archive due to the long histories that are built and are unwilling, particularly if the On Line Analytical Processing (OLAP) sources have dropped records, to see the data warehouse engage in archiving. (See Chapter 6.)

2.6.4 Monitor and Tune BI Activity and Performance

A best practice for BI monitoring and tuning is to define and display a set of customer-facing satisfaction metrics. Average query response time and the number of users per day, week, or month are examples of useful metrics. In addition to the statistical measures available from the systems, it is useful to survey DW/BI customers regularly.

Regular review of usage statistics and patterns is essential. Reports providing frequency and resource usage of data, queries, and reports allow prudent enhancement. Tuning BI activity is analogous to the principle of profiling applications in order to know where the bottlenecks are and where to apply optimization efforts. The creation of indexes and aggregations is most effective when done according to usage patterns and statistics. Tremendous performance gains can come from simple solutions such as posting the completed daily results to a report that runs hundreds or thousands of times a day.

Transparency and visibility are the key principles that should drive DW/BI monitoring. The more one can expose the details of the DW/BI activities, the more data consumers can see and understand what is going on (and have confidence in the BI), and less direct end-customer support will be required. Providing a dashboard that exposes the high-level status of data delivery activities, with drill-down capability, is a best practice that allows an on-demand-pull of information by both support personnel and customers.

The addition of data quality measures will enhance the value of this dashboard where performance is more than just speed and timing. Use heat maps to visualize workload on infrastructure, data throughput, and compliance to operating agreement levels.

3. Tools

Choosing the initial set of tools can be a long process. It includes attempting to satisfy near-term requirements, non-functional specifications, and the as-yet to be created next generation requirements. Decision criteria tool sets, process implementation tools, and professional services offerings can facilitate and expedite this activity. It is critical to evaluate not only the conventional build or buy positions, but also the rent option provisioned as Software-as-a-Service. Renting SaaS tools and the associated expertise is weighed against the cost of building from scratch or deploying purchased products from vendors. Consider ongoing upgrade and potential replacement costs as well. Alignment to a set OLA (Operational Level Agreement) can bridge forecasted costs, and provide input into setting compelling fees and penalties for term violations.

3.1 Metadata Repository

Large organizations often find themselves with many tools from different vendors, each deployed potentially at differing versions. Key to this effort is the ability to stitch Metadata together from a variety of sources. Automating and integrating population of this repository can be achieved with a variety of techniques. (See Chapter 13.)

3.1.1 Data Dictionary / Glossary

A data dictionary is necessary to support the use of a DW. The dictionary describes data in business terms and includes other information needed to use the data (e.g., data types, details of structure, security restrictions). Often the content for the data dictionary comes directly from the logical data model. Plan for high quality Metadata by ensuring modelers take a disciplined approach to managing definitions as part of the modeling process.

In some organizations, business users actively participate in the development of the data dictionary by supplying, defining, and then stewarding corrections to definitions of subject area data elements. Embrace this activity through a collaboration tool, monitor activities through a Center of Excellence, and ensure that content created through this activity is retained in the logical model. Ensuring agreement between the business-facing content and the technical-facing physical data model will reduce the risk of downstream errors and rework. (See Chapter 13.)

3.1.2 Data and Data Model Lineage

Many data integration tools offer lineage analysis that considers both the developed population code and the physical data model and database. Some offer web interfaces to monitor and update definitions and other Metadata. Documented data lineage serves many purposes:

- Investigation of the root causes of data issues
- Impact analysis for system changes or data issues·
- Ability to determine the reliability of data, based on its origin

Look to implement an integrated impact and lineage tool that can understand all the moving parts involved in the load process, as well as end user reporting and analytics. Impact analysis reports will outline which components are affected by a potential change, expediting and streamlining estimating and maintenance tasks.

Many key business processes, relationships, and terminologies are captured and explained during development of the data model. The logical data model holds much of this information, which is often lost or ignored during development or production deployment. It is critical to ensure that this information is not discarded and that the logical and physical models are updated after deployment and are in sync.

3.2 Data Integration Tools

Data integration tools are used to populate a data warehouse. In addition to doing the work of integrating data, they enable scheduling of jobs in ways that account for complex data delivery from multiple sources. In selecting a tool, also account for these features that enable management of the system:

- Process audit, control, restart, and scheduling
- The ability to selectively extract data elements at execution time and pass that extract to a downstream system for audit purposes
- Controlling which operations can or cannot execute and restarting a failed or aborted run (see Chapter 8)

A variety of data integration tools also offer integration capabilities with the BI portfolio, supporting import and export of workflow messages, email, or even semantic layers. Workflow integration can drive data quality defect identification, resolution, and escalation processes. Messaging through email or alert processing driven from email is a common practice especially for mobile devices. In addition, the ability to provision a data target as a semantic layer can be a data virtualization candidate for agile implementations.

3.3 Business Intelligence Tools Types

The maturity of the BI market, and a wide range of available BI tools, makes it rare for companies to build their own BI tools.[68] The purpose of this section is to introduce the types of tools available in the BI marketplace, and provide an overview of their chief characteristics with information to help match the tools to the appropriate customer-level capabilities. BI tools are evolving quickly, enabling a transition from IT-led, standardized reporting to self-service, business-driven data exploration.[69]

- **Operational reporting** is the application of BI tools to analyze business trends, both short-term (month-over-month) and longer-term (year-over-year). Operational reporting can also help discover trends and patterns. Use Tactical BI to support short-term business decisions.

- **Business performance management (BPM)** includes the formal assessment of metrics aligned with organizational goals. This assessment usually happens at the executive level. Use Strategic BI to support long-term corporate goals and objectives.

- **Descriptive, self-service analytics** provides BI to the front lines of the business, where analytical capabilities guide operational decisions. Operational analytics couples BI applications with operational functions and processes, to guide decisions in near-real-time. The requirement for low latency (near real-time data capture and data delivery) will drive the architectural approach to operational analytics solutions. Service-oriented Architecture (SOA) and Big Data become necessary to support operational analytics fully (see Chapters 8 and 15).

3.3.1 Operational Reporting

Operational Reporting involves business users generating reports directly from transactional systems, operational applications, or a data warehouse. This is typically an application functionality. Often business areas will start to

---

[68] The material in this section is primarily from "The Business Intelligence Market" by Cindi Howson, BIScorecard®, http://bit.ly/2tNirv5; used by permission, with minor changes and additions.

[69] Dataversity refers to this trend as the "democratization of data technologies." See Ghosh, Paramita. "A Comparative Study of Business Intelligence and Analytics Market Trends." Dataversity. January 17, 2017. http://bit.ly/2sTgXTJ (accessed 2017-01-22).

use a DW for operational reporting, especially if DW/BI governance is poor, or the DW contains additional data that enhances the operational, transaction data. Often the reports will appear as ad-hoc queries, when in fact they are simple reports or are used to initiate workflow. From a data management perspective, the key is to understand if the data necessary for this reporting exists within the application itself, or if it requires data enhancements from the DW or operational data store.

Data exploration and reporting tools, sometimes called ad-hoc query tools, enable users to author their own reports or create outputs for use by others. They are less concerned with the precise layout because they are not trying to generate an invoice or the like. However, they do want to include charts and tables quickly and intuitively. Often the reports created by business users become standard reports, not exclusively used for ad hoc business questions.

The needs within business operations reporting are often different from the needs within business query and reporting. With business query and reporting, the data source is usually a data warehouse or data mart (though not always). While IT develops production reports, power users and ad hoc business users develop their own reports with business query tools. Use reports generated with business query tools individually, departmentally, or enterprise-wide.

Production reporting crosses the DW/BI boundary and often queries transactional systems to produce operational items such as invoices or bank statements. The developers of production reports tend to be IT personnel.

Traditional BI tools cover some data visualization methods such as tables, pie charts, line charts, area charts, bar charts, histograms, turnkey box (candlestick) as examples fairly well. Data visualizations can be delivered in a static format, such as a published report, or a more interactive online format; and some support end-user interaction where drilling or filtering capabilities facilitate analysis of data within the visualization. Others allow the visualization to be changed by the user on demand. (See Chapter 14.)

3.3.2 Business Performance Management

Performance management is a set of integrated organizational processes and applications designed to optimize execution of business strategy; applications include budgeting, planning, and financial consolidation. There have been a number of major acquisitions in this segment, as ERP vendors and BI vendors see great growth opportunities here and believe BI and Performance Management are converging. How frequently customers buy BI and performance management from the same vendor depends on product capabilities.

Broadly speaking, Performance Management technology enables processes to help meet organizational goals. Measurement and a feedback loop with positive reinforcement are key elements. Within the BI space, this has taken the form of many strategic enterprise applications, such as budgeting, forecasting, or resource planning. Another specialization has formed in this area: creating scorecards driven by dashboards for user interaction. Dashboards, like those found in automobiles, provide the necessary summary or aggregate information to the end user with most recent updates (Eckerson, 2005).

3.3.3 Operational Analytic Applications

Henry Morris of IDC coined the term *Analytic Applications* in the 1990s, clarifying how they are different from general OLAP and BI tools (Morris, 1999). Analytic applications include the logic and processes to extract data from well-known source systems, such as vendor ERP systems, a data model for the data mart, and pre-built reports and dashboards. They provide businesses with a pre-built solution to optimize a functional area (people management, for example) or industry vertical (retail analytics, for example). Different types of analytic applications include customer, financial, supply chain, manufacturing, and human resource applications.

3.3.3.1 Multi-dimensional Analysis – OLAP

Online Analytical Processing (OLAP) refers to an approach to providing fast performance for multi-dimensional analytic queries. The term OLAP originated, in part, to make a clear distinction from OLTP, Online Transactional Processing. The typical output of OLAP queries are in a matrix format. The dimensions form the rows and columns of the matrix, and the factors, or measures, are the values inside the matrix. Conceptually, this illustrates as a cube. Multi-dimensional analysis with cubes is particularly useful where there are well-known ways analysts want to look at summaries of data.

A traditional application is financial analysis, where analysts want to repeatedly traverse known hierarchies to analyze data; for example, date (such as Year, Quarter, Month, Week, Day), organization (such as Region, Country, Business Unit, Department), and product hierarchy (such as Product Category, Product Line, Product). Many tools today embed OLAP cubes into their software footprint and some even seamlessly automate and integrate the definition and population process. This means that any user in any business process can slice and dice their data. Align this capability with the power users in the subject area communities and deliver it along a self-service channel empowering these selected users to analyze their data their way.

Typically, OLAP tools have both a server component and an end user client-facing component installed on the desktop, or available on the web. Some desktop components are accessible from within a spreadsheet appearing as an embedded menu or function item. The architecture selected (ROLAP, MOLAP, HOLAP) will guide the development efforts but common to all will be definition of cube structure, aggregate needs, Metadata augmentation and analysis of data sparsity.

Structuring the cube to provision desired functional requirements may require splitting larger dimensions into separate cubes to accommodate storage, population, or calculation requirements. Use levels of aggregation to ensure calculation and retrieval of desired formulas occurs within agreed upon response times. End user augmentation of hierarchies enable fulfillment the aggregation, calculation, or population requirements. In addition, sparsity of cube data may require addition or removal of aggregate structures or refine materialization needs in the warehouse data layer provisioning it.

Provisioning role-based security or multi-language text within the cube may require extra dimensions, additional functions, calculations, or sometimes creating separate cube structures. Striking a balance between end user flexibility, performance, and server workloads means some negotiating is to be expected. The negotiation typically occurs during the loading processes and may require hierarchy changes, aggregate structure changes or additional warehouse materialized data objects. Strike the right balance among cube count, server workload, and delivered flexibility, so that the refresh occurs in a timely manner, and cubes provide reliable and consistent queries without high storage or server utilization costs.

The value of On Line Analytical Processing (OLAP) Tools and cubes is reduction of the chance of confusion and erroneous interpretation, by aligning the data content with the analyst's mental model. The analyst can navigate through the database and screen for a particular subset of the data, changing the data's orientation and defining analytical calculations. Slice-and-dice is the user-initiated process of navigation by calling for page displays interactively, through the specification of slices via rotations and drill down / up. Common OLAP operations include slice and dice, drill down, drill up, roll up, and pivot.

- **Slice**: A slice is a subset of a multi-dimensional array corresponding to a single value for one or more members of the dimensions not in the subset.

- **Dice**: The dice operation is a slice on more than two dimensions of a data cube, or more than two consecutive slices.

- **Drill down / up**: Drilling down or up is a specific analytical technique whereby the user navigates among levels of data, ranging from the most summarized (up) to the most detailed (down).

- **Roll-up**: A roll-up involves computing all of the data relationships for one or more dimensions. To do this, define a computational relationship or formula.

- **Pivot**: A pivot changes the dimensional orientation of a report or page display.

Three classic implementation approaches support Online Analytical Processing.

- **Relational Online Analytical Processing (ROLAP)**: ROLAP supports OLAP by using techniques that implement multi-dimensionality in the two-dimensional tables of relational database management systems (RDBMS). Star schema joins are a common database design technique used in ROLAP environments.

- **Multi-dimensional Online Analytical Processing (MOLAP)**: MOLAP supports OLAP by using proprietary and specialized multi-dimensional database technology.

- **Hybrid Online Analytical Processing (HOLAP)**: This is simply a combination of ROLAP and MOLAP. HOLAP implementations allow part of the data to be stored in MOLAP form and another part of the data to be stored in ROLAP. Implementations vary on the control a designer has to vary the mix of partitioning.

4. Techniques

4.1 Prototypes to Drive Requirements

Quickly prioritize requirements before the implementation activities begin by creating a demonstration set of data and applying discovery steps in a joint prototype effort. Advances in data virtualization technologies can alleviate some of the traditional implementation pains through collaborative prototyping techniques.

Profiling the data contributes to prototyping and helps reduces risk associated with unexpected data. The DW is often the first place where the pain of poor quality data in source systems or data entry functions becomes apparent. Profiling also discloses differences between sources that may present obstacles to data integration. Data may be of high quality within its sources, but because sources, differ the data integration process becomes more complicated.

Evaluation of the state of the source data leads to more accurate up-front estimates for feasibility and scope of effort. The evaluation is also important for setting appropriate expectations. Plan to collaborate with the Data Quality and Data Governance team(s) and to draw on the expertise of other SMEs to understand data discrepancies and risks. (See Chapters 11 and 13.)

4.2 Self-Service BI

Self-service is a fundamental delivery channel within the BI portfolio. This typically funnels user activity within a governed portal where, depending on the privileges of the user, a variety of functionality is provided ranging from messaging, alerts, viewing scheduled production reports, interacting with analytic reports, developing ad hoc reporting and of course dash boarding and score carding. Reports can be pushed to the portal on standard schedules, to be retrieved by the users at their leisure. Users can also pull data by executing reports from within the portal. These portals share content across organizational boundaries. Extending the collaboration tool outwards toward the user community can also provide self-service tips and tricks, an integrated communique on load status, overall performance, and release progress as well as dialog forums. Mediate forum content through the support channel and then facilitate with user group sessions through the maintenance channel.

Visualization and statistical analysis tooling allows for rapid data exploration and discovery. Some tools allow for business-centric construction of dashboard like objects that can be rapidly shared, reviewed, and revitalized. Once the domain of IT and developers only, many data shaping, calculation, and visualization techniques can now be employed by the business community. This offers a degree of workload distribution and integration efforts can be feasibly prototyped through business channels and then materialized and optimized by IT.

4.3 Audit Data that can be Queried

In order to maintain lineage, all structures and processes should have the capability to create and store audit information at a grain useful for tracking and reporting. Allowing users to query this audit data enables the users to verify for themselves the condition and arrival of the data, which improves user confidence. Audit information also allows for more detailed trouble-shooting when data issues arise.

5. Implementation Guidelines

A stable architecture that can scale to meet future requirements is paramount to the success of a data warehouse. A production support team capable of dealing with the daily loading, analysis and end user feedback is mandatory. In addition, to sustain success, ensure that the warehouse and the business unit teams are aligned.

5.1 Readiness Assessment / Risk Assessment

There may be a gap between when an organization embraces a new venture, and when it has the ability to sustain that venture. Successful projects start with a Prerequisite Checklist. All IT projects should have business support, be aligned with strategy, and have a defined architectural approach. In addition, a DW should:

- Define data sensitivity and security constraints

- Perform tool selection

- Secure resources

- Create an ingestion process to evaluate and receive source data

Identify and inventory sensitive or restricted data elements in the warehouse. This data will need to be masked or obfuscated to prevent access by unauthorized personnel. Additional constraints may apply when considering outsourcing for implementation or maintenance activities.

Account for security constrains before selecting tools and assigning resources. Ensure data governance processes for review and approval have been followed. DW/BI projects risk refocus or total cancellation due to these overarching factors.

5.2 Release Roadmap

Because they require a large development effort, warehouses are built incrementally. Whatever method chosen to implement, be it waterfall, iterative or agile, it should account for the desired end state. That is why a roadmap is a valuable planning tool. The method combined with the maintenance processes can be both flexible and adaptive to balance the pressures of individual project delivery with overall goals of re-usable data and infrastructure.

An incremental approach leveraging the DW bus matrix as a communication and marketing tool is suggested. Use business-determined priorities tethered by exposure metrics to determine how much rigor and overhead to apply to each increment; a small single-sourced delivery may afford rule relaxation especially when limited exposure is felt should those issues be realized by the organization. Each increment will modify existing capabilities or add brand new capabilities typically aligned with a newly onboarded business unit. Apply a consistent needs and abilities process to determine the next business unit to onboard. Maintain a back-order or work item list to identify outstanding capabilities and the business-facing priorities. Determine any technical dependencies that require delivery in a different order. Then package this work into a software release. Each release can be delivered at an agreed-upon pace: quarterly, monthly, weekly, or even faster when appropriate. Manage the releases with the business partners by assembling a roadmap: a listing of releases by date by capabilities.

5.3 Configuration Management

Configuration management aligns with the release roadmap and provides the necessary back office stitching and scripts to automate development, testing, and transportation to production. It also brands the model by the release at the database level, and ties the codebase to that brand in an automated manner so that manually coded, generated programs and semantic layer content is harmonized across the environment and is versioned controlled.

5.4 Organization and Cultural Change

Starting with and keeping a consistent business focus throughout the DW/BI lifecycle is essential to success. Looking at the value chain of the enterprise is a good way to understand the business context. The specific business processes in a company's value chain provide a natural business-oriented context in which to frame areas of analysis.

Most importantly, align projects behind real business needs and assess the necessary business support, considering these critical success factors:

- **Business sponsorship**: Is there appropriate executive sponsorship, i.e., an identified and engaged steering committee and commensurate funding? DW/BI projects require strong executive sponsorship.

- **Business goals and scope**: Is there a clearly identified business need, purpose, and scope for the effort?

- **Business resources**: Is there a commitment by business management to the availability and engagement of the appropriate business subject matter experts? The lack of commitment is a common point of failure and a good enough reason to halt a DW/BI project until commitment is confirmed.

- **Business readiness**: Is the business partner prepared for a long-term incremental delivery? Have they committed themselves to establishing centers of excellence to sustain the product in future releases? How broad is the average knowledge or skill gap within the target community and can that be crossed within a single increment?

- **Vision alignment**: How well does the IT Strategy support the Business Vision? It is vital to ensure that desired functional requirements correspond to business capabilities that are or can be sustained in the immediate IT roadmap. Any significant departures or material gaps in capability alignment can stall or stop a DW/BI program.

5.4.1 Dedicated Team

Many organizations have a dedicated team to manage the ongoing operations of the production environment. (See Chapter 6). A separate set of hands operating the delivered data product is beneficial to workload optimization as this group has repeating tasks on a calendar cycle and may be further used for any escalation items whereas the maintenance channel will see workload spikes aligned to specific deliverables.

A front office support group interacts with the maintenance team to foster inter-department relationships and ensure critical activities are addressed in upcoming releases. It notifies the team of any deficiencies to be addressed. A back office support team in operations will ensure that production configuration has executed as required. They will escalate alerts and report on throughput status.

6. DW/BI Governance

Industries that are highly regulated and need compliance-centric reporting will benefit greatly from a well-governed data warehouse. Critical to ongoing support and vital to release planning is ensuring that governance activities are completed and addressed during the implementation. More and more organizations are extending their Software Development Lifecycle with specific deliverables aimed at addressing governance needs. Warehouse governance processes should be aligned with risk management. They should be business-driven, since different kinds of businesses have different needs (e.g., marketing and advertising companies will use their data differently from financial institutions). Governance processes should mitigate risk, not curtail execution.

The most critical functions are those that govern the business-operated discovery or refinement area, and those that ensure pristine quality within the warehouse itself. As the refinement area leads all initiative boundaries, handshaking and well running procedures are necessary to instantiate, operate, transfer, and discard the data in these areas. Data archival and time horizons are key elements in boundary agreements as they help avoid sprawl. Monitoring of these environments and schedules to determine longevity terms are included in user group sessions as well as management meetings. Loading data into the warehouse means assigning time, resources, and programming efforts to see remediated, credible, high quality data arrive to the end user community, in a timely manner of course.

Consider one-off or limited-use events as part of the lifecycle, and perhaps curtail them within the pilot area itself, or within a user-controlled 'sandbox' area. Real-time analysis processes can feed time-aligned aggregate results back into the data warehouse through an automated process. Policy is defined for the procedures enacted upon the real-time environment, and governance applies to the brokerage of results into the warehouse for organizational consumption.

Apply data discrimination to known or cataloged items managed through a risk exposure mitigation matrix. Those items with a deemed high exposure, and low mitigation or difficult early detection, warrant governance functions to curtail the associated risk. Depending on the sensitivity of the data being examined, a separate workspace for selected local personnel may also be required. A thorough review with corporate security and legal personnel during policy formation creates a final safety net.

6.1 Enabling Business Acceptance

A key success factor is business acceptance of data, including the data being understandable, having verifiable quality, and having a demonstrable lineage. Sign-off by the Business on the data should be part of the User Acceptance Testing. Perform structured random testing of the data in the BI tool against data in the source systems over the initial load, and after a few update load cycles, to meet sign-off criteria. Meeting these requirements is paramount for every DW/BI implementation. Consider, up-front, a few critically important architectural sub-components, along with their supporting activities:

- **Conceptual Data Model**: What information is core to the organization? What are the key business concepts and how are they related to each other?

- **Data quality feedback loop**: How are data issues identified and remediated? How are owners of the systems in which issues originate informed about problems and held accountable for fixing them? What is the remediation process for issues that are caused by the DW data integration processes?

- **End-to-end Metadata**: How does the architecture support the integrated end-to-end flow of Metadata? In particular, is access to meaning and context designed into the architecture? How do data consumers answer basic questions like "What does this report mean?" or "What does this metric mean?"

- **End-to-end verifiable data lineage**: Are the items exposed to business users traceable to the source systems in an automated, maintained manner? Is a system of record identified for all data?

6.2 Customer / User Satisfaction

Perceptions of the quality of data will drive customer satisfaction but satisfaction is dependent on other factors as well, such as data consumers' understanding of the data and the operations team's responsiveness to identified issues. Collecting, understanding, and acting on customer feedback can be facilitated through regularly scheduled meetings with user representatives. Such interaction can also help the warehouse team share information about the release roadmap and understand how data consumers are using the warehouse.

6.3 Service Level Agreements

Business and technical expectations for the environments should be specified in Service Level Agreements (SLAs). Often the response time, data retention, and availability requirements differ greatly between classes of business needs and their respective supporting systems (e.g., ODS versus DW versus data mart).

6.4 Reporting Strategy

Ensure that a reporting strategy exists within and across the BI Portfolio. A reporting strategy includes standards, processes, guidelines, best practices, and procedures. It will ensure users have clear, accurate, and timely information. The reporting strategy must address

- Security access to ensure that only entitled users will gain access to sensitive data elements
- Access mechanisms to describe how users want to interact, report, examine or view their data
- User community type and appropriate tool to consume it with
- Nature of the reports summary, detailed, exception as well as frequency, timing, distribution and storage formats
- Potential use of visualization capabilities to provision graphical output
- Trade-offs between timeliness and performance

Standard reports should be evaluated periodically to ensure they are still providing value, as just executing reports incurs cost in storage and processing. Implementation and maintenance processes and management activities are critical. Aligning the appropriate reporting tools to the business community is a critical success factor. Depending on the size and nature of the organization, there are probably many different reporting tools used in a variety of processes. Ensure that the audience is capable of making the best use of the reporting tools; users that are more sophisticated will have increasingly complex demands. Maintain a decision matrix based on these demands to determine upgrades or future tool selection.

Data source governance monitoring and control are also vital. Ensure that appropriate levels of data are provisioned securely for authorized personnel, and that subscription data is accessible according to agreed-upon levels.

A Center of Excellence can provide training, start-up sets, design best practices, data source tips and tricks and other point solutions or artifacts to help empower business users towards a self-service model. In addition to knowledge management, this center can provide timely communications across the developer, designer, analyst and subscribing user communities.

6.5 Metrics

6.5.1 Usage Metrics

DW usage metrics typically include the number of registered users, as well as connected users or concurrent connected users. These metrics show how many people within the organization are using the data warehouse. How many user accounts are licensed for each tool is a great start, especially for the auditors. However, how many actually connect with that tool is a better measurement, and how many queries (or query equivalents) are dispatched by a user community per timeframe is an even better technical measurement, especially for capacity planning. Allow for multiple analysis metrics such as audit users, generated user query capacity, and consuming users.

6.5.2 Subject Area Coverage Percentages

Subject area coverage percentages measure how much of the warehouse (from a data topology perspective) is being accessed by each department. They also highlight which data is shared across departments, and which is not, but could be.

Mapping operational source(s) to targets is another natural extension, which enforces and validates the lineage and Metadata already collected, and can provide penetration analysis for which source systems are in analytical use by which departments. This can help focus tuning efforts on those high impact analytic queries by mitigating any changes to heavily used sourced objects.

6.5.3 Response and Performance Metrics

Most query tools measure response time. Retrieve response or performance metrics from tools. This data will inform metrics about the number and type of users.

Harvest load times for each data product in raw format from the population processes. These should also be expressed as a percentage of expected support: so a mart that is expected to be refreshed daily and loaded in a four-hour window is 100% supported when it loads in four hours. Apply this process to any extracts generated for downstream processing too.

Most tools will retain, in a log or repository, query records, data refresh, and data extract times for the objects provided to the users. Divide this data into scheduled and executed objects, and express as raw counts both attempted and succeeded. Highly popular objects or queries performing poorly are likely in-need of attention before satisfaction metrics suffer. This can guide defect analysis, maintenance planning, as well as capacity planning if a group of objects is failing regularly. Remediation may vary depending on the tool, but sometimes creating or dropping one index can result in great improvements. (See Chapter 6.)

A natural follow on for this is the validation and adjustment of service levels. Adjust items that have consistently failed in the next release, or in the absence of necessary funding, the support level must be reduced.

7. Works Cited / Recommended

Adamson, Christopher. *Mastering Data Warehouse Aggregates: Solutions for Star Schema Performance*. John Wiley and Sons, 2006. Print.

Adelman, Sid and Larissa T. Moss. *Data Warehouse Project Management*. Addison-Wesley Professional, 2000. Print.

Adelman, Sid, Larissa Moss and Majid Abai. *Data Strategy*. Addison-Wesley Professional, 2005. Print.

Adelman, Sid, et al. *Impossible Data Warehouse Situations: Solutions from the Experts*. Addison-Wesley, 2002. Print.

Aggarwal, Charu. *Data Mining: The Textbook*. Springer, 2015. Print.

Biere, Mike. *Business Intelligence for the Enterprise*. IBM Press, 2003. Print.

Biere, Mike. *The New Era of Enterprise Business Intelligence: Using Analytics to Achieve a Global Competitive Advantage*. IBM Press, 2010. Print. IBM Press.

Brown, Meta S. *Data Mining for Dummies*. For Dummies, 2014. Print. For Dummies.

Chorianopoulos, Antonios. *Effective CRM using Predictive Analytics*. Wiley, 2016. Print.

Delmater, Rhonda and Monte Hancock Jr. *Data Mining Explained; A Manager's Guide to Customer-Centric Business Intelligence*. Digital Press, 2001. Print.

Dyche, Jill. E-Data: *Turning Data Into Information With Data Warehousing*. Addison-Wesley, 2000. Print.

Eckerson, Wayne W. *Performance Dashboards: Measuring, Monitoring, and Managing Your Business*. Wiley, 2005. Print.

Han, Jiawei, Micheline Kamber and Jian Pei. *Data Mining: Concepts and Techniques*. 3rd ed. Morgan Kaufmann, 2011. Print. The Morgan Kaufmann Ser in Data Management Systems.

Hastie, Trevor, Robert Tibshirani, and Jerome Friedman. *The Elements of Statistical Learning: Data Mining, Inference, and Prediction*. 2nd ed. Springer, 2011. Print. Springer Series in Statistics.

Hill, Thomas, and Paul Lewicki. *Statistics: Methods and Applications*. Statsoft, Inc., 2005. Print.

Howson, Cindi. *Successful Business Intelligence: Unlock the Value of BI and Big Data*. 2nd ed. Mcgraw-Hill Osborne Media, 2013. Print.

Imhoff, Claudia, Lisa Loftis, and Jonathan G. Geiger. *Building the Customer-Centric Enterprise: Data Warehousing Techniques for Supporting Customer Relationship Management*. John Wiley and Sons, 2001. Print.

Imhoff, Claudia, Nicholas Galemmo, and Jonathan G. Geiger. *Mastering Data Warehouse Design: Relational and Dimensional Techniques*. John Wiley and Sons, 2003. Print.

Inmon, W. H., Claudia Imhoff, and Ryan Sousa. *The Corporate Information Factory*. 2nd ed. John Wiley and Sons, 2000. Print.

Inmon, W.H., and Krish Krishnan. *Building the Unstructured Data Warehouse*. Technics Publications, LLC., 2011. Print.

Josey, Andrew. *TOGAF Version 9.1 Enterprise Edition: An Introduction*. The Open Group, 2011. Kindle. Open Group White Paper.

Kaplan, Robert S and David P. Norton. *The Balanced Scorecard: Translating Strategy into Action*. Harvard Business Review Press, 1996. Kindle.

Kimball, Ralph, and Margy Ross. *The Data Warehouse Toolkit: The Definitive Guide to Dimensional Modeling*. 3d ed. Wiley, 2013. Print.

Kimball, Ralph, et al. *The Data Warehouse Lifecycle Toolkit*. 2nd ed. Wiley, 2008. Print.

Kimball, Ralph. *The Data Warehouse ETL Toolkit: Practical Techniques for Extracting, Cleaning, Conforming, and Delivering Data*. Amazon Digital Services, Inc., 2007. Kindle.

Linoff, Gordon S. and Michael J. A. Berry. *Data Mining Techniques: For Marketing, Sales, and Customer Relationship Management*. 3rd ed. Wiley, 2011. Print.

Linstedt, Dan. *The Official Data Vault Standards Document (Version 1.0) (Data Warehouse Architecture)*. Amazon Digital Services, Inc., 2012. Kindle.

Loukides, Mike. *What Is Data Science?* O'Reilly Media, 2012. Kindle.

Lublinsky, Boris, Kevin T. Smith, and Alexey Yakubovich. *Professional Hadoop Solutions*. Wrox, 2013. Print.

Malik, Shadan. *Enterprise Dashboards: Design and Best Practices for IT*. Wiley, 2005. Print.

Morris, Henry. "Analytic Applications and Business Performance Management." *DM Review Magazine*, March, 1999. http://bit.ly/2rRrP4x.

Moss, Larissa T., and Shaku Atre. *Business Intelligence Roadmap: The Complete Project Lifecycle for Decision-Support Applications*. Addison-Wesley Professional, 2003. Print.

Ponniah, Paulraj. *Data Warehousing Fundamentals: A Comprehensive Guide for IT Professionals*. Wiley-Interscience, 2001. Print.

Provost, Foster and Tom Fawcett. *Data Science for Business: What you need to know about data mining and data-analytic thinking*. O'Reilly Media, 2013. Print.

Reeves, Laura L. *A Manager's Guide to Data Warehousing*. Wiley, 2009. Print.

Russell, Matthew A. *Mining the Social Web: Data Mining Facebook, Twitter, LinkedIn, Google+, GitHub, and More*. 2nd ed. O'Reilly Media, 2013. Print.

Silverston, Len, and Paul Agnew. *The Data Model Resource Book Volume 3: Universal Patterns for Data Modeling*. Wiley, 2008. Print.

Simon, Alan. *Modern Enterprise Business Intelligence and Data Management: A Roadmap for IT Directors, Managers, and Architects*. Morgan Kaufmann, 2014. Print.

Thomsen, Erik. *OLAP Solutions: Building Multidimensional Information Systems*. 2nd ed. Wiley, 2002. Print.

Vitt, Elizabeth, Michael Luckevich and Stacia Misner. *Business Intelligence*. Microsoft Press, 2008. Print. Developer Reference.

WAGmob. *Big Data and Hadoop*. WAGmob, 2013. Kindle.

Wremble, Robert and Christian Koncilia. *Data Warehouses and Olap: Concepts, Architectures and Solutions*. IGI Global, 2006. Print.

CHAPTER 12

Metadata Management

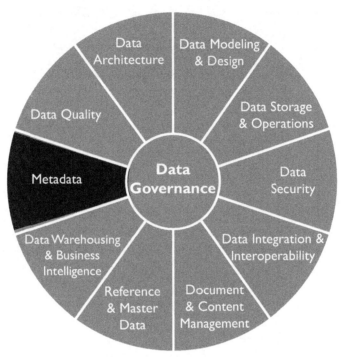

DAMA-DMBOK2 Data Management Framework

Copyright © 2017 by **DAMA International**

1. Introduction

The most common definition of *Metadata*, "data about data," is misleadingly simple. The kind of information that can be classified as Metadata is wide-ranging. Metadata includes information about technical and business processes, data rules and constraints, and logical and physical data structures. It describes the data itself (e.g., databases, data elements, data models), the concepts the data represents (e.g., business processes, application systems, software code, technology infrastructure), and the connections (relationships) between the data and concepts. Metadata helps an organization understand its data, its systems, and its workflows. It enables data quality assessment and is integral to the management of databases and other applications. It contributes to the ability to process, maintain, integrate, secure, audit, and govern other data.

To understand Metadata's vital role in data management, imagine a large library, with hundreds of thousands of books and magazines, but no card catalog. Without a card catalog, readers might not even know how to start looking for a specific book or even a specific topic. The card catalog not only provides the necessary information (which books and materials the library owns and where they are shelved) it also enables patrons to find materials using different starting points (subject area, author, or title). Without the catalog, finding a specific book would be difficult if not impossible. An organization without Metadata is like a library without a card catalog.

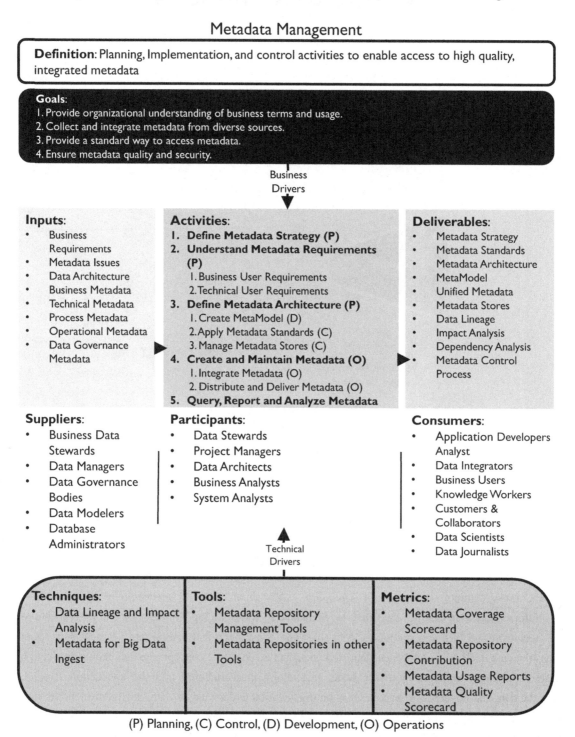

Metadata Management

Definition: Planning, Implementation, and control activities to enable access to high quality, integrated metadata

Goals:
1. Provide organizational understanding of business terms and usage.
2. Collect and integrate metadata from diverse sources.
3. Provide a standard way to access metadata.
4. Ensure metadata quality and security.

Business Drivers

Inputs:
- Business Requirements
- Metadata Issues
- Data Architecture
- Business Metadata
- Technical Metadata
- Process Metadata
- Operational Metadata
- Data Governance Metadata

Activities:
1. **Define Metadata Strategy (P)**
2. **Understand Metadata Requirements (P)**
   1. Business User Requirements
   2. Technical User Requirements
3. **Define Metadata Architecture (P)**
   1. Create MetaModel (D)
   2. Apply Metadata Standards (C)
   3. Manage Metadata Stores (C)
4. **Create and Maintain Metadata (O)**
   1. Integrate Metadata (O)
   2. Distribute and Deliver Metadata (O)
5. **Query, Report and Analyze Metadata**

Deliverables:
- Metadata Strategy
- Metadata Standards
- Metadata Architecture
- MetaModel
- Unified Metadata
- Metadata Stores
- Data Lineage
- Impact Analysis
- Dependency Analysis
- Metadata Control Process

Suppliers:
- Business Data Stewards
- Data Managers
- Data Governance Bodies
- Data Modelers
- Database Administrators

Participants:
- Data Stewards
- Project Managers
- Data Architects
- Business Analysts
- System Analysts

Consumers:
- Application Developers Analyst
- Data Integrators
- Business Users
- Knowledge Workers
- Customers & Collaborators
- Data Scientists
- Data Journalists

Technical Drivers

Techniques:
- Data Lineage and Impact Analysis
- Metadata for Big Data Ingest

Tools:
- Metadata Repository Management Tools
- Metadata Repositories in other Tools

Metrics:
- Metadata Coverage Scorecard
- Metadata Repository Contribution
- Metadata Usage Reports
- Metadata Quality Scorecard

(P) Planning, (C) Control, (D) Development, (O) Operations

Figure 84 Context Diagram: Metadata

Metadata is essential to data management as well as data usage (see multiple references to Metadata throughout the DAMA-DMBOK). All large organizations produce and use a lot of data. Across an organization, different individuals will have different levels of data knowledge, but no individual will know everything about the data. This information must be documented or the organization risks losing valuable knowledge about itself. Metadata provides the primary means of capturing and managing organizational knowledge about data. However, Metadata management is not only a knowledge management challenge; it is also a risk management necessity. Metadata is necessary to ensure an organization can identify private or sensitive data and that it can manage the data lifecycle for its own benefit and in order to meet compliance requirements and minimize risk exposure.

Without reliable Metadata, an organization does not know what data it has, what the data represents, where it originates, how it moves through systems, who has access to it, or what it means for the data to be of high quality. Without Metadata, an organization cannot manage its data as an asset. Indeed, without Metadata, an organization may not be able to manage its data at all. As technology has evolved, the speed at which data is generated has also increased. Technical Metadata has become integral to the way in which data is moved and integrated. ISO's Metadata Registry Standard, ISO/IEC 11179, is intended to enable Metadata-driven exchange of data in a heterogeneous environment, based on exact definitions of data. Metadata present in XML and other formats enables use of the data. Other types of Metadata tagging allow data to be exchanged while retaining signifiers of ownership, security requirements, etc. (See Chapter 8.)

Like other data, Metadata requires management. As the capacity of organizations to collect and store data increases, the role of Metadata in data management grows in importance. To be data-driven, an organization must be Metadata-driven.

1.1 Business Drivers

Data cannot be managed without Metadata. In addition, Metadata itself must be managed. Reliable, well-managed Metadata helps:

- Increase confidence in data by providing context and enabling the measurement of data quality
- Increase the value of strategic information (e.g., Master Data) by enabling multiple uses
- Improve operational efficiency by identifying redundant data and processes
- Prevent the use of out-of-date or incorrect data
- Reduce data-oriented research time
- Improve communication between data consumers and IT professionals
- Create accurate impact analysis thus reducing the risk of project failure
- Improve time-to-market by reducing system development life-cycle time
- Reduce training costs and lower the impact of staff turnover through thorough documentation of data context, history, and origin
- Support regulatory compliance

Metadata assists in representing information consistently, streamlining workflow capabilities, and protecting sensitive information, particularly when regulatory compliance is required.

Organizations get more value out of their data assets if their data is of high quality. Quality data depends on governance. Because it explains the data and processes that enable organizations to function, Metadata is critical to data governance. If Metadata is a guide to the data in an organization, then it must be well managed. Poorly managed Metadata leads to:

- Redundant data and data management processes
- Replicated and redundant dictionaries, repositories, and other Metadata storage
- Inconsistent definitions of data elements and risks associated with data misuse
- Competing and conflicting sources and versions of Metadata which reduce the confidence of data consumers
- Doubt about the reliability of Metadata and data

Well-executed Metadata management enables a consistent understanding of data resources and more efficient cross-organizational development.

1.2 Goals and Principles

The goals of Metadata management include:

- Document and manage organizational knowledge of data-related business terminology in order to ensure people understand data content and can use data consistently
- Collect and integrate Metadata from diverse sources to ensure people understand similarities and differences between data from different parts of the organization
- Ensure Metadata quality, consistency, currency, and security
- Provide standard ways to make Metadata accessible to Metadata consumers (people, systems, and processes)
- Establish or enforce the use of technical Metadata standards to enable data exchange

The implementation of a successful Metadata solution follows these guiding principles:

- **Organizational commitment**: Secure organizational commitment (senior management support and funding) to Metadata management as part of an overall strategy to manage data as an enterprise asset.

- **Strategy**: Develop a Metadata strategy that accounts for how Metadata will be created, maintained, integrated, and accessed. The strategy should drive requirements, which should be defined before evaluating, purchasing, and installing Metadata management products. The Metadata strategy must align with business priorities.

- **Enterprise perspective**: Take an enterprise perspective to ensure future extensibility, but implement through iterative and incremental delivery to bring value.

- **Socialization**: Communicate the necessity of Metadata and the purpose of each type of Metadata; socialization of the value of Metadata will encourage business use and, as importantly, the contribution of business expertise.

- **Access**: Ensure staff members know how to access and use Metadata.

- **Quality**: Recognize that Metadata is often produced through existing processes (data modeling, SDLC, business process definition) and hold process owners accountable for the quality of Metadata.

- **Audit**: Set, enforce, and audit standards for Metadata to simplify integration and enable use.

- **Improvement**: Create a feedback mechanism so that consumers can inform the Metadata Management team of Metadata that is incorrect or out-of-date.

1.3 Essential Concepts

1.3.1 Metadata vs. Data

As stated in the chapter introduction, Metadata is a kind of data, and it should be managed as such. One question that some organizations face is where to draw the line between data that is not Metadata and data that is Metadata. Conceptually, this line is related to the level of abstraction represented by the data. For example, in reporting on the release of the US National Security Administration's surveillance of the phone usage of people in the US, phone numbers and times of calls were routinely referred to as 'Metadata', implying that the 'real' data comprised only the content of the phone conversations. Common sense recognizes that telephone numbers and duration of phone calls are also just plain data.[70]

A rule of thumb might be that one person's Metadata is another's data. Even something that seems like Metadata (e.g., a list of column names) may be just plain data – if, for instance, this data was the input for an analysis aimed at understanding data content across different organizations.

To manage their Metadata, organizations should not worry about the philosophical distinctions. Instead they should define Metadata requirements focused on what they need Metadata for (to create new data, understand existing data, enable movement between systems, access data, to share data) and source data to meet these requirements.

1.3.2 Types of Metadata

Metadata is often categorized into three types: business, technical, and operational. These categories enable people to understand the range of information that falls under the overall umbrella of Metadata, as well as the functions through which Metadata is produced. That said, the categories could also lead to confusion, especially if people get caught up in questions about which category a set of Metadata belongs or who is supposed to use it. It is best to think of these categories in relation to where Metadata originates, rather than how it is used. In relation to usage, the distinctions between Metadata types are not strict. Technical and operational staff use 'business' Metadata and vice versa.

Outside of information technology, for example, in library or information science, Metadata is described using a different set of categories:

- Descriptive Metadata (e.g., title, author, and subject) describes a resource and enables identification and retrieval.

---

[70] Cole, David. "We kill people based on metadata." New York Review of Books. 10 May 2014. http://bit.ly/2sV1ulS.

- Structural Metadata describes relationships within and among resources and their component parts (e.g., number of pages, number of chapters).
- Administrative Metadata (e.g., version numbers, archive dates) is used to manage resources over their lifecycle.

These categories can helpful inform the process of defining Metadata requirements.

1.3.2.1 Business Metadata

Business Metadata focuses largely on the content and condition of the data and includes details related to data governance. Business Metadata includes the non-technical names and definitions of concepts, subject areas, entities, and attributes; attribute data types and other attribute properties; range descriptions; calculations; algorithms and business rules; valid domain values and their definitions. Examples of Business Metadata include:

- Definitions and descriptions of data sets, tables, and columns
- Business rules, transformation rules, calculations, and derivations
- Data models
- Data quality rules and measurement results
- Schedules by which data is updated
- Data provenance and data lineage
- Data standards
- Designations of the system of record for data elements
- Valid value constraints
- Stakeholder contact information (e.g., data owners, data stewards)
- Security/privacy level of data
- Known issues with data
- Data usage notes

1.3.2.2 Technical Metadata

Technical Metadata provides information about the technical details of data, the systems that store data, and the processes that move it within and between systems. Examples of Technical Metadata include:

- Physical database table and column names
- Column properties
- Database object properties
- Access permissions
- Data CRUD (create, replace, update and delete) rules
- Physical data models, including data table names, keys, and indexes
- Documented relationships between the data models and the physical assets
- ETL job details
- File format schema definitions
- Source-to-target mapping documentation
- Data lineage documentation, including upstream and downstream change impact information

- Program and application names and descriptions
- Content update cycle job schedules and dependencies
- Recovery and backup rules
- Data access rights, groups, roles

1.3.2.3 Operational Metadata

Operational Metadata describes details of the processing and accessing of data. For example:

- Logs of job execution for batch programs
- History of extracts and results
- Schedule anomalies
- Results of audit, balance, control measurements
- Error Logs
- Reports and query access patterns, frequency, and execution time
- Patches and Version maintenance plan and execution, current patching level
- Backup, retention, date created, disaster recovery provisions
- SLA requirements and provisions
- Volumetric and usage patterns
- Data archiving and retention rules, related archives
- Purge criteria
- Data sharing rules and agreements
- Technical roles and responsibilities, contacts

1.3.3 ISO / IEC 11179 Metadata Registry Standard

ISO's Metadata Registry Standard, ISO/IEC 11179, provides a framework for defining a Metadata registry. It is designed to enable Metadata-driven data exchange, based on exact definitions of data, beginning with data elements. The standard is structured in several parts:

- Part 1: Framework for the Generation and Standardization of Data Elements
- Part 3: Basic Attributes of Data Elements
- Part 4: Rules and Guidelines for the Formulation of Data Definitions
- Part 5: Naming and Identification Principles for Data Elements
- Part 6: Registration of Data Elements

1.3.4 Metadata for Unstructured Data

By its nature, all data has some structure, though not all of it is formally structured in the familiar rows, columns, and records of relational databases. Any data that is not in a database or data file, including documents or other media, is considered unstructured data. (See Chapters 9 and 14.)

Metadata is as essential to the management of unstructured data as it is to the management of structured data – perhaps even more so. Think again about the card catalog analogy from the chapter introduction. Books and magazines in a library are good examples of unstructured data. The primary use of the Metadata in a card catalog is to find the materials one is looking for, whatever their format.

Metadata for unstructured data includes descriptive Metadata, such as catalog information and thesauri keywords; structural Metadata such as tags, field structures, format; administrative Metadata, such as sources, update schedules, access rights, and navigation information; bibliographic Metadata, such as library catalog entries; record keeping Metadata, such as retention policies; and preservation Metadata, such as storage, archival condition, and rules for conservation. (See Chapter 9.)

While most assertions about Metadata for unstructured data are connected to traditional content management concerns, new practices are emerging around managing unstructured data in data lakes. Organizations wanting to take advantage of data lakes, using Big Data platforms such as Hadoop, are finding that they must catalog ingested data in order to enable later access. Most put in place processes to collect Metadata as part of data ingestion. A minimum set of Metadata attributes needs to be collected about each object ingested in the data lake (e.g., name, format, source, version, date received, etc.). This produces a catalog of data lake contents.

1.3.5 Sources of Metadata

As should be clear from the types of Metadata, Metadata can be collected from many different sources. Moreover, if Metadata from applications and databases has been well-managed, it can simply be harvested and integrated. However, most organizations do not manage Metadata well at the application level, because Metadata is often created as a by-product of application processing rather than as an end product (i.e., it is not created with consumption in mind). As with other forms of data, there is a lot of work in preparing Metadata before it can be integrated.

The majority of operational Metadata is generated as data is processed. The key to using this Metadata is to collect it in a usable form, and to ensure that those responsible for interpreting it have the tools they need to do so. Keep in mind that interpreting data in places like error logs itself requires Metadata that describes the logs. Similarly, a large portion of technical Metadata can be harvested from database objects.

It is possible to reverse engineer knowledge about data from existing systems and to harvest business Metadata from existing data dictionaries, models, and process documentation (Loshin, 2001; Aiken, 1995), but there are risks in doing so. The biggest risk is not knowing how much care was taken to develop and refine the definitions in the first place. If definitions are underdeveloped or ambiguous, then they will not provide data consumers with the information they need to understand the data they are using.

It is better to be intentional about developing definitions than to simply accept existing ones. Development of definitions takes time and the right skill set (e.g., writing and facilitation skills). This is why the development of business Metadata requires stewardship. (See Chapter 3.)

Much of the technical Metadata required to manage databases and the business Metadata required to use data can be collected and developed as part of project work. For example, the process of modeling data requires discussions on the meaning of data elements and the relation between them. Knowledge shared during such discussions should be captured and groomed for use in Data Dictionaries, Business Glossaries, and other repositories. The data models themselves include important details about the physical characteristics of data. Time should be allocated to ensure that project artifacts contain high quality Metadata that aligns with enterprise standards.

Well-defined business Metadata is reusable from project-to-project and can drive a consistent understanding of how business concepts are represented in different data sets. As part of developing Metadata intentionally so that it can be reused, an organization can also plan for the integration of Metadata. For example, it can develop an inventory of systems, and all Metadata related to particular system can be tagged with the same system identifier.

Creating Metadata for its own sake rarely works well. Most organizations will not fund this type of effort and, even when they do, they are unlikely to put in place processes for maintenance. In this respect, as in others, Metadata is like other data: It should be created as the product of a well-defined process, using tools that will support its overall quality. Stewards and other data management professionals should ensure that there are processes in place to maintain Metadata related to these processes. For example, if an organization harvests critical Metadata from its data models, it should ensure that there is a change management process in place to keep models current.

To give a sense of the breadth of Metadata in any organization, a range of sources is outlined here, in alphabetical rather than priority order.

1.3.5.1 Application Metadata Repositories

A Metadata repository refers to the physical tables in which the Metadata is stored. Often these are built into modeling tools, BI tools, and other applications. As an organization matures, it will want to integrate Metadata from repositories in these applications to enable data consumers to look across the breadth of information.

1.3.5.2 Business Glossary

The purpose of a business glossary is to document and store an organization's business concepts and terminology, definitions, and the relationships between those terms.

In many organizations, the business glossary is merely a spreadsheet. However, as organizations mature, they often purchase or build glossaries that contain robust information and the capability to manage it over time. As with all data-oriented systems, business glossaries should be architected to account for hardware, software, database, processes, and human resources with differing roles and responsibilities. The business glossary application is structured to meet the functional requirements of the three core audiences:

- **Business users**: Data analysts, research analysts, management, and executive staff use the business glossary to understand terminology and data.

- **Data Stewards**: Data Steward use the business glossary to manage the lifecycle of terms and definitions and to enhance enterprise knowledge by associating data assets with glossary terms; for example, linking terms to business metrics, reports, data quality analysis, or technology components. Data stewards raise terminology and usage issues and help resolve differences across the organization.

- **Technical users**: Technical users use the business glossary to make architecture, systems design, and development decisions, and to conduct impact analysis.

The business glossary should capture business terms attributes such as:

- Term name, definition, acronym or abbreviation, and any synonyms
- Business unit and or application responsible for managing the data associated with the terminology
- Name of the person identifying the term, and date updated
- Categorization or taxonomy association for the term (business functional association)
- Conflicting definitions that need resolution, nature of the problem, action timeline
- Common misunderstandings in terms
- Algorithms supporting definitions
- Lineage
- Official or authoritative source for the data supporting the term

Every business glossary implementation should have a basic set of reports to support the governance processes. It is recommended that organizations do not 'print the glossary' because glossary content is not static. Data stewards are generally responsible for glossary development, use, operations, and reporting. Reporting includes, tracking for new terms and definitions that have not been reviewed yet, those in a pending status, and those that are missing definitions or other attributes. (See Section 6.4.)

Ease of use and functionality can vary widely. The simpler and easier business glossary search, the more likely the glossary content will be used. However, the most important characteristic of a glossary is that it contains robust content.

1.3.5.3 Business Intelligence (BI) Tools

Business Intelligence tools produce various types of Metadata relevant to the Business Intelligence design including overview information, classes, objects, derived and calculated items, filters, reports, report fields, report layout, reports users, report distribution frequency, and report distribution channels.

1.3.5.4 Configuration Management Tools

Configuration management tools or databases (CMDB) provide the capability to manage and maintain Metadata specifically related to the IT assets, the relationships among them, and contractual details of the asset. Each asset in the CMDB database is referred to as a configuration item (CI). Standard Metadata is collected and managed for each CI type. Many organizations integrate the CMDB with the change management processes to identify the related assets or applications impacted by a change to a specific asset. Repositories provide mechanisms to link the assets in the Metadata repository to the actual physical implementation details in CMDB to give a complete picture of the data and the platforms.

1.3.5.5 Data Dictionaries

A data dictionary defines the structure and contents of data sets, often for a single database, application, or warehouse. The dictionary can be used to manage the names, descriptions, structure, characteristics, storage requirements, default values, relationships, uniqueness, and other attributes of every data element in a model. It should also contain table or file definitions. Data dictionaries are embedded in database tools for the creation, operation, manipulation of data contained in them. To make this Metadata available to data consumers, it must be extracted from the database or modeling tools. Data dictionaries can also describe in business terminology what data elements are available to the community, provisioned under what security restrictions, and applied in which business process. Time can be saved when defining, publishing, and maintaining a semantic layer for reporting and analysis by leveraging the content directly from the logical model. However, as noted earlier, existing definitions should be used with caution, especially in an organization with a low level of maturity around Metadata management.

Many key business processes, relationships, and terminologies are explained during the development of the data model. This information, captured in the logical data model, is often lost when physical structures are deployed to production. A data dictionary can help ensure that this information is not lost entirely to the organization and that the logical and physical models are kept in agreement after production deployment.

1.3.5.6 Data Integration Tools

Many data integration tools are used for executables to move data from one system to another or between various modules within the same system. Many of these tools generate transient files, which might contain copies or derived copies of the data. These tools are capable of loading data from various sources and then operating on the loaded data, through grouping, remediation, re-formatting, joining, filtering, or other operations, and then generating output data, which is distributed to the target locations. They document the lineage as data as it moves between systems. Any successful Metadata solution should be able to use the lineage Metadata as it is moves through the integration tools and expose it as a holistic lineage from the actual sources to the final destinations.

Data integration tools provide application interfaces (API) to allow external Metadata repositories to extract the lineage information and the transient files Metadata. Once the Metadata repository collects the information, some tools can generate a holistic lineage diagram for any data element. Data integration tools also provide Metadata about the execution of the various data integration jobs, including last successful run, duration, and job status. Some Metadata repositories can extract the data integration runtime statistics and Metadata and expose it alongside the data elements. (See Chapters 6 and 8.)

1.3.5.7 Database Management and System Catalogs

Database catalogs are an important source of Metadata. They describe the content of databases, along with sizing information, software versions, deployment status, network uptime, infrastructure uptime, availability, and many other operational Metadata attributes. The most common form of database is relational. Relational databases manage the data as a set of tables and columns, where a table contains one or more columns, indexes, constraints, views, and procedures. A Metadata solution should be able to connect to the various databases and data sets and read all of the Metadata exposed by the database. Some of the Metadata repository tools can integrate the exposed Metadata from the system management tools to provide a more holistic picture about the captured physical assets.

1.3.5.8 Data Mapping Management Tools

Mapping management tools are used during the analysis and design phase of a project to transform requirements into mapping specifications, which can then be consumed directly by a data integration tool or used by the developers to generate data integration code. Mapping documentation is also often held in excel documents across the enterprise. Vendors are now considering centralized repositories for the mapping specifications with capabilities to perform version control and change analysis between versions. Many mapping tools integrate with data integration tools to automate the generation of the data integration programs and most can exchange data with other Metadata and Reference Data repositories. (See Chapter 8.)

1.3.5.9 Data Quality Tools

Data quality tools assess the quality of data through validation rules. Most of these tools provide the capability to exchange the quality scores and profiles patterns with other Metadata repositories, enabling the Metadata repository to attach the quality scores to the relevant physical assets.

1.3.5.10 Directories and Catalogs

While data dictionaries and glossaries contain detailed information about terminology, tables, and fields, a directory or catalog contains information about systems, sources, and locations of data within an organization. A directory of Metadata is particularly useful to developers and data super users, such as data stewardship teams and data analysts, to understand the scope of data in the enterprise, whether to research issues or to find information about sourcing new applications.

1.3.5.11 Event Messaging Tools

Event messaging tools move data between diverse systems. To do so, they require a lot of Metadata. They also generate Metadata that describes this movement. These tools include graphic interfaces through which they manage the logic of data movement. They can export the interfaces implementation details, movement logic, and processing statistics to other Metadata repositories.

1.3.5.12 Modeling Tools and Repositories

Data modeling tools are used to build various types of data models: conceptual, logical, and physical. These tools produce Metadata relevant to the design of the application or system model, like subject areas, logical entities, logical attributes, entity and attribute relationships, super types and subtypes, tables, columns, indexes, primary and foreign keys, integrity constraints, and other types of attribution from the models. Metadata repositories can ingest the models created by these tools and integrate the imported Metadata into the repository. Modeling tools are often the source of data dictionary content.

1.3.5.13 Reference Data Repositories

Reference Data documents the business values and descriptions of the various types of enumerated data (domains) and their contextual use in a system. Tools used to manage Reference Data are also capable of managing relationships between the various codified values within the same or across domains. These suites of tools normally provide capabilities to send the collected Reference Data to a Metadata repository, which in turn will provide mechanisms to associate the Reference Data to the business glossary and to the locations where it is physically implemented like columns or fields.

1.3.5.14 Service Registries

A service registry manages and stores the technical information about services and service end-points from a service oriented architecture (SOA) perspective. For example, definitions, interfaces, operations, input and output parameters, policies, versions, and sample usage scenarios. Some of the most important Metadata related to services includes service version, location of service, data center, availability, deployment date, service port, IP address, stats port, connection timeout, and connection retry timeout. Service registries can be interrogated to satisfy various needs like displaying a list of all available services, services with a specific version, obsolete services, or details about a specific service. Services can also be reviewed for potential re-use. The information contained in these repositories provides important facts on what data exists and how it moves between various systems or applications. Metadata in service repositories can be extracted and incorporated with Metadata collected from other tools to provide a complete picture of how data is moving between the various systems.

1.3.5.15 Other Metadata Stores

Other Metadata stores include specialized lists such as event registries, source lists or interfaces, code sets, lexicons, spatial and temporal schema, spatial reference, and distribution of digital geographic data sets, repositories of repositories, and business rules.

1.3.6 Types of Metadata Architecture

Like other forms of data, Metadata has a lifecycle. Conceptually, all Metadata management solutions include architectural layers that correspond to points in the Metadata lifecycle:

- Metadata creation and sourcing
- Metadata storage in one or more repositories
- Metadata integration
- Metadata delivery
- Metadata usage
- Metadata control and management

Different architectural approaches can be used to source, store, integrate, maintain, and make Metadata accessible to consumers.

1.3.6.1 Centralized Metadata Architecture

A centralized architecture consists of a single Metadata repository that contains copies of Metadata from the various sources. Organizations with limited IT resources, or those seeking to automate as much as possible, may choose to avoid this architecture option. Organizations seeking a high degree of consistency within the common Metadata repository can benefit from a centralized architecture.

Advantages of a centralized repository include:

- High availability, since it is independent of the source systems
- Quick Metadata retrieval, since the repository and the query reside together
- Resolved database structures not affected by the proprietary nature of third party or commercial systems
- Extracted Metadata may be transformed, customized, or enhanced with additional Metadata that may not reside in the source system, improving quality

Some limitations of the centralized approach include:

- Complex processes are necessary to ensure that changes in source Metadata are quickly replicated into the repository
- Maintenance of a centralized repository can be costly
- Extraction could require custom modules or middleware
- Validation and maintenance of customized code can increase the demands on both internal IT staff and the software vendors

Figure 85 shows how Metadata is collected in a standalone Metadata repository with its own internal Metadata store. The internal store is populated through a scheduled import (arrows) of the Metadata from the various tools. In turn, the centralized repository exposes a portal for the end users to submit their queries. The Metadata portal passes the request to the centralized Metadata repository. The centralized repository will fulfill the request from the collected Metadata. In this type of implementation, the capability to pass the request from the user to various tools directly is not supported. Global search across the Metadata collected from the various tool is possible due to the collection of various Metadata in the centralized repository.

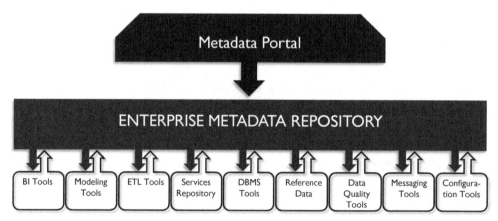

Figure 85 Centralized Metadata Architecture

1.3.6.2 Distributed Metadata Architecture

A completely distributed architecture maintains a single access point. The Metadata retrieval engine responds to user requests by retrieving data from source systems in real time; there is no persistent repository. In this architecture, the Metadata management environment maintains the necessary source system catalogs and lookup information needed to process user queries and searches effectively. A common object request broker or similar middleware protocol accesses these source systems.

Advantages of distributed Metadata architecture include:

- Metadata is always as current and valid as possible because it is retrieved from its source
- Queries are distributed, possibly improving response and process time
- Metadata requests from proprietary systems are limited to query processing rather than requiring a detailed understanding of proprietary data structures, therefore minimizing the implementation and maintenance effort required
- Development of automated Metadata query processing is likely simpler, requiring minimal manual intervention
- Batch processing is reduced, with no Metadata replication or synchronization processes

Distributed architectures also have limitations:

- No ability to support user-defined or manually inserted Metadata entries since there is no repository in which to place these additions
- Standardization of presenting Metadata from various systems
- Query capabilities are directly affected by the availability of the participating source systems
- The quality of Metadata depends solely on the participating source systems

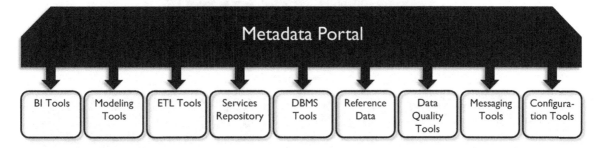

Figure 86 Distributed Metadata Architecture

Figure 86 illustrates a distributed Metadata architecture. There is no centralized Metadata repository store and the portal passes the users' requests to the appropriate tool to execute. As there is no centralized store for the Metadata to be collected from the various tools, every request has to be delegated down to the sources; hence, no capability exist for a global search across the various Metadata sources.

1.3.6.3 Hybrid Metadata Architecture

A hybrid architecture combines characteristics of centralized and distributed architectures. Metadata still moves directly from the source systems into a centralized repository. However, the repository design only accounts for the user-added Metadata, the critical standardized items, and the additions from manual sources.

The architecture benefits from the near-real-time retrieval of Metadata from its source and enhanced Metadata to meet user needs most effectively, when needed. The hybrid approach lowers the effort for manual IT intervention and custom-coded access functionality to proprietary systems. The Metadata is as current and valid as possible at the time of use, based on user priorities and requirements. Hybrid architecture does not improve system availability.

The availability of the source systems is a limitation, because the distributed nature of the back-end systems handles processing of queries. Additional overhead is required to link those initial results with the Metadata augmentation in the central repository before presenting the result set to the end user.

Many organizations can benefit from a hybrid architecture, including those that have rapidly-changing operational Metadata, those that need consistent, uniform Metadata, and those that experience substantial growth in Metadata and Metadata sources. Organizations with more static Metadata and smaller Metadata growth profiles may not see the maximum potential from this architecture alternative.

1.3.6.4 Bi-Directional Metadata Architecture

Another advanced architectural approach is bi-directional Metadata architecture, which allows Metadata to change in any part of the architecture (source, data integration, user interface) and then feedback is coordinated from the repository (broker) into its original source.

Various challenges are apparent in this approach. The design forces the Metadata repository to contain the latest version of the Metadata source and forces it to manage changes to the source, as well. Changes must be trapped systematically, and then resolved. Additional sets of process interfaces to tie the repository back to the Metadata source(s) must be built and maintained.

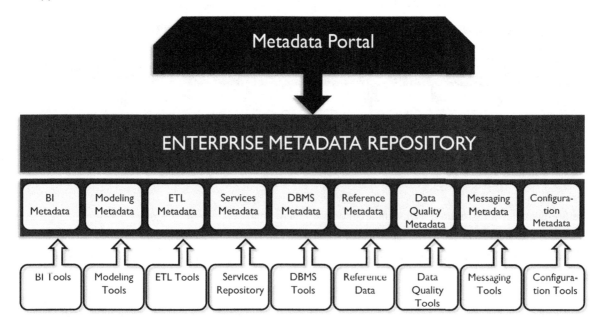

Figure 87 Hybrid Metadata Architecture

Figure 87 illustrates how common Metadata from different sources is collected in a centralized Metadata store. Users submit their queries to the Metadata portal, which passes the request to a centralized repository. The centralized repository will try to fulfill the user request from the common Metadata collected initially from the various sources. As the request becomes more specific or the user needs more detailed Metadata then the centralized repository will delegate down to the specific source to research the specific details. Global search across the various tools is available due to the common Metadata collected in the centralized repository.

2. Activities

2.1 Define Metadata Strategy

A Metadata strategy describes how an organization intends to manage its Metadata and how it will move from current state to future state practices. A Metadata strategy should provide a framework for development teams to improve Metadata management. Developing Metadata requirements will help clarify the drivers of the strategy and identify potential obstacles to enacting it.

The strategy includes defining the organization's future state enterprise Metadata architecture and the implementation phases required to meet strategic objectives. Steps include:

- **Initiate Metadata strategy planning**: The goal of initiation and planning is to enable the Metadata strategy team to define its short- and long-term goals. Planning includes drafting a charter, scope, and objectives aligned with overall governance efforts and establishing a communications plan to support the effort. Key stakeholders should be involved in planning.

- **Conduct key stakeholder interviews**: Interviews with business and technical stakeholder provide a foundation of knowledge for the Metadata strategy.

- **Assess existing Metadata sources and information architecture**: Assessment determines the relative degree of difficulty in solving the Metadata and systems issues identified in the interviews and documentation review. During this stage, conduct detailed interviews of key IT staff and review documentation of the system architectures, data models, etc.

- **Develop future Metadata architecture**: Refine and confirm the future vision, and develop the long-term target architecture for the managed Metadata environment in this stage. This phase must account for strategic components, such as organization structure, alignment with data governance and stewardship, managed Metadata architecture, Metadata delivery architecture, technical architecture, and security architecture.

- **Develop a phased implementation plan**: Validate, integrate, and prioritize findings from the interviews and data analyses. Document the Metadata strategy and define a phased implementation approach to move from the existing to the future managed Metadata environment.

The strategy will evolve over time, as Metadata requirements, the architecture, and the lifecycle of Metadata are better understood.

2.2 Understand Metadata Requirements

Metadata requirements start with content: What Metadata is needed and at what level. For example, physical and logical names need to be captured for both columns and tables. Metadata content is wide-ranging and requirements will come from both business and technical data consumers. (See Section 1.3.2.)

There are also many functionality-focused requirements associated with a comprehensive Metadata solution:

- **Volatility**: How frequently Metadata attributes and sets will be updated

- **Synchronization**: Timing of updates in relation to source changes

- **History**: Whether historical versions of Metadata need to be retained

- **Access rights**: Who can access Metadata and how they access, along with specific user interface functionality for access

- **Structure**: How Metadata will be modeled for storage

- **Integration**: The degree of integration of Metadata from different sources; rules for integration

- **Maintenance**: Processes and rules for updating Metadata (logging and referring for approval)

- **Management**: Roles and responsibilities for managing Metadata

- **Quality**: Metadata quality requirements

- **Security**: Some Metadata cannot be exposed because it will reveal the existence of highly protected data

2.3 Define Metadata Architecture

A Metadata Management system must be capable of extracting Metadata from many sources. Design the architecture to be capable of scanning the various Metadata sources and periodically updating the repository. The system must support the manual updates of Metadata, requests, searches, and lookups of Metadata by various user groups.

A managed Metadata environment should isolate the end user from the various and disparate Metadata sources. The architecture should provide a single access point for the Metadata repository. The access point must supply all related Metadata resources transparently to the user. Users should be able to access Metadata without being aware of the differing environments of the data sources. In analytics and Big Data solutions, the interface may have largely user-defined functions (UDF) to draw on various data sets, and the Metadata exposure to the end user is inherent to those customizations. With less reliance on UDF in solutions, end users will be gathering, inspecting, and using data sets more directly and various supporting Metadata is usually more exposed.

Design of the architecture depends on the specific requirements of the organization. Three technical architectural approaches to building a common Metadata repository mimic the approaches to designing data warehouses: centralized, distributed, and hybrid (see Section 1.3.6). These approaches all take into account implementation of the repository, and how the update mechanisms operate.

2.3.1 Create MetaModel

Create a data model for the Metadata repository, or metamodel, as one of the first design steps after the Metadata strategy is complete and the business requirements are understood. Different levels of metamodel may be developed as needed; a high-level conceptual model, that explains the relationships between systems, and a lower level metamodel that details the attributions, to describe the elements and processes of a model. In addition to being a planning tool and a means of articulating requirements, the metamodel is in itself a valuable source of Metadata.

Figure 88 depicts a sample Metadata repository metamodel. The boxes represent the high-level major entities, which contain the data.

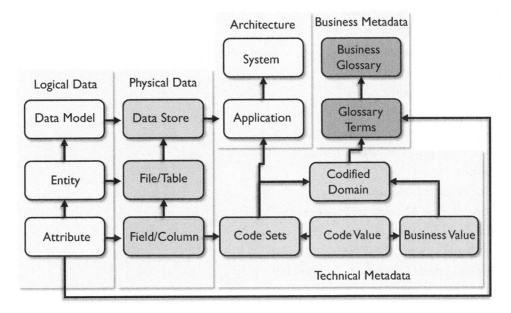

Figure 88 Example Metadata Repository Metamodel

2.3.2 Apply Metadata Standards

The Metadata solution should adhere to the agreed-upon internal and external standards as identified in the Metadata strategy. Metadata should be monitored for compliance by governance activities. Organization internal Metadata standards include naming conventions, custom attributions, security, visibility, and processing documentation. Organization external Metadata standards include the data exchange formats and application-programming interfaces design.

2.3.3 Manage Metadata Stores

Implement control activities to manage the Metadata environment. Control of repositories is control of Metadata movement and repository updates performed by the Metadata specialist. These activities are administrative in nature and involve monitoring and responding to reports, warnings, job logs, and resolving various issues in the implemented repository environment. Many control activities are standard for data operations and interface maintenance. Control activities should have data governance oversight.

Control activities include:

- Job scheduling and monitoring
- Load statistical analysis
- Backup, recovery, archive, purging
- Configuration modifications
- Performance tuning
- Query statistics analysis
- Query and report generation
- Security management
- Quality control activities include:
- Quality assurance, quality control
- Frequency of data update – matching sets to timeframes
- Missing Metadata reports
- Aging Metadata report
- Metadata management activities include:
- Loading, scanning, importing and tagging assets
- Source mapping and movement
- Versioning
- User interface management
- Linking data sets Metadata maintenance – for NOSQL provisioning
- Linking data to internal data acquisition – custom links and job Metadata
- Licensing for external data sources and feeds
- Data enhancement Metadata, e.g., Link to GIS
- And training, including:
- Education and training of users and data stewards
- Management metrics generation and analysis
- Training on the control activities and query and reporting

2.4 Create and Maintain Metadata

As described in Section 1.3.5, Metadata is created through a range of processes and stored in many places within an organization. To be of high quality, Metadata should be managed as a product. Good Metadata is not created by accident. It requires planning. (See Chapter 13.)

Several general principles of Metadata management describe the means to manage Metadata for quality:

- **Accountability**: Recognize that Metadata is often produced through existing processes (data modeling, SDLC, business process definition) and hold process owners accountable for the quality of Metadata.

- **Standards**: Set, enforce, and audit standards for Metadata to simplify integration and enable use.

- **Improvement**: Create a feedback mechanism so that consumers can inform the Metadata Management team of metadata that is incorrect or out-of-date.

Like other data, Metadata can be profiled and inspected for quality. Its maintenance should be scheduled or completed as an auditable part of project work.

2.4.1 Integrate Metadata

Integration processes gather and consolidate Metadata from across the enterprise, including Metadata from data acquired outside the enterprise. The Metadata repository should integrate extracted technical Metadata with relevant business, processes, and stewardship Metadata. Metadata can be extracted using adapters, scanners, bridge applications, or by directly accessing the Metadata in a source data store. Adapters are available with many third party vendor software tools, as well as from Metadata integration tools. In some cases, adapters will be developed using the tool API's.

Challenges arise in integration that will require governance. Integrating internal data sets, external data such as government statistics, and data sourced from non-electronic forms, such as white papers, articles in magazines, or reports, can raise numerous questions on quality and semantics.

Accomplish repository scanning in two distinct approaches.

- **Proprietary interface**: In a single-step scan and load process, a scanner collects the Metadata from a source system, then directly calls the format-specific loader component to load the Metadata into the repository. In this process, there is no format-specific file output and the collection and loading of Metadata occurs in a single step.
- **Semi-proprietary interface**: In a two-step process, a scanner collects the Metadata from a source system and outputs it into a format-specific data file. The scanner only produces a data file that the receiving repository needs to be able to read and load appropriately. The interface is a more open architecture, as the file is readable by many methods.

A scanning process uses and produces several types of files during the process.

- **Control file**: Containing the source structure of the data model
- **Reuse file**: Containing the rules for managing reuse of process loads
- **Log files**: Produced during each phase of the process, one for each scan or extract and one for each load cycle
- **Temporary and backup files**: Use during the process or for traceability

Use a non-persistent Metadata staging area to store temporary and backup files. The staging area supports rollback and recovery processes, and provides an interim audit trail to assist repository managers when investigating Metadata source or quality issues. The staging area may take the form of a directory of files or a database.

Data Integration tools used for data warehousing and Business Intelligence applications are often used effectively in Metadata integration processes. (See Chapter 8.)

2.4.2 Distribute and Deliver Metadata

Metadata is delivered to data consumers and to applications or tools that require Metadata feeds. Delivery mechanisms include:

- Metadata intranet websites for browse, search, query, reporting, and analysis
- Reports, glossaries and other documents
- Data warehouses, data marts, and BI (Business Intelligence) tools
- Modeling and software development tools
- Messaging and transactions
- Web services and Application Programming Interfaces (APIs)
- External organization interface solutions (e.g., supply chain solutions)

The Metadata solution often links to a Business Intelligence solution, so that both the scope and the currency of Metadata synchronize with the BI content. A link provides a means of integration into the delivery of BI to the end user. Similarly, some CRM (Customer Relationship Management) or other ERP (Enterprise Resource Planning) solutions may require Metadata integration at the application delivery layer.

Metadata is exchanged with external organizations using files (flat, XML, or JSON structured) or through web services.

2.5 Query, Report, and Analyze Metadata

Metadata guides the use of data assets. Use Metadata in Business Intelligence (reporting and analysis), business decisions (operational, tactical, strategic), and in business semantics (what they say, what they mean – business lingo'). A Metadata repository must have a front-end application that supports the search-and-retrieval functionality required for all this guidance and management of data assets. The interface provided to business users may have a different set of functional requirements than that for technical users and developers. Some reports facilitate future development such as change impact analysis, or trouble shoot varying definitions for data warehouse and Business Intelligence projects, such as data lineage reports.

3. Tools

The primary tool used to manage Metadata is the Metadata repository. This will include an integration layer and often an interface for manual updates. Tools that produce and use Metadata become sources of Metadata that can be integrated into a Metadata repository.

3.1 Metadata Repository Management Tools

Metadata Management tools provide capabilities to manage Metadata in a centralized location (repository). The Metadata can be either manually entered or extracted from various other sources through specialized connecters. Metadata repositories also provide capabilities to exchange Metadata with other systems.

Metadata management tools and repositories themselves are also a source of Metadata, especially in a hybrid Metadata architectural model or in large enterprise implementations. Metadata management tools allow for the exchange of the collected Metadata with other Metadata repositories, enabling the collection of various and diverse Metadata from different sources into a centralized repository, or enabling the enriching and standardization of the diverse Metadata as it moves between the repositories.

4. Techniques

4.1 Data Lineage and Impact Analysis

A key benefit of discovering and documenting Metadata about the physical assets is to provide information on how data is transformed as it moves between systems. Many Metadata tools carry information about what is happening to the data within their environments and provide capabilities to view the lineage across the span of the systems or applications they interface. The current version of the lineage based on programming code is referred to as 'As Implemented Lineage'. In contrast, lineage describe in mapping specification documents is referred to as 'As Designed Lineage'.

The limitations of a lineage build are based on the coverage of the Metadata management system. Function-specific Metadata repositories or data visualization tools have information about the data lineage within the scope of the environments they interact with but will not provide visibility to what is happening to the data outside their environments.

Metadata management systems import the 'As Implemented' lineage from the various tools that can provide this lineage detail and then augment the data lineage with the 'As Designed' from the places where the actual implementation details is not extractable. The process of connecting the pieces of the data lineage referred to as *stitching*. It results in a holistic visualization of the data as it moves from its original locations (official source or system of record) until it lands in its final destination.

Figure 89 shows a sample data element lineage. In reading this, the 'Total Backorder' business data element, which is physically implemented as column zz_total, depends on 3 other data elements: 'Units Cost in Cents' physically implemented as 'yy_unit_cost', 'Tax in Ship to State' implemented in 'yy_tax' and 'Back Order Quantity' implemented in 'yy_qty'.

Although a lineage graphic, such as in Figure 89, describes what is happening to a particular data element, not all business users will understand it. Higher levels of lineage (e.g., 'System Lineage') summarize movement at the system or application level. Many visualization tools provide zoom-in / zoom-out capability, to show data element lineage in the context of system lineage. For example, Figure 90 shows a sample system lineage, where at a glance, general data movement is understood and visualized at a system or an application level.

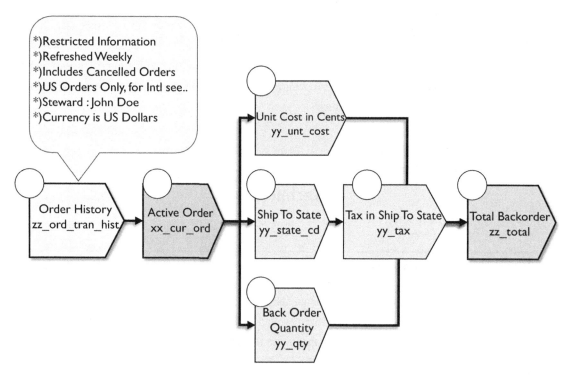

Figure 89 Sample Data Element Lineage Flow Diagram

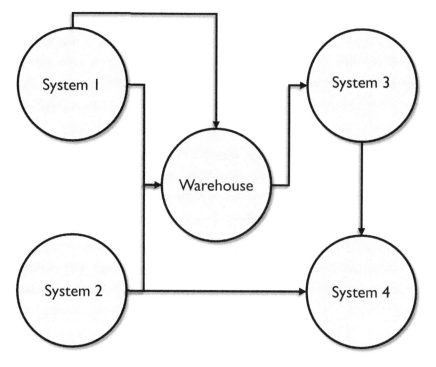

Figure 90 Sample System Lineage Flow Diagram

As the number of data elements in a system grows, the lineage discovery becomes complex and difficult to manage. In order to successfully achieve the business goals, a strategy for discovering and importing assets into the Metadata repository requires planning and design. Successful lineage discovery needs to account for both business and technical focus:

- **Business focus**: Limit the lineage discovery to data elements prioritized by the business. Start from the target locations and trace back to the source systems where the specific data originates. By limiting the scanned assets to those that move, transfer, or update the selected data elements, this approach will enable business data consumers to understand what is happening to the specific data element as it moves through systems. If coupled with data quality measurements, lineage can be used to pinpoint where system design adversely impacts the quality of the data.

- **Technical focus**: Start at the source systems and identify all the immediate consumers, then identify all the subsequent consumers of the first set identified and keep repeating these steps until all systems are identified. Technology users benefit more from the system discovery strategy in order to help answer the various questions about the data. This approach will enable technology and business users to answer question about discovering data elements across the enterprise, like "Where is social security number?" or generate impact reports like "What systems are impacted if the width of a specific column is changed?" This strategy can, however, be complex to manage.

Many data integration tools offer lineage analysis that considers not only the developed population code but the data model and the physical database as well. Some offer business user facing web interfaces to monitor and update definitions. These begin to look like business glossaries.

Documented lineage helps both business and technical people use data. Without it, much time is wasted in investigating anomalies, potential change impacts, or unknown results. Look to implement an integrated impact and lineage tool that can understand all the moving parts involved in the load process as well as end user reporting and analytics. Impact reports outline which components are affected by a potential change expediting and streamlining estimating and maintenance tasks.

4.2 Metadata for Big Data Ingest

Many data management professionals are familiar and comfortable with structured data stores, where every item can be clearly identified and tagged. Nowadays, though, much data comes in less structured formats. Some unstructured sources will be internal to the organization, and some will be external. In either case, there is no longer a need to physically bring the data to one place. Through the new technologies, the program will go to the data as opposed to moving the data to the program, reducing the amount of data movement, and speeding up the execution of the process. Nevertheless, successful data management in a data lake depends on managing Metadata.

Metadata tags should be applied to data upon ingestion. Metadata then can be used to identify data content available for access in the data lake. Many ingestion engines profile data as it is ingested. Data profiling can identify data domains, relationships, and data quality issues. It can also enable tagging. On ingestion, Metadata tags can be added to identify sensitive or private (like Personally Identifiable Information – PPI) data, for example. Data scientists may add confidence, textual identifiers, and codes representing behavior clusters. (See Chapter 14.)

5. Implementation Guidelines

Implement a managed Metadata environment in incremental steps in order to minimize risks to the organization and to facilitate acceptance. Implement Metadata repositories using an open relational database platform. This allows development and implementation of various controls and interfaces that may not be anticipated at the start of a repository development project.

The repository contents should be generic in design, not merely reflecting the source system database designs. Design contents in alignment with the enterprise subject area experts, and based on a comprehensive Metadata model. Planning should account for integrating Metadata so that data consumers can see across different data sources. The ability to do so will be one of the most valuable capabilities of the repository. It should house current, planned, and historical versions of the Metadata.

Often, the first implementation is a pilot to prove concepts and learn about managing the Metadata environment. Integration of Metadata projects into the IT development methodology is necessary. There will be variations depending on architecture and types of storage.

5.1 Readiness Assessment / Risk Assessment

Having a solid Metadata strategy helps everyone make more effective decisions. First and foremost, people should be aware of the risks of not managing Metadata. Assess the degree to which the lack of high quality Metadata might result in:

- Errors in judgment due to incorrect, incomplete or invalid assumptions or lack of knowledge about the context of the data

- Exposure of sensitive data, which may put customers or employees at risk, or impact the credibility of the business and lead to legal expenses

- Risk that the small set of SMEs who know the data will leave and take their knowledge with them

Risk is reduced when an organization adopts a solid Metadata strategy. Organizational readiness is addressed by a formal assessment of the current maturity in Metadata activities. The assessment should include the critical business data elements, available Metadata glossaries, lineage, data profiling and data quality processes, MDM (Master Data Management) maturity, and other aspects. Findings from the assessment, aligned with business priorities, will provide the basis for a strategic approach to improvement of Metadata Management practices. A formal assessment also provides the basis for a business case, sponsorship and funding.

The Metadata strategy may be part of an overall data governance strategy or it may be the first step in implementing effective data governance. A Metadata assessment should be conducted via objective inspection of existing Metadata, along with interviews with key stakeholders. The deliverables from a risk assessment include a strategy and roadmap.

5.2 Organizational and Cultural Change

Like other data management efforts, Metadata initiatives often meet with cultural resistance. Moving from an unmanaged to a managed Metadata environment takes work and discipline. It is not easy to do, even if most people recognize the value of reliable Metadata. Organizational readiness is a major concern, as are methods for governance and control.

Metadata Management is a low priority in many organizations. An essential set of Metadata needs coordination and commitment in an organization. It can be structures of employee identification data, insurance policy numbers, vehicle identification numbers, or product specifications, which if changed, would require major overhauls of many enterprise systems. Look for that good example where control will reap immediate quality benefits for data in the company. Build the argument from concrete business-relevant examples.

Implementation of an enterprise data governance strategy needs senior management support and engagement. It requires that business and technology staff be able to work closely together in a cross-functional manner.

6. Metadata Governance

Organizations should determine their specific requirements for the management of the Metadata lifecycle and establish governance processes to enable those requirements. It is recommended that formal roles and responsibilities be assigned to dedicated resources, especially in large or business critical areas. Metadata governance processes themselves depend on reliable Metadata, so the team charged with managing Metadata can test principles on the Metadata they create and use.

6.1 Process Controls

The data governance team should be responsible for defining the standards and managing status changes for Metadata – often with workflow or collaboration software – and may be responsible for promotional activities and training development or actual training across the organization.

More mature Metadata governance will require business terms and definitions to progress through varying status changes or governance gates; for example, from a candidate term, to approved, to published, and to a final point in the lifecycle of replaced or retired. The governance team may also manage business term associations such as related terms, as well as the categorization of and grouping of the terms.

Integration of the Metadata strategy into the SDLC is needed to ensure that changed Metadata is collected when it is changed. This helps ensure Metadata remains current.

6.2 Documentation of Metadata Solutions

A master catalog of Metadata will include the sources and targets currently in scope. This is a resource for IT and business users and can be published out to the user community as a guide to 'what is where' and to set expectations on what they will find:

- Metadata implementation status
- Source and the target Metadata store
- Schedule information for updates
- Retention and versions kept
- Contents

- Quality statements or warnings (e.g., missing values)
- System of record and other data source statuses (e.g., data contents history coverage, retiring or replacing flags)
- Tools, architectures, and people involved
- Sensitive information and removal or masking strategy for the source

In documents and content management, data maps show similar information. Visualizations of the overall Metadata integration systems landscape are also maintained as part of Metadata documentation. (See Chapter 9.)

6.3 Metadata Standards and Guidelines

Metadata standards are essential in the exchange of data with operational trading partners. Companies realize the value of information sharing with customers, suppliers, partners, and regulatory bodies. The need for sharing common Metadata to support the optimal usage of shared information has spawned many sector-based standards.

Adopt industry-based and sector-sensitive Metadata standards early in the planning cycle. Use the standards to evaluate Metadata Management technologies. Many leading vendors support multiple standards, and some can assist in customizing industry-based and sector-sensitive standards.

Tool vendors provide XML and JSON or REST support to exchange data for their data management products. They use the same strategy to bind their tools together into suites of solutions. Technologies, including data integration, relational and multidimensional databases, requirements management, Business Intelligence reporting, data modeling, and business rules, offer import and export capabilities for data and Metadata using XML. Vendors maintain their proprietary XML schemas and document type definitions (DTD) or more commonly the XML schema definitions (XSD). These are accessed through proprietary interfaces. Custom development is required to integrate these tools into a Metadata management environment.

Guidelines include templates and associated examples and training on expected inputs and updates including such rules as 'do not define a term by using the term' and completeness statements. Different templates are developed for different types of Metadata, and are driven in part by the Metadata solution selected. Ongoing monitoring of guidelines for effectiveness and necessary updates is a governance responsibility.

The ISO standards for Metadata provide guidance for tool developers but are unlikely to be a concern for organizations who implement using commercial tools, since the tools should meet the standards. Regardless, it can be helpful to have a good understanding of these standards and their repercussions.

6.4 Metrics

It is difficult to measure the impact of Metadata without first measuring the impact of the lack of Metadata. As part of risk assessment, obtain metrics on the amount of time data consumers spend searching for information, in order to show improvement after the Metadata solution is put in place. The effectiveness of the Metadata implementation can also be measured in terms of the completeness of the Metadata itself, of the management routines associated it with it, and of Metadata usage. Suggested metrics on Metadata environments include:

- **Metadata repository completeness**: Compare ideal coverage of the enterprise Metadata (all artifacts and all instances within scope) to actual coverage. Reference the strategy for scope definitions.

- **Metadata Management Maturity**: Metrics developed to judge the Metadata maturity of the enterprise, based on the Capability Maturity Model (CMM-DMM) approach to maturity assessment. (See Chapter 15.)

- **Steward representation**: Organizational commitment to Metadata as assessed by the appointment of stewards, coverage across the enterprise for stewardship, and documentation of the roles in job descriptions.

- **Metadata usage**: User uptake on the Metadata repository usage can be measured by repository login counts. Reference to Metadata by users in business practice is a more difficult measure to track. Anecdotal measures on qualitative surveys may be required to capture this measure.

- **Business Glossary activity**: Usage, update, resolution of definitions, coverage.

- **Master Data service data compliance**: Shows the reuse of data in SOA solutions. Metadata on the data services assists developers in deciding when new development could use an existing service.

- **Metadata documentation quality**: Assess the quality of Metadata documentation through both automatic and manual methods. Automatic methods include performing collision logic on two sources, measuring how much they match, and the trend over time. Another metric would measure the percentage of attributes that have definitions, trending over time. Manual methods include random or complete survey, based on enterprise definitions of quality. Quality measures indicate the completeness, reliability, currency, etc., of the Metadata in the repository.

- **Metadata repository availability**: Uptime, processing time (batch and query).

---

7. Works Cited / Recommended

Aiken, Peter. *Data Reverse Engineering: Slaying the Legacy Dragon*. 1995.

Foreman, John W. Data Smart: *Using Data Science to Transform Information into Insight*. Wiley, 2013. Print.

Loshin, David. *Enterprise Knowledge Management: The Data Quality Approach*. Morgan Kaufmann, 2001.

Marco, David. *Building and Managing the Meta Data Repository: A Full Lifecycle Guide*. Wiley, 2000. Print.

Milton, Nicholas Ross. *Knowledge Acquisition in Practice: A Step-by-step Guide*. Springer, 2007. Print. Decision Engineering.

Park, Jung-ran, ed. *Metadata Best Practices and Guidelines: Current Implementation and Future Trends*. Routledge, 2014. Print.

Pomerantz, Jeffrey. *Metadata*. The MIT Press, 2015. Print. The MIT Press Essential Knowledge ser.

Schneier, Bruce. *Data and Goliath: The Hidden Battles to Collect Your Data and Control Your World*. W. W. Norton and Company, 2015. Print.

Tannenbaum, Adrienne. *Implementing a Corporate Repository: The Models Meet Reality*. Wiley, 1994. Print. Wiley Professional Computing.

Warden, Pete. *Big Data Glossary*. O'Reilly Media, 2011. Print.

Zeng, Marcia Lei and Jian Qin. *Metadata*. 2nd ed. ALA Neal-Schuman, 2015. Print.

CHAPTER 13

Data Quality

DAMA-DMBOK2 Data Management Framework

Copyright © 2017 by DAMA International

1. Introduction

Effective data management involves a set of complex, interrelated processes that enable an organization to use its data to achieve strategic goals. Data management includes the ability to design data for applications, store and access it securely, share it appropriately, learn from it, and ensure it meets business needs. An assumption underlying assertions about the value of data is that the data itself is reliable and trustworthy. In other words, that it is of high quality.

However, many factors can undermine that assumption by contributing to poor quality data: Lack of understanding about the effects of poor quality data on organizational success, bad planning, 'siloed' system design, inconsistent development processes, incomplete documentation, a lack of standards, or a lack of governance. Many organizations fail to define what makes data fit for purpose.

All data management disciplines contribute to the quality of data, and high quality data that supports the organization should be the goal of all data management disciplines. Because uninformed decisions or actions by anyone who interacts with data can result in poor quality data, producing high quality data requires cross-functional commitment and coordination. Organizations and teams should be aware of this and should plan for high quality data, by executing processes and projects in ways that account for risk related to unexpected or unacceptable conditions in the data.

Because no organization has perfect business processes, perfect technical processes, or perfect data management practices, all organizations experience problems related to the quality of their data. Organizations that formally manage the quality of data have fewer problems than those that leave data quality to chance.

Formal data quality management is similar to continuous quality management for other products. It includes managing data through its lifecycle by setting standards, building quality into the processes that create, transform, and store data, and measuring data against standards. Managing data to this level usually requires a Data Quality program team. The Data Quality program team is responsible for engaging both business and technical data management professionals and driving the work of applying quality management techniques to data to ensure that data is fit for consumption for a variety of purposes. The team will likely be involved with a series of projects through which they can establish processes and best practices while addressing high priority data issues.

Because managing the quality of data involves managing the data lifecycle, a Data Quality program will also have operational responsibilities related to data usage. For example, reporting on data quality levels and engaging in the analysis, quantification, and prioritization of data issues. The team is also responsible for working with those who need data to do their jobs to ensure the data meets their needs and working with those who create, update, or delete data in the course of their jobs to ensure they are properly handling the data. Data quality depends on all who interact with the data, not just data management professionals.

As is the case with Data Governance and with data management as a whole, Data Quality Management is a program, not a project. It will include both project and maintenance work, along with a commitment to communications and training. Most importantly, the long-term success of data quality improvement program depends on getting an organization to change its culture and adopt a quality mindset. As stated in *The Leader's Data Manifesto*: fundamental, lasting change requires committed leadership and involvement from people at all levels in an organization. People who use data to do their jobs – which in most organizations is a very large percentage of employees – need to drive change. One of the most critical changes to focus on is how their organizations manage and improve the quality of their data.[71]

---

[71] For the full text of *The Leader's Data Manifesto*, see http://bit.ly/2sQhcy7.

Data Quality Management

Definition: The planning, implementation, and control of activities that apply quality management techniques to data, in order to assure it is fit for consumption and meets the needs of data consumers.

Goals:
1. Develop a governed approach to make data fit for purpose based on data consumers' requirements.
2. Define standards, requirements, and specifications for data quality controls as part of the data lifecycle.
3. Define and implement processes to measure, monitor, and report on data quality levels.
4. Identify and advocate for opportunities to improve the quality of data, through process and system improvements.

Business
Drivers

Inputs:
- Data Policies and Standards
- Data Quality Expectations
- Business Requirements
- Business Rules
- Data Requirements
- Business Metadata
- Technical Metadata
- Data Sources and Data Stores
- Data Lineage

Activities:
1. **Define High Quality Data (P)**
2. **Define a Data Quality Strategy (P)**
3. **Define Scope of Initial Assessment (P)**
   1. Identify Critical Data
   2. Identify Existing Rules and Patterns
4. **Perform Initial Data Quality Assessment (P)**
   1. Identify and prioritize issues
   2. Perform root cause analysis of issues
5. **Identify & Prioritize Improvements**
   1. Prioritize Actions based on Business Impact
   2. Develop Preventative and Corrective Actions
   3. Confirm Planned Actions
6. **Develop and Deploy Data Quality Operations (D)**
   1. Develop Data Quality Operational Procedures
   2. Correct Data Quality Defects
   3. Measure and Monitor Data Quality
   4. Report on Data Quality levels and findings

Deliverables:
- Data Quality Strategy & framework
- Data Quality Program organization
- Analyses from Data Profiling
- Recommendations based on root cause analysis of issues
- DQM Procedures
- Data Quality Reports
- Data Quality Governance Reports
- Data Quality Service Level Agreements
- DQ Policies and Guidelines

Suppliers:
- Business Management
- Subject Matter Experts
- Data Architects
- Data Modelers
- System Specialists
- Data Stewards
- Business Process Analysts

Participants:
- CDO
- Data Quality Analysts
- Data Stewards
- Data Owners
- Data Analysts
- Database Administrators
- Data Professionals
- DQ Managers
- IT Operations
- Data Integration Architects
- Compliance Team

Consumers:
- Business Data Consumers
- Data Stewards
- Data Professionals
- IT Professionals
- Knowledge Workers
- Data Governance Bodies
- Partner Organizations
- Centers of Excellence

Technical
Drivers

Techniques:
- Spot-Checking using Multiple Subsets
- Tags and Notes to Mark Data Issues
- Root Cause Analysis
- Statistical Process Control

Tools:
- Profiling engines, query tools
- Data Quality Rule Templates
- Quality Check and Audit Code Modules

Metrics:
- Governance and Conformance Metrics
- Data Quality Measurement Results
- Improvement trends
- Issue Management Metrics

(P) Planning, (C) Control, (D) Development, (O) Operations

Figure 91 Context Diagram: Data Quality

1.1 Business Drivers

The business drivers for establishing a formal Data Quality Management program include:

- Increasing the value of organizational data and the opportunities to use it
- Reducing risks and costs associated with poor quality data
- Improving organizational efficiency and productivity
- Protecting and enhancing the organization's reputation

Organizations that want to get value out of their data recognize that high quality data is more valuable than low quality data. Poor quality data is risk-laden (see Chapter 1). It can damage an organization's reputation, resulting in fines, lost revenue, lost customers, and negative media exposure. Regulatory requirements often demand high quality data. In addition, many direct costs are associated with poor quality data. For example,

- Inability to invoice correctly
- Increased customer service calls and decreased ability to resolve them
- Revenue loss due to missed business opportunities
- Delay of integration during mergers and acquisitions
- Increased exposure to fraud
- Loss due to bad business decisions driven by bad data
- Loss of business due to lack of good credit standing

Still high quality data is not an end in itself. It is a means to organizational success. Trustworthy data not only mitigates risk and reduces costs, but also improves efficiency. Employees can answer questions more quickly and consistently, when they are working with reliable data. They spend less time trying to figure out if the data is right and more time using the data to gain insight, make decisions, and serve customers.

1.2 Goals and Principles

Data Quality programs focus on these general goals:

- Developing a governed approach to make data fit for purpose based on data consumers' requirements
- Defining standards and specifications for data quality controls as part of the data lifecycle
- Defining and implementing processes to measure, monitor, and report on data quality levels
- Identifying and advocating for opportunities to improve the quality of data, through changes to processes and systems and engaging in activities that measurably improve the quality of data based on data consumer requirements

Data Quality programs should be guided by the following principles:

- **Criticality**: A Data Quality program should focus on the data most critical to the enterprise and its customers. Priorities for improvement should be based on the criticality of the data and on the level of risk if data is not correct.

- **Lifecycle management**: The quality of data should be managed across the data lifecycle, from creation or procurement through disposal. This includes managing data as it moves within and between systems (i.e., each link in the data chain should ensure data output is of high quality).

- **Prevention**: The focus of a Data Quality program should be on preventing data errors and conditions that reduce the usability of data; it should not be focused on simply correcting records.

- **Root cause remediation**: Improving the quality of data goes beyond correcting errors. Problems with the quality of data should be understood and addressed at their root causes, rather than just their symptoms. Because these causes are often related to process or system design, improving data quality often requires changes to processes and the systems that support them.

- **Governance**: Data Governance activities must support the development of high quality data and Data Quality program activities must support and sustain a governed data environment.

- **Standards-driven**: All stakeholders in the data lifecycle have data quality requirements. To the degree possible, these requirements should be defined in the form of measurable standards and expectations against which the quality of data can be measured.

- **Objective measurement and transparency**: Data quality levels need to be measured objectively and consistently. Measurements and measurement methodology should be shared with stakeholders since they are the arbiters of quality.

- **Embedded in business processes**: Business process owners are responsible for the quality of data produced through their processes. They must enforce data quality standards in their processes.

- **Systematically enforced**: System owners must systematically enforce data quality requirements.

- **Connected to service levels**: Data quality reporting and issues management should be incorporated into Service Level Agreements (SLA).

1.3 Essential Concepts

1.3.1 Data Quality

The term *data quality* refers both to the characteristics associated with high quality data and to the processes used to measure or improve the quality of data. These dual usages can be confusing, so it helps to separate them and clarify what constitutes high quality data.[72]

Data is of high quality to the degree that it meets the expectations and needs of data consumers. That is, if the data is fit for the purposes to which they want to apply it. It is of low quality if it is not fit for those purposes. Data quality is thus dependent on context and on the needs of the data consumer.

---

[72] In the DAMA-DMBOK2, we have tried to avoid using the words data quality without clarifying their context. For example, referring to *high quality data* or *low quality data*, and to *data quality work efforts* or *data quality activities*.

One of the challenges in managing the quality of data is that expectations related to quality are not always known. Customers may not articulate them. Often, the people managing data do not even ask about these requirements. However, if data is to be reliable and trustworthy, then data management professionals need to better understand their customers' quality requirements and how to measure them. This needs to be an ongoing discussion, as requirements change over time as business needs and external forces evolve.

1.3.2 Critical Data

Most organizations have a lot of data, not all of which is of equal importance. One principle of Data Quality Management is to focus improvement efforts on data that is most important to the organization and its customers. Doing so gives the program scope and focus and enables it to make a direct, measurable impact on business needs.

While specific drivers for criticality will differ by industry, there are common characteristics across organizations. Data can be assessed based on whether it is required by:

- Regulatory reporting
- Financial reporting
- Business policy
- Ongoing operations
- Business strategy, especially efforts at competitive differentiation

Master Data is critical by definition. Data sets or individual data elements can be assessed for criticality based on the processes that consume them, the nature of the reports they appear in, or the financial, regulatory, or reputational risk to the organization if something were to go wrong with the data.[73]

1.3.3 Data Quality Dimensions

A *Data Quality dimension* is a measurable feature or characteristic of data. The term *dimension* is used to make the connection to dimensions in the measurement of physical objects (e.g., length, width, height). Data quality dimensions provide a vocabulary for defining data quality requirements. From there, they can be used to define results of initial data quality assessment as well as ongoing measurement. In order to measure the quality of data, an organization needs to establish characteristics that are both important to business processes (worth measuring) and measurable. Dimensions provide a basis for measurable rules, which themselves should be directly connected to potential risks in critical processes.

For example, if the data in the customer email address field is incomplete, then we will not be able to send product information to our customers via email, and we will lose potential sales. Therefore, we will measure the percentage of customers for whom we have usable email addresses, and we will improve our processes until we have a usable email address for at least 98% of our customers.

---

[73] See Jugulum (2014), Chapters 6 and 7 for an approach to rationalizing critical data.

Many leading thinkers in data quality have published sets of dimensions.[74] The three most influential are described here because they provide insight into how to think about what it means to have high quality data, as well as into how data quality can be measured.

The Strong-Wang framework (1996) focuses on data consumers' perceptions of data. It describes 15 dimensions across four general categories of data quality:

- Intrinsic DQ
    - Accuracy
    - Objectivity
    - Believability
    - Reputation
- Contextual DQ
    - Value-added
    - Relevancy
    - Timeliness
    - Completeness
    - Appropriate amount of data
- Representational DQ
    - Interpretability
    - Ease of understanding
    - Representational consistency
    - Concise representation
- Accessibility DQ
    - Accessibility
    - Access security

In *Data Quality for the Information Age* (1996), Thomas Redman formulated a set of data quality dimension rooted in data structure.[75] Redman defines a data item as a "representable triple": a value from the domain of an attribute within an entity. Dimensions can be associated with any of the component pieces of data – the model (entities and attributes) as well as the values. Redman includes the dimension of representation, which he defines as a set of rules for recording data items. Within these three general categories (data model, data values, representation), he describes more than two dozen dimensions. They include the following:

Data Model:

- Content:
    - Relevance of data
    - The ability to obtain the values
    - Clarity of definitions
- Level of detail:

---

[74] In addition to the examples detailed here and numerous academic papers on this topic, see Loshin (2001), Olson (2003), McGilvray (2008), and Sebastian-Coleman (2013) for detailed discussions on data quality dimensions. See Myers (2013) for a comparison of dimensions.

[75] Redman expanded and revised his set of dimensions in *Data Quality: The Field Guide* (2001).

- o   Attribute granularity
- o   Precision of attribute domains
- **Composition:**
  - o   Naturalness: The idea that each attribute should have a simple counterpart in the real world and that each attribute should bear on a single fact about the entity
  - o   Identify-ability: Each entity should be distinguishable from every other entity
  - o   Homogeneity
  - o   Minimum necessary redundancy
- **Consistency:**
  - o   Semantic consistency of the components of the model
  - o   Structure consistency of attributes across entity types
- **Reaction to change:**
  - o   Robustness
  - o   Flexibility

Data Values:

- Accuracy
- Completeness
- Currency
- Consistency

Representation:

- Appropriateness
- Interpretability
- Portability
- Format precision
- Format flexibility
- Ability to represent null values
- Efficient use of storage
- Physical instances of data being in accord with their formats

Redman recognizes that consistency of entities, values, and representation can be understood in terms of constraints. Different types of consistency are subject to different kinds of constraints.

In *Improving Data Warehouse and Business Information Quality* (1999), Larry English presents a comprehensive set of dimensions divided into two broad categories: inherent and pragmatic.[76] Inherent characteristics are independent of data use. Pragmatic characteristics are associated with data presentation and are dynamic; their value (quality) can change depending on the uses of data.

- **Inherent** quality characteristics
  - o   Definitional conformance
  - o   Completeness of values

---

[76] English expanded and revised his dimensions in *Information Quality Applied* (2009).

- o Validity or business rule conformance
- o Accuracy to a surrogate source
- o Accuracy to reality
- o Precision
- o Non-duplication
- o Equivalence of redundant or distributed data
- o Concurrency of redundant or distributed data
- **Pragmatic** quality characteristics
    - o Accessibility
    - o Timeliness
    - o Contextual clarity
    - o Usability
    - o Derivation integrity
    - o Rightness or fact completeness

In 2013, DAMA UK produced a white paper describing six core dimensions of data quality:

- **Completeness**: The proportion of data stored against the potential for 100%.
- **Uniqueness**: No entity instance (thing) will be recorded more than once based upon how that thing is identified.
- **Timeliness**: The degree to which data represent reality from the required point in time.
- **Validity**: Data is valid if it conforms to the syntax (format, type, range) of its definition.
- **Accuracy**: The degree to which data correctly describes the 'real world' object or event being described.
- **Consistency**: The absence of difference, when comparing two or more representations of a thing against a definition.

The DAMA UK white paper also describes other characteristics that have an impact on quality. While the white paper does not call these dimensions, they work in a manner similar to Strong and Wang's contextual and representational DQ and English's pragmatic characteristics.

- **Usability**: Is the data understandable, simple, relevant, accessible, maintainable and at the right level of precision?

- **Timing issues** (beyond timeliness itself): Is it stable yet responsive to legitimate change requests?
- **Flexibility**: Is the data comparable and compatible with other data? Does it have useful groupings and classifications? Can it be repurposed? Is it easy to manipulate?
- **Confidence**: Are Data Governance, Data Protection, and Data Security processes in place? What is the reputation of the data, and is it verified or verifiable?
- **Value**: Is there a good cost / benefit case for the data? Is it being optimally used? Does it endanger people's safety or privacy, or the legal responsibilities of the enterprise? Does it support or contradict the corporate image or the corporate message?

While there is not a single, agreed-to set of data quality dimensions, these formulations contain common ideas. Dimensions include some characteristics that can be measured objectively (completeness, validity, format conformity) and others that depend on heavily context or on subjective interpretation (usability, reliability, reputation). Whatever names are used, dimensions focus on whether there is enough data (completeness), whether it is right (accuracy, validity), how well it fits together (consistency, integrity, uniqueness), whether it is up-to-date (timeliness), accessible, usable, and secure. Table 29 contains definitions of a set of data quality dimensions, about which there is general agreement and describes approaches to measuring them.

Table 29 Common Dimensions of Data Quality

Dimension of Quality	Description
Accuracy	Accuracy refers to the degree that data correctly represents 'real-life' entities. Accuracy is difficult to measure, unless an organization can reproduce data collection or manually confirm accuracy of records. Most measures of accuracy rely on comparison to a data source that has been verified as accurate, such as a system of record or data from a reliable source (e.g., Dun and Bradstreet Reference Data).
Completeness	Completeness refers to whether all required data is present. Completeness can be measured at the data set, record, or column level. Does the data set contain all the records expected? Are records populated correctly? (Records with different statuses may have different expectations for completeness.) Are columns/attributes populated to the level expected? (Some columns are mandatory. Optional columns are populated only under specific conditions.) Assign completeness rules to a data set with varying levels of constraint: Mandatory attributes that require a value, data elements with conditional and optional values, and inapplicable attribute values. Data set level measurements may require comparison to a source of record or may be based on historical levels of population.
Consistency	Consistency can refer to ensuring that data values are consistently represented within a data set and between data sets, and consistently associated across data sets. It can also refer to the size and composition of data sets between systems or across time. Consistency may be defined between one set of attribute values and another attribute set within the same record (record-level consistency), between one set of attribute values and another attribute set in different records (cross-record consistency), or between one set of attribute values and the same attribute set within the same record at different points in time (temporal consistency). Consistency can also be used to refer to consistency of format. Take care not to confuse consistency with accuracy or correctness.

Characteristics that are expected to be consistent within and across data sets can be used as the basis for standardizing data. Data Standardization refers to the conditioning of input data to ensure that data meets rules for content and format. Standardizing data enables more effective matching and facilitates consistent output. Encapsulate consistency constraints as a set of rules that specify consistent relationships between values of attributes, either across a record or message, or along all values of a single attribute (such as a range or list of valid values). For example, one might expect that the number of transactions each day does not exceed 105% of the running average number of transactions for the previous 30 days. |
| Integrity | Data Integrity (or Coherence) includes ideas associated with completeness, accuracy, and consistency. In data, integrity usually refers to either referential integrity (consistency between data objects via a reference key contained in both objects) or internal consistency within a data set such that there are no holes or missing parts. Data sets without integrity are seen as corrupted, or have data loss. Data sets without *referential* integrity have 'orphans' – invalid reference keys, or 'duplicates' – identical rows which may negatively affect aggregation functions. The level of orphan records can be measured as a raw count or as a percentage of the data set. |
| Reasonability | Reasonability asks whether a data pattern meets expectations. For example, whether a distribution of sales across a geographic area makes sense based on what is known about the customers in that area. Measurement of reasonability can take different forms. For example, reasonability may be based on comparison to benchmark data, or past instances of a similar data set (e.g., sales from the previous quarter). Some ideas about reasonability may be perceived as subjective. If this is the case, work with data consumers to articulate the basis of their expectations of data to formulate objective comparisons. Once benchmark measurements of reasonability are established, these can be used to objectively compare new instances of the same data set in order to detect change. (See Section 4.5.) |

Dimension of Quality	Description
Timeliness	The concept of data Timeliness refers to several characteristics of data. Measures of timeliness need to be understood in terms of expected volatility – how frequently data is likely to change and for what reasons. Data currency is the measure of whether data values are the most up-to-date version of the information. Relatively static data, for example some Reference Data values like country codes, may remain current for a long period. Volatile data remains current for a short period. Some data, for example, stock prices on financial web pages, will often be shown with an as-of-time, so that data consumers understand the risk that the data has changed since it was recorded. During the day, while the markets are open, such data will be updated frequently. Once markets close, the data will remain unchanged, but will still be current, since the market itself is inactive. Latency measures the time between when the data was created and when it was made available for use. For example, overnight batch processing can give a latency of 1 day at 8am for data entered into the system during the prior day, but only one hour for data generated during the batch processing. (See Chapter 8.)
Uniqueness / Deduplication	Uniqueness states that no entity exists more than once within the data set. Asserting uniqueness of the entities within a data set implies that a key value relates to each unique entity, and only that specific entity, within the data set. Measure uniqueness by testing against key structure. (See Chapter 5.)
Validity	Validity refers to whether data values are consistent with a defined domain of values. A domain of values may be a defined set of valid values (such as in a reference table), a range of values, or value that can be determined via rules. The data type, format, and precision of expected values must be accounted for in defining the domain. Data may also only be valid for a specific length of time, for example data that is generated from RFID (radio frequency ID) or some scientific data sets. Validate data by comparing it to domain constraints. Keep in mind that data may be valid (i.e., it may meet domain requirements) and still not be accurate or correctly associated with particular records.

Figure 92 aligns data quality dimensions and concepts associated with those dimensions. The arrows indicate significant overlaps between concepts and also demonstrate that there is not agreement on a specific set. For example, the dimension of accuracy is associated with 'agrees with real world' and 'match to agreed source' and also to the concepts associated with validity, such as 'derivation correct'.

1.3.4 Data Quality and Metadata

Metadata is critical to managing the quality of data. The quality of data is based on how well it meets the requirements of data consumers. Metadata defines what the data represents. Having a robust process by which data is defined supports the ability of an organization to formalize and document the standards and requirements by which the quality of data can be measured. Data quality is about meeting expectations. Metadata is a primary means of clarifying expectations.

Well-managed Metadata can also support the effort to improve the quality of data. A Metadata repository can house results of data quality measurements so that these are shared across the organization and the Data Quality team can work toward consensus about priorities and drivers for improvement. (See Chapter 12.)

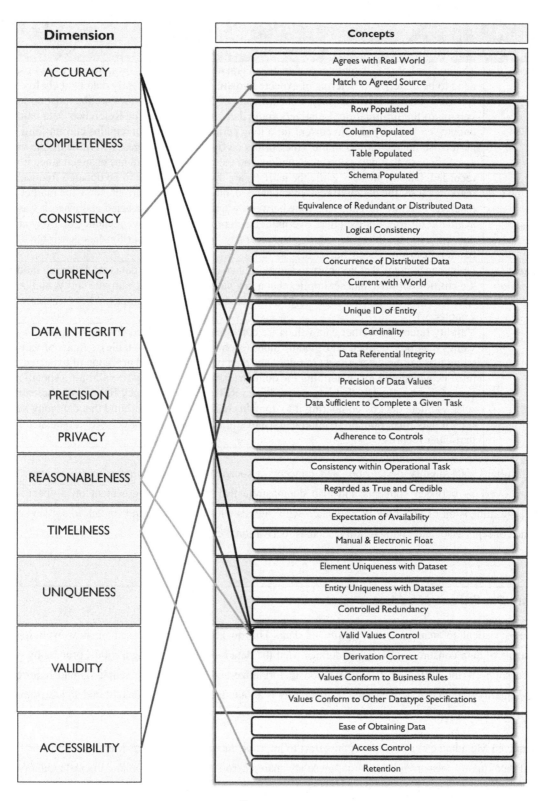

Figure 92 Relationship Between Data Quality Dimensions[77]

---

[77] Adapted from Myers (2013), used with permission.

1.3.5 Data Quality ISO Standard

ISO 8000, the international standard for data quality, is being developed to enable the exchange of complex data in an application-neutral form. In the introduction to the standard, ISO asserts: "The ability to create, collect, store, maintain, transfer, process and present data to support business processes in a timely and cost effective manner requires both an understanding of the characteristics of the data that determine its quality, and an ability to measure, manage and report on data quality."

ISO 8000 defines characteristics that can be tested by any organization in the data supply chain to objectively determine conformance of the data to ISO 8000.[78]

The first published part of ISO 8000 (part 110, published in 2008) focused on the syntax, semantic encoding, and conformance to the data specification of Master Data. Other parts projected for the standard include part 100 - Introduction, part 120 - Provenance, part 130 -Accuracy, and part 140 - Completeness.[79]

ISO defines quality data as "portable data that meets stated requirements."[80] The data quality standard is related to the ISO's overall work on data portability and preservation. Data is considered 'portable' if it can be separated from a software application. Data that can only be used or read using a specific licensed software application is subject to the terms of the software license. An organization may not be able to use data it created unless that data can be detached from the software that was used to create it.

To meet stated requirements requires that these requirements be defined in a clear, unambiguous manner. ISO 8000 is supported through ISO 22745, a standard for defining and exchanging Master Data. ISO 22745 defines how data requirement statements should be constructed, provides examples in XML, and defines a format for the exchange of encoded data.[81] ISO 22745 creates portable data by labeling the data using an ISO 22745 compliant Open Technical Dictionary such as the ECCMA Open Technical Dictionary (eOTD).

The intention of ISO 8000 is to help organizations define what is and is not quality data, enable them to ask for quality data using standard conventions, and verify that they have received quality data using those same standards. When standards are followed, requirements can be confirmed through a computer program.

ISO 8000 - Part 61 Information and data quality management process reference model is under development.[82] This standard will describe the structure and organization of data quality management, including:

- Data Quality Planning
- Data Quality Control
- Data Quality Assurance
- Data Quality Improvement

---

78 http://bit.ly/2ttdiZJ.

79 http://bit.ly/2sANGdi.

80 http://bit.ly/2rV1oWC.

81 http://bit.ly/2rUZyoz.

82 http://bit.ly/2sVik3Q.

1.3.6 Data Quality Improvement Lifecycle

Most approaches to improving data quality are based on the techniques of quality improvement in the manufacture of physical products.[83] In this paradigm, data is understood as the product of a set of processes. At its simplest, a process is defined as a series of steps that turns inputs into outputs. A process that creates data may consist of one-step (data collection) or many steps: data collection, integration into a data warehouse, aggregation in a data mart, etc. At any step, data can be negatively affected. It can be collected incorrectly, dropped or duplicated between systems, aligned or aggregated incorrectly, etc. Improving data quality requires the ability to assess the relationship between inputs and outputs, in order to ensure that inputs meet the requirements of the process and that outputs conform to expectations. Since outputs from one process become inputs to other processes, requirements must be defined along the whole data chain.

A general approach to data quality improvement, shown in Figure 93, is a version of the Shewhart / Deming cycle.[84] Based on the scientific method, the Shewhart / Deming cycle is a problem-solving model known as 'plan-do-check-act'. Improvement comes through a defined set of steps. The condition of data must be measured against standards and, if it does not meet standards, root cause(s) of the discrepancy from standards must be identified and remediated. Root causes may be found in any of the steps of the process, technical or non-technical. Once remediated, data should be monitored to ensure that it continues to meet requirements.

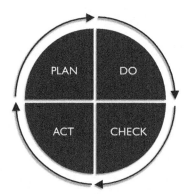

Figure 93 The Shewhart Chart

For a given data set, a Data Quality Management cycle begins by identifying the data that does not meet data consumers' requirements and data issues that are obstacles to the achievement of business objectives. Data needs to be assessed against key dimensions of quality and known business requirements. Root causes of issues will need to be identified so that stakeholders can understand the costs of remediation and the risks of not remediating the issues. This work is often done in conjunction with Data Stewards and other stakeholders.

In the *Plan* stage, the Data Quality team assesses the scope, impact, and priority of known issues, and evaluates alternatives to address them. This plan should be based on a solid foundation of analysis of the root causes of issues. From knowledge of the causes and the impact of the issues, cost / benefit can be understood, priority can be determined, and a basic plan can be formulated to address them.

---

[83] See Wang (1998), English (1999), Redman (2001), Loshin (2001), and McGilvray (2008). See Pierce (2004) for an overview of literature related to the concept of data as a product.

[84] See American Society for Quality: http://bit.ly/1lelyBK Plan-Do-Check-Act was originated by Walter Shewhart and popularized by W. Edwards Deming. 6 Sigma's Measure, Analyze, Improve, Control (DMAIC) is a variation on this cycle.

In the *Do* stage, the DQ team leads efforts to address the root causes of issues and plan for ongoing monitoring of data. For root causes that are based on non-technical processes, the DQ team can work with process owners to implement changes. For root causes that require technical changes, the DQ team should work with technical teams to ensure that requirements are implemented correctly and that technical changes do not introduce errors.

The *Check* stage involves actively monitoring the quality of data as measured against requirements. As long as data meets defined thresholds for quality, additional actions are not required. The processes will be considered under control and meeting business requirements. However, if the data falls below acceptable quality thresholds, then additional action must be taken to bring it up to acceptable levels.

The *Act* stage is for activities to address and resolve emerging data quality issues. The cycle restarts, as the causes of issues are assessed and solutions proposed. Continuous improvement is achieved by starting a new cycle. New cycles begin as:

- Existing measurements fall below thresholds
- New data sets come under investigation
- New data quality requirements emerge for existing data sets
- Business rules, standards, or expectations change

The cost of getting data right the first time is cheaper than the costs from getting data wrong and fixing it later. Building quality into the data management processes from the beginning costs less than retrofitting it. Maintaining high quality data throughout the data lifecycle is less risky than trying to improve quality in an existing process. It also creates a far lower impact on the organization. Establishing criteria for data quality at the beginning of a process or system build is one sign of a mature Data Management Organization. Doing so takes governance and discipline, as well as cross-functional collaboration.

1.3.7 Data Quality Business Rule Types

Business rules describe how business should operate internally, in order to be successful and compliant with the outside world. Data Quality Business Rules describe how data should exist in order to be useful and usable within an organization. These rules can be aligned with dimensions of quality and used to describe data quality requirements. For example, a business rule that all state code fields must comply with the US State Abbreviations can be enforced by data entry pick lists and data integration lookups. The level of valid or invalid records can then be measured. Business rules are commonly implemented in software, or by using document templates for data entry. Some common simple business rule types are:

- **Definitional conformance**: Confirm that the same understanding of data definitions is implemented and used properly in processes across the organization. Confirmation includes algorithmic agreement on calculated fields, including any time, or local constraints, and rollup and status interdependence rules.

- **Value presence and record completeness**: Rules defining the conditions under which missing values are acceptable or unacceptable.

- **Format compliance**: One or more patterns specify values assigned to a data element, such as standards for formatting telephone numbers.

- **Value domain membership**: Specify that a data element's assigned value is included in those enumerated in a defined data value domain, such as 2-Character United States Postal Codes for a STATE field.

- **Range conformance**: A data element assigned value must be within a defined numeric, lexicographic, or time range, such as greater than 0 and less than 100 for a numeric range.

- **Mapping conformance**: Indicating that the value assigned to a data element must correspond to one selected from a value domain that maps to other equivalent corresponding value domain(s). The STATE data domain again provides a good example, since State values may be represented using different value domains (USPS Postal codes, FIPS 2-digit codes, full names), and these types of rules validate that 'AL' and '01' both map to 'Alabama.'

- **Consistency rules**: Conditional assertions that refer to maintaining a relationship between two (or more) attributes based on the actual values of those attributes. For example, address validation where postal codes correspond to particular States or Provinces.

- **Accuracy verification**: Compare a data value against a corresponding value in a system of record or other verified source (e.g., marketing data purchased from a vendor) to verify that the values match.

- **Uniqueness verification**: Rules that specify which entities must have a unique representation and whether one and only one record exists for each represented real world object.

- **Timeliness validation**: Rules that indicate the characteristics associated with expectations for accessibility and availability of data.

Other types of rules may involve aggregating functions applied to sets of data instances (see Section 4.5). Examples of aggregation checks include:

- Validate reasonableness of the number of records in a file. This requires keeping statistics over time to generate trends.

- Validate reasonableness of an average amount calculated from a set of transactions. This requires establishing thresholds for comparison, and may be based on statistics over time.

- Validate the expected variance in the count of transactions over a specified timeframe. This requires keeping statistics over time and using them to establish thresholds.

1.3.8 Common Causes of Data Quality Issues

Data quality issues can emerge at any point in the data lifecycle, from creation to disposal. When investigating root causes, analysts should look for potential culprits, like problems with data entry, data processing, system design, and manual intervention in automated processes. Many issues will have multiple causes and contributing factors (especially if people have created ways to work around them). These causes of issues also imply ways to prevent issues: through improvement to interface design, testing of data quality rules as part of processing, a focus on data quality within system design, and strict controls on manual intervention in automated processes.

1.3.8.1 Issues Caused by Lack of Leadership

Many people assume that most data quality issues are caused by data entry errors. A more sophisticated understanding recognizes that gaps in or poor execution of business and technical processes cause many more problems than mis-keying. However, common sense says and research indicates that many data quality problems are caused by a lack of organizational commitment to high quality data, which itself stems from a lack of leadership, in the form of both governance and management.

Every organization has information and data assets that are of value to its operations. Indeed, the operations of every organization depend on the ability to share information. Despite this, few organizations manage these assets with rigor. Within most organizations, data disparity (differences in data structure, format, and use of values) is a larger problem than just simple errors; it can be a major obstacle to the integration of data. One of the reasons data stewardship programs focus on defining terms and consolidating the language around data is because that is the starting point for getting to more consistent data.

Many governance and information asset programs are driven solely by compliance, rather than by the potential value to be derived from data as an asset. A lack of recognition on the part of leadership means a lack of commitment within an organization to managing data as an asset, including managing its quality (Evans and Price, 2012). (See Figure 94.)

Barriers to effective management of data quality include:[85]

- Lack of awareness on the part of leadership and staff
- Lack of business governance
- Lack of leadership and management
- Difficulty in justification of improvements
- Inappropriate or ineffective instruments to measure value

These barriers have negative effects on customer experience, productivity, morale, organizational effectiveness, revenue, and competitive advantage. They increase costs of running the organization and introduce risks as well. (See Chapter 11.)

1.3.8.2 Issues Caused by Data Entry Processes

- **Data entry interface issues**: Poorly designed data entry interfaces can contribute to data quality issues. If a data entry interface does not have edits or controls to prevent incorrect data from being put in the system data processors are likely to take shortcuts, such as skipping non-mandatory fields and failing to update defaulted fields.

- **List entry placement**: Even simple features of data entry interfaces, such as the order of values within a drop-down list, can contribute to data entry errors.

---

[85] Adapted from *The Leader's Data Manifesto*. https://dataleaders.org/.

- **Field overloading**: Some organizations re-use fields over time for different business purposes rather than making changes to the data model and user interface. This practice results in inconsistent and confusing population of the fields.

- **Training issues**: Lack of process knowledge can lead to incorrect data entry, even if controls and edits are in place. If data processors are not aware of the impact of incorrect data or if they are incented for speed, rather than accuracy, they are likely to make choices based on drivers other than the quality of the data.

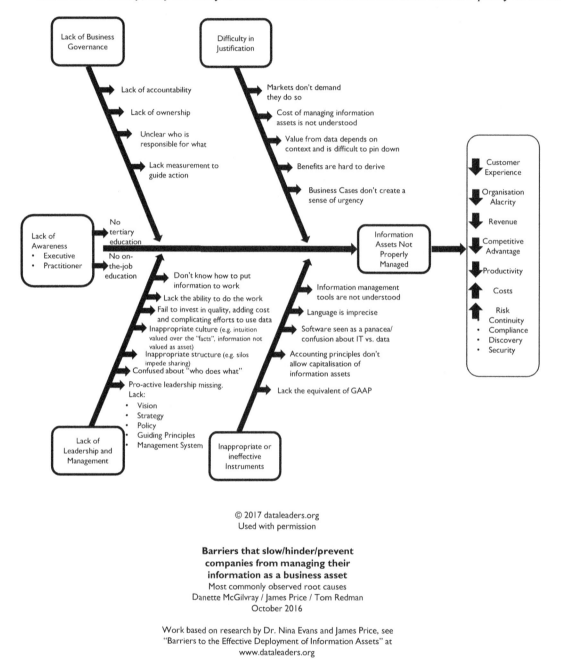

© 2017 dataleaders.org
Used with permission

**Barriers that slow/hinder/prevent
companies from managing their
information as a business asset**
Most commonly observed root causes
Danette McGilvray / James Price / Tom Redman
October 2016

Work based on research by Dr. Nina Evans and James Price, see
"Barriers to the Effective Deployment of Information Assets" at
www.dataleaders.org

Figure 94 Barriers to Managing Information as a Business Asset[86]

---

[86] Diagram developed by Danette McGilvray, James Price, and Tom Redman. Used by permission. https://dataleaders.org/.

- **Changes to business processes**: Business processes change over time, and with these changes new business rules and data quality requirements are introduced. However, business rule changes are not always incorporated into systems in a timely manner or comprehensively. Data errors will result if an interface is not upgraded to accommodate new or changed requirements. In addition, data is likely to be impacted unless changes to business rules are propagated throughout the entire system.

- **Inconsistent business process execution**: Data created through processes that are executed inconsistently is likely to be inconsistent. Inconsistent execution may be due to training or documentation issues as well as to changing requirements.

1.3.8.3 Issues Caused by Data Processing Functions

- **Incorrect assumptions about data sources**: Production issues can occur due to errors or changes, inadequate or obsolete system documentation, or inadequate knowledge transfer (for example, when SMEs leave without documenting their knowledge). System consolidation activities, such as those associated with mergers and acquisitions, are often based on limited knowledge about the relationship between systems. When multiple source systems and data feeds need to be integrated there is always a risk that details will be missed, especially with varying levels of source knowledge available and tight timelines.

- **Stale business rules**: Over time, business rules change. They should be periodically reviewed and updated. If there is automated measurement of rules, the technical process for measuring rules should also be updated. If it is not updated, issues may not be identified or false positives will be produced (or both).

- **Changed data structures**: Source systems may change structures without informing downstream consumers (both human and system) or without providing sufficient time to account for the changes. This can result in invalid values or other conditions that prevent data movement and loading, or in more subtle changes that may not be detected immediately.

1.3.8.4 Issues Caused by System Design

- **Failure to enforce referential integrity**: Referential integrity is necessary to ensure high quality data at an application or system level. If referential integrity is not enforced or if validation is switched off (for example, to improve response times), various data quality issues can arise:

  - Duplicate data that breaks uniqueness rules
  - Orphan rows, which can be included in some reports and excluded from others, leading to multiple values for the same calculation
  - Inability to upgrade due to restored or changed referential integrity requirements
  - Inaccurate data due to missing data being assigned default values

- **Failure to enforce uniqueness constraints**: Multiple copies of data instances within a table or file expected to contain unique instances. If there are insufficient checks for uniqueness of instances, or if the unique constraints are turned off in the database to improve performance, data aggregation results can be overstated.

- **Coding inaccuracies and gaps**: If the data mapping or layout is incorrect, or the rules for processing the data are not accurate, the data processed will have data quality issues, ranging from incorrect calculations to data being assigned to or linked to improper fields, keys, or relationships.

- **Data model inaccuracies**: If assumptions within the data model are not supported by the actual data, there will be data quality issues ranging from data loss due to field lengths being exceeded by the actual data, to data being assigned to improper IDs or keys.

- **Field overloading**: Re-use of fields over time for different purposes, rather than changing the data model or code can result in confusing sets of values, unclear meaning, and potentially, structural problems, like incorrectly assigned keys.

- **Temporal data mismatches**: In the absence of a consolidated data dictionary, multiple systems could implement disparate date formats or timings, which in turn lead to data mismatch and data loss when data synchronization takes place between different source systems.

- **Weak Master Data Management**: Immature Master Data Management can lead to choosing unreliable sources for data, which can cause data quality issues that are very difficult to find until the assumption that the data source is accurate is disproved.

- **Data duplication**: Unnecessary data duplication is often a result of poor data management. There are two main types of undesirable duplication issues:

  - **Single Source – Multiple Local Instances**: For example, instances of the same customer in multiple (similar or identical) tables in the same database. Knowing which instance is the most accurate for use can be difficult without system-specific knowledge.
  - **Multiple Sources – Single Instance**: Data instances with multiple authoritative sources or systems of record. For example, single customer instances coming from multiple point-of-sale systems. When processing this data for use, there can be duplicate temporary storage areas. Merge rules determine which source has priority over others when processing into permanent production data areas.

1.3.8.5 Issues Caused by Fixing Issues

Manual data patches are changes made directly on the data in the database, not through the business rules in the application interfaces or processing. These are scripts or manual commands generally created in a hurry and used to 'fix' data in an emergency such as intentional injection of bad data, lapse in security, internal fraud, or external source for business disruption.

Like any untested code, they have a high risk of causing further errors through unintended consequences, by changing more data than required, or not propagating the patch to all historical data affected by the original issue. Most such patches also change the data in place, rather than preserving the prior state and adding corrected rows.

These changes are generally NOT undo-able without a complete restore from backup as there is only the database log to show the changes. Therefore, these shortcuts are strongly discouraged – they are opportunities for security breaches and business disruption longer than a proper correction would cause. All changes should go through a governed change management process.

1.3.9 Data Profiling

Data Profiling is a form of data analysis used to inspect data and assess quality. Data profiling uses statistical techniques to discover the true structure, content, and quality of a collection of data (Olson, 2003). A profiling engine produces statistics that analysts can use to identify patterns in data content and structure. For example:

- **Counts of nulls**: Identifies nulls exist and allows for inspection of whether they are allowable or not
- **Max/Min value**: Identifies outliers, like negatives
- **Max/Min length**: Identifies outliers or invalids for fields with specific length requirements
- **Frequency distribution** of values for individual columns: Enables assessment of reasonability (e.g., distribution of country codes for transactions, inspection of frequently or infrequently occurring values, as well as the percentage of the records populated with defaulted values)
- **Data type and format**: Identifies level of non-conformance to format requirements, as well as identification of unexpected formats (e.g., number of decimals, embedded spaces, sample values)

Profiling also includes cross-column analysis, which can identify overlapping or duplicate columns and expose embedded value dependencies. Inter-table analysis explores overlapping values sets and helps identify foreign key relationships. Most data profiling tools allow for drilling down into the analyzed data for further investigation.

Results from the profiling engine must be assessed by an analyst to determine whether data conforms to rules and other requirements. A good analyst can use profiling results to confirm known relationships and uncover hidden characteristics and patterns within and between data sets, including business rules, and validity constraints. Profiling is usually used as part of data discovery for projects (especially data integration projects; see Chapter 8) or to assess the current state of data that is targeted for improvement. Results of data profiling can be used to identify opportunities to improve the quality of both data and Metadata (Olson, 2003; Maydanchik, 2007).

While profiling is an effective way to understand data, it is just a first step to data quality improvement. It enables organizations to identify potential problems. Solving problems requires other forms of analysis, including business process analysis, analysis of data lineage, and deeper data analysis that can help isolate root causes of problems.

1.3.10 Data Quality and Data Processing

While the focus of data quality improvement efforts is often on the prevention of errors, data quality can also be improved through some forms of data processing. (See Chapter 8.)

1.3.10.1 Data Cleansing

Data Cleansing or *Scrubbing* transforms data to make it conform to data standards and domain rules. Cleansing includes detecting and correcting data errors to bring the quality of data to an acceptable level.

It costs money and introduces risk to continuously remediate data through cleansing. Ideally, the need for data cleansing should decrease over time, as root causes of data issues are resolved. The need for data cleansing can be addressed by:

- Implementing controls to prevent data entry errors
- Correcting the data in the source system
- Improving the business processes that create the data

In some situations, correcting on an ongoing basis may be necessary, as re-processing the data in a midstream system is cheaper than any other alternative.

1.3.10.2 Data Enhancement

Data enhancement or enrichment is the process of adding attributes to a data set to increase its quality and usability. Some enhancements are gained by integrating data sets internal to an organization. External data can also be purchased to enhance organizational data (see Chapter 10). Examples of data enhancement include:

- **Time/Date stamps**: One way to improve data is to document the time and date that data items are created, modified, or retired, which can help to track historical data events. If issues are detected with the data, timestamps can be very valuable in root cause analysis, because they enable analysts to isolate the timeframe of the issue.

- **Audit data**: Auditing can document data lineage, which is important for historical tracking as well as validation.

- **Reference vocabularies**: Business specific terminology, ontologies, and glossaries enhance understanding and control while bringing customized business context.

- **Contextual information**: Adding context such as location, environment, or access methods and tagging data for review and analysis.

- **Geographic information**: Geographic information can be enhanced through address standardization and geocoding, which includes regional coding, municipality, neighborhood mapping, latitude / longitude pairs, or other kinds of location-based data.

- **Demographic information**: Customer data can be enhanced through demographic information, such as age, marital status, gender, income, or ethnic coding. Business entity data can be associated with annual revenue, number of employees, size of occupied space, etc.

- **Psychographic information**: Data used to segment the target populations by specific behaviors, habits, or preferences, such as product and brand preferences, organization memberships, leisure activities, commuting transportation style, shopping time preferences, etc.

- **Valuation information**: Use this kind of enhancement for asset valuation, inventory, and sale.

1.3.10.3 Data Parsing and Formatting

Data Parsing is the process of analyzing data using pre-determined rules to define its content or value. Data parsing enables the data analyst to define sets of patterns that feed into a rule engine used to distinguish between valid and invalid data values. Matching specific pattern(s) triggers actions.

Data parsing assigns characteristics to the data values appearing in a data instance, and those characteristics help in determining potential sources for added benefits. For example, if an attribute called 'name' can be determined to have values belonging to 'business name' embedded within it, then the data value is identified as the name of a business rather than the name of a person. Use the same approach for any situation in which data values organize into semantic hierarchies such as sub-parts, parts, and assemblies.

Many data quality issues involve situations where variation in data values representing similar concepts introduces ambiguity. Extract and rearrange the separate components (commonly referred to as 'tokens') can be extracted and rearranged into a standard representation to create a valid pattern. When an invalid pattern is recognized, the application may attempt to transform the invalid value into one that meets the rules. Perform standardization by mapping data from some source pattern into a corresponding target representation.

For example, consider the different ways telephone numbers expected to conform to a numbering plan are formatted. While some have digits, some have alphabetic characters, and all use different special characters for separation. People can recognize each one as a telephone number. However, to determine if these numbers are accurate (perhaps by comparing them to a master customer directory), or to investigate whether duplicate numbers exist when there should be only one for each supplier, the values must be parsed into their component segments (area code, exchange, and line number) and then transformed into a standard format.

Another good example is a customer name, since names may be represented in thousands of different forms. A good standardization tool will be able to parse the different components of a customer name, such as given name, middle name, family name, initials, titles, generational designations, and then rearrange those components into a canonical representation that other data services will be able to manipulate.

The human ability to recognize familiar patterns contributes to an ability to characterize variant data values belonging to the same abstract class of values; people recognize different types of telephone numbers because they conform to frequently used patterns. An analyst describes the format patterns that all represent a data object, such as **Person Name**, **Product Description**, and so on. A data quality tool parses data values that conform to any of those patterns, and even transforms them into a single, standardized form that will simplify the assessment, similarity analysis, and remediation processes. Pattern-based parsing can automate the recognition and subsequent standardization of meaningful value components.

1.3.10.4 Data Transformation and Standardization

During normal processing, data rules trigger and transform the data into a format that is readable by the target architecture. However, readable does not always mean acceptable. Rules are created directly within a data integration stream, or rely on alternate technologies embedded in or accessible from within a tool.

Data transformation builds on these types of standardization techniques. Guide rule-based transformations by mapping data values in their original formats and patterns into a target representation. Parsed components of a pattern are subjected to rearrangement, corrections, or any changes as directed by the rules in the knowledge base. In fact, standardization is a special case of transformation, employing rules that capture context, linguistics, and idioms recognized as common over time, through repeated analysis by the rules analyst or tool vendor. (See Chapter 3.)

2. Activities

2.1 Define High Quality Data

Many people recognize poor quality data when they see it. Fewer are able to define what they mean by high quality data. Alternatively, they define it in very general term: "The data has to be right." "We need accurate data." High quality data is fit for the purposes of data consumers. Before launching a Data Quality program, it is beneficial to understand business needs, define terms, identify organizational pain points, and start to build consensus about the drivers and priorities for data quality improvement. Ask a set of questions to understand current state and assess organizational readiness for data quality improvement:

- What do stakeholders mean by 'high quality data'?
- What is the impact of low quality data on business operations and strategy?
- How will higher quality data enable business strategy?
- What priorities drive the need for data quality improvement?
- What is the tolerance for poor quality data?
- What governance is in place to support data quality improvement?
- What additional governance structures will be needed?

Getting a comprehensive picture of the current state of data quality in an organization requires approaching the question from different perspectives:

- An understanding of business strategy and goals
- Interviews with stakeholders to identify pain points, risks, and business drivers
- Direct assessment of data, through profiling and other form of analysis
- Documentation of data dependencies in business processes
- Documentation of technical architecture and systems support for business processes

This kind of assessment can reveal a significant number of opportunities. These need to be prioritized based on the potential benefit to the organization. Using input from stakeholders, including Data Stewards and business and technical SMEs, the Data Quality team should define the meaning of data quality and propose program priorities.

2.2 Define a Data Quality Strategy

Improving data quality requires a strategy that accounts for the work that needs to be done and the way people will execute it. Data quality priorities must align with business strategy. Adopting or developing a framework and methodology will help guide both strategy and tactics while providing a means to measure progress and impacts. A framework should include methods to:

- Understand and prioritize business needs
- Identify the data critical to meeting business needs
- Define business rules and data quality standards based on business requirements
- Assess data against expectations
- Share findings and get feedback from stakeholders
- Prioritize and manage issues
- Identify and prioritize opportunities for improvement
- Measure, monitor, and report on data quality
- Manage Metadata produced through data quality processes
- Integrate data quality controls into business and technical processes

A framework should also account for how to organize for data quality and how to leverage data quality tools. As noted in the chapter introduction, improving data quality requires a Data Quality program team to engage business and technical staff and define a program of work that addresses critical issues, defines best practices, and puts in place operational processes that support ongoing management of data quality. Often such a team will be part of the Data Management Organization. DQ analysts will need to work closely with Data Stewards at all levels. They should also influence policy, including policy about business processes and systems development. However, such a team will not be able to solve all of an organization's data quality challenges. DQ work and a commitment to high quality data need to become embedded in organizational practices. The DQ Strategy should account for how to extend best practices. (See Chapter 17.)

2.3 Identify Critical Data and Business Rules

Not all data is of equal importance. Data Quality Management efforts should focus first on the most important data in the organization: data that, if it were of higher quality, would provide greater value to the organization and its customers. Data can be prioritized based on factors such as regulatory requirements, financial value, and direct impact on customers. Often, data quality improvement efforts start with Master Data, which is, by definition, among the most important data in any organization. The result of the importance analysis is a ranked list of data, which the Data Quality team can use to focus their work efforts.

Having identified the critical data, Data Quality analysts need to identify business rules that describe or imply expectations about the quality characteristics of data. Often rules themselves are not explicitly documented. They may need to be reverse-engineered through analysis of existing business processes, workflows, regulations, policies, standards, system edits, software code, triggers and procedures, status code assignment and use, and plain old common sense. For example, if a marketing company wants to target efforts at people in a specific demographic, then potential indexes of data quality might be the level and reasonability of population in demographic fields like birth date, age, gender, and household income.

Most business rules are associated with how data is collected or created, but data quality measurement centers around whether data is fit for use. The two (data creation and data use) are related. People want to use data because of what it represents and why it was created. For example, to understand an organization's sales performance during a specific quarter or over time depends on having reliable data about the sales process (number and type of units sold, volume sold to existing customers vs. new customers, etc.).

It is not possible to know all the ways that data might be used, but it is possible to understand the process and rules by which data was created or collected. Measurements that describe whether data is fit for use should be developed in relation to known uses and measurable rules based on dimensions of data quality: completeness, conformity, validity, integrity, etc. that provide the basis for meaningful metrics. Dimensions of quality enable analysts to characterize both rules (field X is mandatory and must be populated) and findings (e.g., the field is not populated in 3% of the records; the data is only 97% complete).

At the field or column level, rules can be straightforward. Completeness rules are a reflection of whether a field is mandatory or optional, and, if optional, the conditions under which it should be populated. Validity rules are dependent on stipulating the domain of valid values and, in some cases, the relationship between fields. For example, a US ZIP Code needs to be valid, in and of itself, and correctly associated with a US State code. Rules should also be defined at the data set level. For example, every customer must have a valid mailing address.

Defining data quality rules is challenging because most people are not used to thinking about data in terms of rules. It may be necessary to get at the rules indirectly, by asking stakeholders about the input and output requirements of a business process. It also helps to ask about pain points, what happens when data is missing or incorrect, how they identify issues, how they recognize bad data, etc. Keep in mind that it is not necessary to know all the rules in order to assess data. Discovery and refinement of rules is an ongoing process. One of the best ways to get at rules is to share results of assessments. These results often give stakeholders a new perspective on the data from which they can articulate rules that tell them what they need to know about the data.

2.4 Perform an Initial Data Quality Assessment

Once the most critical business needs and the data that supports them have been identified, the most important part of the data quality assessment is actually looking at that data, querying it to understand data content and relationships, and comparing actual data to rules and expectations. The first time this is done, analysts will discover many things: undocumented relationships and dependencies within the data, implied rules, redundant data, contradictory data, etc., as well as data that actually does conform to rules. With the help of data stewards, other SMEs, and data consumers, DQ analysts will need to sort out and prioritize findings.

The goal of an initial data quality assessment is to learn about the data in order to define an actionable plan for improvement. It is usually best to start with a small, focused effort – a basic proof of concept – to demonstrate how the improvement process works. Steps include:

- Define the goals of the assessment; these will drive the work
- Identify the data to be assessed; focus should be on a small data set, even a single data element, or a specific data quality problem
- Identify uses of the data and the consumers of the data

- Identify known risks with the data to be assessed, including the potential impact of data issues on organizational processes
- Inspect the data based on known and proposed rules
- Document levels of non-conformance and types of issues
- Perform additional, in-depth analysis based on initial findings in order to
  - Quantify findings
  - Prioritize issues based on business impact
  - Develop hypotheses about root causes of data issues
- Meet with Data Stewards, SMEs, and data consumers to confirm issues and priorities
- Use findings as a foundation for planning
  - Remediation of issues, ideally at their root causes
  - Controls and process improvements to prevent issues from recurring
  - Ongoing controls and reporting

2.5 Identify and Prioritize Potential Improvements

Having proven that the improvement process can work, the next goal is to apply it strategically. Doing so requires identifying and prioritizing potential improvements. Identification may be accomplished by full-scale data profiling of larger data sets to understand the breadth of existing issues. It may also be accomplished by other means, such as interviewing stakeholders about the data issues that impact them and following up with analysis of the business impact of those issues. Ultimately, prioritization requires a combination of data analysis and discussion with stakeholders.

The steps to perform a full data profiling and analysis are essentially the same as those in performing a small-scale assessment: define goals, understand data uses and risks, measure against rules, document and confirm findings with SMEs, use this information to prioritize remediation and improvement efforts. However, there are sometimes technical obstacles to full-scale profiling. And the effort will need to be coordinated across a team of analysts and overall results will need to be summarized and understood if an effective action plan is to be put in place. Large-scale profiling efforts, like those on a smaller scale, should still focus on the most critical data.

Profiling data is only the first step in analysis of data quality issues. It helps identify issues, but does not identify root causes, nor does it determine the impact of issues to business processes. Determining impact requires input from stakeholders along the data chain. When planning large scale profiling, ensure that time is allocated to share results, prioritize problems, and determine which issues require in-depth analysis.

2.6 Define Goals for Data Quality Improvement

The knowledge obtained through the preliminary assessments forms the basis for specific Data Quality program goals. Improvement can take different forms, from simple remediation (e.g., correction of errors on records) to remediation of root causes. Remediation and improvement plans should account for quick hits – issues that can be addressed immediately at low cost – and longer-term strategic changes. The strategic focus of such plans should be to address root causes of issues and to put in place mechanisms to prevent issues in the first place.

Be aware that many things can get in the way of improvement efforts: system constraints, age of data, ongoing project work that uses the questionable data, overall complexity of the data landscape, cultural resistance to change. To prevent these constraints from stalling the program, set specific, achievable goals based on consistent quantification of the business value of the improvements to data quality.

For example, a goal may be to improve the completeness of customer data from 90% to 95% based on process improvements and system edits. Obviously, showing improvement will involve comparing initial measurements and improved results. But the value comes with benefits of the improvement: fewer customer complaints, less time spent correcting errors, etc. Measure these things to explain the value of the improvement work. No one cares about levels of field completeness unless there is a business impact. There must be a positive return on investment for improvements to data. When issues are found, determine ROI of fixes based on:

- The criticality (importance ranking) of the data affected
- Amount of data affected
- The age of the data
- Number and type of business processes impacted by the issue
- Number of customers, clients, vendors, or employees impacted by the issue
- Risks associated with the issue
- Costs of remediating root causes
- Costs of potential work-arounds

In assessing issues, especially those where root causes are identified and technical changes are required, always seek out opportunities to prevent issues from recurring. Preventing issues generally costs less than correcting them – sometimes orders of magnitude less. (See Chapter 11.)

2.7 Develop and Deploy Data Quality Operations

Many Data Quality programs get started through a set of improvement projects identified via results of the data quality assessment. In order to sustain data quality, a DQ program should put in place a plan that allows the team to manage data quality rules and standards, monitor data's ongoing conformance with rules, identify and manage data quality issues, and report on quality levels. In support of these activities, DQ analysts and Data Stewards will also be engaged in activities such as documenting data standards and business rules and establishing data quality requirements for vendors.

2.7.1 Manage Data Quality Rules

The process of profiling and analyzing data will help an organization discover (or reverse engineer) business and data quality rules. As the data quality practice matures, the capture of such rules should be built into the system development and enhancement process. Defining rules upfront will:

- Set clear expectations for data quality characteristics

- Provide requirements for system edits and controls that prevent data issues from being introduced

- Provide data quality requirements to vendors and other external parties

- Create the foundation for ongoing data quality measurement and reporting

In short, data quality rules and standards are a critical form of Metadata. To be effective, they need to be managed as Metadata. Rules should be:

- **Documented consistently**: Establish standards and templates for documenting rules so that they have a consistent format and meaning.

- **Defined in terms of Data Quality dimensions**: Dimensions of quality help people understand what is being measured. Consistent application of dimensions will help with the measurement and issue management processes.

- **Tied to business impact**: While data quality dimensions enable understanding of common problems, they are not a goal in-and-of-themselves. Standards and rules should be connected directly to their impact on organizational success. Measurements that are not tied to business processes should not be taken.

- **Backed by data analysis**: Data Quality Analysts should not guess at rules. Rules should be tested against actual data. In many cases, rules will show that there are issues with the data. But analysis can also show that the rules themselves are not complete.

- **Confirmed by SMEs**: The goal of the rules is to describe how the data should look. Often, it takes knowledge of organizational processes to confirm that rules correctly describe the data. This knowledge comes when subject matter experts confirm or explain the results of data analysis.

- **Accessible to all data consumers**: All data consumers should have access to documented rules. Such access allows them to better understand the data. It also helps to ensure that the rules are correct and complete. Ensure that consumers have a means to ask questions about and provide feedback on rules.

2.7.2 Measure and Monitor Data Quality

The operational Data Quality Management procedures depend on the ability to measure and monitor the quality of data. There are two equally important reasons to implement operational data quality measurements:

- To inform data consumers about levels of quality
- To manage risk that change may be introduced through changes to business or technical processes

Some measurements serve both purposes. Measurements should be developed based on findings from data assessment and root cause analysis. Measurements intended to inform data consumers will focus on critical data elements and relationships that, if they are not sound, will directly impact business processes. Measurements related to managing risk should focus on relationships that have gone wrong in the past and may go wrong in the future. For example, if data is derived based on a set of ETL rules and those rules may be impacted by changes to business processes, measurements should be put in place to detect changes to the data.

Knowledge of past problems should be applied to manage risk. For example, if numerous data issues are associated with complex derivations, then all derivations should be assessed – even those that have not been associated with data issues. In most cases, it is worthwhile to put in place measurements that monitor functions similar to those that have had problems.

Measurement results can be described at two levels: the detail related to the execution of individual rules and overall results aggregated from the rules. Each rule should have a standard, target, or threshold index for comparison. This function most often reflects the percentage of correct data or percentage of exceptions depending on the formula used. For example:

$$ValidDQI(r) = \frac{\big(TestExecutions(r) - ExceptionsFound(r)\big)}{TestExecutions(r)}$$

$$InvalidDQI(r) = \frac{\big(ExceptionsFound(r)\big)}{TestExecutions(r)}$$

R represents the rule being tested. For example, 10,000 tests of a business rule (r) found 560 exceptions. In this example, the ValidDQ result would be 9440/10,000 = 94.4%, and the Invalid DQ result would be 560/10,000 = 5.6%.

Organizing the metrics and results as shown in Table 30 can help to structure measures, metrics, and indicators across the report, reveal possible rollups, and enhance communications. The report can be more formalized and linked to projects that will remediate the issues. Filtered reports are useful for data stewards looking for trends and contributions. Table 30 provides examples of rules constructed in this manner. Where applicable, results of rules are expressed in both positive percentages (the portion of the data that conforms to rules and expectations) and negative percentages (the portion of the data that does not conform to the rule).

Data quality rules provide the foundation for operational management of data quality. Rules can be integrated into application services or data services that supplement the data lifecycle, either through Commercial Off The Shelf (COTS) data quality tools, rules engines and reporting tools for monitoring and reporting, or custom-developed applications.

Table 30 DQ Metric Examples

Dimension and Business Rule	Measure	Metrics	Status Indicator
Completeness Business Rule 1: Population of field is mandatory	Count the number of records where data is populated, compare to the total number of records	Divide the obtained number of records where data is populated by the total number of records in the table or database and multiply it by 100 to get to percentage complete	Unacceptable: Below 80% populated Above 20% not populated
Example 1: Postal Code must be populated in the address table	Count populated: 700,000 Count not populated: 300,000 Total count: 1,000,000	Positive measure: 700,000/1,000,000*100 = 70% populated Negative measure: 300,000/1,000,000 *100 = 30% not populated	Example result: Unacceptable
Uniqueness Business Rule 2: There should be only one record per entity instance in a table	Count the number of duplicate records identified; report on the percentage of records that represent duplicates	Divide the number of duplicate records by the total number of records in the table or database and multiply it by 100	Unacceptable: Above 0%

Dimension and Business Rule	Measure	Metrics	Status Indicator
Example 2: There should be one and only one current row per postal code on the Postal Codes master list	Count of duplicates: 1,000 Total Count: 1,000,000	10,000/1,000,000*100 = 1.0% of postal codes are present on more than one current row	Example result: Unacceptable
Timeliness Business Rule 3: Records must arrive within a scheduled timeframe	Count the number of records failing to arrive on time from a data service for business transactions to be completed	Divide the number of incomplete transactions by the total number of attempted transactions in a time period and multiply by 100	Unacceptable: Below 99% completed on time Above 1% not completed on time
Example 3: Equity market record should arrive within 5 minutes of being transacted	Count of incomplete transactions: 2000 Count of attempted transactions: 1,000,000	Positive: (1,000,000 – 2000) / 1,000,000*100 = 99.8% of transaction records arrived within defined timeframe Negative: 2000/1,000,000*100 = 0.20% of transactions did not arrive within defined timeframe	Example Result: Acceptable
Validity Business Rule 4: If field X = value 1, then field Y must = value 1-prime	Count the number of records where the rule is met	Divide the number of records that meet the condition by the total number of records	Unacceptable : Below 100% adherence to the rule
Example 4: Only shipped orders should be billed	Count of records where status for shipping = Shipped and status for billing = Billed: 999,000 Count of total records: 1,000,000	Positive: 999,000/1,000,000*100 = 99.9% of records conform to the rule Negative: (1,000,000-999,000) / 1,000,000 *100 = 0.10% do not conform to the rule	Example Result: Unacceptable

Provide continuous monitoring by incorporating control and measurement processes into the information processing flow. Automated monitoring of conformance to data quality rules can be done in-stream or through a batch process. Measurements can be taken at three levels of granularity: the data element value, data instance or record, or the data set. Table 31 describes techniques for collecting data quality measurements.

Table 31 Data Quality Monitoring Techniques

Granularity	In-stream (In-Process Flow) Treatment	Batch Treatment
Data Element	Edit checks in application Data element validation services Specially programmed applications	Direct queries Data profiling or analyzer tool
Data Record	Edit checks in application Data record validation services Specially programmed applications	Direct queries Data profiling or analyzer tool
Data set	Inspection inserted between processing stages	Direct queries Data profiling or analyzer tool

In-stream measurements can be taken while creating data or handing data off between processing stages. Batch queries can be performed on collections of data instances assembled in a data set, usually in persistent storage. Data set measurements generally cannot be taken in-stream, since the measurement may need the entire set.

Incorporating the results of the control and measurement processes into both the operational procedures and reporting frameworks enables continuous monitoring of the levels of data quality for feedback and improvement to the data generation/collection activities.

2.7.3 Develop Operational Procedures for Managing Data Issues

Whatever tools are used to monitor data quality, when results are assessed by Data Quality team members, they need to respond to findings in a timely and effective manner. The team must design and implement detailed operational procedures for:

- **Diagnosing issues**: The objective is to review the symptoms of the data quality incident, trace the lineage of the data in question, identify the problem and where it originated, and pinpoint potential root causes of the problem. The procedure should describe how the Data Quality Operations team would:

  - Review the data issues in the context of the appropriate information processing flows and isolate the location in the process where the flaw is introduced
  - Evaluate whether there have been any environmental changes that would cause errors entering into the system
  - Evaluate whether or not there are any other process issues that contributed to the data quality incident
  - Determine whether there are issues with external data that have affected the quality of the data

  NOTE: The work of root cause analysis requires input from technical and business SMEs. While the DQ team may lead and facilitate this kind of work effort, success requires cross-functional collaboration

- **Formulating options for remediation**: Based on the diagnosis, evaluate alternatives for addressing the issue. These may include:

  - Addressing non-technical root causes such as lack of training, lack of leadership support, unclear accountability and ownership, etc.
  - Modification of the systems to eliminate technical root causes
  - Developing controls to prevent the issue
  - Introducing additional inspection and monitoring
  - Directly correcting flawed data
  - Taking no action based on the cost and impact of correction versus the value of the data correction

- **Resolving issues**: Having identified options for resolving the issue, the Data Quality team must confer with the business data owners to determine the best way to resolve the issue. These procedures should detail how the analysts:

  - Assess the relative costs and merits of the alternatives
  - Recommend one of the planned alternatives
  - Provide a plan for developing and implementing the resolution
  - Implement the resolution

Decisions made during the issue management process should be tracked in an incident tracking system. When the data in such a system is managed well, it can provide valuable insight about the causes and costs of data issues. Include a description of the issue and the root causes, options for remediation, and the decision on how to resolve the issue.

The incident tracking system will collect performance data relating to issue resolution, work assignments, volume of issues, frequency of occurrence, as well as the time to respond, diagnose, plan a solution, and resolve issues. These metrics can provide valuable insights into the effectiveness of the current workflow, as well as systems and resource utilization, and they are important management data points that can drive continuous operational improvement for data quality control.

Incident tracking data also helps data consumers. Decisions based upon remediated data should be made with knowledge that it has been changed, why it has been changed, and how it has been changed. That is one reason why it is important to record the methods of modification and the rationale for them. Make this documentation available to data consumers and developers researching code changes. While changes may be obvious to the people who implement them, the history of changes will be lost to future data consumers unless it is documented. Data quality incident tracking requires staff be trained on how issues should be classified, logged, and tracked. To support effective tracking:

- **Standardize data quality issues and activities**: Since the terms used to describe data issues may vary across lines of business, it is valuable to define a standard vocabulary for the concepts used. Doing so will simplify classification and reporting. Standardization also makes it easier to measure the volume of issues and activities, identify patterns and interdependencies between systems and participants, and report on the overall impact of data quality activities. The classification of an issue may change as the investigation deepens and root causes are exposed.

- **Provide an assignment process for data issues**: The operational procedures direct the analysts to assign data quality incidents to individuals for diagnosis and to provide alternatives for resolution. Drive the assignment process within the incident tracking system by suggesting those individuals with specific areas of expertise.

- **Manage issue escalation procedures**: Data quality issue handling requires a well-defined system of escalation based on the impact, duration, or urgency of an issue. Specify the sequence of escalation within the data quality Service Level Agreement. The incident tracking system will implement the escalation procedures, which helps expedite efficient handling and resolution of data issues.

- **Manage data quality resolution workflow**: The data quality SLA specifies objectives for monitoring, control, and resolution, all of which define a collection of operational workflows. The incident tracking system can support workflow management to track progress with issues diagnosis and resolution.

2.7.4 Establish Data Quality Service Level Agreements

A data quality Service Level Agreement (SLA) specifies an organization's expectations for response and remediation for data quality issues in each system. Data quality inspections as scheduled in the SLA help to identify issues to fix, and over time, reduce the number of issues. While enabling the isolation and root cause analysis of data flaws, there is an expectation that the operational procedures will provide a scheme for remediation of root causes within an agreed timeframe. Having data quality inspection and monitoring in place increases the likelihood of detection and remediation of a data quality issue before a significant business impact can occur. Operational data quality control defined in a data quality SLA includes:

- Data elements covered by the agreement
- Business impacts associated with data flaws
- Data quality dimensions associated with each data element
- Expectations for quality for each data element for each of the identified dimensions in each application or system in the data value chain
- Methods for measuring against those expectations
- Acceptability threshold for each measurement
- Steward(s) to be notified in case the acceptability threshold is not met
- Timelines and deadlines for expected resolution or remediation of the issue
- Escalation strategy, and possible rewards and penalties

The data quality SLA also defines the roles and responsibilities associated with performance of operational data quality procedures. The operational data quality procedures provide reports in conformance with the defined business rules, as well as monitoring staff performance in reacting to data quality incidents. Data stewards and the operational data quality staff, while upholding the level of data quality service, should consider their data quality SLA constraints and connect data quality to individual performance plans.

When issues are not addressed within the specified resolution times, an escalation process must exist to communicate non-observance of the level of service up the management and governance chain. The data quality SLA establishes the time limits for notification generation, the names of those in that management chain, and when escalation needs to occur. Given the set of data quality rules, methods for measuring conformance, the acceptability thresholds defined by the business clients, and the service level agreements, the Data Quality team can monitor compliance of the data to the business expectations, as well as how well the Data Quality team performs on the procedures associated with data errors.

SLA reporting can be on a scheduled basis driven by business and operational requirements. Particular focus will be on report trend analysis in cases focused on periodic rewards and penalties if such concepts are built into the SLA framework.

2.7.5 Develop Data Quality Reporting

The work of assessing the quality of data and managing data issues will not benefit the organization unless the information is shared through reporting so that data consumers understand the condition of the data. Reporting should focus around:

- Data quality scorecard, which provides a high-level view of the scores associated with various metrics, reported to different levels of the organization within established thresholds
- Data quality trends, which show over time how the quality of data is measured, and whether trending is up or down

- SLA Metrics, such as whether operational data quality staff diagnose and respond to data quality incidents in a timely manner
- Data quality issue management, which monitors the status of issues and resolutions
- Conformance of the Data Quality team to governance policies
- Conformance of IT and business teams to Data Quality policies
- Positive effects of improvement projects

Reporting should align to metrics in the data quality SLA as much as possible, so that the team's goals are aligned with those of its customers. The Data Quality program should also report on the positive effects of improvement projects. It is best to do this in business terms to continually remind the organization of the direct effect that data has on customers.

3. Tools

Tools should be selected and tool architectures should be set in the planning phase of the enterprise Data Quality program. Tools provide a partial rule set starter kit but organizations need to create and input their own context specific rules and actions into any tool.

3.1 Data Profiling Tools

Data profiling tools produce high-level statistics that enable analysts to identify patterns in data and perform initial assessment of quality characteristics. Some tools can be used to perform ongoing monitoring of data. Profiling tools are particularly important for data discovery efforts because they enable assessment of large data sets. Profiling tools augmented with data visualization capabilities will aid in the process of discovery. (See Chapters 5 and 8, and Section 1.3.9.)

3.2 Data Querying Tools

Data profiling is only the first step in data analysis. It helps identify potential issues. Data Quality team members also need to query data more deeply to answer questions raised by profiling results and find patterns that provide insight into root causes of data issues. For example, querying to discover and quantify other aspects of data quality, such as uniqueness and integrity.

3.3 Modeling and ETL Tools

The tools used to model data and create ETL processes have a direct impact on the quality of data. If used with the data in mind, these tools can enable higher quality data. If they are used without knowledge of the data, they can have detrimental effects. DQ team members should work with development teams to ensure that data quality risks are addressed and that the organization takes full advantage of the ways in which effective modeling and data processing can enable higher quality data. (See Chapters 5, 8, and 11.)

3.4 Data Quality Rule Templates

Rule templates allow analyst to capture expectations for data. Templates also help bridge the communications gap between business and technical teams. Consistent formulation of rules makes it easier to translate business needs into code, whether that code is embedded in a rules engine, the data analyzer component of a data-profiling tool, or a data integration tool. A template can have several sections, one for each type of business rule to implement.

3.5 Metadata Repositories

As noted in Section 1.3.4, defining data quality requires Metadata and definitions of high quality data are a valuable kind of Metadata. DQ teams should work closely with teams that manage Metadata to ensure that data quality requirements, rules, measurement results, and documentation of issues are made available to data consumers.

4. Techniques

4.1 Preventive Actions

The best way to create high quality data is to prevent poor quality data from entering an organization. Preventive actions stop known errors from occurring. Inspecting data after it is in production will not improve its quality. Approaches include:

- **Establish data entry controls**: Create data entry rules that prevent invalid or inaccurate data from entering a system.

- **Train data producers**: Ensure staff in upstream systems understand the impact of their data on downstream users. Give incentives or base evaluations on data accuracy and completeness, rather than just speed.

- **Define and enforce rules**: Create a 'data firewall,' which has a table with all the business data quality rules used to check if the quality of data is good, before being used in an application such a data warehouse. A data firewall can inspect the level of quality of data processed by an application, and if the level of quality is below acceptable levels, analysts can be informed about the problem.

- **Demand high quality data from data suppliers**: Examine an external data provider's processes to check their structures, definitions, and data source(s) and data provenance. Doing so enables assessment of how well their data will integrate and helps prevent the use of non-authoritative data or data acquired without permission from the owner.

- **Implement Data Governance and Stewardship**: Ensure roles and responsibilities are defined that describe and enforce rules of engagement, decision rights, and accountabilities for effective management of data and information assets (McGilvray, 2008). Work with data stewards to revise the process of, and mechanisms for, generating, sending, and receiving data.

- **Institute formal change control**: Ensure all changes to stored data are defined and tested before being implemented. Prevent changes directly to data outside of normal processing by establishing gating processes.

4.2 Corrective Actions

Corrective actions are implemented after a problem has occurred and been detected. Data quality issues should be addressed systemically and at their root causes to minimize the costs and risks of corrective actions. 'Solve the problem where it happens' is the best practice in Data Quality Management. This generally means that corrective actions should include preventing recurrence of the causes of the quality problems.

Perform data correction in three general ways:

- **Automated correction**: Automated correction techniques include rule-based standardization, normalization, and correction. The modified values are obtained or generated and committed without manual intervention. An example is automated address correction, which submits delivery addresses to an address standardizer that conforms and corrects delivery addresses using rules, parsing, standardization, and reference tables. Automated correction requires an environment with well-defined standards, commonly accepted rules, and known error patterns. The amount of automated correction can be reduced over time if this environment is well-managed and corrected data is shared with upstream systems.

- **Manually-directed correction**: Use automated tools to remediate and correct data but require manual review before committing the corrections to persistent storage. Apply name and address remediation, identity resolution, and pattern-based corrections automatically, and use some scoring mechanism to propose a level of confidence in the correction. Corrections with scores above a particular level of confidence may be committed without review, but corrections with scores below the level of confidence are presented to the data steward for review and approval. Commit all approved corrections, and review those not approved to understand whether to adjust the applied underlying rules. Environments in which sensitive data sets require human oversight (e.g., MDM) are good examples of where manual-directed correction may be suited.

- **Manual correction**: Sometimes manual correction is the only option in the absence of tools or automation or if it is determined that the change is better handled through human oversight. Manual corrections are best done through an interface with controls and edits, which provide an audit trail for changes. The alternative of making corrections and committing the updated records directly in production environments is extremely risky. Avoid using this method.

4.3 Quality Check and Audit Code Modules

Create shareable, linkable, and re-usable code modules that execute repeated data quality checks and audit processes that developers can get from a library. If the module needs to change, then all the code linked to that module will get updated. Such modules simplify the maintenance process. Well-engineered code blocks can prevent many data quality problems. As importantly, they ensure processes are executed consistently. Where laws or policy mandate reporting of specific quality results, the lineage of results often needs to be described. Quality check modules can provide this. For data that has any questionable quality dimension and that is highly rated, qualify the information in the shared environments with quality notes, and confidence ratings.

4.4 Effective Data Quality Metrics

A critical component of managing data quality is developing metrics that inform data consumers about quality characteristics that are important to their uses of data. Many things can be measured, but not all of them are worth the time and effort. In developing metrics, DQ analysts should account for these characteristics:

- **Measurability**: A data quality metric must be measurable – it needs to be something that can be counted. For example, data relevancy is not measurable, unless clear criteria are set for what makes data relevant. Even data completeness needs to be objectively defined in order to be measured. Expected results should be quantifiable within a discrete range.

- **Business relevance**: While many things are measurable, not all translate into useful metrics. Measurements need to be relevant to data consumers. The value of the metric is limited if it cannot be related to some aspect of business operations or performance. Every data quality metric should correlate with the influence of the data on key business expectations.

- **Acceptability**: The data quality dimensions frame the business requirements for data quality. Quantifying along the identified dimension provides hard evidence of data quality levels. Determine whether data meets business expectations based on specified acceptability thresholds. If the score is equal to or exceeds the threshold, the quality of the data meets business expectations. If the score is below the threshold, it does not.

- **Accountability / Stewardship**: Metrics should be understood and approved by key stakeholders (e.g., business owners and Data Stewards). They are notified when the measurement for the metric shows that the quality does not meet expectations. The business data owner is accountable, while a data steward takes appropriate corrective action.

- **Controllability**: A metric should reflect a controllable aspect of the business. In other words, if the metric is out of range, it should trigger action to improve the data. If there is no way to respond, then the metric is probably not useful.

- **Trending**: Metrics enable an organization to measure data quality improvement over time. Tracking helps Data Quality team members monitor activities within the scope of a data quality SLA and data sharing agreement, and demonstrate the effectiveness of improvement activities. Once an information process is stable, statistical process control techniques can be applied to detect changes to the predictability of the measurement results and the business and technical processes on which it provides insight.

4.5 Statistical Process Control

Statistical Process Control (SPC) is a method to manage processes by analyzing measurements of variation in process inputs, outputs, or steps. The technique was developed in the manufacturing sector in the 1920s and has been applied in other industries, in improvement methodologies such as Six Sigma, and in Data Quality Management.[87] Simply defined, a process is a series of steps executed to turn inputs into outputs. SPC is based on the assumption that when a process with consistent inputs is executed consistently, it will produce consistent outputs. It uses measures of central tendency (how values cluster around a central value, such as a mean, median, or mode) and of variability around a central value (e.g., range, variance, standard deviation), to establish tolerances for variation within a process.

The primary tool used for SPC is the control chart (Figure 95), which is a time series graph that includes a central line for the average (the measure of central tendency) and depicts calculated upper and lower control limits (variability around a central value). In a stable process, measurement results outside the control limits indicate a special cause.

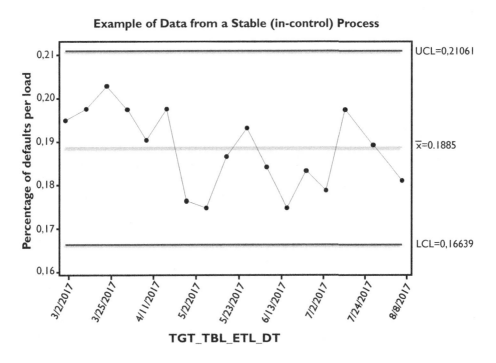

Figure 95 Control Chart of a Process in Statistical Control

SPC measures the predictability of process outcomes by identifying variation within a process. Processes have variation of two types: Common Causes that are inherent in the process and Special Causes that are unpredictable

---

[87] See Redman (1996 and 2001), Loshin (2000), Sebastian-Coleman (2013), Jugulum (2014).

or intermittent. When the only sources of variation are common causes, a system is said to be in (statistical) control and a range of normal variation can be established. This is the baseline against which change can be detected.

Applying SPC to data quality measurement is based on the working assumption that, like a manufactured product, data is the product of a process. Sometimes the process that creates data is very simple (e.g., a person fills out a form). Other times, processes are quite complex: a set of algorithms aggregates medical claim data in order to follow trends related to the effectiveness of particular clinical protocols. If such a process has consistent inputs and is executed consistently, it will produce consistent results each time it is run. However, if the inputs or execution change, then so will the outputs. Each of these components can be measured. The measurements can be used to detect special causes. Knowledge of the special causes can be used to mitigate risks associated with data collection or processing.

SPC is used for control, detection, and improvement. The first step is to measure the process in order to identify and eliminate special causes. This activity establishes the control state of the process. Next is to put in place measurements to detect unexpected variation as soon as it is detectable. Early detection of problems simplifies investigation of their root causes. Measurements of the process can also be used to reduce the unwanted effects of common causes of variation, allowing for increased efficiency.

4.6 Root Cause Analysis

A root cause of a problem is a factor that, if eliminated, would remove the problem itself. Root cause analysis is a process of understanding factors that contribute to problems and the ways they contribute. Its purpose is to identify underlying conditions that, if eliminated, would mean problems would disappear.

A data management example may clarify the definition. Let's say a data process that runs each month requires as input a file of customer information. Measurement of the data shows that in April, July, October, and January, the quality of the data goes down. Inspection of the timing of delivery shows that in March, June, September, and December, the file is delivered on the 30th of the month, whereas at other times it is delivered on the 25th. Further analysis shows that the team responsible for delivering the file is also responsible for closing quarterly financial processes. These processes take precedence over other work and the files are delivered late during those months, impacting the quality. The root cause of the data quality problem turns out to be a process delay caused by a competing priority. It can be addressed by scheduling file delivery and ensuring that resources can deliver within the schedule.

Common techniques for root cause analysis include Pareto analysis (the 80/20 rule), fishbone diagram analysis, track and trace, process analysis, and the Five Whys (McGilvray, 2008).

5. Implementation Guidelines

Improving the quality of data within an organization is not an easy task – even when data quality improvement efforts are launched from within a data governance program and with the support of senior management. A classic academic discussion is whether it is better to implement a Data Quality program top-down or bottom-up. Typically, a hybrid approach works best – top-down for sponsorship, consistency, and resources, but bottom-up to discover what is actually broken and to achieve incremental successes.

Improving data quality requires changes in how people think about and behave toward data. Cultural change is challenging. It requires planning, training, and reinforcement. (See Chapter 17.) While the specifics of cultural change will differ from organization to organization, most Data Quality program implementations need to plan for:

- **Metrics on the value of data and the cost of poor quality data**: One way to raise organizational awareness of the need for Data Quality Management is through metrics that describe the value of data and the return on investment from improvements. These metrics (which differ from data quality scores) provide the basis for funding improvements and changing the behavior of both staff and management. (See Chapter 11.)

- **Operating model for IT/Business interactions**: Business people know what the important data is, and what it means. Data Custodians from IT understand where and how the data is stored, and so they are well placed to translate definitions of data quality into queries or code that identify specific records that do not comply. (See Chapter 11.)

- **Changes in how projects are executed**: Project oversight must ensure project funding includes steps related to data quality (e.g., profiling and assessment, definition of quality expectations, data issue remediation, prevention and correction, building controls and measurements). It is prudent to make sure issues are identified early and to build data quality expectations upfront in projects.

- **Changes to business processes**: Improving data quality depends on improving the processes by which data is produced. The Data Quality team needs to be able to assess and recommend changes to non-technical (as well as technical) processes that impact the quality of data.

- **Funding for remediation and improvement projects**: Some organizations do not plan for remediating data, even when they are aware of data quality issues. Data will not fix itself. The costs and benefits of remediation and improvement projects should be documented so that work on improving data can be prioritized.

- **Funding for Data Quality Operations**: Sustaining data quality requires ongoing operations to monitor data quality, report on findings, and continue to manage issues as they are discovered.

5.1 Readiness Assessment / Risk Assessment

Most organizations that depend on data have a lot of opportunity for improvement. How formal and well-supported a Data Quality program will be depends on how mature the organization is from a data management perspective. (See Chapter 15.) Organizational readiness to adopt data quality practices can be assessed by considering the following characteristics:

- **Management commitment to managing data as a strategic asset**: As part of asking for support for a Data Quality program, it is import to determine how well senior management understands the role that data plays in the organization. To what degree does senior management recognize the value of data to strategic goals? What risks do they associate with poor quality data? How knowledgeable are they about the benefits of data governance? How optimistic about the ability to change culture to support quality improvement?

- **The organization's current understanding of the quality of its data**: Before most organizations start their quality improvement journey, they generally understand the obstacles and pain points that signify poor quality data. Gaining knowledge of these is important. Through them, poor quality data can be directly associated with negative effects, including direct and indirect costs, on the organization. An understanding of pain points also helps identify and prioritize improvement projects.

- **The actual state of the data**: Finding an objective way to describe the condition of data that is causing pain points is the first step to improving the data. Data can be measured and described through profiling and analysis, as well as through quantification of known issues and pain points. If the DQ team does not know the actual state of the data, then it will be difficult to prioritize and act on opportunities for improvement.

- **Risks associated with data creation, processing, or use**: Identifying what can go wrong with data and the potential damage to an organization from poor quality data provides the basis for mitigating risks. If the organization does not recognize these risks, it may be challenging to get support for the Data Quality program.

- **Cultural and technical readiness for scalable data quality monitoring**: The quality of data can be negatively impacted by business and technical processes. Improving the quality of data depends on cooperation between business and IT teams. If the relationship between business and IT teams is not collaborative, then it will be difficult to make progress.

Findings from a readiness assessment will help determine where to start and how quickly to proceed. Findings can also provide the basis for road-mapping program goals. If there is strong support for data quality improvement and the organization knows its own data, then it may be possible to launch a full strategic program. If the organization does not know the actual state of its data, then it may be necessary to focus on building that knowledge before developing a full strategy.

5.2 Organization and Cultural Change

The quality of data will not be improved through a collection of tools and concepts, but through a mindset that helps employees and stakeholders to act while always thinking of the quality of data and what the business and their customers need. Getting an organization to be conscientious about data quality often requires significant cultural change. Such change requires vision and leadership. (See Chapter 17.)

The first step is promoting awareness about the role and importance of data to the organization. All employees must act responsibly and raise data quality issues, ask for good quality data as consumers, and provide quality information to others. Every person who touches the data can impact the quality of that data. Data quality is not just the responsibility of a DQ team or IT group.

Just as the employees need to understand the cost to acquire a new customer or retain an existing customer, they also need to know the organizational costs of poor quality data, as well as the conditions that cause data to be of poor quality. For example, if customer data is incomplete, a customer may receive the wrong product, creating direct and indirect costs to an organization. Not only will the customer return the product, but he or she may call and complain, using call center time, with the potential for reputational damage to the organization. If customer data is incomplete because the organization has not established clear requirements, then everyone who uses this data has a stake in clarifying requirements and following standards.

Ultimately, employees need to think and act differently if they are to produce better quality data and manage data in ways that ensures quality. This requires training and reinforcement. Training should focus on:

- Common causes of data problems
- Relationships within the organization's data ecosystem and why improving data quality requires an enterprise approach
- Consequences of poor quality data
- Necessity for ongoing improvement (why improvement is not a one-time thing)
- Becoming 'data-lingual', about to articulate the impact of data on organizational strategy and success, regulatory reporting, customer satisfaction

Training should also include an introduction to any process changes, with assertions about how the changes improve data quality.

6. Data Quality and Data Governance

A Data Quality program is more effective when part of a data governance program. Often data quality issues are the reason for establishing enterprise-wide data governance (see Chapter 3). Incorporating data quality efforts into the overall governance effort enables the Data Quality program team to work with a range of stakeholders and enablers:

- Risk and security personnel who can help identify data-related organizational vulnerabilities
- Business process engineering and training staff who can help teams implement process improvements
- Business and operational data stewards, and data owners who can identify critical data, define standards and quality expectations, and prioritize remediation of data issues

A Governance Organization can accelerate the work of a Data Quality program by:

- Setting priorities
- Identifying and coordinating access to those who should be involved in various data quality-related decisions and activities
- Developing and maintaining standards for data quality
- Reporting relevant measurements of enterprise-wide data quality
- Providing guidance that facilitates staff involvement
- Establishing communications mechanisms for knowledge-sharing
- Developing and applying data quality and compliance policies

- Monitoring and reporting on performance
- Sharing data quality inspection results to build awareness, identify opportunities for improvements, and build consensus for improvements
- Resolving variations and conflicts; providing direction

6.1 Data Quality Policy

Data Quality efforts should be supported by and should support data governance policies. For example, governance policies can authorize periodic quality audits and mandate compliance to standards and best practices. All Data Management Knowledge Areas require some level of policy, but data quality policies are particularly important as they often touch on regulatory requirements. Each policy should include:

- Purpose, scope and applicability of the policy
- Definitions of terms
- Responsibilities of the Data Quality program
- Responsibilities of other stakeholders
- Reporting
- Implementation of the policy, including links to risk, preventative measures, compliance, data protection, and data security

6.2 Metrics

Much of the work of a Data Quality team will focus on measuring and reporting on quality. High-level categories of data quality metrics include:

- **Return on Investment**: Statements on cost of improvement efforts vs. the benefits of improved data quality

- **Levels of quality**: Measurements of the number and percentage of errors or requirement violations within a data set or across data sets

- **Data Quality trends**: Quality improvement over time (i.e., a trend) against thresholds and targets, or quality incidents per period

- **Data issue management metrics**:
  - Counts of issues by dimensions of data quality
  - Issues per business function and their statuses (resolved, outstanding, escalated)
  - Issue by priority and severity
  - Time to resolve issues

- **Conformance to service levels**: Organizational units involved and responsible staff, project interventions for data quality assessments, overall process conformance

- **Data Quality plan rollout**: As-is and roadmap for expansion

7. Works Cited / Recommended

Batini, Carlo, and Monica Scannapieco. *Data Quality: Concepts, Methodologies and Techniques.* Springer, 2006. Print.

Brackett, Michael H. *Data Resource Quality: Turning Bad Habits into Good Practices.* Addison-Wesley, 2000. Print.

Deming, W. Edwards. *Out of the Crisis.* The MIT Press, 2000. Print.

English, Larry. *Improving Data Warehouse and Business Information Quality: Methods For Reducing Costs And Increasing Profits.* John Wiley and Sons, 1999. Print.

English, Larry. *Information Quality Applied: Best Practices for Improving Business Information, Processes, and Systems.* Wiley Publishing, 2009. Print.

Evans, Nina and Price, James. "Barriers to the Effective Deployment of Information Assets: An Executive Management Perspective." *Interdisciplinary Journal of Information, Knowledge, and Management* Volume 7, 2012. Accessed from http://bit.ly/2sVwvG4.

Fisher, Craig, Eitel Lauría, Shobha Chengalur-Smith and Richard Wang. *Introduction to Information Quality.* M.I.T. Information Quality Program Publications, 2006. Print. Advances in Information Quality Book Ser.

Gottesdiener, Ellen. *Requirements by Collaboration: Workshops for Defining Needs.* Addison-Wesley Professional, 2002. Print.

Hass, Kathleen B. and Rosemary Hossenlopp. *Unearthing Business Requirements: Elicitation Tools and Techniques.* Management Concepts, Inc, 2007. Print. Business Analysis Essential Library.

Huang, Kuan-Tsae, Yang W. Lee and Richard Y. Wang. *Quality Information and Knowledge.* Prentice Hall, 1999. Print.

Jugulum, Rajesh. *Competing with High Quality Data.* Wiley, 2014. Print.

Lee, Yang W., Leo L. Pipino, James D. Funk and Richard Y. Wang. *Journey to Data Quality.* The MIT Press, 2006. Print.

Loshin, David. *Enterprise Knowledge Management: The Data Quality Approach.* Morgan Kaufmann, 2001. Print.

Loshin, David. *Master Data Management.* Morgan Kaufmann, 2009. Print.

Maydanchik, Arkady. *Data Quality Assessment.* Technics Publications, LLC, 2007 Print.

McCallum, Ethan. *Bad Data Handbook: Cleaning Up the Data So You Can Get Back to Work.* 1st Edition. O'Reilly, 2012.

McGilvray, Danette. *Executing Data Quality Projects: Ten Steps to Quality Data and Trusted Information.* Morgan Kaufmann, 2008. Print.

Myers, Dan. "The Value of Using the Dimensions of Data Quality", *Information Management,* August 2013. http://bit.ly/2tsMYiA.

Olson, Jack E. *Data Quality: The Accuracy Dimension.* Morgan Kaufmann, 2003. Print.

Redman, Thomas. *Data Quality: The Field Guide.* Digital Press, 2001. Print.

Robertson, Suzanne and James Robertson. *Mastering the Requirements Process: Getting Requirements Right.* 3rd ed. Addison-Wesley Professional, 2012. Print.

Sebastian-Coleman, Laura. *Measuring Data Quality for Ongoing Improvement: A Data Quality Assessment Framework.* Morgan Kaufmann, 2013. Print. The Morgan Kaufmann Series on Business Intelligence.

Tavares, Rossano. Qualidade de Dados em Gerenciamento de Clientes (CRM) e Tecnologia da Informação [Data Quality in Management of Customers and Information Technology]. São Paulo: Catálise. 2006. Print.

Witt, Graham. *Writing Effective Business Rules: A Practical Method.* Morgan Kaufmann, 2012. Print.

CHAPTER 14

Big Data and Data Science

1. Introduction

Since the early 2000s, the terms *Big Data* and *Data Science* have, unfortunately, been bandied about as buzzwords. The concepts and their implications are misunderstood – or, at least, there is limited consensus on their meaning. Even the meaning of 'Big' is relative. That said, both Big Data and Data Science are connected to significant technological changes that have allowed people to generate, store, and analyze larger and larger amounts of data. More importantly, people can use that data to predict and influence behavior, as well as to gain insight on a range of important subjects, such as health care practices, natural resource management, and economic development.

Big Data refers not only to the volume of data, but also to its variety (structured and unstructured, documents, files, audio, video, and streaming data, etc.), and the speed at which it is produced (velocity). People who mine and develop predictive, machine learning, and prescriptive models and analytics from these and deploy results for analysis by interested parties are called Data Scientists.

Data Science has existed for a long time; it used to be called 'applied statistics'. But the capability to explore data patterns has quickly evolved in the twenty-first century with the advent of Big Data and the technologies that support it. Traditional Business Intelligence provides 'rear-view mirror' reporting – analysis of structured data to describe past trends. In some cases, BI patterns are used to predict future behavior, but not with high confidence. Until recently, in-depth analysis of enormous data sets has been limited by technology. Analyses have relied on sampling or other means of abstraction to approximate patterns. As the capacity to collect and analyze large data sets has grown, Data Scientists have integrated methods from mathematics, statistics, computer science, signal processing, probability modeling, pattern recognition, machine learning, uncertainty modeling, and data visualization in order to gain insight and predict behaviors based on Big Data sets. In short, Data Science has found new ways to analyze and get value from data.

As Big Data has been brought into data warehousing and Business Intelligence environments, Data Science techniques are used to provide a forward-looking ('windshield') view of the organization. Predictive capabilities, real-time and model-based, using different types of data sources, offer organizations better insight into where they are heading. (See Figure 96.)

To take advantage of Big Data, however, requires change in the way that data is managed. Most data warehouses are based on relational models. Big Data is not generally organized in a relational model. Most data warehousing depends on the concept of ETL (Extract, Transform, and Load). Big Data solutions, like data lakes, depend on the concept of ELT – loading and then transforming. As importantly, the speed and volume of data present challenges that require different approaches to critical aspects of data management, such as integration, Metadata Management, and Data Quality assessment.

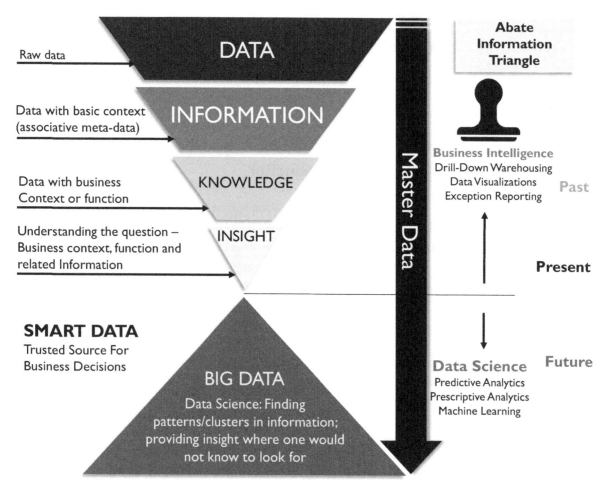

Figure 96 Abate Information Triangle

1.1 Business Drivers

The biggest business driver for developing organizational capabilities around Big Data and Data Science is the desire to find and act on business opportunities that may be discovered through data sets generated through a diversified range of processes. Big Data can stimulate innovation by making more and larger data sets available for exploration. This data can be used to define predictive models that anticipate customer needs and enable personalized presentation of products and services. Data Science can improve operations. Machine learning algorithms can automate complex time-consuming activities, thus improving organizational efficiency, reducing costs, and mitigating risks.

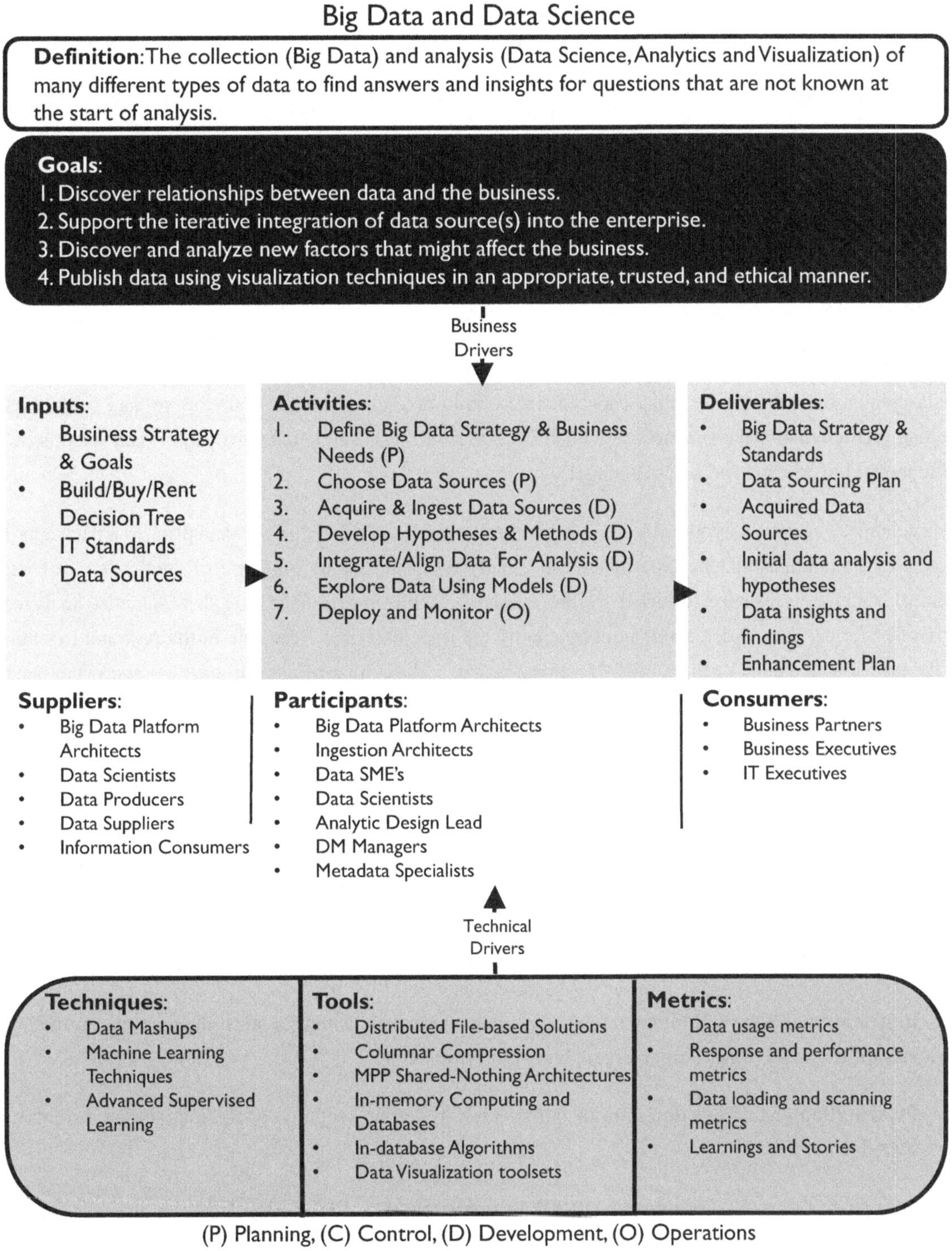

Big Data and Data Science

Definition: The collection (Big Data) and analysis (Data Science, Analytics and Visualization) of many different types of data to find answers and insights for questions that are not known at the start of analysis.

Goals:
1. Discover relationships between data and the business.
2. Support the iterative integration of data source(s) into the enterprise.
3. Discover and analyze new factors that might affect the business.
4. Publish data using visualization techniques in an appropriate, trusted, and ethical manner.

Business
Drivers

Inputs:
- Business Strategy & Goals
- Build/Buy/Rent Decision Tree
- IT Standards
- Data Sources

Activities:
1. Define Big Data Strategy & Business Needs (P)
2. Choose Data Sources (P)
3. Acquire & Ingest Data Sources (D)
4. Develop Hypotheses & Methods (D)
5. Integrate/Align Data For Analysis (D)
6. Explore Data Using Models (D)
7. Deploy and Monitor (O)

Deliverables:
- Big Data Strategy & Standards
- Data Sourcing Plan
- Acquired Data Sources
- Initial data analysis and hypotheses
- Data insights and findings
- Enhancement Plan

Suppliers:
- Big Data Platform Architects
- Data Scientists
- Data Producers
- Data Suppliers
- Information Consumers

Participants:
- Big Data Platform Architects
- Ingestion Architects
- Data SME's
- Data Scientists
- Analytic Design Lead
- DM Managers
- Metadata Specialists

Consumers:
- Business Partners
- Business Executives
- IT Executives

Technical
Drivers

Techniques:
- Data Mashups
- Machine Learning Techniques
- Advanced Supervised Learning

Tools:
- Distributed File-based Solutions
- Columnar Compression
- MPP Shared-Nothing Architectures
- In-memory Computing and Databases
- In-database Algorithms
- Data Visualization toolsets

Metrics:
- Data usage metrics
- Response and performance metrics
- Data loading and scanning metrics
- Learnings and Stories

(P) Planning, (C) Control, (D) Development, (O) Operations

Figure 97 Context Diagram: Big Data and Data Science

1.2 Principles

The promise of Big Data – that it will provide a different kind of insight – depends on being able to manage Big Data. In many ways, because of the wide variation in sources and formats, Big Data management will require more discipline than relational data management. Principles related to Big Data management have yet to fully form, but one is very clear: Organizations should carefully manage Metadata related to Big Data sources in order to have an accurate inventory of data files, their origins, and their value.

1.3 Essential Concepts

1.3.1 Data Science

As noted in the chapter introduction, Data Science merges data mining, statistical analysis, and machine learning with data integration and data modeling capabilities, to build predictive models that explore data content patterns. Developing predictive models is sometimes called *Data Science* because the data analyst, or data scientist, uses the scientific method to develop and assess a model.

The data scientist develops a hypothesis about behavior that can be observed in the data prior to a particular action. For example, the purchase of one type of item is usually followed by the purchase of another type of item (the purchase of a house is usually followed by the purchase of furniture). Then, the data scientist analyzes large amounts of historical data to determine how frequently the hypothesis has been true in the past and to statistically verify the probable accuracy of the model. If a hypothesis is valid with sufficient frequency, and if the behavior it predicts is useful, then the model may become the basis for an operational intelligence process to predict future behavior, even possibly in real time such as suggestive selling advertisements. Developing Data Science solutions involves the iterative inclusion of data sources into models that develop insights. Data Science depends on:

- **Rich data sources**: Data with the potential to show otherwise invisible patterns in organizational or customer behavior

- **Information alignment and analysis**: Techniques to understand data content and combine data sets to hypothesize and test meaningful patterns

- **Information delivery**: Running models and mathematical algorithms against the data and producing visualizations and other output to gain insight into behavior

- **Presentation of findings and data insights**: Analysis and presentation of findings so that insights can be shared

Table 32 compares the role of traditional DW/BI to predictive and prescriptive analytics that can be achieved through Data Science techniques.

Table 32 Analytics Progression

DW / Traditional BI	Data Science	
Descriptive	Predictive	Prescriptive
Hindsight	Insight	Foresight
Based on history: What happened? Why did it happen?	Based on predictive models: What is likely to happen?	Based on scenarios: What should we do to make things happen?

1.3.2 The Data Science Process

Figure 98 illustrates the iterative phases of the Data Science process. The outputs of each step become the inputs into the next. (See Section 2.)

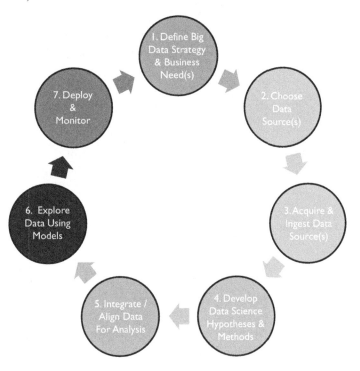

Figure 98 Data Science Process

The Data Science process follows the scientific method of refining knowledge by making observations, formulating and testing hypotheses, observing results, and formulating general theories that explain results. Within Data Science, this process takes the form of observing data and creating and evaluating models of behavior:

- **Define Big Data strategy and business needs**: Define the requirements that identify desired outcomes with measurable tangible benefits.

- **Choose data sources**: Identify gaps in the current data asset base and find data sources to fill those gaps.

- **Acquire and ingest data sources**: Obtain data sets and onboard them.

- **Develop Data Science hypotheses and methods**: Explore data sources via profiling, visualization, mining, etc.; refine requirements. Define model algorithm inputs, types, or model hypotheses and methods of analysis (i.e., groupings of data found by clustering, etc.).

- **Integrate and align data for analysis**: Model feasibility depends in part on the quality of the source data. Leverage trusted and credible sources. Apply appropriate data integration and cleansing techniques to increase quality and usefulness of provisioned data sets.

- **Explore data using models**: Apply statistical analysis and machine learning algorithms against the integrated data. Validate, train, and over time, evolve the model. Training entails repeated runs of the model against actual data to verify assumptions and make adjustments, such as identifying outliers.

Through this process, requirements will be refined. Initial feasibility metrics guide evolution of the model. New hypotheses may be introduced that require additional data sets and results of this exploration will shape the future modeling and outputs (even changing the requirements).

- **Deploy and monitor**: Those models that produce useful information can be deployed to production for ongoing monitoring of value and effectiveness. Often Data Science projects turn into data warehousing projects where more vigorous development processes are put in place (ETL, DQ, Master Data, etc.).

1.3.3 Big Data

Early efforts to define the meaning of Big Data characterized it in terms of the Three V's: Volume, Velocity, Variety (Laney, 2001). As more organizations start to leverage the potential of Big Data, the list of V's has expanded:

- **Volume**: Refers to the amount of data. Big Data often has thousands of entities or elements in billions of records.

- **Velocity**: Refers to the speed at which data is captured, generated, or shared. Big Data is often generated and can also be distributed and even analyzed in real-time.

- **Variety / Variability**: Refers to the forms in which data is captured or delivered. Big Data requires storage of multiple formats; data structure is often inconsistent within or across data sets.

- **Viscosity**: Refers to how difficult the data is to use or integrate.

- **Volatility**: Refers to how often data changes occur and therefore how long the data is useful.

- **Veracity**: Refers to how trustworthy the data is.

Big Data volumes are exceptionally large (greater than 100 Terabyte and often in the Petabyte and Exabyte range). In warehousing and analytic solutions, very large volumes of data pose challenges to data loading, modeling, cleansing, and analytics. These challenges are often solved using massively parallel processing, or parallel processing and distributed data solutions. However, they have much wider implications. The size of data sets requires changes in the overall way that data is stored and accessed, as well as in how data is understood (e.g., much of our current way of thinking about data is based on relational database structures), as well as how data is managed (Adams, 2009). Figure 99 presents a visual summary of the range of data that has become available through Big Data technologies and the implications on data storage options.

1.3.4 Big Data Architecture Components

The selection, installation, and configuration of a Big Data and Data Science environment require specialized expertise. End-to-end architectures must be developed and rationalized against existing data exploratory tools and new acquisitions. Figure 100 describes the DW/BI and Big Data Architecture. (Details about DW/BI components are described in Chapter 11.) The biggest difference between DW/BI and Big Data processing is that in a traditional data warehouse, data is integrated as it is brought into the warehouse (extract, TRANSFORM, load); while in a Big Data environment, data is ingested and loaded before it is integrated (extract, LOAD, transform). In some cases, data may not be integrated at all, in the traditional sense. Instead of being integrated in preparation for use, it is often integrated through particular uses (e.g., the process of building predictive models drives the integration of particular data sets).

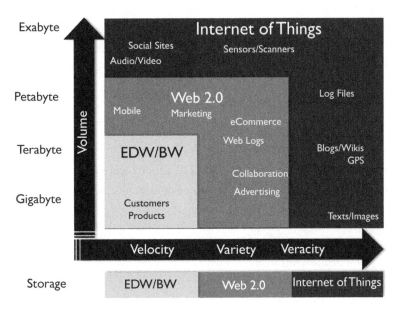

Figure 99 Data Storage Challenges[88]

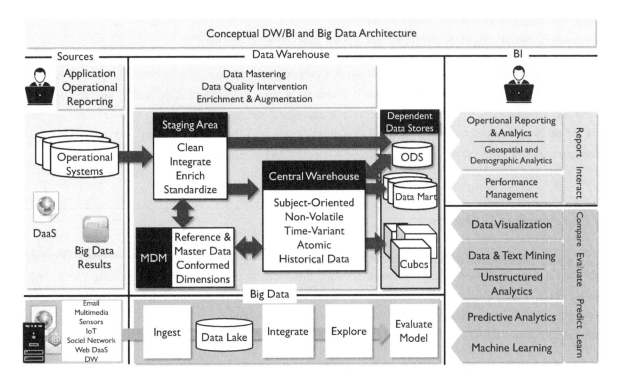

Figure 100 Conceptual DW/BI and Big Data Architecture

---

[88] Sourced and used with permission from Robert Abate / EMC Corporation.

1.3.5 Sources of Big Data

Because so much of human activity is executed electronically, massive amounts of data are accumulating every day as we move through the world, interact with each other, and transact business. Big Data is produced through email, social media, online orders, and even online video games. Data is generated not only by phones and point-of-sale devices, but also by surveillance systems, sensors in transportation systems, medical monitoring systems, industrial and utility monitoring systems, satellites, and military equipment. For example, one airline flight can generate a terabyte of data. Devices that interact directly with the Internet generate a large portion of Big Data. The connections between devices and the Internet are sometimes called the Internet of Things (IoT).

1.3.6 Data Lake

A data lake is an environment where a vast amount of data of various types and structures can be ingested, stored, assessed, and analyzed. Data lakes can serve many purposes. For example, providing

- An environment for Data Scientists to mine and analyze data
- A central storage area for raw data, with minimal, if any, transformation
- Alternate storage for detailed historical data warehouse data
- An online archive for records
- An environment to ingest streaming data with automated pattern identification

A data lake can be implemented as a complex configuration of data handling tools including Hadoop or other data storage systems, cluster services, data transformation, and data integration. These handlers have facilitated cross-infrastructure, analytic facilitation software to bring the configuration together.

The risk of a data lake is that it can quickly become a data swamp – messy, unclean, and inconsistent. In order to establish an inventory of what is in a data lake, it is critical to manage Metadata as the data is ingested. In order to understand how the data in a data lake is associated or connected, data architects or data engineers often use unique keys or other techniques (semantic models, data models, etc.) so that data scientists and other visualization developers know how to use the information stored within the data lake. (See Chapter 9.)

1.3.7 Services-Based Architecture

Services-based architecture (SBA) is emerging as a way to provide immediate (if not completely accurate or complete) data, as well as update a complete, accurate historical data set, using the same source (Abate, Aiken, Burke, 1997). The SBA architecture is similar to the DW architectures which send data directly to an ODS for immediate access, as well as to the DW for historical accumulation. SBA architectures have three main components, a batch layer, a speed layer, and a serving layer. (See Figure 101.)

- **Batch layer**: A data lake serves as the batch layer, containing both recent and historical data
- **Speed layer**: Contains only real-time data
- **Serving layer**: Provides an interface to join data from the batch and speed layers

Data is loaded into both the batch and speed layers. All analytic computations are performed on data in both the batch and speed layers, which most likely requires implementation in two separate systems. Organizations address synchronization issues through trade-offs between completeness, latency, and complexity of merged views defined in the serving layer. Cost/benefit assessment is required to determine whether reducing latency or improving data completeness is worth the associated cost and complexity.

The batch layer is often referred to as the structure-over-time component (here every transaction is an insert), whereas in the speed layer (often referred to as an Operational Data Store or ODS), all transactions are updates (or inserts only if required). In this manner, the architecture prevents synchronization issues while simultaneously creating a current state and a history layer. This architecture usually provides its data through a serving or data services layer that abstracts the data utilizing Metadata. This services layer determines where the data is to be 'served' from and appropriately provides the data requested.

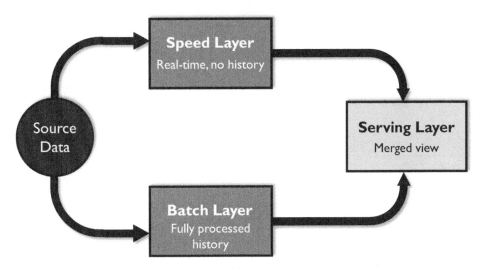

Figure 101 Services-based Architecture

1.3.8 Machine Learning

Machine Learning explores the construction and study of learning algorithms. It can be viewed as a union of unsupervised learning methods, more commonly referred to as data mining, and supervised learning methods deeply rooted in mathematical theory, specifically statistics, combinatorics, and optimization. A third branch is now forming called reinforcement learning, where goal performance is earned but not specifically teacher recognized – driving a vehicle for example. Programming machines to quickly learn from queries and adapt to changing data sets led to a completely new field within Big Data referred to as machine learning.[89] Processes run, and results are stored that are then used in subsequent runs to iteratively inform the process and refine the results.

Machine Learning explores the construction and study of learning algorithms. These algorithms fall into three types:

---

[89] Refer to the Machine Learning resources periodic table at http://bit.ly/1DpTrHC for an interactive guide to the differing platforms available for the machine learning developer, scientist, and practitioner.

- **Supervised learning**: Based on generalized rules; for example, separating SPAM from non-SPAM email
- **Unsupervised learning**: Based on identifying hidden patterns (i.e., data mining)
- **Reinforcement learning**: Based on achieving a goal (e.g., beating an opponent at chess)

Statistical modeling and machine learning have been employed to automate otherwise costly research and development projects, by performing several trial and error passes on a vast set of data, repeating trials with the results collected, analyzed, and errors corrected. This approach can reduce time to answer dramatically and guide organizational initiatives with insights based on cost effective repeatable processes. For example, CIVDDD uses machine learning and complex scientific data visualization techniques to help government agencies and peacekeepers meet the challenge of dealing with the masses of threat-related information.[90]

While it taps into data in new ways, machine learning has ethical implications, especially with respect to the principle of transparency. Evidence shows that deep learning neural networks (DLNN) work. They learn things. However, it is not always clear how they learn. As the algorithms that drive these processes become more complex, they also become more opaque, functioning as 'black boxes'. As they account for a greater number of variables and as those variables themselves are more abstract, algorithms test the limits of human ability to interpret the machine (Davenport, 2017). The need for transparency – the ability to see how decisions are made – will likely increase as this functionality evolves and is put to use in a wider array of situations. (See Chapter 2.)

1.3.9 Sentiment Analysis

Media monitoring and text analysis are automated methods for retrieving insights from large unstructured or semi-structured data, such as transaction data, social media, blogs, and web news sites. This is used to understand what people say and feel about brands, products, or services, or other types of topics. Using Natural Language Processing (NLP) or by parsing phrases or sentences, semantic analysis can detect sentiment and also reveal changes in sentiment to predict possible scenarios.

Consider the case of looking for key words in a posting. If the words *good* or *great* are present, this might be a positive response, versus seeing *awful* or *bad* might be signs that this could be a negative response. Categorizing the data into the types of responses, the 'sentiment' of the whole community or posting (social media such as Twitter, blogs, etc.) is exposed. That said, sentiment is not easily gained, as the words by themselves do not tell the whole story (i.e., I had a *Great* problem with their customer service). Sentiment must interpret words in context. This requires an understanding of the meaning of the post – this interpretation often requires work using NLP functions found in such systems as IBM's Watson.

1.3.10 Data and Text Mining

Data mining is a particular kind of analysis that reveals patterns in data using various algorithms. It began as an offshoot from Machine Learning, a subfield of Artificial Intelligence. The theory is a subset of statistical analysis

---

[90] CIVDDD, the Centre for Innovation in Information and Data-Driven Design, is a research grant in big data analytics and visualization to develop next generation data discovery, design, and visualization techniques for new computational tools, representational strategies, and interfaces.

known as unsupervised learning where algorithms are applied to a data set without knowledge or intent of the desired outcome. While standard query and reporting tools ask specific questions, data mining tools help discover unknown relationships by revealing patterns. Data mining is a key activity during the exploration phase as it facilitates rapid identification of studied data elements, identifies new relationships previously unknown, unclear, or unclassified, and provides structure for the classification of studied data elements.

Text mining analyzes documents with text analysis and data mining techniques to classify content automatically into workflow-guided and SME-directed ontologies. Thus, electronic text media can be analyzed without restructuring or reformatting. Ontologies can be linked into search engines, allowing for web-enabled querying against these documents. (See Chapter 9.)

Data and text mining use a range of techniques, including:

- **Profiling**: Profiling attempts to characterize the typical behavior of an individual, group, or population. Profiling is used to establish behavioral norms for anomaly detection applications, such as fraud detection and monitoring for intrusions to computer systems. Profile results are inputs for many unsupervised learning components.

- **Data reduction**: Data reduction replaces a large data set with a smaller set of data that contains much of the important information in the larger set. The smaller data set may be easier to analyze or process.

- **Association**: Association is an unsupervised learning process to find relationships between studied elements based on transactions involving them. Examples of association include: Frequent item set mining, rule discovery, and market-based analysis. Recommendation systems on the internet use this process as well.

- **Clustering**: Clustering group elements in a study together by their shared characteristics. Customer segmentation is an example of clustering.

- **Self-organizing maps**: Self-organizing maps are a neural network method of cluster analysis. Sometimes referred to as Kohonen Maps, or topologically ordered maps, they aim to reduce the dimensionality in the evaluation space while preserving distance and proximity relationships as much as possible, akin to multi-dimension scaling. Reducing the dimensionality is like removing one variable from the equation without violating the outcome. This makes it easier to solve and visualize.

1.3.11 Predictive Analytics

Predictive Analytics is the sub-field of supervised learning where users attempt to model data elements and predict future outcomes through evaluation of probability estimates. Rooted deeply in mathematics specifically statistics, predictive analytics shares many components with unsupervised learning, with the prescribed difference to the measurement of a desired predictive outcome.

Predictive Analytics is the development of probability models based on variables, including historical data, related to possible events (purchases, changes in price, etc.). When it receives other pieces of information, the model triggers a reaction by the organization. The triggering factor may be an event, such as a customer adding a product to an on-line shopping basket, or it may be data in a data stream, such as a news feed or utility sensor data, or an increased volume of service requests. The triggering factor may be an external event. News being reported about a company is a big predictor of a change in stock price. Predicting stock movement should include monitoring news and determining if news about a company is likely to be good or bad for the stock price.

Frequently, the triggering factor is the accumulation of a large volume of real-time data, such as an extremely high number of trades or requests for service or volatility of the environment. Monitoring a data event stream includes incrementally building on the populated models until a threshold is reached as defined in the model.

The amount of time that a predictive model provides between the prediction and event predicted is frequently very small (seconds or less than a second). Investment in very low latency technology solutions, such as in-memory databases, high-speed networks, and even physically proximity to the source of the data, optimizes an organization's ability to react to the prediction.

The simplest form of predictive model is the forecast. Many techniques exist for trending or forecasting based on regression analysis and benefit from smoothing. The simplest way to smooth data is through a moving average, or even a weighted moving average. More advanced techniques can be useful, like the exponential moving average, which introduces a smoothing factor to be applied. Minimizing the error residual from the least squares can be a starting point, but several runs are necessary to determine and optimize the smoothing factor. Double and triple exponential smoothing models exist to address trend and seasonality components.

1.3.12 Prescriptive Analytics

Prescriptive analytics take predictive analytics a step farther to define actions that will affect outcomes, rather than just predicting the outcomes from actions that have occurred. Prescriptive analytics anticipates what will happen, when it will happen, and implies why it will happen. Because prescriptive analytics can show the implications of various decisions, it can suggest how to take advantage of an opportunity or avoid a risk. Prescriptive analytics can continually take in new data to re-predict and re-prescribe. This process can improve prediction accuracy and result in better prescriptions.

1.3.13 Unstructured Data Analytics

Unstructured data analytics combines text mining, association, clustering, and other unsupervised learning techniques to codify large data sets. Supervised learning techniques can also be applied to provide orientation, oversight, and guidance in the coding process leveraging human intervention to resolve ambiguity when necessary.

Unstructured data analytics is becoming more important as more unstructured data is generated. Some analysis is impossible without the ability to incorporate unstructured data into analytical models. However, unstructured data is difficult to analyze without some way to isolate the elements of interest from extraneous elements.

Scanning and tagging is one way to add 'hooks' to unstructured data that allow filtering and linking to related structured data. However, knowing what tags to generate based on what conditions is difficult. It is an iterative process, from when proposed tag conditions are identified, tags are assigned as data is ingested, then analytics uses those tags to validate the tag condition, and analyze the tagged data, which then leads to potentially changed tag conditions, or more tags.

1.3.14 Operational Analytics

The concept of operational analytics (also known as operational BI or streaming analytics) has emerged from the integration of real-time analytics into operations. Operational analytics includes activities like user segmentation, sentiment analysis, geocoding, and other techniques applied to data sets for marketing campaign analysis, sales penetration, product adoption, asset optimization, and risk management.

Operational analytics involves tracking and integrating real-time streams of information, deriving conclusions based on predictive models of behavior, and triggering automatic responses and alerts. Designing the model, triggers, and responses required for successful analysis takes more analysis on the data itself. An operational analytics solution includes the preparation of historical data for pre-population of the models of behavior. For example, in a retail product model, populating a shopping basket analysis that identifies products often purchased together. In predicting behavior of financial markets, historical price information and historical price rate of change are regularly used. Pre-population calculations are usually performed in advance to enable timely responses to triggering events.

Once predictive models have been determined to be both useful and cost effective, solutions which integrate historical and current data (including real-time and streaming data, structured and unstructured) are implemented to populate the predictive models and trigger actions based on the predictions. The solution must ensure real-time data streams using the model rules are processed correctly and automated responses to meaningful events in the data are generated correctly.

1.3.15 Data Visualization[91]

Visualization is the process of interpreting concepts, ideas, and facts by using pictures or graphical representations. Data visualization facilitates understanding of the underlying data by presenting it in a visual summary, such as a chart or graph. Data visualizations condense and encapsulate characteristics data, making them easier to see. In doing so, they can surface opportunities, identify risks, or highlight messages.

Data visualizations can be delivered in a static format, such as a published report, or a more interactive on-line format; and some support end-user interaction where drilling or filtering capabilities facilitate analysis of data within the visualization. Others allow the visualization to be changed by the user on demand through innovative displays, such as data maps and moving landscapes of data over time.

---

[91] Data visualization is an evolving field. Principles applied in data visualization are based on design principles. See Tufte, 2001 and McCandless 2012. Numerous web-based resources exist with examples and counter examples. See the Periodic Table of Visualization Methods at Visual Literacy.Org http://bit.ly/IX1bvI.

Visualization has long been critical to data analysis. Traditional BI tools include visualization options such as tables, pie charts, lines charts, area charts, bar charts, histograms, and turnkey boxes (candlesticks). To meet the growing need to understand data, the number of visualization tools has increased and techniques have improved.

As data analytics matures, visualizing data in new ways will offer strategic advantages. Seeing new patterns in data can result in new business opportunities. As data visualization continues to evolve, organizations will have to grow their Business Intelligence teams to compete in an increasingly data-driven world. Business analytical departments will seek data experts with visualization skills, including data scientists, data artists, and data vision experts, in addition to traditional information architects and data modelers, especially given the risks associated with misleading visualization. (See Chapter 2.)

1.3.16 Data Mashups

Mashups combine data and services to create visualization for insight or analysis. Many virtualization tools enable mashups through functionality that relates data sources by common data elements, originally used to relate a name or descriptive text to a stored code. This client presentation mashup technique is ideal during discovery or exploration phases as they provide immediate benefits. This technique can be readily applied to the web where secured data mashups enable sharing of personal or confidential information across suppliers or providers. These can couple with artificial intelligence learning algorithms to expose internet-based services with natural language interfaces.

2. Activities

2.1 Define Big Data Strategy and Business Needs

An organization's Big Data strategy needs to be aligned with and support its overall business strategy and business requirements and be part of its data strategy. A Big Data strategy must include criteria to evaluate:

- **What problems the organization is trying to solve. What it needs analytics for**: While one advantage of Data Science is that it can provide a new perspective on an organization, the organization still needs to have a starting point. An organization may determine that the data is to be used to understand the business or the business environment; to prove ideas about the value of new products; to explore something that is unknown; or to invent a new way to do business. It is important to establish a gating process to evaluate these initiatives at several phases during the implementation. The value and feasibility of initiatives need to be evaluated at several points in time.

- **What data sources to use or acquire**: Internal sources may be easy to use, but may also be limited in scope. External sources may be useful, but are outside operational control (managed by others, or not controlled by anyone, as in the case of social media). Many vendors are competing in this space and often multiple sources exist for the desired data elements or sets. Acquiring data that integrates with existing ingestion items can reduce overall investment costs.

- **The timeliness and scope of the data to provision**: Many elements can be provided in real-time feeds, snapshots at a point in time, or even integrated and summarized. Low latency data is ideal, but often comes at the expense of machine learning capabilities – there is a huge difference between computational algorithms directed to data-at-rest versus streaming. Do not minimize the level of integration required for downstream usage.

- **The impact on and relation to other data structures**: There may need to be structure or content changes in other data structures to make them suitable for integration with Big Data sets.

- **Influences to existing modeled data**: Including extending the knowledge on customers, products, and marketing approaches.

The strategy will drive the scope and timing of an organization's Big Data capability roadmap.

2.2 Choose Data Sources

As with any development project, the choice of data sources for Data Science work must be driven by the problems the organization is trying to solve. The difference with Big Data / Data Science development is that the range of data sources is wider. It is not limited by format and can include data both external to and internal to an organization. The ability to incorporate this data into a solution also comes with risks. The quality and reliability of the data needs to be evaluated and a plan for use over time needs to be put into place. Big Data environments make it possible to quickly ingest lots of data, but to use that data and manage it over time, it is still necessary to know basic facts:

- Its origin
- Its format
- What the data elements represent
- How it connects to other data
- How frequently it will be updated

As more data becomes available (like US Census Bureau Statistics, shopping demographics, weather satellite data, research data sets), data needs to be evaluated for worth and reliability. Review the available data sources, and the processes that create those sources and manage the plan for new sources.

- **Foundational data**: Consider foundational data components such as POS (Point of Sale) in a sales analysis.
- **Granularity**: Ideally, obtain data in its most granular form (not aggregated). That way it can be aggregated for a range of purposes.
- **Consistency**: If possible, select data that will appear appropriately and consistently across visualizations, or recognize limitations.
- **Reliability**: Choose data sources that are meaningful and credible over time. Use trusted, authoritative sources.

- **Inspect/profile new sources**: Test changes before adding new data sets. Unexpected material or significant changes in visualization outcomes can occur with the inclusion of new data sources.

Risks associated with data sources include privacy concerns. The ability to rapidly ingest and integrate data from a variety of sources at scale affords communities the ability to recombine data sets that were otherwise secured. Similarly, the published analysis may describe, through summary, aggregate, or modeled state, a sub-set of the public that make it suddenly identifiable; this is a side effect of the ability to perform mass computation on very large populations, but publish to a very specific local or region. For example, when demographics computed at a national or country level quickly become non-identifiable, but not when published after filtering for a postal code or household level.[92]

Criteria used to select or filter data also pose a risk. These criteria should be objectively managed to avoid biases or skews. Filtering can have a material impact on visualization. Discretion is necessary when removing outliers, restricting data sets to a limited domain, or dropping sparse elements. It is common practice to focus the provisioned data to emphasize isolation results, but it must be done objectively and uniformly.[93] (See Chapter 2.)

2.3 Acquire and Ingest Data Sources

Once the sources are identified, they need to be found, sometimes purchased, and ingested (loaded) into the Big Data environment. During this process, capture critical Metadata about the source, such as its origin, size, currency, and additional knowledge about content. Many ingestion engines profile data as it is ingested, providing analysts with at least partial Metadata. Once the data is in a data lake, it can be assessed for suitability for multiple analysis efforts. Because building Data Science models is an iterative process, so is data ingestion. Iteratively identify gaps in the current data asset base and onboard those sources. Explore these data sources using profiling, visualization, mining, or other Data Science methods to define model algorithm inputs, or model hypotheses.

Before integrating the data, assess its quality. Assessment can be as simple querying to find out how many fields contain null values, or as complex as running a data quality toolset or data analytic utility against the data to profile, classify, and identify relationships between data elements. Such assessment provides insight into whether the data provides a valid sample from which to work, and, if so, how the data can be stored and accessed (scattered across logical processing units [MPP], federated, distributed by key, etc.). This work involves SMEs (usually the data scientists themselves) and platform engineers.

The assessment process provides valuable insight into how the data can be integrated with other data sets, such as Master Data or historical warehouse data. It also provides information that can be used in model training sets and validation activities.

---

[92] See Martin Fowler, Datensparsamkeit. Blog, 12 December 2013. Fowler brings into question the assumption that we should always capture as much data as possible. He points out that the "capture it all" approach brings up privacy risks. In its place, he puts forth the idea of data minimization or data sparsity (from the German term *Datensparsamkeit*) http://bit.ly/1f9Nq8K.

[93] For more information on the impact of bias, which can profoundly affect the interpretation of scientific results, consult the following websites: INFORMS is the leading international association for Operations Research and Analytics professionals. http://bit.ly/2sANQRW, Statistical Society of Canada: http://bit.ly/2oz2o5H and American Statistical Association: http://bit.ly/1rjAmHX.

2.4 Develop Data Hypotheses and Methods

Data Science is about building answer sets that can find meaning or insights within the data. The development of Data Science solutions entails building statistical models that find correlations and trends within and between data elements and data sets. There will be multiple answers to a question based upon inputs to a model. For example, one must choose a rate of return to calculate the future value of a financial portfolio. Models often have more than one variable so the best practice is to find deterministic outcomes – or in other words, use best guesses as to the values to be expected. However, best guesses themselves should be educated. Each model will operate depending on the analysis method chosen. It should be tested for a range of outcomes, even the ones that appear least probable.

Models depend on both the quality of input data and the soundness of the model itself. Data models can often give insight into how to correlate the information found. An example of this is using K-Means clustering to determine the number of groupings of data to analyze further. (See Chapter 13.)

2.5 Integrate / Align Data for Analysis

Preparing the data for analysis involves understanding what is in the data, finding links between data from the various sources, and aligning common data for use.

In many cases, joining data sources is more an art than a science. For example, consider one data set based upon daily updates and another based upon monthly updates. The daily data, in order to be aligned, would have to be aggregated so that there would be an alignment pattern that could be used in the Data Science investigation.

One method is to use a common model that integrates the data using a common key. Another way is to scan and join data using indexes within the database engines for similarity and record linkage algorithms and methods. Often data is inspected during the initial phases to understand how the data could be analyzed. Clustering helps determine the grouping of the data outputs. Other methods can find correlations that will be used to build the model to display results. Consider using techniques during the initial phases that will aide in understanding how the model will show results once published.

Most solutions require the integration of Master Data and Reference Data in order to interpret results of the analytics. (See Chapter 10.)

2.6 Explore Data Using Models

2.6.1 Populate Predictive Model

Configuring predictive models includes pre-populating the model with historical information concerning the customer, market, products, or other factors that are included in the model other than the triggering factor. Pre-population calculations are usually performed in advance to enable the fastest response to triggering events. For example, customer purchase history would be needed to pre-populate a retail market-basket recommendation model. In predicting behavior of retail markets, historical price and price change information are combined with customer, demographic, and weather information.

2.6.2 Train the Model

Execute the model against the data in order to 'train' the model. Training includes repeated runs of the model against the data to verify assumptions. Training will result in changes to the model. Training requires balance. Avoid over-fitting by training against a limited data fold.

Model validation must be complete before transitioning to production. Address any population imbalances or data biases with model offsets that are trained and validated; this can be tweaked in production as the initial offset is gradually adjusted through actual population interactions. Optimizing feature mix can be accomplished with Bayesian co-selection, classifier inversion, or rule induction. Models can also be combined for ensemble learning where the predictor model is built by combining the collected strengths of simpler models.

Identifying outliers or anomalies (data objects that do not comply with the general behavior exhibited by the studied elements) is critical to the evaluating the model. For more volatile datasets, apply a variance test based on the average and standard deviation. Both tests can be readily applied on profiled results. It may be that the outliers are the target of the exercise, as opposed to finding and validating trends in the majority of the data.

For predictive analytics, use a real-time data stream to finish the population of the predictive model and trigger a response, which might be an alert or an event. The data stream may require special focus on design and development of an extreme low latency processing capability. In some models, the difference in value of the predictions between fractions of a second is extreme and solutions may require innovative technology with speed of light limitations.

Models can use many statistical functions and techniques that are available in open source libraries, one of which is 'R.' The R Project for Statistical Computing is a free software environment for statistical computing; it contains many functions as service calls.[94] Custom functions can be developed leveraging the scripting language and shared across tools, platforms, and organizations.

Once the solution design has been created and development and operation estimated, the organization may decide whether to develop the solution to predict behavior. Real-time operational analytics solutions frequently require substantial amounts of new architecture and development and could possibly not be cost effective.

2.6.3 Evaluate Model

Once the data is placed onto a platform and ready for analysis, the Data Science begins. The model is constructed, evaluated against training sets, and validated. Refinements to the business requirements are expected at this point and early feasibility metrics can guide the management efforts towards further processing or discarding. It is entirely possible that testing a new hypothesis will require additional data sets.

---

[94] For more information, visit the R-Project website: http://bit.ly/19WExR5.

Data scientists run queries and algorithms against the data to see if any insights become apparent. Often times a number of different mathematical functions will be run to see if any insight is found (clusters in the data, patterns that start to emerge between data element periods, etc.). During this period, data scientists are often building upon insights found in iterative batches. From these, models can be developed that display the correlation between data elements and insights.

There is an ethical component to practicing Data Science and it needs to be applied when evaluating models. Models can have unexpected results or unintentionally reflect the assumptions and biases of the people who create them. Ethical training should be required for all artificial intelligence (AI) practitioners. Ideally, the curriculum for every student learning AI, computer science, or Data Science should include ethics and security topics. However, ethics alone is not sufficient. Ethics can help practitioners understand their responsibilities to all stakeholders, but ethical training needs to be augmented with the technical capability to put good intentions into practice by taking technical precautions as a system is built and tested (Executive Office, 2016). (See Chapter 2.)

2.6.4 Create Data Visualizations

Data visualization based on the model must meet the specific needs related to the purpose of the model. Each visualization should answer a question or provide an insight. Establish the purpose and parameters for the visualization: a point in time status, trends vs. exceptions, relationships between moving parts, geographical differences, or some other point.

Select the appropriate visual to fulfill that purpose. Ensure that the visualization addresses an audience; adjust the layout and complexity to highlight and simplify accordingly. Not all audiences are ready for a complex interactive chart. Support visualizations with explanatory text.

Visualizations should tell a story. Data 'story telling' can link new questions to the context of data exploration. Data stories must be supported by related data visualizations to have the best effect.

2.7 Deploy and Monitor

A model that meets business needs in a feasible manner can be deployed to production for ongoing monitoring. Such models will require refinement and maintenance. Several modeling techniques are available for implementation. Models can serve batch processes as well as real-time integration messages. They can also be embedded into analytics software as input into decision management systems, historical analysis, or performance management dashboards.

2.7.1 Expose Insights and Findings

The presentation of findings and data insights, usually through data visualization, is the final step in a Data Science investigation. Insights should be connected to action items so that the organization benefits from the Data Science work.

New relationships may be explored through data visualization techniques. As a model is used, changes in the underlying data and relationships may surface, telling a new story about the data.

2.7.2 Iterate with Additional Data Sources

The presentation of findings and data insights usually generates questions that start a new process of research. Data Science is iterative, so Big Data development is iterative to support it. This process of learning from a specific set of data sources often leads to the need for different or additional data sources to both support the conclusions found and to add insights to the existing model(s).

3. Tools

Advances in technology (Moore's Law, the proliferation of hand held devices, IOT, to name a few) have created the Big Data and Data Science industry. To understand the industry, one must understand its drivers. This section will explain the tools and technologies that have enabled Big Data Science to emerge.

The advent of Massively Parallel Processing (MPP) was one of the first enablers to Big Data and Data Science as it provided the means to analyze huge volumes of information in relatively short amounts of time. Finding the needle in the haystack of information, or using machinery to plow through tons of dirt to find the gold nuggets is what we are doing today. This trend will continue.

Other advances that have changed the way we look at data and information include:

- Advanced in-database analytics
- Analytics on unstructured data (Hadoop, MapReduce)
- Integration of analytic results with operational systems
- Data visualizations across multiple media and devices
- Linking structured and unstructured information using semantics
- New data sources using IOT
- Advanced visualization capabilities
- Data enrichment capabilities
- Collaboration technologies and toolsets

Existing data warehouses, data marts, and operational data stores (ODS) are being augmented to carry Big Data workload. NoSQL technologies allow storage and query of unstructured and semi-structured data.

Access to unstructured data used to occur largely through a batch query interface that resulted in slow scheduled execution and poor response times. Several NoSQL databases are now available with designs that address specific limitations in this acquisition process. Scalable distributed databases automatically provide sharding capabilities (the ability to scale across servers natively) for parallel query execution. Of course, as with any other database, structural definition and mapping to unstructured data sets remain largely manual processes.

Immediate query, reporting, and analysis capabilities can be satisfied with Big Data in-memory technologies that allow end users to construct SQL-like queries to access unstructured data. There are also adaptors to SQL for some tools that will transmit a NoSQL process and return a SQL compliant query – with limitations and caveats. Adaptor technologies can allow existing tools to be used for unstructured data query.

Decision criteria tool sets, process implementation tools, and professional services offerings can both facilitate and expedite the process of choosing an initial set of tools. As when acquiring BI tools, it is critical to evaluate all options: build, buy, or rent (provisioned as software-as-a-service). As noted in Chapter 11, cloud sourcing tools and the associated expertise should be weighed against the cost of building from scratch or deploying purchased products from vendors. Ongoing upgrade and potential replacement costs must be considered as well. Alignment to a set OLA can bridge forecasted costs and provide input into setting compelling fees and penalties for term violations.

3.1 MPP Shared-nothing Technologies and Architecture

Massively Parallel Processing (MPP) Shared-nothing Database technologies have become the standard platform for Data Science-oriented analysis of Big Data sets. In MPP databases, data is partitioned (logically distributed) across multiple processing servers (computational nodes), with each server having its own dedicated memory to process data locally. Communication between processing servers is usually controlled by a master host and occurs over a network interconnect. There is no disk sharing or memory contention, hence the name, 'shared-nothing'.

MPP has evolved because traditional computing paradigms (indexes, distributed data sets, etc.) did not provide acceptable response times on massive tables. Even the most powerful of computing platforms (Cray computer) would take many hours or even days to compute a complex algorithm against a trillion-row table.

Consider now a number of commodity hardware servers, all lined up in a row and controlled via a host. Each is sent part of the query to run against this segmented or distributed trillion-row table. If there are, for example, 1000 processing servers, the query changes from accessing a trillion rows in one table to accessing 1000 billion-row tables. This type of computing architecture is linearly scalable, which adds to the appeal for data scientist and Big Data users requiring a scalable platform to incorporate growth.

This technology also enabled in-database analytical functions – the ability to execute analytical functions (like K-means Clustering, Regression, etc.) at the processor level. Distribution of workload to the processor level greatly speeds up analytical queries – thereby fueling innovation in Data Science.

A system that automatically distributes data and parallelizes query workloads across all available (localized) hardware is the optimum solution for Big Data analytics.

Data volumes are growing fast. Companies can grow the capacity and performance of their systems over time by adding new nodes. MPP makes it easy to expand the parallelism of hundreds or thousands of cores across an ever-growing pool of machines. A massively parallel, shared-nothing architecture fully uses each core, with linear scalability and increased processing performance on large data sets.

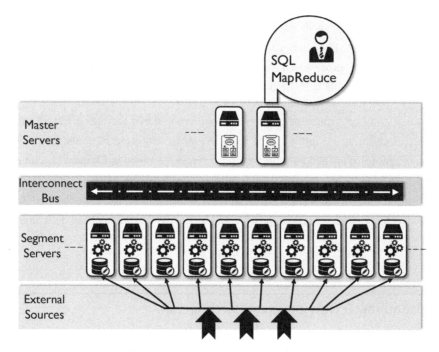

Figure 102 Columnar Appliance Architecture[95]

3.2 Distributed File-based Databases

Distributed file-based solutions technologies, such as the open source Hadoop, are an inexpensive way to store large amounts of data in different formats. Hadoop stores files of any type – structured, semi-structured, and unstructured. Using a configuration similar to MPP Shared-nothing (an MPP foundation for file storage), it shares files across processing servers. It is ideal for storing data securely (as many copies are made), but has challenges when trying to allow access to data via structured or analytical mechanism (like SQL).

Due to its relatively low cost, Hadoop has become the landing zone of choice for many organizations. From Hadoop, data can be moved to MPP Shared-nothing databases to have algorithms run against it. Some organizations run complex Data Science queries in Hadoop, and are not concerned with response times in the order of hours and days (rather than minutes for the former architecture).

The language used in file-based solutions is called MapReduce. This language has three main steps:

- **Map**: Identify and obtain the data to be analyzed
- **Shuffle**: Combine the data according to the analytical patterns desired
- **Reduce**: Remove duplication or perform aggregation in order to reduce the size of the resulting data set to only what is required

These steps can be combined in many different tools in different ways, both in sequence and in parallel, to do complex manipulations.

---

[95] Image Source: "Greenplum Database 4.0: Critical Mass Innovation", White Paper, August 2010.

3.3 In-database Algorithms

An in-database algorithm uses the principle that each of the processors in a MPP Shared-nothing platform can run queries independently, so a new form of analytics processing could be accomplished by providing mathematical and statistical functions at the computing node level. Open-source libraries of scalable in-database algorithms for machine learning, statistics, and other analytical tasks were designed both for in- and out-of-core execution, and for the shared-nothing parallelism offered by modern parallel database engines, ensuring that computation is done close to the data. By moving the computation closer to the data, the computing time is dramatically reduced for complex algorithms (such as K-means Clustering, Logistic or Linear regression, Mann-Whitney U Test, Conjugate Gradient, Cohort Analysis, etc.).

3.4 Big Data Cloud Solutions

There are vendors who provide cloud storage and integration for Big Data, including analytic capabilities. Based on defined standards, customers load their data a cloud environment. The vendor enhances the data, either as open data sets or as provided by other organizations. The customer can do analytics and Data Science using the combined data set. One application uses retail offers as the subject for the data, combines it with geographic and sales data, and offers airline miles for customers who agree to have their data used in this way.

3.5 Statistical Computing and Graphical Languages

R is an open source scripting language and environment for statistical computing and graphics. It provides a wide variety of statistical techniques such as linear and nonlinear modeling, classical statistical tests, time-series analysis, classification, and clustering. Because it is a scripting language, models developed in *R* can be implemented in a variety of environments, differing platforms and collaborated development across multiple geographic and organizational boundaries. The *R* environment can also produce publication-quality plots, including mathematical symbols and formulae, within the control of the end user.

3.6 Data Visualization Tools

Traditional tools in data visualization have both a data and a graphical component. Advanced visualization and discovery tools use in-memory architecture to allow users to interact with the data. Patterns in a large data set can be difficult to recognize in a numbers display. A visual pattern can be picked up quickly when thousands of data points are loaded into a sophisticated display.

Information graphics or infographics are graphical representations stylized for effective interaction and comprehension. Marketing adopted these to provide visual appeal to presentations. Journalists, bloggers, and teachers found infographics useful for trend analysis, presentation, and distribution. Information visualization methods like radar charts, parallel coordinate plots, tag charts, heat maps, and data maps are now supported by many toolsets. These allow users to rapidly discern changes in data over time, gain insights into related items, and understand potential cause and effect relationships before impacts occur. These tools have several benefits over traditional visualization tools:

- Sophisticated analysis and visualization types, such as small multiples, spark lines, heat maps, histograms, waterfall charts, and bullet graphs
- Built-in adherence to visualization best practices
- Interactivity enabling visual discovery

4. Techniques

4.1 Analytic Modeling

Several open source tools are available for development, as well as cloud data processing for model development, for visual development process, for web scraping, and for linear programming optimization. To share and execute models by other applications, look for tools that support the predictive model markup language (PMML), an XML-based file format.

Real-time access can resolve many latency issues from batch processing. The Apache Mahout is an open source project aimed at creating a machine-learning library. Mahout is positioned to automate Big Data exploration through recommendation mining, document classification, and item clustering. This branch of development efforts bypasses the traditional batch query MapReduce data access techniques. Leveraging an API interface directly into the storage layer HDFS, a variety of data access techniques can be provided such as SQL, content streaming, machine learning, and graphics libraries for data visualization.

Analytic models are associated with different depths of analysis:

- **Descriptive modeling** summarizes or represents the data structures in a compact manner. This approach does not always validate a causal hypothesis or predict outcomes. However, it does use algorithms to define or refine relationships across variables in a way that could provide input to such analysis.

- **Explanatory modeling** is the application of statistical models to data for testing causal hypothesis about theoretical constructs. While it uses techniques similar to data mining and predictive analytics, its purpose is different. It does not predict outcomes; it seeks to match model results only with existing data.

Key to predictive analytics is to learn by example through training the model. Performance of a learning method relates its predictive abilities on independent test data. Assessment guides the choice of learning and measures the quality of the chosen model. Model selection estimates performance where assessment evaluates the generalization error on new data.

Avoid over-fitting – a situation that occurs when the model is trained against non-representative datasets, is overly complex in relation to its data, or has described noise instead of the underlying relationship(s). Use additional techniques such as K-fold validation to indicate when training is no longer resulting in better generalization.

Training error consistently decrease with model complexity and can drop off to zero. Therefore, it is not a useful estimate of the test error. Randomly divide the data set into three parts to form training, testing, and validation sets. The training set is used to fit the model, the validation set is used to predict error for selection, and the test set is used for assessment of the generalization error of the final model.

Reusing the same test-set repeatedly can underestimate the true test error. Ideally, perform cross-validation by randomly dividing the data set into a set of K-folds or cross-validation groups. Perform training on all but one set of data based on strongly correlated predictor variables. Test the model on the remaining piece and determine generalization error based on all K-folds. Several statistical tests can be applied and performed to numerically assess contextual model validity.

4.2 Big Data Modeling

Modeling Big Data is a technical challenge but critical if an organization that wants to describe and govern its data. Traditional Enterprise Data Architecture principles do apply; data needs to be integrated, specified, and managed.

The main driver to physically model a data warehouse is to enable population of data for query performance. This driver is not in play for Big Data. This is not an excuse to abandon the modeling process or to hand it off to a developer. The value of modeling the data is that it enables people to understand data content. Apply proven data modeling techniques while accounting for the variety of sources. Develop the subject area model, at least in a summarized way, so it can be related to proper contextual entities and placed into the overall roadmap, just like any other kind of data. The challenge is to make an understandable and useful picture out of these large data sets, and for a justifiable cost.

Understand how the data links between data sets. For data of different granularity, prevent combinations that count data elements or values more than once; for example, don't combine atomic and aggregate sets.

5. Implementation Guidelines

Many of the general principles of managing warehouse data apply to managing Big Data: ensuring that the data sources are reliable, having sufficient Metadata to enable data use, managing the quality of data, figuring out how to integrate data from different sources, and ensuring that data is secure and protected. (See Chapters 6, 7, and 8.) The differences in implementing a Big Data environment are connected to a set of unknowns: how the data will be used, which data will be valuable, how long it needs to be retained.

Data velocity may lead people to think they do not have time to implement controls. This is a dangerous assumption. With larger data sets, managing ingestion and inventorying data in a lake is critical to preventing it from becoming a swamp.

Ingestion may not always require organizational ownership or commitment to the data set being studied. Consider leasing a Big Data platform for finite periods to explore data of interest. Exploration can quickly determine which areas show potential value. Do this before ingesting into the organizational data lake, data store, or data staging area; once landed, it can be awkward to remove.

5.1 Strategy Alignment

Any Big Data / Data Science program should be strategically aligned with organizational objectives. Establishing a Big Data strategy drives activities related to user community, data security, Metadata management, including lineage, and Data Quality Management.

The strategy should document goals, approach, and governance principles. The ability to leverage Big Data requires building organizational skills and capabilities. Use capability management to align business and IT initiatives and project a roadmap. Strategy deliverables should account for managing:

- Information lifecycle
- Metadata
- Data quality
- Data acquisition
- Data access and security
- Data governance
- Data privacy
- Learning and adoption
- Operations

5.2 Readiness Assessment / Risk Assessment

As with any development project, implementation of a Big Data or Data Science initiative should align with real business needs. Assess organizational readiness in relation to critical success factors:

- **Business relevance**: How well do the Big Data / Data Science initiatives and their corresponding use cases align with the company's business? To succeed, they must strongly enforce a business function or process.
- **Business readiness**: Is the business partner prepared for a long-term incremental delivery? Have they committed themselves to establishing centers of excellence to sustain the product in future releases? How broad is the average knowledge or skill gap within the target community and can that be crossed within a single increment?
- **Economic viability**: Has the proposed solution considered conservatively the tangible and intangible benefits? Has assessment of ownership costs accounted for the option of buying or leasing items versus building from scratch?
- **Prototype**: Can the proposed solution be prototyped for a subset of the end user community for a finite timeframe to demonstrate proposed value? Big bang implementations can cause big dollar impacts and a proving ground can mitigate these delivery risks.

Likely the most challenging decisions will be around data procurement, platform development, and resourcing.

- Many sources exist for digital data stores and not all need to be in-house owned and operated. Some can be procured while others can be leased.
- Multiple tools and techniques are on the market; matching to general needs will be a challenge.
- Securing staff with specific skills in a timely manner and retaining top talent during an implementation may require consideration of alternatives including professional services, cloud sourcing or collaborating.
- The time to build in-house talent may well exceed the delivery window.

5.3 Organization and Cultural Change

Business people must be fully engaged in order to realize benefits from the advanced analytics. A communications and education program is required to affect this. A Center of Excellence can provide training, start-up sets, design best practices, data source tips and tricks, and other point solutions or artifacts to help empower business users towards a self-service model. In addition to knowledge management, this center can provide timely communications across the developer, designer, analyst, and data consumer communities.

As with DW/BI, a Big Data implementation will bring together of a number of key cross-functional roles, including:

- **Big Data Platform Architect**: Hardware, operating systems, filesystems, and services.
- **Ingestion Architect**: Data analysis, systems of record, data modeling, and data mapping. Provides or supports mapping of sources to the Hadoop cluster for query and analysis.
- **Metadata Specialist**: Metadata interfaces, Metadata architecture, and contents.
- **Analytic Design Lead**: End user analytic design, best practice guidance implementation in related toolsets, and end user result set facilitation.
- **Data Scientist**: Provides architecture and model design consultation based on theoretical knowledge of statistics and computability, delivery on appropriate tools and technical application to functional requirements.

6. Big Data and Data Science Governance

Big Data, like other data, requires governance. Sourcing, source analysis, ingestion, enrichment, and publishing processes require business as well as technical controls, addressing such questions as:

- **Sourcing**: What to source, when to source, what is the best source of data for particular study
- **Sharing**: What data sharing agreements and contracts to enter into, terms and conditions both inside and outside the organization
- **Metadata**: What the data means on the source side, how to interpret the results on the output side
- **Enrichment**: Whether to enrich the data, how to enrich the data, and the benefits of enriching the data
- **Access**: What to publish, to whom, how, and when

An enterprise view of data should drive decisions on data handling.

6.1 Visualization Channels Management

A critical success factor in implementing a Data Science approach is the alignment of the appropriate visualization tools to the user community. Depending on the size and nature of the organization, there are likely many different visualization tools being applied in a variety of processes. Ensure that users understand the relative complexity of the visualization tools. Sophisticated users will have increasingly complex demands. Coordination between enterprise architecture, portfolio management, and maintenance teams will be necessary to control visualization channels within and across the portfolio. Be aware that changing data providers or selection criteria will likely have downstream impacts to the elements available for visualization, which can impact the effectiveness of tools.

6.2 Data Science and Visualization Standards

It is a best practice to establish a community that defines and publishes visualization standards and guidelines and reviews artifacts within a specified delivery method; this is particularly vital for customer- and regulatory-facing content. Standards may include:

- Tools standards by analytic paradigm, user community, subject area
- Requests for new data
- Data set process standard
- Processes for neutral and expert presentation to avoid biased results, and to ensure that all elements included have been done so in a fair and consistent manner including:
  - Data inclusion and exclusion
  - Assumptions in the models
  - Statistical validity of results
  - Validity of interpretation of results
  - Appropriate methods applied

6.3 Data Security

Having a reliable process to secure data is itself an organizational asset. Policies for handling and securing Big Data should be established and monitored. These policies should account for how to prevent misuse of personal data and to secure it through its overall lifecycle.

Securely provision appropriate levels of data for authorized personnel and make subscription data accessible according to agreed-upon levels. Align services to user communities so that special services can be created to provision private data for those communities allowed to ingest it, and mask the data for others. Often organizations create policies for access to information that are not to be violated (such as no access by name, address, or phone number). In order to secure information that is highly sensitive (social security number, credit card numbers, etc.), data will be stored using encryption techniques that obfuscate the information. Encryption can be chosen that, for example, has the same 'content' when encrypted, so that patterns may be exposed without knowing the actual values.

Recombination measures the ability to reconstitute sensitive or private data. This capability must be managed as part of the Big Data security practice. The outcomes of the analysis may violate privacy, even though the actual data elements can only be inferred. Understanding the outcomes at the Metadata Management level is critical to avoid this and other potential security violations. This requires knowledge of the intended consumption or analysis to be performed and by what role. Some trusted persons within the organization will be granted the ability to read this data when necessary, but not everyone, and certainly not for deep analysis. (See Chapters 2 and 7.)

6.4 Metadata

As part of a Big Data initiative, an organization will bring together data sets that were created using different approaches and standards. Integration of such data is challenging. Metadata related to these data sets is critical to their successful use. Metadata needs to be carefully managed as part of data ingestion, or the data lake will quickly become a data swamp. The user community must have tools that enable them to create a master list of data sets with Metadata that characterizes the structure, content, and quality of the data, including the source and lineage of the data and the definition and intended uses of entities and data elements. Technical Metadata can be harvested from a variety of Big Data tools including data storage layers, data integration, MDM, and even the source filesystems. Consideration of real-time feeds versus data at rest versus computational data elements is necessary to complete the source side lineage.

6.5 Data Quality

Data Quality is a measure of deviation from an expected result: the smaller the difference, the better the data meets expectation, and the higher the quality. In an engineered environment, standards for quality should be easy to define (though practice shows that they are not or that many organizations do not take the time to define them). Some people have raised the question of whether data quality even matters for Big Data. Common sense says it does. For analytics to be reliable, the underlying data must be reliable. In Big Data projects, it may seem very difficult to determine the quality of data, but an effort needs to be made to assess quality in order to have confidence in the analysis. This can be done through an initial assessment, which is necessary to understand the data, and through that, the identification of measurements for subsequent instances of the data set. Data quality assessment will produce valuable Metadata that will be necessary input to any effort to integrate data.

Consider that most mature Big Data organizations scan data input sources using data quality toolsets to understand the information contained within. Most advanced data quality toolsets offer functionality that enables an organization to test assumptions and build knowledge about its data. For example:

- **Discovery**: Where information resides within the data set
- **Classification**: What types of information are present based upon standardized patterns
- **Profiling**: How the data is populated and structured
- **Mapping**: What other data sets can be matched to these values

Just as in DW/BI, it is tempting to put data quality assessment last. Without it, though, it may be difficult to know what Big Data represents or how to make connections between data sets. Integration will be necessary, and the likelihood that data feeds will be provisioned with identical structures and elements is very nearly zero. This means for example, codes and other potential linking data will likely vary from data provider to data provider. Without initial assessment, such conditions will go unnoticed until an analytic need is expressed that attempts to merge or combine those providers.

6.6 Metrics

Metrics are vital to any management process; they not only quantify activity, but can define the variation between what is observed and what is desired.

6.6.1 Technical Usage Metrics

Many of the Big Data tools offer insightful administrator reporting capabilities that interact directly with the contents queried by the user community. Technical usage analysis looks for data hot spots (most frequently accessed data) in order to manage data distribution and preserve performance. Growth rates also feed into capacity planning.

6.6.2 Loading and Scanning Metrics

Loading and scanning metrics define the ingestion rate and interaction with the user community. As each new data source is acquired, loading metrics are expected to spike and then level as that source is fully ingested. Real-time feeds may be served through service queries, but can also appear as scheduled extracts are processed; for these feeds, expect a constant increase in data loading.

The application layer(s) would likely provide the best data usage metrics from execution logs. Monitor the consumption or access through available Metadata, which can guide usage analysis by showing query execution plans that have occurred most frequently.

Scanning metrics should be combined with any query processing that may occur outside of the analytical processing itself. Administrative tools should be able to provide this level of reporting, as well as overall service health.

6.6.3 Learnings and Stories

In order to show value, the Big Data / Data Science program must measure tangible outcomes that justify the cost of developing solutions and managing process changes. Metrics can include quantification of benefits, cost prevention or avoidance, as well as length of time between initiation and realized benefits. Common measurements include

- Counts and accuracy of models and patterns developed
- Revenue realization from identified opportunities
- Cost reduction from avoiding identified threats

Sometimes, the outcomes of the analytics tell stories that can lead to organization re-direction, re-vitalization, and new opportunity. One measurement can be a count of new projects and initiatives generated by marketing and senior executives.

7. Works Cited / Recommended

Abate, Robert, Peter Aiken and Joseph Burke. *Integrating Enterprise Applications Utilizing A Services Based Architecture*. John Wiley and Sons, 1997. Print.

Arthur, Lisa. *Big Data Marketing: Engage Your Customers More Effectively and Drive Value*. Wiley, 2013. Print.

Barlow, Mike. *Real-Time Big Data Analytics: Emerging Architecture*. O'Reilly Media, 2013. Kindle.

Davenport, Thomas H. "Beyond the Black Box in analytics and Cognitive." *DataInformed* (website), 27 February, 2017. http://bit.ly/2sq8uG0 Web.

Davenport, Thomas H. *Big Data at Work: Dispelling the Myths, Uncovering the Opportunities*. Harvard Business Review Press, 2014. Print.

EMC Education Services, ed. *Data Science and Big Data Analytics: Discovering, Analyzing, Visualizing and Presenting Data*. Wiley, 2015. Print.

Executive Office of the President, National Science and Technology Council Committee on Technology. *Preparing for the Future of Artificial Intelligence*. October 2016. http://bit.ly/2j3XA4k.

Inmon, W.H., and Dan Linstedt. *Data Architecture: A Primer for the Data Scientist: Big Data, Data Warehouse and Data Vault*. 1st Edition. Morgan Kaufmann, 2014.

Jacobs, Adam. "Pathologies of Big Data." *AMCQUEU*, Volume 7, Issue 6. July 6, 2009. http://bit.ly/1vOqd80. Web

Janssens, Jeroen. *Data Science at the Command Line: Facing the Future with Time-Tested Tools*. O'Reilly Media, 2014. Print.

Kitchin, Rob. *The Data Revolution: Big Data, Open Data, Data Infrastructures and Their Consequences*. SAGE Publications Ltd, 2014. Print.

Krishnan, Krish. *Data Warehousing in the Age of Big Data*. Morgan Kaufmann, 2013. Print. The Morgan Kaufmann Series on Business Intelligence.

Lake, Peter and Robert Drake. *Information Systems Management in the Big Data Era*. Springer, 2015. Print. Advanced Information and Knowledge Processing.

Lake, Peter. *A Guide to Handling Data Using Hadoop: An exploration of Hadoop, Hive, Pig, Sqoop and Flume*. Peter Lake, 2015. Kindle. Advanced Information and Knowledge Processing.

Laney, Doug. "3D Data Management: Controlling Data Volume, Velocity, and Variety." *The Meta Group* [Gartner]. 6 February 2001. http://gtnr.lt/1bKflKH.

Loshin, David. *Big Data Analytics: From Strategic Planning to Enterprise Integration with Tools*, Techniques, NoSQL, and Graph. Morgan Kaufmann, 2013. Print.

Lublinsky, Boris, Kevin T. Smith, Alexey Yakubovich. *Professional Hadoop Solutions*. Wrox, 2013. Print.

Luisi, James. *Pragmatic Enterprise Architecture: Strategies to Transform Information Systems in the Era of Big Data*. Morgan Kaufmann, 2014. Print.

Marz, Nathan and James Warren. *Big Data: Principles and best practices of scalable realtime data systems*. Manning Publications, 2014. Print.

McCandless, David. *Information is Beautiful*. Collins, 2012.

Provost, Foster and Tom Fawcett. *Data Science for Business: What you need to know about data mining and data-analytic thinking*. O'Reilly Media, 2013. Print.

Salminen, Joni and Valtteri Kaartemo, eds. *Big Data: Definitions, Business Logics, and Best Practices to Apply in Your Business*. Amazon Digital Services, Inc., 2014. Kindle. Books for Managers Book 2.

Sathi, Arvind. *Big Data Analytics: Disruptive Technologies for Changing the Game*. Mc Press, 2013. Print.

Sawant, Nitin and Himanshu Shah. *Big Data Application Architecture Q&A: A Problem - Solution Approach*. Apress, 2013. Print. Expert's Voice in Big Data.

Slovic, Scott, Paul Slovic, eds. *Numbers and Nerves: Information, Emotion, and Meaning in a World of Data*. Oregon State University Press, 2015. Print.

Starbird, Michael. *Meaning from Data: Statistics Made Clear* (The Great Courses, Parts 1 and 2). The Teaching Company, 2006. Print.

Tufte, Edward R. *The Visual Display of Quantitative Information*. 2nd ed. Graphics Pr., 2001. Print.

van der Lans, Rick. Data Virtualization for Business Intelligence Systems: Revolutionizing Data Integration for Data Warehouses. Morgan Kaufmann, 2012. Print. The Morgan Kaufmann Series on Business Intelligence.

van Rijmenam, Mark. *Think Bigger: Developing a Successful Big Data Strategy for Your Business*. AMACOM, 2014. Print.

CHAPTER 15

Data Management Maturity Assessment

1. Introduction

Capability Maturity Assessment (CMA) is an approach to process improvement based on a framework – a Capability Maturity Model (CMM) – that describes how characteristics of a process evolve from ad hoc to optimal. The CMA concept grew out of efforts by the United States Department of Defense to establish criteria through which to evaluate software contractors. In the mid-1980s, the Capability Maturity Model for Software was published by the Software Engineering Institute of Carnegie-Mellon University. While first applied to software development, CMMs have been developed for a range of other fields, including data management.

Maturity models are defined in terms of a progression through levels that describe process characteristics. When an organization gains an understanding of process characteristics, it can evaluate its level of maturity and put in place a plan to improve its capabilities. It can also measure improvement and compare itself to competitors or partners, guided by the levels of the model. With each new level, process execution becomes more consistent, predictable, and reliable. Processes improve as they take on characteristics of the levels. Progression happens in a set order. No level can be skipped. Levels commonly include:[96]

- **Level 0**: Absence of capability
- **Level 1**: Initial or Ad Hoc: Success depends on the competence of individuals
- **Level 2**: Repeatable: Minimum process discipline is in place
- **Level 3**: Defined: Standards are set and used
- **Level 4**: Managed: Processes are quantified and controlled
- **Level 5**: Optimized: Process improvement goals are quantified

Within each level, criteria are described across process features. For example, a maturity model may include criteria related to how processes are executed, including the level of automation of those processes. It may focus on policies and controls, as well as process details.

Such an assessment helps identify what is working well, what is not working well, and where an organization has gaps. Based on the findings, the organization can develop a roadmap to target:

- High-value improvement opportunities related to processes, methods, resources, and automation
- Capabilities that align with business strategy

---

[96] Adapted from Select Business Solutions, "What is the Capability Maturity Model?" http://bit.ly/IFMJI8 (Accessed 2016-11-10).

- Governance processes for periodic evaluation of organizational progress based on characteristics in the model

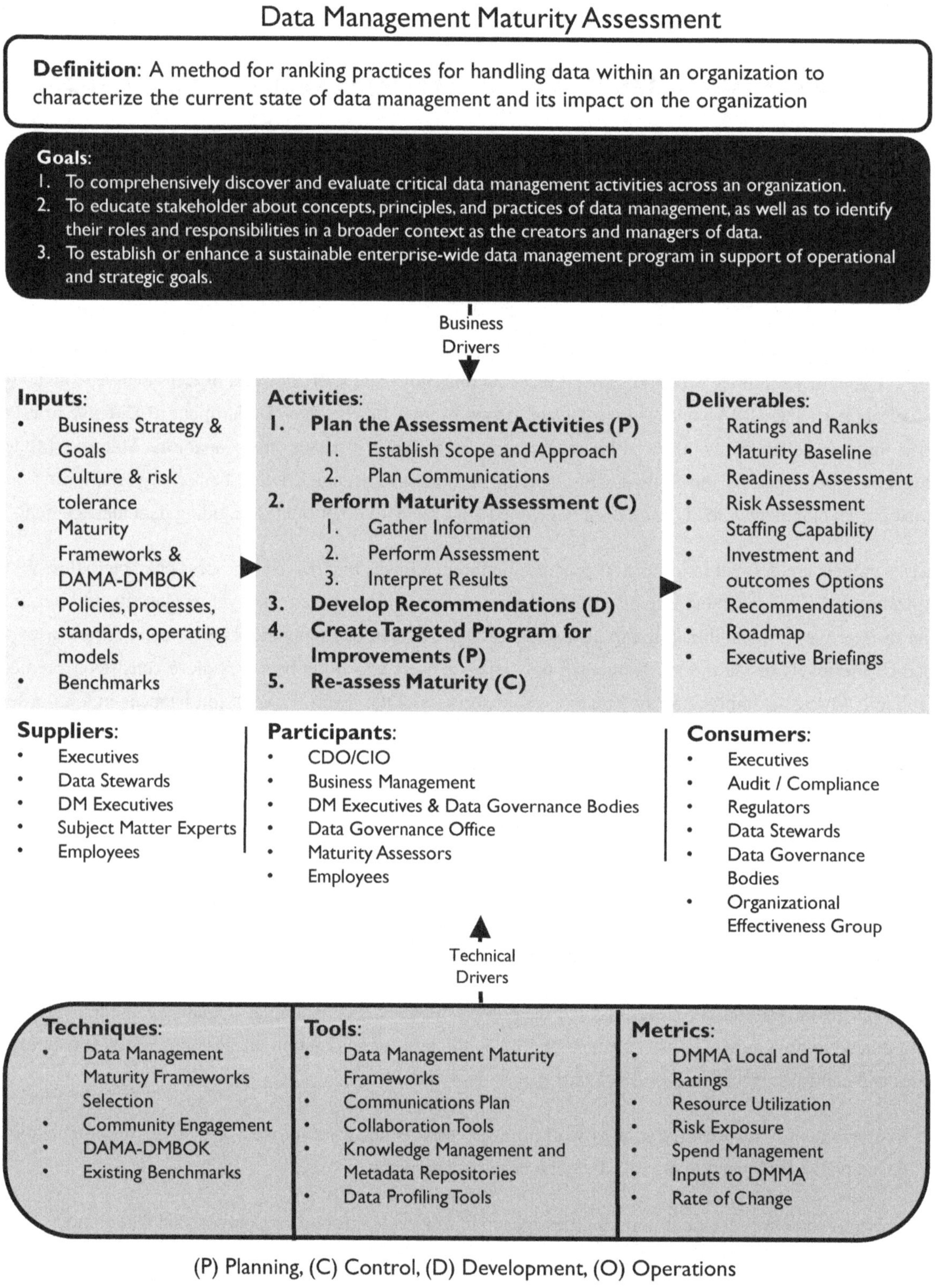

Data Management Maturity Assessment

Definition: A method for ranking practices for handling data within an organization to characterize the current state of data management and its impact on the organization

Goals:
1. To comprehensively discover and evaluate critical data management activities across an organization.
2. To educate stakeholder about concepts, principles, and practices of data management, as well as to identify their roles and responsibilities in a broader context as the creators and managers of data.
3. To establish or enhance a sustainable enterprise-wide data management program in support of operational and strategic goals.

Business Drivers

Inputs:
- Business Strategy & Goals
- Culture & risk tolerance
- Maturity Frameworks & DAMA-DMBOK
- Policies, processes, standards, operating models
- Benchmarks

Activities:
1. **Plan the Assessment Activities (P)**
   1. Establish Scope and Approach
   2. Plan Communications
2. **Perform Maturity Assessment (C)**
   1. Gather Information
   2. Perform Assessment
   3. Interpret Results
3. **Develop Recommendations (D)**
4. **Create Targeted Program for Improvements (P)**
5. **Re-assess Maturity (C)**

Deliverables:
- Ratings and Ranks
- Maturity Baseline
- Readiness Assessment
- Risk Assessment
- Staffing Capability
- Investment and outcomes Options
- Recommendations
- Roadmap
- Executive Briefings

Suppliers:
- Executives
- Data Stewards
- DM Executives
- Subject Matter Experts
- Employees

Participants:
- CDO/CIO
- Business Management
- DM Executives & Data Governance Bodies
- Data Governance Office
- Maturity Assessors
- Employees

Consumers:
- Executives
- Audit / Compliance
- Regulators
- Data Stewards
- Data Governance Bodies
- Organizational Effectiveness Group

Technical Drivers

Techniques:
- Data Management Maturity Frameworks Selection
- Community Engagement
- DAMA-DMBOK
- Existing Benchmarks

Tools:
- Data Management Maturity Frameworks
- Communications Plan
- Collaboration Tools
- Knowledge Management and Metadata Repositories
- Data Profiling Tools

Metrics:
- DMMA Local and Total Ratings
- Resource Utilization
- Risk Exposure
- Spend Management
- Inputs to DMMA
- Rate of Change

(P) Planning, (C) Control, (D) Development, (O) Operations

Figure 103 Context Diagram: Data Management Maturity Assessment

A Data Management Maturity Assessment (DMMA) can be used to evaluate data management overall, or it can be used to focus on a single Knowledge Area or even a single process. Whatever the focus, a DMMA can help bridge the gap between business and IT perspectives on the health and effectiveness of data management practices. A DMMA provides a common language for depicting what progress looks like across Data Management Knowledge Areas and offers a stage-based path to improvement, which can be tailored to an organization's strategic priorities.[97] Thus, it can be used both to set and to measure organizational goals, as well as to compare one's organization against other organizations or industry benchmarks.

Before beginning any DMMA, an organization has to establish a baseline understanding of its current state capabilities, assets, goals, and priorities. A certain level of organizational maturity is required to conduct the assessment in the first place, as well as to effectively respond to the assessment results by setting targets, establishing a roadmap, and monitoring progress.

1.1 Business Drivers

Organizations conduct capability maturity assessments for a number of reasons:

- **Regulation**: Regulatory oversight requires minimum levels of maturity in data management.
- **Data Governance**: The data governance function requires a maturity assessment for planning and compliance purposes.
- **Organizational readiness for process improvement**: An organization recognizes a need to improve its practices and begins by assessing its current state. For example, it makes a commitment to manage Master Data and needs to assess its readiness to deploy MDM processes and tools.
- **Organizational change**: An organizational change, such as a merger, presents data management challenges. A DMMA provides input for planning to meet these challenges.
- **New technology**: Advancements in technology offers new ways to manage and use data. The organization wants to understand the likelihood of successful adoption.
- **Data management issues**: There is need to address data quality issues or other data management challenges and the organization wants to baseline its current state in order to make better decisions about how to implement change.

1.2 Goals and Principles

The primary goal of a data management capability assessment is to evaluate the current state of critical data management activities in order to plan for improvement. The evaluation places the organization on the maturity scale by clarifying specific strengths and weaknesses. It helps the organization identify, prioritize, and implement improvement opportunities. In meeting its primary goal, a DMMA can have a positive impact on culture. It helps:

- Educate stakeholders about data management concepts, principles, and practices
- Clarify stakeholder roles and responsibilities in relation to organizational data
- Highlight the need to manage data as a critical asset

---

[97] http://bit.ly/1Vev9xx July 18 2015.

- Broaden recognition of data management activities across the organization
- Contribute to improving the collaboration necessary for effective data governance

Based on assessment results, an organization can enhance its Data Management program so it supports the organization's operational and strategic direction. Typically, Data Management programs develop in organizational silos. They rarely begin with an enterprise view of the data. A DMMA can equip the organization to develop a cohesive vision that supports overall organizational strategy. A DMMA enables the organization to clarify priorities, crystalize objectives, and develop an integrated plan for improvement.

1.3 Essential Concepts

1.3.1 Assessment Levels and Characteristics

CMMs usually define five or six levels of maturity, each with its own characteristics that span from non-existent or ad hoc to optimized or high performance. See Figure 104 for a sample visualization.

The following is a generic summary of macro states of data management maturity. A detailed assessment would include criteria for sub-categories like strategy, policy, standards, role definition, etc. within each of the Knowledge Areas.

- **Level 0: No Capability**: No organized data management practices or formal enterprise processes for managing data. Very few organizations exist at a Level 0. This level is acknowledged in a maturity model for purposes of definition.

- **Level 1 Initial / Ad Hoc**: General-purpose data management using a limited tool set, with little or no governance. Data handling is highly reliant on a few experts. Roles and responsibilities are defined within silos. Each data owner receives, generates, and sends data autonomously. Controls, if they exist, are applied inconsistently. Solutions for managing data are limited. Data quality issues are pervasive but not addressed. Infrastructure supports are at the business unit level.

Assessment criteria may include the presence of any process controls, such as logging of data quality issues.

- **Level 2 Repeatable**: Emergence of consistent tools and role definition to support process execution. In Level 2, the organization begins to use centralized tools and to provide more oversight for data management. Roles are defined and processes are not dependent solely on specific experts. There is organizational awareness of data quality issues and concepts. Concepts of Master and Reference Data begin to be recognized.

Assessment criteria might include formal role definition in artifacts like job descriptions, the existence of process documentation, and the capacity to leverage tool sets.

- **Level 3 Defined**: Emerging data management capability. Level 3 sees the introduction and institutionalization of scalable data management processes and a view of DM as an organizational enabler. Characteristics include the replication of data across an organization with some controls in place and a general increase in overall data quality, along with coordinated policy definition and management. More formal process definition leads to a significant reduction in manual intervention. This, along with a centralized design process, means that process outcomes are more predictable.

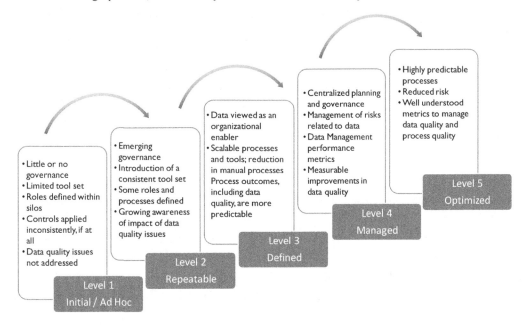

Figure 104 Data Management Maturity Model Example

Assessment criteria might include the existence of data management policies, the use of scalable processes, and the consistency of data models and system controls.

- **Level 4 Managed**: Institutional knowledge gained from growth in Levels 1-3 enables the organization to predict results when approaching new projects and tasks and to begin to manage risks related to data. Data management includes performance metrics. Characteristics of Level 4 include standardized tools for data management from desktop to infrastructure, coupled with a well-formed centralized planning and governance function. Expressions of this level are a measurable increase in data quality and organization-wide capabilities such as end-to-end data audits.

Assessment criteria might include metrics related to project success, operational metrics for systems, and data quality metrics.

- **Level 5: Optimization**: When data management practices are optimized, they are highly predictable, due to process automation and technology change management. Organizations at this level of maturity focus on continuous improvement. At Level 5, tools enable a view data across processes. The proliferation of data is controlled to prevent needless duplication. Well-understood metrics are used to manage and measure data quality and processes.

Assessment criteria might include change management artifacts and metrics on process improvement.

1.3.2 Assessment Criteria

Each capability level will have specific assessment criteria related to the processes being evaluated. For example, if the maturity of the data modeling function is being evaluated, level 1 may ask whether a data modeling practice exists at all and how many systems it extends to; level 2 may ask whether an approach to enterprise data modeling has been defined; level 3 will ask the degree to which the approach has been implemented; level 4 will ask whether modeling standards have been effectively enforced; and level 5 will ask about processes in place to improve modeling practices. (See Chapter 5.)

At any level, assessment criteria will be evaluated along a scale, such as 1 – Not started, 2 – In process, 3 – Functional, 4 – Effective, showing progress within that level and movement toward the next level. Scores can be combined or visually displayed to enable understanding of the variance between current and desired state. When assessing using a model that can be mapped to a DAMA-DMBOK Data Management Knowledge Area, criteria could be formulated based on the categories in the Context Diagram:

- **Activity**: To what degree is the activity or process in place? Are criteria defined for effective and efficient execution? How well defined and executed is the activity? Are best practice outputs produced?

- **Tools**: To what degree is the activity automated and supported by a common set of tools? Is tool training provided within specific roles and responsibilities? Are tools available when and where needed? Are they configured optimally to provide the most effective and efficient results? To what extent is long-term technology planning in place to accommodate future state capabilities?

- **Standards**: To what degree is the activity supported by a common set of standards? How well documented are the standards? Are standards enforced and supported by governance and change management?

- **People and resources**: To what degree is the organization staffed to carry out the activity? What specific skills, training, and knowledge are necessary to execute the activity? How well are roles and responsibilities defined?

Figure 105 illustrates one way of presenting a visual summary of findings from a DMMA. For each of the capabilities (Governance, Architecture, etc.) the outer ring of the display shows the level of capability the organization has determined it needs to compete successfully. The inner ring displays the level of capability as determined via the assessment. Areas where the distance between the two rings is largest represent the greatest risks to the organization. Such a report can help set priorities. It can also be used to measure progress over time.

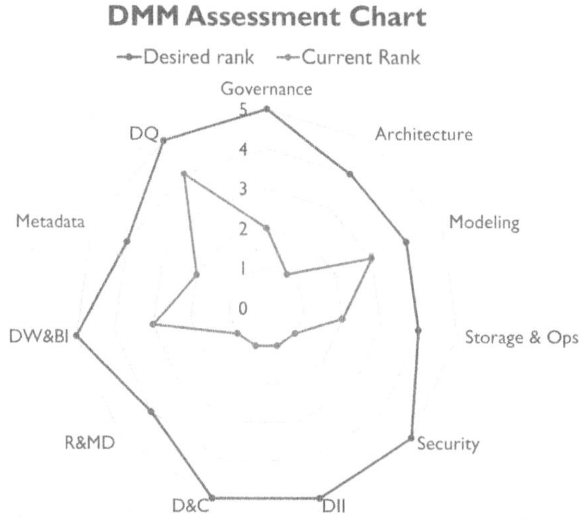

Figure 105 Example of a Data Management Maturity Assessment Visualization

1.3.3 Existing DMMA Frameworks[98]

A data management maturity assessment framework is segmented into discrete data management topics. Framework focus and content vary depending on whether they have a general or industry-specific focus. However, most address subjects that can be mapped to DAMA-DMBOK Knowledge Areas. The examples below are intended to illustrate the range of Capability Maturity Models that have been developed in the data management space. Many vendors have developed their own models. Organizations should evaluate several models before choosing a vendor or before developing their own framework.

1.3.3.1 CMMI Data Management Maturity Model (DMM)

The CMMI (Capability Maturity Model Institute) has developed the CMMI-DMM (Data Management Maturity Model) which provides assessment criteria for the following data management areas:

- Data Management Strategy
- Data Governance
- Data Quality
- Platform and Architecture
- Data Operations
- Supporting Processes

Within each of these processes, the model identifies sub-processes for evaluation. For example, the Data Quality section accounts for Data Quality Strategy and Data Quality Assessment, Profiling, and Cleansing. The model also accounts for the relation between the data management areas. For example the need for stakeholder alignment and the relation between business processes and Data Quality Management.[99]

1.3.3.2 EDM Council DCAM[100]

The Enterprise Data Management Council, an industry advocacy organization for financial services headquartered in the United States, has developed the DCAM (Data Management Capability Assessment Model). The result of a membership-driven effort to get consensus on data management best practices, the DCAM describes 37 capabilities and 115 sub-capabilities associated with the development of a sustainable Data Management program. Scoring focuses on the level of stakeholder engagement, formality of process, and existence of artifacts that demonstrate the achievement of capabilities.

---

[98] For additional information and review of existing Data Management CMMs, see: Alan McSweeney, *Review of Data Management Maturity Models*, SlideShare.net, published 2013-10-23. http://bit.ly/2spTCY9. Jeff Gorball, *Introduction to Data Management Maturity Models*, SlideShare.net, published 2016-08-01. McSweeney includes the DAMA-DMBOK as one of his maturity models, although the DMBOK is not structured as such.

[99] http://bit.ly/1Vev9xx accessed 2015-07-18.

[100] http://bit.ly/2sqaSga accessed 2015-07-18.

1.3.3.3 IBM Data Governance Council Maturity Model[101]

The IBM Data Governance Council Maturity Model was based on input from a council of 55 organizations. Council members collaborated to define a common set of observable and desired behaviors that organizations can use to evaluate and design their own data governance programs. The purpose of the model is to help organizations build consistency and quality control in governance through proven business technologies, collaborative methods, and best practices. The model is organized around four key categories:

- **Outcomes**: Data risk management and compliance, value creation
- **Enablers**: Organizational structure and awareness, policy, stewardship
- **Core disciplines**: Data Quality Management, information lifecycle management, information security and privacy
- **Supporting Disciplines**: Data Architecture, classification and Metadata, audit information, logging and reporting

The IBM model is presented both as a Maturity Framework and as a set of assessment questions with answers constructed to indicate maturity levels.

1.3.3.4 Stanford Data Governance Maturity Model[102]

The Stanford Data Governance Maturity Model was developed for use by the University; it was not intended to be an industry standard. Even still, it serves as a solid example of a model that provides guidance and a standard of measurement. The model focuses on data governance, not data management, but it nevertheless provides a basis for evaluating data management overall. The model differentiates between foundational (awareness, formalization, Metadata) and project (data stewardship, Data Quality, Master Data) components. Within each, it articulates drivers for people, policies, and capabilities. It then articulates characteristics of each level of maturity. It also provides qualitative and quantitative measurements for each level.

1.3.3.5 Gartner's Enterprise Information Management Maturity Model

Gartner has published an EIM maturity model, which establishes criteria for evaluating vision, strategy, metrics, governance, roles and responsibilities, lifecycle, and infrastructure.

2. Activities

Data Management Maturity Assessments require planning. To ensure practical, actionable results, allow time within the plan for preparation of materials and evaluation of results. Assessments should be conducted in a short,

---

[101] https://ibm.co/2sRfBIn (accessed 2016-12-04).

[102] http://stanford.io/2sBR5bZ (accessed 2016-12-04) and http://stanford.io/2rVPyM2 (accessed 2016-12-04).

defined timeframe. The purpose of the evaluation is expose current strengths and opportunities for improvement – not to solve problems.

Evaluations are conducted by soliciting knowledge from business, data management, and information technology participants. The goal is to reach a consensus view of current state capabilities, supported by evidence. Evidence may come from examination of artifacts (such as whether database backups exist), through interviews (verifying someone is performing system of record evaluation for re-use), or both.

Assessments can and should be scaled to fit the needs of the organization. However, amend with care. Models may lose rigor or traceability to original intent if shortened or edited. Keep the integrity of the model intact when customizing.

2.1 Plan Assessment Activities

Planning for an assessment includes defining the overall approach and communicating with stakeholders before and during the assessment to ensure they are engaged. The assessment itself includes collecting and evaluating inputs and communicating results, recommendations, and action plans.

2.1.1 Define Objectives

Any organization that decides it should assess its data management maturity level is already engaged in the effort to improve its practices. In most cases, such an organization will have identified the drivers for the assessment. These drivers must be clarified in the form of objectives that describe the focus and influence the scope of the assessment. The objectives for the assessment must be clearly understood by executives and the lines of business, who can help ensure alignment with the organization's strategic direction.

Assessment objectives also provide criteria by which to evaluate which assessment model to adopt, which business areas to prioritize for assessment, and who should provide direct input to the process.

2.1.2 Choose a Framework

As described in Section 1.3.3, existing frameworks focus on different aspects of data management. Review these frameworks in the context of assumptions about current state and assessment objectives in order to choose one that will inform the organization in meaningful ways. Focus areas of the assessment model can be customized based on organizational focus or scope.

The choice of framework influences how the assessment is conducted. The team working on it should have expertise in the model and the methodology on which it depends.

2.1.3 Define Organizational Scope

Most DMM Frameworks are designed to apply to an entire enterprise. However, an enterprise-wide scope may be impractical. For a first assessment, it is usually best to define a manageable scope, such as a single business area or program. The areas chosen represent a meaningful subset of the organization and participants should be able to influence key business processes that affect the data assets within scope. As part of a phased approach, evaluation can be repeated for other parts of the organization. There are trade-offs between local and enterprise assessments:

- **Localized assessments** can go much deeper into the details. They can also be done more quickly because the scope is contained. To do a localized assessment, select a function that is highly regulated, such as financial reporting within a public company. The inputs, roles, tools, and consumers may be outside of the functions being assessed, which can complicate the scoping and execution of the assessment. Well-planned localized assessments can often be aggregated and weighted to form an enterprise assessment, since many data assets are shared.

- **Enterprise assessments** focus on the broad and sometimes disconnected parts of an organization. An enterprise assessment may be created from localized DMMA's or it can be a separate undertaking. For example, an organization may evaluate different functions (research and development, manufacturing, and financing) based on the same criteria. The inputs, roles, tools, and consumers are typically pan-enterprise and multi-leveled.

2.1.4 Define Interaction Approach

In conducting a DMMA, an organization should follow recommendations for the selected model. Information gathering activities may include workshops, interviews, surveys, and artifact reviews. Employ methods that work well within the organizational culture, minimize the time commitment from participants, and enable the assessment to be completed quickly so that actions from the assessment can be defined while the process is fresh in participants' minds.

In all cases, responses will need to be formalized by having participants rate the assessment criteria. In many cases, assessment will also include actual inspection and evaluation of artifacts and other evidence.

If there are delays in completing the assessment, stakeholders are likely to lose enthusiasm for the Data Management program and the impetus for contributing to positive change. It is advisable to avoid detailed and comprehensive analysis and to emphasize sound judgment based on the expertise of the assessment leaders. The DMM Frameworks provide the measurement criteria and an embedded path to improvement. These enable synthesis of a complete picture of the current Data Management program and its parts.

2.1.5 Plan Communications

Communications contribute to the overall success of the assessment and the action items coming out of it. Communication will be directed at participants and other stakeholders. Findings may impact people's jobs, through changes in methodology and organizational alignment, so it is important to communicate clearly about the purpose, the process, and specific expectations for individuals and groups. Ensure participants understand the assessment model, as well as how the findings will be used.

Before the assessment begins, stakeholders should be informed about expectations for the assessment. Communications should describe:

- The purpose of the DMMA
- How it will be conducted
- What their involvement may be
- The schedule of assessment activities

During any activity of the assessment (for example, a focus group meeting), ensure there is a clear agenda, including a plan to answer any follow up questions. Continually remind participants of the goals and objectives. Always thank the participants and describe next steps.

Determine if the planned approach is likely to be successful across the targeted business scope, including such factors as resistance / cooperation, possible internal legal concerns about exposure to outside inspection if troubling gaps are found, or possible Human Resources concerns.

The communications plan should include a schedule to report on findings and recommendations at all levels, including general reports and executive briefings.

2.2 Perform Maturity Assessment

2.2.1 Gather Information

The next step is to gather appropriate inputs for the assessment, based on the interaction model. At a minimum, the information gathered will include formal ratings of assessment criteria. It may also include input from interviews and focus groups, system analysis and design documentation, data investigation, email strings, procedure manuals, standards, policies, file repositories, approval workflows, various work products, Metadata repositories, data and integration reference architectures, templates, and forms.

2.2.2 Perform the Assessment

The overall rating assignments and interpretation are typically multi-phased. Participants will have different opinions generating different ratings across the assessment topics. Discussion and rationalization will be needed to reconcile the ratings. Input is provided by the participants and then refined through artifact reviews or examination by the assessment team. The goal is to come to a consensus view of current state. This view should be supported by evidence (i.e., proof of practice demonstrated by behavior and artifacts). If stakeholders do not have consensus on current state, it is difficult to have consensus on how to improve the organization.

The refinement generally works as follows:

- Review results against the rating method and assign a preliminary rating to each work product or activity.
- Document the supporting evidence.
- Review with participants to come to consensus on a final rating for each area. If appropriate, use weight modifiers based on the importance of each criterion.
- Document the interpretation of the rating using the model criteria statements and assessor comments.
- Develop visualizations to illustrate results of the assessment.

2.3 Interpret Results

Interpretation of the results consists of identifying improvement opportunities aligned with organizational strategy and recommending actions required to take advantage of these opportunities. In other words, interpretation defines next steps toward a target state. When the assessment is complete, organizations need to plan for the target state that they aspire to achieve in data management. The amount of time and effort required to achieve the desired target will vary, depending on the starting point, the culture of the organization, and the drivers for change.

When presenting assessment results, start with the meaning of the ratings for the organization. The ratings can be expressed with respect to organizational and cultural drivers as well as business goals, such as customer satisfaction or increased sales. Illustrate the linkage between the current capabilities of the organization and the business processes and strategies that they support, and the benefits of improving these capabilities by moving to the target state.

2.3.1 Report Assessment Results

The assessment report should include:

- Business drivers for the assessment
- Overall results of the assessment
- Ratings by topic with gaps indicated
- A recommended approach to close gaps
- Strengths of the organization as observed
- Risks to progress
- Investment and outcomes options
- Governance and metrics to measure progress
- Resource analysis and potential future utilization
- Artifacts that can be used or re-used within the organization

The assessment report is an input to the enhancement of the Data Management program, either as a whole or by Data Management Knowledge Area. From it, the organization can develop or advance its data management strategy. Strategy should include initiatives that further business goals through improved governance of processes and standards.

2.3.2 Develop Executive Briefings

The assessment team should prepare executive briefings that summarize findings – strengths, gaps, and recommendations – that executives will use as input to decisions about targets, initiatives, and timelines. The team must tailor the messages to clarify likely impacts and benefits for each executive group.

Often executives wish to aim higher than the assessment recommendations. In other words, they want to skip levels in the maturity model. Targeting a higher level of maturity has to be reflected in the impact analysis for the recommendations. There is a cost to this kind of acceleration, and costs must be balanced against benefits.

2.4 Create a Targeted Program for Improvements

The DMMA should have a direct impact on data strategy and IT governance, as well as the Data Management program and strategy. Recommendations from the DMMA should be actionable. These should describe capabilities the organizational requires. In doing so, an assessment can be a powerful tool for IT and business leaders to set organizational priorities and allocate resources.

2.4.1 Identify Actions and Create a Roadmap

DMMA ratings highlight items for management attention. Initially, a rating is likely to be used as a standalone metric to determine how well an organization is doing a specific activity. However, ratings can be quickly operationalized into ongoing measures, especially for activities where change is desired (e.g., "The target is level 'n' because we need or want to be able to do something 'z'"). If the assessment model is used for ongoing measurement, its criteria not only guides the organization to higher levels of maturity, its criteria also keeps organizational attention on improvement efforts.

The DMM assessment results should be detailed and comprehensive enough to support a multiple year data management improvement program, including initiatives that will build data management capability as the organization adopt best practices. Since change largely happens in organizations through projects, new projects must be influenced to adopt better practices. The roadmap or reference plan should contain:

- Sequenced activities to effect improvements in specific data management functions
- A timeline for implementing improvement activities
- Expected improvements in DMMA ratings once activities have been implemented
- Oversight activities, including the maturing this oversight over the timeline

The roadmap will give targets and a pace for change within prioritized work streams, and accompanied by an approach for measuring progress.

2.5 Re-assess Maturity

Re-assessments should be conducted at regular intervals. They are part of the cycle of continuous improvement:

- Establish a baseline rating through the first assessment
- Define re-assessment parameters, including organizational scope
- Repeat DMM assessment as necessary on a published schedule
- Track trends relative to the initial baseline
- Develop recommendations based on the re-assessment findings

Re-assessment can also re-invigorate or refocus effort. Measurable progress assists in maintaining commitment and enthusiasm across the organization. Changes to regulatory frameworks, internal or external policy, or innovations that could change the approach to governance and strategies are additional reasons to re-assess periodically.

3. Tools

- **Data Management Maturity Framework**: The primary tool used in a maturity assessment is the DMM framework itself.

- **Communication Plan**: A communication plan includes an engagement model for stakeholders, the type of information to be shared, and the schedule for sharing information.

- **Collaboration Tools**: Collaboration tools allow findings from the assessment to be shared. In addition, evidence of data management practices may be found in email, completed templates, and review documents created via standard processes for collaborative design, operations, incident tracking, reviews, and approvals.

- **Knowledge Management and Metadata Repositories**: Data standards, policies, methods, agendas, minutes of meetings or decisions, and business and technical artifacts that serve as proof of practice may be managed in these repositories. In some CMMs, lack of such repositories is an indicator of lower maturity in the organization. Metadata repositories can exist in several constructs, which may not be obvious to the participants. For example, some Business Intelligence applications rely completely on Metadata to compile their views and reports, while not referring to it as a separate distinct repository.

4. Techniques

Many techniques related to executing a DMMA are defined by the methodology of the DMM framework chosen. Techniques that are more general are described here.

4.1 Selecting a DMM Framework

The following criteria should be considered when selecting a DMM framework.

- **Accessibility**: Practices are stated in non-technical terms that convey the functional essence of the activity.

- **Comprehensiveness**: The framework addresses a broad scope of data management activities and includes business engagement, not merely IT processes.
- **Extensible and flexible**: The model is structured to enable enhancement of industry-specific or additional disciplines and can be used either in whole or in part, depending on the needs of the organization.
- **Future progress path built-in**: While specific priorities differ from organization to organization, the DMM framework outlines a logical way forward within each of the functions it describes.
- **Industry-agnostic vs. industry-specific**: Some organizations will benefit from an industry-specific approach, others from a more generic framework. Any DMM framework should also adhere to data management best practices that cross verticals.
- **Level of abstraction or detail**: Practices and evaluation criteria are expressed at a sufficient level of detail to ensure that they can be related to the organization and the work it performs.
- **Non-prescriptive**: The framework describes what needs to be performed, not how it must be performed.
- **Organized by topic**: The framework places data management activities in their appropriate context, enabling each to be evaluated separately, while recognizing the dependencies.
- **Repeatable**: The framework can be consistently interpreted, supporting repeatable results to compare an organization against others in its industry and to track progress over time.
- **Supported by a neutral, independent organization**: The model should be vendor neutral in order to avoid conflicts of interest, and widely available to ensure a broad representation of best practices.
- **Technology neutral**: The focus of the model should be on practices, rather than tools.
- **Training support included**: The model is supported by comprehensive training to enable professionals to master the framework and optimize its use.

4.2 DAMA-DMBOK Framework Use

The DAMA-DMBOK can be used to prepare for or establish criteria for a DMMA. Execution owners will see a direct linkage between segmented functions (the Knowledge Areas) and the corresponding tasks (activities). The DMBOK Knowledge Areas, activities, and deliverables (work products) can be configured to a specific DMM framework based on the areas measured, their supporting activities, relevancy, and time available. This fast, checklist approach can be used to determine areas that need deeper analysis, represent gaps, or point to hot spots for remediation. The DMBOK offers an additional advantage as an assessment-planning tool: There is a large community of knowledge professionals using the DMBOK as a guide across multiple industries, creating a community of practice around its use.

5. Guidelines for a DMMA

5.1 Readiness Assessment / Risk Assessment

Before conducting a maturity assessment, it is helpful to identify potential risks and some risk mitigation strategies. Table 33 summarizes risks and mitigation approaches.

Table 33 Typical Risks and Mitigations for a DMMA

Risk	Mitigation
Lack of organizational buy-in	Socialize the concepts related to the assessment. Establish benefit statements before conducting the assessment. Share articles and success stories. Engage an executive sponsor to champion the effort and review the results.
Lack of DMMA expertise Lack of time or in-house expertise Lack of communication planning or standards	Use third party resources or specialists. Require knowledge transfer and training as part of the engagement.
Lack of 'Data Speak' in the organization; Conversations on data quickly devolve into discussions about systems	Relate the DMMA to specific business problems or scenarios. Address in the communications plan. The DMMA will educate all participants regardless of background and technical experience. Orient participants to key concepts prior to the DMMA.
Incomplete or out-of-date assets for analysis	Flag 'as of' or balance the rating accordingly. For example, give a -1 to everything that is over 1 year out-of-date.
Narrow focus	Reduce the investigation depth to a simple DMMA and go to other areas for a quick assessment to establish ratings for a later comparative baseline. Conduct the first DMMA as a pilot, then apply lessons learned to address a broader scope. Present in-scope focus of proposed assessment in context of DAMA-DMBOK Knowledge Areas. Illustrate what is being left out of scope and discuss the need to include.
Inaccessible staff or systems	Reduce the horizontal scope of the DMMA by focusing only on available Knowledge Areas and staff
Surprises arise such as a regulation changes	Add flexibility into the assessment work stream and focus.

5.2 Organizational and Cultural Change

Establishing or enhancing a Data Management program includes changes to processes, methods, and tools. With these changes, culture must also change. Organizational and cultural transformation begins with acknowledging that things can be better. Measurement functions typically usher in meaningful change. The DMMA locates the organization on a maturity scale and provides a roadmap for improvement. Doing so, it can point an organization forward through change. The DMMA results should be part of a larger discussion within an organization. When properly supported by effective data governance, DMMA results can coalesce differing perspectives, result in a shared vision, and accelerate an organization's progress. (See Chapter 17.)

6. Maturity Management Governance

Typically, a DMMA is part of an overall set of data governance activities, each of which has a lifecycle. The lifecycle of a DMMA consists of the initial planning and initial assessment, followed by recommendations, an action plan, and periodic re-evaluation. The lifecycle itself should be governed.

6.1 DMMA Process Oversight

Oversight for the DMMA process belongs to the Data Governance team. If formal Data Governance is not in place, then oversight defaults to the steering committee or management layer that initiated the DMMA. The process should have an executive sponsor, ideally the CDO, to ensure improvements in data management activities map directly to business objectives.

The breadth and depth of oversight depend on the DMMA's scope. Each function involved in the process has a voice in the execution, method, results, and roadmaps coming from the overall assessment. Each involved data management area and organization function will have an independent view, but also will have a common language through the DMM framework.

6.2 Metrics

In addition to being a core component of any improvement strategy, metrics are a key communications tool. Initial DMMA metrics are the ratings representing the current state of data management. These can be periodically reassessed to show improvement trends. Each organization should develop metrics tailored to its target state roadmap. Sample metrics could include:

- **DMMA ratings**: DMMA ratings present a snapshot of the organization's capability level. The ratings may be accompanied by a description, perhaps a custom weighting for the rating across an assessment or specific topic area, and a recommended target state.

- **Resource utilization rates**: Powerful examples of metrics that help express the cost of data management in the form of head count. An example of this type of metric is: "Every resource in the organization spends 10% of their time manually aggregating data."

- **Risk exposure** or the ability to respond to risk scenarios expresses an organization's capabilities relative to their DMMA ratings. For example, if an organization wanted to begin a new business that required a high level of automation but their current operating model is based on manual data management (Level 1), they would be at risk of not delivering.

- **Spend management** expresses how the cost of data management is allocated across an organization and identifies the impacts of this cost on sustainability and value. These metrics overlap with data governance metrics.

  - Data management sustainability
  - Achievement of initiative goals and objectives
  - Effectiveness of communication
  - Effectiveness of education and training
  - Speed of change adoption
  - Data management value
  - Contributions to business objectives
  - Reductions in risks
  - Improved efficiency in operations

- **Inputs to the DMMA** are important to manage as they speak to the completeness of coverage, level of investigation, and detail of the scope relevant for interpretation of the scoring results. Core inputs could include the following: count, coverage, availability, number of systems, data volumes, teams involved, etc.

- **Rate of Change** The rate at which an organization is improving its capability. A baseline is established through the DMMA. Periodic reassessment is used to trend improvement.

7. Works Cited / Recommended

Afflerbach, Peter. *Essential Readings on Assessment*. International Reading Association, 2010. Print.

Baskarada, Sasa. *IQM-CMM: Information Quality Management Capability Maturity Model*. Vieweg+Teubner Verlag, 2009. Print. Ausgezeichnete Arbeiten zur Informationsqualität.

Boutros, Tristan and Tim Purdie. *The Process Improvement Handbook: A Blueprint for Managing Change and Increasing Organizational Performance*. McGraw-Hill Education, 2013. Print.

CMMI Institute (website). http://bit.ly/1Vev9xx.

Crawford, J. Kent. *Project Management Maturity Model*. 3rd ed. Auerbach Publications, 2014. Print. PM Solutions Research.

Enterprise Data Management Council (website).

Freund, Jack and Jack Jones. *Measuring and Managing Information Risk: A FAIR Approach*. Butterworth-Heinemann, 2014. Print.

Ghavami, Peter PhD. *Big Data Governance: Modern Data Management Principles for Hadoop, NoSQL and Big Data Analytics*. CreateSpace Independent Publishing Platform, 2015. Print.

Honeysett, Sarah. *Limited Capability - The Assessment Phase*. Amazon Digital Services LLC., 2013. Social Insecurity Book 3.

IBM Data Governance Council. https://ibm.co/2sUKIng.

Jeff Gorball, *Introduction to Data Management Maturity Models*. SlideShare.net, 2016-08-01. http://bit.ly/2tsIOqR.

Marchewka, Jack T. *Information Technology Project Management: Providing Measurable Organizational Value*. 5th ed. Wiley, 2016. Print.

McSweeney, Alan. *Review of Data Management Maturity Models*. SlideShare.net, 2013-10-23. http://bit.ly/2spTCY9.

Persse, James R. *Implementing the Capability Maturity Model*. Wiley, 2001.Print.

Saaksvuori, Antti. *Product Management Maturity Assessment Framework*. Sirrus Publishing Ltd., 2015. Print.

Select Business Solutions. "What is the Capability Maturity Model?" http://bit.ly/IFMJI8 (Accessed 2016-11-10).

Stanford University. *Stanford Data Governance Maturity Model*. http://stanford.io/2ttOMrF.

Van Haren Publishing. *IT Capability Maturity Framework IT-CMF*. Van Haren Pub, 2015. Print.

CHAPTER 16

Data Management Organization and Role Expectations

1. Introduction

The data landscape is quickly evolving and with it, organizations need to evolve the ways they manage and govern data. Most organizations today are faced with an increasing volume of data captured through a wide range of processes in a range of formats. The increase in volume and variety adds complexity to data management. At the same time, data consumers now demand quick and easy access to data. They want to be able to understand data and use it to address critical business questions in a timely manner. Data management and data governance organizations must be flexible enough to work effectively in this evolving environment. To do so, they need to clarify basic questions about ownership, collaboration, accountability, and decision-making.

This section will describe a set of principles that should be considered when putting together a data management or data governance organization. It refers to both data governance and data management because data governance provides the guidance and business context for the activities executed by the Data Management Organization. There is no perfect organizational structure for either. While common principles should be applied to organizing around data governance and data management, much of the detail will depend on the drivers of that enterprise's industry and the corporate culture of the enterprise itself.

2. Understand Existing Organization and Cultural Norms

Awareness, ownership, and accountability are the keys to activating and engaging people in data management initiatives, policies, and processes. Before defining any new organization or attempting to improve an existing one, it is important to understand current state of component pieces, related to culture, the existing operating model, and people. See Figure 106. For example:

- **The role of data in the organization**: What key processes are data-driven? How are data requirements defined and understood? How well-recognized is the role that data plays in organizational strategy?

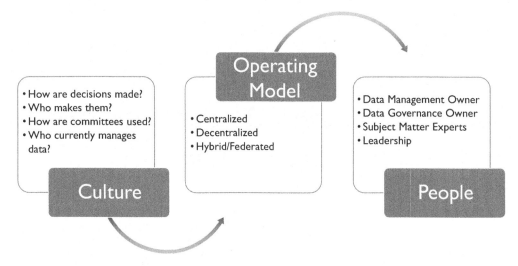

Figure 106 Assess Current State to Create an Operating Model

- **Cultural norms about data**: Are there potential cultural obstacles to implementing or improving management and governance structures?
- **Data management and data governance practices**: How and by whom is data-related work executed? How and by whom are decisions about data made?
- **How work is organized and executed**: For example, what is the relation between project-focused and operational execution? What committee structures are in place that can support the data management effort?
- **How reporting relationships are organized**: For example, is the organization centralized or decentralized, hierarchical or flat?
- **Skill levels**: What is the level of data knowledge and data management knowledge of SMEs and other stakeholders, from line staff to executives?

After forming a picture of current state, assess the level of satisfaction with current state in order to gain insight into the organization's data management needs and priorities. For example:

- Does the organization have the information it needs to make sound, timely business decisions?
- Does the organization have confidence in its revenue reports?
- Can it track the organizational key performance indicators?
- Is the organization in compliance with all laws regarding management of data?

Most organizations that seek to improve their data management or governance practices are in the middle of the capability maturity scale (i.e., they are neither 0's nor 5's on the CMM scale). (See Chapter 15.) To craft a relevant Data Management Organization, it is important to understand and accommodate the existing company culture and organizational norms. If the Data Management Organization is not aligned to the existing decision-making and committee constructs, it will be challenging to sustain it over time. Therefore, it makes sense to evolve these organizations, rather than imposing radical changes.

A Data Management Organization should align with a company's organizational hierarchy and resources. Finding the right people requires an understanding of both the functional and the political role of data management within an organization. The aim should be cross-functional participation from the various business stakeholders. To accomplish this:

- Identify employees currently performing data management functions; recognize and involve them first. Hire additional resources only as data management and governance needs grow.
- Examine the methods the organization is using to manage data and determine how processes can be improved. Determine how much change is likely to be required to improve data management practices.
- Roadmap the kinds of changes that need to take place from an organizational perspective to better meet requirements.

3. Data Management Organizational Constructs

A critical step in Data Management Organization design is identifying the best-fit operating model for the organization. The operating model is a framework articulating roles, responsibilities, and decision-making processes. It describes how people and functions will collaborate.

A reliable operating model helps create accountability by ensuring the right functions within the organization are represented. It facilitates communication and provides a process to resolve issues. While it forms the basis for the organizational structure, the operating model is not an org chart – it is not about putting names in boxes, but about describing the relationship between the component pieces of the organization.

This section will present a high-level overview of the pros and cons of decentralized, network, hybrid, federated, and centralized operating models.

3.1 Decentralized Operating Model

In a decentralized model, data management responsibilities are distributed across different lines of business and IT (see Figure 107). Collaboration is committee-based; there is no single owner. Many Data Management programs start as grass root efforts to unify the data management practices across an organization and therefore have a decentralized structure.

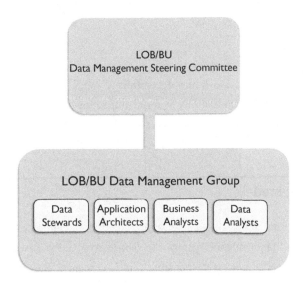

Figure 107 Decentralized Operating Model

The benefits of this model include its relatively flat structure and its alignment of data management to lines of business or IT. This alignment generally means there is a clear understanding of data requirements. It is also relatively easy to implement or improve.

The drawbacks include the challenge of having many participants involved with governance bodies and in decision-making. It is generally harder to implement collaborative decisions than centralized edicts. Decentralized models are generally less formal and because of this, they can be harder to sustain over time. To be successful, they need to have ways to enforce consistency of practices. This can be difficult to coordinate. It is also often difficult to define data ownership with a decentralized model.

3.2 Network Operating Model

Decentralized informality can be made more formal through a documented series of connections and accountabilities via a RACI (Responsible, Accountable, Consulted, and Informed) matrix. This is called a networked model because it operates as a series of known connections between people and roles and can be diagrammed as a 'network.' (See Figure 108.)

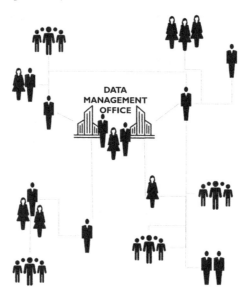

Figure 108 Network Operating Model

A network model's benefits are similar to those of a decentralized model (flat structure, alignment, quick set up). The addition of a RACI helps create accountability without impacting the organizational charts. The additional drawback is the need to maintain and enforce expectations related to the RACI.

3.3 Centralized Operating Model

The most formal and mature data management operating model is a centralized one (see Figure 109). Here everything is owned by the Data Management Organization. Those involved in governing and managing data report directly to a data management leader who is responsible for Governance, Stewardship, Metadata Management, Data Quality Management, Master and Reference Data Management, Data Architecture, Business Analysis, etc.

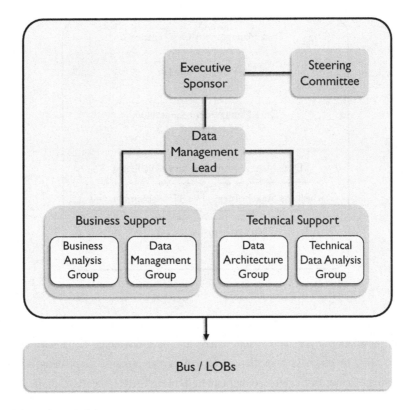

Figure 109 Centralized Operating Model

The benefit of a centralized model is that it establishes a formal executive position for data management or data governance. There is one person at the top. Decision-making is easier because accountability is clear. Within the organization, data can be managed by type or subject area. The drawback is that implementation of a centralized model generally requires significant organizational change. There is also a risk that formal separation of the data management role moves it away for core business processes and can result in knowledge being lost over time.

A centralized model generally requires a new organization. The question arises: Where does the Data Management Organization fit within the overall enterprise? Who leads it and to whom does the leader report? It is becoming more common for a Data Management Organization *not* to report to the CIO because of the desire to maintain a business, rather than IT, perspective on data. These organizations are also commonly part of a shared services or operations team or part of the Chief Data Officer's organization. (See Section 6.1.)

3.4 Hybrid Operating Model

As its name implies, the hybrid operating model encompasses benefits of both the decentralized and centralized models (see Figure 110). In a hybrid model, a centralized data management Center of Excellence works with decentralized business unit groups, usually through both an executive steering committee representing key lines of business and a set of tactical working groups addressing specific problems.

In this model, some roles remain decentralized. For example, Data Architects may stay within an Enterprise Architecture group; lines of business may have their own Data Quality teams. Which roles are centralized and which stay decentralized can vary widely, depending largely on organizational culture.

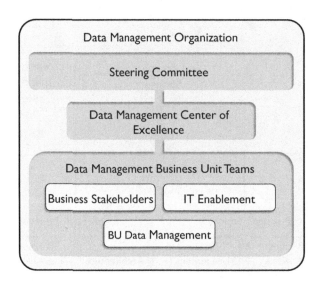

Figure 110 Hybrid Operating Model

The primary benefit of a hybrid model is that it establishes appropriate direction from the top of the organization. There is an executive accountable for data management and/or governance. Business Unit teams have broad accountability and can align to business priorities to provide greater focus. They benefit from the support of a dedicated data management Center of Excellence that can help bring focus to specific challenges.

The challenges include getting the organization set up, since doing so generally requires additional headcount to staff a Center of Excellence. Business Unit teams may have different priorities, and these will need to be managed from an enterprise perspective. In addition, there are sometimes conflicts between the priorities of the central organization and those of the decentralized organizations.

3.5 Federated Operating Model

A variation on the hybrid operating model, the federated model provides additional layers of centralization / decentralization, which are often required in large global enterprises. Imagine an enterprise Data Management Organization with multiple hybrid data management models delineated based on division or region. (See Figure 111.)

A federated model provides a centralized strategy with decentralized execution. Therefore, for large enterprises it may be the only model that can work. A data management executive who is accountable across the organization runs the enterprise Center of Excellence. Of course, different lines of business are empowered to meet requirements based on their needs and priorities. Federation enables the organization to prioritize based on specific data entities, divisional challenges, or regional priorities.

The main drawback is complexity. There are a lot of layers, and there needs to be a balance between autonomy for lines of business and the needs of the enterprise. This balance can impact enterprise priorities.

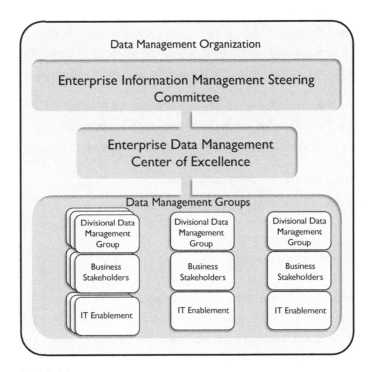

Figure 111 Federated Operating Model

3.6 Identifying the Best Model for an Organization

The operating model is a starting point for improving data management and data governance practices. Introducing it requires an understanding of how it may impact the current organization and how it will likely need to evolve over time. Since the operating model will serve as the structure through which policies and processes will be defined, approved, and executed, it is critical to identify the best fit for an organization.

Assess whether the current organizational structure is centralized, decentralized, or a combination, hierarchical or relatively flat. Characterize how independent divisions or regions are. Do they operate almost self-sufficiently? Are their requirements and goals very different from each other? Most importantly, try to determine how decisions are made (e.g., democratically or by fiat), as well as how they are implemented.

The answers should give a starting point to understand the organization's location on the spectrum between decentralized and centralized.

3.7 DMO Alternatives and Design Considerations

Most organizations start with a decentralized model before they move toward a formal Data Management Organization (DMO). As an organization sees the impact of improvements in data quality, it may start to formalize accountability through a data management RACI matrix and evolve into a network model. Over time, synergies between the distributed roles will become more obvious and economies of scale will be identified that will pull some roles and people into organized groups. Eventually, this can morph into a hybrid or federated model.

Some organizations don't have the luxury of going through this maturity process. They are forced to mature quickly based on a market shock or new government regulations. In such a case, it is important to proactively address the discomfort associated with the organizational change if it is to be successful and sustainable. (See Chapter 17.)

Whichever model is chosen, remember that simplicity and usability are essential for acceptance and sustainability. If the operating model fits the culture of a company, then data management and proper governance can be embedded in operations and aligned with strategy. Keep these tips in mind when constructing an Operating Model:

- Determine the starting point by assessing current state
- Tie the operating model to organization structure
- Take into account:
    - Organization Complexity + Maturity
    - Domain Complexity + Maturity
    - Scalability
- Get executive sponsorship – a **must** for a sustainable model
- Ensure that any leadership forum (steering committee, advisory council, board) is a decision-making body
- Consider pilot programs and waves of implementation
- Focus on high-value, high-impact data domains
- Use what already exists
- Never take a One-Size-Fits-All approach

4. Critical Success Factors

Ten factors have been consistently shown to play a key role in the success of effective Data Management Organizations, regardless of their structure:

1. Executive sponsorship
2. Clear vision
3. Proactive change management
4. Leadership alignment
5. Communication
6. Stakeholder engagement
7. Orientation and training
8. Adoption measurement
9. Adherence to guiding principles
10. Evolution not revolution

4.1 Executive Sponsorship

Having the right executive sponsor ensures that stakeholders affected by a Data Management program receive the necessary guidance to transition efficiently and effectively through the changes needed to put the new data-focused organization together and sustain it for the long term. The executive sponsor should understand and believe in the initiative. He or she must be able to effectively engage other leaders in support of the changes.

4.2 Clear Vision

A clear vision for the Data Management Organization, along with a plan to drive it, is critical to success. Organizational leaders must ensure that all stakeholders who are affected by data management – both internal and external – understand and internalize what data management is, why it is important, and how their work will affect and be affected by it.

4.3 Proactive Change Management

Managing the change associated with creating a Data Management Organization requires planning for, managing, and sustaining change. Applying organizational change management to the establishment of a Data Management Organization addresses the people challenges and increases the likelihood that desired Data Management Organization is sustainable over time. (See Chapter 17.)

4.4 Leadership Alignment

Leadership alignment ensures that there is agreement on – and unified support for – the need for a Data Management program and that there is agreement on how success will be defined. Leadership alignment includes both the alignment between the leaders' goals and the data management outcomes and value *and* alignment in purpose amongst the leaders.

If leaders are not aligned with each other, they will end up sending mixed messages that can lead to resistance and eventually derail the change. Therefore, it is critical to assess – and regularly re-assess – leaders at all levels to identify disconnects and take steps to quickly address them.

4.5 Communication

Communication should start early and continue openly and often. The organization must ensure that stakeholders have a clear understanding of what data management is and why it is important to the company, what is changing, and what changes in behavior are required. People can't improve the way they manage data if they don't know what they are supposed to do differently. Creating a story around the data management initiative and building key messages around it helps these processes.

Messages must be consistent, underscoring the importance of data management. In addition, they should be customized according to stakeholder group. For example, the level of education or amount of training needed by different groups concerning data management will vary. Messages should be repeated as needed and continually tested over time to ensure they are effectively getting out there and that awareness and understanding are building.

4.6 Stakeholder Engagement

Individuals, as well as groups, affected by a data management initiative will react differently to the new program and their role within it. How the organization engages these stakeholders – how they communicate with, respond to, and involve them – will have a significant impact on the success of the initiative.

A stakeholder analysis helps the organization better understand those affected by data management changes. By taking that information and mapping stakeholders according to level of influence within the organization and level of interest in (or affect due to) the data management implementation, the organization can determine the best approach to engaging different stakeholders in the change process. (See Section 5.3.)

4.7 Orientation and Training

Education is essential to making data management happen, although different groups will require different types and levels of education.

Leaders will need orientation to the broader aspects of data management and the value to the company. Data stewards, owners, and custodians (i.e., those on the frontlines of change) will require in-depth understanding of the data management initiative. Focused training will allow them to perform their roles effectively. This means training on new policies, processes, techniques, procedures, and even tools.

4.8 Adoption Measurement

It is important to build metrics around the progress and adoption of the data management guidelines and plan to know that the data management roadmap is working and that it will continue working. Plan to measure:

- Adoption
- Amount of improvement, or the delta from a previous state
- The enabling aspects of data management – how well does data management influence solutions with measurable results?
- Improved processes, projects
- Improved identification and reaction to risk
- The innovation aspect of data management – how well does data management fundamentally change how business is conducted?
- Trusted analytics

The enabling aspect of data management could focus on the improvement of data-centric processes, such as month-end closing, identification of risk, and efficiency of project execution. The innovation aspect of data management could focus on improvement in decision-making and analytics through improved and trusted data.

4.9 Adherence to Guiding Principles

A guiding principle is a statement that articulates shared organizational values, underlies strategic vision and mission, and serves as a basis for integrated decision-making. Guiding principles constitute the rules, constraints, overriding criteria, and behaviors by which an organization abides in its daily activities in the long term. Regardless of whether there is a decentralized or centralized operating model, or anything in between, it is critical to establish and agree upon guiding principles so that all participants behave in synchronistic ways. The guiding principles serve as the reference points from which all decisions will be made. Establishing them is an important first step in creating a Data Management program that effectively drives changes in behavior.

4.10 Evolution Not Revolution

In all aspects of data management, the philosophy of 'evolution not revolution' helps to minimize big changes or large-scale high-risk projects. It is important to establish an organization that evolves and matures over time. Incrementally improving the way that data is managed and prioritized by business objectives will ensure that new policies and processes are adopted and behavioral change is sustained. Incremental change is also much easier to justify so it is easier to gain stakeholder support and buy-in, and get those critical participants involved.

5. Build the Data Management Organization

5.1 Identify Current Data Management Participants

When implementing the operating model, start with teams already engaged in data management activities. This will minimize the effect on the organization and will help to ensure that the focus of the team is data, not HR or politics.

Start by reviewing existing data management activities, such as who creates and manages data, who measures data quality, or even who has 'data' in their job title. Survey the organization to find out who may already be fulfilling needed roles and responsibilities. Such individuals may hold different titles. They are likely part of a distributed organization and not necessarily recognized by the enterprise. After compiling a list of 'data people,' identify gaps. What additional roles and skill sets are required to execute the data strategy? In many cases, people in other parts of the organization have analogous, transferrable skill sets. Remember, people already in the organization bring valuable knowledge and experience to a data management effort.

Once an inventory is complete, and people are assigned to the roles, review their compensation and align it with the expectations of data management. Likely, the Human Resources department will get involved to validate the titles, roles, compensation, and performance objectives. Ensure that the roles are assigned to the right people at the right level within the organization, so that when they are involved in decision-making, they have the credibility to make decisions that stick.

5.2 Identify Committee Participants

No matter which operating model an organization chooses, some governance work will need to be done by a Data Governance Steering Committee and by working groups. It is important to get the right people on the Steering Committee and to use their time well. Keep them well-informed and focused on the ways that improved data management will help them reach business objectives, including strategic goals.

Many organizations are reluctant to start yet another committee since there are so many already existing. It is often easier to take advantage of existing committees to advance data management topics than it is to start a new one. But take this route cautiously. The main risk in using an existing committee is that data management may not get the attention it requires, especially in the early stages. The process to staff either a senior steering committee or a more tactical working group requires conducting stakeholder analysis and, through that, identifying executive sponsors.

5.3 Identify and Analyze Stakeholders

A stakeholder is any person or group who can influence or be affected by the Data Management program. Stakeholders can be internal to or external to the organization. They include individual SMEs, senior leaders, teams of employees, committees, customers, government or regulatory agencies, brokers, agents, vendors, etc. Internal stakeholders can come from IT, operations, compliance, legal, HR, finance or other lines of business. External stakeholders can be influential, and it is important that their needs be accounted for by the Data Management Organization.

A stakeholder analysis can help the organization determine the best approach to engaging participants in the data management process and leveraging their roles within the operating model. Insight gained from the analysis is also helpful in determining how to best allocate time and other limited resources. The earlier this analysis is conducted, the better, since the more the organization is able to anticipate reactions to change, the more it can plan for them. A stakeholder analysis will help answer questions like:

- Who will be affected by data management?
- How will roles and responsibilities shift?
- How might those affected respond to the changes?
- What issues and concerns will people have?

The analysis will result in a list of stakeholders, their goals and priorities, and why those goals are important to them. Figure out what actions are needed for stakeholders based on the analysis. Pay particular attention to what needs to be done to bring along critical stakeholders, those that can make or break an organization's data management success, especially its initial priorities. Consider:

- Who controls critical resources
- Who could block data management initiatives, either directly or indirectly
- Who could influence other critical constituents
- How supportive stakeholders are of the upcoming changes

Figure 112 provides a simple map to help prioritize stakeholders based on their influence, their level of interest in the program, or the degree to which the program will impact them.

5.4 Involve the Stakeholders

After identifying the stakeholders and a good Executive Sponsor, or a short list from which to choose, it is important to clearly articulate why each of the stakeholders should be involved. They may not jump at the chance. The person or team driving the data management effort should articulate the reasons each stakeholder is necessary to the success of the program. This means understanding their personal and professional goals, and being able to link the output from data management processes to their goals, so they can see a direct connection. Without an understanding of this direct connection, they may be willing to help out in the short term, but they will not provide long-term support or assistance.

Figure 112 Stakeholder Interest Map

6. Interactions Between the DMO and Other Data-oriented Bodies

Once the operating model is established and participants are identified, it is time to move the people into the newly authorized roles. Operationalizing the organization means establishing the committees and engaging with stakeholders. In a centralized model, most of the data management activity will be controlled within one organization. With a decentralized or network model, though, the Data Management Organization will need to work with other groups that have a significant impact on the way that data is managed. Those groups are typically:

- Chief Data Officer Organization
- Data Governance Bodies
- Data Quality
- Enterprise Architecture

6.1 The Chief Data Officer

While most companies recognize at some level that data is a valuable corporate asset, only a few have appointed a Chief Data Officer (CDO) to help bridge the gap between technology and business and evangelize an enterprise-wide data management strategy at a senior level. This role is on the rise, however, with Gartner estimating that half of all regulated companies will employ a CDO by 2017 (Gartner, 2015).

While the requirements and functions of a CDO are specific to each company's culture, organizational structure, and business needs, many CDOs tend to be part business strategist, adviser, data quality steward and all around data management ambassador.

In 2014, Dataversity published research outlining common mandates for a CDO.[103] These included:

- Establishing an organizational data strategy
- Aligning data-centric requirements with available IT and business resources
- Establishing data governance standards, policies and procedures
- Providing advice (and perhaps services) to the business for data-dependent initiatives, such as business analytics, Big Data, data quality, and data technologies
- Evangelizing the importance of good information management principles to internal and external business stakeholders
- Oversight of data usage in analytics and Business Intelligence

Dataversity's findings also highlighted shifting focuses across different industries.

Regardless of industry, it is common for a Data Management Organization to report up through the CDO. In a more decentralized operating model, the CDO is responsible for the data strategy, but resources that are in IT, operations, or other lines of business *execute* that strategy. Some DMOs are established initially with the CDO just determining the strategy, and over time other aspects of data management, governance, and analytics are folded under the CDO umbrella as efficiencies and economies of scale are identified.

6.2 Data Governance

Data Governance is the organizing framework for establishing the strategy, objectives, and policy for effectively managing corporate data. It consists of the processes, policies, organization, and technologies required to manage and ensure the availability, usability, integrity, consistency, auditability, and security of data. Since a Data Governance Program consists of the inter-workings of strategy, standards, policies and communication regarding data, it has a synergistic relationship with data management. Governance provides a framework for data management to engage and align with the business priorities and stakeholders.

Within a centralized model, the Data Governance Office can report to the Data Management Organization or vice versa. When a Data Management program is focused on establishing policies and guidelines needed to manage data as an asset, the Data Governance Office can act as the lead, and the Data Management Organization reports to (or is matrixed to) the Data Governance Office. This occurs many times in highly regulated environments where the emphasis is on policy and accountability.

Even in a very decentralized model, there should be a tight partnership between the Data Governance Office, which creates the guidelines and policies for how data should be managed, and the Data Management Organization that

---

[103] http://bit.ly/2sTf3Cy.

implements them. John Ladley succinctly clarifies this relationship: data governance is about 'Doing the right things' and data management is about 'Doing things right' (Ladley, 2012). They are two sides of the equation needed to produce valuable data. In this way, data governance provides the marching orders for data management.

Most importantly, there needs to be an understanding of this synergy and agreement upon roles, responsibilities, and accountabilities that support the guidelines of data governance and the efficiencies of data management. Participants in a Data Governance Working Group can be drawn from a Data Management Organization, and a Data Management Organization can use the mandate and 'air cover' provided by the governance oversight.

6.3 Data Quality

Data Quality Management is a key capability of a data management practice and organization. Many Data Management Organizations start with a focus on the quality of data because there is a desire to measure and improve the quality of data across the organization. It is possible to address Data Quality within a line of business, or even within an application, without having to involve other groups or manage cross-functional complexities. However, as a data quality practice matures, the organization will benefit from a unified approach to data quality; for example, by establishing a Center of Excellence. The goal shifts to improving the quality of data that is shared across lines of business or applications, often with a focus on Master Data Management. It is common that a Data Management Organization develops organically out of a Data Quality initiative as the investment in improving data quality adds value across the company, and efforts associated with improving quality expand into other disciplines like Master, Reference, and Metadata Management.

A Data Quality program can evolve into similar operating models as an over-arching Data Management program, although it is rare for Data Quality functions to become completely centralized in any sizable company because there is most often aspects of data quality that are executed on a line-of-business or application level. Because a Data Quality program can be decentralized, networked, or a hybrid (using a Center of Excellence approach), align the Data Quality operating model to that of the overall Data Management Organization, in order to use consistent stakeholders, relationships, accountabilities, standards, processes, and even tools.

6.4 Enterprise Architecture

An Enterprise Architecture group designs and documents the master blueprints for an organization to articulate and optimize how to meet its strategic objectives. The disciplines within an Enterprise Architecture practice include:

- Technology Architecture
- Application Architecture
- Information (or Data) Architecture
- Business Architecture

Data Architecture is a key capability of an effective Data Management Organization. Therefore, Data Architects can sit in either group, with a dotted line to the other group. When Data Architects sit within a Data Management Organization, typically they interface with the rest of their architecture peers via Architecture Review Boards (ARB), committees that review and give guidance on the way that architecture standards are implemented or affected by projects and programs. An ARB can approve or disapprove new projects and systems based on their level of adherence to architectural standards. When an organization does not have Data Architects, Data Management can interface with the Architecture organization in a few ways:

- **Through Data Governance**: Since both Data Management and Enterprise Architecture participate in a Data Governance program, the governance working group and committee structure can provide a platform for aligning goals, expectations, standards, and activities.

- **Through the ARB**: As data management projects are brought to the ARB, the Architecture group would provide guidance, feedback, and approvals.

- **Ad-hoc**: If there are no formal committees, then the Data Management Lead should periodically meet with the Architecture Lead to ensure there is shared knowledge and understanding of projects and processes that impact the other party. Over time, the difficulty of managing this ad hoc process will likely lead to the development of a formal role or committee to facilitate discussions and decisions.

If there were Data Architects, then they would represent architecture in governance discussions and would lead the discussions in the ARB.

6.5 Managing a Global Organization

Global companies face complex data management challenges based on the volume and variety of country-specific laws and regulations, especially those regarding the privacy and security of certain types of data. Add these issues to the typical management challenges of a global organization (distributed work force, systems, time zones, and languages), and the task of efficiently and effectively managing data can seem like an endless exercise of herding cats. Global organizations need to pay special attention to:

- Adhering to standards
- Synchronizing processes
- Aligning accountability
- Training and communication
- Monitoring and measuring effectively
- Developing economies of scale
- Reducing duplication of effort

As Data Management programs and Organizations become more global, the networked or federated models become more attractive where accountabilities can be aligned, standards can be followed, and regional variations can still be accommodated.

7. Data Management Roles

Data management roles can be defined at the functional or individual level. Names for the roles will differ between organizations and some organizations will have greater or lesser need for some of the roles.

All IT roles can be mapped to points in the data lifecycle, so they all impact the management of data, whether directly (as with a Data Architect who designs a data warehouse) or indirectly (as with a Web Developer who programs a website). Likewise, many business roles create, access, or manipulate data. Some roles, such as Data Quality Analyst, require a mix of technical skills and business knowledge. The functions and roles described below focus on those that are directed engaged in the management of data.

7.1 Organizational Roles

IT Data Management Organizations provide a range of services from data, application, and technical architecture to database administration. A centralized Data Management Services Organization is focused solely on data management. This team may include a DM Executive, other DM Managers, Data Architects, Data Analysts, Data Quality Analysts, Database Administrators, Data Security Administrators, Metadata Specialists, Data Modelers, Data Administrators, Data Warehouse Architects, Data Integration Architects, and Business Intelligence Analysts.

A federated Data Management Services approach will include a set of IT units, each focused on a facet of data management. Especially in large organizations, IT functions are often decentralized. For example, each business function may have its own team of Software Developers. A hybrid approach is also taken. For example, while each business function may have its own developers, the DBA function may be centralized.

Business functions focused on data management are most often associated with Data Governance or Enterprise Information Management teams. For example, Data Stewards are often part of a Data Governance Organization. Such an organization will facilitate Data Governance bodies, such as the Data Governance Council.

7.2 Individual Roles

Individual roles may be defined under business or IT. Some are hybrid roles that require knowledge of systems and business processes.

7.2.1 Executive Roles

Data Management executives may be on the business or technology side of the house. Chief Information Officer and Chief Technology Officer are well-established roles in IT. The concept of Chief Data Officer on the business-side has gained a lot of credibility in the past decade and many organizations have hired CDOs.

7.2.2 Business Roles

Business roles focus largely on data governance functions, especially stewardship. Data Stewards are usually recognized subject matter experts who are assigned accountability for Metadata and data quality of business entities, subject areas, or databases. Stewards play different roles, depending on organizational priorities. The initial focus of stewardship is often on defining business terms and valid values for their subject areas. In many organizations, Stewards also define and maintain data quality requirements and business rules for assigned data attributes, help identify and resolve data issues, and provide input into data standards, policies, and procedures. Stewards may function at the enterprise, business unit, or functional level. Their role may be formal ('data steward' is part of the title) or informal (they steward data, but have another job title). In addition to Data Stewards, Business Process Analysts and Process Architects contribute to ensuring that business process models and the actual processes that create data are sound and support downstream uses. Other business-based knowledge workers, such as business analyst consumers of data and information who add value to the data for the organization, contribute to the overall management of data.

7.2.3 IT Roles

IT Roles include different types of architects, developers at different levels, database administrators, and a range of supporting functions.

- **Data Architect**: A senior analyst responsible for data architecture and data integration. Data Architects may work at the enterprise level or a functional level. Data Architects may specialize in data warehousing, data marts, and their associated integration processes.

- **Data Modeler**: Responsible for capturing and modeling data requirements, data definitions, business rules, data quality requirements, and logical and physical data models.

- **Data Model Administrator**: Responsible for data model version control and change control.

- **Database Administrator**: Responsible for the design, implementation, and support of structured data assets and the performance of the technology that makes data accessible.

- **Data Security Administrator**: Responsible for ensuring controlled access to data requiring different levels of protection.

- **Data Integration Architect**: A senior data integration developer responsible for designing technology to integrate and improve the quality of enterprise data assets.

- **Data Integration Specialist**: A software designer or developer responsible for implementing systems to integrate (replicate, extract, transform, load) data assets in batch or near-real-time.

- **Analytics / Report Developer**: A software developer responsible for creating reporting and analytical application solutions.

- **Application Architect**: Senior developer responsible for integrating application systems.

- **Technical Architect**: Senior technical engineer responsible for coordinating and integrating the IT infrastructure and the IT technology portfolio.

- **Technical Engineer**: Senior technical analyst responsible for researching, implementing, administering, and supporting a portion of the information technology infrastructure.

- **Help Desk Administrator**: Responsible for handling, tracking, and resolving issues related to use of information, information systems, or the IT infrastructure.

- **IT Auditor**: An internal or external auditor of IT responsibilities, including data quality and data security.

7.2.4 Hybrid Roles

Hybrid roles require a mix of business and technical knowledge. Depending on the organization, people in these roles may report through the IT or business side.

- **Data Quality Analyst**: Responsible for determining the fitness of data for use and monitoring the ongoing condition of the data; contributes to root cause analysis of data issues and helps the organization identify business process and technical improvements that contribute to higher quality data.

- **Metadata Specialist**: Responsible for integration, control, and delivery of Metadata, including administration of Metadata repositories.

- **Business Intelligence Architect**: A senior Business Intelligence analyst responsible for the design of the Business Intelligence user environment.

- **Business Intelligence Analyst / Administrator**: Responsible for supporting effective use of Business Intelligence data by business professionals.

- **Business Intelligence Program Manager**: Coordinates BI requirements and initiatives across the corporation and integrates them into a cohesive prioritized program and roadmap.

8. Works Cited / Recommended

Aiken, Peter and Juanita Billings. *Monetizing Data Management: Finding the Value in your Organization's Most Important Asset*. Technics Publications, LLC, 2013. Print.

Aiken, Peter and Michael M. Gorman. *The Case for the Chief Data Officer: Recasting the C-Suite to Leverage Your Most Valuable Asset*. Morgan Kaufmann, 2013. Print.

Anderson, Carl. *Creating a Data-Driven Organization*. O'Reilly Media, 2015. Print.

Arthur, Lisa. *Big Data Marketing: Engage Your Customers More Effectively and Drive Value*. Wiley, 2013. Print.

Blokdijk, Gerard. *Stakeholder Analysis - Simple Steps to Win, Insights and Opportunities for Maxing Out Success*. Complete Publishing, 2015. Print.

Borek, Alexander et al. *Total Information Risk Management: Maximizing the Value of Data and Information Assets*. Morgan Kaufmann, 2013. Print.

Brestoff, Nelson E. and William H. Inmon. *Preventing Litigation: An Early Warning System to Get Big Value Out of Big Data*. Business Expert Press, 2015. Print.

Collier, Ken W. Agile *Analytics: A Value-Driven Approach to Business Intelligence and Data Warehousing*. Addison-Wesley Professional, 2011. Print. Agile Software Development Ser.

Dean, Jared. *Big Data, Data Mining, and Machine Learning: Value Creation for Business Leaders and Practitioners*. Wiley, 2014. Print. Wiley and SAS Business Ser.

Dietrich, Brenda L., Emily C. Plachy and Maureen F. Norton. *Analytics Across the Enterprise: How IBM Realizes Business Value from Big Data and Analytics*. IBM Press, 2014. Print.

Freeman, R. Edward. *Strategic Management: A Stakeholder Approach*. Cambridge University Press, 2010. Print.

Gartner, Tom McCall, contributor. "Understanding the Chief Data Officer Role." 18 February 2015. http://gtnr.it/1RIDKa6.

Gemignani, Zach, et al. *Data Fluency: Empowering Your Organization with Effective Data Communication*. Wiley, 2014. Print.

Gibbons, Paul. *The Science of Successful Organizational Change: How Leaders Set Strategy, Change Behavior, and Create an Agile Culture*. Pearson FT Press, 2015. Print.

Harrison, Michael I. *Diagnosing Organizations: Methods, Models, and Processes*. 3rd ed. SAGE Publications, Inc, 2004. Print. Applied Social Research Methods (Book 8).

Harvard Business Review, John P. Kotter et al. *HBR's 10 Must Reads on Change Management*. Harvard Business Review Press, 2011. Print. HBR's 10 Must Reads.

Hatch, Mary Jo and Ann L. Cunliffe. *Organization Theory: Modern, Symbolic, and Postmodern Perspectives*. 3rd ed. Oxford University Press, 2013. Print.

Hiatt, Jeffrey and Timothy Creasey. *Change Management: The People Side of Change*. Prosci Learning Center Publications, 2012. Print.

Hillard, Robert. *Information-Driven Business: How to Manage Data and Information for Maximum Advantage*. Wiley, 2010. Print.

Hoverstadt, Patrick. *The Fractal Organization: Creating sustainable organizations with the Viable System Model*. Wiley, 2009. Print.

Howson, Cindi. *Successful Business Intelligence: Unlock the Value of BI and Big Data*. 2nd ed. Mcgraw-Hill Osborne Media, 2013. Print.

Kates, Amy and Jay R. Galbraith. *Designing Your Organization: Using the STAR Model to Solve 5 Critical Design Challenges*. Jossey-Bass, 2007. Print.

Kesler, Gregory and Amy Kates. *Bridging Organization Design and Performance: Five Ways to Activate a Global Operation Model*. Jossey-Bass, 2015. Print.

Little, Jason. *Lean Change Management: Innovative practices for managing organizational change*. Happy Melly Express, 2014. Print.

National Renewable Energy Laboratory. *Stakeholder Analysis Methodologies Resource Book*. BiblioGov, 2012. Print.

Prokscha, Susanne. *Practical Guide to Clinical Data Management*. 2nd ed. CRC Press, 2006. Print.

Schmarzo, Bill. *Big Data MBA: Driving Business Strategies with Data Science*. Wiley, 2015. Print.

Soares, Sunil. *The Chief Data Officer Handbook for Data Governance*. Mc Press, 2015. Print.

Stubbs, Evan. *The Value of Business Analytics: Identifying the Path to Profitability*. Wiley, 2011. Print.

Tompkins, Jonathan R. *Organization Theory and Public Management*. Wadsworth Publishing, 2004. Print.

Tsoukas, Haridimos and Christian Knudsen, eds. *The Oxford Handbook of Organization Theory: Meta-theoretical Perspectives*. Oxford University Press, 2005. Print. Oxford Handbooks.

Verhoef, Peter C., Edwin Kooge and Natasha Walk. *Creating Value with Big Data Analytics: Making Smarter Marketing Decisions*. Routledge, 2016. Print.

Willows, David and Brian Bedrick, eds. *Effective Data Management for Schools*. John Catt Educational Ltd, 2012. Print. Effective International Schools Ser.

CHAPTER 17

Data Management and Organizational Change Management

1. Introduction

For most organizations, improving data management practices requires changing how people work together and how they understand the role of data in their organizations, as well as the way they use data and deploy technology to support organizational processes. Successful data management practices require, among other factors:

- Learning to manage on the horizontal by aligning accountabilities along the Information Value chain
- Changing focus from vertical (silo) accountability to shared stewardship of information
- Evolving information quality from a niche business concern or the job of the IT department into a core value of the organization
- Shifting thinking about information quality from 'data cleansing and scorecards' to a more fundamental organizational capability
- Implementing processes to measure the cost of poor data management and the value of disciplined data management

This level of change is not achieved through technology, even though appropriate use of software tools can support delivery. It is instead achieved through a careful and structured approach to the management of change in the organization. Change will be required at all levels. It is critical to manage and coordinate change to avoid dead-end initiatives, loss of trust, and damage to the credibility of the information management function and its leadership.

Data management professionals who understand formal change management will be more successful in bringing about changes that will help their organizations get more value from their data. To do so, it is important to understand:

- Why change fails
- The triggers for effective change
- The barriers to change
- How people experience change

2. Laws of Change

Experts in organizational change management recognize a set of fundamental 'Laws of Change' that describe why change is not easy. Recognizing these at the beginning of the change process enables success.

- **Organizations don't change, people change**: Change does not happen because a new organization is announced or a new system is implemented. It takes place when people behave differently because they recognize the value in doing so. The process of improving data management practices and implementing formal data governance will have far-reaching effects on an organization. People will be asked to change how they work with data and how they interact with each other on activities involving data.

- **People don't resist change. They resist being changed**: Individuals will not adopt change if they see it as arbitrary or dictatorial. They are more likely to change if they have been engaged in defining the change and if they understand the vision driving the change, as well as when and how change will take place. Part of change management for data initiatives involves working with teams to build organizational understanding of the value of improved data management practices.

- **Things are the way they are because they got that way**: There may be good historic reasons for things being the way they are. At some point in the past, someone defined the business requirements, defined the process, designed the systems, wrote the policy, or defined the business model that now requires change. Understanding the origins of current data management practices will help the organization avoid past mistakes. If staff members are given a voice in the change, they are more likely to understand new initiatives as improvements.

- **Unless there is push to change, things will likely stay the same**: If you want an improvement, something must be done differently. As Einstein famously said: "You can't solve a problem with the level of thinking that created it in the first place."

- **Change would be easy if it weren't for all the people**: The 'technology' of change is often easy. The challenge comes in dealing with the natural variation that arises in people.

Change requires Change Agents, people who pay attention to the people and not just the systems. Change Agents actively listen to employees, customers, and other stakeholders to catch problems before they arise and execute the change more smoothly.

Ultimately, change requires a clear VISION of Change Goals communicated vividly and regularly to stakeholders to get engagement, buy-in, backing, and (importantly) continued support when challenges arise.

3. Not Managing a Change: Managing a Transition

Change management expert William Bridges emphasizes the centrality of transition in the change management process. He defines *transition* as the psychological process that people go through to come to terms with the new situation. While many people think of change solely in terms of a new beginning, Bridges asserts that change involves moving through three distinct phases, starting with the ending of the existing state. Endings are difficult because people need to let go of existing conditions. People then enter the Neutral Zone, in which the existing state has not quite ended and the new state has not quite begun. Change is complete when the new state is established (see Table 34). Of these three, the Neutral Zone is the least predictable and most confusing, because it is a mix of old and new. If the people in the organization do not transition through the Neutral Zone, then the organization is at risk of slipping back into old habits and failing to sustain the change.

Bridges maintains that the single biggest reason organizational changes fail is that people driving change rarely think about endings and therefore do not manage the impact of endings on people. He states: "Most organizations try to start with a beginning, rather than finishing with it. They pay no attention to endings. They do not acknowledge the existence of the neutral zone, and then wonder why people have so much difficulty with change" (Bridges, 2009). When experiencing a change, all individuals go through all three phases, but at different speeds. Progression depends on factors such as past experience, personal preferred style, the degree of involvement in recognizing the problem and developing possible solutions, and the extent to which they feel pushed towards a change rather than moving towards it voluntarily.

Table 34 Bridges's Transition Phases

Transition Phase	Description
The Ending	• When we acknowledge that there are things we need to let go of. • When we recognize that we have lost something. • Example: Changing jobs – even when an individual chooses to change jobs, there are still losses such as losing close working friends.
The Neutral Zone	• When the old way has finished but the new way isn't here yet. • When everything is in flux and it feels like no one knows what they should be doing. • When things are confusing and disorderly. • Example: Moving to a new house. The first few days or even months after moving, the new house is not home yet and things are quite probably in turmoil.
The New Beginning	• When the new way feels comfortable, right, and the only way. • Example: Having a baby. After a few months in the neutral zone of turmoil, you come to a stage when you cannot imagine life without your new baby.

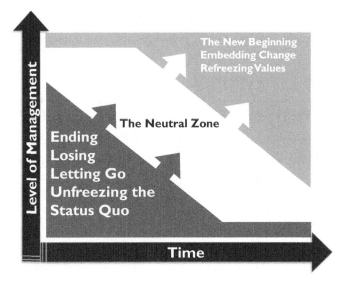

Figure 113 Bridges's Transition Phases

Bridges emphasizes that while the first task of the Change Manager is to understand the Destination (or VISION) and how to get there, the ultimate goal of transition management is to convince people that they need to start the journey. When managing change and transition, the role of the Change Agent, and of any manager or leader in the process, is to help people recognize that the process and the stages of a transition are perfectly natural.

The following checklist for managing transition summarizes key point managers should be aware of as they help people transition.

- The Ending

    o   Help everyone to understand the current problems and why the change is necessary.

    o   Identify who is likely to lose what. Remember that loss of friends and close working colleagues is as important to some as the loss of status and power is to others.

    o   Losses are subjective. The things one person grieves about may mean nothing to someone else. Accept the importance of subjective losses. Don't argue with others about how they perceive the loss, and don't be surprised at other people's reactions to loss.

    o   Expect and accept signs of grieving and acknowledge losses openly and sympathetically.

    o   Define what is over and what is not. People must make the break at some time and trying to cling on to old ways prolongs difficulties.

    o   Treat the past with respect. People have probably worked extremely hard in what may have been very difficult conditions. Recognize that and show that the work is valued.

    o   Show how ending something ensures the things that matter to people are continued and improved.

    o   Give people information. Then do it again and again and again in a variety of ways – written information to go away and read, as well as the opportunity to talk and ask questions.

    o   Use the stakeholder analysis to map out how best to approach different individuals – understand how their perspectives might need to be engaged to initiate the change and what likely points of resistance might be.

- The Neutral Zone

    o   Recognize this as a difficult phase (mix of old and new) but that everyone must go through it.

    o   Get people involved and working together; give them time and space to experiment and test new ideas.

    o   Help people to feel that they are still valued.

    o   Praise people with good ideas, even if not every good idea works as expected. The Plan, Do, Study, Act (PDSA) model encourages trying things out, and learning from each cycle.

    o   Give people information; do it again and again and again in a variety of ways.

    o   Provide feedback about the results of the ideas being tested and decisions made.

- The New Beginning

    o   Do not force a beginning before its time.

    o   Ensure people know what part they are to play in the new system.

    o   Make sure policies, procedures, and priorities are clear; do not send mixed messages.

    o   Plan to celebrate the new beginning and give the credit to those who have made the change.

    o   Give people information; do it again and again in a variety of ways.

4. Kotter's Eight Errors of Change Management

In *Leading Change,* John P. Kotter, one of the most respected researchers in the field of Change Management, outlines eight reasons why organization fail to execute change. These provide perspective on issues that commonly arise in the context of information and data management.

4.1 Error #1: Allowing Too Much Complacency

According to Kotter, the biggest mistake people make when trying to change organizations is plunging ahead without first establishing a high enough sense of urgency among their peers and superiors. (This is related to the need to drive up dissatisfaction with the status quo identified in the Gleicher formula; see Section 6.) Kotter's analysis provides valuable pointers for Change Managers looking to avoid the errors of others. Change Agents often:

- Overestimate their ability to force big changes on the organization
- Underestimate how difficult it can be to shift people out of their comfort zones
- Don't see how their actions and approach might reinforce the status quo by driving up defensiveness
- Rush in where angels fear to tread – kicking off change activities without sufficient communication of what change is required or why change is required (the Vision)
- Confuse urgency with anxiety, which in turn leads to fear and resistance as stakeholders retrench (often quite literally) in their silos

While it is tempting to think that in the face of organizational crisis, complacency would not be a problem, often the opposite is the case. Stakeholders often cling to the status quo in the face of too many (often conflicting) demands for change (which are often processed as 'if everything is important, then nothing is important').

4.1.1 Examples in Information Management Context

Table 35 describes examples of how complacency can manifest in an information management context:

Table 35 Complacency Scenarios

Example Scenario	How it might manifest
Response to a Regulatory Change	"We're OK. We haven't been fined under the current rules."
Response to Business Change	"We've been supporting the business successfully for years. We'll be OK."
Response to Technology Change	"That new technology is unproven. Our current systems are stable and we know how to work around issues."
Response to Problems or Errors	"We can assign a troubleshooting team to that and patch the issues up. There are bound to be some people available in [Insert name of Department or Team here]."

4.2 Error #2: Failing to Create a Sufficiently Powerful Guiding Coalition

Kotter identifies that major change is almost impossible without the active support from the head of the organization and without a coalition of other leaders coming together to guide the change. Leadership engagement is especially important in data governance efforts, as these require significant behavioral changes. Without commitment from top leaders, short-term self-interest will outweigh the argument for the long-term benefits of better governance.

A Guiding Coalition is a powerful and enthusiastic team of volunteers from across the organization that helps to put new strategies into effect and transform the organization. A key challenge in developing a Guiding Coalition is identifying who needs to be involved. (See Section 5.2.)

4.3 Error #3: Underestimating the Power of Vision

Urgency and a strong guiding team are useless without a clear, sensible vision of the change. The vision provides the context of the change effort. It helps people understand the meaning of any individual component. A well-defined and communicated vision can help drive the level of energy required to properly implement the change. Without a public statement of vision to guide decision-making, every choice risks becoming a debate and any action could derail the change initiative or undermine it.

Vision is not the same thing as planning or program management. The vision is not the project plan or project charter or a detailed breakdown of all the components of the change.

A Vision is a Clear and Compelling Statement of where the Change is leading.

Communicating vision means connecting with people. For data management initiatives, the vision must articulate the challenges with existing data management practices, the benefits of improvement, and the path to get to a better future state.

4.3.1 Example in Information Management

All too often in information management, the vision for a particular project is presented as the implementation of a new technology. The technology, while important, is not the change and not the vision. What the organization can do with the technology constitutes the vision.

For example, stating, "*We will implement a new integrated financial reporting and analytics suite built on [insert name of technology here] by the end of Quarter 1*" is a laudable and measurable goal. However, it does little to communicate a clear and compelling statement of where the change will lead.

On the other hand, asserting, "*We will improve the accuracy and timeliness of financial reports and make them more readily available to all stakeholders. Improved understanding of how data flows into and out of our reporting processes will support trust in our numbers, save time, and reduce unnecessary stress during end-of-period processes. We will take our first step to achieve this by implementing [System X] by the end of Q1*" clarifies what will be done, and why it is being done. If you can point out the benefits of the change to the organization, you will build support for change.

4.4 Error #4: Under Communicating the Vision by a Factor of 10, 100, or 1000

Even if everyone agrees that the current situation is unsatisfactory, people will still not change unless they perceive the benefits of change as a significant improvement over the status quo.

Consistent, effective communication of the vision, followed by action, is critical to successful change management. Kotter advises that communication comes in both words and deeds. Congruence between the two is critical for success. Nothing kills a change effort as fast as a situation where people receive the message: 'Do as I say, not as I do.'

4.5 Error #5: Permitting Obstacles to Block the Vision

New initiatives fail when people feel disempowered by huge obstacles in their path, even when they fully embrace the need for and direction of the proposed change. As part of its transformation, the organization must identify and respond to different kinds of roadblocks:

- **Psychological**: Roadblocks that exist in people's heads must be addressed based on their causes. Do they stem from fear, lack of knowledge, or some other cause?

- **Structural**: Roadblocks due to organizational structures such as narrow job categories or performance appraisal systems that force people to choose between the Vision and their own self-interest must be addressed as part of the change management process. Change management should address structural incentives and disincentives to change.

- **Active resistance**: What roadblocks exist due to people who refuse to adapt to the new set of circumstances and who make demands that are inconsistent with the Transformation? If key members of the organization make the right noises about the change vision but fail to alter their behaviors or reward the required behaviors or continue to operate in incompatible ways, the execution of the vision will falter and could fail.

Kotter calls on "smart people" in organizations to confront these obstacles. If they do not, others will feel disempowered and change will be undermined.

4.6 Error #6: Failing to Create Short-Term Wins

Real change takes time. Anyone who has ever embarked on a fitness regime or a weight-loss plan knows that the secret to keeping going is to have regular milestone targets that keep up momentum and motivation by marking progress. Anything that involves a long-term commitment and investment of effort and resources requires some element of early and regular feedback of success.

Complex change efforts require short-term goals in support of long-term objectives. Meeting these goals allows the team to celebrate and maintain momentum. The key thing is to **create** the short-term win rather than merely hoping for it. In successful transformations, managers actively establish early goals, achieve these goals, and reward the team. Without systematic efforts to guarantee success, change is likely to fail.

4.6.1 Examples in Information Management Context

In an information management context, the short-term wins and goals often arise from the resolution of an identified problem. For example, if the development of a Business Glossary is a key deliverable of a data governance initiative, a short-term win might come from solving a problem related to inconsistent understanding of data (i.e., two business areas report different KPI results because they used different rules in their calculations). Identifying the problem, solving it, and linking the solution to the overall long-term vision for the change allow the team to celebrate that goal and demonstrate the vision in action. It also provides valuable collateral for communication about the vision and helps to reinforce the change message.

4.7 Error #7: Declaring Victory Too Soon

All too often in Change projects, particularly ones stretching over several years, there is a temptation to declare success at the first major performance improvement. Quick wins and early wins are powerful tools to keep up momentum and morale. However, any suggestion that the job is done is usually a mistake. Until the changes are embedded in the culture of the organization new approaches are fragile and old habits and practices can reassert themselves. Kotter suggests that changing an entire company can take between three and ten years.

4.7.1 Example in Information Management Context

The classic example of 'Mission Accomplished' syndrome is the scenario where the implementation of a technology is viewed as the route to improving the management of information or resolving an issue with the quality or reliability of data. Once the technology has been deployed, it can be difficult to keep the project moving towards the goal, particularly if the overall vision has been poorly defined. Table 36 captures several examples related to the consequences of declaring victory too soon.

Table 36 Declaring Victory Too Soon Scenarios

Example Scenario	How it might manifest
Addressing Data Quality	"We've bought a Data Quality tool. That's fixed that now." <ul><li>No one in the organization is reviewing or acting on data quality reports</li></ul>
Confusing capability delivery with implementation and operation	"We've implemented the reporting stack for Regulation X. We are now compliant with the legislation." <ul><li>Regulatory requirement changes</li><li>Nobody is reviewing or acting on issues identified in reporting</li></ul>
Migration of data	"All the data in System X is now in System Y." <ul><li>Record counts match, but the data in System Y is incomplete, or truncated due to failures in the migration process. Manual interventions needed</li></ul>

4.8 Error # 8: Neglecting to Anchor Changes Firmly in the Corporate Culture

Organizations don't change, people change. Until new behaviors are embedded in to the social norms and shared values of an organization, they are subject to decay and degradation as soon as the focus of the change effort is removed. Kotter is clear: You ignore culture at your peril when engaging in any change activity.

The two keys to anchoring the change in the culture of the organization are:

- Consciously showing people how specific behaviors and attitudes have influenced performance.
- Taking sufficient time to embed the change of approach in the next generation of management.

4.8.1 Example in Information Management Context

This risk highlights the importance of human factors in the overall change that might be implemented to bring about improvements in data governance execution, Metadata management and use, or data quality practices (to name but three).

For example, an organization may have introduced a Metadata tagging requirement on all documentation to support automated classification and archiving processes in their content management system. Staff begin to comply in the first few weeks, but as time passes, they revert to old habits and do not correctly tag documents, leading to a massive backlog of unclassified records that needs to be reviewed manually to bring them into line with requirements of the technology solution.

This highlights the simple fact that improvements in Information Management are delivered through a combination of processes, people, and technology. Very often that middle component is missed, leading to sub-optimal delivery and backsliding on progress made. It is important when introducing new technology or new processes to consider how the people will carry the change forward and sustain the gains.

5. Kotter's Eight Stage Process for Major Change

In addition to the Eight Errors of Change Management, Kotter recognizes a set of common obstacles to change:

- Inward focused cultures
- Paralyzing bureaucracy
- Parochial politics
- Low levels of trust
- Lack of team work
- Arrogance
- Lack of or failure of leadership
- Fear of the unknown

To combat these, he proposes an eight-step model for major change. Kotter's model provides a framework within which each of these issues can be addressed in a way that supports sustainable long-term change. Each step is associated with one of the fundamental errors that undermine transformation efforts.

The first four steps of the model soften entrenched status quo positions. As Kotter says, this effort is only needed because change is not easy.

The next three steps (5 to 7) introduce new practices and ways of working. The last step locks the changes in place and provides the platform for future gains and improvement.

Kotter advises that there is no short cut in following these steps. All successful change efforts must go through all eight steps. Focusing on steps 5, 6, and 7 is tempting. However, that does not provide a solid foundation for sustaining the change (no vision, no Guiding Coalition, no dissatisfaction with the status quo). Likewise, it is important to reinforce each step of as you move through the process, using quick wins to bolster the vision and the communication and highlight the problems with the status quo.

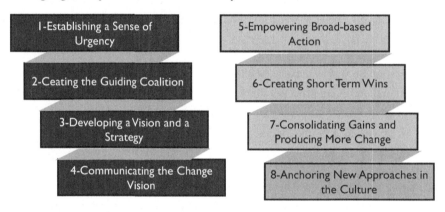

Figure 114 Kotter's Eight Stage Process for Major Change

5.1 Establishing a Sense of Urgency

People will find a thousand ways to withhold cooperation from something they think is unnecessary. A clear and compelling sense of urgency is required to motivate a sufficient critical mass of people to support a change effort. Winning co-operation and collaboration requires a rallying call.

The opposite of urgency is complacency. When complacency is high, it is difficult if not impossible to put together a sufficiently powerful group to create the change vision and guide the change effort. In rare instances, individuals can make some headway in the face of complacency but this is almost inevitably unsustainable.

In the information management context, several factors can create a sense of urgency:

- Regulatory changes
- Threats to security of information
- Risks to business continuity
- Changes to business strategy
- Mergers and acquisitions
- Regulatory audit or litigation threats

- Changes to technology
- Changes to capability of competitors in the market
- Media commentary about an organization's or an industry's information management issues

5.1.1 Sources of Complacency

Kotter identifies nine reasons why organizations and people can be complacent. (See Figure 115)

- In the absence of a visible crisis, it is difficult to raise a sense of urgency.
- The trappings of success can drown out the urgency of some situations.
- Measuring staff against low performance standards or standards that don't compare against external benchmarks or internal long-term trends.
- Overly narrow functional goals, with different performance metrics for different functional units, can lead to a situation where no one is responsible when overall organizational performance is poor or suffering.
- If internal planning and control systems are (or can be) rigged or gamed to make it easy for everyone to reach their goals, it is easy to be complacent.
- If the only source of performance feedback is from the faulty internal systems, there is no sanity check of the correctness of complacency.
- Where problems are identified or where external performance feedback is gathered, it is often attacked as being damaging to morale, hurtful to others, or likely to cause an argument. Rather than take the information as an input into an evaluation of organization performance, the culture is to 'kill the messenger'.
- For very simple psychological reasons people don't accept things they don't want to hear. When evidence of a big problem appears, people will often ignore the information or reinterpret it in a less painful way.
- Even in organizations where the first eight challenges are not significant, there is a risk that 'happy talk' from senior management or senior figures in the organization can create an unwarranted sense of security and success. Often this 'happy talk' is the result of a history of past successes. Past success can give individuals an ego and create an arrogant culture. Both factors can keep the sense of urgency low and hamper change.

A good rule of thumb in any change initiative is never to underestimate the power of forces that might reinforce complacency and promote the status quo. The challenge of complacency must be addressed. An organization can't make any important decisions without tackling the real issues.

5.1.2 Pushing up the Urgency Level

To push up the urgency level requires removal of the sources of complacency or reduction of their impact. Creating a strong sense of urgency requires that leaders take bold or even risky actions. It is worth recalling how Deming admonished management to institute leadership as part of his 14 Points of Transformation.[104]

---

[104] In *Out of the Crisis* (1982), W. Edwards Deming published his 14 Points for Management Transformation. http://bit.ly/1KJ3JIS.

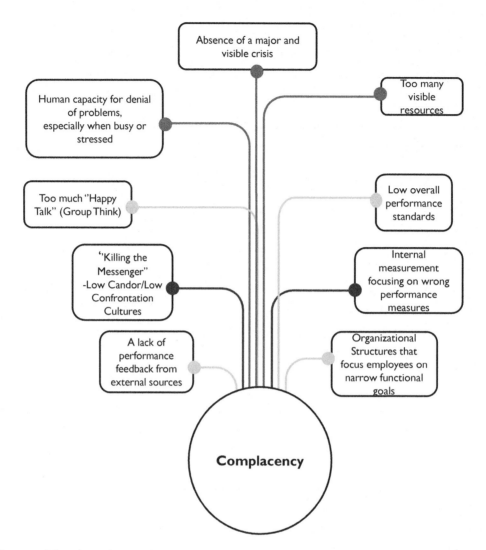

Figure 115 Sources of Complacency

Bold means doing something that might cause short term pain, not just something that looks good in a marketing email. In other words, it requires an *adoption of the new philosophy* (to borrow again from Deming). Moves bold enough to reduce complacency tend to cause short-term conflict and anxiety. However, if the conflict and anxiety can be channeled towards the change vision then a leader can capitalize on the short-term discomfort to build the long-term goals.

Bold moves are difficult in the absence of supported and supportive leadership. Cautious senior managers who are unable to increase the sense of urgency will reduce the ability of an organization to change.

5.1.3 Using Crisis with Care

One way to push up urgency levels is to latch on to a visible crisis. It is sometimes said that major change is not possible until the very economic survival of the organization is at risk. However, it is not necessarily that the change comes even then. An economic or financial crisis in an organization can often result in scarce but necessary resources being difficult to come by to support the change vision.

It is possible to create a perceived crisis by bombarding the organization with information about problems, potential problems, potential opportunities, or by setting ambitious goals that disrupted the status quo. Kotter suggests that it is often easier to create a problem that (coincidentally) you have the plan to address.

5.1.4 The Role of Middle and Lower-level Managers

Depending on the scale of the target for the change (e.g., a department or business unit versus an entire organization), the key players will be the managers in charge of that unit. They will need to be able to reduce complacency in the teams under their direct control. If they have enough autonomy, they may be able to do this regardless of the pace of change in the rest of the organization.

If there is not sufficient autonomy, then a change effort in a small unit can be doomed from the start as the external forces of inertia come to bear. Often senior executives need to reduce those forces. However, middle or lower-level managers can drive this kind of change if they act in a strategic way. For example, if they use analysis to clearly show the impact of not making the required change on a key strategic project. This is particularly effective when the debate can be diffused by directing it onto an external group such as an external consultancy who may have helped with the analysis.

5.1.5 How Much Urgency is Enough?

A sense of urgency about a problem leads people to conclude that the status quo is unacceptable. To sustain transformation for the long term, support from a critical mass of managers is required. Kotter suggests 75%. However, creating too much urgency can be counterproductive. Too much urgency may result in competing visions of change or cause a focus on 'firefighting'.

A sufficiently compelling sense of urgency will help get the change process started and give it momentum. Sufficient urgency will also help in getting the right level of leadership in the Guiding Coalition. Ultimately, the sense of urgency needs to be strong enough to prevent complacency from reasserting itself after initial successes are achieved. One key approach is to tap into the 'voice of the customer' and speak to external customers, suppliers, shareholders, or other stakeholders about their perspective on the level of urgency that is being created.

5.2 The Guiding Coalition

No one person has all the answers, or all the insights necessary to create a vision, or has the right range and variation of connections to support the effective communication of a vision. For successful change, two specific scenarios must be avoided:

- The Lone CEO / Lone Champion
- The Low Credibility Committee

The Lone CEO scenario puts the success or failure of the change effort in the hands of one person. The pace of change in most organization these days is such that one person cannot possibly manage it all. The pace of decision-making and communication slows, unless decisions are being taken without a full assessment of the issues. Either option is a recipe for failure.

The Low Credibility Committee arises where a capable champion is given a 'task force' with representatives from a variety of functional departments (and perhaps some external consultants). What the task force lacks is sufficient representation (if any) from people at a senior level on the executive pecking order. If it is seen as "important but not *that* important" (again, because of the lack of commitment from top brass), people don't feel motivated to get a true understanding of the situation. Inevitably, the task force fails.

It is essential to create a suitable Guiding Coalition that has the necessary management commitment to support the urgency of the need for change. In addition, the team has to support effective decision-making – which requires high levels of trust within the team. A Guiding Coalition that works as a team can process more information faster. It also speeds the implementation of ideas because the decision-makers with power are truly informed and committed to key decisions.

An effective Guiding Coalition has four key characteristics:

- **Position Power**: Are enough key players on board, especially main line managers, so that those who are left out can't easily block progress?
- **Expertise**: Are relevant points of view adequately represented so that informed and intelligent decisions will be made?
- **Credibility**: Are enough people with good reputations in the organization on the team so that it will be taken seriously?
- **Leadership**: Does the team have enough proven leaders on board to drive the change process?

Leadership is a key concern. There must be a good balance between management and leadership skills on the Guiding Coalition. Management keeps the whole process under control. Leadership drives the change. One without the other will not achieve a sustainable result.

Key issues that arise in the context of a building your Guiding Coalition include:

How many people do I need to help me define and guide this change?

The answer to this is a painfully consultant-like "It depends", but the size of the coalition relates to the size of the overall group being influenced. A balance needs to be struck between having a group that is too big and having a group that leaves key stakeholders feeling left 'outside the tent'.

Who should be involved or invited to join the Guiding Coalition?

The Guiding Coalition differs from a formal project or program steering committee in that it needs to provide a platform for influence throughout the organization. As such, the coalition needs to include representatives from different stakeholder communities. However, it is not a general stakeholder requirements gathering forum either. Seek perspectives from people who may be impacted in the information value chain of the organization.

One key attribute of the members of the Guiding Coalition is their ability to influence their peers, either through formal authority in the hierarchy or through their status and experience in the organization.

Behavior is key in the Guiding Coalition.

In the formulation of the Guiding Coalition, change leaders need to avoid behaviors that weaken the effectiveness, function, and reach of the team. For example, avoid:

- **Naysaying**: Naysayers can hamper positive and open dialogue needed for the Guiding Coalition to develop creative ideas, to refine, implement, and evolve the change vision and identify opportunities for growth.
- **Distraction**: Guiding Coalition team members need to be focused on the change activity. Unfocussed individuals can take the team off course, leading to delays or the failure to capitalize on early wins.
- **Selfishness**: The Guiding Coalition's efforts move the organization as a whole and affect everyone. Hidden agendas must not be allowed to derail the team's efforts.

5.2.1 The Importance of Effective Leadership in the Coalition

There is a difference between management and leadership. A Guiding Coalition with good managers but no leaders will not succeed. Missing leadership can be addressed by hiring from the outside, promoting leaders from within, and encouraging staff to step up to the challenge of leading.

When putting your coalition together you need to be wary of what Kotter terms 'Egos', 'Snakes', and 'Reluctant Players'. 'Egos' are individuals who fill up the room and do not let others contribute. 'Snakes' are people who create and spread mistrust and distrust. 'Reluctant Players' are (usually) senior figures who see a moderate need for the change but don't fully grasp the urgency.

Any of these personality types can hijack or undermine the change effort. Efforts should be made to keep them off the team or manage them closely to keep them on message.

5.2.2 Example in Information Management Context

In the context of an information management change initiative, the Guiding Coalition can help the organization identify opportunities to link initiatives in different areas that are engaged in different aspects of the same overall change.

For example, in response to a regulatory requirement, a firm's in-house counsel may have begun to develop a map of data flows and processes in the organization. At the same time, a data warehousing initiative may have begun to map the lineage of data for verification of reporting accuracy and quality.

A data governance change leader might bring the head of legal and the head of reporting together on their Guiding Coalition to improve documentation and control of information processes in the context of data governance. This in turn might require input from the front-line teams using and creating data to understand the impacts of any proposed changes.

Ultimately, a good understanding of the information value chain will help identify potential candidates to include in the Guiding Coalition.

5.2.3 Building an Effective Team

An effective team is based on two simple foundations: trust and a common goal. An absence of trust is often caused by a lack of communications and other factors such as misplaced rivalry. The classic 'Business vs. IT' divide is a good example of where trust breaks down. To build trust, engage in team building activities that create and promote mutual understanding, respect, and caring. In achieving that mutual understanding, though, care should be taken to avoid 'Group Think'.

5.2.4 Combating Group Think

'Group Think' is a psychological effect that arises in highly coherent and cohesive groups, particularly ones that are isolated from sources of information that might contradict their opinions, or those that are dominated by a leader who encourages people to agree with his or her position rather than opening up discussion.

In Group Think, everyone goes along with a proposal even where they have reservations about it. Group Think is probably operating if:

- No one raises objections
- No alternatives are offered
- Different perspectives are quickly dismissed and die forever
- Information that might challenge the thinking is not actively sought

To prevent Group Think it is important to:

- Encourage all participants to follow the scientific method of gathering data to help understand the nature and causes of a problem
- Develop a list of criteria for evaluating all decisions
- Learn to work together efficiently so that Group Think is not the short cut to getting things done faster
- Encourage brainstorming
- Leaders should speak last
- Actively search for outside knowledge and input into meetings
- Once a solution has been identified, have the team develop not just one plan but also a 'Plan B' (which forces them to rethink assumptions in the original plan)

5.2.5 Examples in Information Management Context

Group Think can arise in a variety of contexts. One potential area is the traditional 'Business vs IT divide', in which different parts of the organization are resistant to changes proposed by the other. Another potential scenario is where the organization's goal is to become data-driven with a focus on analytics and data gathering, which may result in privacy, security, or ethical issues in relation to information handling being discounted or deprioritized in the overall work plan.

There are many reasons to apply data governance discipline in organizations. One key function is to ensure clarity about models and methods to be applied. This clarity will allow issues such as the Business / IT divide or balancing of competing priorities to be addressed appropriately and consistently.

5.2.6 Common Goals

If every member of the Guiding Coalition is pulling in a different direction, trust will break down.

Typical goals that bind people are a commitment to excellence or a desire to see the organization perform at the highest level possible in a given area. These goals should not be confused with the vision for change but should be complementary to it.

5.3 Developing a Vision and Strategy

A common mistake in change management efforts is to rely on either authoritarian decree or micromanagement to get the change moving. Neither approach is effective if the change situation is complex.

If the goal is behavior change, unless the boss is very powerful, authoritarian decree approaches work poorly even in simple situations. Without 'the power of kings' behind it, an authoritarian decree is unlikely to break through all the forces of resistance. The Change Agents tend to be ignored, undermined, or worked around. Almost inevitably, some change resister will call the Change Agent's bluff to test the authority and clout behind the change process.

Micromanagement tries to get around this weakness by defining in specific detail what employees should do and then monitoring compliance. This can overcome some of the barriers to change but will, over time, take increasing lengths of time as management have to spend more time detailing the work practices and methods for the new changed behaviors as the level of complexity associated with the change increases.

The only approach that consistently allows Change Agents to break through the status quo is to base change on a clear and compelling vision that provides momentum.

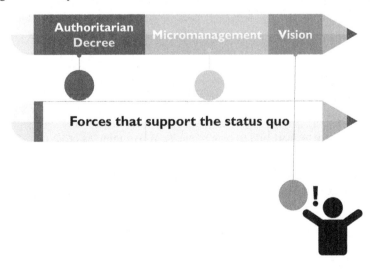

Figure 116 Vision Breaks Through Status Quo

5.3.1 Why Vision is Essential

A vision is a picture of the future with some implicit or explicit commentary about why people should strive to create that future. A good vision shares three important purposes: Clarification, motivation, and alignment.

- **Clarification**: A good vision clarifies the direction of change and simplifies a range of more detailed decisions by setting key parameters. An effective vision (and supporting back up strategies) helps resolve issues that arise out of disagreements about direction or confusion about the motivation or drivers for the change. Endless debates can be avoided with a simple question: Is the planned action in line with the vision? Similarly, the vision can help clear the decks of clutter, allowing the team to focus efforts on priority projects that are contributing to the transformation effort.

- **Motivation**: A clear vision motivates people to take steps in the right direction, even if the initial steps are personally painful. This is particularly true in organizations where people are being forced out of their comfort zones on a regular basis. When the future is depressing and demoralizing, the right vision can give the people an appealing cause to fight for.

- **Alignment**: A compelling vision helps to align individuals and coordinate the actions of motivated people in an efficient way. The alternative is to have a flurry of detailed directives or endless meetings. Experience shows that without a shared sense of direction interdependent people can end up in cycles of constant conflict and nonstop meetings.

5.3.2 The Nature of an Effective Vision

A vision can be mundane and simple. It doesn't need to be grand or overarching. It is one element in the system of tools and processes for change; this system also includes strategies, plans, budgets, and more. Nevertheless, a vision is a very important factor because it demands that teams focus on tangible improvements.

A effective vision has several key characteristics:

- **Imaginable**: It conveys a picture of what the future looks like.
- **Desirable**: It appeals to the *long-term* interests of employees, customers, shareholders, and other stakeholders.
- **Feasible**: It comprises realistic and attainable goals.
- **Focused**: It is clear enough to provide guidance in decision-making.
- **Flexible**: It is general enough to allow individuals to take the initiative and to allow for alternative plans and responses when conditions or constraints change.
- **Communicable**: It is easy to share and to communicate in five minutes or less.

The key test for the effectiveness of a vision is how easy it is to imagine it and for it to be desirable. A good vision can demand sacrifice but must keep the long-term interests of the people involved in scope. Visions that don't focus for the long term on the benefits to people are eventually challenged. Likewise, the vision must be rooted in the reality of the product or service market. In most markets, reality is that the end customer needs to be considered constantly.

Key questions to ask are:

- If this became real, how would it affect customers (internal and external)?
- If this became real how would it affect shareholders? Will it make them happier? Will it deliver longer-term value for them?
- If this became real, how would it affect employees? Would the work place be better, happier, less stressed, more fulfilling? Will we be able to become a better place to work in?

Another key test is the strategic feasibility of the vision. A feasible vision is more than a wish. It may stretch resources and stretch capabilities but people recognize that is can be reached. Feasible does not mean easy, however. The vision must be challenging enough to force fundamental rethinking. Regardless of which stretch goals are set, the organization must ground that vision in a rational understanding of the market trends and the organization's capability.

The vision must be focused enough to guide people but not so rigid that it handcuffs staff to increasingly irrational modes of behavior. Often the best approach is to aim for simplicity of vision while at the same time embedding enough specific hooks that the vision is still a valuable cornerstone and reference point for decision-making:

It is our goal to become the world leader in our industry within 5 years. In this context, leadership means managing information more effectively to deliver greater revenues, more profit, and a more rewarding place for our people to work. Achieving this ambition will require a solid foundation of trust in our ability to make decisions, clarity in our internal and external communications, an improved understanding of the information landscape in which we operate, and rational investments in appropriate tools and technologies to support a data-driven culture and ethos. This culture will be trusted and admired by shareholders, customers, employees, and communities.

5.3.3 Creating the Effective Vision

Kotter advises that creating an effective vision is an iterative process that must have several clear elements to be successful.

- **First draft**: A single individual makes an initial statement reflecting their dreams and the needs of the market place.
- **Role of the Guiding Coalition**: The Guiding Coalition reworks the first draft to fit the wider strategic perspective.
- **Importance of teamwork**: The group process never works well without teamwork. Encourage people to engage and contribute.
- **Role of the head and heart**: Both analytical thinking and 'blue sky dreaming' are required throughout the activity.
- **Messiness of the process**: This won't be a straightforward procedure; there will be much debate, rework, and change. If there isn't, something is wrong with the vision or the team.
- **Time frame**: The activity is not a one meeting deal. It can take weeks, months, or even longer. Ideally, the vision should be constantly evolving.
- **End product**: A direction for the future that is desirable, feasible, focused, flexible, and can be conveyed in five minutes or less.

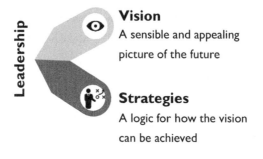

Figure 117 Management/Leadership Contrast

5.4 Communicating the Change Vision

A vision only has power when those involved in the change activity have a common understanding of its goals and direction, a common outlook on the desired future. Problems that commonly arise with communicating the vision include:

- **Failure to communicate,** or to communicate enough.
- **Poor communication**: Cumbersome or unwieldy wording that hides the sense of urgency; as a result, people don't listen carefully.
- **Not communicating far enough**: Managers are trained to communicate up and down. Leaders need to communicate out and into broader constituencies. This range of communication requires leaders to have a clear sense of the problem and how it can be solved.

Another challenge is dealing with the questions that are about the vision, from stakeholders, the Guiding Coalition, and the team implementing the change itself. Often the Guiding Coalition spends a lot of time working out these questions and preparing answers to them only to dump them on the organization in one quick hit (an FAQ page, notes to a briefing). The resulting information overload clouds the vision, creates short-term panic and resistance.

Given that, in the average organization, the change message will account for not much more than one-half of one percent of the total communication going to an employee it is clear that simply dumping information will not be effective. The message needs to be communicated in a way that increases its effectiveness and amplifies the communication.

Kotter identifies seven key elements in effective communication of vision:

- **Keep it simple**: Strip out the jargon, internal vocabulary, and complex sentences.

- **Use metaphor, analogy, and example**: A verbal picture (or even a graphical one) can be worth a thousand words.
- **Use multiple forums**: The message needs to be communicable across a variety of different forums from elevator pitch to broadcast memo, from small meeting to an all-hands briefing.
- **Repeat, repeat, repeat**: Ideas have to be heard many times before they are internalized and understood.
- **Lead by example**: Behavior from important people needs to be consistent with the vision. Inconsistent behavior overwhelms all other forms of communication.
- **Explain seeming inconsistencies**: Loose ends and unaddressed disconnects undermine the credibility of all communication.
- **Give and take**: Two-way communication is always more powerful than one-way communication.

5.4.1 Examples in Information Management Context

In an information management context, the failure to define or communicate a clear and compelling vision for a change can often be seen in initiatives where a new technology or capability is being rolled out driven by a focus on technology deployment. In the absence of an understanding or appreciation of the potential information-handling benefits from the new technology or methods, there may be resistance on the part of stakeholders to adopt new ways of working.

For example, if an organization is implementing Metadata-driven document and content management processes, business stakeholders may not engage with the up-front effort of understanding or applying Metadata tagging or classification of records if there is no clearly communicated vision of how this will be a benefit to the organization *and to them*. Absent that, the otherwise valuable initiative may get bogged down with lower than required levels of adoption and compliance.

5.4.2 Keeping it Simple

It is hard to emotionally connect with language that is unnatural, densely written, or difficult to understand.

These examples illustrate the communication problems that can arise when the vision is not kept simple. The example below illustrates this point.

Our goal is to reduce our mean 'time to repair' parameter so that it is demonstrably lower than all major competitors in our target geographic and demographic markets. In a similar vein, we have targeted new-product development cycle times, order processing times, and other customer-related process vectors for change.

Translation: *"We're going to become faster than anyone in our industry at meeting customer needs."*

When the vision is articulated in a simple way, it is easier for teams, stakeholders, and customers to understand the proposed change, how it might affect them, and their role in it. This, in turn, helps them to more easily communicate it to their peers.

5.4.3 Use Many Different Forums

The communication of vision is usually more effective when different channels are used. There are various reasons for this, ranging from the fact that some channels can be overloaded with information or with 'baggage' of previous change initiatives, to the fact that different people interpret and process information differently. If people are being hit with the same message through different channels, it increases the likelihood that the message will be heard, internalized, and acted on. Related to this 'multi-channel / multi-format' approach is the need to keep repeating the vision and communicating progress.

5.4.4 Repetition, Repetition, Repetition

In many respects, change vision and change messages are like water in a river that encounters a boulder that must be overcome. The water does not burst through the dam immediately (unless it has a lot of force behind it, in which case it tends to do so destructively) but over time, through iterative erosion the water wears down the boulder so it can flow around it.

In the same way, change initiatives have to apply iterative retellings of the change vision in different forums and formats to engender a change that is 'sticky'. Which of these scenarios would be more effective?

- Senior management put out a video message to all staff and a voicemail drop announcement to brief everyone on the change. Details on execution will follow from line managers. The intranet carries three articles over the next six months about the Vision, and there is a briefing session at the quarterly management conference (delivered at the end of the day). The plan includes six instances of communication with no fleshing out of details.

- Senior management undertake to find four chances each day to have a change conversation and tie it back to the 'Big Picture'. They in turn task their direct reports with finding four chances, and with tasking their direct reports to find four chances. So, when Frank is meeting Product Development, he asks them to review their plans in the context of the Big Vision. When Mary is presenting a status update she ties it back to the contribution to the Vision. When Garry is presenting negative internal audit findings, he explains the impact in terms of the Vision. At each level of management, per manager there are countless opportunities for communication per year where the vision can be referenced. (This is also known as "Adopting the New Philosophy" and "Instituting Leadership", which are key points in W. Edwards Deming's 14 Points for Transformation in Quality Management.)

5.4.5 Walking the Talk

There is no substitute for leadership by example. It makes the values and cultural aspects of the desired change tangible in a way that no amount of words can do. If for no other reason than that senior managers walking the talk engenders the development of stories about the vision and triggers discussion about the vision, this is an exceptionally powerful tool. The corollary is that telling people one thing and doing the opposite sends a clear message that the vision isn't that important and can be ignored when push comes to shove. Nothing undermines the change vision and efforts more than a senior member of the Guiding Coalition acting incongruently to the vision.

5.4.6 Example in Information Management Context

In information management context, failure to 'Walk the Talk' can be as simple as a senior manager sending files containing personal information about customers by an unsecured or unencrypted email channel in contravention of the information security policy, but receiving no sanction.

It can also be as simple as the team leading an information governance initiative applying the principles and rigor they are asking the rest of the organization to adopt to their own activities, information handling, reporting, and responses to issues and errors.

Consider the impact in the implementation of a Metadata management project if the team were to apply Metadata standards and practices to their own internal project records. If nothing else, it would help them to understand the practicalities of the change, but would also provide them with a good demonstration for others of the benefits of properly tagged and classified records and information.

5.4.7 Explaining Inconsistencies

Sometimes the inconsistency is unavoidable. It may be that, for tactical or operational reasons, or simply to get things moving within the overall organization system, a Change Agent might need to take an action that looks at variance with the stated vision. When this happens, it must be handled and addressed carefully to ensure the vision is sustained, even if a 'scenic route' is being taken. Examples of inconsistencies that can arise might include the use of external consultants when the organization is seeking to reduce costs or headcount. "Why is the organization bringing in these expensive suits when we're rationing printer paper?" people may ask. There are two ways to deal with apparent inconsistency. One of them is guaranteed to kill your vision. The other gives you a fighting chance of being able to keep things on track.

The first option is to either ignore the question or react defensively and shoot the messenger. Invariably this winds up in an embarrassing climb down where the inconsistency is removed, and not always in a manner that is beneficial to the long-term objectives of the change. The second option is to engage with the question and explain the rationale for the inconsistency. The explanation must be simple, clear, and honest. For example, an organization bringing in consultants might respond like this:

We appreciate that it looks odd spending money on consultants when we are shaving costs everywhere else to achieve our vision of being lean, mean, and sustainably profitable. However, to make the savings sustainable we need to break out of old habits of thinking and learn new skills. That requires us investing in knowledge. And where we don't have that knowledge internally we must buy it in in the short term, and use that opportunity to build the knowledge up internally for the future. Every consultant is assigned to a specific project. And every project team has been tasked with learning as much as possible about their new function through shadowing the consultants and using them for formal training. In this way, we will make sure that we will have sustainable improvements into the future.

The key thing is to be explicit about the inconsistency and explicit about why the inconsistency is valid, and how long it will exist for if it is only a transient inconsistency.

5.4.8 Example in Information Management Context

Explaining inconsistencies is a very good example of the importance of data governance models that create agreed upon protocols for decision-making and promote the formal recognition and control of exceptions to rules.

For example, if a governance standard requires that no testing should be done with live production data but a project requires this to verify data matching algorithms or to prove the effectiveness of data cleansing routines, then there must be a clear and explicit explanation of this variance from the expected standard. That is arrived at through appropriate governance controls. Where that project executes testing using live data *without* having appropriate approvals and risk assessments in place, then there should be a sanction ('walk the talk') or the basis for the non-application of the sanction should be equally clearly and explicitly explained.

5.4.9 Listen and Be Listened To

Stephen Covey advises people who want to be highly effective to "Seek first to understand, then to be understood." In other words, listen so that you will be listened to (Covey, 2013).

Often the leadership team don't quite get the vision right, or they encounter a barrier or bottle neck that could have been avoided if they had been better informed. This lack of information leads to expensive errors and weakens the buy-in to and commitment to the Vision. Two-way conversations are an essential method of identifying and answering concerns people have about a change or about a vision for change. The Voice of the Customer is as important to the definition of and development of the vision as it is to any metric of quality in the data itself. And if every conversation is regarded as an opportunity to discuss the vision and to illicit feedback then, without having to formally tie people up in meetings, it is possible to have thousands of hours of discussion and to evolve the vision and how to execute it effectively.

5.4.10 Example in Information Management Context

In an information management context, two-way communication is best illustrated by a scenario where the IT function's view is that all data that is needed by key business stakeholders is available in a timely and appropriate manner, but business stakeholders are consistently expressing frustration at delays in getting information they require to do their jobs and so they have developed a cottage industry in spreadsheet-based reporting and data marts. A vision to improve the information management and governance capability that doesn't identify and address the gap in perception between the IT function's view of the information environment and the business stakeholders' perception of their information environment will inevitably falter and fail to gain the broad-based support needed to ensure effective and sustainable change is delivered.

6. The Formula for Change

One of the most famous methods for describing the 'recipe' required for effective change, the Gleicher Formula, describes factors that need to be in place to overcome the resistance to change in the organization.

$$C = (D \times V \times F) > R$$

According to the Gleicher Formula, Change (C) occurs when the level of dissatisfaction with the status quo (D) is combined with a vision of a better alternative (V) and some actionable first steps to get there (F) and the product of the three is enticing enough to overcome resistance (R) in the organization.

Influencing any of the four variables in the Gleicher formula increases the effectiveness and success of the change effort. However, as with any complex machine, it is important to be aware of the risks inherent in pushing buttons and pulling levers:

- Increasing dissatisfaction within the organization with the way things are working is a powerful tool and needs to be wielded with care lest it increases Resistance.
- Developing a vision of the future will require a concrete and vivid vision of what people will do differently, what people will stop doing, or what they will start doing that they aren't doing now. Ensure that people can appreciate the new skills, attitudes, or work methods that will be required. Present these in a way that doesn't scare people away or create political barriers to the change by causing people to defend the status quo.
- When describing the first steps to change, ensure they are achievable and explicitly tie them back to the vision.
- Act to reduce resistance and avoid increasing resistance to change. To be blunt: Avoid alienating people. This requires a good understanding of the Stakeholders.

7. Diffusion of Innovations and Sustaining Change

Ultimately, training and education must be put in place to deliver a sustainable information quality and data management change in an organization. Implementing change requires understanding how new ideas spread around the organization. This aspect of change is known as Diffusion of Innovations.

Diffusion of Innovations is a theory that seeks to explain how, why, and at what rate new ideas and technology spread through cultures. Formulated in 1962 by Everett Rogers, it is related to the pop culture concept of the Idea Virus (http://bit.ly/2tNwUHD) as popularized by Seth Godin. Diffusion of Innovations has been applied consistently across a diverse range of fields from medical prescribing, to changes in farm husbandry methods, to the adoption of consumer electronics.

The Diffusion of Innovations theory asserts that changes are initiated by a very small percentage (2.5%) of the total population, the Innovators, who tend (in the context of the society being examined) to be young, high in social class, and financially secure enough to absorb losses on bad choices. They have contact with technological innovators and a high risk tolerance. These are then followed by a further 13.5% of the population, Early Adopters, who share traits with Innovators, but are less tolerant of risk. Early Adopters understand how getting the choice right can help them maintain a central role in the society as people to be respected. Change is adopted next by the largest segments of the population, the Early and Late Majorities, which comprise 68% in total. Laggards are the last to adopt any specific innovation. (See Figure 118 and Table 37.)

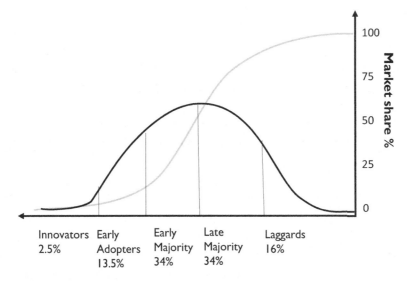

Figure 118 Everett Rogers Diffusion of Innovations

Table 37 Diffusion of Innovations Categories Adapted to Information Management[105]

Adopter Category	Definition (Information Management Perspective)
Innovators	Innovators are the first individuals to spot a better way to tackle problems with the quality of information. They take risks trying to develop profiling of data, build tentative scorecards, and begin to put the symptoms experienced by the business into the language of Information Management. Often these innovators will use their own resources to get information and develop skills about best practices.
Early Adopters	Early Adopters are the second fastest category of individuals to adopt an innovation. These individuals have the highest degree of opinion leadership among the other adopter categories. They are perceived as 'visionary' managers (or experienced managers, or managers responsible for emergent business strategy areas) who have realized information quality issues are a barrier to their success. Often they piggy back on the initial work of the Innovators to develop their business case and begin to formalize information practices.
Early Majority	It takes the Early Majority significantly longer than the Early Adopters to adopt an innovation. Early Majority tend to be slower in the adoption process, have above average social status, contact with early adopters, and seldom hold positions of opinion leadership in a system. They could be in the 'traditional core' areas of the organization where the impact of poor quality data is masked as the 'cost of business'.
Late Majority	Individuals in the Late Majority approach an innovation with a high degree of skepticism and after most society has adopted the innovation. Late Majority typically have below average social status, very little financial lucidity, in contact with others in late majority and early majority, very little opinion leadership. In Information Management terms, these can be areas of the organization where tight budgets might combine with skepticism about the proposed changes to generate resistance.
Laggards	Laggards are the last to adopt an innovation. Individuals in this category show little to no opinion leadership. They are typically averse to change-agents and tend to be advanced in age. Laggards tend to focus on 'traditions'. In Information Management, terms these are often the people or areas of the business who resist because the 'new thing' means having to do the 'old thing' differently or not at all.

---

105 © 2014 Daragh O Brien. Used with permission.

7.1 The Challenges to be Overcome as Innovations Spread

Two key challenge areas exist with the spread of innovations through the organization. The first is breaking past the Early Adopter stage. This requires careful management of change to ensure that the Early Adopters can identify a sufficient level of dissatisfaction with the status quo that they will make and persist with the change. This step is needed to reach the 'Tipping Point' where the innovation is adopted by enough people that it begins to become mainstream.

The second key challenge point is as the innovation moves out of the Late Majority stage into the Laggards stage. The team needs to accept that they cannot necessarily convert 100% of the population to the new way of doing things. A certain percentage of the group may continue to resist change and the organization will need to decide what to do about this element of the group.

7.2 Key Elements in the Diffusion of Innovation

Four key elements need to be considered when looking at how an innovation spreads through an organization:

- **Innovation**: An idea, practice, or object that is perceived as new by an individual or other unit of adoption
- **Communication channels**: The means by which messages get from one individual to another
- **Time**: The speed at which the innovation is adopted by members of the social system
- **Social system**: The set of interrelated units that are engaged in joint problem solving to accomplish a common goal

In the context of information management, an innovation could be something as simple as the idea of the role of a Data Steward and the need for Stewards to work cross-functionally on common data problems rather than traditional 'silo' thinking.

The process by which that innovation is communicated, and the channels through which it is communicated most effectively, are the communication channels which must be considered and managed.

Finally, the idea of the Social System as a set of interrelated units that are engaged towards a joint venture. This is reminiscent of the System as described by W. Edwards Deming which must be optimized as a whole rather than piece-by-piece in isolation. An innovation that doesn't spread outside of a single business unit or team is not a well diffused change.

7.3 The Five Stages of Adoption

The adoption of any change tends to follow a five-step cycle. It starts with individuals becoming aware of the innovation (Knowledge), being persuaded as to the value of the innovation and its relevance to them (Persuasion), and reaching the point of making a Decision about their relation to the innovation. If they do not reject the innovation, they then move Implement and finally Confirm the adoption of the innovation. (See Table 38 and Figure 119.)

Of course, because an idea can always be Rejected rather than adopted, the Tipping Point of critical mass of the Early Adopters and Early Majority is important.

Table 38 The Stages of Adoption (Adapted from Rogers, 1964)

Stage	Definition
Knowledge	In the knowledge stage the individual is first exposed to an innovation but lacks information about the innovation. During this stage the individual has not yet been inspired to find more information about the innovation.
Persuasion	In the persuasion stage the individual is interested in the innovation and actively seeks information about the innovation.
Decision	In the Decision stage the individual weighs the advantages and disadvantages of using the innovation and decides whether to adopt or reject it. Rogers notes that the individualistic nature of this stage makes it the most difficult stage about which to acquire empirical evidence.
Implementation	In the Implementation stage the individual employs the innovation and determines its usefulness or searches for further information about it.
Confirmation	In the Confirmation stage, the individual finalizes his/her decision to continue using the innovation and may end up using it to its fullest potential.

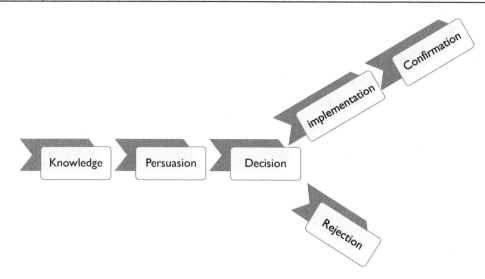

Figure 119 The Stages of Adoption

7.4 Factors Affecting Acceptance or Rejection of an Innovation or Change

People make largely rational choices when accepting or rejecting an innovation or change. Key to these is whether the innovation offers any relative advantage over the previous way of doing things.

Consider the modern smartphone. It presented a clear advantage over previous smartphones because it was easy to use, stylish to look at, and has an App store where the product's capabilities could be extended quickly and easily. Likewise, implementation of data management tools, technologies, and techniques have relative advantages over manual rekeying of data, bespoke coding, or resource intensive manual data search and discovery activities.

For example, in many organizations there can be resistance to simple document and content management changes such as tagging files with Metadata to provide context. However, the use of that Metadata in turn provides a relative advantage in terms of supporting security controls, retention schedules, and simple tasks such as information search and retrieval. Linking the hassle of tagging to the time saved either searching for information or dealing with issues where information is shared or disclosed without authorization can help demonstrate this relative advantage.

Once individuals see that an improvement is proposed, they will ask whether the improvement is compatible with their life, their way of working, etc. Returning to the smartphone example, the fact that it blended a high quality mp3 player, email, phone, etc., meant that it was compatible with the lifestyle and ways of working of its target users.

To understand compatibility, a consumer will (consciously or sub-consciously) consider several factors. For example, the complexity or simplicity of the change. If the innovation is too difficult to use, then it is less likely to be adopted. Again, the evolution of smartphone and tablet platforms is littered with failed attempts that didn't achieve the goal of a simple user interface. The ones that did so redefined the expectation of the market and inspired similar interfaces on other devices.

Trialability refers to how easy it is for the consumer to experiment with the new tool or technology. Hence freemium offers for tools. The easier it is to 'kick the tires' the more likely the user will adopt the new tool or innovation. The importance of this is that it helps establish the understanding of relative advantage, the compatibility with the life style and culture of the organization, and the simplicity of the change. As a set of first steps towards a change vision, iterative prototyping and 'trying it out' with stakeholders is essential and can help cement the Guiding Coalition as well as ensuring early adopters are on-board.

Observability is the extent that the innovation is visible. Making the innovation visible will drive communication about it through formal and personal networks. This can trigger negative reactions as well as positive reactions. Plan on how to handle negative feedback. The experience of seeing people using a new technology or working with information in a particular way (e.g., visualization of traditionally 'dry' numbers) can influence how to better communicate back the experience.

---

8. Sustaining Change

Getting change started requires a clear and compelling vision and clear and immediate first steps, a sense of urgency or dissatisfaction with the status quo, a Guiding Coalition, and a plan to avoid the pitfalls and traps that Change Agents can fall into as they begin their change journey.

However, a common problem in information management initiatives (e.g., Data Governance programs) is that they are initiated in response to a specific driver or to a particular symptom of sub-optimal capability in the organization. As the symptom is addressed, the sense of dissatisfaction and urgency lessens. It becomes harder to sustain political or financial support, particularly when competing with other projects.

It is outside the scope of this work to provide detailed analysis or tools for how these complex issues might be addressed. However, in the context of a Body Of Knowledge it is appropriate to refer back to the change management principles outlined in this chapter to provide some insight as to how solutions might be found.

8.1 Sense of Urgency / Dissatisfaction

It is important to maintain the sense of urgency. The corollary of this is to be alert to emerging areas of dissatisfaction in the organization and how the information management change might help support improvement.

For example, the scope of a data governance initiative that has been implemented to support a data privacy regulatory requirement can be broadened to address information quality issues in relation to personal data. That can be related back to the primary scope of the initiative, as most data privacy regulations have a data quality component and provide a right of access to data to individuals, so there is a risk of poor quality data being exposed. However, it opens the vision of the data governance program up to include information quality methods and practices which can be implemented as a 'second wave' once the core data privacy governance controls are in place.

8.2 Framing the Vision

A common mistake is to confuse project scope with change vision. Many projects may be required achieve the vision. It is important the vision be set in a way that allows broad based action and does not create a cul-de-sac for the change leaders once the initial 'low hanging fruit' projects are delivered.

There is a difference between a vision that says:

We will implement a structured governance framework for personal data to ensure compliance with EU Data Privacy rules.

and one that says:

We will lead our industry in repeatable and scalable approaches and methods for managing our critical information assets to ensure profits, reduce risks, improve quality of service, and balance our ethical obligations as stewards of personal information.

The first is, more or less, an objective. The second provides direction for the organization.

8.3 The Guiding Coalition

Restricting the membership of the Guiding Coalition to the most immediately affected stakeholders will restrict change effectiveness. As with vision, it is important not to confuse project steering groups who are overseeing the delivery of specific deliverables with the coalition who are guiding and evolving the vision for change in the organization.

8.4 Relative Advantage and Observability

While the specific application or focus of a change initiative might be narrow, in most cases the principles, practices, and tools that are applied may be transferrable to other initiatives. Being able to demonstrate how the approach and methods can give a relative advantage to other initiatives in the organization can help extend the Guiding Coalition and identify new areas of urgency or dissatisfaction that the change initiative can support. For example, in a utility company, data quality profiling and score-carding methods and tools that are implemented for a single view of customer implementation may be directly transferrable to a regulatory billing compliance program. Linking the two would lend itself to an Enterprise Data Quality Scorecard and associated data governance and remediation initiatives, particularly where sub-optimal approaches such as manual data clean-up might be the default option for billing data.

9. Communicating Data Management Value

Helping an organization understand the importance of data management often requires a formal organizational change management plan, as described in this chapter. Such a plan helps the organization recognize the value of its data and the contribution of data management practices to that value. Once a Data Management program is established, however, it is also necessary to cultivate ongoing support. Ongoing communication promotes understanding and sustains support. If communications are structured as a two-way channel, a communications plan can help strengthen partnerships by enabling stakeholders to share concerns and ideas. This kind of communications effort requires planning.

9.1 Communications Principles

The purpose of any communication is to send a message to a receiver. When planning communications, one needs to account for the message, the media used to convey it, and the audiences for which it is intended. To support this basic structure, certain general principles apply to any formal communications plan, regardless of topic. These are very important when communicating about data management because many people do not understand the importance of data management to organizational success. An overall communications plan and each individual communication should:

- Have a clear objective and a desired outcome
- Consist of key messages to support the desired outcome
- Be tailored to the audience / stakeholders
- Be delivered via media that are appropriate to the audience / stakeholders

While communications may be on a range of topics, the general goals of communicating boil down to:

- Informing
- Educating
- Setting goals or a vision
- Defining a solution to a problem
- Promoting change
- Influencing or motivating action
- Gaining feedback
- Generating support

Most importantly, in order to communicate clearly, it is necessary to have substantive messages to share with people. Overall communications about data management will be more successful if the data management team understands the current state of data management practices and has a vision and mission statement that connects improvement in data management practices directly to the strategic goals of the organization. Data management communications should strive to:

- Convey the tangible and intangible value of data management initiatives

- Describe how data management capabilities contribute to business strategy and results

- Share concrete examples of how data management reduces costs, supports revenue growth, reduces risk, or improves decision quality

- Educate people on fundamental data management concepts to increase the base of knowledge about data management within the organization

9.2 Audience Evaluation and Preparation

Communications planning should include a stakeholder analysis to help identify audiences for the communications that will be developed. Based on results of the analysis, content can be then tailored to be relevant, meaningful, and at the appropriate level, based on the stakeholder needs. For example, if the goal of the communications plan is to gain sponsorship for an initiative, target the communications to the highest possible influencers, usually executives who want to know the bottom line benefit of any program they fund.

Tactics for persuading people to act on communications include various ways of getting people to see how their interests align with the goals of the program.

- **Solve problems**: Messages should describe how the data management effort will help solve problems pertinent to the needs of the stakeholders being addressed. For example, individual contributors have needs different from executives. IT has needs that are different from those of business people.

- **Address pain points**: Different stakeholders will have different pain points. Accounting for these pain points in communications materials will help the audience understand the value of what is being proposed. For example, a compliance stakeholder will be interested in how a Data Management program will reduce risk. A marketing stakeholder will be interested in how the program helps them generate new opportunities.

- **Present changes as improvements**: In most cases, introducing data management practices requires that people change how they work. Communications need to motivate people to desire the proposed changes. In other words, they need to recognize changes as improvements from which they will benefit.

- **Have a vision of success**: Describing what it will be like to live in the future state enables stakeholders to understand how the program impacts them. Sharing what success looks and feels like can help the audience understand the benefits of the Data Management program.

- **Avoid jargon**: Data management jargon and an emphasis on technical aspects will turn some people off and detract from the message.

- **Share stories and examples**: Analogies and stories are effective ways to describe and help people remember the purposes of the Data Management program.

- **Recognize fear as motivation**: Some people are motivated by fear. Sharing the consequences of not managing data (e.g., fines, penalties) is a way to imply the value of managing data well. Examples of how the lack of data management practices has negatively affected a business unit will resonate.

Effective delivery of communications involves monitoring the listeners' reactions to the message. If a given tactic is not working, adapt and try a different angle.

9.3 The Human Element

The facts, examples, and stories shared about a Data Management program, are not the only things that will influence stakeholder perceptions about its value. People are influenced by their colleagues, and leaders. For this reason, communication should use the stakeholder analysis to find where groups have like interests and needs. As support broadens for the data management effort, supporters can help share the message with their peers and leadership.

9.4 Communication Plan

A communication plan brings planning elements together. A good plan serves as a roadmap to guide the work towards the goals. The communication plan should include elements listed in Table 39.

Table 39 Communication Plan Elements

Element	Description
Message	The information that needs to be conveyed.
Goal / Objective	The desired outcome of conveying a message or set of messages (i.e., why the message needs to be conveyed).
Audience	Group or individual targeted by the communication. The plan will have different objectives for different audiences.
Style	Both the level of formality and the level of detail in messages should be tailored to the audience. Executives need less detail than teams responsible for implementation of projects. Style is also influenced by organizational culture.
Channel, Method, Medium	The means and format through which the message will be conveyed (e.g., web page, blog, email, one-on-one meetings, small group or large group presentations, lunch and learn sessions, workshops, etc.) Different media have different effects.
Timing	How a message is received may be influenced by when it is received. Employees are more likely to read an email that comes out first thing Monday morning than one that comes out last thing on Friday afternoon. If the purpose of a communication is to gain support in advance to a budget cycle, then it should be timed in relation to the budget cycle. Information about impending changes to processes should be shared in a timely manner and in advance of a change taking place.

Element	Description
Frequency	Most messages need to be repeated in order to ensure all stakeholders hear them. The communications plan should schedule the sharing of messages so that repetition is helpful in getting the message across and does not become an annoyance. In addition, ongoing communications (for example, a newsletter) should be published based on an agreed-to schedule.
Materials	The communications plan should identify any materials that need to be created to execute the plan. For example, short and long versions of presentation and other written communications, elevator speeches, executive summaries, and marketing materials like posters, mugs, and other means of visual branding.
Communicators	The communications plan should identify the person or people who will deliver communications. Often the person delivering the message has a profound influence on the target audience. If the data management sponsor or other executive delivers a message, stakeholders will have a different response than if a lower level manager delivers it. Decisions about who will communicate which messages to which stakeholders should be based on the goals of the message.
Expected Response	The communications plan should anticipate how different stakeholder groups, and sometimes how individual stakeholders, will respond to communications. This work can be accomplished by anticipating questions or objections and formulating responses. Thinking through potential responses is a good way to clarify goals and build robust messages to support them.
Metrics	The communications plan should include measures of its own effectiveness. The goal is to ensure that people have understood and are willing and able to act on the messages in the plan. This can be accomplished through surveys, interviews, focus groups, and other feedback mechanisms. Changes in behavior are the ultimate test of a communications plan's success.
Budget and Resource Plan	The communications plan must account for what resources are needed to carry out goals within a given budget.

9.5 Keep Communicating

A Data Management program is an ongoing effort, not a one-time project. Communications efforts that support the program need to be measured and sustained for ongoing success.

New employees are hired and existing employees change roles. As changes happen, communication plans need to be refreshed. Stakeholder needs change over time as Data Management programs mature. Time is needed for people to absorb messages, and hearing messages multiple times helps stakeholders to retain this knowledge. The methods of communication and messages will also need to be adapted over time as understanding grows.

The competition for funding never goes away. One goal of a communications plan is to remind stakeholders of the value and benefits of the Data Management program. Showing progress and celebrating successes is vital to gaining continued support for the effort.

Effective planning and ongoing communication will demonstrate the impact that data management practices have had on the organization over time. Over time, knowledge of data's importance changes the organization's way of thinking about data. Successful communication provides a better understanding that data management can generate business value from information assets and have a long lasting impact on the organization.

10. Works Cited / Recommended

Ackerman Anderson, Linda and Dean Anderson. *The Change Leader's Roadmap and Beyond Change Management*. Two Book Set. 2nd ed. Pfeiffer, 2010. Print.

Ackerman Anderson, Linda, Dean Anderson. *Beyond Change Management: How to Achieve Breakthrough Results Through Conscious Change Leadership*. 2nd ed. Pfeiffer, 2010. Print.

Ackerman Anderson, Linda, Dean Anderson. The *Change Leader's Roadmap: How to Navigate Your Organization's Transformation*. 2nd ed. Pfeiffer, 2010. Print.

Barksdale, Susan and Teri Lund. *10 Steps to Successful Strategic Planning*. ASTD, 2006. Print. 10 Steps.

Becker, Ethan F. and Jon Wortmann. *Mastering Communication at Work: How to Lead, Manage, and Influence*. McGraw-Hill, 2009. Print.

Bevan, Richard. *Changemaking: Tactics and resources for managing organizational change*. CreateSpace Independent Publishing Platform, 2011. Print.

Bounds, Andy. *The Snowball Effect: Communication Techniques to Make You Unstoppable*. Capstone, 2013. Print.

Bridges, William. *Managing Transitions: Making the Most of Change*. Da Capo Lifelong Books, 2009. Print.

Center for Creative Leadership (CCL), Talula Cartwright, and David Baldwin. *Communicating Your Vision*. Pfeiffer, 2007. Print.

Contreras, Melissa. *People Skills for Business: Winning Social Skills That Put You Ahead of The Competition*. CreateSpace Independent Publishing Platform, 2013. Print.

Covey, Stephen R. Franklin Covey Style Guide: *For Business and Technical Communication*. 5th ed. FT Press, 2012.Print.

Covey, Stephen R. *The 7 Habits of Highly Effective People: Powerful Lessons in Personal Change*. Simon and Schuster, 2013. Print.

Franklin, Melanie. *Agile Change Management: A Practical Framework for Successful Change Planning and Implementation*. Kogan Page, 2014. Print.

Garcia, Helio Fred. Power of Communication: The: Skills to Build Trust, Inspire Loyalty, and Lead Effectively. FT Press, 2012. Print.

Godin, Seth and Malcolm Gladwell. *Unleashing the Ideavirus*. Hachette Books, 2001.

Harvard Business School Press. *Business Communication*. Harvard Business Review Press, 2003. Print. Harvard Business Essentials.

HBR's 10 Must Reads on Change Management. Harvard Business Review Press, 2011. Print.

Hiatt, Jeffrey, and Timothy Creasey. *Change Management: The People Side of Change*. Prosci Learning Center Publications, 2012. Print.

Holman, Peggy, Tom Devane, Steven Cady. *The Change Handbook: The Definitive Resource on Today's Best Methods for Engaging Whole Systems*. 2nd ed. Berrett-Koehler Publishers, 2007. Print.

Hood, J H. *How to book of Interpersonal Communication: Improve Your Relationships*. Vol. 3. WordCraft Global Pty Limited, 2013. Print. "How to" Books.

Jones, Phil. *Communicating Strategy*. Ashgate, 2008. Print.

Kotter, John P. *Leading Change*. Harvard Business Review Press, 2012. Print.

Locker, Kitty, and Stephen Kaczmarek. *Business Communication: Building Critical Skills*. 5th ed. McGraw-Hill/Irwin, 2010. Print.

Luecke, Richard. *Managing Change and Transition*. Harvard Business Review Press, 2003. Print. Harvard Business Essentials.

Rogers, Everett M. *Diffusion of Innovations*. 5th Ed. Free Press, 2003. Print.

Acknowledgements

Developing the second edition of the DAMA-DMBOK has been a labor of love for many people. The work started late in 2011 with the first revision of the Framework Paper, released in 2012. The DAMA-DMBOK Editorial Committee devoted many hours to produce the draft DMBOK2. They include:

Patricia Cupoli (DAMA Philadelphia) was the editor-in-chief for the majority of this work, finding authors and helping them develop their chapters. Sadly, Pat passed away in Summer 2015, while still engaged in the project.

Deborah Henderson (IRMAC – Toronto DAMA affiliate), Program Director for the DAMA-DMBOK products since their inception in 2005, was a dedicated sponsor of the project, and worked to ensure its completion after Pat's passing.

Susan Earley (DAMA Chicago), who drafted the DAMA-DMBOK2 framework, was the primary editor for the DMBOK2 draft. She edited and organized content and incorporated the extensive public comments from DAMA Members.

Eva Smith (DAMA Seattle), Collaboration Tool Manager, handled logistics, including enabling DAMA members to access and comment on chapters.

Elena Sykora (IRMAC – Toronto DAMA affiliate), Bibliographer Researcher, compiled the DMBOK2's comprehensive bibliography.

The Editorial Committee also appreciated the particular support of Sanjay Shirude, Cathy Nolan, Emarie Pope, and Steve Hoberman.

Laura Sebastian-Coleman (DAMA New England), DAMA Publications Officer and Production Editor, shaped, polished, and finalized the manuscript for publication. In this effort, she was guided by an advisory committee that included Peter Aiken, Chris Bradley, Jan Henderyckx, Mike Jennings, Daragh O Brien, and myself, with lots of help from Lisa Olinda. Special thanks also go to Danette McGilvray.

DMBOK2 would not have been possible without the primary contributing authors who gave substance to the vision defined in the Framework. All contributors are volunteers who shared not only their knowledge but also their time. They are credited for their contributions below. The many DAMA Members who provided feedback on chapters are listed as well.

DAMA International, the DAMA International Foundation, and the DAMA Chapter Presidents' Council sponsored the DMBOK project. Their vision, insight, patience, and continued support enabled this project to be successful.

Finally, we want to recognize the families of all the volunteers on this project, who gave of their personal time to complete this work.

Sue Geuens, President, DAMA International

Primary Contributors

#	Chapter	Primary Contributors
1	Introduction: Data Management	Editorial Advisory Committee, DMBOK editors, Chris Bradley, Ken Kring
2	Data Handling Ethics	
3	Data Governance and Stewardship	John Ladley, Mark Cowan, Sanjay Shirude
4	Data Architecture	Håkan Edvinsson
5	Data Modeling and Design	Steve Hoberman
6	Data Storage and Operations	Sanjay Shirude
7	Data Security	David Schlesinger, CISSP
8	Data Integration and Interoperability	April Reeve
9	Documents and Content	Pat Cupoli
10	Reference and Master Data	Gene Boomer, Mehmet Orun
11	Data Warehouse and Business Intelligence	Martin Sykora, Krish Krishnan, John Ladley, Lisa Nelson
12	Metadata	Saad Yacu
13	Data Quality	Rossano Tavares
14	Big Data and Data Science	Robert Abate, Martin Sykora
15	Data Management Maturity Assessment	Mark Cowan, Deborah Henderson
16	Data Management Organizations and Roles	Kelle O'Neal
17	Data Management and Organizational Change Management	Micheline Casey, Andrea Thomsen, Daragh O Brien
	Bibliography	Elena Sykora

Reviewers and Commenters

The following people provided valuable feedback at various stages of the DMBOK2:

Khalid Abu Shamleh	Mike Beauchamp	Susan Burk
Gerard Adams	Chan Beauvais	William Burkett
James Adman	Glen Bellomy	Beat Burtscher
Afsaneh Afkari	Stacie Benton	Ismael Caballero
Zaher Alhaj	Leon Bernal	Peter Campbell
Shahid Ali	Luciana Bicalho	Betty (Elizabeth) Carpenito
Suhail Ahmad AmanUllah	Pawel Bober	Hazbleydi Cervera
Nav Amar	Christiana Boehmer	Indrajit Chatterjee
Samuel Kofi Annan	Stewart Bond	Bavani Chaudhary
Ivan Arroyo	Gene Boomer	Denise Cook
Nicola Askham	Taher Borsadwala	Nigel Corbin
Juan Azcurra	Antonio Braga	James Dawson
Richard Back	Ciaran Breen	Elisio Henrique de Souza
Carlos Barbieri	LeRoy Broughton	Patrick Derde
Ian Batty	Paul Brown	Tejas Desai
Steve Beaton	Donna Burbank	Swapnil Deshmukh

Cynthia Dionisio

Shaun Dookhoo

Janani Dumbleton

Lee Edwards

Jane Estrada

Adrianos Evangelidis

William Evans

Mario Faria

Gary Flye

Michael Fraser

Carolyn Frey

Alex Friedgan

Lowell Fryman

Shu Fulai

Ketan Gadre

Oscar Galindo

Alexandre Gameiro

Jay Gardner

Johnny Gay

Sue Geuens

Sumit Gupta

Gabrielle Harrison

Kazuo Hashimoto

Andy Hazelwood

Muizz Hassan

David Hay

Clifford Heath

Jan Henderyckx

Trevor Hodges

Mark Horseman

Joseph Howard

Monica Howat

Bill Huennekens

Mark Humphries

Zoey Husband

Toru Ichikura

Thomas Ihsle

Gordon Irish

Fusahide Ito

Seokhee Jeon

Jarred Jimmerson

Christopher Johnson

Wayne Johnson

Sze-Kei Jordan

George Kalathoor

Nicholene Kieviets

Jon King

Richard King

Bruno Kinoshita

Yasushi Kiyama

Daniel Koger

Katarina Kolich

Onishi Koshi

Edwin Landale

Teresa Lau

Tom LaVerdure

Richard Leacton

Michael Lee

Martha Lemoine

Melody Lewin

Chen Liu

Manoel Francisco Dutra Lopes Jr

Daniel Lopez

Karen Lopez

Adam Lynton

Colin Macguire

Michael MacIntyre

Kenneth MacKinnon

Colin Maguire

Zeljko Marcan

Satoshi Matsumoto

George McGeachie

Danette McGilvray

R. Raymond McGirt

Scott McLeod

Melanie Mecca

Ben Meek

Steve Mepham

Klaus Meyer

Josep Antoni Mira Palacios

Toru Miyaji

Ademilson Monteiro

Danielle Monteiro

Subbaiah Muthu Krishnan

Mukundhan Muthukrishnan

Robert Myers

Dean Myshrall

Krisztian Nagy

Kazuhiro Narita

Mohamad Naser

Susana Navarro

Gautham Nayak

Erkka Niemi

Andy O'Hara

Katherine O'Keefe

Hirofumi Onozawa

Mehmet Orun

Matt Osborn

Mark Ouska

Pamela Owens

Shailesh Paliwal

Mikhail Parfentev

Melanie Parker

John Partyka

Bill Penney

Andres Perez

Aparna Phal

Jocelyn Sedes

Mark Segall

Ichibori Seiji

Brian Phillippi

R. Taeza Pittman

Edward Pok

Emarie Pope

David Quan

K Rajeswar Rao

April Reeve

Todd Reyes

Raul Ruggia-Frick

Scott Sammons

Pushpak Sarkar

John Schmidt

Nadine Schramm

Toshiya Seki

Rajamanickam Senthil Kumar

Sarang Shah

Gaurav Sharma

Vijay Sharma

Stephen Sherry

Jenny Shi

Satoshi Shimada

Sandeep Shinagare

Boris Shuster

Vitaly Shusterov

Abi Sivasubramanian

Alicia Slaughter

Eva Smith

Tenny Soman

José Antonio Soriano Guzmán

Donald Soulsby

Erich Stahl

Jerry Stembridge

James Stevens

Jan Stobbe

Santosh Subramaniam

Motofusa Sugaya

Venkat Sunkara

Alan Sweeney

Martin Sykora

Akira Takahashi

Steve Thomas

Noriko Watanabe

Joseph Weaver

Christina Weeden

Alexander Titov

Steven Tolkin

Toshimitsu Tone

Juan Pablo Torres

David Twaddell

Thijs van der Feltz

Elize van der Linde

Peter van Nederpelt

Peter Vennel

Roy Verharen

Karel Vetrovsky

Gregg Withers

Michael Wityk

Marcin Wizgird

Benjamin Wright-Jones

Teresa Wylie

Hitoshi Yachida

Saad Yacu

Hiroshi Yagishita

Harishbabu Yelisetty

Taisei Yoshimura

Index

Made in the USA
Middletown, DE
27 April 2023

29540943R00329